The Reception of Sir Walter Scott in Euro

The Athlone Critical Traditions Series: The Reception of British and Irish Authors in Europe

Series Editor: Elinor Shaffer
School of Advanced Study, University of London

Published Volumes

All the volumes in the Series are published in paperback as well as e-books.

The Athlone Critical Traditions Series:
The Reception of British and Irish Authors in Europe

Series Editor: Elinor Shaffer
School of Advanced Study, University of London

The Reception of Sir Walter Scott in Europe

Edited by Murray Pittock

B L O O M S B U R Y

LONDON · NEW DELHI · NEW YORK · SYDNEY

Bloomsbury Academic
An imprint of Bloomsbury Publishing Plc

50 Bedford Square   1385 Broadway
London   New York
WC1B 3DP   NY 10018
UK   USA

www.bloomsbury.com

Bloomsbury is a registered trade mark of Bloomsbury Publishing Plc

First published in 2007 by the Continuum International Publishing Group Ltd
Paperback edition first published by Bloomsbury Academic 2014

© Murray Pittock and contributors, 2006
Series concept and Series Editor's Preface © Elinor Shaffer

British Library Cataloguing-in-Publication Data
A catalogue record for this book is available from the British Library.

ISBN: HB: 978-0-8264-7410-0
      PB: 978-1-4725-3547-4
      EPDF: 978-1-4411-9281-3
      EPUB: 978-1-4411-9808-2

Library of Congress Cataloging-in-Publication Data
A catalog record for this book is available from the Library of Congress.

Typeset by RefineCatch Limited, Bungay, Suffolk

Contents

Series Editor's Preface

The reception of British authors in Britain has in good part been studied; indeed, it forms our literary history. By contrast, the reception of British authors in Europe has not been examined in any systematic, long-term or large-scale way. With our volume on Jonathan Swift (2005), we altered our Series title to 'The Reception of British and Irish Authors in Europe', as a reminder that many writers previously travelling under the British flag may now be considered or claimed as belonging to the Republic of Ireland, or Eire.

If Swift's career in England was as prominent and embattled as his career in Ireland, while Joyce in 'silence, exile, and cunning' recreated himself as a European, it is the name of William Butler Yeats that has come by his own fierce choice to stand for 'his country's biography', the life history of Ireland, as his most recent biographer has put it. (R. F. Foster, I, xviii). In his lifetime the crucial moment was the founding of the Irish Free State in 1921 as a full member of the Commonwealth, though the Republic of Ireland did not come into being until 1948.

Walter Scott has stood both as British, and as Scottish, both in the British Isles and abroad. He also represented a European movement, the ballad revival, with his collections of 'border ballads' joining forces with the nascent Romantic movement, and as an original poet renewing an ancient vein, while in his historical writings and most of all in his immensely popular and widely read novels he established a Scottish history both heroic and ordinary, the common and the romantic life of a region. In confirming the existence of an authentic Scottish tradition within the Union, he renewed and set the course of that tradition. If Macpherson's Ossian, the ancient Gaelic bard, the supposed 'Homer of the North', had sung the heroic and tragic loss of the past, and moved many others across Europe who had suffered such losses, Scott re-established the possibility of a present and a future life.

It is the aim of this Series to initiate and forward the study of the reception of British authors in continental Europe, or, as we would now say, the other parts of the Europe to which we also belong, rather than as isolated national histories with a narrow national perspective. The perspectives of other nations greatly add to our understanding of individual contributors to that history. The history of the reception of authors of the British Isles extends our knowledge of their capacity to stimulate and to call forth new responses, not only in their own disciplines but in wider fields and to diverse publics in a variety of historical circumstances. Often these responses provide quite unexpected and enriching insights into our own history, politics and culture. Individual works and personalities take on new dimensions and facets. They may also be subject to enlightening critiques. Our knowledge of our own writers is simply incomplete and inadequate without these reception studies.

By 'authors' we intend writers in any field whose works have been recognized as making a contribution to the intellectual and cultural history of our society. Thus the Series includes literary figures such as Laurence Sterne, Virginia Woolf and James Joyce; philosophers such as Francis Bacon and David Hume; historians and political figures such as Edmund Burke; and scientists such as Charles Darwin and Isaac Newton, whose works have had a broad impact on thinking in every field. In some cases individual works of the same author have dealt with different subjects, each with virtually its own reception history; so Burke's *Reflections on the French Revolution* (1790) was instantaneously translated and moulded thinking on the power struggles in the Europe of his own day; while his youthful 'Essay on the Feeling of the Beautiful and Sublime' exerted a powerful influence on aesthetic thought and the practice of writing and remains a seminal work for certain genres of fiction. Similarly, each of Laurence Sterne's two major works of fiction, *Tristram Shandy* and *A Sentimental Journey*, has its own history of reception, giving rise to a whole line of literary movements, innovative progeny and concomitant critical theory in most European countries. In the case of Scott, individual works struck out a line in different directions, with *Ivanhoe* and its Romantic medievalism perhaps being the most popular single volume, yet the Waverley Novels as a group modelling the ambitious historical and realist novel of the nineteenth century. Virtually all of the major novelists of the century are indebted to him: Manzoni, Balzac, Galdòs, Tolstoy, Dostoevsky, Fontane, and further to Thomas Mann. Scott firmly becomes a 'classic', so that even if some claimed to move on from him, and the so familiar novels, ingrained in childhood, are declared 'childish things', still the editions go on, permitting new generations of children to absorb the stories. If Swift's powerful adult satire was rendered more palatable through children's versions, Scott's permanent allure resided in the childhood experience of value laid on a remote place that nevertheless could be claimed as one's own. As childhood experience it could never lose its power.

The research project examines the ways in which selected authors have been translated, published, distributed, read, reviewed and discussed on the continent of Europe. In doing so, it throws light not only on specific strands of intellectual and cultural history but also on the processes involved in the dissemination of ideas and texts. The project brings to bear the theoretical and critical approaches that have characterized the growing fields of reader response theory and reception studies in the last quarter of the twentieth century and into the twenty-first century. These critical approaches have illuminated the activity of the reader in bringing the text to life and stressed the changing horizons of the reading public or community of which the reader is a part. Here Scott offers another rich field: as with most English-language authors before 1945, his French translator provided the medium in which he was experienced by the majority of his readers abroad and he was passed through the prism of French thought; Defauconpret, a prolific translator of English works, at first followed the traditional method of 'la belle infidèle', rewriting in a more refined style considered fit for an educated and genteel public; but he altered his style in line with new Romantic canons of translation stemming from Schleiermacher calling for the representation of 'difficulty' and 'strangeness', allowing the source text (beginning with the 1830 *Old Mortality*) to alter the target language's range and texture. Scottish regionalisms, for example, were permitted to make themselves felt.

The project also takes cognizance of the studies of the material history of the book that have begun to explore the production, publication and distribution of manuscripts and books. Here again a popular author (in 1830 more than one-third of the novels published in France were by Scott) offers an especially rich field of inquiry, as his works were pirated (undercutting their publishers), or they were packaged and marketed in a variety of ways, and imitators entered the lists, sometimes borrowing his name (for example, circulating a spurious *Robin Hood* that is still catalogued in Spanish libraries under his name). Increasingly, other media too are playing a role in these processes, and to the history of book illustration must be added lantern slides (as in the popular versions of both Scott's and Dickens's works), cinema (whose early impact forms an important part of our H. G. Wells volume), and more recently television (as recounted in the Jane Austen volume). Scott's writings, like Ossian's and Byron's, have almost as extensive a history in images and in sound as in prose and poetry. Many artists were called to illustrate him. Performance history requires strenuous tracing, beyond the texts, whether for works written for the stage or for adaptations, but Scott leaves a rich trail; and his presence as the source of the libretti of major operas is phenomenal.

The study of material history forms a curious annexe, that is, of the objects that form durable traces of the vogue for a particular author, which may be parts of himself (as with the macabre story told in our Shelley volume of the wish to possess the poet's heart), or souvenir objects associated with his characters, or the more elaborate memorial gardens and graveyards such as those linked to Rousseau and Sterne in France. The Czartorysky princes acquired a blade of dried grass said to be from Ossian's battlefield. Scott's spanking new Romantic 'castle' at Abbotsford (like those more ancient piles named in his novels) became a place of pilgrimage. The author's own image may achieve iconic status, as with Byron 'in Albanian dress'. The significance of such cults and cult objects requires further analysis as the examples multiply and diversify.

The Series as published first by Continuum and now by Bloomsbury is open-ended and multi-volumed, with each volume based on a particular author. The authors may be regarded according to their discipline, or looked at across disciplines within their period. Thus the reception of philosophers Bacon and Hume may be compared; or Hume may be considered as belonging to an eighteenth-century group that includes writers like Swift and Sterne, historians and political figures such as Gibbon and Burke. As the volumes accumulate they enrich each other and our awareness of the full context in which an individual author is received. The Swift volume shows that in many places Swift and Sterne were received at the same time, and viewed sometimes as a pair of witty ironists, and sometimes as opposites representing traditional satire on the one hand (Swift) and modern sentimentalism on the other (Sterne), and equally or diversely valued as a result. The Romantic poets, Byron, Shelley, Coleridge and not least Scott himself, were carried forward into mid-century nationalist movements and late nineteenth-century symbolist movements. The *fin-de-siècle* aspects of Pater, early Yeats, Woolf and Joyce are interwoven in a wider European experience. In the twentieth century, Sterne was paired with Joyce as subversive of the novel form; and Joyce and Woolf became Modernists.

These chronological shifts, bringing different authors and different works into view together, are common to the reception process, so often displacing or delaying them into an entirely new historical scene or set of circumstances. Thus Byron's two major works, *Childe Harold* and *Don Juan*, came to stand, after his death, for whole epochs of feeling in Europe: first the melancholic, inward post-Napoleonic *Weltschmerz*, then the bitter and disillusioned mocking tones of the failed Revolution of 1848. So writers, historians and political parties continued to invent, recreate and fight over the significance of past history, and to wrest Scott and his followers from one another. The kaleidoscope of reception displays and discovers new pairings and couplings, new milieux, new matches and mismatches, and, of course, new valuations.

In period terms one may discern within the Series a Romantic group; a Victorian group; a *fin-de-siècle* group; and an early Modernist group. Period designations differ from discipline to discipline, and are shifting even within a discipline: Blake, who was a 'Pre-Romantic' poet a generation ago, is now considered a fully fledged Romantic, and Beckford is edging in that direction. Virginia Woolf may be regarded as a *fin-de-siècle* aesthete and stylist whose affinities are with Pater, or as an epoch-making Modernist like Joyce. Terms referring to period and style often vary from country to country. What happens to a 'Victorian' author transplanted to 'Wilhelmine' Germany? Are the English Metaphysical poets to be regarded as 'baroque' in continental terms, or will that term continue to be borrowed in English only for music, art and to an extent architecture? Is the 'Augustan' Swift a classicist in Italian terms, or an Enlightenment thinker in French terms? Is Scott a Romantic poet and regional singer, or is he an astute Realist, in art as in politics? It is most straightforward to classify them simply according to century, for the calendar is for the most part shared. But the various possible groupings will provide a context for reception and enrich our knowledge of each author.

Division of each volume by country or by linguistic region is dictated by the historical development of Europe; each volume necessarily adopts a different selection of countries and regions, depending on period and on the specific reception of any given author. Countries or regions are treated either substantially, in several chapters or sections where this is warranted, (for example the French reception of Yeats, Woolf or Joyce), or on a moderate scale, or simply as a brief section. In some cases, where a rich reception is located that has not been reported or of which the critical community is not aware, more detailed coverage may be justified. In general, comparative studies have neglected Spain in favour of France, Germany and Italy, and this imbalance needs to be righted. For example, we have shown the reception of Woolf in the different linguistic communities of the Iberian peninsula, and given a detailed treatment of a play of Yeats in Catalan, Galician and Basque. Scott's presence in Spain is remarkably extensive and enduring. But brevity does not indicate lack of interest. Where separate coverage of any particular country or region is not justified by the extent of the reception, relevant material is incorporated into the bibliography and the Timeline. Thus an early translation may be noted, although there was subsequently a minimal response to the author or work, or a very long gap in the reception in that region.

It is, of course, always possible, and indeed to be hoped and expected, that further aspects of reception will later be uncovered, and the long-term research project forwarded, through this initial information. Reception studies often display an author's intellectual and political impact and reveal effects abroad that are unfamiliar to the author's compatriots. Thus, Byron, for example, had the power of carrying and incarnating liberal political thought to regimes and institutions to whom it was anathema; it is less well known that Sterne had the same effect, and that both were charged with erotically tinged subversion; and that Pater suggested a style of aesthetic sensibility in which sensation took precedence over moral values. Scott, on the other hand, was often taken up by those who found Byron too much the egotist. Woolf came to be an icon for women writers in countries where there was little tradition of women's writing. By the same token, the study of censorship, or more broadly impediments to dissemination, and of modes of circumventing control, becomes an important aspect of reception studies. In Bacon studies, the process of dissemination of his ideas through the private correspondence of organized circles was vital. Certain presses and publishers also play a role, and the study of modes of secret distribution under severe penalty is a particularly fascinating subject, whether in Catholic Europe or Soviet Russia. Much translation was carried out in prisons. Irony and aesopian devices, and audience alertness to them, are highly developed under controlling regimes. A surprising number of authors live more dangerously abroad than at home. Where Yeats was at home was a moot point; some Irish groups attacked him as aristocratic, elitist, even 'fascistic'; yet he has been seen as the first prominent Western advocate of decolonization, and *The Tower* (1928) as advancing the prophetic perception that 'colonial violence has to be counteracted by a politics of reason'. Scott's central figures, like Waverley, who were able to see both sides, were attacked as gentry standing above conflict, but also embraced as vital 'focal consciences'.

Translation itself may provide a mode of evading censure. There is probably no more complex and elaborated example in the annals of Europe of the use of translation to invent new movements, styles, and political departures than that of Ossian, which became itself a form of 'pseudo-translation', that is, works by writers masquerading under pseudonyms suggestive of 'dangerous' foreigners but providing safety for mere 'translators'. 'Ossian' became the cover name for new initiatives, as 'Byron' flew the flag of liberation.

New electronic technology makes it possible to undertake reception studies on this scale. 'Some authors live in the citations and imitations or reworkings by others, including satire and pastiche.' Some, like Pater, live in the echoes of their style as understood in another language. Some authors achieve the status of fictional characters in other writers' works; in other cases, their characters do, like Sterne's uncle Toby, Trim and his own alter ego Yorick; or even their characters' family members, as in the memorable tale by a major Hungarian contemporary writer chronicling the early career and writings of the (Hungarian) father of Joyce's Leopold Bloom. No one was so often mistaken for a character in his own works than Byron.

The Project website www.clarehall.cam.ac.uk/rbae provides further information about the Project's history, advisory board, conferences, colloquia and seminars, and reviews of its volumes. The Project database is an open-access bibliographical resource, available online via the Project website and containing all the bibliographies published so far in the Series as well as supplementary information and bibliography relating to the authors.

Dr Elinor Shaffer, FBA
Director, Research Project
The Reception of British and Irish Authors in Europe

Acknowledgements

The Research Project on the Reception of British and Irish Authors in Europe is happy to acknowledge the support of the British Academy, the Leverhulme Trust, the Arts and Humanities Research Board, the Modern Humanities Research Association and other funding bodies. The project is a response to the British Academy's call to its Fellows in 1996 for new and substantial research projects in the modern period.

We are also greatly indebted to the School of Advanced Study, University of London, where the research project was based during the early preparation of this volume, to the Institute of Germanic Studies, and the Institute of Romance Studies (now merged as the Institute of Germanic & Romance Studies), the Institute of English Studies, and the Institute of Historical Research, with whom we have held a series of seminars, colloquia and conferences on Reception Studies since 1998. We are grateful to Clare Hall College, Cambridge, which has provided the project with a second institutional home since 2003.

We are very grateful to Professor Silvia Mergenthal of the University of Konstanz for supporting the launch of the Scott Reception project at the International Conference on Walter Scott that she organized in July 2003 in Konstanz, where the project held a session on Scott's Reception in Europe, and a number of colleagues expressed interest in contributing to the volume. We would again like to express our thanks to Clare Hall College, Cambridge, where the Colloquium on 'Sir Walter Scott's European Reception and the Question of Nationality' was held 28–29 May 2005, and to Dr Alessandra Tosi, Dr Lachlan Moyle and the staff of Clare Hall College for their help in organizing it.

We also gratefully acknowledge the advice and guidance of the Advisory Board of the project, which has met regularly since the launch of the Project. The Research Director, Dr Elinor Shaffer, is also pleased to acknowledge the indispensable services of the staff of the research project during the preparation of this volume: the AHRB Research Fellow, Dr Paul Barnaby, and Dr Wim Van Mierlo; the MHRA Research Associate, Dr Alessandra Tosi; and the Project Officer, Dr Lachlan Moyle.

The project would also like to express its gratitude for invaluable advice and assistance on individual chapters and topics to our contributors, and to Dr Neil Stewart, for his translation of Mark Altshuller's chapter on the Russian reception of Scott into English; and to Dr Alessandra Tosi for her substantial contribution to the Russian bibliography. We would also like to express our grateful thanks to Dr Paul Barnaby for his initial bibliography of European research on Scott, incorporated here, and for his expert construction of the Timeline to the volume. Acknowledgement is also made to the BOSLIT Project on the Translation of Scottish Authors in Twentieth-Century Europe of the University of Edinburgh and the Edinburgh University Library for making available its resources on Scott, and to the National Portrait Gallery London for permission to use Sir William Allan's portrait of Scott on the cover of the volume.

List of Contributors

Mark Altshuller gained his PhD in Russian Literature from Leningrad University. He emigrated to the US in 1978 and was appointed to a professorship at the University of Pittsburgh from 1986. He is the author of numerous articles and several books. Among the latter (in Russian) are: *Precursors of Slavophilism in Russian Literature. The Colloquy of Lovers of the Russian Word* (1984); *The Path of Renunciation. Russian Literature in the Period 1953–1968* (with Elena Dryzhakova) (1984); *The Era of Sir Walter Scott in Russian Literature. The Historical Novel of the 1830s* (1996); and *Between Two Czars. Pushkin 1824–1836* (2003).

Norbert Bachleitner is Associate Professor of Comparative Literature at the University of Vienna. His fields of research include reception and translation studies, sociology of literature, intertextuality, book history, especially censorship, and hypertext. His recent publications include *Kleine Geschichte des deutschen Feuilletonromans* (1999); *Beiträge zur Rezeption der britischen und irischen Literatur des 19. Jahrhunderts im deutschsprachigen Raum* (2000); *Geschichte des Buchhandels in Österreich* (2000), co-authored with Franz M. Eybl and Ernst Fischer; and *Soziologie der literarischen Übersetzung* (2004), co-edited with Michaela Wolf.

Paul Barnaby gained his PhD (Edinburgh) on the reception of French Naturalism in Italy; he was Bibliographer/Researcher for BOSLIT (Bibliography of Scottish Literature in Translation), a joint project of the University of Edinburgh and the Scottish National Library. He was AHRB Research Fellow to the Research Project on the Reception of British Authors in Europe, 1999–2000; and is currently Project Officer, Walter Scott Digital Archive, an online resource based around the Corson Collection of Walter Scott materials at Edinburgh University Library. He has published articles on the Italian reception of French Naturalism, and the translation and reception of Scottish literature; and recently co-wrote with Tom Hubbard the chapters on 'Scotland in World Literature' for the *Edinburgh History of Scottish Literature*. He has contributed the Timeline to most of the volumes in the present Series.

Annika Bautz is Lecturer in Nineteenth-Century Literature at the University of Plymouth. Her research interests are in Romantic and Victorian fiction, the history of the book and reception studies. Her publications include *The Reception of Jane Austen and Walter Scott: A Comparative Longitudinal Study*

(Continuum 2007) and *Reader's Guide to Essential Criticism of Jane Austen's Pride and Prejudice, Emma and Sense and Sensibility* (Palgrave Macmillan 2010).

Alastair Durie has taught at the universities of Aberdeen, Glasgow and most recently Stirling. His past publications have included works on textiles, sport, photography and banking, but his main teaching and research interests now lie in the history of tourism. Amongst publications in this area are *Scotland for the Holidays: Tourism in Scotland 1780–1939* (2003) and *Water is Best: The Hydros and Health Tourism* (2006).

José Enrique García-González wrote his MA thesis on the translation of newspaper articles, with a focus on the language transfer phenomenon between English and Spanish. His doctoral thesis was on the translation and reception of Walter Scott in Spain, with special reference to the translations of *Waverley*. He teaches English and English–Spanish Translation at the Department of English Language of the University of Seville. He is a member of the University of Seville Research Group 'Translation Theory, Practice and Teaching'. His main areas of research are Descriptive Translation Studies, Reception Studies, Translation and Culture and Translation and Censorship. He has published several papers related to these fields.

Tom Hubbard, poet and translator, was Visiting Professor in Scottish Literature and Culture at the University of Budapest (2006). The first Librarian of the Scottish Poetry Library (1984–92), he was Editor of the Bibliography of Scottish Literature in Translation (BOSLIT) (2000–04). His critical works include *Seeking Mr Hyde* (1995), *The Integrative Vision* (1997) and *Michael Scot: Myth and Polymath* (2006). The most recent collections of his poetry are *Scottish Faust* (2004) and *From Soda Fountain to Moonshine Mountain* (2004). In addition to *The New Makars* (1991), an anthology of contemporary poetry in Scots, he has edited an anthology of translations, *Poetry from Switzerland* (2002), and (with Zsuzsanna Varga) he made Scots versions of seven contemporary Hungarian poems for the anthology *At the End of the Broken Bridge* (2005). With Duncan Glen he co-edited the prose selection *Stevenson's Scotland* (2003). His CD anthology of readings by twelve contemporary Scottish writers, *Border Crossings*, appears from Scottish PEN (2006); with R. D. S. Jack he has co-edited an essay collection, *Scotland in Europe* (Rodopi, 2006).

Richard Maxwell (1948–2010) was Senior Lecturer in Comparative Literature at Yale University, the author of *The Mysteries of Paris and London* (1992) and *The Historical Novel in Europe, 1650–1850* (2009), and editor of *The Victorian Illustrated Book* (2001).

Mirosława Modrzewska teaches nineteenth century British literature and culture at the Institute of English at the University of Gdańsk, Poland. She has published articles concerning the works of Romantics, such as Robert Burns, Lord Byron, Walter Scott, Juliusz Słowacki, and has also contributed chapters to the *Byron* (2004; pb 2014) and *Burns* (2013) volumes in this Series. She co-edited and translated with Peter Cochran, Bill Johnston, and Catherine O'Neil

Poland's Angry Romantic: Two Poems and a Play by Juliusz Słowacki (2009). Dr Modrzewska is an author of the Polish section of *European Romanticism* (ed. Stephen Prickett) and has recently published *Byron the Baroque* (2013) in *Gdańsk Transatlantic Studies in British and North American Culture*, edited by Marek Wilczyński.

Andrew Monnickendam is Professor of English Literature at the Universitat Autònoma de Barcelona. His major research area is Scottish literature. The chapter on Burns represents his second contribution to this series, the first being on the reception of Walter Scott in Catalonia. Recent publications include *The Novels of Walter Scott and his Literary Relations – Mary Brunton, Susan Ferrier and Christian Johnstone* (2013) and 'The Scottish National Tale' in *The Edinburgh Companion to Scottish Romanticism* (2011). At present, he is writing a book on literature and war.

The late **Jørgen Erik Nielsen** (1933–2007) was a graduate of the University of Copenhagen and received his DPhil degree in 1976 for a dissertation on the reception in Denmark of English literature in the period 1800–40. He was the author of a number of books and articles on the Danish reception of English and Russian literature and on the history of English studies in Denmark. His most recent publication was the entry on Byron's reception in Denmark in vol. II of *The Reception of Byron in Europe* in the present Series on the Reception of British and Irish Authors in Europe (2004). He was Reader in English at the University of Copenhagen until his retirement in 2002.

Murray Pittock is Bradley Professor of English Literature at the University of Glasgow, a Fellow of the Royal Society of Edinburgh, and a prizewinner of that society and of the British Academy, as well as winning or being nominated or shortlisted for over ten other literary prizes. He has previously held chairs or other senior appointments at Strathclyde, Edinburgh and Manchester universities. He is the author or editor of a number of prominent works on Jacobitism and Romanticism, including *James Boswell* (2007), *Scottish and Irish Romanticism* (2008, 2011), The *Edinburgh Companion to Scottish Romanticism* (2011), *Robert Burns in Global Culture* (2011), *Material Culture and Sedition: Treacherous, Objects, Secret Places* (2013) and *The Reception of Robert Burns in Europe* in this Series (2014). He is currently editing the *Scots Musical Museum* in the AHRC Collected Burns edition. His annotated web resource on Burns can be found at http://www.gla.ac.uk/schools/critical/research/researchcentres andnetworks/robertburnsstudies/majorresearchprojects/burns/

Martin Procházka, Professor of English, American and Comparative Literature, is the Head of the Department of English and American Studies at Charles University, Prague. He is the author of *Romantismus a osobnost* (Romanticism and Personality, 1996), a critical study of English Romantic aesthetics, Coleridge and Byron, and a co-author (with Zdenek Hrbata) of *Romantismus a romantismy* (Romanticism and Romanticisms, 2005), a comparative study on the chief discourses in the West European, American and Czech Romanticism. He has published book chapters and articles on Shakespeare, Romanticism and

Poststructuralism, and translated Byron's *Manfred* into Czech. He is the founding editor of an international academic journal *Litteraria Pragensia*. He has contributed to the volumes on Byron and Coleridge, as well as Scott, in the present Series on the Reception of British and Irish Authors in Europe.

Frauke Reitemeier is an Assistant Lecturer at the Department of English at Göttingen University. Her main areas of interest include early modern and eighteenth-century British literature, with a special interest in the reception and perception of Scotland. Her previous publications include books on Shakespeare's *A Midsummer Night's Dream* and on German and English predecessors of Sir Walter Scott, as well as articles on diverse subjects from Scott and music to rhetorical strategies of emancipation in early eighteenth-century English literature.

Elinor Shaffer, FBA, is Senior Research Fellow, Institute of Modern Languages Research, School of Advanced Study, University of London, and Director of the Research Project on the Reception of British and Irish Authors in Europe. The author of *The Fall of Jerusalem: The Mythological School in Biblical Criticism and Secular Literature 1770–1880* (1975), and *Erewhons of the Eye: Samuel Butler as Painter, Photographer, and Art Critic* (1988), she was a founder member of the British Comparative Literature Association and editor of the annual journal *Comparative Criticism*.

Tone Smolej is an Assistant Lecturer at the Department of Comparative Literature and Literary Theory of the Arts Faculty, University of Ljubljana (Slovenia). His main research interests include French–Slovene relations, imagology, and the history of comparative literature.

Neil Stewart is an Assistant at the Slavic Department of the University of Bonn (Germany). His research interests include comparative literature and literary theory. He is the author of 'Vstan' i vspominaj: Auferstehung als Collage in V. Erofeevs Moskva-Petuski' (Frankfurt 1999), and 'Glimmerings of Wit: Laurence Sterne und die russische Literatur von 1790 bis 1840' (Heidelberg 2005). He contributed 'From Imperial Court to Peasant's Cot: Sterne in Russia' to *The Reception of Laurence Sterne in Europe* (2003) in the present Series. He has also edited (with J. Fritz) *Das schlechte Gewissen der Moderne: Kulturtheorie und Gewaltdarstellung in Literatur und Film nach 1968* (Cologne; Vienna; Weimar 2006).

Emilia Szaffner is a Lecturer at the Institute of English and American Studies, Pannon University, Veszprém, Hungary. She obtained her PhD degree at Eötvös Lóránd University in Budapest in 2002 for her thesis on the nineteeenth-century Hungarian reception of Walter Scott. Several of her publications have focused on the picturesque, the sublime and Romantic nationalism in the novels of Walter Scott and Hungarian writers of the nineteeenth century. She has published comparative studies in literature and painting, and her research is focused on both Scottish and Hungarian culture.

Gertrud Szamosi holds a doctorate from Eötvös Lóránd University in Budapest and lectures in English Literatures and Cultures at Pécs University. She has published in the fields of Scottish and Postcolonial Literatures and edited a volume of *Contemporary Scottish Short Stories in Hungarian*. Her book on the *Changing Models of National and Regional Identification at the Time of the Scottish Enlightenment* will be published in 2006.

Jeremy Tambling is Professor of Literature at Manchester University and writes on nineteenth- and twentieth-century literature, on opera, and on opera on film. He has written on 'James and Opera' for the volume on Henry James in the present Series on the Reception of British and Irish Authors in Europe.

Fernando Toda wrote his doctoral dissertation on the function of linguistic variety in the novels of Walter Scott. He taught History of the English Language at the University of Seville, and is currently a Professor in the Department of Translation and Interpreting of the University of Salamanca. He translated Scott's *The Heart of Midlothian* (El corazón de Midlothian, Madrid 1988), and was translator and editor of 'The Highland Widow' and 'The Two Drovers' (La viuda montañesa / Los dos arreadores, Seville 1991). He carried out the first translation into Spanish of *The Letters of Malachi Malagrowther* (Defensa de la nación escocesa: las cartas de Malachi Malagrowther, Malaga 2004), which he edited. He is also the translator and editor of the first Spanish version of Barbour's *Bruce* (La gesta de Roberto de Bruce, Salamanca 1998).

Beth S. Wright, Professor of Art History and Dean of the College of Liberal Arts at the University of Texas at Arlington, wrote her doctoral dissertation on the influence of Scott's historical novels on French historical painting. Her research on French eighteenth and nineteenth-century art centres on historical representation and the relationship between text and image, most recently 'literature and the arts' in M. A. R. Habib (ed.) *The Cambridge History of Literary Criticism, 6: The Nineteenth Century c. 1830–1914* (Cambridge University Press 2013). Her publications on Scott's impact on French art include catalogues of French paintings with Paul Joannides for the *Bulletin de la Société de l'Histoire de l'Art Français,* a catalogue of French prints for *Nouvelles de l'Estampe*; articles which have appeared in *Art Bulletin, Nouvelles de l'Estampe, Word & Image* and elsewhere; and an essay in the exhibition catalogue *Romance & Chivalry: History and Literature Reflected in Early Nineteenth-Century French Painting* (1996). She is the author of *Painting and History during the French Restoration: Abandoned by the Past* (Cambridge University Press 1997) and editor of *The Cambridge Companion to Delacroix* (Cambridge University Press 2001).

Abbreviations

The following abbreviations of titles of works by Scott can be found in this book:

A	The Antiquary
AB	The Abbot
AG	Anne of Geierstein
AMM	Aunt Margaret's Mirror
AU	Auchindrane
BD	Black Dwarf
BET	The Betrothed
BL	Bride of Lammermoor
BT	The Bridal of Triermain
CC	Chronicles of the Canongate
CD	Castle Dangerous
CRP	Count Robert of Paris
DD	The Doom of Devorgoil
FMP	Fair Maid of Perth
FN	Fortunes of Nigel
FW	The Field of Waterloo
GM	Guy Mannering
HA	The House of Aspen
HD	Harold the Dauntless
HH	Halidon Hill
HM	Heart of Midlothian
HS	The History of Scotland
HW	'Highland Widow'
I	Ivanhoe
IB	Il Bizzarro
J	The Journal of Sir Walter Scott
K	Kenilworth
LDW	Letters on Demonology and Witchcraft
LI	The Lord of the Isles
LL	Lady of the Lake
LLM	Lay of the Last Minstrel
LM	Legend of Montrose
LN	Lives of the Novelists
M	Marmion

MAMM	'My Aunt Margaret's Mirror'
MC	*Macduff's Cross*
MDY	*Memoir of the Duke of York*
MJD	*Memoirs of John Dryden*
MJS	*Memoirs of Jonathan Swift*
MM	*Malachi Malagrowther*
MO	*The Monastery*
MSB	*Minstrelsy of the Scottish Border*
NB	*The Life of Napoleon Bonaparte*
OM	*Old Mortality*
P	*The Pirate*
PLK	*Paul's Letters to His Kinfolk*
PP	*Peveril of the Peak*
QD	*Quentin Durward*
R	*Redgauntlet*
RD	*Religious Discourses*
RO	*Rokeby*
RR	*Rob Roy*
SD	*The Surgeon's Daughter*
SRW	*St Ronan's Well*
T	*The Talisman*
TC	'The Tapestried Chamber'
TD	'Two Drovers'
TE	*Tales and Essays*
TG	*Tales of a Grandfather*
TML	*Tales of my Landlord*
VDR	*The Vision of Don Roderick*
W	*Waverley*
WN	*The Waverley Novels*
WO	*Woodstock*

Timeline of the European Reception of Sir Walter Scott, 1802–2013

Paul Barnaby

Under 'Translations', the Timeline records for each European country the first translation of individual works by Scott. Under 'Criticism', it lists all European book-length monographs on Scott plus significant reviews, articles, chapters and theses. 'Other' covers literary, artistic, and musical works inspired by Scott, adaptations into other media, and miscellaneous events connected to Scott's life and works. The Timeline draws on the Bibliography of Scottish Literature in Translation (BOSLIT) and on the following work, to which the reader is directed for fuller bibliographical details:

Benedetti, Anna (1974) *Le traduzioni italiane da Walter Scott e i loro anglicismi*. Florence: Olschki.

Draper, Frederick William Marsden (1923) *The Rise and Fall of the French Romantic Drama, with Special Reference to the Influence of Shakespeare, Scott, and Byron*. New York: Dutton; London: Constable.

Hartland, Reginald William (1928) *Walter Scott et le roman 'frénetique': contribution à l'étude de leur fortune en France*. Paris: Champion.

Maigron, Louis (1912) *Le Roman historique à l'époque romantique: essai sur l'influence de Walter Scott*. Paris: Champion.

Massmann, Klaus (1972) *Die Rezeption der historischen Romane Sir Walter Scotts in Frankreich, 1816–1832*. Heidelberg: Carl Winter Universitätsverlag.

Pires, Maria Laura Bettencourt (1979) *Walter Scott e o romanticismo português*. Lisbon: Universidade Nova.

Ruggieri Punzo, Franca (1975) *Walter Scott in Italia: 1821–1971*. Bari: Adriatica.

Sigmann, Luise (1918) *Die englische Literatur von 1800–1850 im Urteil der zeitgenossischen deutschen Kritik*, Heidelberg: C. Winter.

Vissink, Hendrik (1922) *Scott and his Influence on Dutch Literature*. Zwolle: W. J. Berends J. Jzn.

Date	Translations	Criticism	Other
1802		**Denmark:** First reference to Scott in Danish press	Scott publishes first two vols of *MSB*
1803			Scott publishes third vol. of *MSB*
1805			Scott publishes *LLM*
1808			Scott publishes *M*
1810	**First German translation:** 'The Gas Gos-Hawk' and 'The Lass of Lochryan' from *MSB*	**Germany:** J. Grimm discusses *MSB* in letter to G. F. Benecke	Scott publishes *LL*
1811	**First Portuguese translation:** Extracts from *VDR*	**Germany:** J. Grimm sends Benecke copy of *LL*; WS discussed in *Morgenblatt* and *Elegante Welt* **Russia:** First reference to Scott in press (*Vestnik Evropy*) **Sweden:** First reference to Scott in press	Scott publishes *VDR*
1813	**First French translation and first European book-length translation:** *LL* **Austria:** Extracts from *VDR* in *Wiener Allgemeine Literaturzeitung* **Germany:** Four ballads from *MSB* (W. Grimm)	**Austria:** *VDR* reviewed in *Wiener Allgemeine Literaturzeitung* **Denmark:** Nyerup refers to *MSB* in *Udvalgte Danske Viser fra Middelalderen*	Scott publishes *BT*, *RO*
1814		**Germany:** Notice of *LI* in *Morgenblatt* **Switzerland:** C. Pictet de Rochemont, 'Coup d'œil sur la littérature anglaise' in *Bibliothèque britannique* (Geneva)	Scott publishes *W*
1815	**Austria:** Extracts from *LI* in *Wiener Allgemeine Literaturzeitung* **Germany:** *LL* in *Journal des Luxus und der Moden*	**Austria:** *LI* reviewed in *Wiener Allgemeine Literaturzeitung* **France:** Stendhal alludes to *W* in MS note on Knight's *Analytical Inquiry*	Scott publishes *FW*, *GM*, *LI*; visits Belgium and France **Denmark/ Germany:** Scott included in Wiedemann's *Modern English Poems* (publ. Kiel; through 1816) **France:** L. Simond, *Journal of a Tour and Residence in Great Britain*

Date	Translations	Criticism	Other
1815 (Cont.)			**Germany:** Beethoven's *25 Scottish Songs, op. 108*, includes settings of Scott's 'Enchantress, Farewell', 'The Maid of Isla', and 'Sunset' (through 1816)
1816	**Austria:** Extracts from *GM* **France:** *GM* **Germany:** Extracts from *GM*; 'The Fire-King', 'The Maid of Neidpath' **Switzerland (French):** Extracts from *A*	**France:** *GM* reviewed in *Annales*; Stendhal refers to Scott in 'Note sur le genre romantique' **Germany:** *A* reviewed in *Jenaische Literatur-Zeitung*; *W* & *GM* discussed in *Morgenblatt* **Poland:** Translation of Pictet de Rochemont's 'Coup d'œil' (see below) in *Pamiętnik Warszawski* **Sweden:** Atterbom mentions Scott as a ballad collector in his *Poetisk kalender* **Switzerland:** Pictet de Rochemont, 'Coup d'œil sur la littérature anglaise en 1815', *Bibliothèque universelle* (expanded version of 1814)	Scott publishes *A*, *BD*, *OM*, *PLK*
1817	**First Danish translations:** 'The Last Words of Cadwallon', 'The Palmer', 'The Resolve' (all trans. Rahbek) **First German book-length translations:** *GM*, *MSB* **France:** *A*, *BD*, *OM*	**France:** Nodier reviews *BD* and *OM* in *Journal des débats* **Germany:** Platen discusses Scott in his *Tagebuch*	Scott publishes *HD*, *RR* **Germany:** A. von Arnim's uncompleted novel cycle *Die Kronenwächter*
1818	**First Dutch translation:** 'The Orphan Maid', from *LM*, trans. H. Tollens **France:** *HM*, *RR*, *W* **Germany:** Extracts from *RR* and *M*; 'The Eve of St John', 'The Maid of Toro' **Switzerland (French):** Extracts from *HM*, *LL* and *RR*	**France:** Stendhal, *Pages d'Italie* **Germany:** *RR* reviewed in *Weimarische Journal* **Spain:** First Spanish reference to Scott in *Crónica científica y literaria*	Scott publishes *HM* **Russia:** Karamzin, *Istoriya gosudarstva rossiiskogo* (through 1824)

Date	Translations	Criticism	Other
1819	**Austria:** 'Alice Brand' **Denmark:** Extracts from *BL* **France:** *BL, LM* **Germany:** *BD, RR*; first book-form version of *LL*; extracts from *BL, LM* and *OM* **Switzerland (French):** Extracts from *BL*	**France:** Hugo reviews *LM* and *BL* in *Le Conservateur littéraire*; Stendhal praises *BD* and *OM* in correspondence **Germany:** Tieck praises Scott in letter to Solger	Scott publishes *BL, I, LM* **Italy:** Rossini's opera *La donna del lago* (libretto: Tottola) based on *LL*
1820	**Denmark:** Selections from *LLM*, 'Rosabelle', 'The Twa Corbies' from *MSB* **France:** *AB, HD, I, M, MO, RO* **Germany:** *BL, I, LLM, OM*; extracts from *A, RO, W* **Switzerland (French):** Extracts from *AB, I, LL, LLM,* and *MO*	**Austria:** *I* reviewed in *Jahrbücher der Literatur* **Denmark:** Rahbek, 'Strøetanker' and 'Om Englands nyere poetiske Litteratur' (through 1821) **Denmark/Germany:** F.J. Jacobsen, *Briefe an eine deutsche Edelfrau über die neuesten englischen Dichter* **France:** Hugo reviews *I* in *Le Conservateur littéraire*; Thierry, *Lettres sur l'histoire de France* and review of *I* in *Censeur Européen* **Germany:** Hoffmann praises *GM* in letter to Hitzig; Series of articles on Scott in *Jenaische Literatur-Zeitung*	Scott publishes *AB, MO* **France:** Galignani Brothers begin publishing *WN* in English in Paris **Germany:** Haug's poem 'An Englands Dichter'
1821	**First Italian translations:** *K, LL* **First Polish translation:** *LLM* **First Swedish translation:** *I* (through 1822) **First book-length Danish translation:** *RR* **Austria:** Extracts from *HD* **France:** *K, BT, FW, LI, LLM, VDR,* and selected shorter poems (all trans. Pichot) **Germany:** *A, AB, FW, HM, K, LI, LM, MO, W*; extracts from *PLK*; 'The Violet'; C.I. Johnstone's *Clan-Albin* erroneously attributed to Scott **Switzerland (French):** 'Rosabelle'	**Austria:** *Literarischer Anzeiger* publishes review of *LL* and *LLM* and comprehensive bibliography **Austria/Germany:** Alexis reviews Scott and Byron in Viennese *Jahrbücher der Literatur* **France:** Balzac praises *K* in correspondence; Nodier reviews *WN* to date in *La Quotidienne*; Pétigny reviews *AB* & *K* in *Annales de la littérature et des arts*; Pichot, *Notice sur Sir Walter Scott et ses écrits*; Letter from Stendhal to Scott praising *AB* (possibly unsent) **Germany:** *I* reviewed in *Weimarische Journal*; *AB, MO* and *HH* reviewed in *Conversationsblatt*; *A* reviewed in *Elegante Welt*	Scott publishes *K, P* **France:** Delacroix, *Self-Portrait as Ravenswood* (approx. date); Ducange's melodrama *La Sorcière, ou, L'Orphelin écossais* (from *GM*); Nodier's travelogue *Promenade de Dieppe aux montagnes d'Ecosse*

Date	Translations	Criticism	Other
1821 (Cont.)		**Hungary:** Scott first mentioned in letter from Count J. Dessewffy to F. Kazinczy **Sweden:** V.F. Palmblad mentions Scott in *Swensk literatur-tidning*	
1822	**First Russian translations:** 'The Dreary Change', 'The Dying Bard', 'Glenfinlas', 'Helvellyn'; extracts from *LLM* **First Swedish translation:** *GM* **Denmark:** *HH, HM, I; K* (through 1825); 'The Search after Happiness' **France:** *FN, HH, P, PLK* **Germany:** *FN, HH, M, P, PLK, RO, SRW*; extracts from *LN* **Italy:** *BD, I, LM, OM, W* **Netherlands:** Extracts from *LL* (trans. Geel), 'The Fire-King' (trans. Bilderdijk) **Poland:** *LL*	**Bohemia:** Čelakovský praises Scott's poetry in a letter to Kamarýt **Denmark:** Ingemann discusses Scott in a letter to Tieck; Rahbek, 'Brev fra Senior om en Brevveksling med W. Scott' **France:** Anon, 'De Walter Scott et de ses Traducteurs' in *Miroir des Spectacles*; Chateaubriand discusses Scott in his *Mémoires d'Outretombe*; Mignet, 'Walter Scott', in Le *Courrier Français* **Germany:** *K* reviewed in *Conversationsblatt*; *FN* reviewed in *Weimarische Journal* **Slovenia:** Čop discusses Scott in correspondence	Scott publishes *FN, HH* **Austria:** Stage adaptations of *K* by Lembert and Lenz **Denmark:** Scott writes to thank Rahbek for sending a copy of *Udvalgte Danske Viser fra Middelalderen*; correspondence between Scott and Oehlenschläger **France:** Balzac, *L'Héritière de Birague* and *Clothilde de Lusignan*; Delacroix's watercolour *Abduction of Rebecca* (from *I*); Dumas's stage adaptation of *I*; Gosselin edn of works, ill. Desenne (through 1829) **Poland:** Mickiewicz's verse collection *Ballady i romanse* **Spain:** J.M. Blanco-White's novel *Vargas*
1823	**First Spanish translation:** Extracts from *I* in *Las Variedades o El Mensajero de Londres* (London) by J.-M. Blanco White **First book-length Russian translations:** *K, LLM, RO* **Denmark:** *AB, BL, FN GM, HD; MO* (through 1824); selections from *PLK*	**Austria/Germany:** Alexis reviews Zwickau edition of 'The Romances of Walter Scott' in *Jahrbücher der Literatur* **Catalonia/Spain:** López Soler, 'Análisis de la cuestion agitada entre románticos y clasicistas' **France:** Bodin reviews *QD* in *Mercure du XIXe siècle*; F. B. Hoffman, 'Des romans de Sir	Scott publishes *MC, PP, QD, SRW* **Belgium:** Prince and Princess of Orange give an *I*-themed costume ball **France:** Blanqui's travelogue *Voyage d'un jeune Français en Angleterre et en*

Date	Translations	Criticism	Other
1823 (Cont.)	**France:** *PP, QD* **Germany:** *HD, PP, QD, VDR* **Italy:** *AB, HM, MO; A* (through 1824)	Walter Scott'; Hugo reviews *QD* in *La Muse Française*; Nodier, '"Oeuvres Complètes" de Walter Scott, 2ᵉ article'; Stendhal, *Racine et Shakespeare, La Vie de Rossini*, and correspondence with Byron on Scott **Germany:** K.G. Jacobs ranks Scott alongside Goethe, Homer, Ossian, and Shakespeare in *Conversationsblatt*; Oelsner praises Scott in letter to R. Varnhagen; *QD* praised in *Conversationsblatt* **Italy:** S. Uzielli, 'Del romanzo storico di WS' (through 1824) **Norway:** M. C. Hansen discusses Scott in a letter to C. N. Schwach	*Ecosse pendant l'automne de 1823*; Delacroix, *Rebecca and the Wounded Ivanhoe* **Hungary:** Kisfaludy's short story 'A vérpohár' **Poland:** Lach-Szyrma, *Letters Literary and Political in Poland* (publ. Edinburgh); Mickiewicz's poem *Grażyna*
1824	**First book-length Dutch translations:** *BD, OM, QD, W; GM, I* (both through 1825) **Denmark:** *A, OM, M; R* (through 1825); 'The Character of the Late Lord Byron'; *Pontefract Castle* erroneously attributed to Scott **France:** *R, SRW* **Germany:** *MC, R, SRW*; 'Fielding' and 'Smollett' from *LN* **Italy:** *BL, GM, QD* **Russia:** *BD, GM, LM, OM*; 'The Wild Huntsman' **Sweden:** *HM, OM, QD; K, RR* (both through 1825); *W* (through 1826)	**Austria:** Grillparzer, 'Erinnerungsblätter' **France:** Barante, preface to *Histoires des Ducs de Bourgogne* **Germany:** Anon., 'Zur Charakteristik Walter Scotts' in *Weimarische Journal*; Anon., 'Noch ein Urteil über Walter Scott als Romandichter' in *Conversationsblatt*; *MC* reviewed in *Conversationsblatt*; *SRW* unfavourably reviewed in *Conversationsblatt* and *Wegweiser* **Italy:** S. Uzielli, 'Su *Waverley* e *Quintino Durward*'	Scott publishes *R* **Austria:** Pichler's novel *Die Belagerung Wiens* **Denmark:** Ingemann's narrative poem *Valdemar den Store og hans Mænd*; Lenz's *Das Gericht der Templer* performed in Danish (Copenhagen) **France:** Delacroix's sketch *Lucy Ashton's Bridal Night* (from *BL*) and lost painting *Leicester* (from *K*); Scheffer's painting *The Death of the Fisherman's Son* (from *A*); Thierry's essay 'Sur l'histoire d'Ecosse, et sur le caractère national des Ecossais' **Germany:** Alexis's novel *Walladmor* (attributed to Scott)

Date	Translations	Criticism	Other
1824 (Cont.)			**Poland:** K. Hoffman's novel *Listy Elżbiety Rzeczyckiej* **Russia:** Glinka's song-setting of 'The Harp' (text: Bakhturin)
1825	**First Czech translation:** 'The Fire King' (trans. Macháček) **First book-length Spanish translation:** Complete *I* (publ. London) **Denmark:** *BD, HD, LM, PP, QD* **France:** *LN, MJD, T, BET*; selections from *MSB* **Germany:** *BET, LN, T* **Italy:** *R, RR, SRW* **Netherlands:** *K, SRW; A, BET, HM, P, R, T* (all through 1826); *PP* (through 1827) **Russia:** *AB, BT, HM; A* (through 1826); 'The Character of the Late Lord Byron' **Sweden:** *BD, HH, MO; BL, PLK, PP* (all through 1826)	**Austria:** Anon., 'Literatur', in *Wiener Zeitschrift für Kunst, Literatur, Theater und Mode* **Bohemia:** Čělakovský discusses *I* and compares German and Polish translations of *LL* in letters to Kamarýt **France:** Stendhal reviews *T* and *BET* for *London Magazine* **Germany:** Gentz expresses disappointment with *K* in letter to von Pilat; W. von Humboldt recommends *GM, HM* and *I* in letter to C. Diede **Slovenia:** Short biography of Scott in *Illyrisches Blatt*	Scott publishes *BET, LN, T* **Austria:** Lembert's stage adaptation of *AB* **France:** Boieldieu's opera *La Dame Blanche* (libretto: Scribe; from *MO* and *GM*); Pichot, *Voyage historique et littéraire en Angleterre et en Écosse*; Thierry, *Histoire de la Conquête de l'Angleterre par les Normands* **Germany:** Tieck's short story 'Der Geheimnisvolle' **Norway:** M. C. Hansen's novel *Keadan eller Klosterruinen* **Poland:** A. Bronikowski's novel *Hippolyt Boratyński* (through 1826); Hoffman's novel *Dziennik Franciszki Krasińskiej*; Niemcewicz's novel *Jan z Tęczyna* **Portugal:** Garrett's poem *Camões* **Russia:** Bestuzhev's story 'Revelsky turnir'

Date	Translations	Criticism	Other
1826	**First book-length Czech translation:** *LL* (trans. Čelakovský) **Denmark:** *SRW, T; W* (through 1827); extracts from *RO*, 'Lochinvar' **France:** *MJS, MSB; WO*; 'Chivalry', 'Drama', 'Romance' **Germany:** *WO*; Immermann's translation of *I* with important preface **Italy:** *BET, T, WO* **Netherlands:** *LM, LN, RR; BL* (through 1827); 'The Eve of St John', 'The Bloody Vest' from *T* (both trans. van Lennep) **Poland:** *BD, HM, LI, RO, T* **Russia:** *I; QD* (through 1827) **Spain:** *BD, OM* (publ. France); *T* (Barcelona and London) **Sweden:** *BET, LM, SRW, R, T*, 'The Maid of Neidpath'; *AB, WO* (both through 1827); translation of Alexis's *Walladmor* (attributed to Scott)	**France:** Bazard, 'Considérations sur l'Histoire'; Jouffroy reviews Scott's complete works in *Le Globe* **Germany:** S. von G., *Walter Scott: ein romantisch-kritisirendes Gemälde seines schriftstellerischen Geistes*; Unfavourable notice of *MJS* in Gentz's diaries; *LN* praised in *Wegweiser* **Slovenia:** Longer biography and article on *NB* in *Illyrisches Blatt* **Spain:** Translations of *I* and *T* praised by A. Bello in *Repertorio Americano* (London)	Scott publishes *MJD, MJS, MM, WO*; makes second trip to Paris **Austria:** Schubert, *op. 52* (settings of seven songs from *LL*) **Denmark:** Ingemann's novel *Valdemar Seier* **France:** A. Carrel, *Résumé de l'histoire d'Ecosse*, Delacroix's watercolour *Lucy Ashton's Bridal Night*; Gosselin edition of the Waverley Novels, ill. Desenne, Lami, C-H-A. and T. Johannot (through 1828); Roqueplan's painting *Equinox Tide* (from *A*); Vigny's novel *Cinq-Mars*; *Vues pittoresques de l'Ecosse*, ill. Pernot, text Pichot **Germany:** Auffenberg's stage adaptation of *T, Der Löwe von Kurdistan* performed in Karslruhe Hauff's novel *Lichtenstein*; Heine's travel writings *Reisebilder* (through 1831); Tieck's unfinished novella *Der Aufruhr in den Cevennen* **Italy:** T. Grossi's poem *I Lombardi alla prima crociata* **Poland:** Bronikowski's novel *Mysza Wieża*; F. Bernatowicz's novel *Pojata córka Lezdejki*; F. Skarbek's novel *Tarło*

Date	Translations	Criticism	Other
1826 (Cont.)			**Portugal:** Garrett's poem *Dona Branca* **Russia:** Pushkin begins first (aborted) attempt to write a historical novel
1827	**First Hungarian translation:** *I* **Austria:** Speech revealing authorship of *WN* **Denmark:** *BET, MDY, WO,* TD; *P* (through 1828), *NB* (through 1830) **France:** *CC, NB* **Germany:** *MDY; NB* (through 1828); TD; Goethe translates 'On the Supernatural in Fictitious Composition'; extracts from *TG* **Italy:** *LI, WO; NB* (through 1828) **Netherlands:** *NB,* 'The Palmer' **Poland:** *QD*; selections from *CC* and *NB* **Russia:** *BL, LI, T, W, FW* and other poems; 'The Eve of Saint John' (trans. Zhukovskii); extracts from *NB* **Spain:** *LM, QD* (both publ. France) **Sweden:** *A, FN, P, RO; NB* (through 1830)	**Austria:** *LN* reviewed in *Wiener Zeitschrift für Kunst, Literatur, Theater und Mode* **Bohemia:** Čelakovský's letter to J. Bowring on naive and sentimental poetry **Denmark:** Article on *CC* in *Kjøbenhavnsposten* (with a translation of the introduction) **France:** J. F. Caze, *Réfutation de la 'Vie de Napoléon' de sir Walter Scott*; Gen. Gourgaud, *Réfutation de la 'Vie de Napoléon par sir Walter Scott'*; Jouy, Preface to *Cécile ou les passions*; Sainte-Beuve reviews *NB* in *Journal des débats*; Thierry's essay 'Sur les trois grandes méthodes historiques'; Vigny, 'Réflexions sur la vérité dans l'art' **Germany:** Alexis, 'Scott als Kritiker und Biograph'; C. N. Gebhardt, *Sir Walter Scott und seine deutschen Übersetzer*; Goethe expresses disappointment with *NB; WO* & *LN* praised in *Conversationsblatt* **Italy:** P. Zaiotti, 'Del romanzo in generale e dei *Promessi sposi* in particolare' **Russia:** On reading *Boris Godunov,* Tsar Nicholas I remarks that Pushkin should have written a novel in the manner of Scott; M. M. Pogodin, 'Pis'mo o russkikh romanakh'; Vyazemsky, 'Retsenziya na al'manakhi 1827 goda: Severnaya lira i dr' **Slovenia:** Notice of *CC* in *Illyrisches Blatt*	Scott publishes *CC* (HW, TD, *SD*), *MDY,* MAMM, TC, *NB* (through 1828) **Austria:** Lembert's stage adaptation of *T* **Denmark:** Blicher's short story 'Røverstuen' **France:** Stage adaptation of *OM* by Dumas and F. Soulié; Hugo's play *Cromwell* (and Preface); Roqueplan's painting *Death of the Spy Morris* (from *RR*) **Germany:** Alexis's novel *Schloß Avalon* (attributed to Scott) **Italy:** G. Bazzoni's novel *Il castello di Trezzo;* F. D. Guerrazzi's novel *La battaglia di Benevento;* Manzoni's novel *I Promessi Sposi;* C. Varese's novel *Sibilla Odaleta* **Norway:** Wergeland's poem 'Napoleon' **Poland:** Bronikowski's novel *Zawieprzyce;* Skarbek's novel *Damian Ruszczyc*

Date	Translations	Criticism	Other
1827 (Cont.)			**Russia:** I. I. Kireevsky's prose sketch 'Tsaritsynskaya noch'
1828	**Austria:** *LL* **Denmark:** *CC*, *RO*, abridged *NB*; *FMP* (through 1829) **France:** *FMP*, *RD*, 'The Cypress Wreath'; *TG* (through 1831) **Germany:** *CC*, *FMP*, *TG* (1830); MAMM **Italy:** *CC*, *LLM*, *M*, *P*, *PLK*, *PP*; *FN* (through 1829) **Netherlands:** *CC*, *RD*, 'The Crusader'; *FMP* (through 1829) **Poland:** *A*, *BL*, *GM*, *K*, *LM*, *OM* **Russia:** *BET*, *HH*, *LL*, *M*, *R*, *SRW*, *VDR*; 'The Twa Corbies' (trans. Pushkin) **Spain:** *A*, *RR* (publ. France), *BL* (Madrid) **Sweden:** *CC*, *LL*; *TG* (through 1833)	**Denmark:** Molbech's review of Ingemann's *Valdemar Seier* **France:** L. Bonaparte, *Réponse à sir Walter Scott, sur son 'Histoire de Napoléon'* **Germany:** Heine criticizes *NB* in *Neue allgemeine politische Annalen*; *CC* unfavourably reviewed in *Jenaische Zeitung* **Italy:** Mazzini reviews Zaiotti's 1827 essays on Scott and the historical novel	Scott publishes *FMP*, *RD*, *TG* (through 1831) **Bohemia:** Scott writes to thank Čelakovský for sending a copy of his translation of *LL*; Klicpera's novel *Točník* **Denmark:** Ingemann's novel *Erik Menveds Barndom* **France:** Dartois's play *Le Caleb de Walter Scott* (after *BL*); Ducange's theatrical adaptation of *BL*; Hugo's play *Amy Robsart* (with costumes by Delacroix) **Italy:** G. Bazzoni's novel *Falco della Rupe* (through 1829); Hayez's lithographs illustrating *I* (through 1829); Varese's novel *La fidanzata ligure* **Netherlands:** Van Lennep's ballad collection *Nederlandsche Legenden* **Poland:** Bernatowicz's novel *Nałęcz*; Bronikowski's novel *Kazimierz i Esterka*; Mickiewicz's poem *Konrad Wallenrod*; F. Wężyk's novel *Władysław Łokietek*

Date	Translations	Criticism	Other
1828 (Cont.)			**Portugal:** Garrett's poems *Adosinda* and *Bernal Francês* **Russia:** Pushkin's poems *Graf Nulin* and *Poltava* **Spain:** Trueba y Cossío's novel *Gómez Arias* **Sweden:** Gumælius's novel *Thord Bonde*
1829	**Denmark:** *LI*; MAMM **France:** *AG*, MAMM, TC, 'On the Supernatural in Fictitious Compostion', 'The Eve of St John' **Germany:** *AG*, *BT*, TC **Italy:** *FMP*, *RO*, 'Thomas the Rhymer' **Poland:** *BET*, *I* **Russia:** *FMP*, *FN*, *MO*, *P*, *RR*, *WO*; 'On the Supernatural in Fictitious Composition' **Spain:** *RO*, *VDR* **Sweden:** *FMP* **Switzerland (French):** TC	**France:** Balzac, 'Du roman historique et de *Fragoletta*' **Germany:** *CC* and *TG* praised in *Conversationsblatt* **Italy:** V. T., *Primo cenno storico sulla vita e sulle opere di Sir Walter Scott* **Spain:** J. Donoso Cortés recommends Scott to students in his lecture at the Colegio de Humanidades (Cáceres)	Scott publishes *AG*, *HA*, *TE*, *HS* (through 1830) **Bohemia:** Čelakovský's verse collection, *Ohlas písní ruských* **Denmark:** *TG*, vol. I publ. in English **France:** Balzac, *Les Chouans*; Gaugain publishes the lithograph suite *Illustrations de Walter Scott*, incl. contributions by Delacroix, Devéria, and Roqueplan; Delacroix's *The Murder of the Bishop at Liège* and *Quentin and the Balafré* (based on *QD*); Dumas's play *Henri III e sa cour*; P. Lacroix ('le bibliophile Jacob'), *Soirées de Walter Scott à Paris, I*; Merimée's novel *Chronique du temps de Charles IX*; Duchesse de Berry gives costume ball *Quadrille de Marie Stuart* (based on *AB*), subsequently depicted in lithographs by Lami

Date	Translations	Criticism	Other
1829 (Cont.)			**Germany:** H. Marschner's opera *Der Templer und die Jüdin* (based on *I*, libretto: W. A. Wohlbrück) **Italy:** Carafa's opera *Le nozze di Lammermoor* (libretto: Balocchi) **Poland:** Wężyk's novel *Zygmunt z Szamotuł* **Russia:** Bulgarin's novel *Dmitry Samozvanets*; Zagoskin's novel *Iurii Miloslavski* **Spain:** Trueba y Cossío's novel *The Castilian*
1830	**Denmark:** *AG*; Galt's *The Omen* erroneously attributed to Scott **France:** *HA* **Germany:** *HS* **Italy:** *AG* (through 1831), *AU*, *HA*, *MAMM*, *TC*, 'On the Supernatural in Fictitious Composition', 'On Planting Waste Lands' **Netherlands:** *AG* (through 1834) **Poland:** *MO*, *P*, *RR*, *W*; *AB* (through 1832) **Russia:** *AG*, *LDW*, *PP*, *SD* **Spain:** *BT*, *LI*, *LL*, *P*, *MAMM*, *TC*; ecclesiastical censor refuses Morales Pantoja permission to publish translation of *I* **Sweden:** *FW*	**France:** A. de Custine, *Mémoires et voyages*; Stendhal, 'Walter Scott et la *Princesse de Clèves*' **Hungary:** Széchenyi's treatise *Hitel* **Italy:** G. Bianchetti, 'Del romanzo storico'; Zaiotti, 'Del romanzo storico' and 'Delle descrizioni ne' romanzi, sulla *Battaglia di Benevento*'	Scott publishes *AU*, *LDW*; appeals to citizens of Edinburgh to tolerate presence of Bourbon Court **France:** Delacroix's lithograph *Ravenswood and Lucy by the Fountain* (based on *BL*); Furne edn of Works, ill. C-H-A. and T. Johannot (through 1832); Stendhal's novel *Le Rouge et le Noir* **Italy:** Varese's novel *Folchetto Malaspina* **Poland:** Bronikowski's novel *Jan III Sobieski i dwór jego*; Z. Krasiński's novel *Władysław Herman i dwór jego* **Spain:** López Soler's novel *Los bandos de Castilla*

Date	Translations	Criticism	Other
1830 (Cont.)			**Sweden:** C. Graffman's paintings *Skottska vuer* (pub. as lithographs, 1832)
1831	**France:** *CD*, *CRP* **Italy:** *FW*, 'The Dance of Death' **Russia:** *CRP* **Spain:** *AG*, *HM*, *WO* (Madrid), *K* (France)	**France:** P. Chasles, 'Chefs-d'oeuvre des romanciers anglais'; Stendhal, 'Sur le *Rouge et le Noir*' **Italy:** G. Scalvini, 'Alessandro Manzoni, *I Promessi Sposi*'	Scott publishes *CD*, *CRP*; travels to Italy **Denmark:** Gibbons's *The Cavalier* misattributed to Scott in Danish translation **France:** Delacroix's painting *Cromwell at Windsor* (from *WO*); Hugo, *Notre-Dame de Paris*; Lacroix, *Soirées de Walter Scott à Paris, II*; Roqueplan's painting and lithograph *The Pardon Refused* (from *K*); Sue's novel *Plik et Plok* **Russia:** Gogol's short-story collection *Vechera na khutore bliz Dikan'ki* (through 1832); Kornilovich's short story 'Andrei Bezymennyi'; Lazhechnikov's novel *Poslednik novik* (through 1832); Lermontov's poem 'Zhelanie'; Pushkin's poems *Boris Godunov* and 'Shumit Kustarnik'; Zagoskin's novel *Roslavlev* **Sweden:** *Snapphanarne*, novel by 'O.K.'

Date	Translations	Criticism	Other
1832	**Denmark:** *CRP*, Collected Works (through 1856; various translators) **France:** *LDW* **Italy:** *CRP* (through 1833) **Netherlands:** *HS* (through 1834) **Sweden:** *AG*, 'On Planting Waste Lands'	**France:** Obituaries by Lamartine, Pichot, and Sainte-Beuve **Germany:** Alexis, 'Walter Scott'; *NB* unfavourably reviewed in *Jenaische Literatur-Zeitung*; obituary in *Elegante Welt* **Hungary:** Obituary in *Társalkodó* **Italy:** F. Beltrame, 'Alcuni cenni sui romanzi di W. Scott al chiarissimo signore Defendente Sacchi di Pavia'; C. Varese, 'Di Rossini e di Walter Scott messi a confronto come genii di indole identica'	Scott dies 21 September **Bohemia:** Mácha's prose fragments *Pout' krkonošská* and *Kláster sázavsky* **Bohemia/ Germany:** Prague-born Karl Herloßsohn's novel *Der Ungar* **Denmark:** *Bruden fra Lammermoor*, Bredal's operatic version of *BL* (libretto: H. C. Andersen, including a translation of 'The Twa Corbies') **France:** Delavigne's painting *Louis XI* (from *QD*); Lamartine's poem 'Réponse aux adieux de Walter Scott à ses lecteurs' **Italy:** Varese's novel *Preziosa di Sanluri* **Poland:** J. Słowacki's drama *Maria Stuart* **Russia:** Lermontov's poem *Izmail-Bei* **Spain:** P. de Escosura's novel *El conde de Candespina* **Sweden:** Sparre's novel *Den siste friseglaren*
1833	**Denmark:** *TG* (through 1839) **France:** *MC*; *HS* (through 1835) **Germany:** *LDW* **Italy:** *BT*, *HD*, 'Cadyow Castle' **Mexico:** First Spanish translation of *W* (Heredia)	**Denmark:** J. L. Heiberg, *Om Philosophiens Betydning for den nuværende Tid*; Oehlenschläger, 'Om det Musikalske, det Philophiske, det Maleriske og det Historiske i Poesien' **France:** Chasles, 'L'Influence exercée par Walter Scott sur la richesse, la moralité et le	**Catalonia:** Aribau's poem 'La pàtria' **Denmark:** Ingemann's novel *Kong Erik og de Fredløse*; Translation of Bulwer-Lytton's 'Death of Sir Walter Scott'

Date	Translations	Criticism	Other
1833 (Cont.)	**Netherlands:** *FN* **Poland:** *NB* (selections) **Russia:** *CD*, *NB* **Spain:** *R* (through 1834)	bonheur de la société actuelle' (adaptation of H. Martineau's 'Achievements of the Genius of Scott'); H. Fortoul, 'De l'art actuel'; J. M. F. Frantine, *Walter Scott*; D. Nisard, 'D'un commencement de réaction contre la littérature facile' **Germany:** K. A. von Varnhagen, *Zur Geschichtschreibung und Literatur*, G. von Kraemer, *Leben und Werke Walter Scott's* **Hungary:** J. Bajza, 'A románköltésről' **Russia:** O. Senkovskii, 'Istoricheskii roman: po povodu romana *Mazepa* F. Bulgarina' **Spain:** Anon., 'Influencia de las obras de Walter Scout en la generación actual' in *El vapor*	**France:** P. Barbot's painting *The Forest of Woodstock*; Delacroix's painting *The Knight and the Hermit of Copmanhurst* (from *I*); Gigoux's painting *Elizabeth of England* (from *K*); A. Lavaudan's painting *Abdication of Mary Stuart* (from *AB*); A. J. Régnier's painting *Landscape (Old Mortality)* **Italy:** M. D'Azeglio's novel *Ettore Fieramosca* **Netherlands:** Van Lennep's novel *De Pleegzoon* **Poland:** J. I. Kraszewski's novels *Rok ostatni panowania Zygmunta III* and *Kościół Święto-Michalski w Wilnie* **Russia:** Bulgarin's novel *Mazepa* (through 1834) **Spain:** Duque de Rivas's poem *El moro expósito*
1834	**First book-length Portuguese translation:** *W* **Denmark:** 'Fielding' and 'Smollett' from *LN* **Netherlands:** *AB*; extracts from *HD*, *LLM*, and from *RO*, 'The Eve of St John', 'The Maid of Toro', 'Song of the Dawn' (all trans. Beets) **Spain:** *CRP*	**France:** J. Janin, 'Manifeste de la jeune littérature'; Thierry, Preface to *Dix ans d'études historiques* **Sweden:** Bremer discusses Scott in letter to Böklin	**Bohemia:** Mácha's novel *Křivoklad* **Denmark:** Hauch's novel *Vilhelm Zabern* **France** Pichot's collection of tales *Le Perroquet de Walter Scott* **Germany:** Translation of Cunningham's *Biographical and Critical History* **Hungary:** F.S. Bölöni's travelogue *Napnyugati utazás*

Date	Translations	Criticism	Other
1834 (Cont.)			**Italy:** Grossi's novel *Marco Visconti* **Poland:** Mickiewicz's poem *Pan Tadeusz* **Russia:** Gogol's novel *Taras Bulba*; Pushkin's essay *Istoriya Pugachova* **Spain:** Espronceda's novel *Sancho Saldaña*
1835	**France:** 'The Palmer' (trans. Antony-Béraud) **Italy:** *TG* **Portugal:** *T* (through 1836) **Spain:** *GM* (France)	**Hungary:** G. Czuczor, 'Szellemi mozgás Angliában, s annak haladása, tekintettel más európai nemzetekre' **Spain:** Bergnes de la Casa's translation of Chasles's 'L'Influence exercée par Walter Scott'	**Bohemia:** Mácha's novel *Cikáni*; Filípek translates Auffenberg's German adaptation of *T* **Denmark:** Ingemann's novel *Prins Otto af Danmark og hans Samtid* **France:** Translations of Washington Irving's *Abbotsford and Newstead Abbey* and L. Ritchie's *Scott and Scotland* **Germany:** Translation of extracts from Hogg's *Domestic Manners and Private Life of Sir Walter Scott* **Hungary:** J. Gaal's short story 'Gyűlölség és szerelem' **Italy:** Donizetti's opera *Lucia di Lammermoor* (libretto: Cammarano) **Russia:** Lazhechnikov's novel *Ledianoi dom*

Date	Translations	Criticism	Other
1836	**Bohemia (Czech):** *LLM* **Denmark:** *LL* **Hungary:** *TC* **Netherlands:** *LDW* **Poland:** *SD* **Portugal:** *BL*; 'Alice Brand' **Spain:** *FMP, FN, PP* (all publ. France)	**Austria:** Feuchtersleben, 'Scott und Bulwer' and 'Moderne poetische Literatur'; A. Schöll, 'Joseph Freyherr von Eichendorff's Schriften' **France:** J. M. Quérard, 'Walter Scott' in *La France littéraire* **Russia:** M. I. Lunin, 'O vliyanii Val'ter Skotta na noveishie izyskaniya po chasti srednei istorii'	**Bohemia:** Mácha's epic poem *Máj* and prose fragment *Valdice* **Denmark:** H. C. Andersen's novel *O.T.*; Blicher's novella 'Fjorten Dage i Jylland'; Ingemann's novel *Dronning Margrethe*; *Festen paa Kenilworth*; Weyse's operatic version of *K* (libretto: H.C. Andersen) **France:** N. E. Maurin's lithograph suite *Ivanhoe*; Pourrat edn of Works, ill. Raffet **Germany:** Immermann's novel *Die Epigonen* **Hungary:** Gaal's novel *Szirmay Ilona*; Jósika's novel *Abafi*; L. Nagy's short story 'Ida'; Petrichevich's novel *Az elbujdosott* **Italy:** Guerrazzi's novel *L'assedio di Firenze* **Netherlands:** Van Lennep's novel *De Roos van Dekama* **Russia:** Lazhechnikov's novel *Basurman*; Pushkin's novella *Kapitanskaya dochka* (*The Captain's Daughter*)
1837	**Bohemia:** Extracts from *T* translated into Czech verse by J. K. Tyl **Netherlands:** 'Lay of the Imprisoned Huntsman', 'Rebecca's Hymn' **Poland:** *WO* **Portugal:** *I, OM, T* (all publ. Paris); *BET, LM,* 'The Fire-King'; 'The Fiery Cross' from *LL* (all publ. Portugal)	**Italy:** G. B. Nicolini, *Sul romanzo storico*	**Bohemia:** Six *tableaux vivantes* inspired by *I* and *T* produced in Prague **France:** Balzac, *Illusions perdues*; Devéria's lithograph *Minna and Brenda*

Date	Translations	Criticism	Other
1837 (Cont.)			**Hungary:** S. Hegedűs's poem 'Walter Scotthoz' **Sweden:** Bremer's novel *Grannarne*
1838	**Netherlands:** 'Jock of Hazeldean', 'Lochinvar' (trans. Tollens) **Poland:** 'Cadyow Castle', 'The Eve of St. John'	**France:** Thiébault, *Trois jours passés à Abbotsford*	**France:** Balzac, *Le Cabinet des antiques; Splendeurs et Misères des Courtisanes* (through 1847); Pourrat edn of *QD*, ill. Fragonard
1839	**Portugal:** *BD, HM* (both publ. Paris); *QD* (Lisbon, through 1839) **Italy:** *LDW* **Portugal:** *LI*; extracts from *LL* **Russia:** 'Jock of Hazeldean', 'Macgregor's Gathering', 'Rosabelle' (trans. Pavlova)	**Germany:** Mörike praises Scott in letter to H. Kurz **Sweden:** E. G. Geijer reviews Lockhart's biography	**Italy:** Cantù's novel *Margherita Pusterla*; Guerrazzi's novel *Veronica Cybo* **Switzerland:** Extracts from Lockhart's *Memoirs* in *Bibliothèque universelle* **Ukraine:** H. Kvitka-Osnovianenko's short story 'Kozyr-Divka' **France:** Stendhal's novel *La Chartreuse de Parme* **Germany:** Translation of Lockhart's *Memoirs*
1840	**Bohemia (Czech):** *OM* **Netherlands:** *LLM* **Portugal:** *FMP* **Spain:** *AB, BET, CD, M* (all publ. France)	**France:** Balzac, 'Fenimore Cooper et Walter Scott' and 'Etudes sur M. Beyle' **Italy:** Nicolini, 'Gualtiero Scott' **Russia:** Belinskii, 'Mentsel' kritik Gete' **Spain:** A. Lista, 'De la novela'	**Austria:** Production of ballet *Das Schloß Kenilworth* (based on *K*) **France:** Roqueplan's painting *Lucy Ashton and the Master of Ravenswood* (from *BL*); spurious *Allan Cameron* **Germany/Italy:** C. O. Nicolai's opera *Il templario* (based on *I*, libretto: G. M. Marini) **Poland:** M. Grabowski's novel *Stanica hulajpolska* (through 1841)

Date	Translations	Criticism	Other
1840 (Cont.)			**Romania:** Negruzzi's short story 'Alexandru Lapusneanu' **Russia:** Lermontov's novel *A Hero of Our Time* and poem 'Kazach'ya kolybel'naya pesnya'
1841	**Bohemia (Czech):** Extract from *I* (Tyl) **Italy:** *VDR* **Portugal:** *K*; 'The Maid of Toro' **Spain:** *SRW* (publ. France)	**Germany:** Schlegel, *Geschichte der alten und neuen Literatur*	**Austria:** Sealsfield's novel *Das Cajütenbuch* **France:** Balzac, *Le Martyr calviniste* **Italy:** D'Azeglio's novel *Niccolò de' Lapi*
1842	**Poland:** *LLM* **Portugal:** *CD, GM, LL, MO*	**France:** Balzac, 'Avant-propos' to *La Comédie Humaine* **Catalonia/Spain:** Milà Fontanals, 'Moral literaria: contraste entre la escuela escéptica y Walter Scott'	**France:** Balzac's 'Avant-propos' to the *Comédie humaine* **Russia:** Gogol's novel *Mertyve dushi* (Dead souls)
1843	**Italy:** *CD* **Portugal:** *AG; WO* (through 1843) **Spain:** *LLM*	**Hungary:** Petrichevich, 'Jósika Miklós regényeiről s a regényirodalomrúl általában'	**France:** Spurious *Aymé Verd*; Balzac, *Les Illusions perdues*, *La Muse du Département*; De Rudder's painting *John Balfour de Burley* (from *OM*); Dumas's novel *Le Chevalier d'Harmental*
1844	**Germany:** Selected poems in Freiligrath's *Gedichte* **Portugal:** *AB* **Spain:** Translation of Jules Antoine David's *La Pythie des Highlands* credited to Scott	**Austria:** Bauerfeld, Introduction to *The Pickwick Papers* **Catalonia/Spain:** Milà Fontanals, *Compendio del arte poética* and review of *SRW* in *El imparcial*	**France:** Dumas's novels *Les Trois Mousquetaires* and *Le Comte de Monte Cristo* (through 1845); Barba edn of Works, ill. Jaque; *Huit pièces sur des thèmes de Walter Scott*, ill. C. Jacquand and H. Lecomte **Hungary:** I. Gorove's travelogue *Nyugot* **Spain:** Gil y Carrasco's novel *El señor de Bembibre*

Date	Translations	Criticism	Other
1845	**Russia:** Aborted attempt to bring out newly translated critical edition of *WN*	**Bohemia:** K. Sabina, 'Úvod povahopisny' (incl. Mácha's possibly apocryphal remarks on Scott) **Italy:** Manzoni, 'Del romanzo storico e, in genere, dei componimenti misti di storia e d'invenzione'	**France:** Dumas's novel *Vingts ans après* **Poland:** H. Rzewuski's novel *Listopad* **Portugal:** Garrett's novel *O Arco de Santana* (through 1850) **Russia:** Dostoevsky's novel *Bedn'ie liudi* (Poor folk) **Spain:** V. Boix's poem 'A la memoria de Walter Scott'
1846			**France:** Delacroix's second *Abduction of Rebecca*; Scheffer's painting *The Bride of Lammermoor* **Hungary:** Jókai's novel *Hétköznapok*
1847	**First Greek translation:** *I* (publ. Izmir, Turkey)	**Hungary:** I. Zilahy, 'A történeti regény' **Spain:** J.E. Hartzenbusch, 'Apuntes sobre el carácter de la literatura contemporánea'	**France:** Balzac, *Le Cousin Pons* **Hungary:** Eötvös's novel *Magyarország 1514-ben* **Spain:** F. Navarro Villoslada's novel *Doña Blanca de Navarra*
1848			**Denmark:** H. C. Andersen's novel *De to Baronesser* **France:** Balzac, *L'Envers de l'histoire contemporaine*; Dumas's novel, *Le Vicomte de Bragelonne* (through 1849) **Portugal:** Herculano's novel *O Monge de Cister* **Russia:** Dostoevsky's novellas *Bel'ikh*

Date	Translations	Criticism	Other
1848 (Cont.)			nochakh (White nights) and *Netochka Nezvanova* (through 1849); Zagoskin's novel *Russkie v nachale os'mnadtsatogo stoletiia* **Spain:** Navarro Villoslada's novel *Doña Urraca de Castilla*
1849	**France:** Complete works, trans. L. Barré (through 1857)	**Denmark/Sweden:** Molbech, Letter to Atterbom on historical novels **Russia:** T. N. Granovskii, *Lektsii po istorii Srednevekov'ya* (through 1850)	**Spain:** Fernán Caballero's novel *La Gaviota*
1850		**France:** Chasles, *Etudes sur la littérature et les moeurs de l'Angleterre au 19ᵉ siècle*	**France:** Dumas's novel *La Tulipe Noire* **Spain:** P. de Escosura's novel *La conjuración de Méjico*
1852	**Portugal:** 'The Gray Brother'		**France:** Barbey d'Aurevilly's novel *L'Ensorcelée*; Government commissions Pottin to portray *The Devotion of Lady Catherine Douglas* (from *TG*) **Hungary:** Jókai's novel *Erdély aranykora*
1853	**Hungary:** 'Sir Patrick Spens' from *MSB* (trans. Arany) **Sweden:** Complete *WN* (through 1858)		**Catalonia:** Milà Fontanals's traditional ballad collection *Romancerillo catalán* **Germany:** Selections from Scott in Freiligrath's English-language anthology *The Rose, Thistle and Shamrock* **Hungary:** Jókai's novels *Egy magyar nabob* and *Török világ Magyarországon*

Date	Translations	Criticism	Other
1854		**Catalonia/Spain:** Milà Fontanals, 'Poemas de Walter Scott'	**Austria:** Breier's novel *Die beiden Grasel* **France:** Balzac, *Les Petits Bourgeois* (posthumous publication) **Hungary:** Jókai's novels *Janicsárok végnapjai* and *Fehér rózsa* **Italy:** Signorini's painting *The Puritans of the Castle of Tillietudlem*
1855	**Denmark:** New edition of Collected Novels (some newly translated; through 1871)	**France:** Delécluze, *David, son école et son temps* **Italy:** Bianchetti, *Dello scrittore italiano*	**Denmark:** H. C. Andersen's autobiography *Mit Livs Eventyr*; Winther's poem *Hjortens Flugt* **Germany:** J. V. von Scheffel's novel *Ekkehard* **Hungary:** Kemény's novel *Özvegy és leánya* (through 1857)
1857	**First Romanian translations:** *BL, T* **France:** *AU, DD, IB*	**Italy:** Tommaseo, *Bellezza e civiltà*	**France:** Flaubert, *Madame Bovary* **Hungary:** Gyulai's novella *Egy régi udvarház utolsó gazdája* **Norway:** Ibsen's play *Fru Inger til Østråt*
1858			**France:** Delacroix's second *Rebecca and the Wounded Ivanhoe* and third *Abduction of Rebecca* **Hungary:** Kemény's novel *A rajongók*
1859		**France:** Delacroix critical of Scott in *Journal*	**Russia:** Goncharov's novel *Oblomov*
1860		**Germany:** F. Eberty, *Walter Scott* **Spain:** Duque de Rivas praises WS in his inaugural speech at the Real Academia	**France:** Pichot's collection of tales *L'Ecolier de Walter Scott*

Date	Translations	Criticism	Other
1860 (Cont.)			**Germany:** Fontane's travelogue *Jenseits des Tweed: Bilder und Briefe aus Schottland* **Romania:** Odobescu's novels *Mihnea Vodă cel Rău* and *Doamna Chiajna*
1861	**Germany:** Fontane translates 'The Twa Corbies' from *MSB*	**Austria:** Heckenast discusses Scott in his correspondence **Slovenia:** Jurčič records reading Scott in his notebooks	**Hungary:** Jókai's novel *Szegény gazdagok* **Norway:** Munch's novel *Pigen fra Norge* **Russia:** Dostoevsky, *Peterburgskie snovideniya*
1862	**France:** Dumas's translation of *I*	**France:** Vallès, 'Les Victimes du Livre'	**France:** Verne, *Voyage à reculons en Angleterre et en Ecosse* (published 1989) **Hungary:** Kemény's novel *Zord idő* **Russia:** A.K. Tolstoy's novel *Kniazia Serebrianogo*
1863		**France:** Taine, *Histoire de la littérature anglaise*	**France:** Barbey d'Aurevilly's novel, *Le Chevalier des Touches* **Russia:** Tolstoy's novel *Kazaki* (The Cossacks)
1864	**Greece:** *T*	**Germany:** K. Elze, *Sir Walter Scott*	**Norway:** Ibsen's play *Kongsemnere* **Slovenia:** Jurčič's novella *Jurij Kozjak*
1865	**First Croatian translation:** Selections from *M* **First Slovenian translation:** Jurčič translates incipit to *K* in his notebooks **Bohemia (Czech):** *I* **Greece:** *BL, GM*	**Bohemia:** Neruda reviews Czech translation of *I*	**Austria:** Stifter's novel *Witiko* (through 1867) **Russia:** Tolstoy's novel *Voyna i mir* (War and Peace)
1866		**Slovenia:** Levec praises *A* in his correspondence	**Slovenia:** Jurčič's novel *Deseti brat* and novella *Hči mestnega sodnika*

Date	Translations	Criticism	Other
1867	**First Serbian translation:** *LL*		**France:** Bizet's opera *La Jolie Fille de Perth*, based on *FMP* (libretto: Vernoy de Saint-Georges & Adenis)
1868	**Greece:** *HD, LI* (both through 1869)		
1869			**France:** Flaubert, *L'Education Sentimentale* **Netherlands:** Translation of Eberty's *Walter Scott* **Russia:** Dostoevsky's unfinished novel *Zhitie velikogo greshnika*; Turgenev's short story 'Neschastnaya'
1870	**First Finnish translation:** *I* **Spain:** *LDW* (approx. date; publ. between 1870 and 1880)		**Spain:** Galdós's novel *La fontana de oro*
1871	**First Norwegian translation:** *LL* **Finland:** *BL, LM* **Hungary:** 'Jock of Hazeldean'	**Hungary:** T. Szana, 'Walter Scott' **Russia:** Turgenev gives speech in praise of Scott during Centenary festivities in Edinburgh	Centenary of Scott's birth
1872	**Sweden:** *LLM*		**Germany:** Freytag's novel cycle *Die Ahnen* (through 1880) **Spain:** Galdós's novel *El audaz*
1873			**Hungary:** Translation of Carlyle's 'Walter Scott' **Spain:** Galdós's novel *Trafalgar*
1874	**Finland:** *BD* **Hungary:** *BL, PP*	**Germany:** S. Gätschenberger, *Geschichte der Englischen Dichtkunst* (publ. London); J. Scherr, *Geschichte der Englischen Literatur*	
1875	**Bohemia (Czech):** *W*	**Denmark:** Brandes, *Naturalismen i England* (German translation: 1876) **Hungary:** T. Szana, 'A történelmi regény és Walter Scott'	

Date	Translations	Criticism	Other
1876	**Finland:** *QD*	**Germany:** K. Bandow, *Charakterbilder aus der Geschichte der Englischen Litteratur*; B. Tschischwitz, 'Introduction' to his new translation of *QD*	**Germany:** F. Dahn's novel *Ein Kampf um Rom*
1877	**Bohemia (Czech):** *K*	**Hungary:** F. Riedl, 'Kemény Zsigmond és Walter Scott'	**France:** Verne, *Les Indes-Noires* **Italy:** Carducci's poem 'Alle fonti del Clitumno' **Norway:** Bjørnson's play *Kongen* **Spain:** A. de Escalante's novel *Ave Maris Stella*
1878	**Finland:** *FMP*		**Denmark:** Translation of Elze's *Sir Walter Scott* **Germany:** Fontane's novel *Vor dem Sturm*
1879		**Italy:** E. Solazzi, *Letteratura inglese*	**Switzerland:** Meyer's novella *Der Heilige*
1880	**Finland:** *T* **Romania:** 'The Maid of Toro'		**Sweden:** Fröding's poems 'Claverhouse' and 'Abbotsford'
1881	**First Latvian translation:** *AG*	**Germany:** J. Scherr, *Allgemeine Geschichte der Literatur*	**France:** Flaubert, *Bouvard et Pécuchet* **Italy:** Signorini's painting *Leith* **Russia:** V. S. Solovev's novel *Sergei Gorbatov*
1882	**Spain:** *TD*	**Germany:** L. Hierthes, *Wörterbuch des schottischen Dialekts in den Werken von Walter Scott und Burns* **Sweden:** G. Lunggren, *Några anmärkningar om Walter Scott och hans romandiktning*	**Germany:** Fontane's novel *Schach von Wuthenow* **Russia:** Turgenev's short story 'Klara Milich'
1883		**Germany:** E. Engel, *Geschichte der Englischen Literatur*; O. von Leixner, *Illustrirte Geschichte der fremden Literaturen* **Slovenia:** Celestin, 'Naše obzorje V.'	**Hungary:** Jókai's novel *Bálványosvár*

Date	Translations	Criticism	Other
1884		**France:** W. Sime, 'Scott's Influence in French Literature' **Italy:** A. Borgognoni, 'Alessandro Manzoni'	**Poland:** Sienkiewicz's novel *Ogniem i mieczem*
1885		**Italy:** F. D'Ovidio, 'Appunti per un parallelo tra Manzoni e Walter Scott'; G. M. Gamna, 'Tommaso Grossi e i *Lombardi alla prima crociata*'; F. Torraca, 'Di alcune fonti dei *Promessi Sposi*'	**France:** Coppée's play *Les Jacobites*
1886		**Germany:** O. Wiencke, *Über Walter Scotts 'The Lady of the Lake'*	**France:** Vallès's autobiographical novel *L'Insurgé* **Poland:** Sienkiewicz's novel *Potop*
1887		**Germany:** K. Bleibtreu, *Geschichte der englischen Litteratur im neunzehnten Jahrhundert*	**Poland:** Sienkiewicz's novel *Pan Wołodyjowski*
1888	**First Estonian translation:** QD **Hungary:** 'Lochinvar'	**Sweden:** G. H. J. Ljunggren, *Några anmärkningar om Walter Scott och hans romandiktning*	**Germany:** Raabe's novel *Das Odfeld*
1889		**Italy:** F. De Sanctis, *La giovinezza*; G. Fenaroli, *Svaghi letterari*	
1890	**Croatia:** *I* (abridged) **Hungary:** 'The Fire-King'		
1891	**Spain:** Collected Novels (publ. France, through 1920) **Switzerland:** Extracts from *J* in *Bibliothèque universelle*	**Italy:** G. Brognoligo, '*Ivanhoe* e i *Lombardi alla prima crociata*' **Russia:** A. I. Kirpichnikov, *Val'ter Skott i Viktor Giugo*; A. Paevskaya, *Valter Skott: ego zhizn i literaturnaya deyatelnost biograficheskii ocherk*	Publication of *J*
1893		**Germany:** G. Opitz, *Die stabreimenden Wortbindungen in den Dichtungen Walter Scotts*	
1894	**Estonia:** *T*	**France:** G. Saintsbury, 'The Historical Novel: Scott and Dumas'	**Russia:** Translation of Elze's *Sir Walter Scott*
1895		**Russia:** P. D. Boborykin, 'Angliiskoe vliyanie v Rossii'	
1896	**Bohemia (Czech):** *QD* (or 1897) **Hungary:** *LL* **Poland:** Extracts from *J*	**Germany:** R. Wülcker, *Geschichte der Englischen Litteratur*	
1897		**Italy:** A. Dobelli, 'Di alcune fonti manzoniane'; C. Segrè, *Profili storici e letterari*	

Date	Translations	Criticism	Other
1898	**Bohemia (Czech):** Selected poems in J. Vrchlický's *Moderní básníci angličtí*	**France:** L. Maigron, *Le Roman historique à l'époque romantique: essai sur l'influence de Walter Scott* **Italy:** P. Bellezza, *Intorno ai presunti convegni del Chaucer col Petrarca e del Manzoni collo Scott*	
1899	**First Bulgarian translation:** *BL* **Latvia:** *T* (abridged)	**Germany:** Leixner, *Geschichte der fremden Literaturen*	
1900	**Serbia:** *I*	**Italy:** G. Burgada, '*Il Talismano* di W. Scott e i *Promessi Sposi*'; M. Dotti, 'Derivazioni nei *Promessi Sposi* di A. Manzoni dai romanzi di W. Scott'	
1901		**Germany:** C. Gaebel, *Beiträge zur Technik der Erzählung in den Romanen Walter Scotts*	
1902		**Denmark:** A. Hansen, *Den engelske og den nordamerikanske Litteraturs Historie i Omrids* **Germany:** R. Ackermann, *Kurze Geschichte der englischen Litteratur in den Grundzügen ihrer Entwicklung*; J. S. Henderson, 'Heine and Sir Walter Scott' **Italy:** A. Albertazzi, *Il romanzo*	
1903		**Germany:** R. Abramczyk, *Über die Quellen zu Walter Scotts Roman 'Ivanhoe'*; A. Siebert, *Untersuchungen zu Walter Scotts 'Waverley'* **Italy:** L. Darchini, *Storia della letteratura inglese*	
1904	**Finland:** *W*	**Germany:** J. Gaerdes, *Walter Scott als Charakterzeichner in 'The Heart of Midlothian'*	
1905	**Hungary:** *QD*	**Germany:** K. Wenger, *Historische Romane deutscher Romantiker* (publ. Switzerland) **Italy:** P. Adiletta, *Le fonti del 'Marco Visconti' in alcuni romanzi storici di Walter Scott* **Slovenia:** D. Šanda, 'Jurčič–Scott'	
1906		**France:** V. E. Frangois, 'Sir Walter Scott and Alfred de Vigny' **Italy:** G. Agnoli, *Gli albori del romanzo storico in Italia e i primi imitatori di Walter Scott*; L. Fassò, 'Saggio di ricerche intorno alla fortuna di Walter Scott in Italia'	

Date	Translations	Criticism	Other
1907	**Spain:** *CC*	**Germany:** H. A. Korff, *Scott und Alexis*	
1908		**Catalonia:** Menéndez Pelayo, *El Doctor Manuel Milá y Fontanals* **France:** D. Gunnel, *Stendhal et l'Angleterre*	
1909	**Bohemia (Czech):** Prose abridgements of *LI, LL*	**Germany:** P. W. Franke, *Der Stil in den epischen Dichtungen Walter Scotts*	
1910	**First Icelandic translation:** *I* **Norway:** *K*	**Germany:** G. Körting, *Grundriss der Geschichte der englischen Literatur;* C. Wegmann, *Theodor Fontane als Ubersetzer englischer und schottischer Balladen*	
1911	**Romania:** HW	**Germany:** A. Petri, *Über Walter Scotts Dramen;* G. W. Thompson, 'Wilhelm Hauff's Specific Relation to Walter Scott'	
1912	**Finland:** *K* **Norway:** *I* (through 1913)	**France:** Saintsbury, 'Scott and Balzac' **Italy:** F. Flamini, 'Walter Scott e il romanzo storico in Italia'	
1913	**Finland:** *HW* **Norway:** *T*	**France/Russia:** E. Haumant, *La Culture française en Russie* **Germany:** F. Hackenberg, *Elise von Hohenhausen* (on an early translator of Scott); F. Knothe, *Untersuchungen zu 'Redgauntlet' von Walter Scott;* A. W. Porterfield, '*Ivanhoe* Translated by Immermann' **Hungary:** A. Yolland, 'Walter Scott's Influence on Jósika'; Z. Ferenc, 'Scott és Jósika' **Italy:** R. Ripari, *Romantic and Non-Romantic Elements in the Works of Walter Scott*	**Sweden:** Posthumous publication of Fröding's poem 'Den kuvade klanen'
1914	**Finland:** *FN, GM*	**France:** H. Brémond, 'Walter Scott et le Romantisme conservateur' **Germany:** H. Rhyn, *Die Balladendichtung Theodor Fontanes: mit bes. Berücks. seiner Bearb. altengl. u. altschott. Balladen aus d. Sammlungen von Percy u. Scott* **Italy:** F. Olivero, *Studi sul romanticismo inglese* **Poland:** S. Windakiewicz, *Walter Scott i Lord Byron w odniesieniu do polskiej poezji romantycznej*	

Date	Translations	Criticism	Other
1915	**Finland:** *WO*	**Germany:** D. Binkert, *Historische Romane von Walter Scott*; H. F. Kohler, *'Walladmor' von Willibald Alexis: Untersuchung des Romans in seinem Verhältnis zu Walter Scott*; W. A. Paterna, *Das Übersinnliche im englischen Roman: von Horace Walpole bis Walter Scott* **Hungary:** Z. Ferenczi, 'A százéves Waverley' **Italy:** E. Cecchi, *Storia della letteratura inglese nel secolo XIX*	**Germany:** Döblin's novel *Die drei Sprünge des Wang-lun*
1916	**Iceland:** *CRP*		
1918		**Germany:** L. Sigmann, *Die englische Literatur von 1800– 1850 im Urteil der zeitgenössischen deutschen Kritik* **Italy:** G. Brognoligo, 'Traduttori italiani di Walter Scott'	
1919		**Catalonia:** A. Rubió Lluch and C. Parpal Marqués, *Milá y Fontanals y Rubió y Ors* **France:** J. M. Devonshire, 'The "Decline" of Sir Walter Scott in France' **Norway:** E. Høye, *Sir Walter Scott: nogen bemerkninger om hans historiske roman* **Poland:** K. Wojciechowski, *'Pan Tadeusz' Mickiewicza a romans Waltera Scotta*	
1920	**Serbia:** *A* (approx. date)	**Denmark:** J. Martensen, *Walter Scott: En Fortælling om hans Liv* **France:** B. M. Woodbridge, 'The Scotts in France' **Scandinavia (General):** P. R. Leeder, *Scott and Scandinavian Literature*	**Germany:** Döblin's novel *Wallenstein*
1921	**Bosnia:** *K* (reprinted Serbia, 1927) **Hungary:** *BD*	**Hungary:** G. Voinovich, 'Scott Walter'	**France:** Proust, *Sodome et Gomorrhe* (through 1822) **Russia:** M. Aldonov's fictional tetralogy *Myslitel'* (through 1927)

Date	Translations	Criticism	Other
1922	**First Catalan translation:** *T* **First Lithuanian translation:** *I*	**Germany:** W. Dibelius, *Englische Romankunst*; L. A. Shears, *The Influence of Sir Walter Scott on the Novels of Theodor Fontane* **Netherlands:** H. Vissink, *Scott and his Influence on Dutch Literature* **Romania:** M. Beza, 'Percy's *Reliques*, Sir Walter Scott's *Minstrelsy* and the Roumanian Ballads' **Spain:** P. H. Churchman and E. A. Peers, 'A Survey of the Influence of Sir Walter Scott in Spain' **Sweden:** O. Sylwan, *Walter Scott och hans romaner*	
1923	**Norway:** *GM*	**France:** F. W. M. Draper, *The Rise and Fall of the French Romantic Drama* **Italy:** Croce, 'Walter Scott' **Poland:** J. Ujejski, *Byronizm i skottyzm w (Konradzie Wallenrodzie)*	**Germany:** Feuchtwanger's novel *Die häßliche Herzogin Margarete Maultasch*
1924	**Croatia:** *BD*, *I* (complete)	**France:** E. Partridge, *The French Romantics' Knowlege of English Literature* **Netherlands:** P. Fijn van Draat, *The Poetry of Walter Scott*	
1925	**Czechoslovakia (Czech):** *CRP*, *R*	**Finland:** E. Railo, *Haamulinna: aineistohistoriallinen tutkimus Englannin kauhuromantiikasta* **France:** H. Bordeaux, *Le Walter Scott normand: Barbey d'Aurevilly* **Germany:** F. Sommerkamp, 'Walter Scotts Kenntnis und Ansicht von deutscher Literatur' **Spain:** M. Nuñez de Arenas, 'Simples notas acerca de W. Scott en España' **Sweden:** E. Lindström, *Walter Scott och den historiska romanen och novellen i Sverige intill 1850*	**Germany:** Feuchtwanger's novel *Jud Süß*
1926	**Czechoslovakia (Czech):** *CD*, *T* **Estonia:** *I*	**Denmark:** T. Lundbeck's entry on Scott in *Salmonsens Konversationsleksikon* (rev. I. Ottesen)	

Date	Translations	Criticism	Other
1926 (Cont.)		**France:** H. J. Garnand, *The Influence of Walter Scott on the Works of Balzac* **Germany:** W. Macintosh, *Scott and Goethe* **Spain:** Peers, *Studies in the Influence of Sir Walter Scott in Spain* **Spain (Catalonia):** F. Soldevila, 'Walter Scott y el Renacimiento literario catalán'	
1927	**Serbia:** *K*	**General:** H. A. White, *Sir Walter Scott's Novels on the Stage* **France:** F. Baldensperger, 'La Grande communion romantique de 1827: sous le signe de Walter Scott' **Germany:** E. Bode, *Einführung in die Geschichte der englischen Literatur besonders der Neuzeit*; C. Bröker, *Scott's 'Anne of Geierstein'*; J. Koch, 'Sir Walter Scotts Beziehungen zu Deutschland' **Italy:** A. Salaroli, *Carlo Varese, il vessillifero del romanzo storico e degli scottiani in Italia* **Spain:** A. González-Palencia, *Walter Scott y la censura gubernativa*	
1928	**Italy:** *HA* (complete) **Russia:** ZIF publish new edition of *WN*, with translations revised by Mandel'stam	**France:** Baldensperger, 'Walter Scott et le pittoresque des moeurs: les années 1827–8 en France et au dehors'; R. K. Gordon: 'Sir Walter Scott and the Comédie Humaine'; R. W. Hartland, *Walter Scott et le roman 'frénetique'* **Germany/Poland:** A. Weimar, *Die Naturschilderungen in den Romanen Walter Scotts und seiner Vorläufer* (publ. Breslau/Wroclaw) **Sweden:** S. Blöndal, 'Scott in Swedish literature'; S. Segerström, 'Frödings beroende av Walter Scott' **Switzerland:** H. Perrochon, 'Un admirateur suisse de Walter Scott: Emmanuel Develey'	

Date	Translations	Criticism	Other
1929	**First Slovak translation:** *K* **Hungary:** *T* **Spain (Catalan):** *I* (abridged)	**France:** A. Chesnier du Chesne, 'Les Voyages de Walter Scott en France'; Devonshire, *The English Novel in France, 1830–1870* **Poland:** A. Tretiak, Introduction to new translation of *W*	
1930	**First Ukrainian translation:** *RR* **Estonia:** *MO* **Slovenia:** *I*	**Italy:** Praz, *La carne, la morte e il diavolo nella letteratura romantica* **Russia:** D. Yakubovich, 'Rol' Frantsii v znakomstve Rossii s romanami Val'ter Skotta'	
1931		**Finland:** R. Koskimies, *Walter Scottin mestarivuodet: (1814–1819)* **Germany:** B. Fehr, *Die englische Literatur des 19. und 20. Jahrhunderts*; B. Kothen, *Quellenuntersuchungen zu Walter Scotts Romanen 'The Monastery' und 'The Abbot'* **Italy:** W. Owen, 'Scott in Italian' **Spain:** G. G. Zellars, 'Influencia de Walter Scott en España'	
1932		**General:** H. Glaesener, 'Walter Scott et son influence' **France:** G. Roth, 'Walter Scott et la France de son temps' **Germany:** O. Burdett, 'Goethe and Scott' **Italy:** L. D. Grillo, 'Il diario di Walter Scott'; Praz, 'Walter Scott' **Russia:** P. Struve, 'Walter Scott and Russia'	Centenary of Scott's death
1933	**Serbia:** *W*	**Belgium:** M. Cordemans, *Sir Walter Scott, 1832–1932* **Germany:** F. W. Bachmann, *Some German Imitators of Walter Scott*; W. Keller, *Walter Scott*; D. M. Mennie, 'Sir Walter Scott's Unpublished Translations of German Plays'; G. W. Spink, 'Fontane's Poem "Walter Scott in Westminster-Abtei"' **Italy:** P. Bardi, *La storia della letteratura inglese* **Norway:** T. Fladsrud, *Walter Scott: 'Ivanhoe'*	

Date	Translations	Criticism	Other
1933 (Cont.)		**Poland**: J. Krzyżanowski, 'Scott in Poland' (through 1934)	
1934		**France:** E. P. Dargan, 'Scott and the French Romantics' **Germany:** A. Paul, *Der Einfluß Walter Scotts auf die epische Technik Theodor Fontanes* (publ. Breslau/Wrocław) **Italy:** C. Alvaro, 'Nota a *Waverley*'	
1935	**First Belarusian translation:** *I* **Lithuania:** *QD*	**Austria:** R. Wild, 'Die historischen Romane der Caroline Pichler mit Rücksicht auf die Einflüsse Walter Scott's' (unpublished thesis) **Catalonia/Spain:** A. Par, *Shakespeare en la literatura española* **France:** P. Genévrier, *Walter Scott historien français, ou, Le Roman tourangeau de 'Quentin Durward'* **Hungary:** G. Laczkó, 'Walter Scott *Ivanhoe*' **Russia:** D. L. Jakubovich, 'Lermontov i Val'ter Skott'; E. J. Simmons, *English Literature and Culture in Russia (1552–1840)*	
1936	**Spain (Catalan):** *BD*	**Germany:** W. Kühne, 'Alexander Bronikowski und Walter Scott'; J. Moeller, *Die romantische Landschaft bei Walter Scott*	
1937	**Slovakia:** *BL*	**Germany:** W. F. Schirmer, *Geschichte der englischen Literatur*; A. Schlösser, *Die englische Literatur in Deutschland von 1895 bis 1934* **Hungary:** Lukács, *The Historical Novel* (publ. Moscow) **Italy:** Praz, *Storia della letteratura inglese* **Spain:** S. Cuthbertson, 'Scott's Influence on José Marmol's *El cruzado*'	
1938		**France:** E. Latham, 'Dumas et Sir Walter Scott'	

Date	Translations	Criticism	Other
1938 (Cont.)		**Hungary:** O. Elek, 'Scott Walter a magyar irodalmi köztudatban' **Italy:** Praz, 'Vite duplici'; J. Rossi, 'Scott and Carducci' **Spain:** Zellers, *La novela histórica en España (1828–1850)*	
1939	**Poland:** *R*	**Italy:** F. Lopez-Celly, *Il romanzo storico in Italia* **Russia:** W. M. Parker, 'Burns, Scott and Turgenev'	
1940	**Norway:** *QD*	**France:** Gordon, 'Le Voyage d'Abbotsford' **Italy:** S. Policardi, *Panorama della letteratura inglese* **Russia:** Z. Rozov, 'Denis Davydov and Walter Scott'; D. P. Yakubovitch, '*The Captain's Daughter* and the Novels of Walter Scott'	
1941	**Portugal:** MAMM		
1942		**France:** R. Caillois, *Puissances du roman* **Russia:** A. Novikov, 'Denis Davydov and Walter Scott'	
1943	**Slovakia:** *T*	**Switzerland:** R. T. Hardaway, 'C. F. Meyers's *Der Heilige* in Relation to its Sources'	
1945		**Catalonia:** R. F. Brown, 'The Romantic Novel in Catalonia' **Russia:** G. Struve, *Scott Letters Discovered in Russia*	
1946		**Slovenia:** A. J. Klančar, 'Josip Jurčič, the Slovene Scott'; Trdina, *Spomini* (written 1860s)	
1947	**Serbia/Croatia:** *QD* **Slovakia:** *I*	**France:** A. L. Sells, 'Leconte de Lisle and Sir Walter Scott'	
1948	**Finland:** *HM*	**Germany:** Schirmer, *Kurze Geschichte der englischen Literatur* **Spain:** R. Ricard, 'Walter Scott et Bernal Díaz del Castillo' **Sweden:** F. G. Bengtsson, 'Walter Scott' in *Litteratörer och militärer* **Yugoslavia:** A. J. Klančar, 'Scott in Yugoslavia' (through 1949)	
1949	**Finland:** *RR* **Hungary:** *W* **Norway:** *HM* (abridged)		

Date	Translations	Criticism	Other
1950		**France:** J. Pommier, 'Les Préfaces de Balzac: Balzac et W. Scott' **Germany:** G. H. Needler, *Goethe and Scott* **Italy:** A. Gibboni, *Parallelo tra Alessandro Manzoni e Walter Scott* **Russia:** G. Struve, 'Russian Friends and Correspondents of Sir Walter Scott' **Spain:** S. A. Stoudemire, 'A Note on Scott in Spain'	
1951	**Greece:** *LL*	**France:** P.-G. Castex, 'Walter Scott contre Hoffmann: les épisodes d'une rivalité littéraire en France' **Norway:** I. Moksnes, *Main Features in the Waverley Novels*	
1952	**Serbia:** *GM* **Slovakia:** *RR*	**Italy:** Praz, *La crisi dell'eroe nel romanzo vittoriano*	
1953	**Greece:** *K* **Portugal:** *P* **Serbia:** *AG*	**General:** F. C. Roe, 'La découverte de l'Ecosse entre 1760 et 1830'	
1954	**Czechoslovakia (Czech):** *LM* **Portugal:** *RR* **Slovakia:** *OM*	**Croatia:** M. Jankovic, *Tri engelska prijevoda 'Hasanaginice' u Skotskoj* **Russia:** M. Grinsbergs, 'Some Aspects of Scottish Authors in Russian Literature in the First Half of the Nineteenth Century' (thesis, Edinburgh)	
1955	**Montenegro:** *BL* **Romania:** *I* **Slovenia:** *A*	**Italy:** Croce, *Poesia e non poesia* **Spain:** J. F. Montesinos, *Introducción a una história de la novela en España en el siglo XIX*	
1956	**Lithuania:** *RR* **Serbia/Bosnia/Croatia:** *SD* **Slovakia:** *W* **Ukraine:** *QD*	**Germany:** J. Hennig, 'Goethe's Translation of Scott's Criticism of Hoffmann'	
1957	**First Moldovan translation:** *I* **Estonia:** *RR* **Greece:** *RR* **Romania:** *RR* **Serbia:** *RR* **Slovenia:** *QD*	**France:** F. C. Green, 'Scott's French Correspondence' **Italy:** M. P. Helder, *Storia della letteratura inglese*; M. F. M. Meiklejohn, 'Sir Walter Scott and Alessandro Manzoni'	
1958	**Czechoslovakia (Czech):** *HM* **Serbia:** *FN*	**Italy:** A. Zanco, *Storia della letteratura inglese* **Russia:** M. P. Alekseev, *Val'ter*	

Date	Translations	Criticism	Other
1958 (Cont.)	**Slovakia:** *QD*	*Skott i 'Slovo o polku Igoreve';* A. A. Bel'skii, *Val'ter Skott: ocherk tvorchestva*; I. M. Levidova, *Val'ter Skott : bio-bibliograficheskii ukazatel' k 125-letiyu so dnya smert*	
1959	**First Albanian translation (Kosovo):** *I* (abridged) **First Macedonian translation:** *W* **Czechoslovakia (Czech):** *RR* **Hungary:** *RR*	**Russia:** N. M. Eishiskina, *Val'ter Skott; kritiko-biograficheskii ocherk*	
1960	**Greece:** *QD* **Russia:** Complete works (through 1965)	**France:** N. Rinsler, 'Gérard de Nerval and Sir Walter Scott's *Antiquary*' **Germany:** P. M. Ochojski's thesis 'Walter Scott and Germany' (Columbia) **Russia:** S. A. Orlov, *Istoricheskii roman Val'tera Skotta*	
1961		**France:** S. Kozuchowska, 'O ludowosci Waltera Scotta i George Sand' **Germany:** H. Knorr, 'Theodor Fontane und England' (thesis, Göttingen)	
1962	**Bulgaria:** *RR*	**Norway:** L. Hartveit, *Scott's 'The Bride of Lammermoor': An Assessment of Attitude*	
1963	**Bulgaria:** *I* **Romania:** *K* **Serbia:** *LM*	**Czechoslovakia:** Wellek, 'Mácha and English Literature' (publ. The Hague) **France:** E. Johnson, 'Sceptred Kings and Laureled Conquerors: Scott in London and Paris, 1815' **Italy:** F. R. Hart, 'The Fair Maid, Manzoni's *Betrothed*, and the Grounds of Waverley Criticism'; C. Izzo, *Storia della letteratura inglese* **Poland:** W. Ostrowski, 'Walter Scott w Polsce 1816–1830' **Spain:** G. Moldenhauer, 'Estudio filológico de una traducción española de "The Wild Huntsman" de Sir Walter Scott'	

Date	Translations	Criticism	Other
1964	**Albania:** *I* (complete) **Greece:** *AB* **Hungary:** *OM* **Portugal:** *A* **Slovakia:** *GM*	**Germany:** W. Iser, 'Möglichkeiten der Illusion im historischen Roman: Sir Walter Scotts *Waverley*' **Poland:** Ostrowski, 'Walter Scott in Poland' **Russia:** Y. D. Levin, 'V. K. Kyukhel'beker o poezii Val'tera Skotta'	
1965	**Croatia:** *HM* **Norway:** *RR* **Poland:** *FMP*	**Poland:** Ostrowski, 'Walter Scott in Poland, Part II: Adam Mickiewicz and Walter Scott' **Russia:** M. Greene, 'Pushkin and Sir Walter Scott'; B. G. Reizov, *Tvorchestvo Val'tera* *Skotta*	
1966	**Iceland:** *T* **Macedonia:** *T*	**France:** J. C. Alciatore, 'Quelques remarques sur Stendhal et les héroines de Walter Scott' **Germany:** Ochojski, 'Sir Walter Scott's Continuous Interest in German' **Russia:** A. A. Gozenpud, 'Val'ter Skott i romanticheskie komedii A. A. Shakhovskogo'; Reizov, 'V. A. Zhukovskii, perevodchik Val'tera Skotta: "Ivanov vecher"' **Spain:** A. Regalado García, *Benito Pérez Galdos y la novela* *histórica española*	
1967	**Bulgaria:** *QD*	**Poland:** W. Ostrowski, 'Adam Mickiewicz i Walter Scott' **Russia:** Parker, 'Scott and Russian Literature' **Spain:** Peers, *Historia del* *movimiento romántico español*	
1968	**Hungary:** *HW* **Portugal:** *CRP*	**General:** E. Forbes, 'Sir Walter Scott and Opera' **Germany:** A. I. Serdyukov, 'Val'ter Skott i nemetskii roman' (publ. Russia) **Italy:** E. Zantai, 'Confrontando Manzoni e W. Scott'	
1969		**Germany (West):** R. Schüren, 'Die Romane Walter Scotts in Deutschland' (doctoral thesis, Freie Universität, Berlin) **Spain:** E. Pujals, *El* *Romanticismo inglés*	

Date	Translations	Criticism	Other
1970	**Lithuania:** *FMP*	**General:** J. O. Hayden (ed.), *Scott: The Critical Heritage* **Finland:** L. Valkama, 'Kuusi ja seitseman veljesta' **Italy:** L. Bottoni, 'Scott e Manzoni nel 1821: tecniche descrittive e funzioni epistemologiche'	
1971	**Hungary:** *K* **Latvia:** *I*	**France:** V. Del Litto, 'Stendhal et Walter Scott'; H. F. Imbert, 'Conjectures sur l'origine scottienne du titre de *Rouge et Noir*'; E. Legouis, 'La fortune littéraire de Walter Scott en France' **Germany:** H. Eggert, *Studien zur Wirkungsgeschichte des deutschen historischen Romans 1850–1875*; H. Oppel, *Englisch-deutsche Literatur-beziehungen, II. Von der Romantik bis zur Gegenwart*; H. Tippkötter, *Walter Scott, Geschichte als Unterhaltung: Eine Rezeptionsanalyse der Waverley Novels'* **Hungary:** G. Hegedűs, '*Walter Scott* születésének kétszázadik évfordulójára' **Italy:** G. Spina, *Il romanzo storico inglese: Sir Walter Scott* **Russia:** A. Nikolyukin, 'Val'ter Skott v Rossii'; Orlov, 'Russkie druz'ya Val'tera Skotta' **Spain:** I. M. Zavala, *Ideología y política en la novela española del siglo XIX*	Bicentenary of Scott's birth
1972	**Bulgaria:** *K* **Hungary:** *R* (publ. Bratislava)	**France:** K. Massmann, *Die Rezeption der historischen Romans Sir Walter Scotts in Frankreich (1816–1832)* **Germany:** H.-J. Müllenbrock, 'Scott und der historische Roman' **Hungary:** M. Szenczi and T. Szobotka, *Az angol irodalom története* **Italy:** M. E. Ambrose, '*La donna del lago*: The First Italian Translations of Scott'	

Date	Translations	Criticism	Other
1972 (Cont.)		**Sweden:** K. Elert, *Walter Scotts Ivanhoe under 150 år*	
1973	**Slovenia:** *W*	**France:** D. Haggis, 'Scott, Balzac, and the Historical Novel as Social and Political Analysis: *Waverley* and *Les Chouans*'; M. Kemp, 'Scott and Delacroix: With Some Assistance from Hugo and Bonnington' **Germany:** R. F. Holt, 'Achim von Arnim and Sir Walter Scott'; M. Meyer, 'Die Entstehung des historischen Romans in Deutschland' (thesis, Munich); Ochojski, 'Waverley über Alles: Sir Walter Scott's German Reputation'; Schüren, 'Sir Walter Scott als deutscher Jugend-Schriftsteller' **Hungary:** A. Katona, 'The Impact of Sir Walter Scott in Hungary' **Italy:** R. D. S. Jack, 'Scott and Italy' **Romania:** E. Lazu, 'Opera lui Walter Scott in Romania' **Russia:** A. Hewton, 'A Comparison of Sir Walter Scott's "The Eve of St. John" and Zhukovsky's Translation of the Ballad'	
1974	**Serbia:** Selected poems **Slovakia:** *LM*	**General:** N. Diakonova, 'Val'ter Skott i Shekspir: u istokov evropeiiskogo romana XIX v.' **Finland:** K. Viitanen, *Dialectal Forms and Words and Archaisms in Sir Walter Scott's 'Bride of Lammermoor'* **France:** Haggis, 'Fiction and Historical Change in *La Cousine Bette* and the Lesson of Walter Scott' **Italy:** A. Benedetti, *Le traduzioni italiane da Walter Scott e i loro anglicismi* **Italy/France:** W. Hempel, *Manzoni und die Darstellung der Menschenmenge als erzähltechnisches Problem in den*	

Date	Translations	Criticism	Other
1974 (Cont.)		*'Promessi Sposi', bei Scott und in den historischen Romanen der französischen Romantik* **Norway:** Hartveit, *Dream within a Dream: A Thematic Approach to Scott's Vision of Fictional Reality* **Spain:** M. Z. Hafter, 'The Spanish Version of Scott's *Don Roderick*'	
1975	**Hungary:** *FN* **Macedonia:** *I* **Romania:** *FMP*	**Germany:** Müllenbrock, 'Scott's *The Heart of Midlothian*'; P.-J. Rekowski, *Die Erzählhaltung in den historischen Romanen von Walter Scott und Charles Dickens*; H. Steinecke, *Romantheorie und Romankritik in Deutschland* and '*Wilhelm Meister* oder *Waverley?*' **Italy:** F. Ruggieri Punzo, *Walter Scott in Italia, 1821–1971* **Russia:** M. P. Alekseev, 'Prizhiznennaia slava Val'tera Skotta v Rossii'; Levin, *Prizhiznennaia slava Val'tera Skotta v Rossii*	
1976	**Romania:** *GM* **Slovakia:** *BD, FMP*	**Denmark:** J. E. Nielsen, 'Den samtidige engelske litteratur og Danmark 1800–1840' (through 1977) **Germany:** H. V. Geppert, *Der 'andere' historische Roman*; H. Grieve, 'Fontane und Scott' **Russia:** N. G. Zhekulin, 'Turgenev in Scotland, 1871'	
1977	**Portugal:** *LDW* **Romania:** *LM* **Slovakia:** *HM*	**France:** C. A. M. Dimic, 'Stendhal, Walter Scott et la légende de Tristan et Iseut'; H. Teyssandier, *Les Formes de la création romanesque à l'époque de Walter Scott et de Jane Austen* **Russia:** A. Socié, 'Génèse et fonction du héros fictif dans *La Fille du capitaine* de Pouchkine' **Spain:** L. Rovatti, 'Le Débat sur le roman historique en Espagne'; L. Urrutia, 'Walter Scott et le roman historique en Espagne'	

Date	Translations	Criticism	Other
1978	**Hungary:** *WO*	**France:** B. S. Wright, 'The Influence of the Historical Novels of Walter Scott on the Changing Nature of French History Painting, 1815–1855' (unpublished thesis) **Germany (West):** K. Gamerschlag, *Sir Walter Scott und die Waverley Novels* **Italy:** L. Lattarulo, *Il romanzo storico*; R. Zanca Pucci, 'Michele Amari, traduttore di Walter Scott' **Romania:** Lazu, 'Walter Scott si cultura româna' **Russia:** J. West, 'Walter Scott and the Style of Russian Historical Novels of the 1830s and 1840s'	**Russia:** Translation of H. Pearson's *Walter Scott*
1979	**Bulgaria:** *P*	**Germany:** M. Chaléat, 'Un émule prussien de Walter Scott' (on Fontane; publ. France); Gamerschlag, *Die Korrectur der Waverley Novels: Textkritische Untersuchungen zu einer Autor-Korrector-Beziehung* **Switzerland:** G. Sandau, 'Les Historiens suisses romands et le roman historique de Walter Scott'	
1980	**First Basque translation:** *I* (abridged) **Albania:** *RR* **Hungary:** *HM*	**France:** W. Conner, 'Scott and Balzac'; N. Ward, 'The Prison-House of Language: *The Heart of Midlothian* and *La Chartreuse de Parme*' **Germany:** Müllenbrock, *Der historische Roman des 19. Jahrhunderts*; O. W. Johnston, 'Literary Influence as Provocation: Sir Walter Scott's Impact on Heinrich Heine and the Young Germans' **Hungary:** I. Bart, *Walter Scott világa* **Portugal:** M. L. Pires, *Walter Scott e o romanticismo português* **Romania:** Lazu, 'Sadovenau si Scott' **Spain:** J. F. Montesinos, *Introducción a una historia de la novela en España en el siglo XIX*; J.-L. Picoche, 'Ramón López Soler, plagiaire et précurseur'	

Date	Translations	Criticism	Other
1980 (Cont.)		**Ukraine:** L. E. Scheider, 'An Examination of Shevchenko's Romanticism'	
1981	**Lithuania:** Selected poems	**France:** D. Mower, 'Romanticism in France and England'; Wright, 'Scott and Shakespeare in Nineteenth Century France' **Italy:** Ambrose, 'Walter Scott, Italian Opera and Romantic Stage Setting' **Germany:** Müllenbrock, 'Die Entstehung des Scottschen historischen Romans als Problem der Literaturgeschichtsschreibung' **Russia:** S. S. Hoisington, 'Pushkin's "Belkin" and the Mystifications of Sir Walter Scott'; J. H. Raleigh, 'Scott and Pushkin' **Spain:** Pujals, 'Las líneas generales del romanticismo inglés y su repercusión limitada a Byron y Scott en España'	
1982		**Denmark:** A. Talbot, 'H. C. Andersen and Meg Merrilies' **Slovenia:** J. Bogataj, *Sir Walter Scott in slovenska zgodnja pripovedna proza*	
1983	**Italy:** Extracts from 'Essay on Romance' **Serbia:** *BL* **Ukraine:** *FMP*	**Denmark:** Nielsen, 'Sir Walter Scott's Reception in Nineteenth Century Denmark'; V. H. Pedersen, 'Walter Scott in Denmark: The Transfer of Literary Form by a Comparison of *Ivanhoe* and *Valdemar Sej*' **France:** I. Filipowska, '*Waverley* de Walter Scott et *Les Jacobites* de F. Coppée' **Italy:** Ambrose, 'Scott, Sicily and Michele Amari' **Norway:** B. J. Tysdahl, 'Sir Walter Scott and the Beginnings of Norwegian Fiction' **Portugal:** L. N. Raitt, *Garrett and the English Muse* **Spain:** R. Álvarez-Rodríguez, *Origen y evolución de la novela histórica inglesa*	

Date	Translations	Criticism	Other
1984	**Lithuania:** *OM*	**France:** M. Lyons, 'The Audience for Romanticism: Walter Scott in France, 1815–51'; Wright, 'The Auld Alliance in Nineteenth Century French Painting'; Wright/Joannides 'Les Romans historiques de Sir Walter Scott et la peinture française, 1822–1863' (through 1985) **Russia:** A. A. Elistratova, *Nikolai Gogol and the West European Novel*	
1985	**Czechoslovakia (Czech):** *BL*	**France:** Haggis, 'The Popularity of Scott's Novels in France and Balzac's *Illusions perdues*'; M. F. Lukacher, 'Flaubert's Pharmacy'; G. Yost, 'Scott and Sand: Novelists of the Rustic' **Italy:** S. B. Chandler, 'The Motif of the Journey in the Eighteenth-Century Novel in Scott and Manzoni'; A. M. Morace, 'Un intertesto manzoniano: il *Waverley* di Scott'	
1986	**Greece:** 'Chivalry'	**Austria:** H. R. Klieneberger, 'Stifters *Witiko* und die Romane Walter Scotts' **Germany:** R. Humphrey, *The Historical Novel as Philosophy of History: Three German Contributions: Alexis, Fontane, Döblin*; G. R. Kaiser, '"Impossible to Subject Tales of this Nature to Criticism": Walter Scotts Kritik als Schlüssel zur Wirkungsgeschichte E. T. Hoffmanns im 19. Jahrhundert'; E. Mornin, 'A Late German Imitation of Walter Scott'; I. Schwartz, *Narrativik und Historie bei Sir Walter Scott*; L. Tatlock, 'Berlin, Walter Scott and the "Roman des Nebeneinander": Three Novels by Willibald Alexis' **Norway:** Tysdahl, 'Walter Scott og Maurits Hansen'	

Date	Translations	Criticism	Other
1986 (Cont.)		**Romania:** M. Macarie, 'Alexandru Odobescu si Walter Scott'	
1987		**France:** Wright, 'Walter Scott et la gravure française' **Germany:** F. Druffner, *Walter Scotts Romanze in Stein: Abbotsford als pittoreske Dichterresidenz* **Spain:** V. López-Folgado and L. Mora-González, 'La primera traducción de *The Bride of Lammermoor*, de W. Scott'	**Russia:** Translation of Daiches's *Sir Walter Scott and his World*
1988	**Croatia:** *MJS*	**Russia:** M. Altshuller, 'Motifs in Sir Walter Scott's *The Fair Maid of Perth* in Aleksandr Pushkin's *Tazit*'; R. F. Christian, 'Sir Walter Scott, Russia and Tolstoy'; A. A. Dolinin, *Istoriya, odetaya v roman: Val'ter Skott i ego chitateli* **Spain:** R. Marrast, 'Ediciones perpiñanescas de Walter Scott en castellano (1824–1826)'	
1989		**Czechoslovakia (Czech):** R. Nenadál, critical postface to Albatros edn of *I* **Italy:** G. Erasmi, 'Lucy of Lammermoor and Lucia Mondella' **Romania:** D. S. Pavel, 'Natura ironiei la Walter Scott si Mihail Sadoveanu' **Russia:** Altshuller, 'The Walter Scott Motifs in Nikolay Gogol's Story "The Lost Letter"'; J. D. Kornblatt, '"Bez skotov oboidemsia": Gogol and Sir Walter Scott'; L. E. Pinskii, *Magistral'nyi syuzhet: F. Viion, V. Shekspir, B. Grasian, V. Skott*	
1990	**Slovakia:** *FN*	**Austria/Germany:** N. Bachleitner, *Quellen zur Rezeption des englischen und französischen Romans in Deutschland und Österreich im 19. Jahrhundert*	

Date	Translations	Criticism	Other
1990 (Cont.)		**Czech Republic:** Nenadál, critical postface to Albatros edn of *QD* **France:** A. H. Armstrong, 'One of Balzac's Sources for *L'Excommunié*' **Germany:** E. McInnes, 'Realism, History and the Nation: The Reception of the Waverley Novels in Germany in the 19th Century'; Müllenbrock, 'Normans Versus Saxons: Variationen eines Themas im historischen Roman des 19. Jahrhunderts'; M. Reiter, 'Die Bedeutung der historischen Romane Walter Scotts für das deutsche Romanverständnis des 19. Jahrhunderts' (thesis, Leipzig) **Spain:** C. H. Walsh, 'The Sublime in the Historical Novel: Scott and Gil y Carrasco'	
1991	**Italy:** 'Chivalry'	**Austria:** Bachleitner, '". . . der so nachtheiligen Romanen-Lektüre ein Ende zu machen"' (on Austrian censorship of *WO*) **France:** M. Allemano, *Historical Portraits and Visions* **Germany:** S. Pritzkuleit, *Die Wiederentdeckung des Ritters durch den Bürger: Chivalry in englischen Geschichtswerken und Romanen: 1770–1830* **Italy:** M. T. Bindella, *La maschera e il ritratto: nascita e metamorfosi dell'autore anonimo nei romanzi di Walter Scott*; M. Orr, '"The Return of the Different": Rereading in Scott and Calvino' **Poland:** J. Lasecka-Zielak, 'Lektury poety: Adam Mickiewicz o Walterze Scotcie i George'u Gordonie Byronie' **Russia/France:** S. B. Davis, 'From Scotland and Russia via France: Scott, Defauconpret and Gogol'	

Date	Translations	Criticism	Other
1992		**General:** H. P. Bolton, *Scott Dramatized* **Belgium:** J. T. Leerssen, 'Image and Reality – and Belgium' **Denmark:** Nielsen, 'From Wester Haf to Loch Katrine and Thence to Copenhagen' **France:** J. R. Williams, 'Emma Bovary and *The Bride of Lammermoor*' **Germany:** A. Bestek, *Geschichte als Roman . . . Walter Scott, Edward Bulwer-Lytton and George Eliot*; G. Kebbel, *Geschichtengeneratoren*	
1993	**Latvia:** *QD*	**Croatia:** K. Cvrljak, 'Dalmatinski Walter Scott: Marko Kažotić' **Denmark:** Nielsen, 'Scott's Use of Two Danish Ballads in *The Lady of the Lake*' **France:** D. Macmillan, 'Sources of French Narrative Painting: Between Three Cultures'; H. Suhamy, *Sir Walter Scott* **Russia:** I. A. Dubashinskii, *Val'ter Skott: ocherk tvorchestva*; M. Frazier, '*Kapitanskaia dochka* and the Creativity of Borrowing'; Y. Mann, 'Russian Attitudes to the Aesthetics of Walter Scott' **Ukraine:** R. M. Bahry, *Shliakh Sera Val'tera Skotta na Ukrainu*	**General:** First vol. of the Edinburgh Edition of the WN (*OM*)
1994	**Latvia:** *OM*	**Germany:** H. Aust, *Der historische Roman*; F. Burwick, 'How to Translate a Waverley Novel'; Müllenbrock, 'Natur und Geschichte im historischen Roman Sir Walter Scotts'; Steinecke, '"Die Geschichte ist die grösste Dichtung": Willibald Alexis' Scott-Rezeption der 1820er Jahre' **Greece:** S. Denise, *To helleniko historiko mythistorema kai ho Sir Walter Scott (1830–1880)*	

Date	Translations	Criticism	Other
1994 (Cont.)		**Poland:** W. Krajewska, 'Angielsko-polskie zwięzki literackie' **Russia/Germany:** D. G. Kropf, *Authorship as Alchemy: Subversive Writing in Pushkin, Scott, Hoffmann* **Slovenia:** K. Bogataj-Gradisnik, 'Literarne konvencije v slovenskem zgodovinskem romanu 19. Stoletja'	
1995	**Lithuania:** *BL*	**General:** H. Orel, *The Historical Novel from Scott to Sabatini* **Romania:** P. Brînzeu, *The Protean Novelists: The British Novel from Defoe to Scott* **Russia:** Altshuller, '*Roslavlev*: roman i popytka romana: M. Zagoskin, A. Pushkin i Ser Val'ter Scott'; V. E. Vatsuro, 'Iz istorii "goticheski romana" v Rossii: A. A. Bestuzhev-Marlinskii' **Spain:** M. Murphy, 'The Spanish *Waverley*: Blanco White and *Vargas*' **Sweden:** T. Johannson, *Paralleller*	
1996	**Slovenia:** Selected poems	**General:** Mitchell, *More Scott Operas* **Catalonia:** M. Serrahima and M. T. Boada, *La novel·la històrica en la literatura catalana* **France:** A. B. Evans, 'Literary Intertexts in Jules Verne's *Voyages extraordinaires*'; Wright, 'Walter Scott and French Art' **Germany:** K. Habitzel, G. Mühlberger, 'Gewinner und Verlierer: Der historische Roman . . . (1815–1848/49)'; C. Johnson, 'Scott and the German Historical Drama'; J. Kałążny, 'Fiktion und Geschichte' **Italy:** F. Ruggieri, et al., *Romanzo storico e romanticismo: intermittenze del modello scottiano* **Portugal:** Pires, 'Walter Scott and Portugal' **Russia:** Al'tshuller, *Epokha Val'tera Skotta v Rossii*	

Date	Translations	Criticism	Other
1997		**France:** M. Kandji, *Roman anglais et traditions populaires: le folklore et l'imaginaire rural de Walter Scott à Thomas Hardy* **Germany:** W. Engler, 'Geschichtsroman oder historischer Roman: Überlegungen zur Scottrezeption wahrend der Restauration'; J. Holzner, W. Wiesmüller, online *Projekt Historischer Roman* (through 2002) **Italy:** S. Porras Castro, 'Walter Scott en Italia' **Russia:** G. de Vries, 'Nabokov, Pushkin and Scott' **Sweden:** P. Graves, 'Fröding, Burns, Scott and Carlyle'	
1998		**General:** Todd/Bowden, *Sir Walter Scott: A Bibliographical History 1796–1832* **France:** J. M. Bennett, 'Walter Scott, *Waverley*: imaginaire romantique et réalité historique'; G. Lamoine (ed.), *Lectures d'une oeuvre: 'Waverley' de Sir Walter Scott*; V. Moreau, 'Delacroix lecteur de Walter Scott' **Germany:** Müllenbrock, 'Theodor Fontanes historischer Roman *Vor der Sturm* und die Scottische Gattungstradition'; Steinecke, 'Der "reichste, gewandteste, berühmteste Erzähler seines Jahrhunderts": Walter Scott und der Roman in Deutschland', 'E. T. A. Hoffmann und Walter Scott', and 'Willibald Alexis' *Schloss Avalon*'	
2000	**Russia:** First verse translation of *M*	**Austria:** A. Ritter, 'Die Bekannten und die beiden "großen Unbekannten": Scott, der historische Roman und sein Einfluß auf Charles Sealsfield'	

Date	Translations	Criticism	Other
2000 (Cont.)		**France:** J. Berton, '*Waverley* pastiché!: étude de *Allan Cameron* de J. Pagnon and A. Callet'; D. Couégnas, '*Ivanhoe* et *Les Chouans*: lecture des dénouements de deux romans historiques'; J. McLeman-Carnie, 'Sir Walter Scott; E. Roy-Reverzy, 'Balzac et les modèles scottiens: l'exemple des *Chouans*' and the French Press: Paris 1826' and 'Alfred de Vigny à Abbotsford' **Germany:** N. Bachleitner (ed.), *Beiträge zur Rezeption der britischen und irischen Literatur des 19. Jahrhunderts im deutschsprachigen Raum*; W. Dürr, 'Übersetzungen vertonter und Vertonungen übersetzter Texte: Mozarts *La finta gardiniera* und Schuberts Lieder aus Walter Scott's *Fräulein vom See*'; W. Engler, 'Geschichtsroman oder historischer Roman: Überlegungen zur Scottrezeption wahrend der Restauration'; H. V. Geppert, 'Ein Feld von Differenzierungen: Zur kritisch-produktiven Scott-Rezeption von Arnim bis Fontane'; P. Hasubek, 'Das Geheimnis des schwarzen Ritters, oder, Scott und Immermann'; S. Meyer, 'Marschner's Villains, Monomania, and the Fantasy of Deviance' (on *Der Templer und die Jüdin*); S. Neuhaus, '"Sechsunddreissig Könige für einen Regenschirm": Heinrich Heines produktive Rezeption britischer Literatur'; S. Stark (ed.), *The Novel in Anglo-German Context*; Steineke, 'Britische-deutsche Romanlektüren im frühen neunzehnten Jahrhundert: Hoffmann und Scott zum Beispiel'	

Date	Translations	Criticism	Other
2000 (Cont.)		**Russia:** Dolinin, 'Swerving from Walter Scott: *The Captain's Daughter* as a Metahistorical Novel' **Sweden:** Graves, *Fröding, Burns and Scott* **Switzerland/France:** M. Andermatt, '"Engelland" als Metapher: Walter Scott, Augustin Thierry und das mittelalterliche England in Conrad Ferdinand Meyers Novelle *Der Heilige*'	
2001	**Albania:** *HW* and other stories **Norway:** *BL*	**General:** R. Crawford, 'Walter Scott and European Union' **France:** D. Hüe, 'Walter Scott et Jean Giono: une parenté'; A. Hunter, 'The Peregrinations of "Auld Robin Gray" and *Eugénie Grandet*'; P. Joannides, 'Delacroix and Modern Literature'; Macmillan, '"A Journey through England and Scotland": Wilkie and Other Influences on French Art of the 1820s' M. Tilby, 'Sur quelques éléments intertextuels des *Paysans*: Balzac, Walter Scott et Théophile Gautier' **Germany:** O. Durrani, J. Preece (eds), *Travellers in Time and Space: The German Historical Novel*; F. Reitemeier, *Deutsch-englische Literaturbeziehungen: Der historische Roman Walter Scotts und seine deutschen Vorläufer* **Germany/Italy:** E. Szaffner, 'Egy regény metamorfózisa: Nicolai-opera az *Ivanhoe*-ból' (on *Il templario*) **Hungary:** E. Szaffner, 'A Scott-regények kanonizálódása Magyarországon' (through 2002) **Italy:** S. Luttazi, 'Walter Scott in Italia, ossia, Un autore di tendenza nel paese di Corilla Olimpica' **Poland:** D. Siwicka, 'Scott Walter'	

Date	Translations	Criticism	Other
2001 (Cont.)		**Spain:** G. de Cabo Pérez, '*Kenilworth* 1821–¿1999?' (on Spanish translations of *K*); Kloss, 'Die Natur- und Landschaftsschilderung im historischen Roman der spanischen Romantik: Ein Aspekt der Scott-Rezeption?'; C. Mata Induráin, 'El Bardo de Escocia y el Homero de Vasconia: Walter Scott, modelo de Navarro Villoslada'	
2002		**France:** B. Franco, 'La Préface de *Cromwell* entre Friedrich Schlegel et Walter Scott'; Y. Lostourtoff, 'The Pew and the Cigar-Case: Heraldry in the French Realist Novel'; F. McIntosh-Varjabédian, *La Vraisemblance narrative: Walter Scott, Barbey d'Aurevilly* and '*Quatre-vingt-treize*, ou, Le Rejet de l'héritage scottien: une réflexion sur le sens de l'Histoire' **France/Germany/Italy:** F. Lampart, *Zeit und Geschichte: die mehrfachen Anfänge des historischen Romans bei Scott, Arnim, Vigny und Manzoni* **Germany:** Bachleitner, 'Wilhelm Müller und Walter Scott'; M. Niehaus, *Autoren unter sich: Walter Scott, Willibald Alexis, Wilhelm Hauff und andere in einer literarischen Affäre* **Slovenia:** K. Nemec, 'Historizam i povijesni roman'	
2003	**France:** Bibliothèque de la Pléiade edition of *W*, *BD*, and *HM* **Moldova:** *T*	**Catalonia:** F. M. Tubino, *Historia del renacimiento literario contemporáneo de Cataluña, Baleares y Valencia* **France:** D. B. Brown, 'Literature and History: Shakespeare, Scott, Byron and *genre historique*'; M.-B. Diethelm, 'Walter Scott et le jeune Balzac' **Germany:** Müllenbrock, *Der historische Roman*; D. Stechern, *Das Recht in den Romanen von Sir Walter Scott*	**Denmark:** Stage adaptation of *I* by J. Ljungdalh and J. Rohde

Date	Translations	Criticism	Other
2003 (Cont.)		**Germany/Austria:** J. S. Chase, 'The Homeless Nation: The Exclusion of Jews in and from Early Nineteenth-Century German Historical Fiction' **Italy:** V. Poggi, 'Glimpses and Echoes of Scott in *I promessi sposi*' **Russia:** J. Howard, 'Scott, Abbotsford, and the Russian Gothic Revival: Influence and Coincidence'; Jones, 'Scott's Edward Waverley and Tolstoy's Pierre Bezukhov' **Spain:** B. Kloss, *Die Abhängigkeit und Loslösung Larras und Escosuras vom Modell des historischen Romans Walter Scotts*; Cabo Pérez, 'D. P. H. B., traductor de Walter Scott'	
2004	**Spain:** *MM*	**General:** T. Ziolkowski, 'Wavering Heroes, from Scotland to Spain' **France:** A. Hook, 'The French Taste for Scottish Literary Romanticism'; M. Samuels, 'Scott Comes to France' **Germany:** S. Mergenthal, 'Translating the Historical Novel: The Scott Formula in 19th-Century German Literature'; J. Zeune, 'Vom "echten Styl" deutscher Burgen: das Bild der Burg im 19. Jahrhundert' (on Walter Scott and German medievalism) **Hungary:** S. Hites, 'Sir Walter Scott és az *Ivanhoe* magyar fordítói' **Italy:** N. Halmi, 'Lucy, Lucia, and Locke' (on Walter Scott and Donizetti) **Russia:** M. Frazier, 'Personae and Personality in O. I. Senkovskij'; W. G. Jones, '"'Tis Sixty Years Since": Sir Walter Scott's Eighteenth Century and Tolstoy's Engagement with History' **Slovenia:** A. Janko, Sir Walter Scott pri Slovencih	

Date	Translations	Criticism	Other
2005		**Spain:** J. E. García-González's thesis 'Traducción y recepción de Walter Scott en España' **France:** C. Fuhrman, 'Scott Repatriated?: *La Dame blanche* Crosses the Channel' **Germany:** A. S. Anderson, 'Ein Kaufmann "von sehr englischem Aussehen": die literarische und soziokulturelle Funktion Englands in *Soll und Haben*' (on Walter Scott and Freytag); A. Curthoys/J. Docker, 'Leopold von Ranke and Sir Walter Scott'; R. Häfner, 'Heine und der Supernaturalismus: Von Walter Scott zu Charles Baudelaire' **Hungary:** S. Ferguson, 'At the Grave of the Gentile Constitution: Walter Scott, Georg Lukács and Romanticism', 'The Imaginative Construction of Historical Character: What Georg Lukács and Walter Scott Could Tell Contemporary Novelists', and 'Walter Scott and the Construction of Historical Knowledge: A Lukácsian Perspective'; Szaffner, '"Regényes kóborlások": a skót Felföld, Erdély és a nemzettudat' **Russia:** L. Korenowska, *Skott, Dikkens, Dostoevskij: o transformatsii motivov* and 'Transformatsiia motivov tvorchestva Skotta i Dikkensa v proze Dostoevskogo' (both pub. Poland) **Spain:** A. M. Freire López, 'Un negocio editorial romántico: Aribau y Walter Scott'; J. E. García González, *Traducción y recepción de Walter Scott en España* and 'Consideraciones sobre la influencia de Walter Scott en la novela histórica española del siglo XIX'	

Date	Translations	Criticism	Other
2006		**General:** V. Nemoianu, *The Triumph of Imperfection: The Silver Age of Sociocultural Moderation in Europe, 1815–1848*; D. Sassoon, *The Culture of the Europeans: From 1800 to the Present* **France:** R. Grutman, 'Lenguas y lenguajes "excéntricos" en la novela decimonónica' (on Walter Scott, Hugo and Balzac); G. Soubigou, 'French Portraits of Sir Walter Scott: Images of the Great Unknown' **Germany:** A. Eppers, '"Berührungen aus der Ferne": Goethe und Walter Scott' **Russia:** Dolinin, 'Val´ter-skottovskii istorizm i *Kapitanskaia dochka*' **Spain:** E. García Díaz, 'La influencia de las novelas de Walter Scott en la novela histórica española *El señor de Bembibre*' and 'Walter Scott and Spain: The Influence of the Waverley Novels in the Spanish Historical Novel during the Nineteenth Century'; García González, 'Translation, Ideology and Subversion: D. Pablo de Xérica's Spanish Translation of Sir Walter Scott's *Waverley*'	
2007	**France:** Bibliothèque de la Pléiade edition of *I, QD,* and *T*	**General:** T. Hubbard, '"Bright Uncertainty": The Poetry of Walter Scott, Landscape, and Europe' **France:** Soubigou, '"These romantic and wild lands": Scottish Literary Subjects in French Nineteenth-Century Art' **Germany:** R. Lach, 'Historische Stoffe - Walter Scott gegen E. T. A. Hoffmann: Warum jeder Roman ein historischer Roman ist'; P. McIsaac, 'Rethinking Tableaux Vivants	

Date	Translations	Criticism	Other
2007 (Cont.)		and Triviality in the Writings of Johann Wolfgang von Goethe, Johanna Schopenhauer, and Fanny Lewald' **Hungary**: N. A. Fischer, 'Historical Fiction as Oppositional Discourse: A Retrieval of Georg Lukacs' Popular Front Revival of Walter Scott's Historical Novels' **Italy:** M. Mancini, *Immaginando 'Ivanhoe': romanzi illustrati, balli e opere teatrali dell'Ottocento italiano* **Russia:** Dolinin, 'Val´ter-skottovskii istorizm i *Kapitanskaia dochka*'; Korenowska, 'Transformatsiia kriminal´nykh motivov proizvedenii Skotta i Dikkensa v rannem tvorchestve Dostoevskogo (1846–1869)' (publ. Bulgaria) **Spain:** García González, '*Waverley* ve la luz en España: consideraciones sobre la traducción publicada por Oliva'; M. J. Torquemada Sánchez, 'La Corona de Aragón y Escocia: paralelismos al hilo de *Heart of Midlothian*'	
2008		**General:** Nemoianu, 'From Historical Narrative to Fiction and Back: A Dialectical Game'; M. Pittock, 'Scott and the European Nationalities Question' **France:** S. Gemie, 'Walter Scott et Jacques Cambry: deux écrivains régionaux; S. Kleiman-Lafon, 'L'Utopie gothique de Jules Verne au pays de Rob Roy'; F. Lecaplain, *Jules Barbey d'Aurevilly (1808–1889): le Walter Scott normand, le connétable des lettres*; C. Peytavie, 'Frédéric Soulié, le "Walter Scott" du Midi: romancier de la Croisade contre les Albigeois'	

Date	Translations	Criticism	Other
2008 (Cont.)		**Germany/Italy:** Szaffner, 'Romance, Melodrama, and Opera: Scott's *Ivanhoe* and Nicolai's *Il Templario*' **Italy:** W. Bernhart, '"Liebling der ganzen Welt": Sir Walter Scott als Inspiration für die romantische Oper und Donizettis *Lucia di Lammermoor*'; M. Mancini, 'Rebecca: l'eroina del romanzo *Ivanhoe* tra scrittura e illustrazioni' **Portugal:** A. Lopes, 'Liquid Translation: On the Portuguese (Sub)Version of Walter Scott's *The Pirate*' **Russia:** G. Rosenshield, '*Taras Bulba* and the Jewish Literary Context: Walter Scott, Gogol, and Russian Fiction; E. Villari, '"La storia mi salvò la mente dalla completa dissipazione": Scott, Tolstoj, Hardy e la terapia della storia' **Spain:** García González, '*Waverley ó Hace sesenta años* de Walter Scott, en la traducción de Francisco Gutiérrez-Brito e Isidoro López Lapuya (S.A., ¿1910?)'; M. Rodríguez Espinosa, 'Exilio, vocación trasatlántica y mediación paratextual: José Joaquín de Mora y sus traducciones de *Ivanhoe* (1825) y *El talismán* (1826) de Walter Scott'; A. L. Soto Vázquez, *Novela regional inglesa y sus traducciones al español: Henry Fielding y Walter Scott*	
2009		**General:** Geppert, *Der Historische Roman: Geschichte umerzählt von Walter Scott bis zur Gegenwart*; R. Maxwell, *The Historical Novel in Europe, 1650–1950* **France:** A. Glinoer, 'Walter Scott: l'histoire au risque du frénétique'	

Date	Translations	Criticism	Other
2009 (Cont.)		**Hungary:** Ferguson, '"Nostra causa agitur": Walter Scott's *The Heart of Mid-Lothian* and George Lukács's Historical Meta-Text' **Spain:** F. Durán López, 'Blanco White y Walter Scott'; García González, 'Estudio y edición traductológica digital de *Waverley*, de Walter Scott, en traducción anónima, Barcelona, Librería-Imprenta de Oliva, 1836'; Rodríguez Espinosa, 'Estudio y edición traductológica digital de *El Talismán*, de Walter Scott, en traducción de José Joaquín de Mora, Londres, Rudolph Ackermann, 1826' and 'Estudio y edición traductológica digital de *Ivanhoe*, de Walter Scott, en traducción de José Joaquín de Mora, Londres, Rudolph Ackermann, 1825' **Switzerland:** A. Mortimer, 'The Translations of Walter Scott's *Waverley* in the *Bibliothèque Britannique*'	
2010		**General:** J. De Groot, *The Historical Novel* **Finland:** E. Schaad, 'Creative Manipulations of Outlaw Narrative in Aleksis Kivi's *Seitsemän veljestä*' **France:** Berton, 'Translating Scottish Literary Texts: A Linguistic Clover-Leaf'; M. Samuels, *Inventing the Israelite: Jewish Fiction in Nineteenth-century France*; N. Savy, *Les Juifs des romantiques* **Sweden:** A. G. Newby, 'A Swedish View of Scott's Scotland: Carl Graffman's *Skottska vuer* (1830)' **Switzerland:** I. Hernández, '*Der Heilige*: Zu einer Interpretation von Conrad Ferdinand Meyers Novelle in der Tradition Walter Scott's'	

Date	Translations	Criticism	Other
		Ukraine: D. Chyk, 'Retseptsya romanu V. Skotta *The Heart of Mid-Lothian* y povisti H. Kvitki-Osnovianenka "Kozyr-Divka"'	
2011		**General:** G. Gil-Curiel, *A Comparative Approach: The Early European Supernatural Tale*	
		France: P. Barnaby, 'Restoration Politics and Sentimental Poetics in A. J. B. Defauconpret's Translations of Sir Walter Scott'; G. Couderc, '*La Jolie Fille de Perth* de Bizet ou comment trahir et honorer Walter Scott'; C. Newark, 'The Novel in Opera: Residues of Reading in Flaubert'	
		Hungary: Fischer, 'The Modern Meaning of Georg Lukács' Reconstruction of Walter Scott's Novels of Premodern Political Ethics'; J. Marx, 'The Historical Novel after Lukács'	
		Italy: L. Lascoux, '*La Donna del Lago* de Rossini: première entrée en scène de Walter Scott dans l'opéra italien'; E. Valseriati, 'Al cospetto del diavolo zoppo: Camillo Ugoni, Giuseppe Nicolini e Walter Scott'	
		Poland: E. Żyrek, 'Między Byronem a Scottem: Hazlitta i Norwida refleksja nad zadaniami poety'	
		Spain: García González, '*Waverley, ó, Hace sesenta años* de Walter Scott, en traducción de Francisco Gutiérrez-Brito e Isidoro López Lapuya (¿1910?)'	
		Sweden: B. Sundmark, '*Ivanhoe* and the Translation of English Children's Books into Swedish in the Nineteenth Century'	

Date	Translations	Criticism	Other
2012		**General:** A. Rigney, *The Afterlives of Walter Scott: Memory on the Move* **General/Germany:** V. Sage, 'Scott contre Hoffmann: le combat du gothique européen pour la modernité' and 'Scott, Hoffmann, and the Persistence of the Gothic' **France:** I. **Thompson**, 'Jules Verne and the Trossachs: Experience and Inspiration' **Germany:** S. Keppler–Tasaki, 'Britische Bilder aus der deutschen Vergangenheit: Gustav Freytags *Die Ahnen* und der Massstab Walter Scott's'; C. Raakow, *Nach Scott: Textanalysen zum historischen Roman in Frankreich, Vigny, Mérimée, Hugo H. Ullrich, Wilhelm Raabe zwischen Heldenepos und Liebesroman: "Das Odfeld" und "Hastenbeck" in der Tradition der homerisch-vergilischen Epen und der historischen Romane Walter Scott's* **Spain:** García González, 'Sir Walter Scott Translated and (Self-)Censored as Children's and Adolescents' Literature in Franco's Spain' and '*Waverley* de Walter Scott, en la traducción de José María Heredia (1833)'	**General:** Completion of the Edinburgh Edition of the WN
2013		**General:** E. Gottlieb, *Walter Scott and Contemporary Theory*	

Introduction: Scott and the European Nationalities Question

Murray Pittock

Along with Byron and Macpherson, Sir Walter Scott was one of the three Scottish Romantic writers who exerted an immediate and powerful influence on European literature. The reception of Scott in that literature is the subject of the present study: and it is immediately apparent from the chapters which follow both how profound and how diverse that influence is.

One of the main aims of the Reception of British and Irish Authors in Europe series is to identify the reception through translation of internationally renowned and influential authors, and this is amply covered here. Another important goal for the series is to measure the absorption of its authors' ideas and practice in the receiving culture: and here Scott is clearly critical to the development of the historical novel across Europe. *The Reception of Walter Scott in Europe* also examines areas where Scott, more than other authors, was a shaping force in cultural reception beyond the limits of translation and literary influence, by exploring fields such as art, tourism and opera. Much of the present volume concentrates on the nineteenth century, the peak era of Scott's influence on the Continent; but some chapters discuss the twentieth century, the reception of Scott in literary histories and the political pressures and agenda which continue to affect the translation and reception of Scott even down to our own day.

It is a commonplace of the contemporary theoretical era that everything is political, just as everything is ideological. Such premises invite assumptions of equality (no one can escape ideology and all therefore share it), required for the countervailing postmodern precepts of tolerance and diversity, which appear to offer differentiation on condition that it is premised on an underlying homogeneity: the more comprehensive tolerance of difference is, the less the things which differ can differ in value. But ideology and politics are not shared between writers like a cake at a party; and indeed, apparent ideological positions can dissolve into the terms of their own rhetoricization. Dickens appears to be a stern critic of Victorian society, but the texts don't perform their own critiques (Jarndyce *v* Jarndyce consumes money, but Jarndyce always has plenty; trade unions are no answer to exploitation in *Hard Times*); but Scott, who as a rule makes far fewer political statements than many nineteenth-century writers, and who moreover wrote nearly always of the past rather than the present, was politically more dangerous than almost all of them. Any study of his reception must therefore account not only for the particular but also the general: the translation and literary influence of Scott, yes, but also the politics and power struggles attendant on the emplacement of his work in the cultures that received it.

Scott's age was the age of Herder; it was the age of Fichte; of the Irish Rising of 1798; of Napoleon; of the liberation of the Spanish viceroyalties in Latin America; of the end of the Holy Roman Empire; of the French Revolution and the last days of the Spanish Inquisition; of the struggle for Greek independence. It was the age of the Platonization of the nation-state as an expression of value (France) or an incarnation of it (Hegel's Prussia); of the widespread use of history and language as reasons for nationhood among those without a nation-state; of *Räuberomantik* and the idealization of the local, the particular and the primitive against an age of urbanization, better communications and a mass-market newspaper audience: the massification of the bourgeoisie, which in turn was to render it a target for Marx and Engels' substitution of class destiny for the intersection of Hegel's philosophy of history with his philosophy of right. Scott was born thirty-one years after it took Lord Lovat forty days to travel by coach from Inverness to London, twenty-nine from Edinburgh. In Scott's lifetime travel became ten times as fast, and before he died regular rail services had begun. Scott was aware of these changes, of their implications, and of their speed: *'Tis Sixty Years Since*, the subtitle of *Waverley* (1814), was the premise for the whole of his fiction: the mapping of rapid changes across short durations. The primary stage for this was of course early modern Scotland; but equally books like *Ivanhoe* (1820) plot the same pattern of swift modernization and its benefits, while cunningly pleasing the reader with the primitive and local, fated to be destroyed if it fought modernity, but otherwise often accommodated within it. Richard's use of secular power against the Templars in *Ivanhoe* prefigures the Reformation of Henry VIII, just as the Saxons who cannot be reconciled to Norman ways mirror Scott's Jacobites. Scott writes of history as closure, as reconciliation, and as the civic settlement of ethnic differences: themes he borrowed from the historians of the Scottish Enlightenment, David Hume (1711–76) and William Robertson (1721–93) in particular. (Robertson's aestheticization of the defeated Stuart past in the person of Mary Queen of Scots appears to have been particularly influential on Scott). The past may be magnificent, but it is over: the taxonomy of glory in Scottish history has given way under the inexorable pressures of the teleology of civility. Hazlitt saw this from the beginning: Scott emotionally evokes treason, but rationally approves loyalty:

> Through some odd process of *servile* logic . . . in restoring the claims of the Stuarts by the courtesy of romance, the House of Brunswick are more firmly seated in point of fact . . . His [Scott's] loyalty is founded on *would be* treason: he props the actual throne by the shadow of rebellion (Hazlitt 1910, 231).

Hazlitt's evaluation has remained a critical commonplace in discussing Scott, but it will bear finessing.

It is important to recognize that within Great Britain, Scott's fictional presentation of an already influential Enlightenment historiography was bound to be understood as relatively politically conservative. Scottish historiography up to the eighteenth century had largely understood the history of the country in terms of a paradigm of national resistance to invasion, of patriot 'republican' values against the encroachments of Empire. The wording of the Declaration of Arbroath (1320) came from Sallust; in the fifteenth century, knowledge of Tacitus's *Agricola* led to an interpretation of the struggle of Calgacus against Rome in terms of that of Scotland against England. It was thought that the most patriotic Scots were the 'oldest' ones, and these were identified with the men of the northern mountains, the Highlanders. So the image of the patriot Highlander was born, and cultivated throughout the Jacobite period, when Highland dress was used to clothe all troops, irrespective of origin. Scottish identity was seen as particularist, heroic and dedicated to victory against odds in the interests of national self-preservation.

Lord Acton observed that 'knowledge of history means choice of ancestors' (Prentis 1983, 1), and in the aftermath of Culloden, it was an urgent necessity for Lowland Scotland to distance itself from the many patriot Jacobites still in its midst: to disown the ancestry of defeat. So the Rising of 1745 was portrayed (as it still often is) as the last gamble of an outdated and marginal Gaidhealtachd against the forces of modernity, and a new historiography was developed which completely ignored centuries of the Scottish patriot tradition and its exponents (Bisset, Boece, Bower, Fordun down to Abercromby in 1711), and instead stressed the Germanicity of Lowland Scotland and the Celticity of the Highlands. Thus the Lowlands were presented as ethnically kin to England, and England was also depicted as on the whole representing that modernity to which Scotland should aspire. Stadial history, developed by Adam Smith (in his 'Four-Stage Theory of Development' of 1762), Dugald Stewart and others (Pittock 2003a, 262–63), argued that societies pass through various stages on the route to modernity, and that these stages were always broadly the same. In this structure (which later influenced sociology, anthropology and other social sciences), Scottish feudalism gave way for the last time in 1745 before the imperatives of civil and commercial modernity, the history of Redgauntlet before that of Joshua Geddes. Scott's closure of history's political and cultural challenges to modernity took place within this widely accepted historiographical paradigm, one which in the nineteenth century came to be known as Whig history: the ineluctable tendency to improvement, reconciliation and civility in society, all taking place in the context of the growth of liberty. David Hume's *History of England* (1754–62) and William Robertson's *History of Scotland* (1759) had made thousands of pounds for their authors, just as Scott was to do with his fictions. It was a comforting and persuasive narrative of Britishness, which stressed the inevitability and desirability of British unity. Scott adopts the 'Germanic Lowlands' theme very strongly: names such as Bradwardine, Edgar Ravenswood and Fairford are extremely unlikely in Scotland, but are redolent of Saxon roots. Within Great Britain, Scott's use of the Picturesque as a thematic accompaniment to the historic roles of Scotland and Scottishness neatly articulated both with Primitivism and the language of internal British tourism in Scotland: in doing so, he helped create a fictional and poetic framework for both cultural and landscape tourism, which both rendered the Scottish landscape as different and minimized its bad points: it does not, as Jim Alison observes, rain in *The Lady of the Lake*. In fraying the idea of a national boundary between England and Scotland by stressing a common Border culture, Scott also helped to create a 'union landscape' which began to formalize the social construction of a marriage between northern vigour and southern lassitude. In Scottish criticism, it was recognized at the time that Scott's Borderers were unrealistically shorn of their historic identities. His heroes too, are often psychologically borderers, situated to some extent on both sides of a divide that has been closed by the end of the novel. The ability to cross social and political borders (Waverley, Morton, Latimer, Ivanhoe) is a presage of the disappearance of such borders altogether. Scott's novels are formally acts of reconciliation to the historiography which produced them, a 'narrative of freedom . . . down the path of progress' in Jean Francois Lyotard's terms (Ahier and Ross 1995, 16).

Yet this reconciliation is not always complete. In *R* (1824) the status of legality and modernity rest all too clearly on the barely concealed sinews of naked power; in HW (1827), the force of the British state's claims on Scotland's past is not ameliorated by the ahistorical good nature conferred on them in *Waverley*; Ravenswood and Lucy Ashton are alike destroyed, not by modernity, but by a manipulative interpretation of it, in BL (1819). Even in *W* itself, the English court trying Euan MacCombich cannot conceive of his true nobility and misunderstands his motives to the point of contempt, while in *Ivanhoe* the Jews are neither overtaken by history nor reconciled to it, but treated as outcast by Saxon and Norman alike. Rebecca is in her way an eloquent comment on the limitations of Herderian ethnic particularism as the basis for nationality: in Adorno's terms 'the idea of Culture as absolute integration finds its logical expression in genocide' (Eagleton 2000, 44), and Isaac and Rebecca offer both a control and a critique not only of both Saxon and Norman assumptions of ethnic particularism, but also (and here is the key to the greatness of *Ivanhoe*, despite *bêtises* such as the 'resurrection' of Athelstan) to the very limited hybridity achieved by their unity. The fraying of borders of blood, history and ethnicity, Scott's typical themes, still leaves a border that Jews cannot cross. Rebecca's flight to a Muslim country, where she and her father will be more secure, problematizes this 'Tale of the Crusades' even further.

Another interesting case of Scott's reservations concerning the fraying of borders is that of *MM* (1826), in which the language of Swift's *Drapier's Letters* is revisited with an equally patriotic determination, in order 'to see the old red lion ramp a little' (Johnson 1970, 974). Scott was proud that *Malachi* had 'headed back the Southron', and its suggestion of common cause between Scotland and Ireland, combined with Scott's comparison of himself to Cuchulain and his use of Thomas Moore's Irish nationalist 'Minstrel Boy' as an analogue to *Malachi* in his *Journal*, are alike suggestive (*Journal*, 94, 105, 157). Even in his home market, Scott was not quite as reconciled to modernity as his plots suggest, particularly after the early 1820s. A further bout of British centralization, culminating in the transfer of Scottish affairs to the Home Office from 1827, combined with Scott's own ageing and bankruptcy to render his latter work somewhat more pessimistic about Scotland's place within the Union than those written in the heat or the afterglow of the struggle against Napoleon, in which Scottish troops played a major role.

In societies struggling for independence against regional powers or colonial oppressors, with suppressed languages, disordered civic societies and no historiography save that of native resentment and patriot resistance, the radical undertow in Scott's writing could seem more prominent than it did to a British audience. In societies innocent of Enlightenment stadialism, Scott's powerful depictions of the victims of history and society could evoke a sympathy which was more politically profound than the ameliorating aesthetics of Primitivism. To Hungarians in 1848, Scott could be a voice for the rights of national particularism; in Catalonia, he could be read as recommending irridentism. In Frantz Fanon's terms, the development of national literatures in Europe became a form of 'combat' in the struggle for freedom, a 'combat' visible in some of the chapters which follow. Scott offered a model for such engagements: that much of his purpose in deploying it was to celebrate its supersession was of less importance than the deep marks of that deployment in the literary and cultural engagement with the past. In Silvia Mergenthal's terms (taken up in the volume that follows by Emilia Szaffner's chapter, among others), the domestic ecology of fictional subgenres was altered by the influence of Scott. It had of course also influenced him: Maria Edgeworth's *Castle Rackrent* (1800) was the first 'national tale' in a sequence which made the first claims for Irish literature in English being a national literature, as Joep Leerssen and others have pointed out (McCaw 2004). In adopting some of the features of Edgeworth's fiction, Scott, not altogether unwillingly, created a national tale of his own, just as others did who learnt from him. One of the clearest features of the Scottian national tale, like that of Edgeworth but even more so, is the 'decentralized network of accidental voices', which does not merely endorse power (Gamer 2000, 3), but challenges it.

Even in the major settled powers of the world, Scott could appear a very different writer from his respectable British provenance. In the United States, he could be read as justifying either the incorporation or exclusion of Native Americans from the polity; or as a supporter of tradition and thus the Confederacy: famously, he was blamed by Mark Twain for the American Civil War. In France during the Restoration, partly thanks to Defauconpret, as Paul Barnaby points out, Scott could be read as an ardent monarchist whose monitory warnings against revolution and civil war had gone unheeded in the revolutionary period. Comparison between the fate of the Bourbons and that of the Stuarts was commonplace in France, which in the 1790s feared the rise of a Cromwell (cf. Lacretelle's *Parallèle entre César, Cromwell, Monk et Bonaparte* (1802)). Napoleon all too soon filled the role. After 1815, the Stuart comparison continued: in 1824, James VII and II was 'reburied at a splendid ceremony at Saint-Germain' (Mansel 1983, 4); in 1829, the Bal Marie Stuart was held at Court, and Charles X compared himself to James VII and II. It was into this environment that Scott, whose best novels dealt with the Stuarts and their fate, entered in 1826 in his visit to France. Scott was, more than he knew, a highly political and politicized writer whose conclusions were not always as important to his readers as what preceded them. In creating an opposition between Scottish *Gemeinschaft* and the *Gesellschaft* of the contemporary polite and industrializing world of Great Britain, Scott created both a language of Union, and one which could be deployed against it to emphasize marginality, repression and the inherent value of the domestic, autochthonous self. So much of his fiction presents the possibility, and sometimes the fullness, of 'counterpublic spheres capable of embodying ... marginalized and oppressed groups' (McCann 1999, 1). If one sees Scott in postcolonial terms, his fiction can be held to display both 'the mix of attraction and repulsion that may characterize relationships between imperial power and colony' and the 'transcultural' products of hybridity, embodied 'in the contact zone' between the two (e.g. Osbaldistone Hall) (Aaron and Williams 2005, xvi). The b(B)order, as ever, remains important.

Even if he were not used in a crude nationalist way, Scott's devotion to history was, in the age of European Romanticism, a surefire means of his adoption into the debate over the national self, and what constituted it. The taxonomy of glory, the identification of the antiquity of one's own society and culture with their nature, levels of operation and right to exist, and to do so autonomously, was a key element in the desire to form and defend a national self and a national literature in the Romantic period. Jacob and Wilhelm Grimm's view of the inherence of nationality in the stories of the people was only another aspect of the archaeology of national essentialism practised by Scott and influential deep into the twentieth century. Macpherson's Ossian poetry had served to make Scotland the home of a *Kulturvolk* throughout Europe; Scott, who treated Macpherson as inauthentic, promoted what he presented as a reality. Faced with a taxonomy of glory rooted in apparent historical fact, without Macpherson's suggestive yet moody evasions, many drew the inference that Scotland could serve not only as a type of *Kulturvolk* but as an exemplar for the celebration and/or reclamation of a *Reichstaat*. Scott provided a means to make this possible: cleverly, he kept the intensity of the Macphersonian representation of Scottish 'essence', but modified the indefinite extensibility of Ossianism with a sturdy battery of precisely realized locations: locations which were, however, enveloped in the language of the Picturesque to muffle the politics of their appeal, and to render less dangerous the irruptive Gothic features inherent in the Burkean Sublime. It was this generic realization of the particular which internationalized Scott's appeal. In Scott's historical novels, writers across Europe could find analogues for the historic struggles of their own societies, and (in cases like Hungary's) develop a fictional articulation of the anteriority of the national self for the first time in their history.

Translation posed special problems in the case of Scott, not least because of his use of Scots as a guarantor of autocthonous authenticity, loyalty to which (as in the case of Jeanie Deans) can be a mark of personal integrity (Scott even preferred the workmen on his estate to use Scots words (Johnson 1970, 465), and noted in his *Journal* that Sir James Melville in the original Scots shows 'force and firmness' as against 'the mincing English edition in which he has hitherto been alone known' (*Journal*, 287)). It adds to the translator's task to even approximately reproduce the linguistic hybridity and linguistic tension evident in Scott's deployment of Scots and English: this may be one of the reasons why English novels such as *Ivanhoe*, where Scott's thematized code switching was less evident, were often more popular on the Continent, though some of the dilemmas as to what represented a correct literary language were found elsewhere, as when Alessandro Manzoni rewrote *I promessi sposi* (The betrothed) in Tuscan for its 1840 edition. As Fernando Toda has pointed out, however, Scott's movement between English and Scots was itself a strategy designed to depict 'the United Kingdom' as 'a multilingual and multicultural society' which should preserve 'national cultural identities and values' (Toda 2005, 123). The switching of registers between Scots and English was also a way of offering the non-Scottish reader a view into the persistence of a Scots public sphere, albeit one under siege, where 'naebody's nails can reach the length o' Lunnon' (*HM*), but which in its distinctive social diversity and egalitarianism (versus the relationship between Edie Ochiltree and Jonathan Oldbuck in *A* (1816)) is nonetheless not disloyal to the wider British polity.

In the book which follows, Scott's reception is discussed in detail with regard to some of the cultures in which it proved particularly influential: sometimes through more than one chapter on different aspects or periods of its significance. There are omissions: the authors of the Bulgarian, Greek and Low Countries chapters did not complete their work by the deadline for a variety of reasons, while it proved impossible to get satisfactory coverage of Portugal or Italy: the Italian reception in general is covered in a number of chapters, notably those of Tom Hubbard, Jeremy Tambling and Beth Wright, but there is no discussion focused on Alessandro Manzoni (1785–1873). Manzoni's *I promessi sposi* is arguably the greatest novel deriving from the influence of Scott, although it was substantially written (though not published) before Scott's text of the same name, which appeared together with *T* in *Tales of the Crusaders* in 1825. Manzoni was sympathetic to the liberation and unification of Italy; and in creating a novel which went through more than 100 editions in half as many years, proved in many ways to be Scott's most potent heir, although Manzoni's influence on a Catholic view of nationalism was at odds with Scott's sturdy Protestantism, which encountered difficulties with the censor in Catholic countries, particularly in Spain, as Garcia-González and Toda's chapter intriguingly shows. Two of Scott's chief traits, the use of the Picturesque to frame a situation, and the historiographical philosophizing over the problems of a historical era into which he nevertheless enters with gusto, are early evident in Manzoni's text (Manzoni 1972 [1827], 27, 37).

The book which follows opens with discussion of Scott's reception in France, where so many of the events which lent critical historical and political significance to his oeuvre on the Continent took place. Richard Maxwell examines Scott's influence on French writing throughout the nineteenth century as far as the work of Proust, also making clear the extent of initial French influence on Scott. Certain related features (such as the cultural significance of Donizetti's *Lucia di Lammermoor*) are also examined, and discussion of Donizetti's cultural influence can also be found in the chapters by Tom Hubbard and Jeremy Tambling; Maxwell's treatment of Jules Verne can also be profitably compared with Alastair Durie's discussion in his chapter on Scott and tourism. Paul Barnaby's chapter on Defauconpret examines the specific dimension of Scott's reception as it was shaped by this centrally important translator.

In Chapter 3, José Enrique Garcia-González and Fernando Toda examine the reception of Scott in Spain from the 1830s through to the present, showing how certain of his texts remained a hot potato for censors right into the Franco era. Toda and Garcia-Gongález's work should be read in conjunction with the chapter by Andrew Monnickendam, which examines the role played by Scott in Catalonia, significantly different from that which he occupied in Castilian Spain. Catalonia was both the engine of Scott's reception in Spain, and also a place where his work was read in a politicized fashion. Catalonia was one of the cultures where Scott was received as a Romantic figure, and the reception of Scott as a Romantic seems to some extent to be connected to the extent to which he was read in politically radicalized terms. Monnickendam focuses on Scott's reception by two periodicals, *El Europeo* and *El Vapor* (The Steamboat), and three literary figures: Ramón López Soler, who saw Scott as the inventor of the historical novel; Bonaventura Carles Aribau, who saw Scott as discrediting the feudal ideas he appears to celebrate; and Manuel Mila Fontanals, who shows the extent of Scott's cultural impact in the context of the rebirth of Catalonia. Scott was compared with Byron and Cervantes (comparisons which were not uncommon elsewhere), and he was seen, rather intriguingly, in some quarters (for example by Bergnes de Las Casas, editor of *El Vapor*) as a champion of modernity who dignified the artisan.

In Chapter 5, Norbert Bachleitner outlines Scott's importance and reception in nineteenth-century Austria, and the importance of his influence in the characterization of the relationship between Austria and Hungary, which in fiction paralleled the relations between England and 'old', 'Romantic' Scotland in Scott. Again, Scott was seen as potentially subversive, and under the rule of an imperial censorship which sought to deter revolutionary ideas from entering Austria, seventeen of his novels were banned. Bachleitner studies in particular the case of *Woodstock* (1826), where passages critical of the Royalist position were cut. Later in the chapter he goes on to discuss the theatrical adaptations of Scott by Johan Wenzel Tremler and Johann Reinhold Lenz, and the range of influence of his historical novels in Austria.

The Austrian reception is linked both to Germany, which is discussed in Chapters 6 and 7, and to Hungary, the subject of Chapters 8 and 9. In Chapter 6, Frauke Reitemeier examines the reception of Scott in German literary histories from 1820 to c1945, as they constructed the German nation, tracing the development of their response from the 'Scottomania' of the 1820s (a much more enthusiastic response than that common at the time in Austria), and Scott's adaptation as a model for German fiction, into the twentieth century, highlighting the relatively untheorized views of the literary historians. In Chapter 7 Annika Bautz examines the political imperatives involved in publishing Scott (often in revived nineteenth-century translation) in a Germany divided after 1949, stressing the appeal of Scott's 'bias to the poor' as it was read in the German Democratic Republic, and the way in which Scott was taken more seriously as a writer in the east than in the west; like Toda and Garcia-González, Bautz discusses issues of censorship and self censorship in the reception of Scott, evidence of what a politically sensitive writer he remained into the twentieth century. Of particular interest in her argument is the dominance of *Ivanhoe* in the Western and later unified German markets: a dominance which appears to reflect Scott's less serious status as an adventure-story writer there, whereas in the east *Ivanhoe*'s relative weakness seems not just to reflect possible class antipathy to its noble heroes, but acts as a sign of Scott's higher rank as a novelist. We are back with the artisanal modernity of elements of Scott's Catalan reception in the previous century.

In Chapters 8 and 9, Emilia Szaffner and Gertrud Szamosi examine dimensions of Scott's Hungarian impact, including his significant impact on the history and historicity of the Hungarian novel, where Transylvania could seem an apt parallel for Scotland. Szaffner points out that German translations were dominant in the 'Reform Age' leading up to 1848 because of the social status accorded it in the era of the Austrian Empire. Many reformers travelled to Scotland, and Scott became seen as a purveyor of national myth, and was combined with German exemplars in Hungarian fiction. Szamosi traces this story forwards to the present day, where Scott's novels are hardly to be found in Hungarian bookshops.

In Chapter 10, Martin Procházka discusses Scott's importance in the national revival of the Czech lands and the role of his influence in Pan-Slavism. Here, too, German translations were at first influential, as the Czech language was only reviving gradually in the period after 1780, and here as in Germany itself, the past was being used as an engine for the discovery, development, recovery and invention of national identity. Landscape was also important in the definition of self, and here *LL* (1810) was particularly influential; Scott and Macpherson were also read together, and Scott was used by writers such as Karel Hynek Mácha as an intertext between Czech history and his own fiction.

In Chapter 11, Mirosława Modrzewska looks at Scott's 'enormous influence' on Polish Romanticism (a topic also looked at by Tom Hubbard) from before 1820, with special attention to Adam Mickiewicz and Scott's role as reflected in Polish identity, and its struggle with Russia. In Chapter 12, Mark Altshuller focuses on Scott's powerful role in Russian nineteenth-century fiction. Tone Smolej in Chapter 13 examines Scott's role in the representation of Slovenian nationhood, and in the novels of Jurčič in particular.

In Chapter 14, Jørgen Erik Nielsen tackles Scott's importance in Denmark and the rest of Scandinavia to figures such as Andreas Munch and Henrik Wergeland (seen as a totemic forerunner by MacDiarmid) right through to the 2003 production of *I* on stage by Denmark's Royal Theatre. Even in the 1820s, Scott's reception in Denmark was being noted in Scotland, as the *Edinburgh Evening Courant* for 5 January 1829 makes clear.[1] The last chapters examine the generic influence of Scott's poetry in Europe, and his influence on art, opera and tourism: the opera chapter in particular contains significant discussion of Scott's reception in Italy, which it has not proved possible to cover in a separate chapter. Tom Hubbard looks at the role of Scott's poetry across Europe, markets, and discusses elements of Scott's Italian reception in an argument also taken up in Jeremy Tambling's chapter. In Chapter 16, Jeremy Tambling provides an overview of the importance of Scott's work in European opera. In Chapter 17, Beth Wright demonstrates the enormous role played by Scott in

---

[1] I am indebted to Silvia Mergenthal for this reference.

nineteenth-century art, and in the last chapter Alastair Durie gives a sober and informative analysis on the role of Scott in the development of the modern tourist industry. Paul Barnaby provides the Reception Timeline.

The reception of Walter Scott in Europe has often been characterized as important, but seldom closely defined. A great deal of work requires to be done: on sales, on the development of Scott's reputation in other European countries and, looking further afield, on its influence on European empires and on the American perception of Europe. But the chapters collected here give a sense of what is possible, and the scale of the phenomenon to be addressed. Further details on translations of Scott across Europe can be readily found in the more than 2,800 entries in the Bibliography of Scottish Literature in Translation database at www.boslit.nls.uk, while the bibliographies to the volume display the range and depth in which Scott's work has been studied.

1 Scott in France

Richard Maxwell

Early in Marcel Proust's *Sodome et Gomorrhe* (the fourth volume of *A la recherche du temps perdu,* published 1921–22), the narrator describes the hypothetical case of a college student who does not yet realize that he is erotically attracted to others of his own sex. His cognitive disadvantage is that he has been instructed in love by reading Madame de Lafayette, Racine, Baudelaire and Walter Scott. Eventually, Proust observes, this innocent young person will learn that 'if the sentiment is the same the object differs, because that which he desires is Rob Roy and not Diana Vernon.'[1] Proust's placement of Scott probably seems more startling now than it did when it was written, because it locates him within a canon that also includes such figures of power as Lafayette, Racine, and Baudelaire. Proust is making a joke, but not about the Waverley novels; over the course of the nineteenth century, they became an integral part of French literature.

The precondition for Scott's impact on France was France's impact on Scott. From the start of his career until its final years, he wrote at length on French literature, history and culture. The Waverley novels mirror this interest. Some of them are set in French or Burgundian territory. Many also assimilate literary influences from across the Channel; thus, *HM* adapts the plot of Sophie Cottin's *Elisabeth* (Garside 1999), *P* evokes the abbé Prévost's *Cleveland*, and *I* alludes parodically to the voluminous romances of Madeleine de Scudéry. More broadly, even when Scott was not imitating models like these so directly, he often used methods and themes associated with France. *W* demonstrates this tendency by evoking a historiographical form adapted in seventeenth- and eighteenth-century French novels. To quote Prévost:

> A particular history has several characteristics peculiar to it [. . .]. The goal of a particular history being nothing but to make known the action, quality, inclinations and manners of a person of one or the other sex, all the public events that belong to

---

[1] 'Si le sentiment est le même l'objet diffère, que ce qu'il désire c'est Rob Roy et non Diana Vernon' (Proust 1987–89, 3: 25).

general history must not be introduced except when they are found to be mixed with those that one is trying to recount.[2]

'Particular history' is a distinctive kind of biography that effectively doubles as history because of the way that it manipulates effects of foreground (the life of an individual) and background (public events). Public events can come into view sharply and abruptly, then once more recede. Conversely, a hero or heroine can seem to enter or exit history, somewhat as actors go on and off a stage. Particular history is notable for flexibility and openness; writers of prose fiction could use it to accommodate an extraordinarily miscellaneous range of materials within a loosely biographical frame.

W brilliantly takes all this over. Like Madame de Lafayette's *nouvelles*, the novel stages a meeting, indeed a kind of blundering collision, between a life and its times, a meeting that is also conceived as an intersection between fictional and historical elements. As in Prévost's *Cleveland*, the intersection is managed and sustained by means of an attachment, directed – or misdirected – towards a member of the Stuart dynasty, who serves as a figure of political and romantic transgression. Such a figure proves eminently useful for mediating between the hero of the narrative and a larger historical scene. Finally, in accordance with the governing convention of particular history, *W* ends by emphasizing the detachability of its hero. Abandoning the Stuarts therefore means quitting history as well.

When the French encountered the Waverley novels, they absorbed them with dazzling speed. Writing in 1828, Sainte-Beuve could declare that his was an 'epoch in which the imitation of Walter Scott was almost a necessary contagion, even for the very highest talents.'[3] The qualification, 'even', is both a tribute to Scott and an expression of amazement: how could this literary fad from across the Channel have penetrated not only so quickly but deeply into French culture? One reason was that Scott could be easily, fleetly, judged within a pre-existing national frame of reference. The judgement was not always positive. Stendhal complained that whereas Mme de Lafayette could analyse, Scott could only describe (Stendhal 1952, 1959). Others, meanwhile, were celebratory: both Balzac and Dumas argued, with relief, that the Waverley novels had effectively superseded the work of Lafayette's earlier heirs, such as Madame de Genlis, Baculard d'Arnaud, and Cottin, opening up a larger and freer literary approach to history. Either way, nineteenth-century French novelists had little hesitation in linking *W* and other Scott novels with a host of indigenous predecessors.

---

[2] 'Une histoire particulière a plusieurs caractères qui lui sont propres [. . .] le but d'une histoire particulière n'étant que de faire connoître les actions, les qualités, les inclinations et les moeurs d'un personnage de l'un ou de l'autre sexe, tous les événements publics, qui sont la matière de l'histoire générale, n'y doivent entrer qu'autant qu'ils se trouvent mêlés avec ceux qu'on entreprend de raconter.' See Prévost 1810, 14: i–ii.

[3] 'A une époque où l'imitation de Walter Scott est presque une contagion nécessaire, même pour de très hauts talents' (Sainte-Beuve 1956, 1: 301).

The French could respond to Scott with such spontaneity partly because he was already, almost, one of their very own. But this does not tell us quite as much as we might want to know about why they kept on responding to him. The fact is, there was an element in the Waverley novels that did not exist in Lafayette, Prévost, and the others. Scott preserved the basic form of particular history but provided a new way of treating the public events that this genre manipulates. These events came to seem at once more distant – where the distancing was accomplished by antiquarian learning about the past – and more immediate; something like the events of 1745 could now be treated as an all-enveloping emergency happening in a crisis-laden present. Further, if he could stage the '45 after this fashion, he could present any other great historical occurrence in the same learned yet highly vivid manner (Maxwell 2001).

This remarkable intensification of the novelized particular history that had been a French speciality for generations was attractive to many writers all over the world. It was most attractive in France because, between the late eighteenth and the late nineteenth century, France was where history happened. We know, or we think we know, that it happened everywhere and that it is omnipresent, but if we think of European or even world history in terms of spectacular and deeply significant events, France was the centre. Its liveliest years would include 1789, 1814, 1830, 1848, 1851, 1870, and 1871 – in other words, the fall of the Bastille, the fall of Napoleon, the ascension of Louis-Philippe to the throne, his subsequent fall and flight, the *coup d'état of* Napoleon III, the Franco-Prussian War, and the brief career of the Commune, bloodily ended by the troops of Adolphe Thiers. If Germany had been the testing ground of history in seventeenth-century Europe, France was the testing ground for history in the nineteenth. It became, in effect, the *theatre* of history.

Scott's reinvention of the historical novel, his absorption of the French model for it, his transformation of that model, was just what the French themselves needed. From *W*, they got a remarkably deft retooling of a form that they themselves had invented and that nonetheless, in its new guise, seemed alluringly strange, as well as immediately useful. Nobody, except for the most minor writers, imitated Scott wholesale; almost everyone was comfortable enough with the Waverley aesthetic to change it around drastically and at will. Just for this reason, French novelists found it wonderfully suited to their own great century of crisis.

There is a huge accumulation of evidence that writers of fiction between, say, Alfred de Vigny and Marcel Proust not only knew Scott's novels and poems well but expected their readers to do so. Traces of his impact are thus far too common for any one essay to exhaust. The present account focuses first on a group of works associated with the Revolution of 1830 – which occurred at the zenith of French Scottophilia and meshed with it powerfully – then traces the later, more scattered but perhaps even deeper impact his work had in the decades following mid century. If in, say, an English context, it is the sluggish Scott who dominates, the Scott who embodies above all the permanence and stability of property (Welsh 1968), then a French context provides a contrastingly volatile, indeed a histrionic, Scott. All the writers treated here acknowledge the picturesque side of the Waverley novels: the dream of the past, the inheritance of the great estate, the grandeur of family heritage, and (in a slightly different vein) the lure of region or custom (so that George Sand could be thought of as the Walter Scott of Berry). Some liked this traditionalist vision, while others regarded it as a laughable mystification; in both cases, it became a portal through which writers (and readers along with them) could reach another, more volatile Scott, whose tales were designed to evoke turning points in history and (miraculously) to put suspense back into them. The excitement of this second Scott can be associated with the siege of Torquilstone or the last moments of Lucy/Lucia of Lammermoor. The heroine's voice rises to a piercing shriek; the castle collapses in on itself. We are there at the moment of emergency, when history is in progress and all is as yet undecided.

I 1830

Paul Lacroix was 23 years old when, in 1829, he published the first volume of his *Soirées de Walter Scott à Paris*. Throughout the *Soirées*, Lacroix poses as an elderly booklover, 'le bibliophile Jacob'. Jacob is a good deal like one of Scott's supposed antiquarian editors, but less comical, more sympathetic than most of them. As suggested by the book's frontispiece, he has a picturesquely ancient library. (He also seems to have the Bayeux Tapestry, or at least a copy of it.) Jacob's greatest social ambition is to meet Scott, which he manages on the great man's visit to Paris in 1826. Since the bibliophile is seemingly the only French-man conversant with Froissart, the Author of Waverley conceives an instant respect for him and spends the night of their meeting telling tales. Transcribed or reconstructed by Jacob, and relaying striking occurrences from medieval or Renaissance French history, these tales form the substance of the *Soirées*.

The 1829 *Soirées* were followed in 1831 by a second volume. In the interim, the revolution of 1830 took place. It seems that this event made its impression even on the fragile and introverted bibliophile:

> I've been at my window since the popular Fronde of July; I have communicated with the exterior air if not with men of the present, and I have had to forget the only goods which make me regret life: my books and my beautiful retreat, to frequent the unknown world of politics. (1831, 2: 22)[4]

Charles X has been driven out of France and replaced by Louis-Philippe; the Restoration thus went to pieces, revealing that where everything seemed to be settled, nothing was. In the wake of this momentous occurrence, Lacroix stages a defining moment of reception for his own channelling of Scott. He tells us that when audiences opened the *Soirées*, they declared, 'Decidedly, Sir Walter Scott is becoming a romantic! (Décidément Walter Scott devient romantique!' (2: 21)). Moreover, if he is a romantic already in volume one, he is even more

---

[4] 'Je me suis mis à fenêtre depuis la Fronde Populaire du mois de juillet ; j'ai com-muniqué avec l'air extérieur, sinon avec les hommes d'à présent, et j'ai failli oublier les seuls biens que me feront regretter la vie : me livres et ma belle retraite, pour fréquenter le monde inconnu et de la politique.' Soirées vol. 2, 22.

so in Lacroix's second instalment. This intensification can be suggested by the first story of the 1831 volume, about the mad king Charles VI, whose elaborate masquerade costume somehow catches fire. The king runs about in flames, yelling frantically for help, while the clever Duc d'Orléans (evoking Louis-Philippe) plots coolly, just offstage. As the present heats up, the past must be represented ever more frenetically.

Lacroix's conveniently dated *Soirées* describe what it means to finds oneself in the centre of a great historical convulsion: to live through a red-letter year, while coming to grips with Scott. The major novelists of this period communicate the same kind of experience on a larger scale. Stendhal's *Le Rouge et le noir* was published in 1830; it follows the efforts of Julien Sorel, a man of modest birth, to make a place for himself in the upper reaches of French society. The story itself is set in the 1820s; an editorial note by the author suggests that its *terminus ad quem* is 1827. As Erich Auerbach observes, *Le Rouge et le noir* can hardly be understood by a reader who does not grasp this social and historical context; Stendhal is writing about an unsuccessful Restoration, one in which pre-Revolutionary hierarchies cannot be convincingly sustained (Auerbach 1957). The times are not conducive to steady judgements or carefully reasoned attachments.

Scott might seem unhelpful in this context. He is, after all, a great believer in social deference as a desirable feature of life. One has to adapt to new times (and new kings), but such adaptations do not destroy the settled pleasures of hierarchy, even when these pleasures have to reappear in sublimated forms. Though a great Scott enthusiast at the time, and one of the best chroniclers of the French rage for his work, Stendhal will have none of this. In a draft of a proposed essay on *Le Rouge et le noir*, he claims that the only two writers admired by both French provincials and Parisians were Scott and his great Italian disciple Alessandro Manzoni; provincials, he says, loved the elaborate descriptions provided by the Author of Waverley, while Parisians detested them. Stendhal is on the side of the Parisians:

> M. de S, bored with all this medievalism, with the *ogive* and the dress of the fifteenth century, dared to recount an adventure that took place in 1830 [here the 1827 *terminus* is forgotten], and to leave the reader in complete ignorance concerning the kind of dresses worn by Mme de Rênal and Mlle de La Mole.[5]

Too much description, especially in an antiquarian vein, can give the illusion of social stability where none is in practice possible. Stendhal claims to be breaking away from this mannerism.

Stendhal's supposedly unprecedented gesture of using two heroines where one would have sufficed provides an example of how he can acknowledge his

---

[5] 'M. de S, ennuyé de tout ce moyen âge, de l'*ogive* et de l'habillement du xvᵉ siècle, osa raconter une aventure qui eût lieu en 1830 et laisser le lecteur dans une ignorance complète sur la forme de la robe que portent Mme de Rênal et Mlle de La Mole, ses deux héroïnes, car ce roman en a deux, contre toute les règles suivies juqu'ici' (1952, 1: 703).

Scottish predecessor while keeping his distance; the two-heroine gambit was (and is) famously associated with Scott. Nonetheless, *Le Rouge et le noir* succeeds in its effort at mould-breaking, for it deploys its contrasting female leads in a different manner than does *W* or *I*. An anonymous letter from Madame de Rênal, the ineligible heroine (older, already married, dangerously passionate), halts Julien's union to her propertied and legitimate rival, Mademoiselle de La Mole. The way that the novelist plays these women off against each other thus prevents his hero from coming into an estate and a settled place in society. Stendhal evokes the Waverley solution only to affirm its impossibility.

So much for the settled, propertied Scott. The volatile, Gallicized Scott (already encountered in Lacroix's later *Soirées*) is a step harder to banish. His presence is evoked in a peculiar habit of Mademoiselle de La Mole; she wears mourning clothes every 30 April. It turns out that she comes from the family of Boniface de La Mole, the lover of Marguerite, 'La Reine Margot', wife of Henri IV. Julien hears the lurid tale of how this earlier Mole was eventually beheaded and of how Margot repossessed his head, then buried it in a chapel at the foot of Montmartre. Mademoiselle's sense of a solemn family heritage (which she will eventually enact on her own) and her very name (Mathilde-Marguerite) give her a strange appeal. She and Julien take long walks together; she tells him one day that she is deeply familiar with the histories of d'Aubigné and Brantôme (on the fearful sixteenth-century Wars of Religion). Strange, thinks Julien: 'The marquise does not permit her to read the novels of Walter Scott!'[6] It is indeed odd that the marquise has failed to realize how mild Scott can look (especially in his love scenes), compared to the historians. On the other hand, if impressionable French maidens were reading sixteenth-century history during the 1820s, that was largely because of Scott's defining influence; as Lacroix suggests, it was he who brought history for amateurs and general readers back into play. Finally, then, it is as though Mademoiselle did not need to read Scott to have read him. She got her dose of *I* indirectly, even though forbidden to open the book.

Like Stendhal (whose work he admired), Honoré de Balzac disliked both the Restoration and its aftermath. However, his reasons for dissatisfaction were quite different; a confirmed monarchist and a Catholic who had strayed towards Swedenborg (where Stendhal was a rationalist and a follower of Napoleon), Balzac regretted the irreversibility of the changes wrought in France. One of his early responses to these changes was to write about them in what he hoped was the manner of Scott. The latter's impact is already evident in Balzac's juvenilia, especially *Clotilde de Lusignan, ou le Beau Juif, manuscrit trouvé dans les Archives de Provence et publié par Lord R'Hoone* (1822). *Clotilde* adds amorous heat to an *I*-like milieu; a few years later, Balzac's Scott imitations manifest larger ambitions. The first book in the *Comédie Humaine* is *Les Chouans* (1829), a historical novel with links to both *W* (1814) and Fenimore Cooper's *The Last of the Mohicans* (1826); Balzac's subject is guerilla warfare, *Chouannerie*, as practised in the Brittany of the early 1790s against the encroachments of Paris and the Revolution. His

---

[6] 'La marquise ne lui permet pas de lire les romans de Walter Scott!' (1: 504–05).

original idea was to pair *Les Chouans* with a study of urban civil war (the city would be Paris, the time the fifteenth century); related novels would follow, producing a panoramic representation of France through the ages. In practice, as Georg Lukács stresses, Balzac eventually took another course; he passed 'from the portrayal of *past history* to the portrayal of the *present as history*' (Lukács 1983). The young Balzac's relatively conventional aspirations would be memorialized in *Illusions perdues* (1837) as those of Lucien de Rubempré, seeking fame from the publication of a novel in the style of Scott. Balzac's own project, was fresher in kind. Many of his novels include a survey of past decades, in some cases centuries; at a certain point, however, the narrative tends to focus in on a pivotal year or month, typically from the 1820s or 1830s; thus, as Lukács would have it, relatively short periods take on the character of distinctive epochs. The present is treated as though it were the past.

In *Le Cabinet des antiques* (1838) Balzac discovers an especially self-conscious way of pursuing an antiquarianism of the present (or of the very recent past). *Cabinet* chronicles the ordeals of the ancient, proud, and provincial d'Esgrignon family. Loyal to the Bourbon dynasty, even during the worst days of the Revolution, they get little recognition from the restored Louis XVIII; left to their own devices, they manage to gather the local nobility into a self-enclosed social world, whose members can pretend that the cataclysms of the late eighteenth century and the betrayals of their own moment have never occurred. 'The excluded had thus, in scorn of this little *faubourg Saint-Germain* of the provinces, given the nickname *the Cabinet of antiques* to the salon of the marquis d'Esgrignon.'[7] The name is apt; the Cabinet of Antiques they remain. 'Cabinet' signifies a display case for remarkable objects – and indeed, everybody in town can watch the show at the d'Esgrignon *hôtel* through its enormous windows. (The *hôtel* is effectively 'a cage of glass'.) 'Antiques' suggests the world of the Scott-like antiquary; in this instance, however – as Balzac specifies – it is the characters themselves, the Marquis d'Esgrignon and his mummified companions, who constitute a tableau of curiosities, the kind of exhibition that Scott's own antiquarian hero, Jonathan Oldbuck, might have assembled, had he collected human beings instead of objects. In one of the novel's most vivid (and disturbing) passages, Balzac mimes at length the recollections of a man who was a schoolboy in the local village and who recalls observing the Cabinet of Antiques at its grisly business of playing cards or parading back and forth ceremoniously. There is nothing for these people to do; they can only be themselves, or rather, pretend to be what they once were. Inadvertently, they have transformed themselves into museological specimens.

However, one member of this social microcosm grasps what has happened in the world without flagging in his loyalty to the d'Esgrignon name. This is the aged notary Chesnel. 'For him, the Revolution had shaped the spirit of the new generation, it touched the deeds at the bottom of a thousand wounds, it found

---

[7] 'Les exclus avaient donc, en haine de ce petit faubourg Saint-Germain de province, donné le sobriquet de *Cabinet des antiques* au salon du marquis d'Esgrignon' (1999 [1838], 64).

them irrevocably accomplished.'[8] Chesnel is unable to convince the Marquis that times have changed. His failure on this account elicits the novel's most direct and elaborate reference to the Waverley novels:

> Simple soldier, faithful to his post and ready to die, his opinion could never be heard, even at the heart of the storm; at least had chance not placed him, as in *The Antiquary* the king's beggar, at the edge of the sea, when the lord and his daughter were surprised there by the tide.[9]

Balzac alludes to one of the most celebrated incidents in the Waverley novels, when Oldbuck and Lovel rescue Sir Arthur and Isabella Wardour in *A*. Lovel in the end marries Isabella.

Le Cabinet des antiques moves towards an analogous marriage, with several mordant twists. In theory Balzac agrees with Scott that social and political compromise is good; in practice he illustrates how terrible prudential adjustments can be. Lovel and Isabella are a love match. Victurnien's marriage, by contrast, allows him to sustain a life of hopeless and meaningless, though occasionally pleasant, dissipation. That is the dilemma of those who inhabit the Cabinet of Antiques, or who, like Victurnien, were simply educated there. By ignoring the new order, the order of money and liberal self-promotion, this provincial aristocracy assures its own humiliating absorption into the enemy tribe; by not ignoring it, they also betray themselves. Much more than in Scott, history is defined by its losses.

Chesnel and the d'Esgrignons have small parts in *L'Envers de l'histoire contemporaine* (1848), the last novel of the *Comédie Humaine* to be written. In certain ways, *L'Envers* is the mirror image of *Le Cabinet des antiques*. The latter argues that it is the tragedy of the loyal and the heroically stubborn that – no less than other, lower, and more easygoing souls – they must find a way to live in historical time; their purity affords them no respite. *L'Envers* takes the opposite stance; there is, after all, an honourable way to escape the degradations of the post-1830 world of *Enrichissez-vous*, Balzac's most obvious target. The time is 1836. Godefroid is a young man who has failed as a man of the world and lost his taste for life. Quite by accident, he discovers in the centre of Paris (on the *Ile de France*, in the shadow of Notre-Dame) an austere retreat overseen by the beautiful and alluringly mature Madame de la Chanterie. Chesnel turns out to be her notary; she has several other similarly loyal, and loyalist, associates, each with a previous life that he wishes to escape. They are all plotting together, but at what? During the early days of his acquaintance with this group, Godefroid wonders if they might not be some kind of legitimist conspiracy; and

---

[8] 'Pour lui, la Révolution avait composé l'esprit de la génération nouvelle, il en touchait les faits au fond de milles plaies, il les trouvait irrévocablement accomplis.' (1999 [1838], 77)

[9] 'Simple soldat, fidèle à son poste et prêt à mourir, son avis ne pouvait jamais être écouté même au fort de l'orage; à moins que le hasard ne le plaçât, comme dans *L'Antiquaire* le mendiant du Roi au bord de la mer, quand le lord et sa fille y sont surprise par la marée' (1999 [1838], 80).

indeed, as we learn in the course of a lengthy flashback, Madame de la Chanterie served a long prison sentence as punishment for her links to a genuine Royalist plot. Godefroid 'fantastically pictured to himself not the aforementioned Rifoël [one of the plotters], but a chevalier du Vissard, a young man somewhat similar to the Fergus of Walter Scott, in short the French Jacobite.'[10] For a few moments, we seem to be back in the world of *W* or *R*, with Bourbon sympathizers substituting for Stuart adherents. But however dangerous Madame de la Chanterie's past, she is now a conspirator of a spiritual sort: leader of the *Frères de la consolation*, who do good deeds about Paris in a silent, ubiquitous, semi-supernatural way. (One suspects some influence from Eugène Sue's *Mystères de Paris*, with its aristocratic Samaritan Prince Rodolphe.) The second half of *L'Envers* (originally published separately) narrates Godefroid's initiation into this group, whereby he remains within the world, at the heart of the great city, even while transcending it. The novel not only works *towards* contemporary history but provides a *reverse* image of it; thus, both meanings of 'envers' are simultaneously in play (Pingaud in Balzac, 1970).

Le Cabinet des antiques suggests that Balzac is more of a materialist than Scott, *L'Envers de l'histoire contemporaine* that he is more of an idealist too. Both perceptions are accurate; further, the materialism exacerbates the idealism, and vice versa. This arrangement is not so conspicuous so long as one reads only *Les Illusions perdues* or *Cousine Bette*, where the worldly side of Balzac predominates. Further explorations reveal that Balzacian contemporary history has its own internal conflicts. It is, as Lukács argued, an effort to discern a process of social change in the shape, drift, and texture of very short periods. But the more pervasive social change becomes, the more Balzac wants certain favoured protagonists to undergo mystical conversions that will separate them from change altogether. Scott's idea of the End of History is that warring parties should compromise. The virtue of such an agreement is that it facilitates social stability and the transfer of property. Balzac is much less certain that any such arrangement could be desirable.

In their different ways, both Balzac and Stendhal were realists. Victor Hugo was the pre-eminent Romantic writer of France. For this reason – and for others too, as will be seen – he is, in his generation, the most eager of all to evoke Scott, not just for purposes of argument, nor merely as a general precedent but as a direct and pertinent model, to be imitated in the most exacting manner. The best example of all is *Notre-Dame de Paris* (1831). Evoking those ogives that bored Stendhal, and the Middle Ages that both he and Balzac thought they had outgrown, *Notre-Dame* borrows from a generous range of Waverley Novels (*QD* and *FN* prominent among them), eventually, at its climax, attempting what is practically a point-by-point restaging of *I*'s great military conflict, the siege of the Castle of Torquilstone.

---

[10] Godefroid 'se dessina fantastiquement non pas le nommé Rifoël, mais un chevalier du Vissard, un jeune homme quasi semblable au Fergus de Walter Scott, enfin le jacobite français' (Balzac 1970 [1848], 156).

Torquilstone is the site where Richard I, in disguise, banded together with Robin Hood and his Merry Men to rescue some captured maidens and various other victims of the maleficent Norman oppressor Front-de-Boeuf. Scott puts considerable emphasis on the violence of the assault and the desire for revenge that it unleashes in the soul of at least one oppressed Saxon, the ancient Ulrica. The violence is, however, contained and channelled. To be sure, the castle burns down. But the local peasants do not go on a rampage or conduct an untrammelled slaughter of the Norman establishment. And Robin Hood himself reaffirms his loyalty to the monarchy. Torquilstone thus affirms the power of chivalric energy governed by feudal ties of loyalty.

It is important to understand just how closely Hugo works from this model. The parallels can be enumerated systematically. First of all, in *I*, Rebecca – an exotic, fiercely chaste Jewish heroine – is held prisoner in a castle, which is first besieged by her friends, the Saxons, and then set afire by a grotesque pariah (Ulrica) who has been lurking on the premises for many years and knows all their secrets. The fire is intended to help the besiegers get in. It does this, but at a great cost. Amid the ensuing chaos, the heroine is kidnapped by de Bois-Guilbert, only to find herself on trial for the crime of witchcraft. Fortunately, in a last-minute turnabout, she will be saved from execution.

Second, in *Notre-Dame*, Esmeralda – an exotic, fiercely chaste gypsy heroine – finds herself on trial for the crime of witchcraft, then is snatched away, into a medieval cathedral, where she becomes, effectively, a prisoner. The cathedral is later besieged by her friends, the Truands, and then set afire by a grotesque pariah (Quasimodo, her attendant) who has been lurking on the premises for many years and knows all their secrets. The fire is intended to keep the besiegers out. It does this only briefly, and at a great cost. Amidst the ensuing chaos, the heroine is kidnapped by Frollo, like de Bois-Guilbert, a rejected but obsessive suitor. Unhappily, in a last-minute turnabout, she will be executed.

Hugo, like Scott, is writing a historical novel that culminates in a great storming of a spectacular medieval structure, punctuated by historical allusions. Nonetheless, he uses this problematic indulgence to quite a different end than Scott: not to memorialize chivalry, but rather to place it as a force for order conspicuous by its absence. It is symptomatic that the single important chivalric figure in Hugo's novel is a gallant but worthless rake (Phoebus); *Notre-Dame*'s schema can imagine no significant role for knighthood. Indeed, among Esmeralda's many suitors, Quasimodo is the most knightly in his impulses – especially in his humility before the lady and his selfless courage in defending her – yet his spectacular ugliness and lack of socialization set him apart from any recognizable chivalric ethos.

Correspondingly, the siege of Notre-Dame as imagined by Hugo is an effort to explore what might happen if a culturally dominant structure were assaulted without chivalric supervision. Echoing Stendhal's kind of complaint, Lukács observes that *Notre-Dame* depends excessively upon grotesque and picturesque tableaux; the novel's description of the struggle at the cathedral is the outstanding case in point. However, like many other picturesque/grotesque moments in *Notre-Dame*, this sequence is addressed to show how architecture can become not only a stage for history but an actor within it – an actor that both embodies and elicits the power of active multitudes. Both the besiegers and besieged in the conflict take the form of crowds, but crowds so peculiar in nature as to make the incident a crux, a riddle, that even the author himself might have some difficulty in illuminating.

The siege stems from heroic good intentions. Hoping to reclaim Esmeralda from her churchly refuge, whose supposed inviolability they distrust, the Truands (a fellowship of beggars and thieves based at the Court of Miracles) assemble in front of Notre-Dame. They look like a crowd of louts; they even have pitchforks and scythes, like the untutored feudal peasants of *I*. On the other hand, this unpromising group proves surprisingly well-organized, forming a professional wedge formation as it prepares to march on the church. The Truands, then, are not the amateurs they seem; indeed, as Hugo is at pains to suggest, some of them frequently execute mass assaults, bursting into well-appointed homes on a regular basis (unless those homes are guarded by similar ad hoc armies of minor miscreants) and then looting them thoroughly.

As for the church, they have promised not to loot that, as long as the clerics inside yield to them peaceably. The surrender in question is about to occur when Quasimodo steps in. Misunderstanding the intentions of the Truands (who he thinks have come to threaten Esmeralda), the hunchback decides to defy them, all by himself. One hunchback versus a formidable gang of thieves: it seems like a mismatch, but Quasimodo, no less than his opponents, possesses the attributes of collectivity, having become (in an earlier appearance) the King of Carnival, and having sustained, through his bellringing career, the capacity to make the cathedral itself – an embodiment of the whole culture – speak to the city of Paris. Now these same talents of uncanny multiplication are turned to a military end. First he throws down beams and stones onto the besieging Truands, then, when that approach proves insufficient, attempts another defence more spectacular yet:

> An idea occurred to him. He ran and fetched a faggot from the little chamber he occupied, laid over the faggot several bundles of laths and rolls of lead – ammunition he had not yet made use of – and after placing this pile in position in front of the orifice of the gutters, he set fire to it with his lantern.[11]

Soon the fire leaps up between the towers of the great cathedral; from the drainpipes, meanwhile, molten lead engulfs the cathedral's terrified assailants. Thus, through the medium of architecture, Quasimodo seems to become a thousand soldiers; he constitutes an army in himself, eliciting in turn ever more terrifying energies from the Truands beneath.

Hugo provides a commentary on the siege of Notre-Dame in the form of a dialogue occurring across town. As the siege unfolds, Louis XI holds court at the Bastille; when news of the Truands' assault arrives, he attempts to judge the causes and the seriousness of this disturbance. Jacques Coppenole, a Flemish

---

[11] 'Une idée lui vint. Il courut chercher un fagot dans son bouge de sonneur, posa sur ce fagot force bottes de lattes et force rouleaux de plomb, munitions dont il n'avait pas encore usé, et, ayant bien disposé ce bûcher devant le trou des deux gouttières, il y mit le feu avec sa lanterne' (Hugo 1967, 431).

burgher familiar with popular rebellions, describes one to Louis, but agrees with him that the hour has not yet struck for similar events in France. When, in that case, might the time of revolution arrive? It will come, says Coppenole, when citizens and soldiers turn against each other. Louis responds that his good Bastille will not be so easily shattered. The uprising of the Court of Miracles is thus pinpointed as a premature version of the 'siege' (as it is often called) of the Bastille.

It was not that Hugo found the upheavals of 1789 or, by implication, 1830, wrong turns. In the process of moving leftwards, from monarchism towards socialism and a doctrine of eternal historical progress, he acquired a substantial commitment to revolutionary action. However, his point-by-point imitation of Scott's Torquilstone is also a point-by-point refutation of it: if *Notre-Dame* explicitly predicts the Bastille's fall, where the energies of the people will finally prevail, it implicitly worries about the direction in which those energies might take the nation. He fears that no movement of the people can be contained within an orderly, long-term compromise, as Scott had seemed to suggest. Any large-scale release of popular will can yield massively bloody results. Hugo, apostle of progress, is thus simultaneously a prophet of apocalypse. It is Scott who provides him with a narrative language in which he can express this tension.

II After the mid-nineteenth century

The generation of 1830 worshipped Scott, mocked him, or did both at the same time. Beyond the middle of the century, their kind of intensity, their interest in the Waverley novels as a fresh discovery, would have seemed absurd. These books were what people had read at a formative stage of life, before going to more sophisticated or at least more up-to-date forms of literature. But juvenile memories have a way of remaining vivid. Among the writers formed by the uneasy glories of the Second Empire (1851–70), most not only had Scott in their past but also found his image rising up before them when they embarked on their own defining literary projects. In recovering Scott, they also recovered the aesthetic of crisis-within-idyll; only this time, the way that terrorizing emergencies could rise up out of a nostalgic landscape had something oddly intimate about it. Scott had become an integral part of so many private pasts that his historical scheme often took on an autobiographical cast.

Gustave Flaubert's letters of the mid to late 1830s (written in his teens) report his viewing or reading of work by Hugo (especially *Notre-Dame*), Alexandre Dumas (then primarily a playwright), and their esteemed forefather Scott. 'I am going to take away for my trip *The History of Scotland* in three volumes by W. Scott.' 'We have in our town a Norwegian violinist of the Paganini kind [. . .] named Old-Buck.'[12] (Flaubert changes 'Ode Bull' to 'Oldbuck' to make a

---

12   'Je vais emporter pour mon voyage *L'Histoire d'Ecosse* en trois volumes par W. Scott.' 'Nous avons dans notre ville un violiniste norvégien dans le genre de Paganini . . . nommé Old-Buck' (Flaubert 1973–98, 1: 17–20): the quotations are from two letters of 1835. Ole Bull is identified in the annotations. *L'Histoire d'Ecosse* is Defauconpret's translation of *Tales of a Grandfather*.

literary pun on the name of Scott's antiquary.) The novelist's set of Scott's *Oeuvres complètes* is still to be found in the town hall of Cantaleu-Croisset; but even without this material confirmation, one would know that Flaubert began his literary life as an ardent devotee of the Waverley novels.[13]

In *Madame Bovary* (1857), *L'Education Sentimentale* (1869), and *Bouvard et Pécuchet* (1881), Flaubert transfers this early enthusiasm to his protagonists. The most elaborately worked-out instance occurs in *Bovary*. At the age of 15 or 16, Emma encounters Scott for the first time. Under his influence:

> she fell in love with historical events, dreamed of guardrooms, old oak chests and minstrels.[14]

Along with this medievalized Scott, she absorbs *Paul et Virginie*, Chateaubriand's *Génie du Christianisme*, illustrated 'keepsake' volumes, and lending-library narratives of love. (Later on there is also *Notre-Dame*.) In effect, the Waverley novels belong to an integrated romantic curriculum initiating girls into daydreams and desire. Later on, after Emma's marriage, Scott acquires a less dreamy presence in her life. His new role is shaped, first and foremost, by musical fashion. During the nineteenth century, there were about fifty operas based on the Waverley novels (as well as two on *The Lady of the Lake*) (Mitchell, 1977).[15] The most popular of them was Donizetti's *Lucia di Lammermoor* (sixth, last, and best of the *Bride of Lammermoor* adaptations). The first performance of *Lucia* was in 1835, in Naples. When Hector Berlioz was brought to London in 1847, in an early, doomed effort to establish an English tradition of grand opera, he was assigned to conduct *Lucia*, which he did successfully (though probably not enthusiastically). *Lucia* outlasted Donizetti's other tragic works on European stages. It also became a literary point of reference. Looking beyond Flaubert for a moment, *Anna Karenina* (1874–76) has its *Lucia* moment; later yet, E. M. Forster's *Where Angels Fear to Tread* (1905) describes a provincial Italian staging while simultaneously referring back to the opera's previous appearance in *Bovary*.

The *Bovary* treatment is perhaps the richest of all. Emma and her husband Charles have come to Rouen to see a performance of *Lucia*, starring the famous tenor Lagardy. The novelist provides a lively account of her experiences at this event. *Lucia* begins with a hunting song (practically a must in Scott operas). The hunting song recalls the original novel to Emma; her memory of it allows her to make sense of the libretto – which, of course, drops many characters, scenes, and motivations, in order to concentrate on the central love triangle, and is thus occasionally enigmatic or confused in comparison with its more expansive model. However, further bursts of music then reverse this process, obscuring both Emma's memories of Scott's text and her grasp of the words uttered by the performers; now she enters into a state of stunned receptivity, absorbing the

---

[13]   It is Bruneau, the editor of the *Correspondance* (1973–98, 1: 848), who specifies the location of Flaubert's collected Scott (in the Defauconpret translation).

[14]   'Elle s'éprit de choses historiques, rêva bahuts, salle des gardes et ménestrels' (Flaubert 1964, 69). Translated by Paul de Man.

[15]   For a full treatment of Scott's operatic reception see Chapter 17.

production through music and spectacle, overwhelmed by its aura of urgency. At one high point of identification, just as the lovers bid each other farewell, 'Emma gave a sharp cry that mingled with the vibrations of the last chords.'[16] Here the outer and inner operas briefly merge, even harmonize, as Emma seems to join the musical fray.

Following this climax, Emma tries to distance herself from her own swooning ecstasy; she recalls that art deceptively magnifies the passions of life. Even more to the point, Donizetti has magnified Scott; *BL* plus music is a combination that cannot be reasoned away, less soothing, more gripping, than the visions of the Middle Ages Emma once experienced while reading the Waverley novels. Of course, *Lucia*, unlike *I*, say, is not about medieval life; moreover, unlike most other tales by Scott, it features a central couple who end badly. Emma returns to her state of stunned absorption until she is distracted by the coincidental arrival of Léon, a law-clerk with whom she had previously flirted. It is Léon, rather than philosophical reasoning, that punctures the theatrical and musical illusion. Now Lucia does not need to fantasize about Lagardy or someone like him carrying her away. Léon is right there. Under these circumstances, even Lucia's mad scene seems unimpressive; Emma complains that the actress screams too much. She, Charles, and Léon leave the theatre early and go for ice creams. The next day, still in Rouen (though Charles has returned home), Emma spends the afternoon with Léon, in a closed coach that rolls through the city, rocking from side to side.

Emma has stopped thinking about *Lucia*. As we learn much later, Flaubert has not. Towards the end of the novel, Emma will suffer her own deranged, agonized mad scene of a death; she suffers it, moreover, against a raucous musical background provided by a grotesque blind vagrant, who sings a frightful song as she expires. 'And Emma began to laugh, an atrocious, frantic, desperate laugh'.[17] In this retrospective context, her imperviousness to Lucia's fate looks like an inability to imagine her own impending moment of extinction. A desire not to confront the idea of one's own death is a known human weakness. It is far easier to observe that there is too much screaming than to suppose that the screaming might (sooner or later) issue from oneself. But in that case, Flaubert has not so much highlighted Scott's irrelevance or vapidity (which is what we might have supposed earlier on) as his surprising tragic force. If Donizetti magnifies Scott, then Flaubert magnifies Donizetti, providing a real-life version of the sort of thing that (supposedly) only happens in historical romances, or in bel canto operas made from them. We know better; it happens to Emma too. *BL* is more than an artifact of youthful longing; it proves to tell the truth (one truth, at least) about the way that people die.

Madame Bovary uses Scott to stage its heroine's isolated rebellion against a world that she contemplates with horror. That horror is incommunicable.

---

16 'Emma jeta un cri aigu, qui se confondit avec la vibration des derniers accords' (Flaubert 1964, 265).

17 'Et Emma se mit à rire, d'un rire atroce, frénétique, désespéré' (Flaubert 1964, 372–73).

Elsewhere, Scott's force is felt less solipsistically; it becomes a shared project. A remarkable instance is afforded by the work of Barbey d'Aurevilly. In 1835, at the age of 27, Barbey had dismissed the Waverley novels as overly dependent on description – the old Stendhal complaint. As time went by, he changed his mind. His *L'Ensorcelée* (1852) presents itself as the first of a series of tales in the mode of the Waverley novels. 'One asks oneself what the illustrious author of *Chronicles of the Canongate* would have made of the chronicles of *Chouannerie* if, in place of being Scottish, he had been Breton or Norman.'[18] Barbey decided to become the Norman Scott. Claiming to have ancestors who had fought in the provincial monarchist resistance against the Revolution, he planned various novels either set in the milieu of *Chouannerie* or treating it as a subject. A few of them got written. Perhaps the most memorable – and certainly the most Scott-obsessed – is *Le Chevalier des Touches* (1863).

The early chapters of *Chevalier* introduce a group of crotchety, broken-down and grotesque old people who have lived for many decades in the same little Norman village. There is a worldly abbé, a baron with a fiery red nose, Mademoiselle de Percy (the abbé's ugly sister), the doddering Mademoiselles de Touffedelys, and Aimée de Spens (the faded, blushing, and long-deaf beauty of the group). While making his way to the de Touffedelys's hearth one night – he and the others have long been accustomed to gather there – the abbé literally bumps into a terrifying figure from the past, the Chevalier des Touches, who clutches at him, curses the ungrateful world in a demented fashion, and abruptly disappears. The Chevalier is supposed to have perished in Edinburgh, of a sword thrust to the liver. If not, strictly speaking, a ghost, he might as well be one. His bizarre appearance on the scene stirs the abbé and his circle to remember heroic days past. Mademoiselle de Percy determines to tell the tale of how, in 1799, the Chevalier des Touches was captured by the revolutionary enemy (who of course condemned him to death) and then rescued in the nick of time by a heroic group that included herself and eleven others (the twelve, 'les douze').

Her narrative is remarkable in two ways, each suggesting something central about Barbey's use of Scott. Among French readers (there seems to be no English translation and almost no Anglophone reception of the text), *Le Chevalier des Touches* is famous for close-focus savagery. This savagery is intended to evoke epic precedents, in Homer, most obviously, but also in the Waverley novels; as is eventually revealed, the Chevalier's fictional prototype is the dandyish, deadly Claverhouse from *OM* (867). Barbey's critics have made much of the Scott precedents for his most bloodthirsty passages; a close look at these reveals that they have a distinctive flavour of their own. This is perhaps most evident in Mademoiselle de Percy's account of the initial rescue effort, when 'les douze' create a diversion that turns into a mass slaughter. The Chevalier's behaviour after his release is also, in this regard, striking. He makes a beeline for the local

---

[18] 'On se demande ce que l'illustre auteur des *Chroniques de la Canongate* aurait fait des chroniques de la Chouannerie si, au lieu d'etre Ecossais, il avait été Breton ou Normand' (Barbey d'Aurevilly (1964–66) *Le Chevalier des Touches* in *Oeuvres*, 1: 1347).

miller, who seems to have betrayed him to the authorities. The Chevalier beats this contemptible Jacobin squealer half to death. Next he straps him, bleeding profusely, to a blade of the windmill, which is then made to turn: *le moulin bleu* becomes *le moulin rouge*.

Adding to the peculiar flavour of these sequences are the heavily accentuated gender miscues of the tale. Claverhouse-like, the Chevalier is beautiful. 'Les douze' think of him as 'La Belle Hélène', whom they are attempting to repatriate from the treacherous Troy that abducted him (Homer again!). Conversely, Mademoiselle de Percy's mannishness and her consequent ability to keep up with the other (male) guerilla warriors is a leitmotif. All of this somehow comes to a head when we learn, at the end, why and how Aimée de Spens did a striptease for the Armies of the Revolution; a lifetime of blushes could not expunge her shame, nor her pride, for she removed her clothes as a way of distracting the enemy from a fugitive she was hiding. Thus Barbey keeps insisting, via many narrative tricks and from every possible angle, that sex and violence are linked even more intimately than might have been imagined. The Scott influences are real, and proudly acknowledged; they are filtered, however, through Barbey's exemplary decadence.

Aside from its take on violence, the other outstanding feature of *Chevalier* is its deft emphasis on memory. Here again, Barbey has learned from Scott; Old Mortality himself, the obsessive restorer of graves, offers the obvious point of reference. Barbey's equivalent of Mortality is not his title character, the crazed Destouches, but the aged friends who recall his exploits and their own. Moreover, it is not only, or not just, the story of the Chevalier and his rescue, but the story of the story that counts; we are seldom allowed, for long, to forget the teller of the tale or her audience (who frequently question, comment, and otherwise interrupt Mademoiselle de Percy). Even before he goes mad and starts stalking through the night, ranting about ingratitude, the Chevalier is himself an unlovable figure; the most ardent counter-revolutionary might, in retrospect, have second thoughts about saving him from his doom. Barbey's point is that none of this matters. He makes it explicit from the beginning that in 1799 there was no chance of the guerillas winning their war against Paris. Moreover, they themselves realized as much. Barbey is cultivating an idea at once aesthetic and political: that the most futile resistance is also the most heroic. He favours *Chouannerie* for *Chouannerie*'s sake. The Waverley novels are generally sceptical about perishing on principle, in the manner colourfully illustrated by *Chevalier*. However, Barbey has not exactly misinterpreted Scott; rather, he is reading him in a national frame where there have been so many losers, of so many political stripes, in such a quick succession of violent historical turnabouts, that a philosophy of defeat embracing the absurd (a kind of proto-existentialism) becomes a near necessity.

By its nature, and the nature of the times, this philosophy was attractive not only to the Right but to the Left – where it was also framed in terms provided by Scott's fiction. In 1862, for *Le Figaro*, Jules Vallès wrote a lively bit of polemical criticism, 'Les Victimes du Livre'. 'Victimes' develops the argument (which hardly originates with Vallès) that human emotions, far from being fresh or original, stem from literature; those who declare 'Cherchez la femme' (a tag from Dumas's *Les Mohicans de Paris*) should instead propose, 'Cherchez le livre'.

Vallès would seem to suspect that we are all Madame Bovary (though he does not put it that way). In substantiation of this theory, he takes his readers on a whirlwind tour of popular fiction: *Robinson Crusoe* and its many imitations, bluebooks, pirate fantasies, the novels of James Fenimore Cooper, and then – as a first climax – the Waverley novels. Like the ardent French Scottist he is, Vallès singles out *QD* and *I* as the crucial instances; then he embarks upon a fevered fantasy à la Torquilstone. Reading Scott's historical fiction, one dreams of:

> battles from which one always emerges with the sack or the cross, a load of booty or an epaulette. Boats founder, powder speaks, fire blares out; you walk within, like the man of the Circus [Olympique] in his brazier: you can be drilled full of holes, you burn, you split up; get out of there – *since one knows that one will come back.*[19]

The infinitely repeatable fantasy of the foundering, burning, exploding arena of stylized violence, from which both attacked and attackers flee in an ultimate exalted panic, takes hold of the early adolescent mind, remaking it.

Epic violence is Vallès's great subject. Especially in his masterpiece, *L'Insurgé*, on the events of 1870–71, he excels in providing portraits of determined, eccentric plotters, muttering sweetly of murder or martyrdom (and frequently getting their chance to experience both). As in 1789, as in 1848, every marginalized political visionary in Paris comes out of the woodwork; Vallès knows, and loves, them all – if not for their moral qualities, then in any case for their singular enthusiasms. Two-thirds of the way through *L'Insurgé*, the Commune takes command of Paris, and here we learn the limits to the narrator's taste for mayhem. Though he is dedicated to overthrowing governments, as noisily as possible, he wishes himself and other people – even including the Second Empire bourgeoisie – to remain alive in the process. At the same time, he cheerfully accepts a kind of violence that seems to have sprung directly from the siege of Torquilstone and the mind of someone much like *I*'s old Ulrica. 'What were they talking about, then, those wild, distracted women, that "all was to perish"? Someone delivered up two or three buildings to petrol. So what?'[20] Thus Vallès treats the legend of the much-despised *pétroleuses*, whose efforts to incinerate Paris were both widely exaggerated and widely decried. He seems to suggest at once that his screaming comrades are victims of their own delusions of grandeur and that arson, since it is not the end of the world, might not be such a bad idea.[21] After all, 'my last [student] essays were in honour of heroic

---

[19] 'batailles d'où l'on sort toujours avec le sac ou la croix, une cargaison ou une épaulette. Les navires sombrent, la poudre parle, l'incendie éclate; vous promenez là-dedans comme l'homme du *Cirque* dans son brasier: on peut vous trouer, vous brûler, vous fendre; allez-y! – puisqu'on sait qu'on en reviendra' (Vallès, 'Les Victimes du Livre', 67).

[20] 'Que disaient-elles donc, ces éperdues "que tout allait périr"? On a bien livré deux ou trois bâtisses au pétrole. Et après?' (Vallès 1975, 2: 1063).

[21] Citing a discussion by Jules Andrieu, Roger Bellet notes the contemporary 'confusion between a project to incinerate Paris with gas, which never existed, and the project, a real one, to mine certain strategic points of the town' (2: [1947] n. 2).

resistances . . . of Numance in ruins, Carthage in cinders, Saragossa in flames.'[22] Literature, it seemed, showed him what he wanted: a burning castle to fight in, a catastrophe that would tear the world apart, a large-scale opportunity for revenge against an implacably corrupt society. He got it. He lived Scott (in such a manner that the latter must have turned in his grave), and lived as well all his schoolboy patriotic histories.

At the age of 31 (in 1859), Jules Verne visited Scotland and England. Verne's lively account of his trip (*Voyage à reculons en Angleterre et en Ecosse*) was turned down by his publisher, Hetzel, in 1862; the belated twentieth-century publication of the manuscript in 1989 testifies amply to the author's obsession with all things Scottish. He begins by considering Charles Nodier's comment that if you want to visit Scotland, it is easier by far to go to Franche-Comté, where you can get much the same picturesque effects, without nearly so much travelling. For Verne, on the contrary, nothing but the real thing will do. His northern British expedition puts him, of course, 'On the Traces of Walter Scott'.[23] To study Scott, Verne argues, is to get a full initiation into the Middle Ages. Only then is one ready for the tour of Glasgow, Edinburgh, and the Highlands. This Scott-dominated itinerary includes a cruise on 'lac Katrine' and ends with a return to what is now Waverley Station in Edinburgh, near, as Verne notes, the 'monument de Walter Scott' (1989, 179).

Like so much else in his career, Verne's Scottish journey suggests a conflict between romantic daydream (back to the Middle Ages) and scientific daydream (forwards to utopia). Verne explores Lake Katrine on a steam-powered packet; nineteenth-century technology facilitates his return to a past that is both picturesque and sublime (and defined almost entirely by Scott's novels and poems). He takes the tourist's privilege of whisking his way from one attraction to another, condensing his experience of Scotland into a terse form suitable for quick consumption. Progress makes the past easier, gives it the utopian sheen more conspicuously associated with Verne's futuristic *Voyages extraordinaires*.

It is in Verne's (first) Scottish novel that this balance is most instructively complicated. *Les Indes-Noires* (1877; known in English as *Black Diamonds*) follows the fortunes of a Scottish coal-mining family who live in an exhausted and otherwise abandoned mine, hoping for its revival. The industrial future seems in this case to have failed, but then a new vein is discovered. It is so huge that the industrialist who owns the mine builds an entire underground metropolis adjacent to it. 'Coal-city' embodies one of Verne's favorite motifs, the scientific utopia free from the ravages of history. One way of constructing such a fantasy was on the model of *Robinson Crusoe*; Verne used this approach most effectively in *L'Ile mystérieuse* (1873). 'Coal-city' is something else: a whole society designed from scratch and functioning without conflict. The miners love living underground, where there is no unpredictable weather with which to contend. They hardly regret the absence of the sun, so delightful are their subterranean circumstances. Science permits a perfectly regulated existence. During the period

---

[22] 'Mes dernières narrations étaient en l'honneur de résistances héroïques . . . de Numance en ruines, de Carthage en cendres, de Saragosse en flammes' (2: 1063).

[23] 'Sur les traces de Walter Scott': the title of Chapter 28.

of the Commune, Verne had expressed his ardent wish that all the Parisian socialists be extirpated, by whatever means were necessary. 'Coal-city' is a metropolis where nobody needs to be shot, since every worker is uniformly grateful and cooperative.

A hint of conflict enters in the person of a young girl, Nell (borrowed from Dickens). Rescued from a pit, Nell refuses to say who she is or where she has come from; apparently she has never been outside the mine. She would just as soon stay put, but her friends and fiancé determine that she must be given a view of the upper world. They steal out in the night, and ascend to the heights of Arthur's Seat, from which Nell witnesses her first sunrise (a procedure recommended by Scott in *HM*). So begins an enchanted tour of Scotland, deriving largely from *Voyage à reculons*; the *pièce de résistance* is a version of that steamboat tour of 'lac Katrine' on a vessel named the 'Rob Roy' (Verne 1877, 126 ff.).

During this last stage of the journey, a shocking turn occurs. In a surreally abrupt development, 'lac Katrine' loses its waters. There is a thump. The 'Rob Roy,' which a moment before was steaming smoothly along through the picturesque, Scott-sodden landscape, lies stranded on the lake bottom. But this is not the only problem. Verne suddenly reveals that Coal-city lies directly beneath the lake: God save the city now! The illustrator of *Les Indes-Noires* (J. Férat) provides a splendid visualization of Scotland's best-known aquatic landmark crashing into the great cavern where Verne has located his industrial utopia. There is just no getting away from history and social conflict. Coal-city has, in fact, been sabotaged by Nell's mad grandfather, a bard-like wizard with an owl for a familiar – anarchist as enchanter. However, we do not need this murky and somewhat underdeveloped subplot to see where the book is going. Lake Katrine's threat to Coal-city is Verne's acknowledgement of the implicit wildness in what seems a routinized resource. Those apparently stable touristic landmarks (established, largely, by the works of Scott, and savoured by Verne himself on his own Scottish tour) harbour violence and mass cataclysm.

Two generations of French writers retained a vital relation with the works of Scott. The third generation went largely in other directions, but there is *A la recherche* to suggest that Scottophilia post-1900 had not quite run its course. *Recherche* takes more than Marcel's expectations about love from that startling core canon of specialists in love. The novel's defining interest is the alchemy of personal memory, as it works through eros, glamour, and life in Society, set against a background of large-scale social and military catastrophe. This plan powerfully recalls Lafayette's *nouvelles historiques*. But it is also influenced by Scott and a range of his most attentive students – not only Barbey, whose *Chevalier des Touches* Proust much admired, but Baudelaire, who could declare the Waverley novels 'a fastidious heap of descriptions of bric-à-brac', only to adapt this distinctive Scott-identified aesthetic in one of his greatest poems: 'Spleen II', with its extraordinary linkages between a stuffed chest of drawers and a tortured apprehension of the past.[24] Proust's synthesis of these seemingly

---

[24] 'Un fastidieux amas de descriptions de bric-à-brac.' Proust puts his complaint about bric-à-brac into the mouth of Samuel, a character from *La Fanfarlo*; see Baudelaire 1961, 489.

divergent sources and approaches is brilliantly exemplified in a famous evocation of the pearls of Henrietta of England (sister of Charles II, friend of Lafayette), pearls turned black in a disastrous domestic blaze, then retrieved by the indefatigable Madame Verdurin (4: 293–94). The antiquarian, museological fervour with which the author (and his characters) consider the blackened necklace evokes powerfully the side of Scott that conceived of Abbotsford. Like Henrietta's pearls, history is *blackened* by its passage through time – not to mention its passage through Scotland, its best-known novelist, and his multitudinous French admirers in the century before the Second World War.

2 Another Tale of Old Mortality: The Translations of Auguste-Jean-Baptiste Defauconpret in the French Reception of Scott

Paul Barnaby

> We speak of the 'immense influence' of *Werther*, of the ways in which the European awareness of the past was reshaped by the Waverley Novels. What do we remember of those who translated Goethe and Scott, who were in fact the responsible agents of influence? Histories of the novel and of society tell us of the impact on Europe of Fenimore Cooper and Dickens. They do not mention Auguste-Jean-Baptiste Defauconpret through whose translations that impact is made. (Steiner 1975, 270–71)

George Steiner's lament in *After Babel* gains added power when one considers that Auguste-Jean-Baptiste Defauconpret (1767–1843) translated not only Cooper and Dickens, but, first and foremost, Walter Scott. So closely was he associated with the French translation of the Waverley novels, and so eager to reinforce that association, that he signed not only his other translations but even his own works 'the translator of the novels of Sir Walter Scott'. The primacy of Defauconpret's translations over their many rivals is well established. Regularly reprinted throughout the nineteenth and twentieth centuries, they were used in a critical edition of Scott as recently as 1981. The editor Michel Crouzet argued that, whatever Defauconpret's failings by contemporary standards, he deserved credit for turning Scott into a 'French author' (Crouzet 1981) ('[E]lles ont fait de Scott un auteur "français".') One must not overstress Defauconpret's undeniable linguistic and literary merits: command of idiom, grasp of register, narrative flair and ear for dialogue. Equally important is the commercial acumen which saw him negotiate an agreement in 1822 with Scott's London agents Black, Young and Young to receive proof sheets of Scott's novels straight from the press (Green 1957, 39–43). Defauconpret's translation therefore appeared almost simultaneously with the original, and significantly ahead of the English-language versions published by the Galignani Brothers in Paris from 1820 onwards. Consequently, even fluent readers of English (like Stendhal or Vigny) might turn first to the translation. Defauconpret's dominance of the market was further assured when his translations were chosen for the sumptuously illustrated Furne edition of the Waverley novels (1830–32). Long the standard French Scott, the Furne edition was recently digitized by the Bibliothèque de France (French National Library) to become the standard French e-text of the Waverley novels.

Defauconpret, however, is not only the major 'agent of influence' for the French reception of Scott. His translations became familiar, directly or indirectly, to many European readers. In Russia, Poland, Spain and Italy, they were read long before indigenous versions appeared. Pushkin, Manzoni and Mickiewicz all read Scott in Defauconpret's French (Greene 1965, 208; Ruggieri Punzo 1975, 42; Ostrowski 1965, 80). Even when European readers did not read Scott in French, they used translations derived from Defauconpret rather than from Scott's original. When in 1821 Gaetano Barbieri initiated the Italian translation of the Waverley novels, he translated directly from Defauconpret's version. Only in 1827 did he begin working primarily from Scott's text. He continued, though, to refer to Defauconpret, even polemicizing against him in footnotes (Benedetti 1974, 47–55). Similarly, Gogol knew *OM* either in Defauconpret's very free 1817 version or in Vasiliĭ Sots's rendering of Defauconpret's text (Davis 1991). Even translators who worked from English turned to Defauconpret for comprehension of difficult terms, or followed his example in adapting Scott's text. Thus the German W. A. Lindau imitates Defauconpret in omitting Chapter 1 of *OM* (Scott 1820–21). Defauconpret's influence extends even to choice of title. His rendering of *HM* as *La Prison d'Edimbourg* (The Prison of Edinburgh) (Scott 1818) is echoed in Italian (*La prigione di Edimburgo*), Spanish (*La cárcel de Edimburgo*), Portuguese (*A prisão de Edimburgo*), Russian (*Èdinburgskaia tiurma*), Danish (*Fængslet i Edinburgh*) and Polish (*Więzienie w Edymburgu*).

Sanctioned by Scott's London's agent and thus regarded as semi-official, Defauconpret's translations are frequently supposed to be colourless but essentially accurate. Yet Scott often undergoes a startling transformation at Defauconpret's hands. Particularly in his earliest translations, Defauconpret tailors the Waverley novels to a Legitimist, Catholic, post-Napoleonic readership. Abandoning the political impartiality that offended Conservative and Liberal alike, Defauconpret's Scott unreservedly condemns all popular challenges to constituted authority. Martin Lyons (1984) has charted the appropriation of Scott by the Romantic Right in 1820s France. This chapter, focusing on Defauconpret's first Scott translation, *Les Puritains d'Ecosse* (*OM*) (1817), will show that this appropriation began with translation.

Auguste-Jean-Baptiste Defauconpret: Life and Work

Born in Lille in 1767, Defauconpret practised law in Paris until 1814 or 1815, when he fled to London to escape his creditors (J. P. F. 1855; Richardot 1965; Benani 1993). By his own account, the discovery of *OM* while engaged 'on more serious works' ('des travaux plus sérieux') led unexpectedly to a lucrative second career as a translator (Defauconpret 1833, 4). Struck by 'this great historical composition' ('cette grande composition historique'), he circulated a translation among Parisian booksellers until it found favour with the far-sighted

Henri Nicolle (Defauconpret 1833, 4). In reality, the Bibliothèque de France records several earlier translations by Defauconpret, from novelists like Maria Edgeworth, Amelia Opie and Elizabeth Bennett, some published by Nicolle. Indisputably, however, the success of Defauconpret's Scott translations established him in his new career. It is equally certain that his translations first brought Scott to critical and public attention. Defauconpret's 1817 *OM* was preceded by versions of *LL* by Elisabeth de Bon (1813) and *GM* by Joseph Martin (Scott 1816).[1] The latter was reviewed in the *Annales politiques, morales, et littéraires* (Political, moral and literary annals), but both otherwise passed unobserved (Massmann 1972, 16).

Defauconpret went on to translate (or re-translate) all of the Waverley novels. Besides Dickens and Fenimore Cooper, he also specialized in Scottish or Irish 'national tales' by John Galt, Jane Porter, Susan Ferrier, Lady Morgan and the Banim brothers. Towards the end of his career (1835), he produced what long remained the standard French edition of Fielding's *Tom Jones* (republished as recently as 1967). In the early 1840s, free from pursuit, he returned to France, where he died in 1843.

The exceptional number of translations credited to Defauconpret has attracted much amused or sceptical comment. Working on his Scott-influenced historical novel *Chronique du règne de Charles IX* (Chronicle of the reign of Charles IX) in December 1828,[2] Prosper Mérimée declared to Albert Stapfer: 'I'm doing an extraordinary amount of work, not just for a lazybones like me, but even for a man of letters, M. Defauconpret excepted!' (Mérimée 1969, 8).[3] Others openly queried the extent of Defauconpret's involvement. Joseph-Marie Quérard, in particular, in *La France littéraire* (Literary France) (1828) inflicted lasting damage on Defauconpret's reputation by flatly denying Defauconpret's claim that, assisted only by his son Charles-Auguste (1797–1865), he translated 422 volumes of English-language fiction between 1816 and 1828. Rather, he employed a team of assistants. (Quérard 1828, 419–20).

L. A. Bisson (1942) partially restores Defauconpret's reputation. He traces correspondence suggesting that Amédée Pichot, besides translating Scott's narrative poems (Scott 1820–21) and *Paul's Letters to his Kinsfolk* (Scott 1822), was general editor of the *Complete Works of Scott* published by Nicolle's successor Gosselin from 1820 to 1832. For Bisson, Defauconpret was 'translator-in-chief', submitting his versions to Pichot for approval and revision (1942, 340). In support of Quérard's claims that Defauconpret oversaw a team, Bisson quotes correspondence from a translator identified only as 'Brunet' who produces a draft of 'The Two Drovers' for Defauconpret to polish up (341). Yet Bisson equally quotes discussions between Defauconpret and Pichot on the rendering

---

[1] Extracts had also been published in the Genevan *Bibliothèque universelle* (Universal Library), probably translated by Charles Pictet de Rochemont (Scott 1816a).

[2] See Dargan 1934, 609 for this novel's debt to *OM*.

[3] 'Je travaille extraordinairement, non seulement pour un paresseux comme moi, mais même pour un homme de lettres, M. de Fauconpret [sic] excepté!'

of problematic terms, which prove that Defauconpret was intimately involved in the translation process (400–03). These also demonstrate Pichot's professional regard for Defauconpret, further displayed in his *Voyage historique et littéraire en Angleterre et en Ecosse* (Historical and literary tour of a foreigner in England and Scotland) where Pichot acknowledges that Defauconpret's translations 'are doubtless made rapidly' but 'must not be confused with those of certain school-boys' who 'make use of his name to credit their own blunders to his account' (1825, 3: 288n).[4]

F. C. Green (1957) queries Bisson's view of the working relationship between Pichot and Defauconpret. He quotes a letter from Defauconpret to Charles Gosselin dated 4 October 1822 describing the agreement with Black, Young and Young. Black, Defauconpret reports, insisted upon 'inviolable secrecy about the whole business which must only be known to you, him, and me' (Green 1957, 41).[5] Reassuring Gosselin, Defauconpret argues that a single translator would work more efficiently. Pichot, he notes, had committed errors translating the third volume of *FN*, which he would have avoided had he read or translated the previous two. This indicates that, in 1822, Pichot's role involved translation as much as editing and perhaps suggests that Defauconpret was sole translator from 1822 onwards. It might have jeopardized secrecy to involve even his son, then living in Paris. Strikingly, all the correspondence that Bisson quotes dates from 1827, after, that is, the ruin of Scott's publishers and the acknowledgement of his authorship of the Waverley novels. Perhaps, with no further need for 'inviolable secrecy', Defauconpret is again able to call upon collaborators. Perhaps only now, if at all, is Pichot installed as general editor. Moreover, 1827 is an exceptionally busy year for Scott's French translators, who work through ten volumes of his eagerly awaited *Life of Napoleon Bonaparte*.

There is more to suggest that Quérard and Bisson underestimate Defauconpret's industry. Quérard's figure of 422 volumes is misleading, as he counts each volume of a four-volume novel separately. Even before his first Scott translation, Defauconpret translated seven novels in little over a year. Just over 100 novels in twelve years may not, then, be altogether excessive. Nonetheless, Defauconpret is clearly not solely responsible for all the translations bearing his name. At the very least, he collaborated with Pichot, Charles-Auguste Defauconpret and 'Brunet'. For this reason, this chapter will focus on Defauconpret's earliest Scott translation, which is unquestionably his own work.

Old Mortality *in France:* Les Puritains d'Ecosse

Defauconpret's *Les Puritains d'Ecosse* gave Scott his first French success and first major European breakthrough. Although partially obscured by *I* (1820) and *QD* (1823), it remained for many Frenchmen the Scott novel *par excellence.*

---

[4] 'dont les traductions sont faites rapidement sans doute, mais qu'il ne faut pas confondre avec celles de quelques écoliers, qui [. . .] s'emparent de son nom pour faire passer leurs bévues sur son compte.'
[5] Green quotes the letter only in English translation.

Stendhal is among many to call Scott not 'the author of *Waverley*' but 'the author of *Old Mortality*'.[6] Often critical of Scott, Stendhal remained an unswerving admirer of *OM*. In an unpublished addendum to his *Racine et Shakespeare* (Racine and Shakespeare) (1823), he asks, 'Which tragedian, following Aristotle, has produced, over the last century, a work to compare with *Tom Jones*, with *Werther*, with [Lafontaine's] *Leben eines armen Landpredigers*, with *La Nouvelle Héloïse*, or with *Old Mortality*?' (Stendhal 1970, 208).[7] He had earlier written to Adolphe de Mareste on 18 July 1819: 'I have just finished reading *The Black Dwarf* and *Old Mortality* by W. Scott. The last half-volume of *Old Mortality* isn't worth a f★★★, the rest can stand beside *Tom Jones*.' (1962–68, 2: 980).[8] Reading Vigny's *Cinq-Mars* (1826), the first significant attempt to adapt Scott's techniques to French fiction, Stendhal nowhere detects 'the simplicity and profundity that we adore in *Old Mortality*' (1962–68, 2: 86).[9]

Balzac, then, knew how it would please Stendhal, when, in his review of *La Chartreuse de Parme* (The charterhouse of Parma), he named *OM*'s Balfour of Burley as the only character to rival Stendhal's rebel hero Ferrante Palla (Balzac 2001, 787). Yet *OM* was an even more constant point of reference for Balzac himself. Allusions to Scott's novel abound throughout *La Comédie Humaine* (The human comedy), most strikingly in the 'Avant-Propos' (Preface) (1842) where *OM*'s Claverhouse is named among the immortal literary characters that successfully embody an epoch (1976–81, 1: 10). References to *OM* are particularly frequent in Balzac's fiction of the 1840s, two decades after the first encounter with Scott that inspired his juvenile novels *L'Héritière de Birague* (The heiress of Birague) and *Clothilde de Lusignan* (1822). In *La Muse du Département* (The muse of the department) (1843), Balzac calls an antique collector 'this Old Mortality of furniture' ('cet Old Mortality des meubles') (1976–81, 4: 646). In *Le Cousin Pons* (Cousin Pons) (1847), he suggests that Scott might have called a monumental mason 'Young Mortality' ('que Walter Scott eût surnommé le jeune homme des tombeaux') (7: 725). In the unfinished *Les Petits Bourgeois* (The lesser bourgeoisie), he asks why social historians should not rescue demolished buildings from oblivion just as 'Walter Scott's Old Mortality tended his tombs' (8: 22).[10] There are further references in

---

[6]   See his review of Châteaubriand's *Le Dernier des Abencérages* (The last of the Abencerages) (1826) (Stendhal 1959, 90) and letter to Byron of 23 June 1823 (1962–68, 2: 16). The five novels published in French between *OM* (1817) and (1820) are, in fact, credited to 'the author of *OM*'.

[7]   'Quels tragiques, suivants d'Aristote, ont produit, depuis un siècle, quelque oeuvre à comparer à *Tom Jones*, à *Werther*, aux *Tableaux de famille*, à *La Nouvelle Héloïse ou aux Puritains*?'

[8]   'Justement, je viens de finir *The Black Dwarf* et *Old Mortality* de W. Scott. Le dernier demi-vol. d'*Old Mortality* ne vaut pas un f . . ., le reste est à côté de *Tom Jones*.'

[9]   '[L]a simplicité et de la profondeur que nous adorons dans *Old Mortality*.' For more on Scott and Stendhal, see Alciatore 1954, 1966; Del Litto 1971 and Ward 1980.

[10]   'Nouvel Old Mortality, pourquoi l'historien de la société française ne sauverait-il pas ces curieuses expressions du passé, comme le vieillard de Walter Scott rafraîchissait les tombes?'

Splendeurs et Misères des Courtisanes (A harlot high and low) (1838–47) (6: 664) and *Le Martyr calviniste* (The Calvinist martyr) (1841) (11: 341), where the portrayal of Protestant fanaticism draws heavily on *OM*.[11]

Admiration for *Old Mortality* is not restricted to writers and critics. In 1818, the future statesman Charles de Rémusat writes to his mother from Paris that 'you do well to like *Old Mortality*; it is very fashionable here' ('Vous faites bien d'aimer les *Puritains*; cela est de la mode ici') (1883–86, 3: 402). In March 1818 the *Annales Encyclopédiques* (Encyclopaedic Annals) confirm that *BD* and *OM* are widely read in society (Massmann 1972, 16).[12] Indeed, public acclaim preceded critical notice. Nodier, in his review for the *Journal des débats* on 28 November 1817, apologizes for discussing an already successful novel seven months after its first French publication (Massmann 1972, 17–18).[13]

Yet *OM* must seem an unlikely best-seller in early Restoration France. However indirectly, it portrays a successful popular revolution leading to the exile of a restored Catholic dynasty. Its popularity must appear all the more puzzling given the enduring French view of Scott as an arch-Conservative in religion and politics. Thus in 1823, Victor Hugo praises Scott's defence of perennial religious values in the face of superstition and fanaticism (1976, 29).[14] In the same year, Nodier hails Scott as an advocate of 'all the old social doctrines' ('toutes les anciennes doctrines sociales') (quoted Lyons 1984, 36). Shortly after Scott's death, in his essay 'De l'art actuel' ('On contemporary art') (1833) the Saint Simonian Hippolyte Fortoul described Scott as 'the poet of legitimacy' adding, 'almost all of his novels end with a restoration' (quoted Baldensperger 1927, 62).[15] This image of Scott survived into the twentieth century through the abbé Brémond, for whom Scott wrote the 'epic of tradition' ('l'épopée de la tradition') (1924, 87). Although Scott's Tory sympathies emerge from *OM*, few readers would feel that they smother the arguments of the Covenanters. That such was the French perception is predominantly due to Defauconpret.

---

[11] I am indebted here to Gordon 1928. For more on Balzac and Scott, see Conner 1980; Garnand 1926 and Haggis 1973, 1974 and 1985.

[12] 'les *Contes de mon Hôte* [. . .] ont été fort répandus dans la société'

[13] Defauconpret's translation of *BD* and *OM* was also reviewed in the *Annales politiques, morales et littéraires*, 24 July 1817 and *Archives philosophiques, politiques et littéraires* (Philosophical, Political, and Literary Archives), October 1817 (Massmann 1972, 102).

[14] 'Il nous peint nos devanciers avec leurs passions, leurs vices et leurs crimes, mais de sorte que l'instabilité des superstitions et l'impiété du fanatisme n'en fassent que mieux ressortir la pérennité de la religion et la sainteté des croyances.'

[15] 'Scott est le poète de la légitimité; presque tous ses romans aboutissent à une restauration.'

Les Puritains d'Ecosse, *or* Old Mortality

Defauconpret left few published comments on his translating practice. The fullest is a response to Lady Morgan's criticism that he had translated her *Florence Maccarthy* with excessive freedom. In a letter to the *Journal des Débats* (Journal of Debates) dated 3 February 1819, Defauconpret objects that she cannot expect her works to be translated 'with the religious respect accorded to those of Horace or Tacitus' ('avec le même respect religieux que ceux d'Horace ou de Tacite'):

> I believe that in importing a *novel* from one language to another, a translator's first duty is to make it capable of pleasing the new readers that he wishes to acquire for it. The taste of the English does not always conform to our own [. . .]. I have thus suppressed some details which might have appeared otiose to the French reader, and I have abbreviated the portraits of several characters that are quite unconnected to the action. I have taken the same liberty with respect to an author whose reputation, *pace* Lady Morgan, stands infinitely above hers in England, Mr Walter Scott; and the welcome accorded in France to *Old Mortality*, *Rob Roy* and only recently, *The Heart of Mid-Lothian*, has proved that I was not wrong.[16] (quoted in Béreaud 1971, 232)

For the low genre of the novel, then, Defauconpret favours the 'belle infidèle' ('faithless beauty') advocated by French translation theorists from Malherbe (1603) onwards. Throughout the Classical period French translators adopted a common approach to the British novel: reduction of a prolix, digressive original to linear logic, avoidance of excesses of language and behaviour, strict observation of unities and refusal to mingle modes and genres. British authors were thought incapable of mastering their imagination. The translator's task was to impose Gallic restraint.[17]

In many respects, the 1817 *Puritains* is a typical 'belle infidèle'. Descriptive passages are radically reduced. Flashbacks are suppressed and expository passages inserted to secure unity of action. Authorial digressions and passages where characters engage in introspection are sacrificed for rapid forward movement. Language is stripped of local colour or figurative boldness and rendered as smooth Classical French. Yet Defauconpret's interventions extend far beyond the 'improvements' demanded of the 'belle infidèle', refashioning Scott for a conservative, legitimist, Restoration readership.

---

[16] Je crois qu'en faisant passer un *roman* d'une langue dans une autre, le premier devoir d'un traducteur est de le mettre en état de plaire aux nouveaux lecteurs qu'il veut lui procurer. Le goût des Anglais n'est pas toujours conforme au nôtre [. . .]. J'ai donc supprimé quelques détails qui auraient pu paraître oiseux à des lecteurs français et j'ai raccourci les portraits de quelques personnages qui ne sont aucunement liés à l'action. Je me suis permis la même liberté à l'égard d'un auteur dont la reputation, n'en déplaise à Lady Morgan, est infiniment au-dessus de la sienne en Angleterre, M. Walter Scott, et la manière dont on a accueilli en France *Les Puritains d'Ecosse*, *Rob-Roy*, et tout récemment *La Prison d'Edimbourg*, m'a prouvé que je n'avais pas eu tort.

[17] See West 1932, 337–44; Streeter 1936 and Meschonnic 1999, 43–47.

Defauconpret's *Puritains* immediately presents two startling innovations: a drastic abridgement of Jebediah Cleishbotham's Preface and the omission of the first chapter. By abridging Cleishbotham's Preface, Defauconpret excises Scott's nominal narrator Peter Pattieson. The decision to simplify Scott's convoluted framing narrative is perhaps unsurprising. In Scott, Cleishbotham edits manuscripts left by the recently deceased Pattieson, which themselves derive from the village inn-keeper's oral narratives. Defauconpret clearly felt he could remove the middleman Pattieson. Yet Pattieson, a licensed preacher, fulfils a vital ideological function as a Presbyterian who regrets the Kirk's historical divisions. Defauconpret also omits all details indicating that Cleishbotham too is Presbyterian, such as his regular attendance of the Kirk's General Assembly. Although many, from Thomas M'Crie (1817) onwards, have felt that Scott's narrative approaches an Episcopalian position, it is essential to his vision of historical reconciliation that both narrator and editor are moderately disposed Presbyterians. Such a vision is alien to Defauconpret who persistently denies the Presbyterians all ideological authority.

More astonishing than Pattieson's disappearance is that of Old Mortality himself. By removing Chapter 1, Defauconpret entirely omits the preserver of the Covenanters' graves, along with Pattieson's tribute to the misguided bravery of 'those sufferers' (Scott 1816, 2:11). Pattieson accepts too that the Covenanters were genuinely oppressed by the 'persecuting squadrons of Earlshall and Claverhouse' (2:29). Yet his narrative, he insists, will be impartial, recognizing good and ill on both sides. The omission of such material is not simply a side-effect of cuts to the framing narrative. Defauconpret reveals here that impartiality is no part of his policy. Throughout the novel, he deletes all passages where the narrator takes an even-handed view, expresses sympathy for the Covenanters or alludes to instances of persecution such as the summary execution of 'auld deaf John Macbriar' (2:235) and torture of Ephraim Macbriar. In Defauconpret, the Presbyterians are an undifferentiated body of religious fanatics. He initially elides all distinction between their radical and moderate factions, between republican 'Protesters' and monarchist 'Resolutioners', to whom, vitally, Scott's protagonist belongs. 'Covenanters' is translated as 'the Puritans, also called Presbyterians' ('les Puritains, nommés aussi Presbytériens') (Scott 1817, 1:10). Thus Scott's comments on the most radical Presbyterian faction are made to extend to the whole Kirk. When Morton attempts to muster a moderate majority among the Covenanters, Defauconpret is belatedly obliged to distinguish factions, employing 'Puritans' for the Protesters and 'Presbyterians' for the 'Resolutioners'. As, however, he fails to revise the earlier chapters, where these terms are interchangeable, it is questionable how far his readers would have understood the distinction and, by extension, Morton's policy.

Where Scott contrasts 'the elder and more rigid puritans' with 'the generality' of Presbyterians (2:49), Defauconpret contrasts the 'zealous Puritans' ('les zélés Puritains') with a generality of Scots (1:22). He adds that they 'nurtured in their hearts feelings of hatred for royalty' ('dont le coeur nourissoit des sentimens de haine contre la royauté'). Defauconpret's Presbyterians are not only, then, a religious minority but, just as inaccurately, unanimously Republican. They are, moreover, exclusively plebeian. Defauconpert expunges all references to Presbyterian sympathies amongst the gentry. Landowners are unanimously 'well-affected', which Defauconpret translates as 'Royalist' ('royaliste(s)'), reducing complex civil and religious conflict to a battle between cavalier and roundhead.

The peculiarly Scottish dimension of the insurrection is entirely sacrificed. When Burley laments that the Covenanters are persecuted 'for adherence to the Solemn League and Covenant between God and the kingdom of Scotland, to which all of them have sworn in former days' (2: 118), Defauconpret has: 'because we adhere faithfully to laws promulgated after the death of Charles I, which they, like us, swore to bring into force' (1: 69).[18] The Solemn League and Covenant was signed in 1643, six years before Charles's death. In 1647, the predominantly Presbyterian Scottish Parliament made peace with the King, and in 1648 sent an army to fight Cromwell. In 1650 Charles II was crowned King of Scots after taking the Oath of the Covenant. To present the Covenanters, then, as intrinsically anti-Royalist is profoundly misleading. Defauconpret removes all references to the resentment created by Charles II's failure to establish Presbyterianism in England and Wales and his reintroduction of Episcopacy in Scotland, and thus obscures the crux of the Covenanters' political and religious grievances.

Indeed, Defauconpret nowhere employs or directly translates the term 'Covenant', employing the following strategies of circumlocution, substitution, or omission:

Scott 1816	Defauconpret 1817
1. 'tell them that we are this day in arms for a broken Covenant and a persecuted Kirk; tell them that we renounce the licentious and perjured Charles Stuart, whom you call King, even as he renounced the Covenant' (3: 51)	1. 'tell them that as Charles Stuart, whom you call King, has broken the oaths which bind him to us, we are freed from those which bind us to him' (2:2)[19]
2. 'for all the whigs that ever swore the Covenant' (2: 256)	2. 'for all the Puritans of Scotland' (1: 164)[20]
3. 'a champion of the Covenant' (3: 101)	3. '[. . .] the good cause' (2: 35)[21]
4. 'a' that winna take the Covenant' (3: 122)	4. 'anyone who isn't of their party' (2: 55)[22]
5. 'the children of the Covenant' (3: 182)	5. 'true children of the Church' (2: 86)[23]

---

[18] 'Parce que nous adhérons constamment aux lois promulguées après la mort de Charles Ier, et dont ils ont juré comme nous l'exécution.'

[19] 'Dis-leur que comme Charles Stuart, que vous nommez roi, a été parjure aux sermons qui le lioient à nous, nous sommes dégagés de ceux qui nous attachoient à lui.'

[20] 'tous les Puritains d'Ecosse'

[21] 'la bonne cause'

[22] 'tout ce qui n'est pas de leur parti'

[23] 'vrais enfans de l'Eglise'

6. 'the godly army of the Solemn League and Covenant' (3: 243)	6. 'the religious and patriotic army of the Presbyterians' (2: 129)[24]
7. '*She's at the Covenant now*, serjeant, shall we not have her away?' (2: 202)	7. Italicized words omitted (1: 124)

Such reluctance to import an intractably foreign term, whether in its original form or via a neologism, is characteristic of the 'belle infidèle'. Taken individually, the renderings above are perhaps unexceptionable. Collectively, however, they assist in rendering the Puritans of Scotland indistinguishable from their English counterparts. Defauconpret displays an even greater reluctance to translate terms associated with the Covenanters' political enemies. The terms 'Episcopal', 'Episcopacy', 'High Church', or 'prelatic' are either omitted or substituted by 'Royalist'. Rather than bring out the peculiarly Scottish nature of the conflict, Defauconpret translates in terms with which the French reader is already familiar, invoking, turn by turn, the English Civil War and French Revolution. It is unsurprising that Ancelot and Saintine, when adapting Defauconpret's *OM* for the stage, saw little difficulty in transferring the action to Plymouth.[25]

Defauconpret's refusal to differentiate between militant and moderate Covenanters renders Balfour of Burley their unchallenged leader. He cuts an unequivocally sinister figure, lacking the moral complexity and quasi-paternal authority of Scott's original. Where Scott repeatedly describes Burley as 'stern' and 'firm', Defauconpret substitutes 'fierce' ('féroce') and 'wild' ('farouche' or 'sauvage'). 'Wild look' is even inserted among the distinguishing features on Burley's 'Wanted' notice ('le regard farouche') (1: 50). Defauconpret omits all passages where Burley's conscience appears troubled by the murder of Archbishop Sharp. Far from striking Morton 'with a sensation approaching to awe' (2: 122), Burley appals him with unrepentant violence.

This Burley resembles the villain of a Gothic novel or of the French melodrama. Louis Maigron (1898) and Reginald W. Hartland (1928) have argued that, for his first French readers, Scott was less the father of historical fiction than heir to the Gothic tradition. Far from supplanting the Gothic in France, Scott granted it a new lease of life. Novelists like Nodier, Frédéric Soulié, Roger de Beauvoir and the young Victor Hugo abused Scott's 'dramatic form' to stage Manichean conflicts between Good and Evil. Their characters embodied violent, superhuman passions rather than historical forces. F. W. M. Draper (1923) argues that Scott similarly influenced the development of Restoration French melodrama. Such accounts, however, neglect the role of translation in Scott's French reception. Defauconpret's Burley is precisely the personification of a single ruling passion – here religious fanaticism – so frequently encountered in Romantic French literature, from the sensational 'roman noir' to the mature fiction of Hugo and Balzac.

---

[24] 'l'armée religieuse et patriotique des Presbytériens'
[25] Their *Têtes rondes et cavaliers* (1833) forms the basis of Bellini's *I puritani*.

Whereas in Scott, Burley and Claverhouse exert rival paternal claims on the orphaned Morton, in Defauconpret, Claverhouse alone is a father figure. Defauconpret grants him a pivotal role in Morton's decision to join the insurgents. The opening chapters of *Les Puritains* strive to obscure Morton's awkward religious and political sympathies. Where, in Scott, Morton's Presbyterian 'enthusiasm was unsullied by fanatic zeal, and unleavened by the sourness of the puritanical spirit' (2: 314), Defauconpret has: 'His family had embraced Presbyterian dogma, but he did not share their exaggerated opinions, and had not the least spark of the fanaticism of the Puritans' (1: 202).[26] As 'Puritan' and 'Presbyterian' are synonyms in Defauconpret, this suggests that Morton was no Presbyterian at all. Defauconpret creates further confusion by elevating the bourgeois Morton to the aristocracy. His uncle and protector, Old Milnwood, becomes a baronet, and his modest country house a 'château'.

Morton's political awakening is almost entirely expunged. Imprisoned by Claverhouse, Scott's Morton believes himself spurned by Edith for 'one of the pensioned cut-throats of this oppressive government' (2: 323). Her apparent infidelity is 'just punishment on [him] for being dead to public wrongs'. Nothing remains 'but vengeance for [his] own wrongs, and for those which are hourly inflicted on [his] country' (3: 17). All this is omitted in Defauconpret, where amorous rivalry has no political dimension and where Morton equates imprisonment with dishonour. His Morton joins the rebels to seek vengeance on Claverhouse and thereby restore his honour. When Morton finally confronts Claverhouse before the Battle of Bothwell Bridge, Defauconpret inserts: 'You alone, Colonel, have thrown me, without my even having thought about it, into the ranks of people whose principles I approve without approving all their conduct' (2: 238).[27]

In Scott, Morton offers an eloquent apology for armed resistance to an oppressive government, sanctioning not only the moderate Covenanters but also the 'Glorious Revolution' with which the novel concludes. Morton would not deserve 'the name and rights of a freeman' were he to 'withhold his arms from the cause of his country' (3: 246). Defauconpret's Morton is a reluctant rebel. Where Scott's Morton assures Cuddie Headrigg that he will 'resist any authority on earth [. . .] that invades tyrannically [his] chartered rights as a freeman' (3: 18), Defauconpret has: 'No one respects legal authority more than I [. . .] and I shall always be ready to submit to it' (1: 233).[28] As he marshals a moderate majority, Defauconpret's Morton seeks to 'extinguish the flame of rebellion' (2: 209) rather than 'to bring this rebellion to an end' ('à éteindre le feu de la rebellion') (3: 344) through an honourable settlement. The French reader may conclude that the Cameronians rightly view his ambivalent policy as treacherous.

---

[26]   'Sa famille avoit embrassé les dogmes des Presbytériens, mais il ne partageoit pas leurs opinions exagérées, et n'avoit pas la moindre étincelle du fanatisme des Puritains.'

[27]   'Vous seul, colonel, m'avez jeté, sans que j'y songeasse, dans les rangs de gens dont j'approuve les principes sans approuver toute leur conduite.'

[28]   'Personne ne respecte plus que moi l'autorité légale, Cuddie, et je serai toujours disposé à m'y soumettre.'

Scott's Morton is an untypically dynamic, politically engaged protagonist. Defauconpret's is the slave of circumstances, alive only to private passions, honour and romance. Yet he is not simply Waverley Redux. He is a petulant, vacillating, morally ambiguous character, possessed of a gloomy fatalism barely present in Scott. When early French readers found Scott's heroes weak, it was a response to Defauconpret as much as a misunderstanding of Scottian 'mediocrity'. Critics like Maigron, Draper and Hartland regret that French historical dramatists and novelists omit the synthesizing, mediating force represented by Scott's protagonists. Yet, in his early Scott translations, Defauconpret seldom permits the protagonist to adopt that role. There are nonetheless echoes of Morton in those French Romantic heroes, like Hugo's Léopold d'Auvernay (*Bug-Jargal*) and Ordener Guldenlew (*Han d'Islande*) or Vigny's Cinq-Mars, for whom political engagement is inextricably linked to, and undermined by, private passion.

For all Defauconpret's interventions, the conclusion to Scott's *OM* presented a dilemma. He understandably omits all direct references to the Glorious Revolution of 1688 which is, first, inexplicable in his rewriting and, second, a sensitive political issue three years after the Restoration of the Bourbons. Thus no attempt is made to explain the ascent to power of the Whigs. Where Scott portrays them re-establishing Presbyterianism and securing the political independence of the Kirk, Defauconpret merely observes that the Whigs hypocritically defend the throne as passionately as they had attacked it under the Stuarts (3: 82). Only in Defauconpret's rewriting, where Presbyterians are unanimously Republican, is this a *volte-face*. The Jacobites, meanwhile, are forced into hiding, their land seized by Whiggish parvenus. In Scott, they are merely compelled to hold 'private meetings' (4: 150). Defauconpret deletes all references to the marriage of convenience between Jacobites and Cameronians, rendering the final chapters, where Claverhouse fights alongside Burley, politically incomprehensible. It is perhaps unsurprising that Ancelot and Saintine rewrote Defauconpret's conclusion so thoroughly for their stage adaptation as to have Edith marry the Royalist Lord Evandale.

However incoherently, Defauconpret intervenes repeatedly to refashion *OM* for a Restoration French audience, reducing intricate politico-religious conflict to a battle between a sympathetic Royalist majority and a fanatical Republican minority, eliding debates over church government and civil rights, and obscuring the success of a national popular revolution. Such modifications need not reflect Defauconpret's own political views. He remained in Paris throughout the Revolutionary years and, in his *Anecdotes sur la Cour et l'Intérieur de la Famille de Napoléon Bonaparte* (Anecdotes of the court and family of Napoleon Bonaparte), praised Napoleon's civic reforms and military achievements. Although a Catholic and a Royalist, Defauconpret does not appear to have espoused the reactionary authoritarianism of the 'Ultra' party which dominated early Restoration politics. More probably, he sought to flatter or appease an 'Ultra' readership. His translation is unlikely to have been vetted or modified by the Censor, who displayed little interest in fiction. Indeed, living in London, Defauconpret may have overestimated the need for political self-censorship. Rival translators like Joseph Martin and Henri Villemain are notably less cautious.

A New Model of Translation

Defauconpret's *Puritains* several significant revisions in his translation. From the 1821 Nicolle edition onwards, Defauconpret largely restores Scott's descriptive passages and respects breaks in the narrative momentum. The 1830 Lecointe edition, however, most persuasively supports Jacques Béreaud's claim that Defauconpret gradually moved away from the 'belle infidèle' to pioneer modern literal translation (1971, 241). Here Defauconpret restores much of *OM*'s religious and political context. He favours neologisms ('covenantaires', 'caméroniens', 'épiscopaux') or the original term ('les Whigs') over paraphrase or cultural equivalence, and accurately conveys the Covenanters' political and religious grievances.

This is not the place to examine in depth why Defauconpret abandoned the 'belle infidèle'. Patrick Hersant (1999, 87) has suggested the combined action of negative reviews, improved knowledge of English and exposure to the 'foreignizing' theories of translation expounded in Schleiermacher's 'Methoden des Übersetzens' ('On the different methods of translation') (1813) and Goethe's *Noten und Abhandlungen zum bessern Verständnis des 'West-östlichen Divans'* (Notes and papers for a better understanding of the *West-Eastern Divan*) (1819). First introduced to France by Mme de Staël in her 'De l'esprit des traductions' (On the spirit of translations) (1816),[29] these sought to retain difficulty and to gain for the target language new expressive possibilities. Goethe and Schleiermacher argued that by domesticating the foreign, the 'belle infidèle', conversely, destroyed any benefits that translation might bring to the target culture.

Other factors might include the greater press freedom permitted by the 'Serre Laws' (1819) and the more Liberal views and Romantic aesthetics of Defauconpret's co-translators Pichot and Charles-Auguste Defauconpret. Perhaps, though, the 'belle infidèle' was finally destroyed by the industrialization of the fiction market, largely fuelled by Scott's unprecedented commercial success. As rival translators raced to publish first, they could no longer afford the creative engagement with the original which produced the 1817 *Puritains*. Collaborative translation, too, as practised by Defauconpret, often denied the individual translator an overview of the whole text. Following the 1822 agreement with Black, Young and Young, moreover, Defauconpret translated proof-sheets as they arrived, with no knowledge of how the novel would develop.

Nonetheless, it is the 1817 and (slightly revised) 1821 versions of *Les Puritains* that are read by the French Romantic generation of the 1820s. Equally importantly, they provide the source texts for other translations. The 1822 Italian versions and 1824 Russian versions of *OM* are derived from Defauconpret's 1817 and 1821 texts respectively (Davis 1991, 27; Benedetti 1974, 47). The first

---

[29] First published in Italian, this essay only became known in France in the 1820s, after publication in the 'Miscellaneous Essays' section (vol. 17) of her *Oeuvres complètes* in 1821.

Spanish and Polish versions (1826, 1828) are translated from French and must logically be based on one of these two texts.

This perhaps explains the contrast between the novel's fortune in France and elsewhere in Europe. *OM* is not among the small canon of Scott texts regularly reprinted in Europe (*I, QD, T, RR, K, BL, P*). According to BOSLIT, fully twelve Waverley novels were more frequently republished or retranslated in the twentieth century. Strikingly, there were no Italian or Polish editions. Perhaps in countries where Romanticism took a Liberal, nationalist turn, Defauconpret's conservative reworking of *OM* effectively denied it a sympathetic audience. Even twentieth-century France saw only one edition of the novel. Defauconpret, then, retold *OM* for a conservative Restoration audience, producing a text which, with its politically ambiguous hero, colourful melodramatic villain and (from 1821) lavish local colour influenced the development of French Romantic drama and fiction. In the longer term, however, he may have hindered French and European appreciation of one of Scott's major novels.

3 The Reception of Sir Walter Scott in Spain

José Enrique García-González and Fernando Toda

In October 2005, the online catalogue of the Biblioteca Nacional de España (Spanish National Library <www.bne.es>), which starts in 1831, returned 1,862 results for Shakespeare, 1,677 for the Spanish nineteenth-century novelist Benito Pérez Galdós and 1,225 for Dickens; Walter Scott got 623; James Fenimore Cooper 277 (in all cases this includes editions published in and outside of Spain). If that is any indicator of an author's popularity, Scott has certainly been popular in Spain and continues to be so, to judge from the number of recent editions.

This chapter deals with the reception of Walter Scott in Spain in the nineteenth and twentieth centuries, and the beginning of the twenty-first. The essay concentrates on translations and their production and reception (including problems with censorship), and less on the influence of Scott on Spanish authors, though some reference is made to that aspect. The sections related to the nineteenth and the first half of the twentieth century are based on research for García-González 2005.[1] As a translator of Scott, Fernando Toda has focused on aspects of Scott translations from the 1950s up to 2004. This volume includes a chapter on Scott in Catalonia by Andrew Monnickendam, and more detailed information regarding the nineteenth-century reception of the author in that part of Spain is to be found there.

---

[1] 'Traducción y recepción de Walter Scott en España: estudio descriptivo de las traducciones de Waverley al español': doctoral thesis, University of Seville (forthcoming on CD-ROM), supervised by Dr Fernando Toda and Dr Isidro Pliego, on the reception of Scott in Spain, with special reference to the translations of *Waverley*.

The nineteenth century: translations

The first known translation of Walter Scott into Spanish, which was only partial, was published by José María Blanco-White in 1823–24.[2] An émigré in Britain since 1810 on religious and political grounds, this enlightened member of the Spanish Catholic clergy, who later became a Protestant, was the editor of a Spanish-language journal, *Las Variedades o El Mensajero de Londres* (Varieties or the London messenger), published in London by a German printer, Rudolph Ackermann. It was there that Blanco-White published some passages translated from *I*, together with a summary of some chapters, and comments on certain scenes. Perhaps more important than the translation itself are Blanco-White's remarks on how well-received translations of Scott might be in Spain:

> A Spaniard having good taste and a perfect understanding of English could translate this novel in such a way that his fellow countrymen would tear it from each others' hands. But − we would warn translators − let no one attempt it who is not up to the task and on a par with the author who, in this genre, has no equal in Europe.[3]

Ten years after the publication of *Waverley*, this learned Spaniard, writing in Britain, was labelling Scott as the greatest historical novelist in Europe. It should be mentioned that Blanco-White was, in turn, probably the first Spanish writer to imitate Scott: his novel *Vargas, a Tale of Spain* (1822) is largely influenced by *Waverley* (Murphy 1995).

Thus, Scott was first translated outside Spain, and this tendency was to continue. The first full translations, *Ivanhoe* (1825) and *El Talismán* (1826), were both published simultaneously in London and Mexico, but not in Spain, and the publisher was also Ackermann (Churchman and Peers 1922, 268).[4] As we will see, other translations were published in France. The reasons for this partly have to do with the political situation in Spain.

Ferdinand VII came to the throne in 1808, but was soon deposed by Napoleon, who summoned him to France and made him resign, imposing his own brother, Joseph Bonaparte, as King of Spain. This brought about the May

---

[2] For more on this author, see Antonio Garnica (ed.) (2004) *Cartas de España*, Seville: Fundación J. M. Lara; also Martin Murphy (1989) *Blanco White: Self-banished Spaniard*, New Haven: Yale University Press.

[3] 'Un español, de buen gusto, que entendiese el inglés perfectamente, pudiera traducir esta novela de tal modo que sus paisanos se la quitasen unos a otros de las manos. Mas *nadie la mueva*, diremos a los traductores, que *estar no pueda*, si no *a prueba* con el autor, cuyo igual, en este género, no se halla en Europa' (*Las Variedades* (1823), 1.1: 32). Blanco-White makes reference to a phrase in *Don Quijote*, Part II, LXVI: 'Nadie las mueva [las armas] que estar no pueda con Roldán a prueba.'

[4] Menéndez Pelayo held that these two versions, with minor changes, were reprinted by other publishers, with no reference to the original translations: *Ivanhoe* (1833, Bergnes); *The Talisman* (1837, Moquet; 1838, Bergnes; 1849, Oliveres) (Churchman and Peers 1922, 277).

1808 uprising and the ensuing Spanish War of Independence. In 1812, the Spanish Parliament, which had moved to Cadiz to escape from the advance of the Napoleonic army, proclaimed a new liberal Constitution, with Ferdinand VII as the rightful king. In December 1813 the Treaty of Valençay was signed, putting an end to the war. France recognized Ferdinand as King of Spain, and he returned in 1814, but reigned as an absolutist, causing many liberals to flee the country. Some of these exiles would eventually become translators or promoters of translations of books which could not be published in Spain (Ruiz-Casanova 2000). For a brief three-year period (1820–23), Ferdinand had to submit to the precepts of the 1812 Constitution, but from 1823 to his death in 1833 the absolutist regime reverted to a repressive policy which had an impact on the cultural life of the country. During that period, Scott and other foreign authors were less published in Spain than they were in other European countries. Censorship was active during most of Ferdinand's reign (in 1815 he reinstated the Spanish Inquisition, which had been abolished in 1809 under Joseph Bonaparte), and was to reappear at several moments during the nineteenth century. Scott's novels underwent censorship for religious reasons.

As for the first translations of *I* and *T*, neither included the translator's name, but critics like Menéndez-Pelayo (Churchman and Peers 1922, 268) and Montesinos (1980, 59) agree in attributing them to José Joaquín de Mora. Both translations were well received. A good example is the review by Andrés Bello, the renowned Venezuelan lawyer and philologist (1781–1865), who resided in London from 1810 to 1829. Bello, named a representative of the new government after the declaration of independence of Venezuela in 1811, became an exile himself during the Venezuelan War of Independence (1811–23), and was in contact with many of the exiled Spaniards. In 1826 he praised the translations of *I* and *T* in the journal *Repertorio Americano* (American repertory, London, 1826, vol. 1, 139).

Another group of Spanish liberals went into exile in France. Their literary production, including translation, was aimed both at Spaniards residing in that country and at the Spanish-American readership. Some of those publications were smuggled into Spain so as to avoid censorship. In 1824 a pamphlet printed in Perpignan announced the publication of the complete works of Walter Scott, translated into Spanish by 'a society of Spanish literati' (Marrast 1988, 71). However, only a few translations were published: *Ivanhoe, ó el regreso de la Palestina del caballero cruzado* (Ivanhoe, or the return from the Palestine of the knight crusader, 1826), *Los Puritanos de Escocia* (The puritans of Scotland; *OM*) together with *El enano misterioso* (The mysterious dwarf; *BD*) in 1826, and *Quintín Durward, ó el escocés en la corte de Luis XI* (Quentin Durward, or the Scotsman in the court of Louis XI) in 1826. The publisher was Alzine. The titles in Spanish seem to echo almost word for word those in French: *Ivanhoe, ou le Retour du Croisé* (1820), *Les Puritains d'Ecosse et le Nain Mysterieux* (1817), and *Quentin Durward ou l'Ecossais à la Cour de Louis XI* (1823). These were the titles used by A. J. B. Defauconpret (who translated all the Waverley novels), and it seems likely that the Spanish versions were done from the French, or at least with the French texts at hand. Other works of Scott were published in Spanish in different French cities in the late 1820s and early 1830s. Some were translated by Pablo de Xérica, a liberal émigré,[5] and in the late 1830s and early 1840s we find a number of them published in Paris, by Rosa. A few were printed simultaneously in Mexico, by Galván (Churchman and Peers 1922, 282–83). It is not easy to establish whether the translations were done from French, or simply used the French titles because they were already familiar to readers. García-González (2005, 73, note 36) quotes the points of view and evidence given by different authors in trying to establish this. Nevertheless, one might almost speak of a Spanish tradition of translating not from the original but from an existing version in another language, usually French (the most commonly learned foreign language); this was to be especially the case with Russian literature. In most cases the fact was not mentioned in the book, but it seems to have been so common that it is not infrequent, even in the early twentieth century, to find books stating 'translated directly from English', or something to that effect, so as to reassure the reader.[6]

The first Scott novel to be printed in Spain was *El Talismán, o Ricardo en Palestina* (The Talisman, or Richard in Palestine) (1826) and it was published in Barcelona by Piferrer. Churchman and Peers (1922, 269) state that, according to Menéndez-Pelayo, the translators were Juan Nicasio Gallego and Eugenio de Tapia (again, we find something fairly common in Spanish editions: the translator's name is not given in the book). The first Scott translation to be published in Madrid (by Sanz) was *La pastora de Lammermoor o la desposada* (The shepherdess of Lammermoor or the newlywed; *BL*) (1828). All we find are the translator's initials, D. L. C. B., and in the prologue a statement of admiration for Scott which goes so far as to affirm that the translator is fully convinced that only his own 'ineptitude' will be to blame 'if Spain does not find pleasing that which in all other nations has obtained an acceptance which is as widespread as it is deserved'.[7]

The 1830s and the early 1840s saw the peak of Scott's popularity in Spain. Varela-Jacome (1974, 15) refers to the 'Scottism' of the period, made manifest both in the number of translations and the criticism published in those years. An important factor in this rise in popularity was the flourishing of the publishing business after the death of Ferdinand VII in 1833. Madrid and Barcelona were the main centres, followed by Valencia and, much further behind, Seville, Cadiz,

---

[5]   It should be mentioned that Xérica infused his liberal ideology into his texts, making omissions, additions and substitutions to subvert the Spanish dominant milieu on religious, moral and political grounds. This aspect is dealt with in José E. García-González, 'Translation, Ideology and Subversion: D. Pablo de Xérica's Spanish translation of Sir Walter Scott's *Waverley*', *Journal of Romance Studies* 6: 3 (2006), 87–102.

[6]   And this may not always be true. Marrast (1988, 70–71) says that the three Scott novels published by Alzine state on the cover that they are translated from the English, and yet the printer's advertising for the collection affirms that all care has been taken to avoid 'Gallicisms' or 'idioms from the French' in the translations.

[7]   'que su propia ineptitud puede ser la única causa de no agradar en España lo que en todas las demás naciones ha obtenido una aceptación tan general como bien merecida' (as quoted by López-Folgado and Mora-González 1987, 350).

Malaga and Santander (Alonso 1984, 36). Most of Scott's works appear in collections or 'libraries', which often include a motley mixture of authors and titles (Ferreras 1976, 41). The first of these came out in Madrid, published by Federico Moreno between 1830 and 1832. It received the name of 'Nueva Colección de novelas de Sir Walter Scott, traducidas por una Sociedad de litera-tos' (New collection of works by Sir Walter Scott, translated by a society of literati). It consisted of twenty volumes, corresponding to ten works. There were poems – for example *La dama del lago* (*LL*) (1830) – and novels. Among the latter was *HM*, entitled *Las cárceles de Edimburgo* (The prisons of Edinburgh, 1831). It takes its title from the French *La prison d'Edimbourg*, from which it was translated. No other version of it was carried out in Spain until 1988.[8] In fact, all ten works were apparently translated from French. Contemporary criticism made satirical references to this collection and the poor quality of the transla-tions. A reflection of the unsatisfactory evaluation of some contemporaneous versions of Scott is given by the well-known journalist and novelist Mariano José de Larra, who has one of his characters offer the following advice to an aspiring translator:

> Make a deal with a couple of book publishers, who will give you twenty or twenty-five pesetas for each volume of the novels of Sir Walter Scott which you may translate for them in a few hours, and even if they be badly translated, do not worry, for neither the publisher nor anyone else will understand them.[9]

Another publisher, Tomás Jordán, continued Federico Moreno's task and from 1831–32 brought out the 'Nueva colección de novelas de diversos autores, traducidos al castellano por una Sociedad de literatos' (New collection of novels by divers authors, translated into Spanish by a society of literati). The series included James Fenimore Cooper among the historical novelists, together with Scott. In terms of the value given to translations, it is curious to remark how the publishers of the time seem to have been eager to assure their readers that the translations were commissioned from 'literati', and yet the translators' names are sometimes not given, or given in initials, and neither is the information that the books are indirect translations.

In Barcelona, Antonio Bergnes de las Casas published collections in which the translations were done directly from English. He started with a 'Biblioteca selecta, portátil y económica' (Select, portable and inexpensive library), which ran from 1831 to 1833, and followed it with a 'Biblioteca de damas' (Ladies' library) in 1837–39. The translations of Scott's novels in the latter were praised

---

[8] There is a theatrical adaptation of the novel: *Las prisiones de Edimburgo: melodrama semi-serio en tres actos, para representarse en el Teatro Principal* (The prisons of Edin-burgh: a semi-serious melodrama in three acts, to be staged at the Main Theatre), Cadiz: Viuda de Comes, 1841.

[9] 'Ajústese usted con un par de libreros, los cuales le darán a usted cuatro o cinco duros por cada tomo de las novelas de Walter Scott que usted en horas les traduzca, y aunque vayan mal traducidas, usted no se apure, que ni el librero lo entiende, ni ningún cristiano tampoco' (as quoted by Montesinos 1980, 80).

in the journal *El Imparcial* (The impartial press) in 1844 by Milá y Fontanals (1892a, 38–39).

Also in Barcelona, Oliva published a 'Colección de novelas escogidas' (Collection of choice novels), which included Scott among other foreign writers, many of them French (e.g. Mme Genlis, Montesquieu). In Madrid, we find *Guy Mannering, ó El astrólogo* (Guy Mannering, or the astrologer) (1838) translated by Eugenio de Ochoa, who comments on the difficulty of the task and claims his is the first translation into Spanish (in fact it had been rendered by Xérica in Paris in 1835). Ochoa admits that when working from the English text he also made use of the French translation by Defauconpret, whose notes he translated and included in his edition together with Scott's. Ochoa also rendered *El monasterio* (The monastery, Paris: Rosa, 1840) and *Las aguas de San Ronan* (St Ronan's waters, Paris: Rosa, 1841; *SRW*). There are several later editions of these books, printed by other publishers; they appear to be Ochoa's translations. Montesinos comments on the deficient legislation on intellectual property of the time, and mentions 'books which have great success [. . .] which everyone appropriates as soon as they become aware of the public's liking for them; some publishers must even have made use of translations already published by a competitor'.[10]

In the 1840s we continue to find works by Scott in different collections. One of these is the 'Biblioteca popular económica' (Popular inexpensive library), published in Madrid by Mellado between 1844 and 1863. It contained works already published in Spain, and also some which had never been printed but were considered 'important', e.g. Scott's *Las aventuras de Nigel* (The adventures of Nigel, 1845 (*FN*)). The collection included Spanish authors, like Cervantes or Gil y Carrasco (a Romantic writer) and other popular foreign writers like Sue, Dumas, and Hugo. Some 'mistakes' were committed: *La maga de la montaña* (The Highland sorceress) came out in 1844 as a novel by Scott, but the text corresponds to *La pythie des Highlands*, by Jules Antoine David (1844). Perhaps it was felt that Scott's name on the cover would attract readership. Similarly, Mellado's 'Biblioteca de recreo' (Recreational library) included *Allan Cameron*, also attributed to Scott, but in fact a Scott pastiche written in French by Pier Auguste Callet and Javelin Pagnon (the translators of Chatterton's Rowley poems into French).

This tendency to attribute others' works to Scott carried on into the twentieth (in fact, the early twenty-first) century: a search at the Spanish ISBN site, which includes books published since 1972, yields six editions of *Robin Hood* by Walter Scott, by four different publishers.[11] The first corresponds to 1975 (Alcobendas: Círculo de Amigos de la Historia) and the translation is attributed to an 'Equipo de redacción' (Editorial team); the last, dated 2004

---

[10] 'Los libros de gran éxito [. . .] de los que todos se apoderan tan pronto advierten apetencias favorables del público; algún editor hasta debió de aprovecharse de traducciones ya hechas y publicadas por otro competidor' (Montesinos 1982, 120).

[11] Agencia española del ISBN <*www.mcu.es/bases/spa/isbn/ISBN.html*> [accessed 27 September 2005].

(Barcelona: Planeta-De Agostini), attributes the Spanish text to 'Equipo Sape' (Sape Team). None of the entries for the other four editions give a translator's name at all. What is more, of course, Scott did not write *Robin Hood*: we have found it to be a translation of *Robin Hood, prince des voleurs* (1872), attributed to Alexandre Dumas the Elder after his death in 1870. However, Dumas was probably only responsible for finding a translator and adapter (Marie de Fern- and, one of his collaborators, who used the pen name Victor Perceval) for Pierce Egan's *Robin Hood and Little John, or the Merry Men of Sherwood Forest* (serialised in 1838, published as a book in 1840).[12] We have not yet ascertained when the first Spanish translation of this French version came out, or the translator's name. But it has continued to be printed, by various publishers and in different collections, so that for most Spanish readers *Robin Hood* is to all intents and purposes a novel by Walter Scott.

The 1840s also saw the publication of some of Scott's works in the form of newspaper serials and in fascicles. This second option does not appear to have thrived: we find a 'Colección de novelas de Sir Walter Scott' (Madrid: Omaña) of which, according to Montesinos (1980, 242), only one volume was completed: *Ivanhoe* (1841). It was a luxury edition, with beautiful loose illustra- tion plates, and perhaps this made the collection too expensive for its potential customers. *Quintín Durward, episodio de la historia de Luis XI* (Quentin Durward, an episode from the history of Louis XI, 1841) was published in fascicles for sale with the Sunday edition of the newspaper *El Panorama* (The panorama). They could be bound in five volumes.

When we mention 'popular editions' of Scott, talk of his popularity and think of the extent of his readership in Spain, it should not be forgotten that the situation is not comparable to what it was for the source-language reading public. In Britain, *I* is said to have sold 10,000 copies in the first two weeks of its publication: such figures were unimaginable for Spain even twenty years later. Lloréns (1989, 245) states that the vast majority of the population of Spain was illiterate (about 90 per cent in 1841). Among the working classes, the transmission of literature, if any, was mostly oral: one person would read to a group.

Scott continued to be published in different collections throughout the nine- teenth century. In 1857–58 an editorial enterprise called 'La Maravilla: Gran Sociedad Editorial' (The wonder: great publishing society) brought out 'the greatest works of human knowledge' in luxury editions, printed by Luis Tasso in Barcelona (Churchman and Peers 1922, 292). The collection included some works by Scott, among which was *Rob Roy*, translated by 'D. E. de C. V.' (1858; it is the same translation that had been published by Bergnes in Barcelona in 1838). Works by Scott were also published in 1882–84 for the 'Biblioteca Verdaguer' (Verdaguer library) in Barcelona, and for the 'Biblioteca de los novelistas' (Novelists' library) published by the Garnier brothers in Paris. This collection, which began in 1891 with *I* and *QD*, continued up to 1920, and was the first (and the only) collection to include all of the Waverley novels in Spanish.

---

[12] See <*www.dumaspere.com*> [accessed 15 October 2005].

To this overview of nineteenth-century editions of Scott we could add the publication of a number of bilingual Italian-Spanish libretti of operas based on his works. The favourites among these seem to have been *I Puritani* (*OM*) and *Lucia di Lammermoor*. They were first staged in Madrid in the second quarter of the nineteenth century, and remained popular with opera lovers. Stoudemire (1950, 4–5) lists six Italian operas based on works by Scott. The years of their premieres in Spain are: *La Donna del Lago* (*LL*) (1828); *Il Condestabile di Chester* (The constable of Chester (*TB*)) (1831); *Il Castello di Kenilworth* (The castle of Kenilworth (*K*)) (1835); *I Puritani e I Cavalieri* (Puritans and cavaliers (*OM*)) (1836); *Lucia di Lammermoor* (Lucia of Lammermoor (*BL*)) (1837); *Il Templario* (The templar (*I*)) (1841). The publication date of the libretti almost invariably coincides with the year of the premieres in Spain, and most were printed by Sancha in Madrid.

For the nineteenth century, we have found approximately 130 Spanish editions of Scott. This includes translations published in France and Britain. Apocryphal and doubtful editions have been left out, and when the same translation was printed by several publishers, all the editions were counted.

It was basically the novels that were translated. As for the poetry, of the few translations carried out several are presented as novels. Here are a few examples: *Rokeby: A Poem* was published as *Matilde de Rokeby. Novela histórico-poética* (Mathilda of Rokeby. A historical-poetic novel) (1829); *LL* came out as *La dama del lago. Novela histórica* (The lady of the lake: a historical novel) in 1830. *The Lay of the Last Minstrel* was labelled as poetry in the title, *Canto del último trovador: Poema en seis cantos* (Lay of the last minstrel: a poem in six cantos), but it was translated as prose and included in a 'Colección de novelas' (Collection of novels), published by Oliveres in Barcelona, in 1843. Among the novels, the ones most often translated, and so presumably the most popular, were *Ivanhoe* and *Quentin Durward*.

Although a considerable number of editions do not bear the translator's name (a practice that would carry over into the twentieth century), the number of those that do is higher. In the earlier ones, it is fairly common to find only the initials. Some translators, like Eugenio de Ochoa[13] and Pablo de Xérica, rendered as many as three of Scott's works, but they are exceptions. Spain does not have a figure to compare with Defauconpret.

The nineteenth century: criticism and followers

The first allusion to Scott in Spain appeared in the journal *Crónica Científica y Literaria* (Scientific and literary chronicle), no. 160, published in Madrid on 6 October 1818. It was in an article signed by José Joaquín de Mora, later to be one of Scott's first translators. Churchman and Peers (1922, 232) state that it is in fact a translation of an article in French written by a certain Malte-Brun, and the allusion, which refers to Scott's poetry, was not very complimentary: it held

---

[13]   See Lloréns (1989, 259–62) on Ochoa's literary biography.

that Scott, 'wrongly called the Scottish Ariosto, shows nothing but a certain trivial ease, lacking originality'.[14]

The same reasons that retarded Scott's entrance into Spanish literary life also explain the scarcity of critical appraisal until the late 1820s. There was a mistrust of foreign innovations and, as far as literary taste is concerned, there was still a tendency to preserve the Neoclassical spirit. It is not surprising, then, that an article in *El Censor* (The censor) (Madrid, vol. XV, 16 March 1822, 22) about the novel in Europe, which discussed Rousseau and Richardson, did not mention Scott at all, even though by then he had published nine novels. The journal, sponsored by conservative liberals and favourable to Neoclassical aesthetics, gives an idea of the view held by such critics about the historical novel: its value was considered to be mostly moral, not literary, since it was not up to classical standards, and anyone with a certain amount of imagination and style could write in that genre (Zavala 1971,18).

Scott received some criticism on the part of the Neoclassicists, but he was highly praised in Spain, especially from the late 1830s and throughout the 1840s. His name was naturalized as Gualterio Scott (sometimes even Escoto) in some publications, which was the norm in Spain at the time (so, for example, Guillermo Shakespeare), sometimes hyphenated (Walter-Scott) and sometimes simply misspelled (Valter, or Waltlet, Scoot); a number of clichés crop up in relation to him: 'ingenio privilegiado' (privileged mind), 'bienhechor de la humanidad' (benefactor of humanity), 'el Cervantes escocés' (the Scottish Cervantes). Such admiration is mostly related to his work as a historical novelist, and it is found among writers with different ideologies.

As early as 1829 Juan Donoso Cortés (1809–53), a conservative parliamentary statesman, diplomat, government minister, royal counsellor, theologian, and political theorist, recommended Scott to students in his lecture at the opening of the academic year at the Colegio de Humanidades (College of Humanities) in Cáceres (Peers 1967, 2: 150). On his return to Spain, the Romantic playwright and poet Ángel Saavedra (1791–1865), better known in Spanish letters as Duque de Rivas (Duke of Rivas) – one of the liberals who had gone into exile – was made a member of the Real Academia (Royal Academy). In his inaugural speech, he credited Scott, together with Byron and Hugo, with having helped to revive interest in Spanish history. Even some journals which did not side with Romanticism admitted Scott's supremacy, like *Eco del Comercio* (The echo of commerce) (2 March 1835), which called him the father of the historical novel, stating that the most fertile period for this literary genre came with 'the genius of the famous Walter Scott' ('el genio del célebre Walter Scott').

Some were not so laudatory. An 1834 article in *El Correo de las Damas* (The ladies' post) is relevant because in being satirical it enables us to see to what extent Scott had become popular:

---

[14] 'mal apellidado el Ariosto Escocés, no tiene más que cierta facilidad trivial y sin originalidad' (as quoted by Churchman and Peers 1922, 232).

Well, wherever there may be a novel by Walter Scott let everyone fall silent. Admittedly, some of them are very boring, very monotonous, and have nothing good or new to say; but they have the author's name to recommend them, and that is enough.[15]

In 1840 the poet Alberto Lista (1775–1848), a professor at the University of Seville, wrote a series of articles entitled 'De la novela' (On the novel). When he came to the historical novel, he introduced a fictional dialogue in which he has Scott offer his works to the readers:

> 'I have gathered numerous precise observations on the customs of the Middle Ages. I shall give them to you in novels. What do you say?' 'Yes,' answered society, fed up with immorality and exaggeration of feelings. 'At least we will learn something about our ancestors.'[16]

Lista's admiration for the literary value of Scott's work is complemented by that of critics like Andrés Bello, who in his 1825 review of *Ivanhoe* praised not only the novel's capacity to amuse, but also its usefulness in diffusing historical knowledge. He hoped that the book (which had also been published in Mexico) would serve as an example for the peoples of America, some of whom had already gained independence from Spain, so they might learn to 'rectify their ideas' as needed for political reforms, and to appreciate 'the eternal rules of order'.[17] Bello had probably seen that Scott's vision of history, including the need to come to a compromise between the old and the new, and the need to understand the other's position and circumstances, held an important message for the critical moment that Spanish America was going through.

Zavala (1971), who has very interesting observations on the reception of Scott in socio-political terms, notes that his 'pacifism' is one of the aspects that critics tended to enhance, especially during the time of the First Carlist War (1833–39), a civil confrontation over succession which broke out, after the death of Ferdinand VII, between those who supported absolute monarchy in the person of Carlos María Isidro, Ferdinand's brother (hence the name Carlists), and the constitutionalists, who supported liberal monarchy and Isabel II, Ferdinand's daughter. In Zavala's opinion, 'it was necessary to foster humanitarianism and to unite the social classes, and also the country, divided by a fratricidal war.'[18] So, apart from the novelty in style and setting and the moral

---

[15] 'Vaya, donde hay una novela de Walter-Scott calle todo el mundo. Verdad es que las hay muy pesadas, muy monótonas y que nada dicen bueno ni nuevo; pero el nombre del autor las recomienda y esto basta y basta de tal modo' (*El Correo de las Damas*, 20 March 1834).

[16] 'Tengo recogidas observaciones exactas y numerosas sobre las costumbres de la edad media. Os las daré en novelas. ¿Queréis?' 'Sí', respondió la sociedad fastidiada de inmoralidad y de exageración de sentimientos. 'A lo menos sabremos algo de nuestros antepasados' (as quoted by Peers 1926, 153).

[17] 'rectificar sus ideas [. . .] las reglas eternas del orden' (Andrés Bello, *Repertorio Americano*, 1826, 1: 320).

[18] 'era necesario fomentar el humanitarismo y unir las clases sociales, así como el país, dividido por una guerra fratricida' (Zavala 1971, 38).

implications, the political message in Scott was applied by some to current circumstances in Spain and America.

Spanish writers and critics of the nineteenth century made numerous references to Scott. His great popularity made him a point of comparison when considering native and foreign authors. When Cecilia Böhl de Faber, writing under the pen name Fernán Caballero, published her novel *La Gaviota* (The seagull) in 1849, Eugenio de Ochoa (one of Scott's translators) remarked in a review that the author was contributing to a comeback of the autochthonous Spanish novel, and thus doing for Spain something similar to what Scott had done for Britain. If Fernán Caballero continued in that line, 'there is no doubt that *La Gaviota* will be to Spanish literature what *Waverley* was to English literature'.[19]

Manuel Fernández y González (1821–88) was a prolific writer who combined the historical and the adventure genres. From the mid 1840s to the late 1860s, his work was very popular. His were serial novels, and the speed and quantity of production may be to blame for their low quality (Ferreras 1976, 265 ff.). Emilia Pardo Bazán (1851–1921), a major novelist herself, lamented this in a writer whom she considered one of the 'walterscottianos' who, if he had not squandered his talent, 'could have been called, more than anyone else, the rival of the author of *Ivanhoe*'.[20]

A number of Spanish novelists followed in Scott's footsteps and started writing historical novels, as Blanco-White had done with *Vargas*. Peers, who held that in the second quarter of the nineteenth century 'most, if not all, of the principal Spanish novelists were directly or indirectly influenced by the Waverley Novels' (Peers 1926, 3), divided the followers and imitators of Scott into three groups. The first includes those writers whose historical novels followed Scott's model so closely that they went so far as to include passages taken straight from his novels. This is the case of Ramón López Soler with *Los bandos de Castilla o El caballero del Cisne* (The factions of Castile or the knight of the swan, 1830), José de Espronceda with *Sancho Saldaña o el castellano de Cuéllar* (Sancho Saldaña or the Castilian from Cuéllar, 1834) and Enrique Gil y Carrasco with *El señor de Bembibre* (The lord of Bembibre, 1844). A second group includes 'disciples and admirers', and in it are those authors who look to Scott for inspiration and style, but do not actually copy parts of his works. Among them is the liberal exile Telesforo Trueba y Cossío, who wrote in English. His novels *Gómez Arias; or, the Moors of the Alpujarras* (1828) and *The Castilian* (1829) were translated into Spanish: *Gómez Arias, o los moros de las Alpujarras* (1831) and *El castellano o El Príncipe Negro en España* (The Castilian or the Black Prince in Spain, 1845). José García de Villalta, with novels like *El conde de Candespina* (The earl of Candespina, 1832) and *La conjuración de Méjico o Los hijos de Hernán Cortés* (The Mexico conspiracy or the children of Hernán Cortés, 1850) is also in this

---

[19] 'no hay duda de que *La Gaviota* será en la literatura española lo que *Waverley* en la inglesa' (*La España* (Spain), 26 August 1849)

[20] 'pudo llamarse, mejor que nadie, rival del autor de *Ivanhoe*' (quoted by Churchman and Peers 1922, 265).

group. The third includes writers who professed their admiration for Scott (e.g. Milá y Fontanals) and/or incorporated some elements of Scott's aesthetics in their novels at a time when the Spanish Romantic movement was in decline and the author of *Waverley* was losing popularity. Among these are Francisco Navarro Villoslada (*Doña Blanca de Navarra*, 1847; *Doña Urraca de Castilla*, 1848) and Amós de Escalante (*Ave Maris Stella*, 1877).

From the middle of the 1840s, Scott's popularity began to decrease, as that of the social novel, published in serials, increased. In making reference to the most widely read authors in the five years from 1846 to 1850, Joaquín M. Sanromá observed in 1886 that 'Walter Scott had gone out of fashion; D'Arlincourt was becoming outdated; Sue, Dumas and Paul de Kock ruled the roost.'[21] The number of translations published decreased, as did that of critical reviews, although Scott remained popular until the end of the century. The writer and critic Juan Eugenio Hartzenbusch pointed to the renewal in literature in an article published in 1847, 'Apuntes sobre el carácter de la literatura contemporánea' (Notes on the nature of contemporary literature), in which he held that Romantic aesthetics, as exemplified by Scott, Byron, Hugo, or the Spaniards Larra and Espronceda, was 'tediously dragging on into our own time.'[22] Lloréns (1989, 548) considers it significant that most of the narratives published by the journal *Semanario Pintoresco Español* (Picturesque Spanish weekly, 1846–57) are no longer in the Romantic line, but, rather, tend to depict local customs; that literary reviews no longer make reference to Scott; and that the debates over Romanticism have disappeared.

The Duke of Rivas, mentioned earlier, continued to show his admiration for Scott. Apart from the fact that his epic poem *El moro expósito* (The foundling Moor, 1833–34) has similarities with *Ivanhoe*, in his 1860 speech at the Real Academia he exalted Scott's technique in presenting characters (Peers 1926, 9–11).

Marcelino Menéndez-Pelayo (1856–1912), one of the leading figures in Spanish literary studies in the nineteenth century, attacked those who disdained Scott's work and favoured the influence of experimental science on the naturalist novel:

> In vain do today's critics, despite the universal pleasure he gives to readers, try to play down the worth of this wizard of history, basing their disapproval on a poor and sad concept of the novel, from which they would banish by force any poetic element and any traditional sap.[23]

---

[21] 'Walter Scott había pasado de moda; d'Arlincourt se iba anticuando; Sue, Dumas y Paul de Kock eran los amos del cotarro' ('Mis memorias', *Revista Contemporánea* (Contemporary review), 30 November 1886)

[22] '[va] durando trabajosamente hasta hoy' (*El Siglo Pintoresco* (The picturesque century), 1847, 3: 149–52)

[23] 'En vano intentan hoy los críticos, a despecho del placer universal de los lectores, rebajar el mérito de este mago de la historia, fundando sus censuras en una pobre y triste concepción de la novela, de la cual quieren desterrar a viva fuerza todo elemento poético y toda savia tradicional' (Menéndez-Pelayo 1940, 4: 362).

The reasons for Scott's popularity in nineteenth-century Spain are probably similar to those which made him such a favourite with readers in Britain and elsewhere in Europe. A new type of novel, which catered for a new Romantic sensibility and not only included elements of adventure and romance but also exalted values such as chivalry, patriotism, friendship and courage was a welcome change, and Spanish readers were as eager for it as others. Spanish writers, as we have seen, found a model in the historical novel, and the most famous and prolific of them, Benito Pérez Galdós, writing in the late nineteenth century, owes among other things his use of 'average Spaniards' as heroes to the influence of Scott's 'mediocre heroes' (Regalado-García 1966, 135 ff.).

Censorship in the nineteenth and twentieth centuries

The publication of Scott's works in Spain was subjected to censorship at several points over the nineteenth century. During the absolutist reign of Ferdinand VII, and in some later periods, books had to be submitted to censorship before they could be published. In some cases this meant that certain books were banned; in others, they were printed but had to undergo changes or cuts. The first known attempt to translate Scott in Spain, by a Catalan society (including the writer Aribau) that intended to publish a selection of his novels in Spanish, failed in 1828 because the ecclesiastical censor forbade it (Soldevila 1926, 88). In 1830, Gregorio Morales Pantoja applied for a permit to publish his translation *Ivanhoe o la vuelta del desierto* (Ivanhoe or the return from the desert), but after a long process it was not granted, the reasons being that the book contained certain passages which revealed the author's Protestant bias, and offered a poor image of the Catholic religion and clergy (González-Palencia 1927, 3–4). His translation of *LM*, however, was authorized in 1831. Other attempts to publish *I* in those years also met with the censors' refusal. Even French translations of Scott were forbidden to be sold in Spain, since it was felt that works such as *PP, GM, AB, Monastery* or *QD* contained opinions contrary to the Catholic Church, its practices and its clergymen. Not only that, it was feared that these historical novels would cause unhealthy passions in young people (González-Palencia 1927, 16–19).

In some cases, the translators, wary of what the censors might think, manipulated their texts so as to produce 'acceptable' versions. Such was the case of 'A. Tracia', who in his *La visión de Don Rodrigo* (The vision of Don Roderick, 1829), 'translated freely into Spanish' (the only translation that has ever been done), openly admitted in the prologue that he had changed some of Scott's ideas and expressions for the following reasons: 'Walter Sccoth [*sic*] is Scottish and writes basically for the English. I am a Spaniard and a Catholic, and I write only for the Spanish.'[24] Similarly, D. P. H. B., the translator of *Kenilworth*,

---

[24] 'Walter Sccoth es escocés y escribe principalmente para los ingleses: yo soy católico y español y escribo únicamente para los españoles': as quoted by Santoyo (2000, 305), who holds that 'A. Tracia' is an acronym for Agustín Aicart.

identified as Don Pedro Higinio Barinaga by Montesinos (1980, 240), included a 'warning' in his edition (published in Valencia 1831–32), indicating that he had carried out several alterations and suppressions for literary and especially for religious reasons: 'the author being a Protestant, the work contains some paragraphs which should not be passed on through a Catholic's pen, much less circulate in a country of such glorious renown.'[25] Religious reasons were also alleged by the translator of *Woodstock, ó el caballero* (Woodstock, or the knight. Madrid: Jordán, 1831) when he argued that he had had to be careful with some dialogues: 'sometimes when these fanatics talk about Catholicism we shall have to modify their expressions by means of some notes.'[26]

This practice of censorship recommenced in the twentieth century, especially during the Franco regime (1939–66). After 1966, a slight 'opening up' of the regime brought about the Ley de Prensa e Imprenta (Press and Print Law), which eliminated previous censorship (although publishers could still submit works voluntarily for 'counselling') but established methods for post-publication control. If a book, an article, a play, or a film was considered unacceptable in some way (for political, religious or 'moral' reasons), it could be confiscated (in the case of editions of books or periodical publications), and the publishers were held responsible. They risked being tried and fined or sent to prison and/or having their business shut down for a period of time, as well as losing their investment in the edition. Authors were also held responsible. This era of 'self-censorship' lasted until Franco's death in 1975, and indeed a few years longer.[27]

In the nineteenth and twentieth centuries, Scott was censored basically for religious reasons, because he was a Protestant and some aspects in his works were considered anti-Catholic.[28] Even the Catalan writer Milá y Fontanals, a great admirer of Scott, when he wrote a review of *M* in 1854 remarked that 'this is perhaps the work in which one feels most deeply the painful impression of the Protestant cares of the Baronet of Edinburgh.'[29]

Censorship of Scott's novels during the Franco regime was based on religious reasons, too. In the Archivo General de la Administración (General Archive of

---

[25] 'siendo el autor de la obra protestante, hay algunos párrafos en ella, que ni deberían pasar por la pluma de un católico, ni menos circular en un país que tiene tan glorioso renombre' (as quoted by Cabo-Pérez 2001, 790).

[26] 'Alguna vez que estos fanáticos tengan que hablar del Catolicismo tendremos que modificar sus expresiones por medio de alguna nota' (as quoted by López-Folgado and Mora-González 1987, 351).

[27] Though it does not mention Scott, Rabadán 2000 is basic for the history of censorship and translation in Spain after the Civil War. According to her, the last vestiges of Francoist censorship disappeared in 1985.

[28] García-González 2005, Chapter 2, gives a description of the process of censorship in the nineteenth and twentieth centuries, and its effect on Scott.

[29] 'es esta acaso la obra en que más de lleno se siente la penosa impresión de las preocupaciones protestantes del Baronet de Edimburgo' (Milá y Fontanals 1892b, 204). It is striking, however, that Milá made no reference to Scott's anti-Catholic position in *The Monastery*, and in fact praised the forthcoming translation by Eugenio de Ochoa (Milá y Fontanals 1892a, 39).

the Administration) we came across an application to publish five Scott novels in one volume. The censor's report had no objections to four of them (*I, QD, GM, W*) but demanded that three expressions referring to the Catholic religion in *El paje de María Estuardo* (Mary Stuart's page, *AB*) be omitted. When they had been, the volume came out as *Las cinco mejores obras de Walter Scott* (The five best works of Walter Scott, Barcelona: Mateu, 1957).[30]

The twentieth and early twenty-first centuries. Popular and scholarly editions

In the twentieth century, Scott's novels gradually lost interest among readers, but he continued to be translated and published.

One of the most frequent academic debates has to do with the question of the historical accuracy of his novels. With regard to this tension between history and invention, Spanish literary criticism in general seems to hold the view that although the historical aspect of his novels is of great relevance, Scott tends to value the fictional story to the detriment of historical fact. The point is often made that, in spite of this liberty, Scott is careful to create characters and events which appear credible in the context of the past, achieving, in Martín's words, 'a fictional reconstruction as historically authentic as possible'.[31]

With regard to the conflict between history and invention in Scott's novels, Alonso (1984) argues that one should consider the inaccuracies not so much in terms of historical errors but as the conscious alteration of historical fact that is part of literary re-creation: 'Walter Scott used to condense several decades into a few years, and he deliberately shed light and colour on the roughness and barbarism of historical events.'[32]

Although Scott was not as popular as he had been earlier, throughout the twentieth century translations were published in larger numbers than before. In the first quarter of the century the tradition of offering complete versions of the novels, sometimes in more than one volume, persisted. Most books were published in collections, which often included a mixture of earlier and modern writers from several countries. Later on in the century, we begin to find abridged versions in collections. From the 1940s onwards we begin to find that the same translation is reprinted by several publishers.

In 1988 one of the major Spanish publishers, Cátedra (Cathedra), included a scholarly edition of *HM* in their 'Letras Universales' (Universal Letters) series,

---

[30] The censorship file number is 2292/57. The censor's report, dated 29 May 1957, demands that the expressions '*My neighbours were popish and mass-mongers*', '*idolatrous devotion*' and 'the *superstitious* practices of the Catholic religion' be crossed out.

[31] 'Una reconstrucción ficticia lo más históricamente auténtica' (Martín 1988, 193).

[32] 'Walter Scott solía condensar varias décadas en algunos años y deliberadamente iluminaba y coloreaba la crudeza y la barbarie de los sucesos históricos' (Alonso 1984, 42).

giving Scott a place in this collection of world literature.[33] It was edited by Román Álvarez, the author of a book on the historical novel in Britain (Álvarez 1983), and translated by Fernando Toda. The reasons for choosing *HM* were that it is generally considered as one of Scott's best novels, and yet it was practically unknown in Spain: the book (first translated in 1831, probably from French) had not been published again since Garnier's 1907 Paris edition. The initiative was appreciated: *Quimera* (Chimera), a literary journal published in Barcelona, made precisely this last point, and welcomed the publication of a great historical novel.[34] A brief review in *El País* (The nation), Spain's leading daily, called it one of Scott's masterpieces and also remarked that the earlier translation had not been reprinted.[35]

The Highland Widow and 'The Two Drovers' were also scarcely known in Spain. There had been a translation of *CC* by Rafael Mesa López, *Las crónicas de la Canongate* (Paris: Garnier, 1907) and one of HW, *La viuda de las Highlands* (Madrid: Proa, 1945?) by A. Giménez Ortiz, but both were long out of print. In 1991 Publicaciones de la Universidad de Sevilla (Seville University Press) published the two stories, plus the pages that link them in *CC*, in a volume translated by Fernando Toda, who wrote the introduction and notes, with a foreword by Angus McIntosh.[36]

MM (1826) is Scott's most openly political work.[37] It had never been published in Spanish, anywhere in the world. The subject seemed relevant for Spain at the turn of the twentieth century, when some of the autonomous parliaments and governments, and the nationalist parties, claimed that the transfer of competences from the central to the autonomous governments had not yet been completed or did not grant enough home rule, nearly thirty years after Franco's death, the 1978 Constitution and the enactment of the different Statutes of Autonomy. In 2004, Publicaciones de la Universidad de Málaga (Malaga University Press) published a translation, with an introduction and notes, by Fernando Toda.[38] Dr Luis Moreno, an expert on Scottish political history, wrote the foreword.[39] The Spanish title *Defensa de la nación escocesa* (Defence of the

---

[33]   Started in 1973, it had 369 titles up to October 2005. It includes works from all countries and periods, except those written in Spanish, which go in the 'Letras Hispánicas' (Hispanic Letters) series. All the books carry introductions and notes. *HM* is the only work by Scott. There are twelve by Shakespeare, three by Dickens and four by Joyce.

[34]   *Quimera*, no. 86, 64. Review by Ramón Acín.

[35]   *El País*, 8 January 1988. Review by Rafael Conte.

[36]   Walter Scott, *La viuda montañesa / Los dos arreadores*, Seville: Publicaciones de la Universidad de Sevilla, 1991.

[37]   Paul Henderson Scott says of the *Letters* that 'it would be no exaggeration to describe them as the first manifesto of modern Scottish Nationalism'. Walter Scott (1981) *The Letters of Malachi Malagrowther*, Edinburgh: William Blackwood, p. xviii.

[38]   Walter Scott (2004) *Defensa de la nación escocesa* (*Las cartas de Malachi Malagrowther*), Malaga: Publicaciones de la Universidad de Málaga.

[39]   Luis Moreno is the author of *Escocia: nación y razón* (1995) Madrid: CSIC.

Scottish nation) had the obvious intention of making it plain that this was an essay touching on the question of nationalities.

These cases, of which we have direct experience, show that at the academic level support can be found for translations and editions of Scott's less well-known work. However, to judge by the sales and the number of copies printed, it would seem that interest in such work is not high.

And yet the 'classic' Scott still seems to be attractive to publishers, who keep putting out editions of *I*, *QD* and *RR*. In this last case, the 1995 film starring Liam Neeson saw the reissue of a translation by Hipólito García with a new cover illustration that evoked the film. This reissue has already been published in two different series. At the beginning of the twenty-first century, as in the late twentieth, it is still common practice for publishers to buy existing translations of Scott (and other authors in the public domain) from each other, and to publish them, sometimes without the translator's name, and certainly without paying the translator any royalties, if the translation was published before the 1987 Ley de Propiedad Intelectual (Intellectual Property Act), which for the first time in Spain recognized translators' rights to the copyright of their translations.

Malpractice in translation in the 1950s: an example

Further investigation into the translation censored in 1957, *El paje de María Estuardo* (*AB*, see note 30), revealed something about irregular editorial practice in the 1950s. Comparison with a Brazilian version by Coralia Rego Lins bearing the same title (*O pagem de María Stuart*, 1954),[40] showed that the Spanish text, which indicated that it was a translation and adaptation by María Amparo García-Burgos, had been abridged in exactly the same places and by the same methods as the Brazilian one. We eventually discovered that both versions had a common source: *Le Page de Marie Stuart* (1927), an abridged translation into French.[41] Well into the twentieth century, unavowed indirect translation and lack of information about alterations made to the original text were still going on (it should be noted that this would apply equally to the Brazilian translation). Whether the Spanish one was done from the Portuguese or from the French would be hard to establish, but the second possibility seems more likely.

---

[40] Walter Scott (1954) *O Pajem de Maria Stuart*, 3rd edn, Rio de Janeiro: Casa Editorial Vecchi.

[41] Walter Scott, *Le Page de Marie Stuart (L'Abbé) adapté de l'anglais*, Paris: Librairie Delagrave, 1929. The book offers relevant information on the cover, and yet the translator's name does not appear. The initials 'N. d. l. E.' at the end of a one-page introductory note might correspond to the translator. The regard for this profession in France would appear to be as low as in Spain at the time, to judge by this book.

Malpractice in translation in the 1990s: an example

Scott is considered good summer reading, to judge by the decision of the newspaper *El Mundo* (The world) – Spain's second largest-selling daily – to sell, with the paper, a copy of HW as part of their collection 'Novelas de verano' (Summer novels) in 1998. This came out as *La viuda de las montañas* (The widow from the mountains. Barcelona: Bibliotex, 1998), and it would seem that a new translation had been commissioned, since the version is signed by Raquel Luzárraga. Unfortunately, some of the nineteenth-century habits of misappropriating translations seem to have lasted. On examination, the new Spanish version seems to be broadly based on the 1991 translation.[42] Luzárraga's text was reissued in 2000 by another newspaper, *El Periódico de Cataluña* (The Catalonia journal), and made available with the purchase of that and other papers belonging to the same publishing group in a collection also called 'Novelas de Verano'. The authors of the covers of this second printing seem to have done little research, and certainly not to have read the book, since on the back cover one learns that it 'tells the story of a lady who has rights to claim the Crown of Scotland, but meets a very awesome opponent'.[43]

Improved practice in translating and editing

An example of better publishing practice, which illustrates how two translations of the same text will not have as high a number of exact coincidences as the case mentioned above, is *Cuentos sobrenautrales* (Supernatural stories), published by Gaviota (Seagull) in 2000. This translation by Javier Franco-Aixelá includes 'La viuda montañesa' (HW), together with 'La historia de Willie el vagabundo' (Wandering Willie's Tale, from *R*), 'Los dos boyeros' (TD) and 'El espejo de mi tía Margaret' (*AMM*). It carries a ten-page prologue plus brief introductions to each of the stories, presumably by Franco-Aixelá (unfortunately this information is not given). The book is included in the Colección Trébol (Clover collection), aimed at teenagers. It has illustrations and contains no bibliography, but it is not an abridged version. The title of the volume is taken from *The Supernatural Stories of Sir Walter Scott* edited by Michael Hayes in 1977, which included the four stories listed above and in addition 'The Tapestried Chamber'. This Spanish edition was another notable attempt to move away from the staple Scott editions (*I, RR, QD*) and to put in the hands of a wider readership, under the label of 'the supernatural', stories which they might not have bought as scholarly editions (such as HW or TD).

---

[42]   There are many passages which reflect Toda's 1991 translation word for word. There are also mistakes from the 1991 edition that reappear. A misprint of John Bunyan's surname as *Bunvan* in a footnote has been repeated, as has an error in the use of second-person pronouns in one of the dialogues between Elspat and her son.

[43]   'cuenta la historia de una dama que tiene derechos para reclamar la Corona de Escocia, pero que encuentra un adversario muy temible.' This Bibliotex edition, which is page by page the same as the 1998 one, bears no ISBN number.

It should also be said that in the case of *Ivanhoe*, undoubtedly the most frequently printed Scott novel in the twentieth century, there was at least one scrupulous edition which did not merely draw on past translations. In 1990 Ediciones Anaya, in their collection 'Tus libros' (Your books), aimed at young readers, published a new unabridged translation by María del Mar Hernández which also included Scott's 'Dedicatory Epistle' (hardly, if ever, included in the editions). She also wrote the notes and an excellent study aimed at secondary school students, for whom the series is intended.[44]

Recapitulation: Walter Scott in twentieth- and twenty-first-century Spain

In the twentieth century Scott seems to have filled a certain literary void in periods in which, for social and political reasons, literary production in Spain was not particularly buoyant. This was especially the case with literature for children or teenagers. As in other European countries, Scott's novels were published for young readers in shortened editions, either translated from previously abridged texts or adapted in the process of translation.

There is a notable increase in the number of Scott translations in the twentieth century as compared to the nineteenth. Including different editions of the same text by several publishers, the number is about 270. *I*, *RR* and *QD*, in that order, are the most edited works. The Spanish ISBN page, which lists books from 1972 onwards, yields ninety-one, twenty-four and seventeen entries respectively for these three, up to and including 1999. And Scott is definitely still an author on publisher's agendas in the twenty-first century: the same page shows twenty-three editions for the years 2000–05.[45] Of these, fourteen correspond to *I*, of which six are labelled as out of print (this includes an 'Ajvanho' published in Spain but translated into Montenegrin). The rest of the editions correspond to *BL*, *RR* (abridged, published in English, for language learning), *A*, *MM*, *OM*, 'The Tapestried Chamber', and the 'supernatural stories' mentioned above. To them should be added yet another printing of the wrongly attributed *Robin Hood*. We have not been able to ascertain the number of copies printed or sold for each edition, but it seems that, among writers in the public domain, Walter Scott is still a favourite for publishers, and presumably for those who buy their books. The history of his works in Spain is also very revealing in terms of the history of translating and publishing in our country.

---

[44]   Walter Scott (1990) *Ivanhoe*, Madrid: Anaya. The edition is also exemplary in the amount of information provided about the source text and illustrations.

[45]   16 October 2005. See note 10.

4 Ivanhoe, a Tale of the Crusades, or Scott in Catalonia

Andrew Monnickendam

In this chapter, I will describe the influence of Scott in Catalan literature and culture during the nineteenth century, with a particular emphasis on the 1820s and 1830s. I will examine his reception in two Barcelona journals – *El Europeo* (The European) and *El Vapor* (The Steamboat) – from the pens of three literati: Ramón López Soler (1799–1836), Bonaventura Carles Aribau (1798–1862) and Manuel Milà Fontanals (1818–84). This approach allows us to focus, in the case of the first author, on the historical novel; in the case of the second, on poetry; and in the case of the third, on Scott as a wider, cultural figure. The final section will extend this analysis of Scott's importance as a national figure down through the nineteenth century, by which time the links with literature have diminished and his importance as a nationalist has increased. Before addressing these questions, three clarifications need to be made: the first relating to the timescale, the second, to work which has already been done in the field, and the third, a brief note on the historical context.

In the history of Catalan literature, the first half of the nineteenth century is very much a period of beginnings or promise of things to come. The Catalan literary revival known as the *Renaixença* (the Renaissance or re-birth, the term conflates both) dates from 1859, which witnessed the inauguration in Barcelona of the *Jocs Florals* (Floral games), a revival of Medieval literary traditions in the form of a poetry festival. To what extent, then, can we say that the *Renaixença* is a romantic movement influenced by Scott? This is polemical, but it leads us to an equally intriguing issue: to what extent was Spain affected by Romanticism at all? A typical comment is that it 'appears [. . .] with a tardiness regarded by many as characteristic of Iberian cultural development' (King 1962, 1). The fact that it arrived late might be due to tardiness but might be due to other factors; this response is, in my opinion, based on stereotypes of Iberia. Despite differences in many fields, all the contemporary accounts we will read perceive Romanticism as essentially a national movement. Consequently, we participate in a much wider debate on the nature of Romanticism: Catalonia as a culture distinct from or similar to Spain, Germany, France, Scotland, England and so on. This might look initially as a series of binary opposites, but it is wiser to see it as a series of concepts that often overlap and are contiguous, as well, of course, as coming into conflict.

The English Hispanist Edgar Allison Peers (1891–1952), author of the influential and controversial *A History of the Romantic Movement in Spain* (1940), has exhaustively studied the impact of Scott in Spain via translations in 'A Survey of the Influence of Sir Walter Scott in Spain' (1922), co-authored by Philip Churchman. It contains a 'Bibliography of Translations of Scott into Spanish' and the accompanying 'Analysis of Bibliographical Material'. The former has an entry for each translation from 1823 until 1897 with full details, and the latter groups together translations by title, time, publisher, place and so on. For a better understanding of this chapter, two phenomena stand out. First, Barcelona is one of the main centres for translation; Bergnes de las Casas is arguably the most important translator and publisher of Scott's works in Spain. His translations were praised by Milà Fontanals in a review of *St Ronan's Well*, first published in *El Imparcial* in 1844:

> the most fashionable translations have been, until now, except for the occasional one by Cabrerizo and the excellent ones which formed part of Mr. Bergnes *Biblioteca de Damas* (The Ladies' Library), utterly detestable.[1]

Second, all these translations, whether directly from English or from French, are into Spanish. The first complete Catalan translation was Carles Capdevila's *The Talisman*, published in 1922. There is also an undated translation of *Ivanhoe* by C. A. Jordana, which was probably produced at about the same time. It has proved impossible to give it a precise date. Consequently, the information given in the *Gran Enciclopèdia Catalana*, namely that Jordana's 1936 translation of *BD* was the first, is erroneous. This imbalance gives a clear indication of the use and/or literary status and commercial potential of both languages in Catalonia. We should be aware that Catalan nationalism expresses itself in both languages.

Scott's influence in Catalonia springs from a feeling of identification with the national concerns related and debated in the historical novel. After the end of the War of Spanish Succession in 1714, when Barcelona surrendered to the Bourbon army, Philip V replaced a multi-kingdom model with a highly centralized unified state. Through the New Plan Decrees (Decretos de nueva planta) of 1716, the Catalan parliament was abolished and Castilian replaced Catalan as the official language. These events coincide with the Jacobite attempts to recover the British thrones, and consequently national and dynastical paradigms cross cultures. Wolfgang Schivelbusch's aptly named *The Culture of Defeat* (2003) explains with great erudition how defeated nations readjust to loss; reading Scott is one of the principal vehicles for the transfer of allegiance.

---

[1] Las traducciones que más boga han alcanzado hasta ahora, exceptuando alguna de las publicadas por Cabrerizo y las excelentes que formaron parte de la *Biblioteca de Damas* de Sr. Bergnes, son de todo punto detestables (Milà Fontanals 1892a, 38–39).

López Soler

Both López Soler and Aribau were editors of *El Europeo*, along with three other people, two Italians, Luis Monteggia and Galli, and an Austrian, Johannes Ernst Koch, who signed his articles with an anglicised version of his name, 'Ernest Cook'. Peers states that the journal had 'a cosmopolitan character' (1920, 376); in other words it is European in outlook rather than being nationalist or provincial in the narrow-minded, pejorative sense these terms can take on. Its notes and reviews of books include Macpherson, Byron, Scott, Moore, Fenimore Cooper and Washington Irving (Peers 1920, 381). Manzoni is considered an important Romantic, as are the mainstream German figures, Schlegel above all. This broad view of what European literature is affects one's view of literature and culture. In other words, one is not simply looking at Europe to see how Europeans write and perceive themselves, but in doing so, one is forced to consider one's own similarity and difference, and hence specificity.

These abstract ideas take the form of two essays on Romanticism that appear in the earlier numbers of the journal. Of particular interest is one written by López Soler in which he articulates an account of Romanticism that explains and predicts how Scott will later be received in Catalonia. His article has been preceded by an earlier one, written by Monteggia, which delves into ancient history: to the druids, the Greeks, the Romans, to Aristotle's unities. In all, 'it reveals no conception of Romanticism as a revolt, still less as a force which was to dominate the literature of half a century' (Peers 1920, 377). In the seventh number, published on 29 November 1823, López Soler pens an article entitled 'Análisis de la cuestion agitada entre románticos y clasicistas' (Analysis of the Controversy between the Romantics and the Classicists). López Soler sets out his aesthetics in a simple way: 'Three great circumstances have an overwhelming influence on artistic production: religion, customs and nature.'[2] In the original text, religion is written with a capital letter, consequently its importance as being the first of the three circumstances is doubly unequivocal. López Soler believes Christianity, by which he means Catholicism, is the foundation of the modern world, and hence progress.

> This, then, is the origin of Romanticism. The splendid enterprise of the Crusades, the virtue and honour of the knights, together with their gallant, wonderful adventures [. . .] but the metaphysical and sublime aspects came from religion.[3]

Through its moral principles, Christianity heightens our sense of natural beauty and modifies our sense of tragedy. In earlier times, people had less spirituality

---

[2]   'Tres grandes circunstancias influyen sobremanera en las producciones poéticas: la Religion, las costumbres y la naturaleza' (López Soler 1823a, 208).

[3]   He aqui el origen del romanticismo. El esplendoroso aparato de las cruzadas, las virtudes y el pundonor de los caballeros en union con sus galantes y maravillosas aventuras [. . .] pero para su parte metafisica y sublime se recurrió a la Religion (1823a: 209).

because their religion was little more than 'a fabric of outrageous fables'.[4] Consequently, death was simply death, a calamity which afforded no comfort to the soul. López Soler's glorification of Medievalism leads him to argue that tournaments and listening to troubadours were the popular leisure activities at all levels of the Feudal pyramid.

Because they lacked the spiritual dimension of medieval Europe, the customs of Greeks and Romans, including the Olympic Games, were never so poetic; they were essentially violent. Instead of the sophistication of tournaments, gladiatorial combat was brutal and bloody (213). López Soler firmly believes that the unified Christian church brought progress to Europe. It is not very difficult to find holes in López Soler's arguments; indeed, Peers excuses him by stating he was simply 'a literary patriot' (1920, 380). It is of greater importance to understand that his ideas lean very heavily on Chateaubriand's *Le Génie du Christianisme* (1802). However, the fact that Scott – as the most influential medievalist – is from a Presbyterian country is often ignored by his Catalan followers.

These views represent the background of the presence of Scott in *El Europeo*. They have been noted by Churchman and Peers (1922, 234–35). We are told that

> Sir Walter Scott, after having undergone the dangerous trials of exaggerated admiration and excessive critical attention, has finally been recognised as the foremost Romantic of this century.[5]

This graphically demonstrates Scott's stature. Churchman and Peers point out that the 31 January 1824 issue describes *I* as a tale of the crusades, though it 'is not a "tale of the crusades" at all.' (234–35, n. 7). That 'at all' is a bit of a sweeping statement, as it is very much a backdrop, but rather than split hairs, I would point out that this assumption stems from López Soler's remarks about Romanticism being fundamentally medieval and the Crusades being its great scenario.

Another announcement for Scott's complete works is accompanied by a justification for Scott's prestige as the foremost Romantic of the century:

> This author, Lord Byron's rival, has been seen by some as the foremost of the modern romantics, and placed alongside Richard[d]son and Fielding. He is the creator of a new genre, [is] always original, each new work improves on the previous one.[6]

---

[4] 'Un texido de fábulas groseras' (López Soler 1823a: 211).
[5] Sir Walter Scott despues de haber sufrido las peligrosas pruebas de una admiracion exagerada ó de una crítica escesiva está finalmente reconocido por el primer romántico de este siglo (noticias 1824, 198). Note, 'crítica escesiva' could refer to quantity or degree, but as the previous phrase refers to degree – 'admiracion exagerada' – the second probably refers to quantity.
[6] Este autor rival de lord Byron ha sido mirado por algunos come el primero de los románticos modernos, y colocado al lado de Richar[d]son y Fielding. Ha sido el creador de un genero nuevo, siempre original y superior en cada una de sus producciones (anon. 1823, 351).

The comparison with Byron is a subject I will return to. The announcement canonizes Scott, that is clear, but the same cannot be said about what the author meant by 'a new genre'. Bearing in mind López Soler's account of Romanticism, a historical romance of the Middle Ages seems the most satisfactory definition.

López Soler's definition of Romanticism and the journal's praise of Scott as inventor of the historical romance are important because *El Europeo* is itself seen as being central to Spanish Romanticism. A representative comment would be: '*El Europeo* was, without a doubt, the first conscious and organized manifestation of Romanticism in Spain.'[7] Montoliu's emphasis on 'conscious and organized' underlines the belief that the editors formed an enterprise with a distinct purpose. Also, the fact that such an openly nationalist critic as Montoliu[8] places the first stirrings of Romanticism in Barcelona presumably implies that if Romanticism came late to Spain, it was Catalonia that led the way.

In 1830, López Soler publishes his own historical romance, *Los bandos de Castilla ó el caballero del cisne* (The Factions of Castille, or, the Knights of the Swan). Peers (1926b, 13) claims 'it was immediately hailed both as an important historical novel, and as an avowed imitation of Sir Walter Scott'. Today it is virtually unread, known in academia for two reasons: its prologue and its plagiarism. The former begins:

> The novel *The Factions of Castille* has two aims: to make Walter Scott's style well known and show that the history of Spain offers landscapes so beautiful and special that they could capture the attention of readers as have those of Scotland and England.[9]

On first reading, this looks like homage from the disciple to the master; the novel's reputation as foundational, in addition to the author's association with *El Europeo*, reinforce this idea. Before looking at other people's appreciations, from the words on the page, I would draw another conclusion. This opening sentence is odd. If Scott has been so important, then why do readers need to be acquainted with his style? Furthermore, this novel was published by Cabrerizo in Valencia, a firm which had produced several translations of Scott, which, as I have previously mentioned, were approved of by Milà Fontanals. The second objective indicates something different; we have had enough of Scott, Scottish and English landscapes, so it is about time we used our own landscapes for our own literature.

Let us look at two different accounts of the reception of this novel. The first is by Tubino, author of the classic study *Historia del renacimiento contemporáneo*

---

[7] '*El Europeo*, fou, sens dubte, la primera manifestació conscient i organitzada del Romanticisme a Espanya' (Montoliu 1912, 52).

[8] Manuel de Montoliu de Togores (1877–1961), language scholar and translator.

[9] La novela de *Los bandos de Castilla* tiene dos objetos: dar a conocer el estilo de Walter Scott y manifestar que la historia de España ofrece pasajes tan bellos y propios para despertar la atención de los lectores como las de Escocia y de Inglaterra (Buendia 1963, 44).

en Cataluña, Baleares y Valencia (History of the Contemporary Renaissance in Catalonia, the Balearics and Valencia), first published in 1880. He states that:

> It seems obvious that *El Caballero del Cisne* helped to orientate the literary taste of Catalans towards Walter Scott, at the same time it popularized what we could call its aesthetics, by means of an applying them to local or national history. It replaced the indigestible series of Greek and Roman affairs and heroes with the paladins and subjects taken from the western Christian world.[10]

Tubino takes up Chateaubriand and López Soler's line on Classicists and Romantics, insisting that Christianity and the Crusades are the central subjects.

Reginald Brown argues that the influence of Scott is not as obvious as Tubino makes out. He believes that this reference to Scott is simply 'lip service' (1945, 303), before making a huge generalization: 'In brief, López Soler held the general Spanish opinion of the *Waverley Novels*. They were too sane, too discursive and too erudite' (304). Brown goes on to say that in later years his influence was enormous. He believes that his greatest achievement was to open up 'the treasure house of Spanish history' (307).

What Brown did not comment on was the considerable controversy surrounding this novel. López Soler decided to give his readers a hefty taste of Walter Scott. In the opening paragraph of the prologue, he states that he has translated some passages from Scott with this aim in mind. This translation consists of two elements: the use of Scott's style, and chunks of *I*. From his belief in the centrality of tournaments, it is no surprise to learn that it is precisely the tournament chapter that he copied. Peers places text and translations side by side in order to allow us to see the extent of this extensive borrowing. Towards the end of the novel, according to Peers, 'the plot is little less than a continuous plagiarism from *Ivanhoe*'. (1926b, 19) As a result, the reputation of López Soler as a novelist has never been very high. According to Milà Fontanals, indolence turned him into an incurable plagiarist (1892c, 251). To conclude this section, we have to weigh the considerable participation of López Soler in *El Europeo* against his bizarre reputation as a novelist. Both phenomena demonstrate the considerable presence of Scott.

Aribau

El Europeo had a short life. It shut down in 1824 as a result of the changing political climate. In 1833, Aribau founded *El Vapor*, subtitled *Periódico político literario y mercantil de Cataluña* (Political, Literary and Mercantile newspaper of

---

[10] Parécenos evidente que *El Caballero del Cisne* cooperó a llevar el gusto literario de los catalanes al lado de Walter Scott, toda vez que popularizó la que llamaremos su estética, por medido de una aplicación a la historia doméstica o nacional. Sustituía aquella, la serie indigesta de los asunto y héroes de Grecia y Roma, con los paladines y temas del mundo occidental cristiano (Tubino 2003, 13).

Catalonia). A steamboat is drawn above the title. This clearly represents progress. As we shall see, the relationship between economics and literature becomes a central feature of the reception of Scott in Catalonia. Aribau had himself written three articles for *El Europeo* (Montoliu 1936, 150); López Soler was also a contributor. It is therefore understandable to read into this sequence of events a continuation and development of earlier thinking; this is very much the opinion of Montoliu, author of a full-length study of Aribau. Aribau himself is very much a liberal, Enlightenment figure with a strong belief in progress and the use of the press.

I have not been able to discover much material on Scott in this second journal, whose present-day fame rests today largely on the fact that in the edition of March 26, 1833, Aribau published his landmark poem 'La pàtria – trobes' (The Fatherland – verses).[11] This poem is generally recognized as being the single most significant poem of Catalan Romanticism, nothing less than the foundation-stone of the *Renaixença*, basically because it is written in Catalan and expresses a deep attachment to the fatherland. Both the dedication and the article on patriotism which follows are written in Spanish. Consequently, its originality is highlighted simply by this placing. The dedication reads:

> This composition, written to celebrate the saint-days of Sr D. Gaspar Remisa, comes from the elegant pen of D. Buenaventura Carlos Aribau. We present it to our readers with the same patriotic pride as would a Scot in presenting the verses of Sir Walter Scott to the inhabitants of his fatherland.[12]

(Gaspar Remisa was Aribau's wealthy patron.) This is a straightforward declaration of intent. It could be argued that it conveniently forgets that Scott wrote his poems in English, but though that is true, Scott's early career as a collector of folk poems is a more satisfactory parallel. From this dedication, I would only make three brief observations. First, at this key moment in Catalan history, the figure of reference is Scott. Second, the Scott who emerges at this point is primarily a national poet speaking to his ain folk. Third, the important genre is not, as in the case of López Soler, prose, but lyric poetry.

This is not the place to undertake a lengthy analysis of the poem; I will restrict myself to describing those elements which are central to the image of Scott, as he emerges from the poem. For Montoliu (1912, 78), the writings of *El Vapor* form a much clearer declaration of patriotism than those in *El Europeo*. Patriotism – as expressed in the poem – has three components: love of the landscape, love of past history and love of the native language. What Aribau describes in the opening lines is a landscape composed of clouds, mountains and mist, and although these are marked by their exact geographical location, the

---

[11]   Scholars looking for further information about this poem should be aware that it is more than often referred to as 'Oda a la pàtria' or simply 'Oda'.

[12]   Esta composicion, escrita para celebrar los dias del Sr. D. Gaspar Remisa, es obra de la selecta pluma de D. Buenaventura Carles Aribau. La presentamos á nuestros lectores con el patriótico orgullo con que presentaria un escocés los versos de sir Walter Scott á los habitantes de su patria (Aribau 1833, 3).

clouds and mountains could equally belong to the Highlands. As to past history, to a reader unfamiliar with Catalan, its presence is not immediately obvious. Aribau uses a series of linguistic archaisms, the most striking of which is the use of 'llemosí' (Limousin) ('llemosí' is a term used from the sixteenth century onwards to describe medieval Catalan) to construct an ethnographic past. By far the most important of the three components is language. The word 'llemosí' is used four times in the eight lines that make up the ninth and tenth verses. Rather than history, Aribau returns us to infancy, as 'llemosí' is the language not only of his first songs or first prayers, but also the language of his first baby-like cries. This last instance firmly places 'llemosí' as the maternal language of feeling transmitted at the mother's breast, the implication being that everything else is not natural. The boundary between nature and nurture is thus purposefully merged. Consequently, 'llemosí' is the language that speaks – naturally – to the spirit. This is why, according to the poem, it is sweeter than honey.

From this brief explanation, it is hopefully clear why this particular poem has become so influential. The poem is followed by a short article penned by Ayguals entitled 'El patriotismo en ciencias y artes' (Patriotism in the sciences and Arts). The title alludes to Diderot, the subtitle of the *Cyclopedia* reading 'A Universal Dictionary of Arts and Sciences'. Whereas the poem glorifies one's own national roots, the article starts on a different tack:

> True patriotism in our mental operations consists of enriching one's own nation with the good that shines in others.[13]

The article goes on to claim that this is the real nature of patriotism. Greece, it is argued, accepted Egyptian influences and produced its own geniuses as a result of this process of assimilation. Great French literature, that of Corneille or Molière, fed from Lope de Vega and Calderón. National greatness is only achieved after a period of adaptation. Side by side, then, we have two very different accounts of patriotism: a poetical version, based on emotions and the spirit, and a prose version, based more on universalism and the ideas of the encyclopaedists.

Who was responsible for this juxtaposition and for what reason can only be speculated upon, because the article itself is virtually unknown to current readers of the poem. However, what is more tangible is the form that Scott-based Romanticism is beginning to take. Two brief mentions of Scott appear in the editions of June 17, 1834, one in an article on Italian theatre, and another on March 4, 1837, in an address given to young writers, but neither is of much interest. What is, is an extensive article in the edition of 2 November 1833, entitled 'Influencia de las obras de Walter Scott en la generación actual' (Influence of the Works of Walter Scott on the Current Generation). This article is placed on the front page. Scott is lauded as 'protector of humanity,'[14] before

---

13 El verdadero patriotismo en las operaciones mentales consiste en enriquecer la nacion propia con lo bueno que brilla en las agenas (Ayguals 1833, 5).
14 'Benhechor de la humanidad' (anon. 1833, 1).

his virtues are enumerated. Scott's importance as a medievalist is commonplace, but in this article, the idea is given a twist. Scott, we are told, 'evokes the feudal genius in order to discredit it'.[15] This view is incompatible with López Soler's views of Scott as a glorifier of the Middle Ages. At the same time, he is referred to as the Scottish Cervantes, a frequent comparison, weighing one national genius against another. He is also accredited for his depiction of manners and virtue, again, rather ordinary comments, but then comes one which is new; Scott is responsible for 'having contributed to the increase of work'.[16] 'Increase' here could refer to both quantity and/or its importance. What is clear for this author is that Scott, whether as moralist or historian, is basically a pragmatist at the opposite pole from abstraction and casuistry. Consequently, his voice is heard not only in salons but in the workplace.

Many parties appropriate Scott for differing ideological purposes. It is with the writings of Milà Fontanals that these appropriations take on a definitive form.

Milà Fontanals

In approaching the figure and ideas of Milà Fontanals, we move into another dimension, in the sense that his status as an intellectual has been the subject of recent, extensive scholarly work undertaken by Manuel Jorba. Milà, it is claimed, is the 'patriarch of the Catalan literary movement'.[17] His status is partly due to the influence of one of his followers, Marcelino Menéndez Pelayo (1856–1912), an intellectual of much greater standing. Menéndez Pelayo argues that Milà's interest in Scott as a Romantic gave him a healthier and more realistic view of art than the more abstract aesthetics of Schlegel (1908, 31). In the same passage, he tells us that Scott became his favourite author, capable of alleviating his melancholy. Menéndez Pelayo also states that Milà was an enthusiastic reader of both poetry and fiction, fond of *Rokeby* and *The Lady of the Lake*, which Milà judged to be better than commonly believed.

In a tone similar to that employed in 'El patriotismo en ciencias y artes', in his review of *St Ronan's Well*, Milà argues that however gratifying it is to see the publication of contemporary Spanish fiction, people should also read works by contemporary geniuses such as Walter Scott. Milà remarks very favourably on the quality of the translator's – D. E. de Ochoa – work. Milà points out that *St Ronan's Well* is rather different from Scott's previous work, but if the subject matter of this contemporary tale is unexpected, what defines it as a work by Scott is its 'moral depth, its excellent characters and dialogues'.[18] In trying to square the circle, by accounting for a historical novelist writing a

---

[15] 'Evoca el genio feudal para desacreditarlo' (anon. 1833, 1).
[16] 'Haber contribuido al acrecentamiento del trabajo' (anon. 1833, 2).
[17] 'Patriarca del movimiento literario catalán' (Rubió and Parpel 1919, 3).
[18] 'Por su fondo de moral, por sus excelentes caracteres y diálogos' (Milà Fontanals 1892a, 39).

contemporary tale, he says that a French translator observed that *St Ronan's Well's* contemporaneity does not make it an exception; it forms part of Scott's plan to complete 'the portrait of Scottish manners from the Middle Ages till the present day'.[19] The fact that this idea is transferred on to a third person might betray a lack of conviction. The reader of this new model will 'detest the artificial lifestyle, the mean passions and the thirst for pomp and opulence that the author attributes to certain members of the upper class of his time and country'.[20] Milà goes on to propose that whereas Scott looks on the past times with some indulgence, no such leniency is given to present-day Scotland. This interesting thought retains the central idea that Scott's virtue as a novelist is basically that of a moralist. Milà concludes that Scott highlights virtue and resignation. Resignation might sound rather too close to fatalism, but here Milà imbues it with a religious calm. Milà's views are certainly debatable, but he shows himself to be a perspicacious reader.

His most explicit praise for Scott comes in a Socratic dialogue on the novel, first published in 1844. For Milà, there are ten kinds of novels: novels of antiquity, oriental novels, novels of the northern peoples, novels about the Round Table, novels about Charlemagne and his peers, novels after *Amadis*, heroic novels, comic novels, moral, sentimental and psychological novels and, finally, historical novels (1844, 106). Initially, this might seem an unnecessarily obtuse classification, but his description takes on an almost Bahktinian tone, whereby epics become 'novels in verse',[21] engaging in a dialogic relationship with their listeners or readers. For Milà, the historical novel is the glory of contemporary literature (112), though he does cast his net wide by including the works of Walpole and Raccliffe [sic] in this category, due to the setting in old castles: 'the summoning of the frightening Genius of the Gothic centuries'.[22] The final section is dedicated to the glory of modern literature, and the concluding lines to its greatest practitioner. Scott is praised not only for his knowledge of the human heart but also for his constant production. Thus, the dialogue concludes, Scott, 'up to a certain point, could be called *the inventor of the novel*' (1844, 112) (italics in the original).[23] Most surprising in this praise is the conflation of novel and historical novel: contemporary literature is legitimately set in a real or imaginary castle, returning us to the Crusades and the troubadours.

When Milà analyses Scott's poetry, he uses the terms 'poetic novels'.[24] In describing *LLM*, Milà becomes very specific about patriotism. He affirms that the poem contains the bases of Scott's more mature work, a combination of two

---

[19] 'El cuadro de costumbres escoceses desde la Edad media hasta nuestros días' (Milà Fontanals 1892a, 39).

[20] 'La vida facticia, las mezquinas pasiones y la sed de fausto y de opulencia que atribuye el auto á algunos miembros de la alta clase de su época y de su nación' (Milà Fontanals 1892a, 40).

[21] 'Novelas versificadas' (Milà Fontanals 1844, 108).

[22] 'El evocar el pavoroso Genio de los siglos góticos' (Milà Fontanals 1844, 112).

[23] 'Hasta cierto punto puede llamarsele *el inventor de la novela*' (112).

[24] 'Novelas poéticas' (Milà Fontanals 1854a, 976).

elements: 'love for his fatherland and ancient memories'.[25] The links with the preceding account of the historical novel are very clear; it is again the description of character and legends and so on, but in the case of the poetry there is a clear difference. Whereas the novels portray Scotland from the historical past to the present day, in the case of the poems, their greatness lies in their depiction of humanity many centuries ago. In the second part of the article, published a week later, Milà continues his analysis of Scott. He insists that he is 'no less poetic than moral'[26] in order to prevent the reader suffering from what he calls, in an extremely melodramatic coinage, the tyranny of the imagination. For Milà, *Rokeby* teaches us that same lesson, as do the early chapters of *W*. Scott, he argues, is a poet of reason, and in an idiosyncratic image, compares him to preserving salt which purifies and prevents the excesses of the creative imagination (1131). If that is a difficult image to follow, it is worth noting that what Milà is preparing us for is a distinction between what he considers positive and negative values. The positive values of Romanticism are obviously in Scott, in contrast to Cowper, who, according to Milà, was a 'very pure poet, but afflicted by an utterly sickly sensitivity'.[27] Scott's more immediate contemporaries, Shelley, Byron, Coleridge all have some fault. Consequently, he concludes that there are basically two kinds of Romantics: those headed by Scott who subordinate the imagination to reason, and those who let the imagination dominate everything else. The former are healthy, the latter not.

In an article entitled 'Moral literaria. Contraste entre la escuela escéptica y Walter Scott' (Literary Morality. Contrast between the School of Sceptics and Walter Scott), first published in 1842, the national implications of this distinction are made abundantly clear. The opening paragraph is dedicated to the founder of that school, Chateaubriand, which is followed by an attack on Byron, who is

> described by one of his own countrymen as half fatuous and half female, is the person who has most distinguished himself in voicing his grievances against existence and society; the truth is, at least that is what it seems, that he is the person with least motives to complain.[28]

Byron cannot complain because he has everything – looks, wealth and position. Even worse is the fact that he is not alone: other terrible sceptics include Balzac, Victor Hugo and George Sand. All these writers moan and rant, but they offer nothing in exchange for what they want to tear down. Milà contrasts these destructive writers with Scott. He then goes on to say that if

---

[25] 'Con su amor á la patria y á sus antiguos recuerdos' (976).

[26] 'No menos poético que moral' (Milà Fontanals 1854b, 1131).

[27] Poeta muy puro, pero aquejado por una sensibilidad en sumo grado enfermiza (1132).

[28] Calificado por un paisano suyo de medio fatua y medio mujer, es el que más se ha distinguido en levanta al alto quejas contra la existencia y la sociedad, siendo en realidad, ó al menos en apariencia, el que menos motivos tenía de quejarse (Milà Fontanals 1892b, 6).

you could get together a considerable number of young people who shared a solid and revitalizing idea, perhaps rather than put forward a political slogan, what would happen is that they would inscribe on their flag: *Admirers of Sir Walter Scott*.[29] (Italics in original)

These young people would share the virtues that Milà sees in Scott: a person who is Romantic, in the Christian sense of the word used by López Soler; someone who is honest, a lover of virtue, and who favours progress, even though he is aware of the price society has to pay. Scott is not perfect; Milà ticks Scott off for his over-respectful attitude to monarchy. He concludes that readers of Scott always leave his novels with the desire to act, to do good. What is the point of replacing political admiration with Walter Scott? I believe that the answer lies in the use of the flag. The flag, the appeal to young people, the idea of revitalization all point towards renovation and progress on a national level; the young people are the new patriots and the flag, that of Catalonia. To what extent this reading is valid will depend on the final section of this chapter, in which I analyse how these admirers of Scott in Catalonia are themselves, together with Scott, received by their contemporaries and followers.

The consolidation of Scott's reputation

This final section describes how Scott's reputation is consolidated down the nineteenth and into the twentieth century. I will concentrate on three areas: enthronement, healthy Romanticism and economy. Initially, the first topic might seem unnecessary, as through the journals and writings of our three authors, Scott's presence is undeniable. True: but the examples given come from the examination of a large amount of material, so the impression of a widespread acceptance of Scott is biased by the nature of the search. I hope to demonstrate that the dominance of Scott as an inspiration in Catalonia has a considerable amount of hindsight to it. That is to say that later writers, looking back at López Soler, Aribau and Milà Fontanals, link and bring together ideas that are not so closely connected. Peers, for example, argues that 'The native element of Spanish Romanticism, which the works of Scott fostered, was at its strongest in Barcelona' (1926b, 116). This is undoubtedly true.

Rubió Lluch cites the aforementioned remark made by Milà Fontanals about the admirers of Walter Scott (Rubió and Parpal 1919, 27). However, for some unknown reason, he says that this idea was confided to him by Milà Fontanals (27). For him there is no doubt that there was a 'Scottish school in Catalonia'.[30] He later says that 'when the Catalan movement [Renaixença] fulfilled its

---

[29] Si se ofreciese reunir un número considerable de jóvenes ligados con el vínculo común de una idea sólida y vivificadora, más tal vez que invocando un lema político, se lograría con inscribir en la bandera: *Admiradores de Walter Scott*. (8).

[30] 'La escuela escocesa en Cataluña' (Rubió and Parpal 1919, 21).

potential [. . .] it fed fully from the sap of Walter Scott.'[31] Menéndez Pelayo made the following authoritative statement:

> When the history of the influence of Walter Scott in Spanish Romanticism – which was far greater than that of Byron – is written, Barcelona will stand out as one of the principle centres of this literature [. . .] because the aesthetic thought of Walter Scott, more than that of any other, penetrated the soul of its artists and critics.[32]

Menéndez Pelayo goes on to say that Walter Scott also found great favour among readers; he left his mark everywhere. Such statements indicate that however extensive Scott's readership was, his influence spills over into other activities. It is a long way from a historical romance to becoming inscribed on a flag by young Catalans. Consequently, two issues have to be addressed: what precisely was the nature of this extra-literary influence? And is this idea accepted by everyone?

The first question has a simple answer: his influence on nationalism. Tubino states that

> Scottish history, in the way Walter Scott handled it, provided astonishing analogies with specifically Catalan events and situations. The cruel persecution of the Puritans, the accomplishments of the brotherhoods of the Covenant, the martyrdom of the patriots after the battle of Culloden where nationhood was destroyed by the English sword, became events which the Catalans could not look upon indifferently.[33]

This suggests that Catalans identified themselves with the fate of the persecuted. It is curious that Tubino uses two Protestant examples to back up his argument, as initially Puritanism would not seem the most obvious example to cite for identification, much less that of the Covenanters, who, from many points of view, are more likely to be seen as fundamentalists. However, Tubino interestingly uses the word 'handle/manage,' in the original 'manejaba'. That is to say that Tubino is aware that Scott is not primarily a historian but a writer of fiction capable of stirring these emotions. These emotions are nationalist.

Rubió Lluch, from a similar angle, states that the 'the Scottish poet made Catalonia feel, in a kind of reflection, the poetical vision of the Middle Ages and

---

[31] 'Cuando la escuela catalana llegó a la plenitud de su vigor [. . .] se nutrió hondamente de la savia de Walter Scott' (27).

[32] Cuando se haga la historia del influjo de Walter-Scott, que fué mucho más extenso que el de Byrón en el romanticismo español, habrá que señalar á Barcelona como uno de los principales focos de esta literatura [. . .] porque el pensamiento poético de Walter-Scott pen[e]tró más que ningún otro en el alma de los artistas y de los críticos (Menéndez Pelayo 1908, 32–33).

[33] Ofrecía además, la historia escocesa, según Walter Scott la manejaba, pasmosas analogías con acaecimiento y situaciones peculiares a Cataluña. La cruel persecución de los puritanos, las hazañas de los agermanados del *Covenant*, el martirio de los patriotas, después de la batalla de Culloden, donde quedó rota la nacionalidad por la espada de Inglaterra, e[ra]n hechos que los catalanes no podían mirar indiferentes (Tubino 2003, 131).

the consciousness of its national soul'.[34] Whereas Menéndez Pelayo used the word 'soul' as a general term, here there is no doubt that it is specifically national soul. Therefore the Middle Ages should not be understood solely in the sense of the Crusades, of a literary trope, as López Soler stated in *El Europeo*, but as Catalonia's most glorious time in history, as a medieval power and cultural centre in its own right. To return to the Middle Ages is not simply nostalgia.

Menéndez Pelayo states that the return to the Middle Ages has a lot to do with archaeology (1908, 32); Montoliu also uses the term archaeological Romanticism (1936, 147). This emphasis on prehistory might seem even more peculiar to the modern reader than a return to the Middle Ages. But I think that in both cases, it makes more sense to see that the excavation searches for real roots which have lain untouched for several centuries. They constitute, in other words, a real find. Particularly active in this field was Milà Fontanals himself, who published his groundbreaking *Romancerillo catalan* (Little Collection of Catalan Ballads) in 1853. The connection with Scott's early career is thus cemented.

The answer to the second question is that Scott does indeed have a rival, in the figure of Manzoni, who also appears in *El Europeo*. Montoliu states that Aribau was deeply influenced by him as well. He argues that 'La Pàtria', which Aribau dedicates to Scott, is in fact Manzonian (1936, 168). He cites the dramatic farewell address by Lucia at the end of Chapter 8 of *I promessi sposi* (*The Betrothed*) as a close textual influence. I disagree; although it does share some elements (deep feeling, the role of the church), it lacks that one fundamental element which is so essential to Aribau and Montoliu: Manzoni does not mention language in this passage. That does not mean that Manzoni was not a great influence, but that in this particular case, the textual correspondence is debatable. Menéndez Pelayo states that there was indeed a cult of Manzoni.

Two specific reasons for believing that Manzoni was an important influence are his Catholicism and his conservatism. Hence, in a virtually unknown history of the Catalan historical novel, its author confesses that while reading an early Catalan historical novel, *The Little Orphan Girl of Menargues* (La orfaneta de Menargues) (1862) by Antoni Bofarull de Brocá (1821–92), he initially thought of it as a Scott-inspired novel, basically because that was the general belief, before stating that in his own opinion Manzoni is the real source of inspiration because 'we sense the impalpable presence of the Catholic spirit, and all those things which distinguish it from the Protestant feeling of the founder of the school'.[35] This is in direct contradiction to Tubino's cavalier approach to religion. Another reason that might lead us on to Manzoni is that stated by Hans Juretschke, for whom Milà Fontanals should be placed in the historically

---

[34] 'El poeta de Escocia hizo sentir a Cataluña de una manera refleja la visión poética de la Edad Media y la conciencia de su alma nacional' (Rubió and Parpal 1919, 21).

[35] 'Endevinem la presència impalpable de l'esperit catòlic, i de tot allò que el diferencia del sentit protestant del fundador de l'escola' (Serrahima 1966, 55).

conservative, Christian Romanticism, along the lines of Scott, Manzoni and Schlegel (Juretschke 1973–74, 29). From this ideological point of view, then, it makes little difference in distinguishing between the two, as they are both healthy.

Why do I use the term healthy? This is in opposition to sickly Romanticism, in other words Byron and the French Romantics. In short, it is a rejection of the Byronic hero's solipsism and rebellion, which are judged incompatible with the community, whether religious or national. This subject is analysed by Peers (1967). The most striking example I have come across is by Bertrán de Amat in a homage to Milà Fontanals. For him, the encyclopaedists were utopian, cosmopolitan and anti-Christian (1891, 10); they produced not enlightenment but tyranny. He then puts forward the proposition that 'what one might call English Romanticism, which contained such valiant figures as Cooper, Bruns [*sic*] and Walter Scott inoculated it [Spain] against the burning fever of despair and the atheistic rage of Byron.'[36] Whereas for Milà Fontanals Scott was the standard bearer of Catalan nationalism, in this later case, he is now very much a Spanish nationalist in the line that glorifies the Catholic monarchs, Ferdinand and Isabella.

A much more interesting analysis is provided by Alfonso Par, whose three-volume study *Shakespeare en España* (Shakespeare in Spain) has a misleading title, as the third volume is about Romanticism. Thankfully, he makes little use of hyperbole when asking how Catalonia resisted sickly Romanticism (1935, 3: 310). He designs three lines of defence. First, he says that the Catalan national character dislikes outlandishness; this, along with religious faith and its introverted nature meant it had little sympathy with new fashions. The second line of defence which saved Catalan literature from 'Romantic disorder'[37] was its own popular song. As noted, Milà Fontanals played a crucial role. The third, and strongest line of defence was Walter Scott, 'emblem and compendium of all that was beautiful and healthy'.[38] For Par, one cannot begin to understand Catalan romanticism without Walter Scott's presence.

My final example of the influence of Walter Scott comes from Bergnes de las Casas (1801–78), academic, rector of the University of Barcelona, editor of *El Vapor*, responsible for the dissemination of Scott in Spain and a confirmed Anglophile. He was also responsible for the journal *El Museo de las Familias* (The Museum for Families), a nineteenth-century mix of fiction, general knowledge and anything instructive. The title of the article I will refer to gives a clear indication of the magazine's tone: 'Influjo que ha ejercido y está ejerciendo Walter-Scott en las riquezas, la moralidad y la dicha de la sociedad moderna' (The Influence that Walter Scott Has Exerted and Is Exerting on the Wealth, Morality and Happiness of Modern Society). This article is in fact an

---

[36] 'El Romanticismo que pudiera llamarse inglés, que entre elementos de tanta valía como Cooper, Bruns[sic] y Walter Scott, le inoculó la fiebre ardorosa de desesperación y la ira atea de Byron' (Bertrán de Amat 1891, 20).
[37] 'Desquiciamiento romántico' (Par 1935, 3: 314).
[38] 'Cifra y compendio de de cuanto era bello y sano' (3: 315).

unacknowledged translation of an article that appeared in the March 1833 issue of *Revue Britannique*. It argues that 'great moral ideas [. . .] contribute to the activity which constitutes social well-being, to industry'.[39] The example he puts forward, Benjamin Franklin (the self-made man), is understandable, but what about Walter Scott? He has produced an enormous interest in the arts for the serious study of the Middle Ages. The consequences of this are to be found in new architecture, new furniture and new products more in tune with our Christian ideas than classical designs. Scott has dignified the status of the artisan, thus making work the consequence of morality and wealth the consequence of work (356). The logic is perhaps difficult to follow. At the article's end, it is stated more simply. Scott made us believe in a new attitude to work: love (359). Apart from material benefit, Scott has produced a new sense of awareness, for Scots now see that they hold their destiny in their own hands, both poverty and opulence are now options. This awareness has a clear nationalist message to it.

Bergnes then turns to wider considerations. He asks, rhetorically:

> Where, with the possible exception of Shakespeare's plays can be found expressed a more complete and clearer conviction of the universal equality of men than in the novels of Walter Scott?[40]

To a Spanish reader, the only possible answer is Cervantes.

To conclude a chapter with an unacknowledged translation is arguably peculiar. However, I would maintain that it demonstrates, ethics aside, the great interest Scott stirred up all over the continent, crossing over national boundaries and paradoxes with the same nonchalance that turns him into an upholder of medieval chivalric ideology. That is palpably false, and in complete contrast to the extremely critical account of chivalry which Scott himself wrote for the 1824 edition of *Encyclopedia Britannica*. It is tempting to say that reception is too protean to track down, but my conclusion would be a simple one: that in Catalonia, his reception switches back and forward between a more liberal Enlightenment model and a more conservative, strongly Catholic view of nationhood.

---

[39] Las grandiosas ideas morales [. . .] contribuyen á la actividad que constituye el bienestar social, á la industria (1835, 355). The article has quite a history. It claims to be taken from *Tait's Edinburgh Magazine*, but neither the style nor length of the article has much to do with the most obvious candidates, two articles by Harriet Martineau: 'Characteristics of the Genius of Scott,' which appeared in number IX, December 1832, 301–14; and 'The Achievements of the Genius of Scott,' in the following number of January, 1833, 446–60. Dr Paul Barnaby, Project Officer of the Walter Scott Digital Archive, explains that the article is in fact the work of Philarète Chasles, who edited (and wrote most of) the literary section of the *Revue*. His translations were free in the extreme. Paragraphs 1–10 and the concluding paragraph 21 appear to be Chasles's own work. Paragraphs 11–20 of the Scott article are free but recognizable translation of Martineau's 'The Achievements of the Genius of Scott'.

[40] ¿Dónde, esceptuando tal vez los dramas de Shakspeare [sic], se halla profesada con una conviccion mas cabal y de un modo mas claro la igualdad universal de los hombres que en las novelas de Walter-Scott? (3: 357).

5 The Reception of Walter Scott in Nineteenth-Century Austria

Norbert Bachleitner

Introduction

A study of the reception of Walter Scott in nineteenth-century Austria has to take into account a significant reluctance to modernize political structures and cultural life. While it is true that in some provinces like Lower Austria or Bohemia industry prospered and, at least until 1848, economic liberalism was on the advance, it is also true that Metternich's Restoration politics tried to suppress philosophical and political ideas that were believed to support opposistional spirit. In these circumstances the interpretation of history was an important political issue. From the government's point of view, the evil of 'revolutionary' democratic ideas lurking abroad, above all in the German states but also in Great Britain and France, must be strictly controlled lest they sweep the country. Censorship therefore plays a key role in Austrian literary life in the first half of the century, excluding from circulation among Austrian readers not only philosophical, historical and political works but also thousands of novels. Thus Austria was in many respects separated from Western 'progressive' ideas, a fact often deplored by critically minded contemporaries. A number of declared Liberals, among them many literary authors, left the country. Others remained and adapted their works to official political standards or – especially in the 1840s – sought to establish structures of opposition.

The literary scene was controlled or even pervaded by the state. Book production, book shops and circulating libraries were strictly observed, and the possibilities of public discussion were restricted. Leading journals and magazines like the *Jahrbücher der Literatur* (Yearbooks of literature) were directed by state officials, and the other journals tried to survive by avoiding controversial subjects. The majority of authors, approximately two-thirds, were state officials as well; some of them even worked as censors. As concerns aesthetics, a rather epigonal Classicism was reigning, with innovations in genre or style being rare. It is not surprising that in such circumstances a modern literary genre like the novel was regarded very sceptically by the vast majority of critics. If they were considered at all, novels were treated as a trivial genre not worthy of serious literary discussion, and as a typical outcome of the commercialization of literature.

Censorship, translations and adaptations

Seventeen works by Scott were forbidden for Austrian readers. Censors judged *AG, BD, Tales of The Crusades, FMP, FN, I, LM, M, Paul's Letters to his Kinsfolk, PP, P, QD, RR, T, TG, W* and *WO* to contain passages that could do harm to religion, the order of the state or morals.[1] Which passages were considered dangerous can be deduced from a comparison of German and Austrian editions. As an example we have checked the Austrian editions of *WO* (1826) (Bachleitner 1991). This novel puts into question the legitimate king and the Anglican and Catholic Churches. Measures of censorship turn mainly around these two points. In the Strauß edition (Scott 1827a), a censored Austrian reprint of the German translation by C. F. Michaelis which had appeared in Leipzig a year before (Scott 1826a), 120 passages are cut or reformulated. Verbal attacks on the king or his followers and especially representations of their uncivilized behaviour or sexual aggressions are either cut or attenuated. It goes without saying that discussions about the legitimacy of the king and regicide are deleted; for instance, the following passage in which Cromwell argues that the only legitimation kings can actually claim are military victories against competitors:

> Yet what can they see in the longest kingly line in Europe, save that it runs back to a successful soldier? I grudge that one man should be honoured and followed because he is the descendant of a victorious commander, while less honour and allegiance is paid to another, who, in personal qualities, and in success, might emulate the founder of his rival's dynasty.[2]

A number of passages in which Puritanism and Presbyterianism are discussed and Anglicans and Catholics attacked were cut as well. Thus a passage from the first chapter in which Scott describes the religious point of view of the Puritans:

> The presumption of these learned Thebans being in exact proportion to their ignorance, the last was total and the first boundless. Their behaviour in the church was anything but reverential or edifying. Most of them affected a cynical contempt for all

---

[1] See the detailed list of prohibited Scott editions and translations in Bachleitner 1990, 65.

[2] Scott 1871, ch. 37, 463. 'Doch was können sie in der längsten königlichen Linie in Europa erblicken, außer daß sie in einen glücklichen Krieger zurückläuft? Das aber wurmt mich, daß einem Manne darum Ehre und Gehorsam zu Theil werden soll, weil er von einem siegreichen Feldherrn abstammt, dagegen ein Anderer sich mindrer Ehre und Anhänglichkeit erfreut, welcher an persönlichen Eigenschaften und glücklichem Erfolge mit dem Begründer der Dynastie seines Nebenbuhlers zu wetteifern vermöchte?' (Scott 1826a, III, 324; the passage was deleted in Scott 1827a).

that was only held sacred by human sanction – the church was to these men but a steeple-house, the clergyman, an ordinary person; her ordinances, dry bran and sapless pottage, unfitted for the spiritualized palates of the saints, and the prayer, an address to Heaven, to which each acceded or not as in his too critical judgement he conceived fit.[3]

At first sight such corrections may seem of no great importance, but they doubtless destroy the balance between the parties, carefully established by Scott. In his novels history appears as a dynamic interplay of ideas, arguments and principles. In *Woodstock* he locates faults and errors on both sides. Readers of his novel are invited to evaluate the parties, their opinions and actions and draw their own conclusions. In the Austrian version things are less complicated: the moral superiority of the Royalists and their right to regain power cannot be doubted. The censored version presents the victory of monarchy and state religion, that need no justification and are valid beyond time and space. Thus history loses its dynamics, and the Civil War appears as a criminal upsurge that is mainly fuelled by the protagonists' personal ambition. This becomes clear if one regards Everard, a specimen of those Scott heroes who waver undecidedly between the parties. In the course of events he recognizes that the revolution leads only to disorder and this is why he joins the Royalists. In Scott's version his motives for this change of side are clear; he has gone through a development and come to new insights. Since the Austrian version deletes most of his deliberations, critical of both parties, he appears as an opportunist or even as a traitor.

In this context it is only logical that a passage was deleted in which the narrator evaluates the contending parties and recognizes faults on both sides:

> [It was wonderful to behold what a strange variety of mistakes and errors, on the part of the King and his Ministers, on the part of the Parliament and their leaders, on the part of the allied kingdoms of Scotland and England toward each other, had combined to rear up men of such dangerous opinions and interested characters among the arbiters of the destiny of Britain.]
>
> Those who argue for party's sake, will see all faults on the one side, without deigning to look at those on the other; those who study history for instruction, will perceive that nothing but the want of concession on either side, and the deadly height to which the animosity of the King's and Parliament's parties had arisen, could have so totally overthrown the well-poised balance of the English constitution.

---

[3]   Scott 1871, ch. 1, 18. 'Der Eigendünkel dieser gelehrten Thebaner stand in genauem Ebenmaaß zu ihrer Unwissenheit; dieß war eine gänzliche Unwissenheit, und ihr Eigendünkel war grenzenlos. Ihr Benehmen in der Kirche war alles Andre, als andächtig oder erbaulich. Die meisten affectirten eine cynische Verachtung alles dessen, was blos durch menschliche Verfügung als heilig galt; die Kirche war diesen Leuten nur ein Haus mit einem Thurme, der Geistliche ein gewöhnlicher Mann; die Kirchenordnungen gleich trocknen Kleien und geschmacklosen Brühen, unpassend für den geistigen Gaumen der Heiligen; und das Gebet, eine Anrede an Gott, welcher sich Jeder anschloß oder nicht, je nachdem es seinem überkritischen Urtheil angemessen dünkte' (Scott 1826a, I, 6–7; passage deleted in Scott 1827a).

But we hasten to quit political reflections, [the rather that ours, we believe, will please neither Whig nor Tory].[4]

Study history for instruction in order to find faults and avoid them in the future – this enlightening potential of history was not wanted in Austria. It may be surprising that censors cared so much for the details of a fictional representation of seventeenth-century British history. Obviously the line between factual and fictional historiography was not distinctly drawn. In any case one had to reckon with readers who would draw parallels between a historical revolt and the present situation in Austria.

As demonstrated above, most of Scott's novels were only available in bowdlerized versions. They were nevertheless very popular among readers. Three Austrian publishers edited more or less complete works (Scott 1825–30, 1825–31 and 1827–34). In the 1820s the pirating of German editions was still in its heyday. Thus all these editions were reprints of previous German translations, which could be offered rather cheaply to the Austrian public. Strauß's publishing house, for instance, released each month a complete work at the price of half a florin the volume. The demand was great and according to contemporary reports the size of the edition had to be augmented during publication (cf. anon. 1825a, 576, and 1826, 212). In addition to the complete works a publishing house of Brünn/Brno released individual editions of *Old Mortality* (Scott 1820–21), *Kenilworth* (Scott 1825a) and *Lives of the Novelists* (Scott 1829), all of them pirated German translations as well. In the circulating libraries of the capital Scott was the leading author; in the 1840s he is at the top of the number of volumes listed in their catalogues (Martino 1990, 767 and 772).

The only genuine Austrian translations of Scott's works concerned his epic poetry. Caroline Pichler, who distinguished herself as an author of historical novels in the vein of Scott (see below), published a short excerpt from *The Lady of the Lake*, the ballad 'Alice Brand' (Scott 1819). Ferdinand Haas, apparently a dilettante, translated the entire poem, which was published posthumously by his relatives (Scott 1828), and Joseph von Hammer-Purgstall contributed a sample of *Harold the Dauntless* (Scott 1821). Further evidence of the popularity of

---

[4] Scott 1871, 143; passages deleted in Scott 1827a in square brackets. '[Es war seltsam zu betrachten, welche sonderbare Menge von Mißgriffen und Irrthümern, von Seiten des Königs und seiner Minister, von Seiten des Parlaments und seiner Anführer, von Seiten der verbündeten Königreiche England und Schottland gegen einander, sich verbunden hatten, Menschen von so gefährlichen Meinungen und selbstsüchtigen Charakteren zu Schiedsrichtern über das Schicksal Englands empor zu bringen.] Diejenigen, welche für Parteien streiten, werden alle Fehler auf der einen Seite sehen, ohne jene auf der andern eines Blicks zu würdigen. Jene, welche Geschichte zur Belehrung studiren, werden bemerken, daß nichts, als Mangel an Nachgiebigkeit auf beiden Seiten, und die tödtlich gewordene Erbitterung zwischen den Parteien des Königs und des Parlaments, so gänzlich das wohl abgemessene Gleichgewicht der Englischen Constitution erschüttern konnte. Aber wir eilen, politische Reflexionen zu verlassen, [um so mehr, da den Unsrigen, wie wir glauben, weder Whig noch Tory gefallen wird]' (Scott 1826a, I, 264–65).

Scott's epic poetry with the Austrian public is given by Schubert's composition of seven songs from *The Lady of the Lake* (Scott 1826b).

But on the whole, as elsewhere in Europe, Scott's novels were more success-ful than his poetry. In addition to the abundance of editions of his novels, this fact is testified by various dramatic adaptations. In 1822 Johann Wenzel Tremler, an actor at the Vienna Burgtheater, produced an adaptation of *K* under the pseudonym Johann Wilhelm Lembert (Scott 1845). But the Burgtheater pre-ferred another adaptation, submitted by Johann Reinhold Lenz (Scott 1825b), which was staged in November 1822. Curiously enough twelve years later, in 1834, the Burgtheater replaced Lenz's play by Lembert's adaptation. While Lembert's adaptation of *I* was rejected by the Viennese censors he was success-ful abroad with two other plays adapted from novels of Scott. His version of *The Abbot* (Scott 1827b) was staged in 1825 and his adaptation of *The Talisman* in 1827. In addition to dramatic adaptations Donizetti's opera *Il Castello di Kenilworth* was staged at the Schönbrunner Schloßtheater in 1835, and in 1840 the Kärntnertor-Theater produced the historical ballet *Das Schloß Kenilworth* (Castle Kenilworth).

Lembert's dramatic adaptation of *K* is modelled on classical drama. He renders the main plot only and concentrates on the aristocratic and courtly characters. Wayland Smith, for instance, is only granted a marginal appearance. Compared to the novel the most significant change is the happy ending intro-duced by Lembert: in his version Varney is himself killed by the intruding Tresillian; Elizabeth pardons Leicester and announces his marriage with Amy – her appearance in the masquerade as Varney's wife was only for fun.

Criticism

According to a contemporary critic, Napoleon's blockade of Great Britain seriously delayed the reception of Scott's epic poetry on the Continent. Thus *LLM* and *LL* attracted almost no attention until 1813. Only in 1821, in an article reprinted from the *Abendzeitung* (Evening News) [Dresden], does an Austrian journal present a discussion of the two works on the occasion of the German translations by Adam Storck (anon. 1821a). In comparison to these master works his recent poems like *The Vision of Don Roderick* fall under the mark (anon. 1813), the same applies to *The Lord of the Isles* (anon. 1815). By the beginning of the 1820s the interest in Scott was great but reliable information about his work was still lacking. Thus in 1821 the *Literarischer Anzeiger* (Literary Advertiser) printed a comprehensive bibliographical sketch including German translations (anon. 1821b).

Scott's novels were treated as a trivial genre by the majority of the critics. It is hardly surprising that Franz Grillparzer was rather critical of Scott. The Austrian dramatist was generally averse to prose. Perhaps as an answer to Willibald Alexis's review (see below), he compares Scott to Shakespeare in order to demonstrate the former's inferiority. Whereas Shakespeare's characters are organic, Grillparzer argues, Scott constructs his protagonists to suit certain con-cepts and purposes so that they crack to pieces if they start acting. Nevertheless, Grillparzer finds the plots interesting and the descriptive passages lively and impressive. According to Grillparzer the realism of representation is the main reason for Scott's success with the public, but his writing lacks proportion and beauty. In his opinion Scott may not pretend to the higher spheres of literature since he does not strive for poetic independence. In his 'Erinnerungsblätter' (Memorial leaves) of 1824, Grillparzer resumes:

> His main fault is the lack of a sublime and superior spirit hovering high above. Homer seems to be drowned in his own work and to become one with it too, but his subjects are appropriate for that because they encompass everything great on earth. If on the contrary a subject like that of Ivanhoe or Waverley is perfectly identical with the spirit of the author one must assume that the latter is not particularly extensive.[5]

Grillparzer's knowledge of Scott's novels seems to have been limited.[6] But even if he had studied Scott in depth, the Scottish novelist would hardly have matched with his maxims of idealistic aesthetics. The voices of critics that judge Scott from the point of view of idealistic aethetics can be easily multiplied, but we only mention two more. In 1827 Scott is blamed for regarding the novel as a means of providing pleasure to society. In the critic's opinion he should better have taken the point of view of German philosoph, which acknowledges the dignity of art (anon. 1827a). In 1836 Adolf Schöll criticizes Scott's nonchalance in presenting masses of materials that would have needed selection guided by poetic judgement (Schöll 1836, 102–05). As early as 1825 a critic states that *The Talisman* shows marks of hasty production and that the enthusiasm of the public is already vanishing (anon. 1825b).

As demonstrated above by the number of editions and their presence in circulating libraries, Scott *is* popular among Austrian readers. This fact is corroborated by 'background stories' published in Austrian journals, such as the reprinting of Scott's Edinburgh speech, in which he revealed his authorship of the Waverley Novels (anon. 1827b) or the report about the source of the legend of Grizzy Oldbuck, Jonathan Oldbuck's sister, in *The Antiquary* (anon. 1829). Since Scott was more popular than almost any other author before him, the discussion about his novels was also a discussion about the direction literature should take, about classical standards threatened by the demands of the widening reading public.

---

[5] Der Hauptmangel endlich ist der Abgang des Gewahrwerdens eines über dem Ganzen schwebenden erhabenen, überlegenen Geistes. Wenn Homer in seinem Stoff gleichsam unterzugehen, mit ihm Eins zu seyn scheint, so ist der Stoff darnach und alles was die Erde Hohes und Großes kennt, findet darin einen Raum. Wenn aber ein Stoff wie der des Ivanhoe oder Waverley und der Geist eines Verfaßers sich so vollkommen decken, so entsteht für letztern unmöglich die Vermuthung einer besonderen Ausgebreitetheit (Grillparzer, Erinnerungsblätter 55).

[6] A factura of books delivered by the librarian Wallishausser lists for the year 1824 *Ivanhoe* and vols 5 to 8 of 'Scott's works' (Grillparzer, Briefe und Dokumente 43), which, considering the German editions available in 1824, undoubtedly refers to vols 5 to 8 of the edition of Gleditsch in Leipzig, i.e. to *P* and *A*. For Grillparzer's knowledge of English literature cf. Eder 1934.

Scott was esteemed by critics who favoured the concept of a literature that truly depicts history and society and thereby contributes to the solution of current problems. If Scott was not a social realist his work was at least regarded as an important step towards a literature conscious of social problems. Ernst von Feuchtersleben, a medico, state official and author, took an intermediate position. Critical of the commercialization of literary life, he nevertheless maintains that the novel should depict (contemporary) society. In a fictional drawing room discussion he has followers of Scott confront adherents of Bulwer-Lytton. Whereas Scott excels in the representation of material details and leaves the readers to draw their own conclusions, Bulwer-Lytton tends to philosophical deliberation and propaganda for certain ideas. The dispute is unresolved. Feuchtersleben reminds the reader of a difference of temperament which can be observed throughout history and which distinguished Euripides from Sophocles, Schiller from Goethe and Bulwer–Lytton from Scott (1836a). His appreciation of Scott, the 'immortal author', and the historical novel led him to argue against the German philosophical novel. According to Feuchtersleben extensive description, often declared a vice of Scott's novels, is necessary in a historical novel (1836b).[7]

Eduard von Bauernfeld, another Austrian author who excelled in drama, introduced Scott in the prehistory of 'democratic' literature. In the foreword to his translation of four Dickens novels, Bauernfeld attests national fervour for Scott and recognizes his great impact on the development of the novel. Nevertheless he maintains that the heyday of the historical novel is over. According to Bauernfeld it is no longer sufficient to reconstruct the past without drawing conclusions for the present and contributing to the solution of its urgent questions (1844, 324).

The *Jahrbücher der Literatur* was founded in 1818 on the initiative of Metternich and Friedrich Gentz, funded by the state and controlled by the state chancellery. This is why the journal was very close to the government's point of view. It served as a complement to censorship, as an instrument of propaganda addressing an intellectual readership who should be won over to the government's cause. The critics employed by the editors of the *Jahrbücher* usually took a classicist point of view: they professed to the ideal of 'true poesy' (wahre Poesie) which represents moral ideas, particularly patriotic or religious sentiments; on the other hand they strictly opposed plain realism and literature with a (liberal) purpose and the commercialized literature which followed the taste of the mass readership (cf. Lechner 1977).

Considering this background it is rather astonishing that Scott is very favourably reviewed in three articles that appeared in the *Jahrbücher* between 1820 and 1823. The first article, published anonymously, praises *Ivanhoe* as a 'master-piece of the genre of chivalric romance' (Meisterstück der Gattung der Ritterromane) (anon. 1820, 139). In the second article Willibald Alexis compares the poetic works of Byron and Scott, with special reference to *LL* and *LLM* (1821). According to Alexis, Scott and Byron mark the return of 'true

---

[7] Feuchtersleben was an assiduous reader of Scott's novels (cf. Feuchtersleben 2002).

poesy' that had been absent from Great Britain since the days of Shakespeare. Alexis opposes the characteristics of the two poets – subjectivity *vs.* objectivity, use of a few characters in all works *vs.* a multitude of characters, scarcity *vs.* plenitude of action, pessimism and even hatred of the world *vs.* optimism, abroad settings *vs.* concentration on Scotland – which will not be further discussed here. If Byron appears as the major poet, the 'healthy spirit' of Scott's poetry seems clearly preferable because it is lacking ambiguity. In Alexis's eyes Scott is not blind to the faults of the world but he searches for the good at the bottom of every phenomenon. Furthermore he clings to his national environment, does not avoid common people as subjects of his poetry, evokes the contrast between ancient times and the civilized present, between Scotland and England, in order to produce poetic effects. Scott tries to be true to historical manners and costumes, avoids disturbing raisonnement and, all in all, avers himself a true Romantic poet.

The third article, again by Willibald Alexis and dedicated to the novels (1823), is one of the most comprehensive and detailed pieces of Scott criticism in German language in these years. Alexis is convinced that Scott's novels are apt to please the reading masses and the friend of 'true poesy'. He compares Scott with Shakespeare, Cervantes and Goethe and classifies him together with these authors. Alexis begins with the discussion of two complaints directed against Scott's novels. First, the reproach with 'poorness of ideas' (Ideenarmuth), which is a typical offspring of the German preference for artists' novels (Kunstromane) in the vein of *Wilhelm Meister*. According to Alexis the novel must be based on true pictures of life and not on ideas. Even if the novel of ideas has a right of its own he considers a comparison of *The Antiquary* with *Wilhelm Meister* inadequate. Next comes the reproach with 'poorness of thought' (Gedankenarmuth), that is, the scarcity of philosophical reflection. Alexis argues that philosophical novels tend to be boring. In a true work of art inner life will be represented by the actions of the characters. Thus Scott avoids introspection and lets the characters speak for themselves. Sometimes, for instance in *The Antiquary*, he achieves even an equivalent to German homeliness (Gemüthlichkeit). The common reader likes to recognize pictures from life, the connoisseur will discover hidden truths in these pictures. Scott's history, depicted with the help of characters from all classes, is interesting for readers in the whole world. A further attraction of Scott's novels is his objectivity, the lack of partisanship.

Alexis discusses various specific complaints against Scott's novels, most of them of a technical nature. The most interesting points concern the prolixity of his descriptions, the harsh endings and the weak and unattractive heroes.

In Alexis's eyes the charge of prolixity is a charge typical of the common reader, who yearns for action and sensual excitation, while lovers of true poesy cannot object to detailed pictures. Alexis praises, for instance, the detailed descriptions of the political and religious parties in *Waverley*, which are a touchstone that distinguishes the lover of poesy from the common reader. In order to obey poetic justice many of Scott's novels end with executions or other punishments for bad characters. In Alexis's opinion this is untrue to life and poesy because in life misdeeds are not always punished and poesy should not care if good and bad charcters are treated 'justly'. In general, Scott goes too far in the depiction of the horrible, for instance when he describes the details of the execution of Fergus Mac Ivor at the end of *W*. The ending of *HM* seems too harsh as well, moral didacticism and poetic justice expelling poesy. Scott's heroes, mostly young men of no particular character – 'amiable stuffed shirts, leading gentlemen, as they often appear in English novels, particularly in those written by women' (liebenswürdige Nullen, erste Liebhaber, wie sie wohl häufig in englischen Romanen, namentlich denen der Frauen, vorkommen) (Alexis 1823, 29) – are, rather, anti-heroes. These heroes might be interpreted as a consequence of the author's truthfulness to life, which not only produces heroes but a majority of average men; but the main reason for the common characters that appear in the centre of most of Scott's novels is the fact that the author needed a representative of the reader with whom it is easy to identify oneself.

To sum up, Alexis takes a decisive step towards the emancipation of historical subjects in literature; he even calls history 'the most sublime form of poetry' (12). Furthermore he defends Scott's realism against the German tradition of the philosophical novel, including the delight Scott takes in the description of details; the only features of Scott's novels Alexis cannot tolerate are 'ugly' and harsh scenes. Finally the critic praises Scott's choice of heroes who are not important as individuals but as representatives of their people, or at least of a class of their people. The historical novels are thus able to represent history as a complex and dynamic interplay of antagonistic forces, interests and ideas.

It is true that Alexis, a pseudonym of Wilhelm Häring, a Berlin-based critic and author of historical novels who also wrote two parodic novels in Scott's manner, takes a German rather than an Austrian point of view in his articles. Several times he refers to previous German criticism, in particular to objections to Scott's novels. But nevertheless, as his articles appeared in the *Jahrbücher*, they can be read as statements approved by the Austrian Government. By publishing in the *Jahrbücher* an unbiased discussion of a rather dubious literary phenomenon, the Metternich regime could demonstrate tolerance towards a literary hero of the day and counter the verdict of Austria's seclusion from Western European culture. Anyway we have to remember that the readership of a learned journal was extremely restricted in number and consisted almost exclusively of the higher classes. For such a readership no harm was to be feared from praise of the Scottish national novelist. Alexis refers in detail to the conflicts between political parties and religious groups. He even includes some criticism of the Stuarts and Tories, for instance when he refers to the 'cruel despotism of tyranny' (57) that the Presbyterians in *OM* are confronted with – whereas the common reader was only allowed bowdlerized versions of Scott's works.

Scott and the Austrian historical novel

Before 1848 veritable historical novels in general and productive adaptations of Scott's model in particular were extremely scarce. According to Julius Seidlitz, a pseudonym of Ignaz Jeitteles, the reason for this was censorship that disencouraged Austrian authors (1836, I, 26). Controversial political or religious subjects could not be raised, therefore evasion of conflicts and a certain patriotism prevailed. A circumstance that may have contributed to the scarcity of interesting and unbiased historical novels is the fact that most authors were members of the aristocracy, or were state officials. The limits of poetical freedom were set in a review of two historical novels of Caroline Pichler in the *Jahrbücher* in 1828. The anonymous reviewer demands that novels be written from and unmistakably defend a moral point of view (qtd. in Kucher (2002), 50). It goes without saying that besides conforming to morals the historical novel must not contradict the interests of the state.

Caroline Pichler, the first Austrian author who wrote historical novels under the influence of Scott, was a dedicated reader of his works. Already in 1819 she had read his epic poetry (Pichler 1893, 290) and translated a ballad from *LL* (see above). The novels were to follow soon – in a letter of 1821 she mentions the reading of *I* (309) – some of them lent out by Hammer-Purgstall.[8] She praises the plots, the truth of description, the psychology of the characters and their humanity (Pichler 1914, II, 67–69). Without any doubt inspired by Scott she began a long series of historical novels, which started with *Die Belagerung Wiens* (The Siege of Vienna) (1824). This novel, about the war between Austria and the Ottoman Empire and the latter's Hungarian allies, culminating in the siege of Vienna in 1683, touches a key conflict in Austrian history: the relation between the core provinces and the Eastern (Slavic/Hungarian/Islamic) periphery and neighbours. The two daughters of the family Volkersdorf are sent to Preßburg in Hungary and encounter the aristocracy of this country, among them Count Zriny. Ludmilla, the elder daughter, falls in love with Zriny; they marry secretly and flee to Paris because Ludmilla is destined to take the veil. Zriny, an intimate counsellor of Emperor Leopold, gets involved in the movement of the Hungarian malcontents, which is preparing the liberation from Austrian government with the help of the Turks. Zriny is torn between the feeling of loyalty to Austria and his commitment to national emancipation. At last he confesses his conspiracy to the Emperor. His life is spared but his life project is ruined and he dies in mental disorder. Ludmilla returns from Paris and finally takes the veil. This makes possible the marriage of her sister Katharina, who has long been engaged to a brave fighter for the Austrian case.

Like Scott, Pichler studied various historical sources during the preparation of her novel. In the historical setting she places fictional characters, some of them representative of the common people. Pichler introduces us to their feasts, customs and habits (cf. Pichler 1914, II, 175; Pichler 1893, 329). The Hungarians appear as a 'romantic' people, their function can be compared with that of the Highlanders in Scott's novels; Hungarian aristocracy, for instance, resembles the Scottish chiefs, and Pichler dwells amply upon their folklore (cf. Wild 1935, 78–85). The private life of characters stands clearly in the fore and relegates historical events and political action to the background. History is thus

---

[8]   Hammer-Purgstall was one of the earliest readers of Scott in Austria. In his memoirs he mentions readings of *Waverley* (already in 1814!) and *Kenilworth* (Hammer-Purgstall 1940, 221 and 269).

individualized but not explained. Zriny is a typical hero in Scott's manner, torn between the parties, but active as a rebel. The malcontents' upsurge is doomed to failure because in Pichler's perspective rebellion entails moral decline, treason of religion and family tradition and disloyalty to the legal Emperor. In addition to that Pichler introduces some stereotyped images of the enemy. The Turkish and Hungarian allies are qualified as 'hordes of Tartars' and 'Barbarians calling on Allah', and the Christian Habsburg Empire is thus opposed to atheistic Hungary/Asia (cf. Kucher 2002, 281–87).

Pichler's portrayal of characters and local colour is 'true' to life but her representation of the central conflict is lacking any bearing on the present situation because she starts from an immovable set of principles. 'True' religion and form of government must not be put into question. These features are typical of an Austrian historical novel in the age of Metternich. Authors try to imitate Scott's technique but they are not able to follow his model as to a balanced view of historical conflicts.

An exception to this rule is Karl Herloßsohn's novel *Der Ungar* (The Hungarian) (1832). Herloßsohn, born in Prague, went to Leipzig in 1825 and by this step evaded Austrian censorship of his manuscripts. The novel is set in the fifteenth century and revolves around the fight for the throne of King Ladislaus, the last of the Albertinian Habsburgs. All characters are historical, and therefore they have very little liberty of action. The action takes place in Hungary and the rhetoric of national emancipation is given ample space. Parallels to the contemporary Greek liberation movement are obvious; Vienna appears as the city of court intrigues. As in Pichler's novel the alternatives in the history of national upsurge against a central power are loyalty or liberty; political actions are often motivated by erotic attraction and rivalry, which keep history going. But as to the treatment of political questions, Herloßsohn contrasts strongly with Pichler, whose novels are clearly patriotic and pro-Habsburg. Herloßsohn even discusses regicide, which was undoubtedly the main reason for the novel's ban by Austrian censorship. His novels were rightly compared to those of Scott by the critics because of their unbiased approach towards history.

A historical novel with such an approach to history could only be published abroad; *Der Ungar* was published in Leipzig. Another Austrian emigrant is Karl Postl, who in 1823 went to the USA and decided to construct himself a new identity under the name of Charles Sealsfield; later he moved to London and Paris and finally settled down in Switzerland. Like Scott he published his works anonymously and was qualified by critics as the second 'Great Unknown'. Undoubtedly this stratagem helped to enhance the publicity around his novels, but at the same time it was part of his building up a new identity. Sealsfield acknowleges the debt to Scott – together with references to Cooper and Bulwer-Lytton, the other two authors in full vogue in the 1830s – but he rejects the idea of being a simple follower of Scott. What he finds most attractive in Scott is the latter's true and unbiased representation of characters of different social standing and political opinion. Sealsfield subordinates his writing exclusively to the goal of enlightenment and intellectual progress, he wants to make 'sick' European society conscious of its state (1835, preface). Sealsfield's plots are based on historical events and characters. His political credo is anti-monarchical, anti-clerical and republican, but at the same time he praises the virtues of patriarchal landowners. His political programme is clearly modelled on the 'Jacksonian democracy' of the Southern States, which he presents to his European readers as an alternative to monarchy and despotism. He is indebted to Southern novelists such as Paulding, Kennedy, Simms, Flint, Crockett, Bancroft, Caruthers and Ingraham, who were devoted followers of Scott. Sealsfield's reception of Scott's model is thus a second-hand reception (Ritter 2000).

In his novel *Das Cajütenbuch oder Nationale Charakteristiken* (The book of the cabin or national character-sketches) (1841), Sealsfield assembles a series of episodes from the liberation of Texas from Mexican rule (1836) and of various Latin-American states from Spanish domination. The stories are told in Captain Murky's cabin (Cajüte) on the Mississippi in the course of an evening party. The life of North-American settlers, the role of money in society and diverse questions of political morals are discussed. Sealsfield presents his sketches of North- and Latin-American liberation movements as examples of what a small number of determined revolutionaries can achieve. The characters speak for the different parties and points of view, and the author's own view of history and politics is transported by a set of dominant characters. In most of the episodes Sealsfield employs an Ivanhoe-type of character as well: that is, a mediating character who is actively involved in the events.

In the years from 1848 to 1890, 180 historical novels by Austrian authors have been counted (Holzner, Neumayr and Wiesmüller 2000, 456). In these four decades the historical novel was still at the top in lists of authors present in the catalogues of circulating libraries. Between 1849 and 1888 Scott holds the seventh place in the catalogues of Viennese circulating libraries, behind Dumas, de Kock, G. P. R. James, Mühlbach, Sue and Sand and before Spindler and Breier (Martino 1990, 802). It is striking that six of the nine leading authors are historical novelists; only de Kock, Sue and Sand were famous for other novelistic subgenres.

Of the 180 Austrian historical novels mentioned above, two-thirds chose as their subject a chapter of Austrian history. Especially attractive was the era of Joseph II, the hero of the liberal bourgeoisie and of the majority of state officials in the nineteenth century. Even if the Emperor and his mother Maria Theresia are idealized as wise and just regents and the novels appear therefore as clearly pro-Habsburg, there is nevertheless a certain critical undertone in the reminders of an era of enlightenment and fight against clerical obscurantism – the power of the Catholic Church had recently been codified by the concordat of 1855 between Austria and Rome. The vast majority of the novels are popular novels of intrigue and conspiracy, often the clergy and members of religious orders plot against law, order and prosperity of the common people. They were published in popular newspapers like *Morgenpost* (Morning Post), *Stadt- und Vorstadtzeitung* (City and Suburb News) or *Neues Wiener Tagblatt* (New Vienna Daily). Occasionally police seized newspapers because they serialized a novel of this sort (Bachleitner 1999, 48–49), but in general censorship was much more liberal after 1848.

That much of this rich production of popular historical novels received an impulse by Scott can be demonstrated by the example of one of its leading authors. Eduard Breier wrote a plethora of historical novels, most of them on a historical basis, like for instance *Die beiden Grasel* (1854), a novel which recapitulates the deeds of two famous Austrian brigands. In his memoirs Breier relates how in 1839 he and his publisher J. Stöckholzer von Hirschfeld decided to 'cultivate the Austrian historical novel' (1871, 6). Soon Breier was awarded the title of 'the Austrian Scott' because of the detailed descriptions of manners, language, costumes, etc and the comical characters of common people that abound in his novels.

One of the very few historical novels that stand out in this era is Adalbert Stifter's *Witiko* (1865–67). Set in twelfth-century Bohemia the novel deals with the problems of hereditary succession and legitmate power. We do not know very much about Stifter's knowledge of Scott's novels; one of the few hints are two volumes of 'Walter Scott' that were found among the books of his widow (Stifter 1979, 411). Whichever novels these may have been, in his letters to his publisher Gustav Heckenast he reflects on the historical novel and his relation to Scott. Stifter's ambition was not to become a new Scott; he condescends to the popular form of the historical novel modelled on Scott in which, on a historical background, the adventures and loves of one or a few characters are told. As to Scott, Stifter declares that he likes best novels like *Old Mortality*, because they represent not individuals but the life of the masses. In a letter of 8 June 1861 he explains:

> In this kind of novel the peoples appear as products of nature issued from the hand of the creator, their fate demonstrates the effect of a giant law which we call the moral law, and the turmoils of a people's life are idealizations of this law. There is something mysteriously extraordinary in this. Therefore, in historical novels, history is most important, the individual characters are only of minor interest because they are borne by the great stream and help in forming the stream. This is why epic poetry is much more precious to me than drama, and in my mind the so-called historical novel is epic poetry in prose.[9]

With his idealistic and metaphysical view of history, Stifter keeps his distance from the liberal, nationalistic and democratic tendencies prevailing in the contemporary historical novel. His scepticism about the genre, which Stifter bases on arguments derived from classical aesthetics, implies an ideological distance. The history of families and dynasties, favoured by Stifter, is important to him because it demonstrates 'natural' traditions. The rise and fall of dynasties results from their relation – acceptance or neglect – to the moral law. As Stifter explains

---

[9] Es erscheinen da bei dieser Art die Völker als großartige Naturprodukte aus der Hand des Schöpfers hervorgegeangen, in ihren Schiksalen zeigt sich die Abwiklung eines riesigen Gesezes auf, das wir in Bezug auf uns das Sittengesez nennen, und die Umwälzungen des Völkerlebens sind Verklärungen dieses Gesezes. Es hat das etwas geheimnißvoll Außerordentliches. Es erscheint mir daher in historischen Romanen die Geschichte die Hauptsache und die einzelnen Menschen die Nebensache, sie werden von dem großen Strome getragen, und helfen den Strom bilden. Darum steht mir das Epos viel höher als das Drama, und der sogenannte historische Roman erscheint mir als das Epos in ungebundener Rede (Stifter 1929, 282).

in a letter to Heckenast of 10 April 1860, history is also an instance of judgement since it reveals the 'terrific majesty of the moral law' (1929, 231). Considering the majesty of the moral law that reveals itself in history, the historian has to abstain from comments and speculations that would underline his subjective interests. Insight into the dealings of the creator is the only lesson that can be learnt from history.

In fact, in *Witiko*, Stifter's narrator is neutral if not absent from the story. The events speak for themselves. With the demand of total submission to past events that ends in an annihilation of the self, Stifter holds a conservative point of view, which is fuelled by his disappointment in the revolution of 1848 and about the recent Austrian defeat in the battle at Solferino in 1859, to be followed by the defeat at Königgrätz in 1866. Stifter observed the upsurge of the politics of power which left no doubt about the fact that contemporary historical events scorned the moral law and put legitimate government into question. His concept of the historical novel can therefore be interpreted as a silent protest against contemporary politics and as a means of creating a sort of conservative utopia. With the help of this utopia he clings obstinately to the idea of an ultimate victory of the legitimate powers. After all, *Witiko* raises the question whether teleology, and especially a moral law, can still be postulated in recent history (cf. Wiesmüller 1981 and Wiesmüller 1995). Stifter's theory of history and its application in *Witiko* reminds us of the moderately monarchical point of view prevailing among Austrian intellectuals in the era of Metternich, for example of the view taken by Grillparzer, who favoured the utopia of an elective monarchy, in which the one who guarantees the welfare of his subjects is elected legitimate king. One can observe similarities in the aesthetic programmes of Stifter and Grillparzer as well, notably the search for the beautiful and the aversion to any political agitation in art which corresponds to an aversion to upheaval and violent change in society (cf. Lengauer 1989, 55 and 174).

Witiko is not only a novel about Bohemia and the past but about the Holy Roman Empire and the present. If Stifter chooses local history as his subject matter the reader is supposed to think of the whole. In this respect the reminiscences of the past that his characters evoke in their discourses play an important role. Stifter adopts a balanced point of view: Bohemia is an important part of the monarchy and should not try to become politically independent, but on the other hand Austria should not suffocate the national pride and the traditions of the various peoples in its dominion. Significantly the novel ends with an apotheosis of the legitimate Emperor who reigns on the basis of law and order, as the representative of God on earth.

In this utopian aspect Stifter differs widely from the sober and empirically oriented Scottish novelist. In spite of the many differences we should not forget the analogies. *Witiko* revolves around a decisive crisis within the process of modernization in which civil war appears as a necessary step towards a more civilized state. Like Scott, Stifter presents a wide spectrum of opinions on the question of the selection of the monarch and on the best way of government. He includes a variety of oppositional voices with special emphasis on the voices of the 'weak'. After all, the monarch is the only one who cares for the common people, represented in *Witiko* by the 'woodsmen' (Waldleute). The plot is reminiscent of *QD*, a novel in which the authority of a monarch is challenged by local 'warlords', petty tyrants who do not recognize any law. The preference of both authors is on the side of lawful and peaceful government, which replaces fist-law and egotism (cf. Klieneberger 1986). Thus, notwithstanding the important differences, *Witiko* may be called a distant relative of Scott's historical novels.

6 The Reception of Sir Walter Scott in German Literary Histories, 1820–1945

Frauke Reitemeier

Introduction

> Whoever listens to Scott's songs
> (His everlasting fame is based on them)
> And does not wind garlands for him
> Does not deserve his own fame.[1]

Virtually from the publication of *Waverley* onwards, Sir Walter Scott captured the imagination of German readers. His novels were radically new and sharply different from everything written by German novelists of the times. Unsurprisingly, readers reacted with a veritable, unparalleled 'Scottomania' in the 1820s (Bachleitner 1989, 9): Scott appeared as 'the first great migratory element of modern times'[2] (Hackenberg 1913, 11). Although German novelists tried to incorporate Scott's model, German history did not lend itself as easily to historical fiction.

For most of the nineteenth century, there was no 'Germany' to speak of, but numerous principalities of various sizes and importance. In the wake of the French Revolution and the Wars of Liberation, German intellectuals set about creating a unified German nation on the basis of a common language and culture. The formation of a German nation, and with it the creation of a German national literature, remained hotly disputed throughout much of the nineteenth century until, after several failed revolutionary attempts, the German Kaiserreich was founded in 1871.

In order to draw a full picture of Scott's reception in Germany until the end

---

[1] 'Wer Scotts Gesänge hört / (Sein Nachruhm ist gegründet) / Und ihm nicht Kränze windet / Ist nicht des eignen wert.' Haug, 'An Englands Dichter' ('To England's Poet', 1820), quoted in Sigmann 1918, 56.
[2] 'das erste große völkerwandernde Element der neuen Zeit', from Schmidt-Weißenfels's monograph on Rahel Varnhagen.

of the Second World War, several aspects must be taken into account. First, Scott's works proved lastingly popular with German novel readers. This has been analysed at length (Wenger 1905; Sigmann 1918; Price 1953; Schüren 1969), so that an overview emphasizing the distribution of and responses to translations will be given in place of a more detailed account. Reliable data for tracing translations of Scott's novels are, however, hard to come by; while the BOSLIT database (www.boslit.nls.uk) contains a number of translations for the first half of the nineteenth century, many of the later publications have not yet been added. The publication data used in this essay are drawn from BOSLIT where possible and have been correlated with data from the cumulative index of German books (*Gesamtverzeichnis des deutschen Schrifttums*, GV); additional titles were researched in library catalogues and in the main antiquarian and rare books catalogues. As publishers often did not distinguish between a reissue or a simple reprint, a new edition, and the continuation of an already published volume, some publications are not mentioned in catalogues at all (Schlösser 1937, 11). In many cases publishers did not bother to print the publication date on the title pages, so the exact date has to be guessed at; consequently, in several cases, the conjectured publication dates of a series of Scott volumes differ considerably. What data there are for the years 1895 to 1934 have been collected and analysed by Schlösser (1937).

Second, Scott set an example for German authors of historical fiction, who adapted his models for their own purposes. While authors were personally deeply impressed by his novels and tried to imitate them, the readers' enthusiasm for translations of the Waverley novels resulted at the same time in a mass production of historical novels; many of them were not written in a style or on a plan similar to *Waverley*, but were nevertheless brought forth by the German Scottomania. The development of historical novels in Germany after *Waverley* was recently analysed in depth by the Project 'The German Historical Novel' based at Innsbruck (Holzner and Wiesmüller 1997–2002). German historical novels had been written even before the publication of *Waverley* in Britain (Meyer 1973), some of which even seem to have influenced Scott (Reitemeier 2001); Aust gives an overview of the relevant bibliographies (1994, 35–8). But publication data for the decade after the first translations show a sharp rise in the total number of historical novels that were produced as a result of Scott's impact. A first analysis of the findings is published by Habitzel and Mühlberger (1996), and further aspects are discussed in Durrani and Preece (2001).

Tracing the more specific influence of the Waverley novels on specific authors proves more difficult. Some novelists, like Theodor Fontane, openly acknowledged their debts to Scott; with others, a connection seems likely but cannot be proved. Besides, although Scott's model quickly became the standard plan for historical novels in Germany in literary theory, it was not always used by novelists. From the first there was no 'German Scott novel', but a plurality of forms (Aust 1994, 69). While some authors imitated Scott's use of a travelling fictitious hero, others followed his technique in describing landscapes and events. Aust provides a detailed summary both of the imitative qualities of German novels and of the various other forms that become mixed up with Scott's. Further valuable research on all aspects covered can be found in Eggert (1971), Geppert (1976) and Steinecke (1975b), so that only the main developments will be outlined here.

While the readers' and authors' reactions to Scott's novels are clearly very important, a different genre has to be considered, which served to propagate and cement Scott's reputation. This essay aims at charting the reception of Scott's novels in literary histories in Germany as a special case of reception studies. The function of literary histories lies in explaining the development of literature during a specific period that enables readers to understand the respective contexts. They are thus an important factor in forming the readers' knowledge and judgement of authors and works.

The reception of Scott by his readers

In the late eighteenth century, reading circles for English literature had been established throughout Germany. Publications from Britain were hard to come by, both during the French Revolution and immediately afterwards due to the French embargo laid on British trade, but also for much of the nineteenth century (Wittmann 1999). But many readers preferred translations to original editions because of their scanty knowledge of the English language. While there had already been English classes in secondary schools in the eighteenth century (Klippel 1994, 93), English was by no means a school subject taught everywhere and to everyone; although the level and amount of teaching increased in the first third of the nineteenth century, it was only in the latter half that English as a school subject was introduced on a broad scale. Most German readers therefore read Scott's works in German translations. When from 1841 the publishing firm of Bernhard Tauchnitz began to bring out editions of the classic works of English literature in English at moderate prices, German readers were introduced to another and affordable source of foreign-language books. The publication number of Tauchnitz editions proved that there was a market (*Führer* 1927, iv), although, on the whole, translations were in far greater demand even towards the end of the nineteenth century (Schlösser 1937, 36).

The most productive period in the publication of translations was in the early years of the reception of Scott's novels, in the decade between 1821 and 1830 (Sigmann 1918). In 1817, the first complete translation of a Scott novel appeared, *Der Astrolog* (The astrologer, *GM*), but other novels had been reviewed earlier, and some extracts had been printed in magazines. At first, reviewers responded coolly (52–53); only after the translation of *Ivanhoe* had appeared, in 1820, did reactions become much more enthusiastic both on the reviewers' and on the readers' sides (Steinecke 1975b, 32). Some novels appeared in up to four translations at the same time (36); from 1822, seven collected editions were published (Bachleitner 1989, 7). Early reviews stress Scott's ability to create convincing and realistic characters, his use of the historical context and his narrative voice (Sigmann 1918).

At first, publishers partly relied on little-known female translators (Hackenberg 1913). The German versions of Sophie May, Elise von Hohenhausen and Henriette Schubart, for example, were all published by various firms in places such as Berlin (Fleischer), Leipzig (Herbig, Gleditsch), Zwickau (Schumann) and Vienna (Mausberger). In the following decades, their translations would either be reissued or would form the basis for corrected editions by other translators. While there were at the same time highly renowned male translators such as Georg Nikolaus Bärmann, they do not seem to have translated many of Scott's novels, probably for financial reasons (Bachleitner 1989, 9–12) Towards the end of the 1820s, however, Leonhard Tafel worked for the very successful publisher Franck at Stuttgart and thus emerged as a rival; his translations were not only found all over Germany, but were also exported to the German-speaking regions in the Austrian Empire and beyond.

The Pirate and *Rob Roy* were the most popular novels in Germany shortly before Scott's death in 1832, closely followed by *Quentin Durward*, *Kenilworth* and *A Legend of Montrose*:

Number of Editions of Scott's Novels, 1800–30

Title	Number of editions
RR, P (both 18)	12 each
K, LM, QD	10 each
A, HM, I, W	9 each

Readers seem to have been mainly interested in novels that stress picturesque Scottish customs and landscapes (*P, RR, LM*) or colourful historical narratives (*QD, K*), but as the number of editions is close together, a clear picture does not emerge.

The high overall number of publications for the years between 1820 and 1830 was only possible because a new printing method had been invented that enabled publishers to lower publication costs dramatically. The large publishing firms in particular relied on stereotype printing and fast-printing machines (Wittmann 1999, 220–23). The price of the books could thereby be reduced to a highly affordable 15–20 *groschen* – before that, it would have sold at 3–5 *taler* (237–38). Since one *taler* was the equivalent of 30 *groschen*, the fall of prices was dramatic: the same book could now be bought at a veritable cut-throat rate of about one-fifth of its original price. In addition, many of the publishers printed duodecimo, pocket-size volumes that further reduced the cost for paper (237).

Because of the high number of copies, however, the market seems to have become quickly saturated (Schüren 1969, 197). In addition, the readers' interest in Scott's novels obviously waned in the following thirty years up to 1860 – overall, only some seventy-four editions of Scott's novels can be traced, as opposed to 197 for the years between 1800 and 1830 (Sigmann 1918, 73). But precisely because of the high production numbers of the 1820s, earlier editions were still on the market and in the lending libraries; these posed a grave problem for booksellers and continued to do so until the early 1900s (Wittmann 1999, 275).

Readers seemed not only to be less interested in Scott on the whole, but also to take a different kind of interest in his novels; partly this was due to a change in ideas on the genre (Aust 1994, 69). During the years between 1831 and 1860, *Quentin Durward* sold best, followed by *The Talisman*. The attraction of *The Pirate* – one of the favourites in the 1820s – waned, as had the readers' interest in *Rob Roy*. Instead, novels set in the Middle Ages and spiced with romance now excited the readers' interest; another medieval novel, *Ivanhoe*, would soon become even more sought after.

From the mid 1850s, the reputation of the historical novel began to rise again (Eggert 1971, 25–27). During the 1850s, the publishing company Hoffmann in Stuttgart brought out an edition of the collected novels, which was obviously quite popular with readers. In the following decade, between 1861 and 1870, most translations of Scott's novels that were published were printed at Stuttgart, which means Hoffmann had become the leading publishing company for Scott translations.

Again, novels set in the Middle Ages were among the more popular ones, with three editions each of *T* and *AB* and two of *I* and *Quentin Durward*. On the whole, however, Scott's novels did not seem to have drawn many new readers.

Gradually, German authors had become firmly established on the market for historical novels (e.g. Wilhelm Raabe, Karl Gutzkow, Louise Pichler; Habitzel/ Mühlberger 1996), though their reputation was in part tied to Scott's (Eggert 1971, 26); besides, other British authors – like Frederick Marryat, Edward Bulwer-Lytton and Charles Dickens (Bachleitner 1989, 7) – had begun to rival Scott, though they would invariably be compared to him (Sigmann 1918, 75). Publishing firms reacted by bringing out selections of works instead of collected editions.

Between 1871 and 1900 the number of Scott publications rose again; the data show the trend towards medieval novels even more clearly: *W* and *BL* with four editions each rank fifth on the readers' appreciation scale; *T*, by comparison, is brought out three times as often (twelve editions), closely followed by *I* (eleven editions). The list is led by *QD* (fifteen editions). The editions now bear the names of more professional translators, like the philologist Benno Tschischwitz and the literary historians Robert Koenig and Ernst Susemihl.

Tschischwitz comments in 1876 that *QD* deals with many questions relevant for readers in the late nineteenth century (vii); at least the translators still believe in the relevance of Scott's works. Readers' reactions, though, are hard to find; Sigmann mentions a lasting enthusiasm (1918, 313) without giving references.

After 1900, readers' interests did not change materially; it was still the novels set in the Middle Ages that held the greatest fascination. But the most popular novel by far became *I*, with eleven editions up to 1910, and a further twenty-six until 1945; with *Kenilworth* (twenty-two editions, 1900–45), *QD* and *T* (twenty editions each, 1900–45) lagging behind (Schlösser 1937, 69). Judging from the selection of titles, the most attractive feature seems to have been the period in which the novels are set. As many of the publications came out between 1920 and 1930 (thirty-eight publications), politically and economically very difficult years throughout Germany, an escapist yearning for an idealized world somewhere in past times can be assumed as one of the reasons behind that development.

A more practical reason for the large number of *I* editions was the novel's recommendation as a set text at school. The publishing firms of Reclam, Velhagen & Klasing, and Schöningh, all of which were also active in the market for textbooks and teaching material, brought out various editions from the 1880s onwards; three of the eleven editions between 1901 and 1910 and another four until 1945 were published under their auspices. Additionally, a number of editions in English were published, explicitly to be used at school. On the whole, though, editions for adult readers outnumbered children's editions (Schlösser 1937, 68).

The development of Scott's reception, as mirrored by the number of editions, peaked during the 1820s, with two lesser peaks following in the 1860s and 1900s respectively. A comparison with the publication development of the all-time medieval favourites shows some indication that the readers' interest could – at least partly – have been triggered by political events (Tschischwitz 1876). Sales data for *QD* for example first peaked in the 1850s, just after the 1848 Revolution, then reached an even more significant high in the 1870s, after the Franco-Prussian War of 1871, and again in the first decade of the twentieth century. This development is also related to more general sociological and financial changes in the readership (Aust 1994, 63–64); Wittmann (1999) and Eggert (1971) analyse them with respect to the bookmarket and the historical novel respectively.

The reception of Scott by authors

In the nineteenth century the impact of Scott's novels on German literature was already being discussed and analysed. Reviewers pointed out parallels or discrepancies, alternatively praising or deprecating alterations; authors placed their own novels in relation to Scott's. Goethe warmly applauded Scott's *FMP* both as a reader and as an author (Price 1953, 329), while *I*'s translator Karl Immermann criticized and parodied Scott in his own plays (Hasubek 2000). This continued throughout the nineteenth century and even well into the twentieth; until the 1940s, comparisons of German novels to Scott's were still drawn by readers and reviewers alike (Steinecke 1975b, 44).

The main reason for this lay in Scott's status as *the* historical novelist *par excellence*, which he had acquired in Germany soon after the first translations of his works. *W* and *I* were considered suitable models of historical novels (Steinecke 1975b), which invited imitation as well as comparison on the part of readers and reviewers. Four elements, mainly based on the *Waverley* type, were considered the basic ingredients of Scott's novel (Aust 1994, 65–66). These were i) the use of a fictional 'middle' protagonist (characters like Ivanhoe who actively take sides instead of being drawn almost against their will into a conflict are a variant); ii) the middle temporal distance, which shows the past as a time of crisis which still bears on the (readers') present (novels like *I* constitute a different type in this respect as remote past history becomes an adventure rather than a means for understanding the present); iii) on a more abstract level, the relation between fact and fiction, or fiction and history. Scott's many, often ironic remarks on the function of fiction and narrators, his use of iv) contradicting narrative voices, and of poetic mottoes prefixed to chapters all served to define his novels as works of fiction, not as historiography.

Broadly speaking, Scott's influence on German literature was greatest in the 1820s, at the same time that his novels were published in Germany. In 1817, virtually contemporary with the first Scott translation, Achim von Arnim wrote *Die Kronenwächter* (The crown guardians), which, however, remained unfinished, as only the first of four parts was completed; he knew Scott's novels in the English original and at least partly made use of Scott's techniques (Aust 1994, 59–62), though his own style is strongly reminiscent of the early German romanticists and sometimes verges on the grotesque in its combination of fairy tale motifs with historical facts. In 1824, Willibald Alexis, whose real name was Georg Häring, published *Walladmor*, successfully pretending it was the translation of a Scott novel, which imitated most of Scott's model, even including similar footnotes (30). Three years later his far less convincing novel *Schloß Avalon* (Avalon Castle, 1827) followed, expressly in the footsteps of Scott: *Frei nach dem Englischen des Walter Scott vom Übersetzer des Walladmor* (Freely translated from the English of Walter Scott by the translator of Walladmor), as the subtitle states (Steinecke 1975b, 40). Alexis's use of Scott's model for narrating events from the history of the Mark Brandenburg soon earned him the epithet 'der märkische Scott', 'the Scott of the Mark Brandenburg' (Eggert 1971, 156), even 'the German Scott' (Wenger 1905, 44); in spite of that, Alexis's novels are virtually forgotten today, unlike Arnim's decidedly more complex *Kronenwächter*.

Wilhelm Hauff's *Lichtenstein* (1826), like Ludwig Tieck's fragmentary *Der Aufruhr in den Cevennen* (The rebellion in the Cevennes, 1826), are also clearly modelled on Scott's novels. Hauff portrayed an incident in the history of the Lichtenstein family in the Middle Ages; the novel follows the *Ivanhoe* rather than the *Waverley* model (Geppert 2000, 491–92). Hauff saw German regional history as equivalent to the role Scottish history played in Britain (Steinecke 1975b, 41–42); Tieck's (unfinished) 'novella' is set in the Huguenot wars in 1703. Both place at the centre fictional protagonists, who are drawn into history at a moment of crisis; but their protagonists serve different functions from Waverley or Ivanhoe by bringing about some drastic, and ultimately important change in affairs. While Hauff's *Lichtenstein* was enormously successful and strongly influenced later German novels through its structure and use of Scott's model, it was Tieck's novella that contemporaries like Alexis praised for having discovered the true spirit of historical novels. Both Tieck and Alexis also published historical novels after 1830, when the image of genre had deteriorated (73–77), but then they changed the form and structure of the historical novel to render the text more *vaterländisch* (patriotic or national), such as Alexis's *Hans Jürgen und Hans Jochem. Vaterländischer Roman. Erste Abtheilung der Hosen des Herrn von Bredow* (Hans Jürgen and Hans Jochem. A patriotic novel. First part of the Master of Bredow's trousers, 1846) (Geppert 2000, 487–89) or his *Ruhe ist die erste Bürgerpflicht* (A citizen's first duty is to remain calm, 1852) (Eggert 1971, 152–53). Neither of the novels deserves a place in the literary canon, however.

From the middle of the 1850s, a surprising number of authors turned to the historical novel again; in fact, most of the important novels were produced in the second half of the century (Eggert 1971). Joseph Viktor von Scheffel's *Ekkehard* (1855), set in tenth-century Germany, was an enormously popular novel although there is little dramatic tension and no remarkable historical incident; instead, the novel propones a sort of historical idyll where even the Hunnish incursions do not really matter (168). But readers enjoyed the quiet irony as well as the subtle rendering of passions. Ten years later Adalbert Stifter, well-known for his collection of realist novellas and stories which are still read today and even used as set texts in school, published *Witiko* (1865–67), likewise set in the Middle Ages, but stylistically less polished than Scheffel's novel and structurally related to those of Scott's novels that place the social and cultural conditions of a particular period at the centre (191). Besides, unlike Scheffel's *Ekkehard*, Stifter's hero is not the passive or vacillating Waverley-type protagonist; Geppert sees close parallels to *Ivanhoe* (2000, 492–93). But Stifter's main interest lay in the parallel between the Bohemians' rebellion against a foreign ruler and the Revolution of 1848.

In the 1870s, after the German Kaiserreich had been established, a number of historical novels still well-known and read today were published. Gustav Freytag attempted to go beyond Scott by trying to depict the history of a family from fourth-century settlements until present times in six volumes (*Die Ahnen* / *Our Forefathers*, 1872–80); although the first of them, *Ingo und Ingraban* (1872), was rather frowned upon because of its setting in a remote past about which very little was known, the later novels were received more enthusiastically. Freytag's reputation had been already established with *Soll und Haben* (Debit and credit) in 1855. All of his novels are influenced by his political ideas – he had been the editor of the influential liberal newspaper *Die Grenzboten* from 1848 until 1871 – but *Die Ahnen* shows his growing resignation about the future for the German *Bildungsbürgertum* (educated middle classes) most clearly, and this seems to have been a major reason for readers and critics alike to prefer the first novels. On the whole, *Die Ahnen* was a strangely ambiguous project, combining criticism of contemporary developments with historical facts, but in a way that made neither wholly satisifying.

The most representative 'archaeological' novels were written by Georg Ebers, Felix Dahn and Adolf Hausrath; all held various professorships and were passionate historians. The best-known of them and indeed the only one still available today, Dahn's *Ein Kampf um Rom* (A struggle for Rome, 1876), pictures a series of fictional biographies centred around the Ostrogoths' fight for control over the Roman Empire after the death of Theodosius. Dahn presents history as a series of incidents arising mainly from conflicting passions; the political or social basis hardly plays a role in his novels.

The best-known of Scott's German successors is probably Theodor Fontane. Unlike most mid-nineteenth-century German authors of historical novels, Fontane had studied Scott's works intensively and translated many of the *Minstrelsy of the Scottish Border* ballads (Knorr 1961, 100–14), before he set to writing *Vor dem Sturm* (Before the storm, 1878), a 'patriotic' novel set in 1812–13. Like Scott, he described incidents that happened in the middle distance and focused on fictional, middle-class protagonists; and although German history did not lend itself easily to Scott's inherent model of national reconciliation, Fontane adapted it to the Brandenburg society of the Napoleonic Wars (Geppert 2000, 496–97). Partly this was because he knew intimately the region he was writing about; like Scott in Scotland, Fontane had travelled widely around the Mark Brandenburg. *Vor dem Sturm* was Fontane's first historical novel, but more were to follow (e.g. *Schach von Wuthenow* / Schach of Wuthenow, 1882) (Geppert 2000, 498–500). Literary critics were at first not much impressed; Fontane's tendency to focus not on one single protagonist but on several characters and their relations to each other was seen as inappropriate. However, his attempts to move beyond the 'simple' historical novel by attempting to draw a more subtle, intricate picture of society became more appreciated from the mid twentieth century.

After Fontane, few historical novels of any note followed that show evidence of having been influenced by Scott. Only Raabe's *Das Odfeld* (The Odin field, 1888), set in the Seven Years' War (1761), partly follows Scott in his use of dialogues and the historically accurate description of the battle scenes, though his characters and especially his narrator differ greatly from Scott's; *Das Odfeld* does not contain a positive outlook on history or historical developments, quite unlike Scott's novels.

In 1915, Alfred Döblin's *Die drei Sprünge des Wang-lun* (The three leaps of Wang Lun) radically changed the form of the German historical novel by introducing an expressionist style and form. Döblin had studied medicine in Berlin, specializing in neurology and psychiatry. Already during his student years he wrote novellas and novels that were influenced by his psychiatric studies; Döblin came to believe that a more neutral narrative style would have to be developed, which should leave judgements about the characters wholly to the reader. As a consequence, *Die drei Sprünge*, and even more so his later novel *Wallenstein* (1920), virtually 'narrate themselves', almost without order imposed by a narrator. Döblin was presented with the renowned Fontane Prize for his earlier novel; but it was *Wallenstein* that effectively ended the special position of the historical novel in that it is strictly speaking a novel without beginning or end; it has no (historically) dramatic structure, nor a clearly recognizable protagonist (Aust 1994, 116–20). Lion Feuchtwanger's *Die häßliche Herzogin Margarete Maultasch* (The ugly duchess, 1923) follows in Döblin's steps by focusing on a historical person, as does his internationally successful *Jud Süß* (Jew Süss, 1925) (Dietschreit 1988).

Although Scott's novels continued to be read and well-liked by German readers, then, the notable German authors had stepped out of Scott's shadow. Radically new ways of narrating were felt to be necessary for an adequate depiction of history and its relation to society in and after the First World War, at least in the eyes of the most gifted authors. Others (e.g. Georg Kutzleb, Friedrich Blunck, Erwin Guido Kolbenheyer) pursued different directions, partly using themes and motifs as well as structural elements from novels before 1900. During the 1930s and 1940s, historical novels – especially historical biographies as well as nationalistic or *Blut und Boden* (blood and soil) novels – were extremely popular (Westenfelder 1989), showing a specific, often mystified, image of history, which fitted neatly into Nazi ideology.

The reception of Scott in literary histories
Introduction: Reading and assessing English literature in Germany

While some research has been done on the development of histories of English literature in English (Stierstorfer 2000) and of histories of German literature in German (Fohrmann 1989), the historiography of English literature in German has not so far been the focus of much attention.

From the early eighteenth century, English literature had been of great interest to German intellectuals; towards the end of the eighteenth century, the focus of attention for many, if not most, German authors and literary scholars was Shakespeare. Comparisons of authors to Shakespeare, therefore, almost inevitably meant great praise. The first texts in German dealing with the history of British literature were written in the late eighteenth century. Among the most important names that deserve to be mentioned are August Wilhelm Schlegel and Johann Gottfried Eichhorn, who seems to have been the first German to write a history of English literature. Neither Schlegel nor Eichhorn dealt with Scott.

Any analysis of histories of British literature in German – especially in the nineteenth century – has to take the parallel publications in the British Isles into account, as they often set the standard and were used for reference by German authors. The first histories in German were translations of English histories. One of them was William Spalding's highly popular *History of English Literature* (1854). Even later, German authors would often rely on English literary histories, acknowledging the debt in prefaces or lists of sources; among the titles named are the *Cyclopaedia* (1844) and the *History of English Literature* (1837) by Robert and William Chambers.

The 1860s registered a peak in the publication of literary histories in English. Several older histories were reissued, yet new works also appeared, many of which proved to be lastingly popular with the readers; among them are George Lillie Craik's *Compendious History* (1861) and his *Manual of English Literature* (1862), and Thomas Shaw's, as well as William Collier's, *History of Literature* (1864; 1865). At the same time, the total number of literary histories in German that were original works, not translations of English texts, rose steadily until they reached their high-water mark in the 1880s. A total of ten different histories – including republications and reissues – can be traced. Judging from the number of editions during the next decades, the histories of Eduard Engel, Gustav Körting and Johannes Scherr were especially widely read. At the same time, they already show the broad range in style and contents that literary histories covered. While Körting's history consists of compressed facts and very short paragraphs, ideal for private students, Scherr's book represents, rather, the traditional narrative, whereas Engel combines his narration with plenty of references to his personal reading experiences.

The total number of histories in German steadily decreased in the period leading to the First World War. The ranks now also included histories of British literature in English, but written by Germans, for example Emil Penner's *History of English Literature* (1900). The use of literary histories not only for teaching at universities, but also increasingly at schools becomes evident in specifically produced textbooks such as Richard Ackermann's *Kurze Geschichte der englischen Litteratur in den Grundzügen ihrer Entwicklung* (Short history of English literature with the rudiments of Its development) (1902).

During and immediately after the First World War, virtually no new German-language histories were produced. The minor peak registered in the 1920s draws on older histories which were revised and reissued; most notably, Engel's *Geschichte der Englischen Literatur* (History of English literature), first published in 1884, reached its eighth and ninth editions. Georg Morris Cohen Brandes's *History*, however, was also republished (1924), which suggests an ongoing interest in realist historiography. The low number of German-language histories is partly due to the wartime and the post-war difficulties in Germany; however, the publication of the *Cambridge Modern History of English Literature* under the editorship of Adolphus Ward from 1909 onwards has to be taken into account too. It was the most influential and most comprehensive attempt by far to write the history of English literature, and it set new standards for historiography. While no translation into German seems to have been produced, a work of such standing was present in all notable libraries and universities and further decreased the need for new histories in German.

Under the Nazi regime, too, very few literary histories were produced (Hausmann 2003). Apart from Bernhard Fehr's *Die englische Literatur des 19. und 20. Jahrhunderts* (English literature of the 19th and 20th centuries, 1931) the only notable history of English literature was written by Walter Franz Schirmer in 1937. His *Geschichte der englischen Literatur von den Anfängen bis zur Gegenwart* (History of English literature from its beginnings to the present) was hailed by his contemporaries as the epitome of German historiography of English literature (167) for its accurate and perceptive rendering of literary history.

Scott and his works in literary histories
Descriptive techniques and reception patterns

Three basic approaches to Scott and his novels can be distinguished in the literary histories under review: the biographical or Positivist, the contextual, and the systematic or structural approach. While there is some overlap, most literary histories use only one approach. Their judgements on Scott and his novels vary according to the aspects stressed.

Biographical approaches

Early works especially regard literary history mainly as a sequence of authors producing a number of literary works. Literary histories that place Scott's biography at the centre tend to present Scott's literary output as linked to his circumstances in life, both with direct references and in more abstract terms. Examples are:

> The pride he took in descending from the 'noble' border robbers, whose 'nobility' like that of any nobleman in Europe is derived from stealing sheep and thieving, also led him to his literary début. (Bleibtreu 1887, 34)

Walter Scott's main merits, both as an author and as a novelist, consist in his immense naturalness (Wülcker 1896, 463)[3]

Every personal crisis, they claim, is mirrored by his production, as are more positive events. Whatever Scott uses in his novels from his life is duly noted (Bleibtreu 1887; Wülcker 1896). He is shown as a generous and self-effacing person with a strong sense of honour and duty. All biography-centred literary histories comment approvingly on his withdrawal from poetry (e.g. Bandow 1876, 72). His behaviour after the bankruptcy is even more applauded, though the phrasing tends to become less overtly enthusiastic over the years:

> This horrible disaster brought to light Scott's true strength of soul. He boldly confronted the difficulties (Bandow 1876, 73)

> Now, awakened from the dream of outward vanities, the whole high-mindedness of Scott's fundamentally noble nature unfolded (Bleibtreu 1887, 56)

> But Scott now showed his full strength of mind and resolve (Wülcker 1896, 462)[4]

The positive reaction to his personal likeableness, his honourable character and strength of mind is also extended to his work. That many of the later novels fail to convince the reader is more or less openly excused on grounds of his personal crisis.

> Such an over-exertion, increased by the pain about the loss of his wife, soon took its toll both on body and mind (Bandow 1876, 73)

> But Scott exerted himself beyond his limits, and the result was soon evident. [. . .] In April 1831 he suffered another stroke, and as he finished 'Castle Dangerous' and 'Count Robert of Paris' notwithstanding, his strength failed him completely so that he had to remove to a milder climate on the order of his doctors (Wülcker 1896, 462–63)[5]

---

[3] Sein Stolz auf die Abkunft von den adligen Räubern der Grenzdistrikte, deren 'Adel' sich wie der Adel in Europa überhaupt vom Schafestehlen und Räubern herleitet, begeisterte Scott denn auch zu seinem litterarischen Debut (Bleibtreu); Das Hauptverdienst Walter Scotts, des Dichters wie des Romanschriftstellers, war seine große Natürlichkeit (Wülcker).

[4] Diese schreckliche Katastrophe brachte Scotts wahre Seelengröße ans Licht. Er bot den Schwierigkeiten kühn die Stirn (Bandow); Da, aus dem Traum äusserlicher Eitelkeiten erwacht, entfaltete sich die ganze Hochsinnigkeit dieser im Grunde so edeln Natur (Bleibtreu); Aber Scott zeigte nun seine ganze Entschlossenheit und Thatkraft (Wülcker).

[5] Eine solche Ueberanstrengung, wozu noch der Schmerz um den Tod seiner Gattin kam, machte bald auf Geist und Leib ihren Einfluß geltend (Bandow); Doch arbeitete Scott über seine Kräfte, und das zeigte sich bald. [. . .] Im April 1831 traf ihn ein neuer Schlaganfall, und da er trotzdem noch den 'Grafen Robert von Paris' und das 'Gefahrvolle Schloß' vollendete, war er ganz entkräftet und mußte auf den Wunsch seiner Ärzte ein milderes Klima aufsuchen (Wülcker).

Biographically minded authors seem to find it hard to criticize Scott's works precisely because they like and sometimes admire his personality. Authors prefer to dwell on the strengths of the novels. Invariably the Waverley novels are seen as 'a long and splendid series of novels' (Bandow 1876, 75);[6] it is mainly Scott's powers of characterization, both of people and of times, that are singled out (Bandow 1876, 76; Bleibtreu 1887, 44–5; Wülcker 1896, 463–64). Defects or shortcomings in his novels are dismissed as on the whole inconsequential; even Karl Bleibtreu, who regards Scott more critically than do other commentators, finds it hard to stick to his negative opinion for long. A whole page is spent on showing and explaining the strengths, but he needs little more than one paragraph to point out the weaknesses of the novels (Bleibtreu 1887, 44–45). Characteristically Bleibtreu promises to explain the shortcomings by Scott's life and personality (45), but goes on first to quote at length some of Scott's poems, until both he and the reader have forgotten that an explanation is still pending (45 54).

For all authors of this kind of literary history it goes without saying that Scott deserves a place in the canon of English literature. While for some he simply is 'one of the most important authors [. . . and] in the strict sense an English classical author'[7] (Bandow 1876, iii), others are more precise: 'Scott is the founder of the historical novel. He was the first who cultivated the powerful poetry inherent in history.'[8] (Bleibtreu 1887, 59) Few authors single out novels which they regard as his most important or best; Bleibtreu calls *Waverley* one of his best (42), but seems to regard all novels published before 1821 as equally well written; Scherr (1874, 179) mentions Jeanie Deans and Rebecca as two of the most memorable characters. In the end, the authors award Scott his place in the history of literature more for his powers of description and characterization than for any specific work: 'The plastically realistic delineation of men, landscapes, and events is Scott's most characteristic feature, and enters with equal power into the different styles of his works'[9] (Scherr 1882 [1874], 198). More detailed descriptions of how Scott uses landscape in his novels are lacking, however (Müllenbrock 1994, 24). The mistakes Scott makes in an otherwise historically correct depiction of people and events are occasionally negatively noticed (e.g. Bleibtreu 1887, 59), but with regard to his superior powers of characterization usually ignored (e.g. Bandow 1876); Scherr (1874, 176) even

---

[6] 'Wir wenden uns nun zu der langen und glänzenden Reihe von W. Scotts Prosadichtungen.'

[7] '[Scott gehört zu den] bedeutendsten Erscheinungen [. . .] den englischen Classikern im engern Sinne.'

[8] 'Scott ist der Gründer des historischen Romans. Er war der Erste, der die gewaltige Poesie der Geschichte spurbar machte.' Here as elsewhere Bleibtreu echoes Scherr: 'Scott war der erste, welcher die Poesie der Geschichte in all ihrer Macht und Größe aufzeigte' (1874; 'Scott was the first who showed the poetry of history in all its grandeur.' [1882])

[9] 'Die sinnliche Plastik in der Schilderung von Menschen, Landschaften und Begebenheiten ist Scotts eigentlichstes Wesen. Sie tritt einem überall [. . .] gleich mächtig entgegen' (1874, 178). Bleibtreu is happy to echo the sentence (44).

notes that because of his historically faithful description of manners and customs, the historian Schlosser considers him one of the sources for historical
studies. The 1882 English edition of Scherr's history does not contain the
reference.

Contextual approaches

Literary histories using a contextual approach to their subject regard the social,
cultural and historical background of a specific author first, and place him and
his work in that context. As with biographically oriented literary histories, the
structure of literary texts is virtually irrelevant. As far as histories of English
literature in German are concerned, few German authors make full use of this
approach; but translations of two of the internationally important texts were
widely read in Germany: Hippolyte Taine's *Histoire de la littérature Anglaise*
(1906) (Die Neuzeit der englischen Literatur, 1880) and Brandes's lectures on
the main currents in nineteenth-century literature (1871–83) (*Hauptströmungen
der Literatur des neunzehnten Jahrhunderts*, 1872–78).

Both Taine and Brandes are critical of Scott because he does not do full credit
to historical veracity. Partly this is a by-product of his nationality (Taine 1906,
430). Nationality aside, however, Scott is shaped by his country; his tales
originate from the fights and robberies in Scottish history, and the traits of his
characters are influenced by Scottish Presbyterianism (439). Brandes, too,
believes Scott's nationality to be one of the key factors for his success (1876,
171), as Scott is stamped with a love for the geographical and national traits and
people of his country. For Brandes, this is connected to the historical situation:

> And it is therefore not surprising that, at the period when the spirit of nationality was
> breaking forth into poetry all over Europe, this county should produce a great
> descriptive, great narrative, poet – that it should be Scotland which brings forth
> the first and the most vigorous fruits of historical, ethnological Romanticism.
> (1905 [1876], 106)[10]

Körting points out that the situation within Britain also played its part: 'The
poets' minds fled from the narrow-minded and dull present into physically and
temporally remote times and chose the Middle Ages and the Orient for the
poetic setting' (1910, 362).[11] The latent escapism had already been noted by
Cunningham in 1834 and after him by other authors of literary histories, but
had been disregarded for the most part. Contextually minded authors consider

---

[10] 'Es kann also nicht Wunder nehmen, daß Schottland, als in diesem Lande ein
    großer epischer Dichter geboren wird, obendrein zu einer Zeit, wo das National-
    gefühl rings in Europa die Poesie durchdringt, die ersten und kräftigsten Erzeug-
    nisse der historischen und volkspsychologischen Romantik hervorbringt' (1876,
    172–73).
[11] 'Aus der beengten und dumpfen Gegenwart flüchtete der Sinn der Dichter sich in
    die zeitliche und räumliche Ferne, wählte das Mittelalter einerseits, den Orient
    andrerseits zum Schauplatz der poetischen Handlung.'

it a grave fault. It is precisely because Scott is so deeply rooted in his own times and nation that his historical novels fail to convince Taine and like-minded authors. To them, he does not attempt to recreate a past era, but simply uses his contemporaries as models for the past (Taine 1906 [1880], 436; Brandes 1906, 125; Körting 1910, 367). Consequently, though his characters are lively and engaging to the reader, the historical novel is doomed to fail because of its lack of historicity: 'Undoubtedly the faults inherent in the historical novel – which is indisputably a literary cross breed – could already be found in Scott's novels.'[12] (Körting 1910, 336–37). It is no surprise that all of them see the historical novel as antiquated (Taine 1905, 441; Brandes 1906, 125; Engel 1902, 445) and fit only for young readers:

> The author who in the second and third decades of the nineteenth century ruled the book-market [. . .] has become, by the silent, instructive verdict of time, the favourite author of boys and girls of fourteen or thereabouts, an author whom all grown-up people have read, and no grown-up people read.[13] (Brandes 1905, 127)

Yet all authors concede that Scott, as the founder of the historical novel, is entitled to hold a key position in the history of literature, both because he brought history and the novel together (Taine 1905, 434; Brandes 1906, 125) and because he opened up the novel for more realistic treatment of middle-class life – Taine even states that he was 'the Homer of modern citizen life' (440; similarly Brandes 1906, 119) and credits him with having invented the modern realistic novel almost by accident. Additionally, Scott's powers of characterization are pointed out by all the authors as exceptional; at the same time, all of them complain of his lengthy descriptions, which are considered 'tiring' (ermüdend) (Körting 1910, 367) and anyway 'exaggerated beyond measure' ('ins Maßlose gesteigert') (Engel 1902, 445).

As in the biographically oriented literary histories, authors rarely name the Scott novels they think the best, perhaps because all of them have grave faults; only Engel lists his favourites: *W, MO, AB, I, K, QD, GM* and six others, of which he believes only *K, I, QD* and *A* to have any lasting qualities (444–45). It seems, however, that Scott's personality and the overwhelming success of his work with the readers have charmed even critical authors; Taine's history clearly shows the author's fascination with Scott as a literary and cultural phenomenon (438), and Engel cannot help his nostalgia when he thinks back to reading his first Scott novel (444).

---

[12] 'Freilich aber haften die dieser Dichtungsgattung, die ja unleugbar eine Zwittergattung ist, notwendig innewohnenden Mängel auch schon Sc.'s [sic] Romanen an.'

[13] 'Der Dichter, welcher im zweiten und dritten Jahrzehnt unseres Jahrhunderts den literarischen Markt beherrschte [. . .] ist in unseren Tagen durch die stumme, aber lehrreiche Kritik der Zeit der Lieblingsdichter der Knaben und Mädchen von vierzehn Jahren geworden, ein Dichter, den jeder Erwachsene gelesen <u>hat,</u> aber den kein Erwachsener mehr <u>liest.</u>' (1876, 209; underlined words are printed in spaced letters for emphasis in the original.)

Systematic Approaches

Literary histories using a systematic approach consider neither the author's biography nor the social, historical or political contexts to be of great importance. Instead, they examine the texts themselves, dissect their key elements and analyse their relations and use in specific texts. Schirmer is the first to fully use this approach as a basis for his work.

In several literary histories, Scott's novels are classified according to their setting in time or according to their historicity (e.g. Scherr 1882, 196; Bandow 1876, 75–76; Ackermann 1902, 96–98). Schirmer goes beyond that. Unlike his predecessors he refrains from giving even a biographical outline of the author. Instead he divides Scott's life and work into three distinct phases that form the backbone of his text:

> It was by Sir Walter Scott's work that the Romantic movement first gained success and recognition throughout Europe. It can be divided into three periods. In the first, the preparatory phase (1796–1805), Scott was the collector, editor and translator. [. . .] When, almost by accident, he began composing lays, a genre invented by himself, the second, poetic period began (1805–1814). [. . .] Most important, however, both in historical and artistic terms is the third period of Scott's work (1814–1832) in which he wrote his novels.[14] (Schirmer 1937, 464–66)

The main part of Schirmer's text is taken up by an analytical discussion of the novels, beginning chronologically with *W.* Schirmer points out the main elements and shows their connection to each other and their effects on the reader; the contents of the novels are hardly relevant to his discourse:

> Waverley, the 'waverer', reduced the danger of distorting history and introduced the reader plausibly to various situations; it was later taken over by his successors.[15] (466)

Schirmer is clearly impressed by Scott's abilities, but refrains from open commendations. Only in passing does he give critical evaluations. He constantly tries to connect judgement and structure: 'In *Rob Roy* (1818) Scott returns to history. The well-narrated story, the wealth of characters and incidents attain

---

[14] 'Das Schaffen von Sir Walter Scott (1771–1832), das der englischen romantischen Schule Erfolg und europäische Geltung errang, läßt sich in drei Abschnitte gliedern. in der vorbereitenden ersten (1796–1805) war Scott der Sammler, Herausgeber und Übersetzer. [. . .] Als er dann fast zufällig zu der von ihm erfundenen Gattung des Lay [. . .] überging, begann seine zweite, dichterische Epoche (1805–1814). [. . .] Die größte Bedeutung, historisch wie künstlerisch, kommt aber der dritten Epoche in Scotts Schaffen zu (1814–1832), in der die Romane entstanden.'

[15] 'Waverley, den Wankler – die Gefahr historischer Verzeichnung verringerte und den Leser ohne Unwahrscheinlichkeit in die verschiedenartigsten Lagen einzuführen gestattete.'

the same high level as in *Waverley*[16] (467). Unlike many of his predecessors, Schirmer does not hesitate to enumerate Scott's best novels, explaining his choice structurally. While it is the plot in *OM* that is most varied and vivid through the portrait of Claverhouse, *HM* is renowned for Jeanie Deans and the depiction of the Porteus Riots (467). He likewise explains the popularity of the novels set in the Middle Ages by drawing attention to their broad historical pictures (467).

On the whole, Schirmer is favourable towards Scott: he may have made mistakes – especially in writing too quickly and not paying enough attention to plot lines – but he is convincing in his minor characters and a brilliant narrator (468). It is mainly Scott's use of – mostly medieval – history that Schirmer criticizes at the end of his analysis:

> We also take offence at his idea of history; often history is presented with loving care (Quentin Durward), but Scott only saw an ideal image of the Middle Ages, like a boy's dream [. . .] Scott's history is a pageant, on the whole too superficial, even with respect to human nature.[17]

Schirmer is the first to take into consideration that an author's reception and evaluation partly depends on what other authors have achieved in the meantime: '*We who have gone through the Realist school* take offence at the author's many interventions and at the often unrealistic monologues and dialogues'[18] (468). But this is no reason, so Schirmer states, to consider Scott a bad author, quite the contrary: a good novelist is an author whose imagination is full of characters and plots, like Scott (469). At the same time, Schirmer is also the first to emphasize the structural development of literature:

> Literary history has to stress especially that Scott broke with the common idea that a novel needs a moral, that he had very rare narrative powers, and that he was the first to achieve the imaginative revival of the past.[19] (469)

---

[16] 'In *Rob Roy* (1818) taucht das Geschichtliche wieder auf. Die gut erzählte Geschichte, die Fülle von Charakteren und die reiche Szenenfolge zeigt die gleiche Höhe wie Waverley [sic].'

[17] Wir stoßen uns ferner an seiner Auffassung der Geschichte; sie ist oft mit Sorgfalt dargestellt (Quentin Durward), doch sah Scott nur das Wunschbild des Mittelalters, wie ein Knabe es sich erträumen mag [. . .] Scotts Geschichte ist ein Trachtenaufzug, das Ganze ist uns zu sehr Oberfläche, Oberfläche auch im Menschlichen (Schirmer 1937, 468).

[18] '*Wir, die wir durch die realistische Schule gegangen sind*, stoßen uns daran, daß der Autor [. . .] so oft dazwischengreift, daß Monolog und Dialog so oft fern von der Wirklichkeit sind' (Schirmer 1937, 468; my emphasis).

[19] Die Literaturgeschichte vollends muß betonen, daß Scott mit dem Herkommen brach, wonach der Roman einen moralischen Zweck haben müsse, daß er die Gabe des Erzählens in seltenem Maße besaß und daß ihm als erstem die phantasiemäßige Wiederbelebung der Vergangenheit gelang.

Scott and his relations to German literature

Scott began his career as an author with translations from the German, of ballads such as Gottfried August Bürger's 'Lenore' and of plays, most notably Goethe's *Götz von Berlichingen*. Scott also knew several German historical novels; in particular he valued Benedikte Naubert's *Alf von Dülmen* and her *Herrmann von Unna*, both of which had been translated anonymously into English. There are even indications that some of Scott's techniques were borrowings from, or imitations of, Naubert's methods (Reitemeier 2001). Whereas Scott's praise of the anonymous translations was known only to a few, his early predilection for German *Schauerliteratur* (Gothic literature) was well known. Some literary historians took pride in this; others largely ignored the fact.

The earliest literary history, Allan Cunningham's *Biographical and Critical History* (1834a), does not mention German literature at all. Scott's translations in Matthew Gregory Lewis's *Apology for Tales of Terror* (1799) are dismissed as being an irrelevant first attempt: 'there is extant a letter from Monk Lewis, proving that even of that simple kind of stanza he could not be called the master.'[20] Only with 'Glenfinlas' does Scott show 'evidence of [poetical] genius' (42). Although Cunningham devotes a separate chapter to Scott's dramatic works (278–81) he keeps silent about the German source for *The House of Aspen*, Veit Weber's *Lesedrama* (closet drama), *Die Heilige Vehme* (The holy Vehme, 1797). Cunningham's translator Alexander Kaiser does not add remarks or notes of his own.

Twenty years later the translation of Spalding's *History of English Literature* (1854) does not refer to the influence of German literature on Scott either. In the same year, the German author Scherr has more to say about Scott's translations in his literary history. He notes that Scott 'found a spirit similar to his own'[21] (Scherr 1882, 193) in Bürger's and Goethe's texts and mentions the most important translations (193). Many Germans had felt some kind of national kinship with the English from the end of the eighteenth century, and this was even stressed in literary histories in the twentieth century (Engel 1915, 514). In phrases like Scherr's, however, the appeal of German literature to English, or Scottish, authors is predominant, forming a reverse side to that kinship. Scherr even considers the translations as a kind of literary self-education: 'After having gone through school, as it were, Scott began to produce texts of his own'[22] (1874, 174), thereby suggesting the importance of German literature for Scott's own work.

Another twenty years on, Karl Bandow implicitly attributes a far greater influence of German literature to the development of English literature, although he says very little:

---

[20] 'Ein noch vorhandener Brief von Monk Lewis beweist, daß er auch dieser simplen Stanzen nicht Meister war' (Cunningham 1834b, 37).

[21] 'ein der eigenen Dichternatur verwandtes Element' (1874, 174).

[22] 'Als er so gleichsam seine Schule gemacht hatte, verschritt er zur Originaldichtung.' The 1882 English edition does not contain the sentence.

It was precisely in those days that the Edinburgh *literati* became interested in German literature; Bürger, Goethe and other poets began to be well-known and were admired. Scott did not only read them, but even translated several poems, in particular 'Der Wilde Jäger', 'Lenore' and 'Der Erlkönig', and later the complete 'Götz von Berlichingen'.[23] (1876, 71)

Scott is presented as being actively interested in German literature; the fact that Bandow points to the admiration felt by the famous Scottish literati (both authors and historians) for German literature hints at its importance and at the same time at its superior quality. Implicitly he even attributes Scott's *Minstrelsy* to the influence that German literature had had on him (71).

The pride felt by German authors in the fact that Scott began his career with translations from the German is increasingly felt in histories published during the next decades. Engel (1884) refers to them as 'especially affect[ing]' Scott and adds that it is in particular 'their national stamp' which 'pleased their Scotch imitator above all things'[24] (1902, 443). Besides, Engel sees a lasting influence of German literature on Scott's own poems (443). Bleibtreu considers Scott's translations as a kind of literary support for home-grown romantic poetry[25] (1887, 35); Richard Wülcker tries to illustrate a development in Scott's literary abilities by adding that he turned one of Goethe's fragmentary poems, 'Der ungetreue Knabe' ('The faithless boy'), into a fully fledged and thematically and structurally round ballad (449); thus, the translations are presented as a kind of literary apprenticeship for Scott. Similar notions are held by Ackermann (1902, 93).

Later histories are far less interested in Scott's translations from the German. Körting only mentions them in a half-sentence (1910, 364), and the Zurich-based Fehr places the translations of German ballads in the wider context of Scott's preoccupation with foreign literature (1931, 82). Schirmer considers the translations together with Scott's editorial work as belonging to the first period, but does not see Scott's concern for translations as different from his interest in Scottish ballads (1937, 464–65).

A similar pattern can be traced in histories of German literature. Scott's influence on many German authors of historical novels as well as on historians such as Leopold von Ranke was not necessarily referred to at all. The histories of Ludwig Salomon (1881) and Wilhelm Scherer (1883) are hardly concerned

---

[23] Gerade zu jener Zeit war in den gebildeten Kreisen Edinburgs der Geschmack an deutscher Litteratur erwacht; Bürger, Goethe und andere Dichter fingen an bekannt und bewundert zu werden. Scott las sie nicht nur, sondern übersetzte auch mehrere ihrer Gedichte, wie 'den wilden Jäger' [sic], 'Leonore', 'Erlkönig' und später den ganzen 'Götz von Berlichingen'.

[24] 'An Goethes und Bürgers Dichtungen gefiel dem schottischen Nachdichter zumeist ihr nationales Gepräge' (1884, 538).

[25] '1796 hatte er nämlich Balladen von Bürger, besonders "Der wilde Jäger", und 1798 Goethe's [sic] "Götz" übersetzt und hiermit auch die deutsche Spuk- und Ritterromantik zur Verstärkung der heimischen Romantikblüte herangezogen.'

with Scott; neither his name nor titles of his novels or poems are found in the indexes. But Scott is mentioned in the text, especially in the passages on his first German imitator, Alexis. Both literary histories stress Alexis's accomplishments over those of Scott, pointing especially to his successful posing as 'the Great Unknown' himself in *Walladmor* (Salomon 1887, 450; Scherer 1883/[1929], 728). The personal achievement of Alexis is far more important than the imitative character, as it is one of the first landmarks of a 'national' German literature. August Friedrich Vilmar's remarks show this nationalistic attitude even more clearly:

> Wilibald Alexis [. . .] used to be called the German Walter Scott according to the bad habit originating from the times of our literature's dependency [on other literatures]. It would have been better to say that he had the same importance for northern Germany and specially for Prussia and the Mark Brandenburg, from which today's Prussia originated, as Scott had for Scotland and England. (Vilmar 1894, 572)[26]

That Scott's influence on other German authors of historical novels such as Alexis, Tieck, Dahn and Fontane is rarely mentioned in these histories is evidence for the attempt at minimising the dependency of German literary developments on foreign impulses at a time when it could serve to bolster Germany's national self-esteem.

Later histories of German literature treat Scott differently. Oskar Walzel's *Die deutsche Literatur von Goethes Tod bis zur Gegenwart* (German history from Goethe's death until the present, 1918), for example, has six index entries for Scott; in his passages on Charles Sealsfield (20), Scheffel's *Ekkehard* (50–51), Dahn and his fellow authors (70–72), but also on various minor historical novels, Scott constantly serves as a model for comparison. Hermann Ammon's *Deutsche Literaturgeschichte in Frage und Antwort von Luther bis zur Gegenwart* (German literary history: in questions and answers from Luther to the present, 1922) also contains several references, especially on Scott's influence on various authors (Tieck: 152; von Arnim: 153–54; historians: Ranke, von Giesebrecht: 190), although Ammon, too, tends to play it down on occasion:

> What effect has foreign literature on German literature [1850–83]? *As is true for every climax in German literary history, foreign influences are rare*, Classical literature is hardly

---

[26]   *Wilibald Alexis* aus Breslau (mit seinem bürgerlichen Namen *Wilhelm Häring*, 1798–1871) ward nach einer üblen Gewohnheit, die aus den Zeiten der Unselbstständigkeit unserer Litteratur herstammt, nur allzu oft als der deutsche Walter Scott bezeichnet. Besser hätte man gesagt, daß er für Norddeutschland und namentlich für Preußen, für die Mark Brandenburg, aus der Preußen hervorgewachsen ist, eine gleiche Bedeutung habe als Walter Scott für Schottland und England.

important; authors of comic texts are somewhat influenced by Laurence Sterne and Dickens, historical realism by Scott (Ammon 1929, 181; emphasis added).[27]

Conclusion

There are three different strands to the reception of Scott in Germany: German readers very early on appreciated Scott's novels, and it was only over the years that they became more specifically interested in the novels set in the Middle Ages, yet Scott's novels continued to hold a strong appeal for readers. German authors, at first equally enthusiastic, tried to appropriate Scott's model, but found that a full adoption was impossible, and therefore developed the historical novel along specifically German lines. As a result, historical novels varied greatly in quality and texture, from a simple imitation of Scott's basic ingredients to openly nationalistic books, both of which are largely forgotten today. Even major German authors of historical novels in the wake of Scott, such as Hauff or Alexis, were succesful with only one 'true' imitation; quite unlike Scott's, their later novels on a similar plan did not equally catch the readers' interest. Scott's model for literary fame could not simply be copied in Germany; more was needed – such as Fontane's congenial rendering of atmosphere – to ensure a lasting success.

The third strand of Scott's reception centres on the discovery and evaluation of Scott's work in the nascent genre of literary histories, which developed parallel to the rise of interest in English as a subject at school and at university. Literary histories commonly do not single out specific Scott novels for explanation or evaluation. They have little else on offer for German readers than the repetition of phrases that are rarely supported by arguments. Throughout the period under review, literary histories approvingly comment on Scott's use of structural elements that had been pointed out already by the first German reviewers. The evaluation of Scott does not change materially thoughout the nineteenth and early twentieth centuries. One reason lies in the traditional conservativism inherent in literary histories; but especially in the light of the changes in readers' and authors' views, this stagnation of opinions is highly interesting. After all, authors of literary histories were at the same time readers of novels, so it could be expected that the varying fortunes at least of some of Scott's novels would be reflected.

The extent and focus with which German literary histories treat Scott's translations runs parallel to the formation of the German Kaiserreich and can be regarded as a mirror for German self-esteem. As such, they show slight similarities in the reception of Scott to the way German authors change Scott's model. In the decades between the Franco-Prussian War of 1871, which had as its

---

[27] Wie wirkt das Ausland auf die deutsche Litteratur? – Wie an allen Höhepunkten der deutschen Literatur ist der ausländische Einfluß gering. Die Antike wirkt kaum; für die Humoristen sind die Engländer Sterne und Dickens nicht ohne Einfluß, für den geschichtlichen Realismus Scott.

ultimate result the formation of the Kaiserreich, and the turn of the century, the influence of German literature on Scott's own work is increasingly seen as important, until some notion of German model for Scott becomes apparent. After 1900, when the Kaiserreich had become firmly established, the need to mention German literature decreased.

Scott's merits as an author, then, do not undergo a radical change in histories of English literature published between 1820 and 1945; but the Germans' view on his involvement with German literature does, and that in turn has some influence on the perspective taken on Scott's work in histories of German literature. Where one could reasonably expect parallels in the reception of Scott by readers, authors of novels and authors of literary histories alike, few such similarities become visible, as if the three groups had different points of access to Scott's novels.

7 The Reception of Walter Scott in East, West and Reunified Germany (1949–2005)

Annika Bautz

I 1949 to 1990

East and West German literary markets

Between 1949 and 1990, Germany was divided into two separate states with different ideologies. This section investigates differences between the receptions in the two German states: though divided into separate countries, readers share a language and cultural history, which is not that of the author. Differences in reading between the two states indicate the immediate impact of culture, while similarities point to a specifically German reading.

Numbers and kinds of editions published in East and West Germany serve as a measure of public popularity of Scott's works and of the extent to which he was read. Prefaces to his novels indicate ways in which the works were read by the public as well as testifying to the critical literary reputation of the author and his works. Prefaces also give indications of Scott's cultural status through the ways in which preface writers presented him, as well as hinting at the implied readership, and revealing what it was about Scott that was thought noteworthy and appealing in each state. The chapter is therefore concerned with public as well as critical reputation.

Editions as well as prefaces are influenced by the two states' different literary markets, which are determined by their different ideologies: the West German market operated under the conditions of free market capitalism, and was therefore influenced largely by reader selection as one market force, whereas the East German literary market was subject to censorship and material restrictions. The West German market functioned much like the British one, but East German publishing conditions may need some explanation. To establish East German conditions, I have supplemented published accounts[1] with letters I received

---

[1] Barck, Langermann and Lokatis 1997; Emmerich 1989.

from former publishers in response to enquiries, as well as questionnaires I sent to people who used to live in the German Democratic Republic (GDR). Both publishers and general readers were very willing to share information about their past and ways of reading before the reunification.

Education was held high in GDR ideology, as 'the universal and harmonic socialist personality needed to be created and educated'.[2] Education should therefore be understood to contain the shaping of political ideas ('Bewusstseinsbildung'). According to Friedemann Berger, former director of the Gustav Kiepenheuer publishing house, the state 'imputed the central role in the intellectual and emotional education of the human being to literature before all other arts' (2003).[3] Some classic European novels were seen not only as harmless, but also as promoting these educational aims. Following Georg Lukács, the realism of the nineteenth century came to be seen as the highpoint of pre-socialist prose literature. This meant, as Berger points out, that in addition to Russian literature of this time, numerous nineteenth-century British authors were at the centre of the East German translation activities. These three factors were favourable to the publication of Scott: the state emphasized the general and political education of its citizens, it imputed to literature a leading role in this education, and it saw realistic classical novels as part of this educational literature.

There were two main obstacles to be overcome in order to get published in the GDR, censorship and shortage of paper. Elke Maes, citizen of the former GDR, comments that in a centralized state, whose aim it was to get bourgeois thinking out of people's heads and Marxist–Leninist thinking into them, education as well as all other areas of social life were of course centrally managed and controlled.[4]

Censorship arose out of the paradoxical aim to 'promote and at the same time control [literature]' (Barck, Langermann, Lokatis 1997, 12).[5] A publishing house needed a licence from the Ministry of Culture to bring out a book. Few books were rejected each year, not due to literary liberalism, but because censorship began prior to submission of manuscripts. Every author knew the conditions and subjected himself to self-censorship ('Schere im Kopf', scissors in the head).[6] The publishing house's lectors (readers) would usually supervise an author's work in progress, so that authors generally did not present a finished

---

[2]   Dr Elke Maes on East German publishing conditions (2003). See also Barck, Langermann and Lokatis 1997, 12, 'die allseitig und harmonisch entwickelte sozialistische Persönlichkeit galt es zu bilden und erziehen'. All translations from German originals are mine unless otherwise stated.

[3]   'schrieb der Literatur vor allen anderen Künsten die entscheidende Rolle bei der intellektuellen und emotionalen Bildung des Menschen zu'.

[4]   'Selbstverständlich war in einem zentralistischen Staat, dem es darum ging, bürgerliches Gedankengut raus aus den Köpfen und marxistisch-leninistisch geprägtes Gedankengut hinein zu bringen, Bildung wie auch alle anderen Bereiche des gesellschaftlichen Lebens zentralverwaltet und gesteuert.' (2003)

[5]   'zu fördern und gleichzeitig zu kontrollieren'.

[6]   Maes 2003; Baadke 2004b; see also Emmerich 1989, 39–40.

work to a publisher. The director of the publishing house decided whether or not to present the work to the Ministry of Culture and thus served as another filter. The same was true for translations: every publishing house had its authorized translators, whose work was supervised, and their translations needed permission to be printed. Friedrich Baadke, lector of the East German publishing houses Aufbau Verlag and Rütten & Loening, points out that even where a finished manuscript was deemed unsuitable, it would not be rejected. Instead, the publishing house would be asked to withdraw its application, 'so that censorship did not become obvious as such' (Baadke 2004b).[7]

Books were cheap, but due to censorship the choice was limited mainly to Russian and GDR literature as well as classics. Because of paper shortage, there were never enough even of those books that were thought to be harmless – though there was of course always enough paper for the works of Marx and Lenin. Paper shortage thus facilitated censorship, as the size of editions could be controlled through paper contingents. Borrowing and lending were therefore important features, which makes the reception of an author harder to assess. Readers tended to buy a book just because it was uncertain how long it would be possible to do so. In connection with this, readers find that they buy fewer books now, when there is an 'over-supply', than they did when books were more difficult to obtain.

One reply relates an anecdote of a woman who had a conversation with an Englishman in the 1980s about different reading habits. He comments on her being very well-read, before saying that he assumes GDR citizens would read so much because of restrictions in their way of life. She was enraged at this patronizing remark, as she perceived it, but writes that she now believes that the man was partly right. She concludes: 'I realize now that I do read different things since the reunification, read differently, and all in all much less.'[8]

Friedrich Baadke makes similar observations, from a publisher's point of view, about reading patterns before and after the reunification, especially where English authors were concerned: before the reunification, the question had been:

> 'Will we get it through (censorship)?' [. . .] The question after the reunification was 'will it sell?' As regards the last question, we had no experience because we did not have to worry about sales of our limited print runs where authors with an English name were concerned. (2004a)[9]

---

[7] 'so dass die Zensur nicht als solche in Erscheinung trat'.

[8] Questionnaire number 8, filled in by a 51-year-old woman who lived in the GDR from her birth until 1990, 'Ich realisiere jetzt dass ich seit der Wiedervereinigung wirklich andere Dinge lese, anders lese, und überhaupt viel weniger.' (I have numbered the questionnaires in the order I received them, between February and June 2003, and they were anonymous.)

[9] Kriegen wir es durch (die Zensur)? [. . .] Nach der Wende lautete die Frage: läßt es sich verkaufen? Hinischtlich der letzten Frage hatten wir keine Erfahrungen, denn um den Absatz unserer begrenzten Auflagen brauchten wir uns bei Autoren mit englischen Namen keine Soren zu machen.

Quite apart from the state promoting classic authors, this hints at a special taste for English – Western – authors' works among general readers.

Western travellers' observations confirm that East Germans and Russians generally read more books: comparing London to Leningrad underground, or West to East German trains, travellers remarked that the image of the former is dominated by newspapers and magazines, the latter by people reading books.[10] In a state that strongly promotes literature, and whose magazines and newspapers are homogenous because they are controlled by the state ('gleichgeschaltet'), people read more novels. The promotion of literature as well as its limited availability resulted in a nation of readers that were eager to get hold of books.[11]

Editions and reissues of Scott's novels in East and West Germany

East and West German literary markets were independent of one another and therefore featured Scott in different ways and at different times.[12] Thirteen of Scott's novels have been published in translation in Germany since 1949, ten titles in the East and eleven in the West. Table 1 opposite shows which of Scott's novels were published in East and West Germany.

Table 1 indicates that the titles printed in East and West are mostly identical, and comprise Scottish as well as medieval titles. The most significant differences in choice of titles in East and West Germany are the publication of four versions each of *The Tale of Old Mortality* (*OM*) and *The Fair Maid of Perth* (Das schöne Mädchen von Perth) in East Germany and none in West Germany. Prefaces to the former emphasize Scott's being biased 'in favour of the rights of the people' (Baadke 1978, 550)[13] and the people's 'never unimportant role in the great historical events' (Schulz 1955, 857),[14] so that the choice of this novel in a communist state seems no coincidence. *The Fair Maid of Perth* is not accompanied by a preface. Considering that East German prefaces' role was also to ensure that readers read the novel in the correct way, the absence of prefaces to any of the four versions of the novel indicates that it was deemed

---

[10] E.g. Gamerschlag 2003; conversation with Claire Lamont, 21 January 2003.
[11] Wolfgang Emmerich confirms the importance of books (1989, 24): 'The GDR, together with Japan and the Soviet Union, publish[es] more books per head of population than any other nation. About a third of this [is fiction].' 'die DDR, was die Pro-Kopf-Produktion von Büchern angeht, [steht damit] neben der Sowjetunion und Japan an der Spitze in der ganzen Welt. . . etwa ein Drittel davon [ist Belletristik].'
[12] I am looking at translated versions only. There is just one English version of a Scott novel published in Germany, *Ivanhoe* in 1949 by Quelle & Meyer in Heidelberg. This has been left out of my discussion since it is not indicative of how most readers would have read Scott. Especially in West Germany, imported English editions would also have been available, but since it is impossible to determine how many of these were sold in Germany I am excluding them.
[13] 'seine Parteinahme für die Rechte des Volkes [ist] unübersehbar'.
[14] 'ihren nie unwichtigen Platz im großen historischen Geschehen'.

Table 1 *Novels by Scott published in East and West Germany*

	East		West		Britain
					Titles published by Penguin following the Edinburgh Edition of the Waverley Novels (1993–2005)
Title	*Numbers of versions published★*	*Title*		*Numbers of versions published★*	
Ivanhoe	10	Ivanhoe		31	✔
Quentin Durward	4	Quentin Durward		11	✔
The Tale of Old Mortality	4	–		–	✔
The Fair Maid of Perth	4	–		–	–
The Talisman	3	The Talisman		3	–
Kenilworth	3	Kenilworth		1	✔
Rob Roy	1	Rob Roy		3	✔
The Heart of Midlothian	3	The Heart of Midlothian		1	✔
Waverley	2	Waverley		2	✔
The Bride of Lammermoor	2	The Bride of Lammermoor		1	✔
–	–	Legend of Montrose		1	–
–	–	Anne of Geierstein		1	–
–	–	The Black Dwarf		1	–
–	–	–		–	Redgauntlet
–	–	–		–	The Antiquary
–	–	–		–	Guy Mannering
–	–	–		–	Chronicles of the Canongate

★ As it is not always possible to distinguish an edition from a reissue I have used the term 'version', meaning a 'publishing event'. This includes abridgements and children's versions.

self-explanatory. Given its working-class heroism contrasted with the constitutional cowardice and malice of the King and his son, the choice to publish this novel in East Germany again appears obvious.

The general similarities between titles chosen in East and West also coincide with the most popular Scott titles in Britain. The novels selected by Penguin for publication following the Edinburgh Edition of the Waverley Novels are mostly the same as the ones chosen by East and West German publishers: *Ivanhoe, Quentin Durward, The Tale of Old Mortality, Kenilworth, Rob Roy, The Heart of Midlothian, Waverley, The Bride of Lammermoor, Redgauntlet, The Antiquary, Guy Mannering* and *Chronicles of the Canongate*. Regardless of national culture and political ideology, these titles appear to be the ones that most appeal to a late twentieth-century readership.

Counting the number of versions, the most popular novel in East and West is *Ivanhoe*, though in the West this novel was published more often than all other Scott novels taken together. There are thirty-one West German versions of *Ivanhoe*, and apart from *Quentin Durward* (eleven versions), no other novel is issued more than three times. Versions included are those I have seen, or are in the German Library in Frankfurt, or are listed in the Bibliography of Scottish Literature in Translation.[15] One of the three was enough for inclusion; if a version was mentioned anywhere else but did not fulfil any of the above it was ignored. There are bibliographical problems in determining the relative popularity of each Scott title. The novels appeared in different versions, sometimes new editions, but often reissues, and sometimes abridged or in children's versions. It is not always possible to distinguish between an edition and a reissue, and abridgements are sometimes not much abridged at all, so I refer to them as 'versions', meaning by version a 'publishing event'. The size of editions presents another difficulty. In the West, publishers have generally refused to disclose them, though in the East they would probably be determinable, because the 'Druckgenehmigungsakten' (printing-permission files) for each publication are kept in the Federal Archive in Berlin. Just like numbers of editions and reissues, however, sizes of editions cannot necessarily be seen as indicators of popularity of a work in East Germany: as in the system described above, readers' demands were not the deciding factor. The version most often reissued in West Germany is in fact an abridgement, of *Ivanhoe*, though a slight one. First published in 1949 by Hoch-Verlag, in a translation by Carl Mandelartz, it has individual titles for the chapters and includes 43 instead of the original 44 chapters (Chapter 14 being left out completely), as well as abridging many selected passages.

Only *Ivanhoe* and *Quentin Durward* were issued significantly more often in the West than in the East, the other novels existing in equal numbers. In view of a much smaller population and a limited literary market place in the East, equal numbers point towards a relatively higher positioning of Scott in the East than in the West. In the West, *Ivanhoe* was therefore published more often than all other Scott titles taken together. In the East, the novel's percentage of the overall Scott market is about 30 per cent, making *Ivanhoe* a popular Scott title, but one existing within a group of Scott novels.

Especially in the 1950s and 1960s, *Ivanhoe* dominates the West German market and hardly any other Scott titles are published. Even after that however, the increase in titles published is partly due to the three publications by Goverts Verlag of one version each of *The Bride of Lammermoor*, *Waverley*, and *Anne of Geierstein*, none of which have been reissued, and similar non-reissued publications by Ullstein of *The Black Dwarf* and *A Legend of Montrose*. There being more Scott titles available in the East than in the West in spite of the East's more limited literary market, as well as these titles existing in more than one version between 1949 and 1990, shows the author's literary status to have been higher in the East than in the West.

15   BOSLIT; <http://boslit.nls.uk> (accessed 25 March 2005).

Translations

The evidence of translations supports Scott's higher position in the East. Because of the complete division between the East and West German literary markets, the two states usually did not publish and often did not even know of each other's translations, nor did they make each other's publications available. In most cases, translations used in East and West Germany are different ones. While East German editions tend to be based on newly commissioned translations, most of the West German editions are based on nineteenth-century translations. Some of these date from as early as the 1820s, when Scott was first translated into German. Different East German editions are always based on the same translation, whereas there is some variety in the translations used for different editions in West Germany. There are two instances of an East German translation being published in West Germany (*Waverley* 1982 and *The Heart of Midlothian* 1987), and none vice versa. Roland Links (2003), former director of an East German publishing house, explains that as East German currency was not compatible with West German currency, publishers avoided using West German translations, and instead either used one out of copyright for which they would not have to pay, or commissioned a new translation. Friedrich Baadke (2004b) confirms this practice, emphasizing the care that was taken over translations, stating that because of the 'strict criterion of truthfulness to the text' ('Texttreue'), classic authors were almost always newly translated. As a lector, a large part of his job was to edit newly made translations 'in a sentence-by-sentence comparison with the original' ('Satz-für-Satz-Vergleich').

The thirty-one West German versions of *Ivanhoe* are based on ten different translations, whereas the ten versions in the East are all based on the same one (see Table 2 overleaf). In East Germany, a new translation of *Ivanhoe* is commissioned and abided by throughout. In West Germany, a variety of translations used, many of them dating from the nineteenth century. The majority of new translations tend to be abridgements rather than exact translations, testifying to the West-German attitude being the opposite of the East-German emphasis on 'Texttreue'. *Ivanhoe* is extreme in the number of abridgements in which it is published in West Germany, but patterns of translations in East and West Germany for Scott's other novels nevertheless show similar patterns to the one above: East Germany commissions one new translation and bases all editions on that, West Germany reuses the existing nineteenth-century ones and contract very few new translations (*Ivanhoe* and *Rob Roy* are the only two of Scott's novels that are newly translated in West Germany). Sample examinations of translations confirm these findings: East German translations are on the whole close to the text, though occasional slight ideological colourings occur. These differences in translation practice point to East Germans regarding Scott as a more serious author, of higher literary quality.

Table 2 *Translations of* Ivanhoe *published in East and West Germany*

East (10 versions of Ivanhoe)			West (31 versions of Ivanhoe)		
Translator	Year of trans.	Number of versions based on this trans.	Translator	Year of trans.	Number of versions based on this trans.
Christine Hoeppener	1952	10	Carl Mandelartz (slightly abr.)	1949	11
			Rudolf Hermann (abr.)	1973	4
			Leonhard Tafel (edited by Paul Ernst in 1911)	1827/ 1911	3
			Inge Lehmann (abr.)	1968	3
			Ernst Susemihl	1860	1
			Benno Tschischwitz	1880	1
			Burkhard Busse, editing a 19th-c trans.	19th cen- tury/ 1983	1
			Katerina Horbatsch (abr.)	1976	1
			Elisabeth Ciccione	1964	1
			Paul Frischauer (abr.)	1967	1
			Not cited	1953, 1957, 1963, 1981	4

Prefaces/Epilogues

This section addresses the critical reception and representation of Walter Scott in East and West Germany by assessing prefaces to his novels. It discusses what introductions are determined by and to what extent they reflect cultural and critical trends of their period. A discussion of prefaces in connection with the evidence of kinds of editions and versions also illuminates the relation between critical and public popularity of an author, showing whether prefaces reflect or influence developments in an author's public reputation, or whether they do both. Of all scholarly essays on a novel, introductions are most likely to reach general readers. The kind of readership introductions address reveals critics' perceptions of the relation between public and critical readers, as well as to what extent they construct rather than just reflect expected readership, and whether they see themselves as cultural mediators. Prefaces and epilogues show how

Scott was presented in East and West Germany and what about him was thought to appeal, and to what group of readers.[16]

A quantitative comparison of prefaces[17] to Scott's novels in East and West Germany reveals that in the West, only 34 per cent (one-third) of Scott's novels had a preface at all, and the great majority of these were less than three pages long. In the East, 54% (more than half) of Scott's novels had a preface, almost all of which were longer than the ones in the West (the longest consisting of forty-four pages).

The inclusion of a preface indicates that the reader was expected to have an interest in the novel or its author beyond the immediate text, or that this interest needed to be created. In either case, the above data suggests that East German publishers cared more about how a novel was to be read, as well as showing that Scott was taken more seriously as an author of literature that needed an explanation. The majority of West German publishers did not see the need for supplementary explanation, indicating Scott's lower literary rank in the West.

Literature was seen as contributing to the education of GDR citizens and prefaces were one way of ensuring this aim. In the West, prefaces appear to be designed to attract readers to buy and enjoy, whereas East German preface writers direct their essays more towards making sure that the reader reads a book in 'the correct' way, which would also have promoted the book to the Ministry of Culture. That some Scott novels appear in the East without a preface, such as *The Fair Maid of Perth*, reflects the level of acceptance he enjoyed with the censors, while the fact that the majority of his novels in East Germany do include a preface indicates his high literary status.

Most prefaces in East and West Germany are thus not the critical introductions that we now associate with the reprinting of novels: they are not influenced by the demands of education in schools and universities, but are primarily designed for private readers and so arise from the world of publishing.[18]

In the following text, I examine points typically brought up in East or West German prefaces, as well as their general tone and attitude. To illustrate these points I am, wherever possible, using examples from *Ivanhoe* as the most widely read novel, though others are considered as well. There are three East and two West German prefaces to *Ivanhoe*, all of which are representative of East and West German prefaces generally. The two West German ones are short, largely biographical, and do not discuss the novel; the three East German ones are longer and more analytical.

Prefaces of both countries by their very nature generally approve of the book, as their publishers' object is to promote it. In the East, the book had to

---

[16]   For a full list of German prefaces to Scott's novels see the Bibliography.

[17]   Read 'prefaces or epilogues'. For simplicity's sake I refer to them as prefaces.

[18]   The first and only German edition of Scott to have a critical introduction of that sort in either East or West Germany between 1949 and 1990 is Gamerschlag's 1982 edition of *Waverley*, so my discussion of what prefaces typically contain does not consider his.

be recommended to the Ministry of Culture, which may be one reason why East German prefaces are more laudatory than West ones. East and West differ in their attitudes: in the East, Scott is presented as an author of literary works that can be read for both enjoyment and instruction. Bruno Kaiser in his 1952 epilogue to *Ivanhoe* points out that Scott is 'very entertaining' (678)[19] and arrives at an 'impressive critical and truthful superiority' (679)[20] through a thorough study of the historical sources. In the majority of East German prefaces, the main aim is to present Scott as a great writer. This greatness is shown within the framework of a communist ideology; he is great because he is read as promoting communist ideals of literature and society. East German prefaces base this greatness on the combination of realism, accurate and serious representation of the people, and the depiction of the people's role in historical progress. Klaus Udo Szudra in his 1972 epilogue to *Ivanhoe* interprets Scott's view of history from a Marxist perspective, from which 'the people as the epicentre of a coordinate system of unconciliatory historical antagonisms are the power that actually guarantees progress' (600).[21] East German prefaces regard Scott's novels as relevant for today, which is typical of East German prefaces to novels generally and repeatedly emphasized in questionnaires. Thus Kaiser sees 'incessant parallels' between Scott's novels and today's situation (GDR in 1952); just as in *Ivanhoe* the best English people are seen to fight the foreign occupants, so the East German people fight for national independence against imperialistic oppression now. The representatives of oppression today are just as brutal and false as the Norman knights Malvoisin and Front-de-Boef, and the working people were leading the fight for independence centuries ago as well as now. Kaiser makes these statements harder to disagree with by phrasing them as rhetorical questions.[22] He uses abstract parallels and, as has also been pointed out by Rainer Schüren, these mean that 'he can deceive the reader and *not* point out Scott's objective way of presenting history' (1969, 204). All three East German prefaces to *Ivanhoe* gloss over the complexity of the different conflicts. Aristocratic Saxons, serfs, outlaws, and Jews are not distinguished, instead the conflicts are either explicitly or implicitly reduced to 'the people' against the aristocratic Normans. The prefaces ignore Scott's promotion of compromise as a solution to historical antagonisms.

When discussing Scott's hero, a similar technique is applied. East German prefaces commend Scott's hero for being unidealized, an ordinary character who, in Szudra's words, 'does not appear as a larger-than-life maker of history,

---

[19] 'sehr unterhaltsam'

[20] 'erstaunlichen kritischen und wirklichkeitstreuen Überlegenheit'

[21] 'das Volk als Mittelpunkt im Koordinatensystem unversöhnlicher historischer Gegensätze ist die eigentliche, den Fortschritt verbürgende Potenz.'

[22] 'Ist der Kampf der Besten des englischen Volkes gegen die fremden (französischen) Okkupanten nicht gleich dem Kampf des deutschen Volkes für nationale Unabhängigkeit, gegen imperialistische Unterdrückung?' (1952, 679)

continuously committing world-shaking deeds [but who embodies the consciousness of his time] beyond such heroic-legendary stylization' (1972, 610).[23] This is part of Scott's greatness. Szudra again stays abstract, allowing him to be unclear about the distinction between 'ordinary character' and 'the people'. Scott's hero therefore appears to be one of the people, which is of course rarely the case in Scott's novels. Again, the argument shows both perceptive understanding and ideological colouring.

The strategic use of quotations by literary and political authorities emphasizes Scott's greatness. Apart from Karl Marx and Friedrich Engels, who come up in almost every East German preface, important people mentioned include Johann Wolfgang von Goethe, Thomas Mann, Heinrich Heine, Alexander Pushkin, George Sand and George Eliot. They are cited almost irrespective of the content of their judgements, indicating that the people quoted are more important than the quotations themselves. This technique of including important people again hints at preface writers' consideration of the censors during the composition of the essays, as well as showing their ideological colouring. Szudra for example states that Scott's romantic nostalgia for the past, exemplified in the depiction of the Scottish clans, gives some of his novels a 'poetical gleam' ('poetischen Schimmer' (1972, 612)) and blurs his perception of reality. Szudra connects his assertion of Scott's unrealistic romanticism with a quote from Engels, who states that if he himself had been ruler at the time, he would also have had to end 'the infamous actions of these fellows' ('Schindhansentum dieser Burschen' (612)). However, Szudra later states that the romantic elements support the realistic import, as the romantic ones stir "the readers' empathy" ('Teilnahme der Leser' (615)). Szudra's meaning of 'romantic' has shifted from meaning unrealistic to meaning emotional, or evocative of emotion, rather than being biased by emotion. This shift again indicates that Szudra only uses Engels's quotation because it is by Engels, not because of its contents. Also, the quotation's negative impact is lessened by his assertion that Engels, 'like Karl Marx, was a lifelong warm admirer of Scott' ('zeitlebens ein warmer Bewunderer Scotts' (612)).

The general perception of Scott as conservative in personal politics might have presented a problem to East German preface authors. Georg Lukács presents Scott as writing realistically almost against his will:

> Undoubtedly, there is a certain contradiction here between Scott's directly political views and his artistic world picture. He, too, like so many great realists, such as Balzac or Tolstoy, became a great realist despite his own political and social views. In Scott, too, one can establish Engels's 'triumph of realism' over his personal, political and social views. [. . .] [His] great historical art arose precisely out of the interaction, out of the dialectical interpenetration of both these sides of Scott's personality.

---

[23] 'keine zu heroischen Kolossen stilisierten Elitemenschen die in einem fort weltbewegende Taten begehen, sondern schlichte Vertreter des Volkes, die das Bewußtsein ihrer Zeit über eine solche Stilisierung hinaus verkörpern.'

It is precisely because of his character that Scott did not become a Romantic, a glorifier or elegist of past ages. And it was for this reason that he was able to portray objectively [. . .] in a large historical and artistic sense: he saw at one and the same time [the] outstanding qualities [of past social formations] and the historical necessity of their decline. (1989, 54–55)

Scott's political conviction is shown to enhance his art, as his realism and objective historical presentation gain credibility if seen in the context of his personal politics. The people's significance in historical developments thus becomes something anyone possessing 'sober rationality' (54) has to realize, and there can be no doubt of the validity of this interpretation of history if even those, like Scott, who would most likely oppose this view cannot but become its advocates. Scott, a 'sober, conservative petty aristocrat' (54) in his personal life, can thus as an artist be seen as a predecessor to socialist ideology, writing realistically about the major historical developments of his country, in favour of progress, and depicting the people as a major part of these developments. Instead of preventing realism, the two sides of Scott's personality generate it.

Preface writers use Abbotsford to emphasize Scott's personal conservatism. Elisabeth Schulz in her 1956 preface to *Kenilworth* presents Scott as being himself an anachronism, as his social ambitions lead to his attempting to live the life of a 'medieval squire' ('mittelalterlichen Edelmannes', (652)) and to his building 'castle Abbotsford' (653). By not specifying the kind of castle Abbotsford is, she evokes the image of a much grander castle than Scott's home in the readers' mind. However, she also strongly emphasizes Scott's love for the people and realistic way of writing, thereby following Lukács's argument.

Not all East German writers adopt Lukács's view. For some, Scott's personal opinions do not play an important role at all, and these writers focus entirely on the texts. Some stay abstract in their descriptions of Scott's personal politics, calling him 'in no way a revolutionary' ('keineswegs ein Revolutionär') (Ilberg 1965, 541) or 'liberal' (545) to avoid a contradiction between man and art. Some bring in general context without connecting that to Scott in any detail, such as Günther Klotz in his 1959 preface to *HM*, who presents the French Revolution as having made possible Scott's view of history as progress and as history of the people, but does not explain this any further (Klotz, 5). Thus in no East German reading is Scott's greatness as a writer diminished by his perceived personal conservatism, because the focus is on the political dimension of the works. All East German preface writers focus on content as the factor that makes the works great.

West German writers show less interest in Scott's politics and often leave them out completely. If his personal opinions come up they are usually reduced to a nostalgic conservatism, evident in his love of the past and his romanticism, rather than a more political conservatism, though in prefaces of both countries political conservatism, romanticism, and Scott's home Abbotsford are connected. Traude Dienel's epilogue to *Quentin Durward*, published in West Germany in 1976, presents Scott as having wanted to live in the past and 'having dreamt almost since his childhood of gaining back the old glory [of the Scottish aristocracy]. He could finally fulfil his dream by buying the land that had belonged to his ancestors on his father's side (and which had witnessed the obligatory bloodshed) and having his castle Abbotsford built there, which was a mixture of the county seat of a squire, a museum, a national shrine, and a stage set' (Dienel, 599).[24]

Abbotsford is used to illustrate Scott's romanticism: buying his ancestors' land is a romantic and emotional rather than a practical act, having a castle built is an even more romantic step towards the past (especially considering that, like Schulz's readers, Dienel's are likely to picture a castle like one of the great German ones), and her list of Abbotsford's qualities is taking further the same point of proving him to be unrealistic and living in his own fictional world.

While East German prefaces present Scott as idealizing the present, and as believing that the constitutional monarchy is the end-goal of historical progress, West German ones see Scott as romanticizing the present and the past, thereby asserting that his novels are necessarily romantic rather than realistic. Thus in the East his romanticism is in contrast to his novels, whereas in the West it complements them.

Instead of presenting Scott as great, West German authors of prefaces diminish his literary significance. The emphasis is on romanticism and universal accessibility, rather than on realism and topicality. He is presented as a great entertainer whose novels have adventure-story traits. Paul Ernst, in his epilogue to *Ivanhoe*, places Scott in a category below greatness (1984, 617): 'Only very few authors are on [the] highest level, and we will be grateful that there is a lesser level, to which belong so many men who can delight and entertain us. Among these, Scott is one of the best.'[25] His works amuse and are therefore worth reading.

West German prefaces do not provide as deep or as wide an analysis as their East German counterparts do. Their prefaces are less well researched and contain more factual mistakes. One obvious example occurs in Ernst's epilogue to *Ivanhoe*, written as long ago as 1911, and published three times between 1949 and 1990, and twice since then (1984, 1985, 1989, 1993, 1996). The date already shows that the object of including this epilogue cannot be to convey information about issues such as current developments in criticism, or about Scott's specific relevance to today. Ernst misquotes the title of Scott's first novel, calling it 'Waverley, oder so war's vor fünfzig Jahren' ('Waverley, or

---

[24] 'In mittleren Jahren konnte er seinen Jugendtraum verwirklichen: er kaufte jenen Grundbesitz, der seinen Vorfahren von Vaterseite gehört hatte (und auf dem es standesgemäß blutig zugegangen war) und ließ dort sein Schloß Abbotsford errichten, eine Mischung von Herrensitz, Musum, Nationalheiligtum und Bühnendekoration.'

[25] 'Auf [der] höchsten Stufe stehen nur sehr wenige Dichter: wir wollen dankbar sein, daß es noch eine geringere Stufe gibt, auf der sich so viele Männer befinden, die uns erfreuen und unterhalten können. Unter ihnen ist Scott einer der vozüglichsten.'

'tis fifty years since', when it should of course read 'or 'tis sixty years since' (Ernst, 615)).[26] The repeated inclusion of this mistake shows up West German attitudes to Scott, as anyone at all acquainted with Scott's novels would spot it. Not only the publisher in 1911, but also the publisher in 1984 and the publishers of all subsequent editions can either not have realized the mistake, not have heeded it, or not have cared enough about the edition to have such data verified. While Ernst's mistake is more serious because it misquotes the title of Scott's novel, its repeated inclusion bears similarities to the continued use of Andrew Hook's miscalculation in his introduction to *Waverley*, originally published in 1972 and still included unchanged. West German and British publishers thus appear less concerned about the content of the introductions to their editions than the East German publishers, perhaps because the former are motivated by commerce, whereas the latter are subject to more careful readings.

West German prefaces consider hardly any aspects in detail. Scott's view and depiction of history is seldom discussed, nor is the figure of the hero. Leaving out these points leads to a superficial reading which in turn leads to Scott being placed in a category below the 'highest'. Once this view is established, it might prevent any attempt at in-depth analysis, and cause a superficial reading of his novels as adventure stories. Kurt Gamerschlag argues in his epilogue to *Waverley* that such a reading is perfectly possible but misses the point of Scott's novels (1982, 555). His approach is therefore closest to the more elitist attitude of British critical introductions towards the end of the twentieth century. Scott's novels reach West German readers largely without a preface, and even where a preface exists, the editions still exclude the possibility of the novels' possessing any serious literary qualities, suggesting that Scott's main value is as entertainment.

Since a free literary market is largely regulated by customer demand, prefaces stress those qualities about the respective novel that are thought to attract readers – readers only, rather than readers and censors. Entertainment therefore appears to be what appeals most to West German readers. Editions of Scott's novels are close to those of modern novels, in which explanation and historical context are omitted. West German prefaces use the fact that Scott wrote the novels more than 150 years ago to underline their romantic content, and ignore the fact that this in itself may merit some explanation, even apart from literary

---

[26] In the 'General Preface' to the 1829 edition of his novels, Scott writes about the genesis of *Waverley*: '[A]bout the year 1805, I threw together about one-third part of the first volume of Waverley. It was advertised to be published [. . .] under the name of 'Waverley, or 'tis Fifty Years since' – a title afterwards altered to ' 'Tis Sixty Years since', that the actual date of publication [1814] might be made to correspond with the period in which the scene was laid.' Claire Lamont comments: 'Scott's memory is at fault here. 1745 was 'Sixty Years since' in 1805, when he began the novel, [as Peter Garside has argued, *Waverley* is more likely to have been begun in 1808–10] and 'Sixty Years' occurs both in an early part of the manuscript [. . .] and in the advertisement of 1809–10': Walter Scott (1981) *Waverley*, ed. Claire Lamont, Oxford: Clarendon Press, pp. 352 and 465. Ernst was presumably using the 1829 Magnum Edition with the General Preface, without reading it closely.

analysis. Scott is being marketed as unchallenging, towards an audience not necessarily used to reading literature. While East German preface writers emphasize Scott's love for the people and present Scott as challenging but provide guidance to the reader, West German preface writers to a far greater extent present Scott's works as accessible to anyone without providing any guidance, instead using nineteenth-century translations – or abridgements. Christian Berger, reader (Programmlektor) in the West German publishing house Verlag Das Beste (the German arm of *Reader's Digest*), states that his concept for promoting *Ivanhoe* as part of a classics series was to present 'popular and today still easily readable classics to a relatively broad audience not generally used to reading classics' (2003).[27] Similarly, Heinrich Pleticha, author of an *Ivanhoe* preface, states that the intended audience was 'those many readers from 14 years onwards who are interested in challenging adventure books' (2003).[28] In contrast to this, Roland Links, director of the East German Verlagsgruppe Kiepenheuer from 1979 to 1990, states that the target readership was mainly an 'educated audience' ('gebildetes Publikum') (2003). The prefaces themselves confirm these different intended audiences. However, Emmerich points out that the aim of GDR education not to have 'an elitist high-culture and - literature of the few, separated from the trivial culture of the many' was to an extent successful, since in the GDR, 'books that are considered [in the West] to be too demanding [. . .] of the reader and are therefore held to be unsaleable, achieve high print-runs in East Germany' (1989, 26).[29] The reading experience of GDR citizens testified to in the questionnaires confirms this broader appeal of classic literature. 'Educated' (in a literary sense) would therefore have applied to more readers in the East, though Links's statement shows that people did read differently, so that it still addressed a limited audience.

East German reviews of their editions of Scott's novels confirm that entertainment was an aspect of reading, but not the only one. They emphasize the respective novel's historical, geographical, and political background, and commend the combination of fiction with 'longer political and ideological discussions' ('längeren politischen und weltanschaulichen Erörterungen' (*Ihre Brigitte*, June 1968)) as a trait typical of Scott's works. Most importantly, however, all reviews let Scott emerge as a great writer, whose status is beyond dispute. The first sentence of one review reads 'Sir Walter Scott, who is not familiar with this name?' ('Sir Walter Scott, wem ist dieser Name kein Begriff?'

---

[27] 'populäre und auch heute noch gut lesbare Klassiker einem relativ breiten Publikum vorzustellen, das ansonsten eher nicht "Klassiker-affin" ist'. The edition of *Ivanhoe* referred to appeared in 1997, seven years after reunification. Since trends after reunification intensify West German trends and almost entirely supplant the East German approach, I have used it here as an example as it summarizes the attitude that the West German prefaces reveal.

[28] 'die große Zahl von Lesern aller Altersstufen ab 14, die sich für anspruchsvolle Abenteuerbücher interessieren'.

[29] 'In der DDR erreichen Bücher hohe Auflagen, die hierzulande als literarisch zu anspruchsvoll [. . .] und damit tendenziell als unverkäuflich gelten.'

(*Thüringische Landeszeitung*, 8.8.1972)), while the others have similar underlying assumptions, casually referring to him as 'the great English novelist' ('des großen englischen Romanciers' (*Ostsee-Zeitung*, 29.3.1980)), the 'founder of the historical novel' ('Begründer des historischen Romans' (*Der Morgen*, 28.10.1972)), or to 'the great proximity between Scott and Shakespeare's dramatic art' ('die große Nähe Scotts zur dramatischen Kunst Shakespeares' (*Ihre Brigitte*, June 1968)). That there are hardly any West German reviews may be partly due to the lack of a new translation for most West German editions, but is nevertheless telling: the differences between East and West German attitudes to Scott as revealed in prefaces are therefore confirmed by numbers and content of reviews.

East German preface writers connect entertainment to literary value and didacticism. Scott therefore has a higher literary status in the East, as well as being read more widely. Both East and West German prefaces associate popularity with literary quality. In East Germany, preface writers strategically connect Scott's popularity to his greatness, such as Kaiser pointing out that Scott's novels are being published 'again and again in the Soviet Union' ('in immer neuen Ausgaben' (1952, 679)). West Germans could not refer to Scott's popularity in the Soviet Union as something that would recommend him to their readers, nor could they present him as popular in Western nations because he was not. His not being popular therefore confirms him as a second-class author. West Germans frequently bring up his nineteenth-century popularity, so that neglect of an author who had once been considered first rate and had consequently been popular adds to the romantic image of him evoked in their essays.

The contrast in the prefaces to Scott's novels shows East and West Germans' different orientations towards different political ideologies as literary authorities. While in West German prefaces, no deliberate orientation becomes obvious, though similarities among the prefaces indicate the shaping impact of their cultural context, East Germans consciously appropriate Scott to fit in with their political aims, testifying to a conscious choice of influence. In East German prefaces, a development can be traced: Kaiser's and Schulz's essays, published in the 1950s when the GDR was still finding its identity, are more determined by communist ideology than later ones such as Reichel's (1972) or Baadke's (1982). Baadke states in a letter that while he still had to conduct his interpretation 'within the ideological limits, they had already become quite broad by this time [1982]' (2004a).[30] The development in East German prefaces shows their deliberate appropriation of Scott's novels. East German publishers and readers confirm that care was taken as to the quality and ideology of prefaces. Links (2003) stresses that prefaces were written by 'competent authors whose expertise was certain' ('wissenschaftlich ausgewiesen'). This of course did not mean that the social conditions in the novels were not judged from a Marxist point of view. Elke Maes is more extreme and asserts that prefaces 'had to comply with the educational aim required for all citizens of the GDR' in order to get them

---

[30]   'innerhalb der ideologischen Grenzen – die zu diesem Zeitpunkt aber schon ziemlich weit waren'.

published, implying that 'wissenschaftlich ausgewiesen' did not only mean scholarly capable, but also politically recommendable.

Despite some ideological colouring, East German prefaces are informed, scholarly essays that have a more insightful perception of Scott's qualities than their West German counterparts. Holding Scott worthy of analysis shows them to regard Scott as more than an adventure-story author. Scott's greatness is bound up with his being interpreted as an author fitting in with a communist ideology, a revolutionary predecessor who asserted almost 200 years ago the continuous progress of history and the significance of the people in it. Once he is seen as promoting a suitable ideology, the weight of literature generally and its role in educating the readers contribute to regarding him as great.

As we have seen, East and West Germany promote two very different versions of Walter Scott. In the East, he is represented as an author of great literary works; in the West, as an author of adventure stories. This is reflected in East German prefaces being longer and more analytical than West German ones. Scott's literary status was thus higher in the East than in the West. In both countries, his critical reputation corresponds with his public popularity: similar numbers of versions in the two states testify to Scott's being relatively more read in the restricted East German market than in the West. Preface authors in neither country present the author in an objective way, so that both East and West guide their readers. While East German publishers and preface writers do this deliberately, West Germans appear unconscious of abiding by ideas of a general trend.

II 1990 to 2005

The two German states were reunited on 3 October 1990. The West German literary market was comparatively little affected by this, whereas the East German market's structures were fundamentally changed. Hence, in addition to the term 'Wiedervereinigung' (reunification), Germans refer to the 'Wende' – turn, or change. Literature in East Germany had been controlled, but it had also been promoted, and had been regarded as fulfilling a central role in the education of GDR citizens. With the dissolution of the system run by the state and the privatization of publishing houses, the latter had to refocus. As Friedrich Baadke recalls, in the GDR he did not have to worry about selling his limited print runs of British authors, whereas after 1990, his publishing house had to learn how to sell the printed books to the readers. This proved especially difficult with literature, as reading tastes and habits changed immediately, and 'literature (schöne Literatur) was only read by those who were interested in it in a literary way [. . .] [whereas] guide-, hobby-, travel-books and light fiction were now primarily wanted' (Baadke 2004a). More than half the public libraries disappeared within the first two years of reunification, and those that remained changed about 40 per cent of their stock (Emmerich 1996, 437).

The following section discusses the reception of Scott's novels in reunified Germany: in a literary market that is determined by capitalist market forces – in a culture that functions largely under West German conditions – does Scott's reputation bear obvious similarities to what it had been in East or West Germany, or does a new Scott emerge?

The variety of Scott titles published in Germany after 1990 is limited. While titles exist that are published only in East or only in West Germany, no new Scott title is published in reunified Germany:

Table 3 *Novels by Scott published in reunified Germany*

Title	East (1949–1990) Numbers of versions published	West (1949–1990) Numbers of versions published	Reunified (1990–2005) Numbers of versions published
Ivanhoe	10	31	13
Quentin Durward	4	11	1
The Tale of Old Mortality	4	–	1
The Fair Maid of Perth	4	–	–
The Talisman	3	3	1
Kenilworth	3	1	–
Rob Roy	1	3	2
The Heart of Midlothian	3	1	–
Waverley	2	2	–
The Bride of Lammermoor	2	1	2
A Legend of Montrose	–	1	–
Anne of Geierstein	–	1	–
The Black Dwarf	–	1	–

The distribution of numbers of titles is similar to what it had been in West Germany: *Ivanhoe* dominates the market.

In West Germany *Ivanhoe* was published more often than all the other Scott novels put together, while the novel was an integral part of a general Scott market in East Germany. After the reunification, West German trends take over: *Ivanhoe* represents an even larger part of the Scott market than the work had done in West Germany.

Not only are no new Scott titles published after 1990, there are hardly any new editions of those of his texts previously published in German either. Almost all versions of Scott's novels that appear after 1990 are reissues of earlier East or West German editions. Even where a text is marketed as a new edition, it is usually based on an existing one, displaying only slight alterations, such as a new title page. If not based on a specific previous edition, at least the translation used is – with few exceptions – an older one that is not revised.

The only new translation is a version of *The Talisman*, translated and edited by Theresia Leitner, and appearing as *Richard Löwenherz* (Richard the Lionheart) in 1993. The edition represents a heavily altered version of Scott's texts, contains many coloured illustrations, and appears to address a young audience.

Apart from this new translation, there are three instances of an old translation being newly edited: Benno Tschischwitz's 1880 translation of *Ivanhoe* is newly edited by Günther Geisler for Thienemann-Erdmann in 1998, W. Sauerwein's 1851 translation of *The Bride of Lammermoor* is newly edited by Michael Klein and published by Gollenstein as *Das Leid von Lammermoor* (The sorrow of Lammermoor) in 1999, and an anonymous translation is newly edited by Sybil Gräfin Schönefeldt. The last is a children's version: it is heavily abridged, contains many illustrations, and is in a folio format. The first two editions also include illustrations, but both are unabridged (though *Ivanhoe* is published without the dedicatory epistle).

The Thienemann-Erdmann and the Gollenstein editions and one other, *Ivanhoe* in Christine Hoeppener's 1952 translation published in 1997 by Verlag Das Beste, are the only ones after 1990 that include a new preface: Heinrich Pleticha writes an epilogue to Thienemann-Erdmann's *Ivanhoe*, Günther Klotz to Verlag Das Beste's edition of the same novel, and Michael Klein to *Das Leid von Lammermoor*. Apart from these three new essays, just two of the pre-1990 prefaces are reissued: Insel Verlag – previously West German – twice incorporates Ernst's 1911 epilogue to *Ivanhoe* with all its mistakes, and Aufbau Verlag – previously East German – includes Baadke's 1978 essay on *Old Mortality*. Thus of the twenty versions of Scott's texts published between 1990 and 2005, only six include a preface at all, and only three have a new one. Attitudes to Scott as testified to by the inclusion of a preface therefore appear to follow West German rather than East German trends.

The three new epilogues read well and are mostly factually correct, though all contain mistakes. All three emphasize Scott's significance as an author that everyone ought to read by outlining his contemporary popularity, and by referring to him as the 'creator of the historical novel: all later masters of this genre call him their ancestor: Charles Dickens and Victor Hugo, Alexandre Dumas and Wilhelm Hauff, Alessandro Manzoni and Leo Tolstoi' (Klotz 1997, 569).[31] The preface writers also underline Scott's writing about Scotland, and his being concerned with various social classes, their 'living conditions, ways of thinking, and customs' (Lebensumstände, Denkweisen und Sitten) (Klein 1999, 433), thereby giving colourful historical panoramas of 'the social conditions of past eras. [. . .] Scott's historical novels were not merely set in the past, but were concerned precisely with this past.' (433).[32]

There are some differences between the prefaces. The most scholarly introduction to Scott's times, life, and works is Günther Klotz's essay on *Ivanhoe*. He had written an epilogue to *The Heart of Midlothian* for Aufbau Verlag in 1959, and therefore appears to have had some background knowledge about Scott and British literature. Heinrich Pleticha's epilogue emphasizes *Ivanhoe*'s adventure traits much more and is generally less precise than Klotz's. In a letter, written in response to my queries, Pleticha explains that the edition of *Ivanhoe*

---

[31] 'Schöpfer des historischen Romans, und alle späteren Meister dieses Genres nennen ihn als Stammvater'.
[32] 'der gesellschaftlichen Verhältnisse einer vergangenen Epoche.[. . .] Scotts historische Romane spielten nicht mehr einfach in der Vergangenheit, sondern sie machten diese Vergangenheit ganz gezielt zum Inhalt.'

he was introducing was 'part of a series of classic adventure novels' (2003). He describes himself as a 'specialist in adventure literature, rather than specifically a Scott-specialist',[33] and hence it is adventure-novel traits that he most emphasizes. Michael Klein's epilogue to *Das Leid von Lammermoor* reads almost like an adventure story itself, narrating Scott's life and fame in an exciting rather than a strictly factual manner (though he gets the basics right). His essay abounds with quotations from German literary greats of the nineteenth century, such as Goethe, Hauff, Tieck and Fontane, which testify to Scott's greatness.

The three essays are between five and fifteen pages long, and they are informative: if a publisher or editor cares enough about the edition to commission a new preface, this preface needs to be of a certain quality. These three editions represent exceptions among the versions of Scott's texts published in reunified Germany: most publishers do not appear to care about which version of the text or which translation they use, nor do they see the need for an editor or an introductory essay. Chart 1 illustrates this lack of prefaces:

Length of prefaces, 1990–2005 (pages)

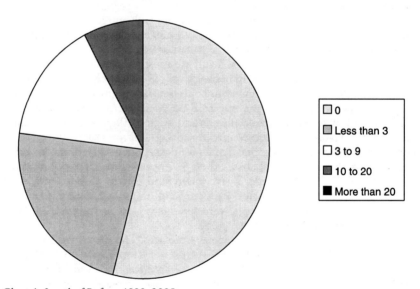

Legend:
- ☐ 0
- ◩ Less than 3
- ☐ 3 to 9
- ◼ 10 to 20
- ■ More than 20

Chart 1 *Length of Prefaces, 1990–2005*

Compared to the length of prefaces in East and West Germany, this evidence again indicates that Scott in a reunified Germany is treated in the way West Germany dealt with him.

The study of the reception of Scott's novels in East, West and reunified Germany has shown that it is not readers' shared national history and identity

---

[33] 'Teil einer Reihe sogenannter klassischer Abenteuerromane'; 'Spezialist für Abenteuerliteratur, eher als ein Scottspezialist'.

but their immediate cultural context that determines interpretation. East Germans read Scott according to the dominant trends of their culture. They deliberately appropriate him to fit their ideology. West Germans, too, read within the values of their culture, so that the reading of an author is necessarily influenced by current cultural trends, whether deliberately, as in East Germany, or not, as in West Germany.

The differences between East and West German receptions of Scott emphasize the impact of readers' context on their reactions to an author: Scott's texts are not intrinsically less attractive now than they have been in the past, but they are so in fast-moving commercial societies. The political, economic, and cultural context of German readers after 1990 is similar to that in former West Germany, and different from East German conditions. Scott's reputation in reunified Germany is akin to his West German, and different from his East German, status, which confirms that a text's reception depends only to a limited extent on the text itself, and largely on current cultural trends in the society that receives it.

8 The Hungarian Reception of Walter Scott in the Nineteenth Century

Emilia Szaffner

The Hungarian reception of Walter Scott is strongly connected to the expansion of a new reading public, the beginnings of literary criticism and the rise of the novel genre in Hungary. Scott's novels had an unsurpassable role in the developmental process of Hungarian national identity.

The Hungarian readership

The authorship of Scott's novels was enigmatic for his British contemporaries, from the first edition of *Waverley* in 1814 to his avowal of authorship in 1827. In Hungary the traces of his impact can be found from the early 1820s, but never did the slightest doubt of his authorship appear there. Scott's name was first mentioned in writing (together with that of Byron) as late as 1821, in a letter written by Count József Dessewffy to Ferenc Kazinczy, as 'a notable poet of contemporary England'[1] (Kazinczy, 17: 429). The term poet may also refer to the author of novels, because the usage did not differentiate between an author of poems and an author of prose fiction, the novel genre being in its infancy in Hungary at that time. Therefore we cannot know if the 'notable poet' meant the anonymously publishing novelist or the minstrel of heroic epics and lays. The first appearance of the names of Scott and Byron together is representative of the paradoxical situation that in spite of the anti-Romantic features of both, they mediated and acted in place of British Romanticism in Hungary (Szegedy-Maszák 1995, 125).

In the so-called 'Reform Age' (as the pre-revolutionary period of the 1820–40s is generally called), the target languages of the reading public were stratified according to social classes. The members of the aristocracy collected books written in German, Latin, or sometimes French. The provincial nobility

---

[1] 'a mostani Anglia nevezetes költője'.

and the lower orders read almost nothing. As Hungary was subordinate to Austria, the developing towns were populated by German-speaking people who read literature mostly in German. The intellectuals began to learn English in growing numbers from the 1820s.

The cultural orientation of the intelligentsia can be exemplified by the small group of ambitious young writers organized around the almanac *Auróra*, and its editor, Károly Kisfaludy. They selected their ideals from the romantic authors, especially Anglophone ones, because they tried to resist the German influence for political reasons. The best known members of the circle were József Bajza, Ferenc Toldy and Mihály Vörösmarty, a triad of a critic, a literary historian and a poet, who were to become the leading personalities of Hungarian literature by the 1830, and 1840s. The members also spent merry evenings together, and they gave themselves funny nicknames, first 'Lumpengesindel', then 'Alsatians'. The latter denomination originated from Walter Scott's novel, *The Fortunes of Nigel*, referring to a district in London where people could find shelter against civil obligations (Fenyő 1983, 118–124).

Walter Scott's impact on Hungarian literature can be detected first in the works of this literary circle: in the short stories of Károly Kisfaludy, Ferenc Kölcsey and László Bártfay in the 1820s, in the poetry of Vörösmarty (Jakabfi 1941, 43–44, 47–49), in the novel theory and prose fiction of Bajza, and the translation projects of Toldy in the 1830s. András Thaisz, the translator of *Ivanhoe*, was also connected to the circle.

From their correspondence written during the November and December of 1823, it is clear that Ferenc Toldy was learning English and József Bajza was learning German. Toldy's original surname was Schedel and his mother tongue was German. He began to learn English in 1823, with the definite aim of reading his favourite authors – Moore, Goldsmith, Byron, Scott and Shakespeare (Toldy 1823a) – in the original. After a few weeks' learning he was able to read in English, and he developed plans for translations. 'I admire the romans [sic] of Sir Walter Scott (it's being translated from a bad German translation by Prepeliczay!), the plays of Schiller, Shakespeare's Othello and Lear. I will never desist from seeing them in my own translation'[2] (Toldy 1823b). Bajza received Toldy's plans for translation with enthusiasm:

> Your effort to translate Othello, the works of Schiller, the romans of Sir Walter Scott etc. deserves credit from our country. [. . .] We would benefit more if you translated the remarkable works of the great foreign spirits into Hungarian, and maybe [. . .] more could be gained from these than if you were to write original works.[3]
> (Bajza 1823)

---

[2] 'Úgy rájok meredtem én a Sir Walter Scott románjaira (Prepeliczay fordítja le, egy gonosz német fordításból!), Schiller teátromára, Shakespeare Othello-Lear-jára [sic!], hogy soha el nem állok a kívánattól magam által másolva látnom őket.'

[3] Hogy tehát te Otellót, Schiller munkáit, Walter Scott románjait stb. fordítani igyekszel, e feltétel nagy hálát érdemel a hazától. [. . .] Annak nagy hasznára fognál lenni, ha a külföldi nagy szellemek remekjeit magyarra ált-tennéd és talán [. . .] nagyobb hasznára, mintha eredetit írnál.

In 1828 Toldy was again planning the translation of one of Scott's works: 'I'm going to translate the Scottish history of Walter Scott from English (30 printed sheets) with the sort of diligence I usually expect from others'[4] (Toldy 1828). The 'Scottish history' could not be the *History of Scotland*, because it appeared a year later, but either the *Border Antiquities of England and Scotland* (Oltványi 1969b) or one of Scott's 'Scottish' novels. But all these plans for translations came to nothing, and Prepeliczay did not translate any Scott novels either (Oltványi 1969a).

Bajza was learning German at that time, with a similar intention to widen his knowledge of literature, so he asked Toldy to send him volumes of drama, novel or criticism. Toldy was obviously enthusiastic about the British writer, therefore he could provide Bajza with Scott's novels in German translation. Bajza read several novels of Walter Scott, which is apparent from the references in his theoretical work and from the characteristics of his own fiction. Soon Bajza became suitable for translating short stories, and he published them in a separate volume titled *Pillangó* (Butterfly, 1836). It is typical of the contemporary attitude towards translation that only one of the novellas was rendered from a German original, and the others from different originals through the mediation of German, but this was not even mentioned by its reviewer (Tornay [Szontagh Gusztáv], 1837). The selection shows that Bajza employed the German language to acquire information, but most of the stories are from English. The story he chose from Scott was 'A kárpitos szoba' (The Tapestried Chamber). In his preface Bajza emphasized that he wanted to set models to be followed by future writers with his selection, especially to achieve more realistic characters and emotions besides modest morals. However, the stories of the volume are not the best of the age, and fall short of the expectations raised by the preface.

The translation of Scott's work in Hungary began with a failure. The enterprise, started under the title *Selected Romances of Walter Scott*, exhausted itself with the publication of the first of the series. *I* appeared in 1827 in the rendering of András Thaisz, and it was the only novel of Walter Scott's which was translated into Hungarian in the first half of the nineteenth century; even that only sold a few copies (Elek 1938). The six-volume edition must have been too expensive for Hungarian readers (György 1941, 81). The quality of the translation was acceptable by contemporary standards: Toldy expressed his contentment with it (Toldy 1829, 455), Bajza labelled it as a 'mediocre translation' (Bajza 1981, 103). Unquestionably its success suffered from the fact that the upper and middle classes in the Habsburg monarchy read mostly in German. Aristocrats did not even speak Hungarian, most of them being resident in other European countries. Even Count István Széchenyi, who won the name 'the greatest Magyar' for initiating several significant national institutions, could not speak Hungarian very well, learning it as an adult.

Széchenyi was apparently well acquainted with the prose fiction of Walter Scott. According to his diary, he read the following Scott novels, all in the original, between 1824 and 1826: *Betrothed*, *T*, *The Monastery*, *SRW*, *WO*,

---

4   'Walter Scottnak skót históriáját fogom lefordítani angolból (30 nyomtatott ív); de olly szorgalommal, melyet én minden[ki] mástól szoktam kívánni.'

and some others where only the author's name was mentioned (Széchenyi 1925–1939, 2: 512, 593, 596, 3: 49, 95). The count read *The Monastery* in August 1825 in English, and copied a few sentences into his diary: 'Such men we have seen marked by a waywardness, and even an obstinacy of character, which hath appeared intractability and stupidity, to those among whom they walked and were conservant, until the very opportunity hath arrived in which it was the will of Providence that they should be the fitting instrument of great things.' (from Chapter 18) – ' "It has been said that sorrow must speak or die" – ich hatte lieber gesagt, "sorrow must speak, or it will kill" ' (from Chapter 23 and Széchenyi's comment) (Széchenyi 1925–39, 2: 596).

Both sentences, torn from their contexts, the latter also transformed, became aphorisms to be used as practical philosophy. This procedure of quoting suggests that contemporary readers demanded aphoristic statements of a principle, wise observations and general truths in prose fiction, breaking the flow of narrative or descriptive passages. This narrative technique was adapted by Bulwer-Lytton, in Hungarian literature by Petrichevich and József Eötvös later employed a similar method.

The long narratives of Scott found favour with the aristocrats of the monarchy. They were especially attracted by the detailed descriptions of costumes, objects, interiors and exteriors, all employed by Scott to support characterization, and to conjure up the spirit of distant times and places. His contemporary audience were captivated by the picturesque and exotic self-contained extracts, which they also enjoyed reproducing visually. In the 1820s countesses and dukes, besides performing short comedies, entertained each other with 'tableaux vivants', representing scenes chosen from their favourite novels, posing silently in costumes, at aristocratic receptions in Vienna and Pest-Buda. According to Count Széchenyi's diary, several 'tableaux vivants' were based on the following Scott's novels: *AB, K, QD* and *I* (Viszota 1925–39, 3: 12, 4: 458). Such 'tableaux' gradually became a widely popular form of entertainment in middle-class social gatherings by the 1840s. Young ladies and gentlemen gave theatrical performances in country mansions and manors, posing as romantic heroines and medieval knights from an especially effective scene of Walter Scott and Miklós Jósika. The numerous examples of amateur performances and 'tableaux' show that the contemporary interpretations arose from the visual nature of Scott's works. Contemporary magazines, private letters and diaries give proof of the fact that by the 1830s and 1840s familiarity with Scott's novels gradually became a precondition of partaking in social life. Thus literary tradition became a customary source of reference for the middle-class readers.

Hungarian reformers from the aristocracy, the landed gentry, the rising bourgeoisie and the intelligentsia soon became mediators of the Scottian patriotism and landscape. Several members of the reform generation travelled to Scotland and recorded their experiences in print. Their enthusiasm about the wild settings of Scott's descriptions can be revealed in a remark made by József Bajza in one of his letters, where he mentioned Scotland as a place you can find in romances and fairy tales ('regényes, tündér Scotia'). (Bajza 1830). However we can explore the real experience in two contemporary travelogues by Farkas Sándor Bölöni and István Gorove.

Bölöni, a Unitarian Secler nobleman, arrived in Scotland at the end of May

1831. First he walked all around Edinburgh, escorted by John Gibson Lockhart, Walter Scott's son-in-law and editor of the *Quarterly Review*. They visited the archives to see the sources Scott employed in his writings. According to Bölöni's travelogue, by the 1830s travellers were received with a whole network of tourism, all because of the literary works of great merit. The passengers searched Scotland for the spots they had known from Shakespeare's *Macbeth* and the *Ossian*, and above all from the epic poetry and the Scottish novels of Sir Walter Scott. Bölöni made the following remark near Loch Katrine:

> We have arrived in the region to see the famous 'Lochs', the most noteworthy beauties of Scotland. Recently they have become so well-known by the novels of Walter Scott that the Scots regard it unpatriotic not to explore them. In the summer there are lots of English and foreign visitors.[5] (Bölöni 1984, 287–88)

Elsewhere he suggested that 'Walter Scott has made these places so famous that all his readers feel bound to visit the localities of his depicted scenes [. . .] Nearly every traveller kept a copy of the *Select Views* or Walter Scott in their hands, dipping into them according to the changes of scenery'[6] (Bölöni 1984, 234, 236). Here, Bölöni probably referred to the *Select Views on the River Clyde*, an album of engraved drawings, with historical and descriptive illustrations, which was published in 1830, a year before Bölöni's journey. This observation of Bölöni suggests that among the possible interpretations of art and literature, the contemporary public employed them as traveller's guides.

Bölöni himself was influenced by memories of his readings, and expected the same from his own readers, when he explored 'the rocky Highlands with its summits in the clouds, which has been renowned by the *Fair Maid of Perth*',[7] or when he recalled *HM* at West Bow, and *A* and *GM* at Queensferry, or when he directed his readers to *RR* for descriptions of Loch Katrine and Loch Lomond. While boating on the Loch Katrine, he is reminded of the scenery in the *LL*, although he observed that the owner of the island had built and furnished a hunting-seat after Scott's description.[8]

---

[5]   felértünk a híres tavakat (Lochs) nézni meg, melyek Skócia nevezetesebb szépségeit teszik. Ezeket közelebbről Walter Scott románjai oly elhíreltté tették, hogy a scotus hazafiságtalanságnak hiszi, ha e helyeket meg nem járta. Nyáron által temérdek az ide utazó angol és idegen.

[6]   'A Loch Katrine keveseknél volt ismeretes W. Scott leírása előtt, most minden utas meglátogatja s bámulja. [. . .] W. Scott oly nevezetessé tette ezen helyeket, hogy minden olvasója szent kötelességének tartja leírt szcénája helyeit is megnézni. [. . .] Majd minden utas és utasné kezében a *Select Views* vagy Walter Scott volt, s a szcénák változása szerint tekingetett belé.'

[7]   'Perthnél már a fellegekkel játszó sziklás Felföldön jártunk, mely a Walter Scott szép poémája, *Fair Maid of Perth* által megint nevezetessé lett'

[8]   'Tudva van, hogy W. Scott *Lady of the Lake* szép poémája szcénáját a Loch Katrine-ra és környékébe tette. [. . .] Beülünk a csónakba, s legelébb is azon szigetbe vitt, mely W. Scottban Kirnan Uriskin név alatt jön elé. Ezen hely tulajdonosa éppen oly vadászházat állított ide, mint W. Scottban le van írva. [. . .] A fal rakva minden vadállatok bőreivel, régi lándzsák, pajzsok, sisakok az asztalon etc.'

The sublime scenery of the Scottish Highlands, the wild mountainous land-scape and the ruinous castles, reminded the Hungarian travellers of Transylvania. Bölöni made several comparing remarks like: 'entering Kinrosshire is just like arriving in Gyergyó'.[9] On leaving the Highlands he was reflecting on the lack of literary descriptions of his homeland, and the apparently concomitant boom of tourism: 'Various beauties are bestowed upon Transylvania by nature, how-ever we do not range our beauteous regions, either for its qualities have not been discovered by any writer, or for not all classes of our nation have taken pleasure in nature yet'[10] (Bölöni 1984).

István Gorove likewise wandered all over Scotland, visited the monuments of Scott and Burns in Edinburgh; moreover he noted the Scottish national cos-tume, which reminded him of the Hungarian dress styles: 'the national costume is worn not only in the mountains, but also in the army. Only our Hungarian costume is more unique'.[11]

The names of British and American novelists appeared in growing num-bers in the library catalogues of diverse collections from the 1830s. In accord-ance with the readers' knowledge of languages, German translations were more numerous than original works. The largest Hungarian bookseller and publisher, Gusztáv Heckenast, opened the first public lending library in Pest in 1839, which contained – besides the prose works of Bulwer-Lytton, Dickens, Fenimore Cooper and Washington Irving – several novels of Scott. British and American literatures are represented by these names as well as by Shakespeare, Milton, Edward Young, Byron and *Ossian* on the catalogues of most student associations, civil societies, reading clubs, and private collections. These show that within the middle class especially the young urban intellectuals had access to Scott's novels in the 1830s and 1840s (Fülöp 1978, 109, 127, 142, 156, 179).

We are offered a more detailed picture of the orientation of readers from the library catalogue of the Fejér County Reading Society. Books in Hungarian from Ann Radcliffe, Sheridan, Shakespeare and Scott; and in German from Shakespeare (six), John Barclay, Milton, Bulwer-Lytton (thirty-four!), Edgeworth, Thomas Moore and Fenimore Cooper (five). Scott was apparently the favourite; he was represented in the collection with 106 volumes in German, and even a copy of the three-volumed *AG* in the original (Murányi 1993).

Contemporary travelogues give a similar account of the reading habits of the day. An English traveller, Robert Walsh, on his way through Transylvania, related an incident in a bookshop in Hermannstadt (Nagyszeben, today Sibiu), a Lutheran Saxon town:

---

[9] 'Kinrosshire-be a bémenetel olyan, mintha Gyergyóba érnénk.'

[10] 'Erdélynek sok szépség van adva a természettől, s azért-e, hogy még író nem támadt felfedezni ennek szépségeit, vagy hogy a nemzet minden osztályánál nem ébredt fel a természet szépségei iránt való érzés, mi még nem járjuk szebb vidékeinket.'

[11] 'nemcsak a hegyek közt, de a katonaságnál is megtarták a nemzeti öltözetet, érdekesb ennél csak a mi magyar öltözetünk lehet.' (Gorove 1844)

The bookseller, who spoke French, directed my attention to a portrait which he had just hung up. I asked him who it was, and he replied, 'Le Sieur Valtere Skote, l'homme le plus célèbre en toute l'Europe'. It was certainly no small proof of his celebrity to have his picture thus exhibited in an obscure town at the remotest confines of civilized Europe: his novels, translated into French and German, formed a considerable part of the books in the shop. (Walsh 1832 302)

John Paget wrote a richly illustrated, monumental account of his travels in Hungary and Transylvania. He started his journey in 1836 in the northern highland of Hungary, where he and his brother struck up a conversation with a poor Jew:

On hearing that we were English, he asked very earnestly if one Walter Scott was yet living, and expressed the greatest regret when he learnt his death. Surprised at such a sentiment from such a man, and suspecting some mistake, I inquired what he knew of Scott, when he pulled from his pocket a well-thumbed German translation of *Ivanhoe*, – the very romance of persecuted Judaism, – and assured me he had read that and many others of his works with great pleasure. I do not know that I ever felt more strongly the universal power of genius that when I found the bard of Scotland worshipped by a poor Jew in the mountains of Hungary. (Paget 1839 120–21)

Afterwards the traveller added that the Hungarians generally possessed a knowledge of several languages and read a lot of literature. In many private collections he saw the English originals, but much more often the 'excellent' German translations of the best known authors like Shakespeare, Byron, Scott and Bulwer-Lytton. He also argued that 'a great cause of this extension of English literature has been the judicious selection and the cheap form in which Galignani and other foreign booksellers have published the standard English works' (Paget 1839 121). Paget himself established a Reading Club in 1843, and later a Conversation Club in Kolozsvár (today Cluj-Napoca), with a library of 2000 books and subscription to English magazines (Ferencz and Tasnádi 2002).

By 1830, Scott had become an unquestionable authority. Scott's novels were so popular that disapproval of them was not proper in company. Count Széchenyi himself lodged a complaint against this phenomenon. He encouraged the readers of his treatise *Hitel* (Credit) to think independently, and declare their views openly. By way of illustration he argued that it would be an insult against the 'immense vogue' to confess that you do not regard Scott as an excellent historian, or his works as highly amusing (Széchenyi 1830).

The usage of cultic terminology also proves that the admiration for Scott culminated in the 1830s. His anonymous obituary in the magazine *Társalkodó* (Conversationalist) in December 1832 started with the announcement: 'England lost its great minstrel', and continued in a like manner, 'all those several volumes of works, with which his genius presented the world of cultivated readers'. The writer placed Scott beside Goethe, employing the following phrases: 'they both stand in mankind as the landmarks of an epoch, for the glory of which they worked much, and both lived to see the same historical phenomenon: the sudden collapse of the political and intellectual Toryism; while they could view around themselves the germination of new mental powers.' A casual remark in the same article brought to light that the contemporary readers kept an eye also on the private life of their favourite authors: 'Walter Scott – as we know – travelled to Italy last summer on his doctors' advice'[12] (*Társalkodó* 1832).

The first modern Hungarian encyclopaedia, called *Közhasznú Esmeretek Tára* (The storehouse of public utility knowledge), was based on the third edition of the German Brockhaus Conversations-Lexikon, but also contained original entries. The writer termed Scott 'the greatest poet of the English' and 'a writer of prolific mind, beautiful spirit and European influence'.[13] The editor, Gábor Döbrentei, apparently avoided neologism, adhering to archaic phrases like 'poet' for a novelist, or 'roman' for a novel (Döbrentei 1831–34, 10: 402–03).

A minor, but fashionable, contemporary writer, Lázár Petrichevich Horváth, referred to Scott in his novel as 'the present-day dictator of the recent Romanticism' (1836, 1: 123), and in 1843 he brought the novelist in focus as a mystic figure:

> And around this time arrived the Great Unknown. Who would not know him, with his endless dialogues, excessively detailed descriptions of landscapes, situations and costumes, his gentle characters, unexpected turns, magnificent style, lifelike pictures, heroic knights and splendid tournaments – so, who would not know the author of Waverley, the founder of the new novel – with all his virtues and weaknesses?[14] (Petrichevich 1843, 1: 125)

Despite the lack of translations into Hungarian, the works of Walter Scott were essential reading for the Hungarian public of the time.

István Gorove, in his travelogue, argued that civilization keeps billowing between east and north. It rose from Byzantium and Athens, nowadays it takes its source from Scotland, the fatherland of Scott, Burns, Adam Smith and Edward Young, and soon it will flow back to the east, flooding Hungary as well. Gorove prophesied that Hungary might have a share in the ensuing cultural

---

[12] 'Anglia elveszíté nagy dalnokát. [. . .] mindazon sok kötet munkák és elmeművek, mellyekkel lángszelleme a mívelt olvasó világot megajándékozta. [. . .] Mindketten úgy állnak az emberi nemzetben, mint egy korszak (Epoche) határoszlopi, mellynek dicsőítésére ők nem keveset munkáltak, s mindketten egy – a világ történetében – egyetlen jelenést értek meg: a politikai és szellemi toryzmus egyazon ponton történt összeomlását; mialatt magok körül már-már új szellemi erők s életmagvak csírázatát szemlélheték. [. . .] Scott Walter – mint tudjuk – legközelébb múlt nyáron orvosainak javaslására Olaszországba utazott.'

[13] 'az angolok legnagyobb költésze' [. . .] 'termékeny elméjű, szép lelkű, s európai hatású író'.

[14] az újabb romantikának ideigleni diktátora' [. . .] 'És e tájt érkezett meg a Nagy Ismeretlen. Ki ne ismerné őt, végtelen párbeszédei, vidékek, helyzetek és ruházatok túlzóan részletes leírásaival, kedves alakjaival, meglepő fordulataival, gyönyörű stíljével, lehelő képei, hősszerű lovagjai és pompás lovagünnepeivel – szóval ki ne ismerné Waverley íróját, amaz új regény alapítóját – az ő minden erényeivel és gyöngeségeivel egyetemben?

development if we prepared the way for it[15] (Gorove 1834, 75–76). Scott's name appears here as the first among the representatives of a scientific and artistic centre, and a model in contemporary Europe.

The exceptional popularity of the writer is obvious: anecdotes about him crossed several frontiers. A Hungarian magazine issued an anecdote which threw into relief Scott's political achievement, by setting the scene at the coronation of George IV in 1821. The story contains more politics than humour. The sergeant of the Scottish armoured forces lets Scott pass through the line of soldiers to the king when he hears the name of his famous compatriot (*Társalkodó* 1838, 15: 60).

References and allusions

Hungarian prose fiction came into being in the 1830s, therefore the early writers imitated the narrative strategies of their favourite novels. They held Scott up as a model writer for themselves.

In the Reform Age a familiarity with the works of Walter Scott was essential in reading contemporary Hungarian poetry and fiction. Readers were supposed to understand the numerous direct and indirect intertextual references, quotations, allusions and analogies.

The monumental oeuvre of Walter Scott also offered structural innovations to later novelists. The idea of novel-sequences appeared in 1832, when József Gaal decided to write a series of novels modelled on the *Tales of my Landlord*, which was published between 1816–37. The planned title referred to the narrator, a jovial councillor from a small country town,[16] which suggests that Gaal wanted to follow the Fieldingesque convention of the armchair narrator in his series. Unfortunately only a fragment was published from the project in the magazine *Athenaeum*, under the title 'Éji lovasok' (Night Riders). Some of his other stories, like 'Badacsonyi Lanka' and 'Portugali gróf', also show the impact of Scott's novels (Ferenczi 1915 99).

A quotation in a private diary is a dialogue between the text and the reader, but a quotation in a published literary work is a complicated, multilateral relationship among the original work, the new narrative and the reader of both. In his novel *Az elbujdosott* (The refugee), Petrichevich employs the narrative technique he learnt from Bulwer-Lytton: he keeps breaking the narrative by directly addressing the reader, making intertextual references and inserting quotes or

---

15　'Mi van [ma] Bizáncban s Athénben, mi lelket emeljen? tudomány és művészet? s Európa legéjszakibb pontja Waltereket [=Scott], Burnsöket, Smitheket, Blaireket, Youngokat, Richardsonokat szült, így látjátok, barátim, a civilizációnak bizonyos hullámzása van, keletről átvonult ide éjszakra, [. . .] s most a világ azt akarja elhitetni magával, hogy újra keletre vonul. Hiszitek-e, hogy hatalmas folyamával bennünket is eláraszt? Én hiszem, s ennek hatalmas öntudatában élek s halok, csakhogy e folyamnak utat készíteni nekünk magunknak kell.'

16　'Pattanházi Pattangi Jób mátészalkai esküdt elbeszélése' (The relation of Job Jumpson of Jumpy, a councillor from Mátészalka).

footnotes. He often borrows an idea from another author instead of confessing his own reflections or descriptions (cf. Szinnyei 1925–26, 1: 135–36). Here the narrator suddenly interrupts the thoughts of the protagonist with wise aphorisms from Scott on the passing of time (Petrichevich 1836, 1: 3–4, 1: 123). He never indicates the location of the Scott quotes, but neither the location nor the authorship is important; these maxims could have been told by anyone. Scott's name is used to increase the value of the Petrichevich text; the author is parading his knowledge of fashionable writers. In spite of the primitive method of addressing the reader, this technique marks a new demand of the reading public, and opens a new dimension of the literary text. It supposes the reader's role as an initiate, and reduces the illusion of reality in the created world of the novel.

In his novel *Abafi* Miklós Jósika employed another form of citing. He cut his book into short chapters, providing them with a title and a motto, a device he had learnt from Walter Scott. The names quoted in the mottoes reveal a comprehensive knowledge of European literature, but also the varying level of his selections. Walter Scott appears with four citations; all the other authors have less quotes. Nevertheless the mottoes of Jósika are telegraphic in comparison with the 8–10 lines in Scott's novels (Nagy Miklós 1968, 348). They are also rather superficial, usually referring to an attribute of the main character of the given chapter, or the situation, in contrast with the profound mottoes of Walter Scott, sometimes written by himself, which interacted with the text, especially in the novels of his earlier period. Similarly to Petrichevich, Jósika wanted to elevate the prestige of his work (Nagy Miklós 1968, 348). But it was only the uncertainty of the beginner; in his later books he could create a greater cohesion between motto and text. The similarity in the form calls our attention to Jósika's attempt to adapt the Scott novel at the summit of Scott's popularity in Hungary, which was advantageous for the young novelist. But the unexploited device soon lost its function; the mottoes gradually disappeared by the end of the 1840s, even from Jósika's novels. The young Mór Jókai experimented with the renovation of the form with quotes from folk songs in his early novel, *Hétköznapok* (Weekdays), but he did not continue his initiative, for fear of imitating Jósika (Nagy Miklós 1968, 348–49).

The abovementioned literal citations built a passive, accepting relationship with the quoted writer, but other intertextual methods create a critical interpretative attitude towards the given writer or text. The inserted commentary was a fashionable poetic–rhetoric device in the contemporary novel, a characteristic of Bulwer-Lytton. The device originated in Scott's prefaces, footnotes and appendices, but they did not thrust themselves on the reader. By separating them from the narrative, the author offers us the possibility to decide if we want to read the additional passages by interrupting the story, or only afterwards, or not at all. Moreover, Scott's notes are rarely personal reflections, but rather historical data or anecdotes related to the historical personalities of the novel. Jósika employed Scott's armchair narrator, whose remarks refer only to the situation of story-telling to create an intimate relationship with the reader, or to the pictures of a well-known painter to enhance the imagination.

In the novels of Bulwer-Lytton the inserted commentaries occur more often, and they become independent of the world of the novel, with references to the external reality and other novels. This model was followed by several Hungarian writers, often referring to the works of Walter Scott, as in the following examples.

The narrator of *Az elbujdosott* (The refugee) by Petrichevich suddenly calls one of the characters, an old gipsy woman, 'our Megmerillis', then adds in a footnote: 'Who would not know Walter Scott's gipsy woman, Megmerillis? Even if it is not a historical name!'[17] (Petrichevich 1836, 1: 47). Petrichevich treats literary characters as historical personalities, or rather as personal acquaintances.

At the end of a third-rate short story of Károly Péter, titled 'Halál szerelemért' ('Death for love'), the protagonist relates his life and poetic ambition to his lover. He describes the artistic work as the eruption of passion and tension in the soul of the poet, and he chooses the admired poets of the romantic era as models, Shakespeare, Lord Byron and Walter Scott. Here, external reality is involved in the monologue of a character.

Another short story, 'Gyűlölség és szerelem' ('Hatred and love'), by József Gaal, depicts an aesthetic debate between a young nobleman and a young lady about the values of Walter Scott and Bulwer-Lytton. The protagonist and mouthpiece of the writer gives precedence to Scott over Bulwer due to his depth in characterization, the versatility of his female figures and a wider view of life: 'Bulwer has more appeal to the heart, Scott to the mind'[18] (Gaal 1835). A twentieth-century critic was pleased to see the nobility of the first decades of the nineteenth century so well-read, so responsive to aesthetic qualities that they are capable of making critical judgements and taking an interest in world literature (Elek 1938). But the girl's interest is said to be a rare exception, and we must mention the third character, an uneducated lieutenant, who regards both Scott and Bulwer-Lytton as boring in comparison with Kotzebue and Clauren. The lower nobility of the day is introduced in Gaal's story as an ignorant dandy.

Petrichevich draws a similar picture of the upper nobility in his novel. He informs the readers ironically about the library of a baroness in the Transylvanian city of Kolozsvár (today Cluj-Napoca): the richly decorated volumes of Racine, Boileau, Scott, Byron, Cooper, Spindler, Mme Staël, Lady Morgan and Schopenhauer lined the mahogany shelves to suggest that the baroness followed the current fashion. But these books were used not only for ornamentation; they were the frequent topics of conversation, and sometimes even their styles were imitated in the small talk of the day. Here a character ends his description of a newcomer with these words: 'whose genuine Scottish cloak is glittering through the dimness of the surrounding area like the last rays of the blood-stained sun beyond the dark peaks in the fading dusk.' The baroness replies: 'the one whom you depicted with the brush of

---

[17] ' "Biz úgy, édes galambom" – e szókkal töré meg a fagyos csöndet Megmeril-liszünk.' Footnote: 'Ki ne ösmerné Walter Scott cigánynéját, Megmerillist? Habár nem históriai név is az!'
[18] 'Bulwerhez inkább vonzódik az olvasó szíve, Scotthoz az esze.'

Walter Scott?'[19] (Petrichevich 1836, 1: 221). In this passage the Scottian depiction obviously means the accumulation of details, conjuring picturesque sights. In a later commentary in the same novel the author did not even exert himself to describe the place thoroughly, he found it sufficient for the readers to say 'Walter Scottian dining room' to recall the spirit of antiquity from long descriptions of old buildings in Scott's novels (1: 231).[20] Petrichevich finished his novel with a dialogue between the 'author' and his friend about the possible impact of the work, recalling the prologue of *FN* (Petrichevich 1836).

In the very same year, however, the circumstantial costume descriptions of Scott were judged superfluous, when the narrator of a short story refused to offer a long introduction of the supporting characters (László Nagy 1836).[21]

It was Mór Jókai who first made the audience realize the absurdity of the epilogue which listed the afterlives of the characters, a favourite device of the time. In his novel *Egy magyar nábob* (A Hungarian nabob),[22] after a minor character has finished an anecdote, one of his listeners puts further inquiries to him. He replies: 'Your lordship wants me to finish an anecdote in the manner Scott finished his novels: who lived till when, and how he died'[23] (Jókai 1853a).

In spite of this observation Jókai finished one and the same novel and even its sequel with an epilogue. In the latter one he omitted the minor characters with the explanation that he regarded this kind of appendage meaningless, without any psychological edification, only to satisfy curiosity (1853a). The omission of the epilogue in his later novels marks the death of the armchair narrator, and the beginning of experiments with new narrative techniques.

The laudatory or, on the contrary, the satirical poem is a special kind of commentary complete in itself. The loquacious poem of Sámuel Hegedűs praises Scott in fifteen stanzas. After making a catalogue of the famous poets and scholars of Caledonia in the first three stanzas, the poet depicts Scott's significance, his merits as a novelist, and even sketches his biography. Scott is introduced as a well-informed and educated man who learnt simplicity and originality from the antique Greek and Latin authors, and also as a man of inspiration who could depict 'the holy mystery of nature' which only Homer and Virgil managed to do before him. His talent in characterization is

---

[19] 'az a [. . .] dandy, [. . .] kinek valóságos skóciai palástja úgy tündöklik a körül vidék homályin ált, mint a vérbe mártott nap utó sugári az el-elhaló estalkony sötétlő bércein.' – 'Az, [. . .] kit olly Walter Scott-i színekkel föste?'

[20] 'egy törpe, keskeny nyílású százados cserajtó nyitott be egy szinte négyszegű, két széles ablakú, gerendákkal bépadlozott Walter Scott-i ebédlőszobába'.

[21] 'Itt még az *Ivanhoe* s régiségek búvára írójaként bővebben is kiereszkedhetnénk; nevezetesen: kik szoktak jelen lenni? millyen ranggal, renddel, öltözettel? nemzetiben-e vagy külföldiben? vendéghajakat viselnek-e, vagy első, középső s harmadik lépcsőn álló háromszegletes kalapokat? sat. – De mind illyen nagy ezekhez közel levő szógarmadákkal élést most sem a hely, sem az idő, sem célunk meg nem engedik. Elegendő legyen az adott rövid rajz.'

[22] London, 1898 (translated by R. Nisbet Bain).

[23] 'A nemes lord azt akarja, hogy az ember úgy végezzen egy anekdotont, mint Scott a regényeit: ki meddig élt, és hogyan halt meg.'

emphasized, as well as in verisimilitude. In the last stanza Hegedűs calls Scott 'the torch-bearer of our time' ('időnk vezérlámpása') (Hegedűs 1837). In this poem Hegedűs also bestowed two stanzas on praising Scott's biography of Napoleon, but the Hungarian critical assessment of this work was not so favourable in the second half of the nineteenth century. Two decades later Gyula Sárosi published a translated satirical poem (from an unidentified English source) which mocked both Napoleon and Scott[24] (Sárosi 1857), and another two decades later Frigyes Riedl accused Scott of belittling and betraying 'the great emperor', who − quoting Heine − was murdered by the Britons (Riedl 1877).[25]

We can discover several cases of intertextuality in the literature of the Reform Age: direct references, allusions (even paraphrases) and less direct influences like similarities in structure, nature description and characterization. But the most striking impact of Scott lies in the historical interest of our novelists.

The beginnings of historical fiction in Hungary

The earliest impact of Scott on Hungarian literature is traceable to the short stories of Károly Kisfaludy, who possessed some of Scott's novels in German in his library. In the story 'A vérpohár' ('The blood-cup'), he made an attempt to write a historical novella as early as 1823. It is set in the picturesque mountains of Abaúj and Zemplén during the civil wars in the beginning of the fourteenth century, but history does not influence the private affairs of the characters. The medieval period is represented as a barbarous and brutal age, set against 'our gentle present time'. But he successfully employed Scott's structural pattern: the slow beginning with carefully detailed historical circumstances as well as the personal characteristics and background of the characters, and the gradual acceleration of the events.

His heroine, the orphaned Hedvig, was brought up by her father to become courageous and patriotic, but also reckless and irascible, therefore possessing masculine features like some memorable Scott heroines such as Flora in *W*, Diana Vernon and Helen MacGregor in *RR*, Rebecca in *I*, or Lilias in *R*. The plot also recalls that of *W*.

Likewise, several pieces of the volume *Beszélyek* (Novellas, 1843) by Nagy Ignác show strong influence of Scott. The 'Hitrabság' (Bondage of faith) also leads the reader back to the fourteenth century. This story offers a variation of the Rebecca–Brian duet of *I*. Regina is an uncommonly beautiful Jewess, who is determined to protect her virtue from Leone Sacchieri, the illegitimate son of the king, but on the verge of jumping out of the window she catches a glimpse of her father and fiancé being dragged towards the torture chamber, and faints

---

[24] 'Győzött Wellington! s a győzelem / Nagyobb volt, mint a veszedelem. / S Waterloonál, bár nem volt ott, / Nem esett el, csak − Walter Scott.'

[25] 'történész is; csakhogy Scott nagy történelmi munkájában, *Napóleon élet*ében, felsőbb parancsra letörpítette a nagy császárt, elárulta pénzért, − Heine fellengős kifejezése szerint − azt, akit az angolok csak megöltek.'

into the arms of the knight. The modest and decent battle of words in Scott's novel develops into a real scuffle, and the open brutality of the erotic scene is a bad omen of the tragic ending. Also in the manner of Rebecca, in the heat of the quarrel she complains bitterly about the hypocrisy of the Christian knights. But the grave sentences of Scott's heroine turn into petty personalities against the illegitimacy of the adventurer. Only the externals of the original characters and plot were borrowed from Scott by Ignác Nagy.

Scott can also be credited with the upgrading of the novel genre into canonized literature all over Europe. The appearance of Hungarian literary criticism intertwined with the spread of Scott's novels, as these initiated theoretical speculation on the problems of genre. Numerous Hungarian critics praised his faithfulness to historical reality, his continuation of the epic traditions, his descriptions of nature and character. The novel genre had not been appropriate for the Neoclassical ideal: it lacked conformity with the established rules. With the breakthrough of Romanticism the popular became part of the elite culture: the previously despised common language and the shapeless prose genre became highly appreciated. The novel transmitted a new worldview, offering a bourgeois model of conduct and social norms to the reading public. The shift in attitude towards the novel is noticeable in the change of the terminology, as 'román', a phrase of German origin, was replaced by an original new term, 'regény' (rooted in 'rege', which means tale or legend in English), in harmony with the language reform movement. The metamorphosis can also be traced in the change of the title of a study by József Bajza: in the 1833 edition it appeared under the title 'A románköltésről' (On the Composition of Romans), but only three years later as 'A regényköltészetről' (On the Composition of Novels). It was the first essay in Hungary which elevated the novel into a critical work, and at that time there was no Hungarian example to refer to. Bajza based his theory on the novels of Scott and Goethe. In a footnote of the second, otherwise unaltered edition of his essay he announced his delight over the rise of the first great Hungarian novel to fulfil the requirements of the genre, *Abafi* by Miklós Jósika.

In his essay Bajza recommended (with Goethe the only exception) mostly British and American writers as models to be followed – Richardson and Fielding (as the creators of the genre), Scott, Irving and Cooper. He mentioned several titles from Scott: *T, K, GM, The Monastery* and *LM*.

In his theory and fiction alike, Bajza is characterized with a mixture of styles and principles. He respected the simplicity, balance and control of Classicism, the emotionalism of Sensibility, the nature and character descriptions of Romanticism, and the lifelike scenes and language of Realism. This kind of amalgamation is a constant feature in the oeuvre of Scott. The Neoclassical principles could not be followed in fiction, but otherwise Bajza's novellas represent this diversity. 'Ottilia' and 'A vándor' (The Wanderer) are written in the manner of Sensibility, reminding the reader of Goethe's *Werther*. 'Rege a hableányról' (A Legend of the Mermaid), 'A fekete lovag' (The Black Knight) and 'Kámor' carry more Romantic as well as Realistic features, and follow the footsteps of Scott. Bajza employed the picturesque and the sublime in his depictions of character and landscape, and he mixed the romance-like imagination with credibility in characterization and dialogues.

The fragmentary 'Kámor' is the closest to historical fiction, but history remains in the background.

The historical truth was a recurring problem in the literary criticism of the day, always connected to Scott's novels. Bajza expected less historical than poetical truth, and wanted to reconcile credibility with idealization. But other critics (Czuczor, Zilahy) definitely missed the historicity from Scott. Petrichevich held a contrary opinion, when he lodged a complaint against the 'penmen growing bold due to the witty painter of Scotland', being in fear of the readers' mixing reality with the tale in the 'hermaphroditic' historical novel[26] (Petrichevich 1843, 332).

The appearance of three important novels made 1836 a significant year in Hungarian fiction: *Abafi* by Jósika (discussed in the next section), *Szirmay Ilona* by József Gaal and *Az elbujdosott* by Lázár Petrichevich Horváth. The strong impact of Walter Scott is visible in the former ones, as well as other short and long stories of the same authors. In the last one, the novel of Petrichevich, the impact is superficial (as we have seen in the previous subchapter), this work is much closer to the 'silverfork novels' of Bulwer-Lytton.

In *Szirmay Ilona* the principal elements of the plot and the leading characters are known from historiography. József Gaal studied several sources to describe real personalities in the sixteenth-century war of independence led by Prince Ferenc Rákóczi, but he did not discover the connection between the fate of the characters and the historical process. This work is regarded as the last romance to bear the marks of the 'Ritter' – and 'Räuberroman' (György 1941, 117–18). However, Gaal managed to transplant Scott's structural innovation, the 'mediocre hero', later to be defined by György Lukács. Ilona, the heroine, is a neutralized, characterless, airy creature, with rare appearances throughout the novel, but still she is in the focus, related to all the important events in the book. In the later development of the Hungarian historical novel this compositional method becomes rare; the personality of the protagonist is more characteristic in the novels of Miklós Jósika, Mór Jókai, or Zsigmond Kemény. But in the second half of the century the genre fused the impact of several novel genres, especially the memoir-novels of Dumas *pére*, which followed the opposite direction, emphasizing the unique character of the protagonists.

Hungarian nationalism and historical fiction

Walter Scott aroused an ever-growing interest in the national myth of the Land of the Gaels, both in the homeland and on the Continent. Likewise in his novels Scott effectively reinforced the renewed sense of Scotland's nationhood. In a search for alternative values in the past to those of the contemporary Habsburg regime, the Hungarian historical novelists also found the Hungarian national

---

[26] 'Skóthon szellemdús festőjének hatására vérszemet kapott tollforgatók' [. . .] 'nem ártalmas-e vajjon a napi irodalomnak ezen hermaphrodit sarja, [. . .] nem téveszti-e össze, tarkán tetszkedő vegyületével, a históriát a mesével?'

stereotypes in the rebellious, untameable historic personalities and the sublime landscapes of Transylvania.

After long decades of experimentation, the first work in Hungarian literature to meet the requirements of the novel genre was published as late as 1836. The writer, Baron Miklós Jósika, a Transylvanian aristocrat (later an exile for his participation in the 1848–49 Hungarian Revolution), was for decades called the 'Hungarian Scott', which first as a beginner he gladly accepted, but later denied. The majority of his numerous works were historical novels, which gained enormous popularity in the period. In his first and best, *Abafi*, he managed to balance imitation of Walter Scott with originality, earning him the name 'the creator of the Hungarian novel'.

Like Scott, Jósika positively depicted a nation which had long lost her independence. The novel is set in Kolozsvár, in 1594, under the principality of Zsigmond Báthori. In the personality of the prince, Jósika continues Scott's line of rulers unfit for their vocation. Abafi, the protagonist, is a descendant of an ancient aristocratic family, who spends his youthful years in dissipation. Then, by a sudden recognition, he finds his vocation, and enters public life to battle for the national cause. Therefore, after the initial wavering between proper and ill behaviour, Abafi becomes a real hero, achieving mental and physical perfection, and always making the right decision in political matters as well as love affairs. For the reader, the acquaintance with the past becomes a source of cultural and moral power. The novel suggests that the rise of the Hungarian historical novel is inseparable from the rising nationalism of the 1820s to 1830s.

Jósika also sought to recreate the environment in a picturesque manner. In *Abafi* he provided details of the mountains and valleys, the caves and fountains of Transylvanian landscape counter to the late sixteenth-century streets and houses, as he noted the human 'physiognomy' of Kolozsvár and of the behaviour of its inhabitants. Similarly, he set the negligence and passivity of several characters and also of the protagonist in the beginning of the novel against his later enthusiasm and endeavour. In this way, the descriptions have various functions: they serve the growing demand of the readers for the '*couleur locale*'; create an atmosphere with the picturesque scenery; portray the personality traits of the character brought into contact with nature, and offer an illusion of credibility. But Jósika's narrator also keeps comparing past and present in customs and morals, drawing contrast between the exemplary period of history and the degenerated present. In short, in the very first Hungarian novel Transylvania emerged as a symbol of the glorious past, independent statehood, and patriotism, analagous to Highland Scotland.

Scott's influence became less direct from the 1840s onwards. References and allusions to his work slowly disappeared from Hungarian literature, although his innovations in fiction were mediated through French writers like Hugo, Dumas and Balzac. Yet the historical novel genre in the middle of the nineteenth century preserved some characteristics of Scott's fiction, especially in the choice of setting and his constant attempt at political compromise. The latter was the main endeavour of the 'Literary Deák Party', a group of thinkers, historians and writers surrounding Ferenc Deák, creator of the Austrian–Hungarian Compromise of 1867.

A member of this group, Baron József Eötvös, coined the phrase 'peaceful co-existence', suggesting that the aspirations of nationalities can be reconciled. In the oeuvre of Baron Eötvös, out of his four longer works of fiction only one is a historical novel, but that one is set in sixteenth-century Hungary and Transylvania, titled *Magyarország 1514-ben* (Hungary in 1514; 1847). The year in the title refers to the great Peasant Revolution, which forms the core of the novel, and the framework of its events. Under the pretence of a 300-year-old uprising the author presented his views of a possible revolution in the light of the problems of his own age, originating the realistic Hungarian historical novel with social purposes. He demystified the leader of the revolt, György Dózsa, representing him as an average man glorified by the ignorant mob. Eötvös had not seen Transylvania before writing this novel, which shows in the lack of nature descriptions. However, he presented wild and fierce Seclers, and the uncontrollability of their passions. While Jósika in the midst of the Reform Age introduced Transylvania as a country which offers a large scope for profitable action, Eötvös, at the premonitory signs of the Revolution, conjured up the dangers of violence, drastic solutions and the mobilization of the masses, even in the case of justified anger.

Zsigmond Kemény, another supporter of Ferenc Deák, also strove for the union between Hungary and Transylvania before the 1867 Compromise. In his two pamphlets after the Revolution, he defined the peculiar situation of Hungary: compared to other nationalities planning to secede from the monarchy, only the Hungarians would remain without allies; placed between the two emerging empires of a united Germany and an expanding Russia, Hungary could mediate between the civilized West and the underdeveloped East. After early attempts at the historical novel, all set in Transylvania, in a few years' interval he elaborated contemporary subjects in his short stories and novels. Then he returned to Transylvanian history in his best works, *Özvegy és leánya* (The Widow and her Daughter, 1857), *Rajongók* (Fanatics, 1859), and *Zord idő* (Severe Times, 1862).

Like Jósika, Kemény was a descendant of an ancient Transylvanian aristocratic family; therefore he had a similarly intimate relationship with the history of the region. He revived the events chosen from genuine chronicles and memoirs to illustrate his tenets about the tragic and unpredictable process of history, and the defencelessness of the individual in the hands of fate. In his world neither reason, nor moral values are valid. Written after the collapse of the revolution, his novels introduce Transylvania as the land of hopelessness and express his despair on the absurdity of man's endeavours.

The most prolific and popular Hungarian novelist, Mór Jókai, tried his hand at most of the styles and subgenres of contemporary fiction. As a law student, and a member of the Protestant lower nobility, his background was similar to that of Walter Scott. In contrast with Eötvös, Kemény, or Gyulai, who strived for realism in their novels, Jókai continued to employ the devices of romantic fiction until his death at the beginning of the twentieth century, to the satisfaction of his readers, but to the irritation of critics. His novels and short stories are filled with exotica and fantasy from all ages and parts of world; they express his optimistic view to sustain Hungarians hopes for a better life.

Jókai was not of Transylvanian origin, but his short travelogues, like 'Úti levelek' (Travel Records 1862), and 'More Patrio: Regényes kóborlások' (More Patrio: Romantic Rambles 1862), give evidence of his journeys of exploration in the region. Here the term 'romantic' is employed in the sense 'suggesting a romance'. Besides the character sketches and townscape descriptions, these accounts offered picturesque and sublime views of ruinous fortresses, the barren salt-mines of Parajd, the legendary and perilous cave of Homoródalmás, the enchanting but sinister St Anna Lake, or the mountain gorge of Torda, providing the prospective visitors with tales and legends related to the beauty spots.

His fiction set in distant times can be easily divided into two periods. The historical novels proper written in the first half of the 1850s: *Erdély aranykora* (The golden age in Transylvania, 1852),[27] *Török világ Magyarországon* (Turkish times in Hungary, 1853),[28] *Fehér rózsa* (White rose, 1854),[29] *Janicsárok végnapjai* (The last days of the Janizaries, 1854)[30] all present chapters from Transylvanian history. The second period, between 1877 and 1893, consists of numerous adventure stories where history remains in the background. He always kept the contemporary reader in mind; the flaws of his historic personalities served as warnings, their virtues as models for the Hungarian community. He returns to the ancient past of the region only in *Bálványosvár* (Idolburgh, 1883). The geographical name in the title refers to one of the seven royal castles of Transylvania (hence its German name 'Siebenbürgen'), and the story evolves in the war between paganism and Christianity as late as the thirteenth century.

Between the two distinct periods Jókai wrote two novels set in the recent past, *Szegény gazdagok* (The poor plutocrats, 1861)[31] and *Egy az Isten* (God's unity, 1877),[32] which reflected his latest personal experience of picturesque landscape, on a journey to the southern part of Transylvania in the summer of 1858. The contrast between the capitalist intrigues in Pest and Vienna and the adventures in a timeless fairytale world is a determining element of both works. In the hands of Jókai history was formed into myth and Transylvania into a 'land of romance' (like the Scottish Highlands for Waverley).

Pál Gyulai, descendant of an impoverished Transylvanian aristocratic family, was one of the leaders of Hungarian literary life in the second half of the nineteenth century, as an outstanding critic and literary historian. His story *Egy régi udvarház utolsó gazdája* (The last master of an old manor, 1857) is set less than a decade earlier than the time of writing. However, it can be classified as a historical novel (or novella) because the reader is made to face a historical phenomenon: the difficulties of the noble middle class after the emancipation of

---

[27] New York, 1898 (trans. S. L. and A. V. Waite), also: *Midst the Wild Carpathians*. London, 1894 (trans. R. Nisbet Bain).

[28] *The Slaves of the Padishah*. London, 1902 (trans. R. Nisbet Bain).

[29] *Halil, the Pedlar*. London, 1892 (trans. R. Nisbet Bain).

[30] *The Lion of Janina, or the Last Days of the Janissaries*. London, 1897, New York, 1898 (trans. R. Nisbet Bain).

[31] New York. 1874. (trans. I. Fretwell), London, 1899 (trans. R. Nisbet Bain).

[32] *Manasseh*. London, 1901 (trans. P. F. Bicknell).

serfs, and their 'passive resistance' to the violent 'civilizers' of the post-revolutionary Austrian government. The protagonist, an old Transylvanian nobleman, represents the pre-revolutionary liberalism of the nobility. During the revolution, while he was in hospital, his Romanian serfs were emancipated and became the new owners of the lands. The old nobleman, like Rip van Winkle in the famous story of Washington Irving, does not understand the historical changes; he cannot accept that his rights and estate have been curtailed.

In the period of Hungarian national revival, before and after the 1848 Revolution, the nationalism of Walter Scott served as an example for Hungarian historical novelists. To the emerging questions of the nation's present and future, they found an answer in the past, particularly in the most troublesome period of Hungarian history. The metamorphosis of the self-image of the nation can be traced in the sequence of the writing of Miklós Jósika, József Eötvös, Zsigmond Kemény, Pál Gyulai and Mór Jókai. The self-esteem and optimism of the Reform Age in Jósika's *Abafi*, the sublime horror of a peasant revolt in *Hungary in 1514*, written a year before the outbreak of the 1848 revolution by Eötvös, the tragic pessimism of both the historical novels of Kemény and the long short story of Gyulai after the defeat, and the optimistic encouragement in the numerous narratives of Jókai to rouse the self-respect and vitality of Hungary. Several of these works show a parallelism in their choice of time and setting: the turning points of Transylvanian past and the magnificent mountains in these novels are comparable to Scottish history and the Highlands as represented by Scott. Sixteenth- and seventeenth-century Transylvania emerged as a symbol of national unity and persistence. The hardships of a small, but independent country were employed for consolation in the desperate post-revolutionary years. By maintaining the cultural memory of the nation it became a device in the service of national survival.

In the second half of the nineteenth century Scott was considered an out-dated 'romantic' by critics, and by the 1880s, under the influence of Hippolyte Taine's literary history, his fiction was judged with disapproval by Frigyes Riedl and Tamás Szana. Scott's novels gradually became adventure stories for youngsters. Although György Lukács's work led to a revival in translating Scott's fiction between 1955 and 1980, he has never regained the popularity he enjoyed in early mid-nineteenth-century Hungary.

9 The Canonization of Walter Scott as the Inventor of the Historical Novel in Twentieth-Century Hungarian Reception

Gertrud Szamosi

From among the many different duties that every generation leaves behind, the saddest one remains the inevitable revision of fame. It seems to be somewhat cruel trying to do justice to somebody posthumously, especially in the case of those who were mostly worshipped and treated with utmost indulgence in their own days. It is a gross injustice to call forth the writer from among his contemporaries, whose feelings and ideas he was one with, and to question him in a hundred years' time on what he has to offer the following generations. Yet mankind cannot possibly preserve everybody for eternity; from time to time a great number of names have to be relegated to the index section of reference books. There is a bitter lesson to be learnt; one should be the most cautious with those who were once greeted with the most thunderous applause.[1]

Changing paradigms in the representation of historical consciousness

This chapter aims to assess Sir Walter Scott's Hungarian reception from the point of the changing perceptions, roles, modes and representations of historical consciousness.

---

[1] A sok mindenféle feladat közt, melyeket az egyes öltők az utókorra hagynak, alig lehet szomorúbb tiszt a népszerűségek átvizsgálásánál. Van abban valami kegyetlenség, ha holtukban igazságot akarunk gyakorolni azokkal szemben, a kik iránt a maguk kora csupa elnézés volt és hódolat. Méltánytalanság, kiszólítani az írót kortársai közül, a kiknek érzései és gondolatai keringtek benne, s számon kérni tőle, hogy van-e mondani-valója egy száz évvel utána élő nemzedék számára is? Csakhogy az emberiség nem őrizhet minden nevet az emlékezetében; időnként egy-egy sereget át kell utalnia a szakkönyvek névmutatóiba. S egy pár keserű leczke

As early as 1874, the Hungarian poet and translator Károly Szász (1829–1905), in his Academy prize-winning essay, praises Shakespeare and Scott for possessing the highest degree of historical consciousness, thus setting an example in showing that: 'artists should study history in great detail in order to provide the most effective illusion with the help of absolute truth' (1875, 240).[2] As for the relationship between art and history, Szász claims that history provides the raw material for art, and artists make use of the methods of historical research. The artist may invent the tale, and therefore, it might be enough if the minor characters and the period are historical, but the description of the age must resort to history:

> The best historical writers like Homer, Shakespeare, Scott, Hugo or our Katona, Arany, Eötvös, Kemény are similarly well trained in the study and research of history, as a result they are capable of deeply penetrating the spirit of the historical age. With a single brush stroke, in the figure of a minor character, in an episode of secondary importance, they provide a more appropriate characterization of a given period than historians do by means of the most thorough and detailed examination.[3] (1875, 241)

Positivist critical attention has proved to be most influential on the Hungarian reception of Sir Walter Scott as a result. It also outlined the focal topics of critical interest. Tamás Szana (1844–1908), the editor of *Figyelő* (Observer), a literary and art critical periodical mostly read by young middle-class intellectuals in the years 1871–76, was one of the earliest representatives of positivist literary criticism. *Törekvésünk* (Our aspirations) is the title of the amateur journalist's manifesto, which outlines the framework of a most ambitious cultural policy. As an ardent Positivist, he celebrates the centenary of Scott's birth with an article (1871) that explains Scott's historical commitment by means of providing biographic information about the writer, who apparently 'developed a keen sense of antiquarian interest for the past as a child collecting ballads and learning many of them by heart' (1871, 366).[4] In line with the middle-class realist aesthetic principles of the time, Szana distinguishes between two types of Romantic literature, which he classifies as historical–realist and philosophical–idealistic trends. He holds that the main objective of science proper and the major attraction of literature should be connected to the study and comparison, in a faithful and colourful manner, of different fashions and ways of thinking.

árán éppen azok a nevek intenek bennünket leghamarabb óvatosságra, a melyek körül a maguk korában sokat zúgott a taps (Voinovich 1921, 131).

[2]   'A történelmet magát kell e végből a legbehatóbban s a legrészletesebben tanulmányoznia, s a legteljesebb illusiót a legteljesebb igazság útján kell keresnie.'

[3]   Az igazi történeti költők: Homér, Shakespeare, Scott Walter, Hugo Victor, nálunk Katona, Arany, Eötvös és Kemény, valóban a legmélyebb történeti tanúlmányok alapján állnak; ők azok, a kik legmélyebben hatolnak a történeti korszakok szellemébe, s néha egy vonással, egy mellékalakban, egy másodrendű epizódban találóbban jellemeznek egy egész kort, mint a történetírók a legbehatóbb elemzésekkel s részletezésekkel.

[4]   'Már mint gyermek gyűjtött régi balladákat, melyeket könyv nélkül tudott.'

In his opinion historical concern should examine the different types and forms of society. He believes that Scott fulfils these requirements as he studies and portrays the different phases of human development in the fields of civilization, the state of human passions and that of the mind (366). Szana also hails Scott's masterly descriptions and compares his genius in characterization to that of the painter Hogarth.

With the help of Scott's characters, Szana defines the concept of the type, observing that: 'Walter Scott knew that certain types were connected to certain periods, as opposed to Smollett and Fielding, who simply copied every interesting character. Scott also examined their origins and tried to establish a coherent relationship between frame and content' (367).[5] Szana uses the concept of the type by calling forth a social model worthy of imitation, as a consequence of which the meaning of the work of art is to be derived from the social, historical, political and moral context of society in order to assist our inner development, the *Bildung* of the individual (367). Positivist critical interest in the epic genres and the novel in particular points towards a new Realist aesthetic that is primarily concerned with the social embeddedness of literature, the reflection of the real, the concepts of type and typicality. In summary it can be concluded that Szana outlines some of the most influential arguments that help to establish and maintain the popularity of the historical novel in subsequent periods.

Scott reception in the first half of the twentieth century

There is little doubt that Walter Scott's literary critics unanimously hail him as the inventor of the new genre of the historical novel. Géza Voinovich (1875–1952), the academically acclaimed literary historian and critic of the period, recognizes the historical atmosphere in the novels of Scott and attributes the writer's unexpectedly sudden fame to the events of the French revolution (1921, 139). With regard to Scott's historical approach, he claims that the writer 'never made use of serious history, but followed in the footsteps of a more poetic tradition; nevertheless Scott coloured his writings with historical characteristics and relics' (135).[6] Scott's antiquarian interest was often regarded as a true sign of his 'fiery Scottish patriotism' (136). His 'serious moral integrity and healthy outlook upon life' (138) were also warmly received at the time. However, Voinovich remarks that Scott often worked too hastily, as a result of which he produced many similar character types. He measures Scott's stature by quoting the *bon mots* of the Hungarian historical novelist Baron József Eötvös (1813–71): 'Whoever flies too high will appear to his fellow men like a tiny spot, but the one who merely mounts a chair will tower over them. Scott's

---

[5] 'Walter Scott tudta azt, hogy bizonyos typusok bizonyos időviszonyokhoz vannak kötve, s míg Smollett, Fielding egyszerűen lemásolt minden érdekes alakot, ő eredetüket vette vizsgálat alá, s azon igyekezett, hogy mindig összefüggésben álljon a keret és a tartalom.'

[6] 'Sohasem épített magára a komoly történelemre, mindig a költőibb hagyományra; de kiszínezte ezt a történelem vonásaival és emlékeivel.'

greatness was of the former' (137).[7] In Voinovich's evaluation, Scott's best novels are to be found among his first attempts: hence he praises *W* and *I* for excelling in legendary features and *R* for being his most lifelike work (141). Voinovich ends his study on a prophetic note by claiming that 'there is no place for him among the greats of world literature' (145), as a result of which 'his fame will not withstand the march of time' (146).

In 1915 an influential periodical paid tribute to Walter Scott on the centenary of the publication of *Waverley*. *Budapesti Szemle* (Budapest review), a monthly periodical founded at the initiative of and subsidized by the Hungarian Academy of Sciences between 1873 and 1944, published the following mission statement on its cover page: '*Budapesti Szemle* tries to inform the Hungarian public of those ideas that occupy the rest of the world; it aims to mediate on the one hand between the academic fields of study and the educated reading public and on the other hand between Hungarian and foreign literatures.'[8] In an inaugural address to members of the Academy in 1915 Zoltán Ferenczi, head of the Academy Library and editor of the Hungarian *Shakespeare Tár* (Shakespeare repository) from 1912 to 1922, claims that the rise of the novel and the beginnings of British literary influence in Hungary are intertwined. He attributes the development of the genre to the influence of Bulwer-Lylton and Scott, some of the most popular British writers of the time.[9] Ferenczi finds it rather disheartening that *W* has not yet been translated into Hungarian. At the same time he also admits that *W* is rarely seen as Scott's best work (1915, 86). Ferenczi gives a detailed account of the plot that primarily takes the form of an 'adventure story' as opposed to being an 'analytical' work of 'character study' (92). According to Ferenczi, Scott's writing style possesses a 'charming sense of reality' (92), but what he admires most is the writer's art of characterization:

> The emphasis falls on those heroes and minor characters who, in spite of not being historical figures, are still able to represent the main ideas of the period.[10] (94)

Ferenczi also draws attention to the minor characters, whose importance becomes a cornerstone for Scott's later reception. The critic makes a most controversial statement by claiming that 'the historical novel is the enemy of history' (95), thereby foreshadowing future debates about historicism.

---

[7]   'Eötvös mondja valahol, hogy a ki nagyon is magasra száll, az embertársai szemében csak egy parányi pontnak látszik; a ki csupán székre áll, az vállal kimagaslik a többiek közül. Scott nagysága ilyen volt.'

[8]   'A *Budapesti Szemle* tájékoztatni igyekszik a magyar közönséget az eszmékről, melyek világszerte foglalkoztatják a szellemeket s mintegy közvetítő kíván lenni egyfelől a szaktudomány és mívelt közönség, másfelől a hazai és a külföldi irodalom között.'

[9]   For a more detailed discussion of the topic see Antal Wéber, *A magyar regény kezdetei* (The beginnings of the Hungarian novel) (1959, 102–61).

[10]   A fősúlyt rendesen egy-egy oly hősre és mellékalakra helyezi, a kik a történelmi korban, tehát a történelemben szerepelnek s a kik a felvett kor eszméjét képviselik ugyan, de nem történelmi alakok.

Another influential Positivist literary historian of the time, Ferenc Szinnyei (1875–1927) predicted that historicism in the period of literary modernism is more likely to be concerned with the investigation of our inner world, hence it is a movement turning towards representations of our consciousness and feelings, in opposition to common historical concern that focuses on the representation of outer experience (1926, 221). The interwar years were marked by a worldwide interest in historical topics that significantly contributed to the growing demand for historical novels. Among the most celebrated Hungarian historical writers of the time were Géza Gárdonyi (1863–1922) and Ferenc Móra (1879–1934), whose books have joined the canon of youth literature. Launched in 1908 *Nyugat* (West), the leading literary journal of the time, became a representative forum for Modernist writers until its cessation in 1938. The paper revealed a marked orientation towards contemporary European and world literature and its contributors set the standards for the reception of new modernist literature. The translator and critic Irma P. Berinkey notes that with the rise of the new genre of historical autobiography, fantasy gives way to historical facts. She finds that in more recent times the romantically decorative hero worship of Scott's and Carlyle's age has been surpassed:

> While historical novels belong with the earlier period of hero-worship, historical biographies are more up to date. In the case of the latter genre, the psychological analysis of historical figures provides a thorough examination of their spiritual inclinations thus revealing their genius and human frailty alike. As a result the remote idols of old times are taken down from their pedestals and become more accessible for the contemporary reader.[11] (1933, 253)

Berinkey connects the inevitable decline of the genre to the common experience that 'the critical, scientific and psychological school of historical biographies is much closer to our world than the Romantic style of the historical novel' (1933, 253).[12]

Another well-known theorist and historical novel writer, translator, critic and member of the *Nyugat* generation, Géza Laczkó (1884–1953), in his study on the historical novel claims that, apart from Scott's highly praised sense of moral consciousness, historical novelists should also possess a 'sense of historical responsibility' (1937, 241).[13] As a Positivist thinker he rejected the Romantic type of historical novels, and in his own works he elaborated on a philologically more exact historical approach. Nevertheless, the *poeta doctus* Laczkó also pays his tribute to Walter Scott as a major representative of the genre. In his view *Waverley* was published at the most appropriate moment:

---

[11] A történelmi regény a hőskultusz korából való. A történelmi életrajz a hőskultusz megfordítottja. A régi korok megközelíthetetlen ideáljait leszállítja piedesztáljukról. Nemcsak zsenijüknek, hanem emberi gyarlóságuknak és egész lelki adottságuknak mélyreható pszichológiai analízisével közelebb hozza őket a mai emberhez.

[12] 'A történelmi életrajz kritikus és tudományos szelleme és lélekelemző irányzata közelebb áll a mai emberhez, mint a történelmi regény romatikája.'

[13] 'történelmi felelősségérzet'.

At the time when the English novel was drowned in the syrup of sentimentalism and Victorian morality, while the reading public, locked in a stuffy room, was kept on a diet of sweetmeats spiced with outrageous adventure, there came an entirely unknown writer who opened the windows, took a hatchet and made his way towards the Scottish woods where, in a moonlit clearing, he found Tale and Nature entangled in each other's arms, fast asleep.[14] (1935, 478)

The critic gives the briefest summary ever written in which he claims that the success of Scott's art stems from the sources of 'outward historical faithfulness, characterization, heroic legends and adventure' (1937, 256).[15] Accordingly Scott's recipe for the novel includes 'one portion fashion, one portion folk element, and two portions of personal novelty' (257).[16]

In the period following the First World War, there was a general spirit of revolt against earlier methods of literary study, namely

against the mere accumulation of unrelated facts, and against the whole underlying assumption that literature should be explained by the methods of natural sciences; by causality, or by other external determining forces that are formulated in Taine's famous slogan of *race, milieu, moment*. (Wellek 1963, 256)

In an attempt to overcome the flat rationalism of the Positivists, German literary historians inspired by Oswald Spengler's *Decline of the West* opened up a new ground of large-scale syntheses in the theoretical and historical fields of the intellectual world. At the very centre of the 'history of the spirit' world-view there is a universal analogizing method that looks for totality behind objects of study and explains them with the Zeitgeist, or spirit of the times (Wellek 1963, 272). By the 1930s the 'history of the spirit' philosophy also became popular in Hungary, one of its major proponents being the Anglophile polymath of the period, Antal Szerb (1901–45). Szerb's concept of historicism refuted the dominant evolutionary theories of the time, as he held that nations and cultures were similar to living organisms, inasmuch as they followed nature's circular life-model in their development.

Since Szerb regarded a work of art as necessarily representative of the spirit of the age in which it was conceived, he held that Scott's central concern for the novel was not primarily historical but stemmed from a more general human interest, not unlike that of Romantic love: 'The sentimental part, concerning the immaculate knight and his blushing lady, together with their conventionally convoluted story, though it may look rather lifeless to a modern audience, conformed entirely to the taste of the period'

---

[14] Amikor az angol regény belefulladt az érzelmesség és erény polgári szirupjába, amelyhez borzalmas kalandokból gyúrt fűszeres süteménykéket ropogtattak négy fal zárt levegőjében, egy ismeretlen szerző kitárta az ablakokat, csákányt ragadott, s elindult a skót erdők felé, amelyek tisztásain holdfényben egymást átölelve aludt a Mese és a Természet.
[15] 'Történelmi külső hűség, természetfestés, hősi legenda, kaland.'
[16] 'Egy rész divat, egy rész népi hozam, két rész egyéni újdonság.'

(1941, 497).[17] He noted that Scott's antiquarian interest did not embrace the spiritual life of those living in the past (498), while for Szerb the centrality of experience is more markedly spiritual than it is material. In Szerb's evaluation, the historical spirit of an age can be caught in the works of genius; therefore, in *A világirodalom története* (The history of world literature) (1941) he looks only at the best writers of the time. Szerb shared the Positivists' biographical concern, but he only focused on events that he believed to have played a formative role in the experience of the writer. In Szerb's final assessment, Scott has two native lands, England and Scotland, and accordingly, his writing is best characterized with 'excellent English realism and a dry Scottish sense of humour' (498). Nevertheless, in his view Scott was a truly Romantic spirit who embraced his native land and its national past with a passionate love:

> It was Macpherson and Burns who transformed Scotland, under influence of the Scottish national renaissance of the eighteenth century, into the favourite haunt of the Romantic imagination, but it was Scott who composed its usable imaginary travel-guide. He was the one to draw the map of its legends. Scott was the first British poet to be inspired by the driving force of the Romantic soul, by the national spirit.[18] (1941, 499)

The newly emerging Romantic–Realist debate becomes crucial from the point of historical representations, as it sets the standards for the future reception of Scott. Szerb's final verdict that Scott's novels were rather naive for the general taste of the contemporary reading public (498) paved the way towards relegating Scott's literary heritage to the shelves of youth literature.

The Lukácsian legacy of Walter Scott's reception

György Szegedy von Lukács, later known as Georg Lukács (1885–1971), was born in Budapest. The Hungarian literary historian, essayist and critic developed an ambiguous reputation for being a highly influential and a most controversial figure of the Marxist tradition at one and the same time, though his stature had already been established with two major works of criticism before he turned towards Marxism in about 1910. Lukács's best-known work on Scott and the genre was undoubtedly *The Historical Novel* (1937), in which the theorist applied an entirely new paradigm to the reception of Scott, as a result of which the genius of Romantic literature was re-evaluated as a major Realist writer. In *The Historical Novel*, Lukács also laid the foundations of Marxist literary criticism

---

[17] 'Ez a szentimentális rész teljesen a kor ízlése szerint íródott, a kifogástalan lovag és szende hölgye és konvencionálisan fordulatos történetük ma sápadtnak tűnik.'

[18] Skóciát Macpherson és Burns tette a romantikus képzelet kedves tartózkodó helyévé, a XVIII. század végén beálló skót nemzeti felújulás hatása alatt, de Scott írta meg használható imaginárius úti kalauzát, ő rajzolta meg legendáinak térképét. Az első brit költő, akit a romantikus lélek egyik legfőbb mozgatója, a nemzeti érzés ihlet.

by providing new means for interpreting nineteenth-century literature in terms of Realism, with special emphasis on its social and ideological implications. Lukács proclaimed that Realist art strove to capture the totality of life, and he advocated the idea that historical processes could be better understood and represented with the help of art. For Lukács, 'the essential aim of the novel is the representation of the way society moves' (1962, 144). Therefore he scrutinized Scott's novels, searching for characteristics that would provide general connections to the development of human societies.

According to Lukács, it was the 'transformation of men's existence and consciousness throughout Europe [that] provided the economic and ideological basis for Scott's historical novel' (31). He held the view that the evolution of the genre of the historical novel was necessarily connected to the socio-historical development of society, for the purpose of which the acquisition of a historical sense, or as he put it, a 'conscious growth of historicism' (22) was vital. Lukács formulated the aesthetic principles of the historical novel in relation to Walter Scott's works, as he held that modern Realism came into being when the Scottish writer started to represent the workings of history in fiction writing. Lukács stated that the first mass experience of history was provided by the French Revolution as 'it strengthened the feeling that there is such a thing as history, that it is an uninterrupted process of changes and finally that it has a direct effect upon the life of every individual' (23). Influenced by Hegelian ideas, he advocated a conception of history according to which 'human progress develops ever increasingly out of the inner conflict of social forces in history itself' (27) and as such, it provides 'the most important theoretical preliminaries for the future transformation of society' (20).

In *The Historical Novel* Lukács identified Realism as the only literary mode capable of representing the totality of society by revealing, through its narrative form, the underlying movement of history. In his view, the greatest artists represent the totality of human life in the most effective way, therefore Scott's characters serve a historically representative function, since their portrayal as historical subjects forms an integral part of the given society they manifest: 'Scott's greatness lies in the capacity to give living human embodiment to historical-social types' (35). 'Typical' characters are microcosms of the prime historical determinants of an age, as they become indicators of the forces that allow us to grasp the movement of history itself. Characterization serves as a major device of Realism, since the best literature of the kind involves characters that have Realist individuality, while embodying larger historical forces. Lukács warns that it is a mistake to see Scott as a Romantic writer, since his national heroes are the most prosaic, decent and average of characters (36). In his argument the paradigmatic figure is Jeanie Deans, 'the Puritan peasant girl' (52) who in *HM* represents the true voice of Scotland. She is a genuinely archetypal heroine for the historical novel, not only because she proves without doubt that real heroism resides in ordinary folk, but because her heroism makes her one of Scott's popular heroes. In other words, the critical acclaim attributed to Scott's popular characters is evidence of the true heroism of such people. Scott's much-debated portrayal of characters comes to fullness with the major figures turning out to be minor ones, despite their social positions, and the minor characters becoming major ones as a result of their fortitude.

Scott is placed in the role of the ardent conservative who 'attempts by fathoming historically the whole of English development to find a "middle way" for himself between the warring extremes' (32). For Lukács, Scott's conception of British history strives towards the 'middle course', the famous English compromise that asserts itself in the struggle of extremes. Like earlier critics, he also believes that plot construction and the selection of the passive, mediocre hero are of major importance among Scott's artistic methods. The advantage of such a hero, according to Lukács, is that in a historical situation involving 'hostile social forces' he can, 'through character and fortune, enter into human contact with both camps' (36–37), because he does not passionately side with either camp; moreover, he 'provide[s] a perfect instrument for Scott's way of presenting the totality of art in transitional stages of history' (35). Lukács illustrates the 'compositional importance of the mediocre hero' (36) with the help of Edward Waverley, who most importantly provides a link between the two competing parties by entering 'through character and fortune into human contact with both camps' (37). The hero of *Waverley* is an English squire in origin, who at the time of the Jacobite rising of 1745 sustains personal relations with both the rebellious Stuart supporters and those on the Hanoverian side. 'In this way Waverley's fortunes create a plot which not only gives us a pragmatic picture of the struggle on both sides, but brings us humanly close to the important representatives of either side' (37).

The 'truthfulness of historical atmosphere' in Scott's case most importantly 'rests on the popular character of his art' (48). The archetypical tragic hero is Euan Dhu, Vich Ian Vohr's fellow clansman who, at the trial where both of them are condemned to death, offers his and other clan members' lives in return for their chief's release (50). According to Lukács 'historical authenticity means for [Scott] the quality of the inner life, the morality, heroism, capacity for sacrifice, steadfastness etc. peculiar to a given age' (50). This is not the over-used 'local colour' that earlier Scott reception dwelt on so extensively:

> It is neither by analysis, nor by psychological explanation of its ideas that Scott familiarizes us with the peculiar historical qualities of the inner life of an age, but by a broad portrayal of its being, by showing how thoughts, feelings, and modes of behaviour grow up out of this basis. (1962, 50)

If it is not the means of antiquarian research and factual analysis of the past, then what provides the bases of historical faithfulness? According to Lukács, the historical necessity embedded in social processes gains representation through particular events in the life of individuals, and the writer presents these in the form of lifelike experience. Through the historical novel readers 'should re-experience the historical period as a phase of mankind's development which concerns and moves us' (42). For Lukács, Walter Scott remains the genius of the new genre, and his greatness lies in paving the way for nineteenth-century Realist art (81). However, Lukács was generally regarded as a problematic thinker, due to his active participation in a number of doomed political factions; for the greater part of his life he was viewed with suspicion by different Communist Party ideologists. Only in the 1980s did the party and academic circles start to integrate Lukács's philosophy into the mainstream of Hungarian culture. The mostly ambivalent evaluation of the Lukácsian oeuvre as a whole has inevitably left its mark on the Hungarian reception of Scott. As a result, some of Lukács's most important Marxist theoretical implications, including the universality of experience, the totality of life, the concept of the type, the dialectical relationship of social and individual existence, and the world-view of the author (Gyáni 2004, 80), did not enter the critical discourse on Walter Scott's art. His work had a powerful reception abroad.

The ideologically ambivalent reception of the historical novel

In the wake of the communist takeover of Hungary, the cultural life of the country was kept under tight control in order to minimize Western influence. There was no hope for revival until the aftermath of the 1956 revolution, when the counter-revolutionary government of János Kádár attempted to pacify Hungarian intellectuals by offering them minor concessions. The best word to characterize the political and ideological situation in Hungary under the Kádárian era is 'ambiguity'. The relative freedom and tolerance shown by the government in the early 1960s did not readily yield to a stable situation; the ideological freedom of the country remained restricted. Curiously enough, the cultural vacuum of the post-war years saw the publication of two Scott novels: in 1949 *W* was first published in a translation by János Bókay (1892–1961); and in 1955 *I* was reprinted in a new translation by the writer Tivadar Szinnai (1894–1972) under the classification of 'youth literature', with a publisher's note stating it was 'for twelve years of age and over'. In the later years of the communist period, book publishing developed into a flourishing industry, and owing to high state subsidies, books were sold for extremely low prices. In spite of heavy censorship, a wide selection of world literature was translated and delivered to the Hungarian reading public. Between 1955 and 1980 seven previously unpublished novels of Scott appeared: *RR* in 1959 and *OM* (Puritánok utódai) in 1964, both translated by Tivadar Szinnai. *BL* (A lammermoori nász) was translated by Ilona Kulin in 1967. In 1971 Balázs László (b. 1944) translated *K* on the basis of the novel's 1906 edition.[19] *R* was translated in 1972 by István Bart (b. 1944). *FN* (Nigel jussa) was translated by Ágota Kászonyi (b. 1942) in 1975, working from the 1905 London Nelson edition. In 1978 György Szegő (1908–69) translated *PP* (A lovag) into Hungarian from the 1906 London Dent edition. Seven new translations of previously translated novels were also reprinted. Altogether thirty-two different Scott editions became available to the general public.

In the second half of the 1960s *Tiszatáj* (Tisza region), one of the highly regarded provincial literary journals in the country, launched a public debate on the historical novel. In his opening article, the literary historian Lajos Csetri (b. 1928) announced the crisis of the genre (1967, 155). The author gives the following outline of the state of affairs:

---

[19]   London; Edinburgh; Dublin; New York: Thomas Nelson and Sons.

Even the best works of the most traditional type of historical fiction barely pass the level of best sellers; indeed, a large proportion of them are little above kitsch. The greatest Romantic historical novelists of the previous century were first downgraded to the level of youth literature, and this was not the end of the process: from one generation to the next, they have entertained an increasingly juvenile public, eventually 'developing' into children's literature.[20] (1967, 155)

Csetri comes to the conclusion that however hard it tries to update itself, there is no future for the 'modern' Romantic historical novel, because 'it is an epigone product that is destined to take over the function of pulp fiction' (155).[21] In a subsequent issue of the review, another critic incredulously wondered which historical novelists Csetri was referring to:

If he was thinking of Jókai, Walter Scott, Dumas, Victor Hugo, he was wrong. All relevant statistical data show that it is not only the young who favour the works of these writers, but they are also notably popular with male intellectuals.[22] (1967, 778)

Another defender of the classical historical novel, the Hungarian academician Béla Pomogáts (b. 1934), emphasized the educational importance of the genre by claiming that the readers' expectations of the historical novel are those of 'guidance', and the interpretation of the past or present (1966, 36). The literary historian and film critic László Nagy (1927–73) shared the prevalent opinion of other intellectuals:

The average reader turns to the historical novel in order to find out more about the national, or the common human historical past; therefore one is more likely to read historical novels that focus on great historical turning points or outstanding historical personalities and speak to us in the most captivating and enjoyable manner.[23] (1968, 170–71)

The attractions of the historical novel are manifold; apart from offering historical and moral education, it also offers fine entertainment. A survey carried

---

[20] A történelmi regény hagyományos típusaiban ma már a legjobb eredmények is csak a bestseller szintjét érik el, a produkció többsége viszont legalábbis a giccs határterületén mozog. A múlt századi romantikus történelmi regény nagyjai századunkban először ifjúsági irodalommá degradálódtak, de a folyamat nem állt meg: nemzedékről nemzedékre egyre éretlenebb korúak olvasmányát képezik, lassan gyermek-irodalommá 'fejlődnek'.

[21] 'eleve epigon produktum, mely a ponyva funkcióját tölti be.'

[22] Ha Jókaira, Walter Scottra, Dumas-ra, Victor Hugóra – tévedett. Valamennyi idevonatkozó statisztika tanúsága szerint e szerzők művei nemcsak ifjúsági, hanem rendkívül erősen favorizált felnőtt olvasmányai az értelmiségi férfirétegeknek is.

[23] Az átlagolvasó a történelmi regényekben a saját nemzeti vagy egyetemes emberi múltját keresi, s elsősorban azokat a történelmi regényeket olvassa szívesen, amelyek nagy történelmi sorsfordulókról vagy kiemelkedő jelentőségű történelmi személyekről szólnak, s amelyek mondanivalójukat a legérdekfeszítőbb módon, a lehető legélvezetesebb stílusban adják elő.

out by the Szolnok County Library in 1966 testifies to the outstanding popularity of the genre. The study found that, in the case of literary works, 24 per cent
of all books borrowed from the library were historical novels. On investigating
the composition of the readership, it found that the majority were secondary-
school students, with manual workers and the elderly a close second (Szathmáry
1967, 585). Scott was placed third on the list of the most popular writers, only
preceded by the most favoured Hungarian Romantic writer Mór Jókai and the
French author Alexander Dumas. In the popularity stakes, *I* stood in fifteenth
place, as it was borrowed twelve times in the course of a month, whilst *T*
(A talizmán) was in nineteenth place, having been borrowed eleven times. The
relatively high popularity rate of the genre with the working classes, who made
up 28 per cent of the total readership in Budapest, called forth a statement from
the Communist Party's Cultural and Theoretical Work Association:

> Considering the traditionally low standard of the newly engaged peasant and other
> layers of society in their relation to the arts, even this petty bourgeois art form can
> present itself as a new 'conquest', a 'higher form of development' that may be read as
> the first sign of their long-awaited 'advancement'.[24] (1966, 48)

The debate on the historical novel, and the inconsistent judgement on the
genre itself, most likely stems from the general ideological repugnance towards
Romanticism. In spite of the Lukácsian legacy, Scott is still seen as an essentially
Romantic writer, and as such he is considered outmoded. On the bicentenary
of his birth, a major Hungarian scholar, Géza Hegedűs (1912–99) confessed,
'I mostly resort to the novels of Jókai, Hugo or Scott, when I am forced to
stay in bed with a light flu, or find myself exhausted by modern literature'
(1971, 1229).[25]

In spite of such remarks, Scott's role as a popular historical novelist and the
extent of his historicity continued to attract attention. The Hungarian Scott
reception of the period is characterized by two recurrent motifs: in the more
positive reviews the Realist aesthetic values of his art are highlighted, while
negative criticism dismisses the outdated principles of Romantic aestheticism.
Tivadar Szinnai, who translated *RR* into Hungarian in 1959, argues that Scott's
main attraction is due to his 'ability to offer a full experience of the past,
providing the reader with a truthful experience of the landscape and the different scenes, and participation in the life of the characters' (1959, 459).[26] At one
and the same time Szinnai draws a comparison between Scott and Thomas

---

[24] A művészetek élvezetébe újonnan bekapcsolódó paraszti és más rétegek számára a
múlt alacsony szintjéről nézve még a kispolgári jellegű művészet is mint újonnan
'meghódított', 'magasabb fejlődési fok', mint régen várt 'emelkedés' jelentkezhet.

[25] 'Én például ha könnyű influenza pihenni kényszerít, vagy ha átmenetileg kimer-
ültem a modern irodalom különböző zsákutcáiban, Jókai, Hugo vagy Scott reg-
ényekhez szoktam fordulni.'

[26] 'az átélés és megelevenítés képessége, segítségével olvasói is átélik a múltat, valóság-
gal látják a leírt tájakat és jeleneteket, részt vesznek a regényalakok életében.'

Mann, concluding that in most of his novels Scott is 'shallow, as he is unable to penetrate beneath the surface of the past as, for example, Thomas Mann could' (460).[27] Bart gives an outline of what he regards as a major representational achievement of Scott's historical fidelity. In the story of *I* Scott was confronted for the first time with the particular challenges involved in dramatizing a period that lay more than a generation in the past and in a setting more remote than late seventeenth-century Scotland (1980, 239). The same critic and Scott translator praises *OM* (Puritánok utódai) for the success of 'a major attempt to portray historical forces' (204).[28] At the other end of the scale, Bart considers *BL* (A lammermoori nász) to be the least historical of Scott's novels, yet he also welcomes the fact that 'for this shortcoming the reader is compensated by the personality of Edgar Ravenswood, who is a real protagonist' (1977, 404).[29]

Apart from Scott's evaluation as a major historical novelist, his reception focuses on a number of different topics, including the skill of his characterization, his optimistic world-view and sense of humour (Elek 1938, 19–21). Several critics from the Hungarian Age of Reform to the most recent times also highlight Scott's role as a moral educator and his unique ability to raise national self-consciousness by revitalizing the readers' interest in the past. The eminent literary historian Mihály Szegedy-Maszák (b. 1943), in his monograph on nineteenth-century British literature, claims that Scott 'wrote his best novels in order to help the development of national self-continuity' (1982, 128). He cites the example of *HM*, which reveals, within the larger historical subtext of Scotland's Anglicization, the problematic character of the newly implemented political and cultural reforms that hint towards assimilation. More recently Walter Scott has also been evaluated as the precursor to the modern psychological novel because *HM* (Midlothian szíve) offers a unique moral and psychological study of the inner development of its characters (Bart 1980, 693). Bart's postscript to *BD* (A fekete törpe) (1974) connects Scott with the mainstream of twentieth-century Eastern European literature by praising *HW* and 'The Two Drovers' for their balladistic intensity and poetically folkloristic style:

> Something similar is to be created in Eastern Europe in the course of the twentieth century, when the Hungarian writer Zsigmond Móricz will compose a fateful drama out of the ruins of a disintegrating world-order with its no longer meaningful, yet still murderous traditions.[30] (1974, 443)

---

[27] 'felszínes, a múlt lényegébe nem tudott olyan mélyen behatolni, mint például Thomas Mann.'

[28] 'legnagyobb szabású kísérlete a történelem mozgásának ábrázolására.'

[29] 'Kárpótlásul azonban ennek a regénynek igazi főhőse van Edgar Ravenswood személyében.'

[30] A huszadik századi Kelet-Európa teremt majd hasonlót. A széthulló régi világ értelmüket, hitüket vesztett, ám még gyilkos erejű tradícióit Móricz Zsigmond-i végzetdrámává komponálja.

It is hard to predict what kind of future awaits Walter Scott's Hungarian reception. Tamás Ungvári (b. 1939), a learned critic of Scott, presents an optimistic outlook:

> It is not inconceivable that his 'renaissance' will eventually arrive. His volumes have been neglected for long enough. Occasionally one of his works manages to keep the young spellbound; thus his magic has not worn off entirely. Yet, he does not glow with full radiance anymore. His plunge was sudden, and his rise will be slow. He is waiting for someone to discover him, and this person cannot be a literary historian. Scott rediscovery is to come from a literary movement able to draw inspiration at his inexhaustible source.[31] (1964, 1)

Walter Scott's decline into light reading

Though Scott's literary prestige was left more or less intact for almost a hundred years, his reputation started rapidly to decline at the beginning of the twentieth century, when he was increasingly relegated to the shelves of youth literature. In 1905, when the first Hungarian translation of *QD* was published, the work of the poet and translator Béla Telekes (1873–1960), it took the form of an edition 'revised for young people'. At the beginning of the twentieth century Scott's role as youth educator is still being emphasized by Ferenczi:

> Walter Scott's reception suffers at the cruel hands of literary history. Scott, in his own time, undoubtedly ruled the literary world and attained unprecedented success both in his literary and publishing career. Yet a hundred years after his death, Scott's books are placed on the highest shelves of libraries, which can only be reached with a ladder, with the exception of those volumes put on the lowest ones, so as to be within the reach of children.[32] (1915, 96)

When trying to assess Scott's reputation as a writer of youth literature, one needs to consider his role in the literary education of Hungarian pupils. Arthur Yolland (1874–1956), a young Englishman who received his degree in philology at Cambridge, arrived in Hungary in the year of the millennium festivities and founded the Department of English Studies at Péter Pázmány University of Budapest in 1899, where he lectured until 1936. In 1924, when the new school-law was drafted, he proposed the introduction of English-language teaching in Hungarian high schools and wrote a series of

---

[31] Elképzelhető, hogy lesz reneszánsza. Oly régen pihennek kötetei olvasatlan. Egy-egy munkája megbabonázza az ifjúságot, a teljes varázslat nem múlt el. Igazi fényében mégsem ragyog. Magasról zuhant le, lassan emelkedik fel ismét. Felfedezőjére vár, s ez nem lehet irodalomtörténész. Csak egy írói mozgalom, mely újra merít kiapadhatatlan forrásából.

[32] Mostoha irodalomtörténeti sors jutott Walter Scottnak. , aki a maga idején valóban fejedelme volt az irodalomnak, addig példátlan irodalmi-és könyvkiadói-sikereket aratott, halála után száz évvel a könyvtárak legmagasabb polcaira került, ahonnan csak létrán állva lehet levenni a köteteket-annak a néhánynak a kivételével, amely viszont a legalacsonyabb polcokon rakódott le a gyerekek keze ügyébe.

textbooks for secondary education. Yolland compiled a schoolbook, *Szemelvények a XIX.század angol remekíróiból: Angol olvasókönyv* (Anthology of the best writing in nineteenth-century English literature: English reader) (1928), in which he devoted an entire chapter to the literary oeuvre of Sir Walter Scott. He provided biographical information and a brief selection of poetical and prose works,[33] and supplemented them with explanatory footnotes in Hungarian. From among Scott's writings Yolland expresses his deepest admiration for *The Antiquary*, as it 'contains the best description of Scottish life and character ever written' (1928, 8). Unfortunately the collection of textbooks from the period before the 1960s is rather sparse, as books of the time were either destroyed by the wars or 'picked apart' by political propagandists. In most recent literary textbooks, the novels of Scott are mostly classified as 'light reading' if they are mentioned at all.

Any attempt to assess Walter Scott's popularity with the Hungarian reading public would be incomplete without consulting the existing publication records. *I* has undoubtedly been among the most widely published of Scott novels in Hungary, as in other European countries: it has been translated into Hungarian seven times and printed in thirteen different editions. It is most likely to remain the one novel to have challenged so many translators from different historical periods; the earliest one being the work of András Thaisz (1789–1840) in 1829, to be followed by the 'over-ornamented' translation by a Hungarian writer who had settled in England, a certain Mrs Ginever, Ilona Győry (1868–1926) in 1906. In his 1935 edition Ernő Salgó (1873–1946), journalist and translator, must have relied heavily on Győry's version. The most recent and complete version is that of István Bart, from 1993. Bart remains the only Hungarian to have translated the 'Dedicatory Epistle', including Scott's introduction to the novel written in 1830. Thaisz, Győry and Szinnai did not translate Scott's notes; Salgó included some of them; while Bart translated them all. Curiously enough, in place of Scott's historical explanations, Szinnai included his own, while Győry backed up the text with historical linguistic remarks and notes on puns (155). Even the most recent translation's language remains rather archaic, and in line with the earlier translations it entirely ignores the different linguistic registers used by Scott. In 1993 the writer and translator Zoltán Majtényi (b. 1933) translated Scott's *Richard Coeur de Lion* from an Italian publication. This richly illustrated self-conscious imitation of a historical romance is intentionally marketed for young readers. With the liberalization of Hungarian book publishing in the 1990s, many publishers unearthed some of the best-known works by Scott. Owing to prevailing copyright regulations, most of them opted for the texts of early twentieth-century translations, and in order to counterbalance the curiously archaic language the novels have often been packaged under attractive cover designs that market *I* (2000) and *T* (1999) in the guise of enticing historical adventure stories.

---

[33] These are the following: 1. 'Trial and Execution of Mary Queen of Scots', 2. 'Lullaby', 3. From 'The Lay of the Minstrel', 4. 'The Death of Marmion', 5. 'Sir Walter Scott to his son Charles' by Lockhart (1928, 9–25).

QD is among the earliest translations of the Scott novels. It was published in six different editions; first translated in 1905 by Béla Telekes, to be followed in 1928 by the Transylvanian critic Kálmán Csillay's version (b. 1863). The most enduring attempt has been the 1957 translation by Elek Máthé (1895–1968), reprinted in 1966 and again in 1999. Máthé worked with the British edition of 1908 (London: Macmillan). Last in line was Ágnes Katona's translation published in 1982, based on the 1907 London Everyman Library's edition. The following Scott novels have, however, never been translated for a Hungarian readership: *GM*, *A*, *The Monastery*, *AB*, *P*, *SRW*, *WO* and *AG*.

Conclusion

When trying to assess Walter Scott's Hungarian reception, we find that most critics deal with Scott and his novels in a rather superficial way, the single book-length biographical work on Scott was published by István Bart: Walter Scott világa (The World of Walter Scott) (1980). As a result, the bulk of Scott's Hungarian reception is concentrated in the prefaces or postscripts of his novels and a few lines of general introduction in different volumes on the history of 'English' literature. Walter Scott's influence on Hungarian literature in general, and on the development of the novel in particular was also discussed with admiration in a number of Hungarian literary historical volumes. Taking into account the limited critical acclaim to which the above examples testify to, it turns out that Walter Scott's literary evaluation was rather ambivalent in the course of the twentieth century. He was either seen as a writer 'struggling with Romantic extravagance' (Szász 1963, 289), or as 'the "pioneer" of Realist novel writing' (Szenczi 1972, 415). What remains obvious is that, in spite of Party directives, his novels continued to be widely read and published during the communist regime. Owing to the very powerful Positivist legacy of Hungarian literary criticism, that measures the generic characteristics of the historical novel on a scale moving down from the portrayal of historical reality to the arbitrary workings of fantasy, Scott was placed at the bottom end of the hierarchy. As for the present state of affairs, the reputation of Scott's novels remains rather precarious, as his works are not shelved any longer under the heading of canonical writers but are most commonly marketed in the form of light entertainment. At the beginning of the year 2006 neither the earlier nor the more recently published novels of Scott were available in any of the country's major bookshops.

10 From Romantic Folklorism to Children's Adventure Fiction: Walter Scott in Czech Culture

Martin Procházka

Walter Scott's work entered Czech culture relatively late, in the mid 1820s.[1] One of the first mentions of Scott's writings had appeared several years earlier in a letter written in November 1822 by František Ladislav Čelakovský (1799–1852), the leading poet of that time, to his fellow-patriot and friend Vlastimil Kamarýt (1797–1833). Čelakovský introduces Scott to his correspondent as 'the most recent English poet, and what a Romantic! A true Ossian of our times' (1907, 162).[2] Interestingly, he refers to Scott's poetry as the 'most recent' ('nejnovější'), when it was almost a matter of the past, and he does not mention at all the tremendous popularity of Scott's historical novels. Moreover, the title of Scott's verse tale Čelakovský had just finished reading, *The Lady of the Lake*, is given in Polish – '*Pani Jeżióra*' – and mistranslated into a macaronic German–English: 'The Lady of the *See*' (162; my emphasis).

---

[1] The research for this chapter was financed from Grant No. 405-06-239 of the Czech Science Foundation. Before the appearance of F. L. Čelakovský's translation of *LL* (Scott 1826, 1828) only one poem was translated, 'The Fire-King' by Simeon Karel Macháček (1799–1848), and published, in an adapted version (the changes included renaming the main heroes) as 'Ohenník' in the *Čechoslav* magazine (Scott 1825) (I am grateful to my colleague, Professor Bohuslav Mánek, for this reference). The ballad (collected by Scott in 1796 under the title *Ballads from the German*) was written at the request of Matthew Gregory Lewis and does not seem to have any specific model in German literature. The poem was most probably chosen for its exotic character (see below on the Czech adaptations of *T*) and its similarity to German and Czech folklore ballads in which demonic forces make the hero or heroine renounce Christian faith (or try to seduce them into doing so). It may also have had an impact on the leading Czech Romantic Karel Hynek Mácha (1810–36), specifically on his fragment of a verse tale *Mnich* (The Monk, 1833).
[2] 'Nejnovější anglický básník, – ale jaký to romantik! pravý Ossian našich časů' (all translations from Czech and German are mine).

These details do not only demonstrate the prevailing orientation of the Romantic nationalist movement known as the Czech National Revival[3] towards Slavonic literatures and folklore, but they also prove the weakness of the influence of the contemporary British literary production in the Czech lands during the first half of the 1820s. Only after the appearance of German translations of Scott's collected works, *Walter Scott's Romane* in Zwickau (Scott 1822–29), *Walter Scott's Werke* (Scott 1825–30) in Vienna and Graz (Scott 1827–34), *Walter Scott's sämmtliche Werke* in Stuttgart (Scott 1826–32) and Gotha (Scott 1826–34), and of selected writings (Scott, 1825–31), did the knowledge of Scott's oeuvre start to increase.

Čelakovský's choice of the Polish translation of Karol Szienkiewicz (1792–1860) (1907, 247)[4] is no mere mark of his insufficient knowledge of English. In another letter to Kamarýt of 20 January 1825 Čelakovský compares the original text of *The Lady of the Lake* with its German and Polish translations. While in the German verse translation 'thoughts appear that Scott had never dreamt of' (247–48),[5] Szienkiewicz's prose translation is, in Čelakovský's opinion, more faithful to the orginal. Moreover, translating Scott's poem into prose gives Čelakovský a chance to overcome what he calls the 'brevity' of the 'English language, especially that of Scott' (247):[6] that is, to keep the typical rhythm of Czech, in which trochaic and dactyllic feet prevail. Another reason for using the Polish translation is the Panslavic orientation of the nationalist movement at that time. From this point of view the Polish translation presented Scott's poem as a close analogue of the poetry of the Slavonic folklore, which represented a universal value for the nationalists. This is implied in Čelakovský's letter to Kamarýt, written on 25 September 1825:

> Having collected a good supply of Serbian folksongs, I am now dealing with some Russian songs for the 3rd volume [of my collection] [. . .]; it is really the most beautiful branch of poetry. Only when the Slavs have all these treasures gathered

---

[3]   The Czech National Revival (or Renascence) was a protracted process of cultural and political emancipation of the Czechs from Austrian domination, starting in the 1780s under the influence of the reforms of Maria Theresa (1740–80) and Joseph II (1780–90), interrupted by the Austrian reprisals after the revolution of 1848 and continuing until the First World War. The first three phases (1780–1848) are characterized mainly by the recovery of the Czech language, which lost its administrative, cultural and partially also its socially communicative functions after 1627 when the country had been virtually deprived of its autonomy in the aftermath of the unsuccessful uprising of Czech estates (1619–20) against the Habsburg Emperor Ferdinand II (1618–37). The last phase, starting in the late 1850s, is marked by the struggle for an adequate political representation of Czechs in the Austrian Empire, concluded only after the downfall of Austria–Hungary and the formation of independent Czechoslovakia in 1918.

[4]   Karol of Kalinówka [Karol z Kalinówki] mentioned by Jiří Levý (1957, 130, 132) is identical with Karol Sienkiewicz (Čelakovský 1907, 326; Levý 1957, 261), a translator, renowned historian and a librarian of the Czartorysky library in Puławy (Čelakovský 1907, 326).

[5]   'myšlenky přicházejí, o nichž se Skotovi ani nesnilo.'

[6]   'jazyk anglický, zvláště Skotův, tuze stručný.'

together, will the beautiful nature of this folk come to light everywhere! In my view, there cannot be a more beautiful and truer mirror of it than the folksong. I would like to send you two cantos of my Scott (1907, 264).[7]

A similar understanding of the function of Čelakovský's translation is evident in a short laudatory poem of 12 October 1825 dedicated to the translator by Josef Jungmann (1773–1847), a Czech nationalist leader referred to as 'the batyushka' (Čelakovský 1907, 264),[8] that is, by the popular appelation of the Russian Tsar, meaning 'Father' or 'venerable man'. According to Jungmann, Čelakovský's 'art', 'warbling Walter's tones in a pleasurable Slavonic way', should 'enter the temple of Czech history, / To find Slavonic Malcolms and Slavonic Ellens' (265),[9] that is, to discover universal Slavonic features in Czech historical personages resembling Scott's heroes.

A corresponding tendency to emphasize the universality of folklore was typical of John Bowring (1792–1872), a Unitarian adherent of Jeremy Bentham, and a co-editor of the *Westminster Review* since 1820, who became interested in Russian, Polish, Serbian[10] and Czech literature after his visit to St Petersburg in 1819–20, where he learned Russian and met some leading writers of that time, including Krylov and Karamzin. In a letter to Čelakovský of 28 June 1827 Bowring maintained that all poetry had 'a national character' and contrasted the limitations of great authors, to whose praise 'nothing can be added', to the 'boundless field of folk culture' (Čelakovský 1907, 314). According to Bowring, there was a closer resemblance of the Czech folksongs to the English folk ballads than to the Ossian poems, whose authenticity he disputed.

As a result, the link between *LL* and chiefly Slavonic folklore was all but arbitrary. Apart from the evidence in the works of individual writers it can also be established from the contemporary aesthetic theory of the Czech nationalists, influenced by Schiller's notions of the 'naive' and the 'senti-mental' in art. According to Čelakovský, only 'naive' ('naivní') poetry can produce immediate sensuous beauty of aesthetic form, while the 'sentimental poet' ('Básník sentymentální') runs into problems in dealing with its 'matter'

---

[7] Maje již zásobu srbsk. písní obírám se zas s někt. ruskými pro 3 díl [. . . .]; jest to opravdu nejpěknější větev básnictví. Až jen budou Slované všecky tyto drahocen-nosti pohromadě míti – jaká to krásná povaha toho lidu všudy vysvítá, a nemůž, podlé mého nynějšího nahlednutí pěknějšího a věrnějš. zrcadla býti jako zpěv nár. Skota mého 2 zp. rád bych ti poslal, [. . . .]. (The words abbreviated in the Czech original are given in full in the English translation. The syntax of the last two sentences has been modified to reproduce the emphatic nature of Čelakovský's letter.)

[8] Significantly, Čelakovský writes Jungmann's nickname in original Cyrillic as 'батюшка'.

[9] 'Ty, jenž slovensky líbezně hlaholíš Waltrové zvuky, / [. . . .] / Ó! do českých dějin chrámu nech vstoupí tvoje Uměna, / Slovenské najde Malcolmy, slovenské najde Elleny.' (The original is in clumsy quantitative hexameters.)

[10] Bowring's translations from Russian, Polish and Serbian poetry appeared in London in 1820 (2nd edn 1821) and 1827, respectively (cf. Chudoba 1912, 6, 7).

('námět', 'materye') which always needs some rational structuring (27). To this, Kamarýt added that while the 'sentimental' ('sentimentální') Schiller was 'in a good deal' ('z většího dílu') a follower of 'the English poets' ('Angličanů'), Goethe, as a genuine 'naive' ('naivní') artist, followed 'the divine Greeks' ('jest následovník božských Řeků') (34).[11] In this aesthetic system, Scott's poetry in Čelakovský's translation functioned as a mediator between the 'naive' poetry of the Slavs and the 'sentimental' poetry of the British, and also between folklore, called 'the poetry of nature' ('Naturpoesie'), and modern literature, called 'the poetry of art' ('Kunstpoesie') (Čelakovský 1910, 590).[12] It also bridged the gap between the ancient heroic poetry of Ossian and modern pre-Romantic and Romantic poetry inspired by folk songs.[13]

The support for this conclusion can be found in the genre structure of other works of that time: a good instance is the forged medieval Czech *Manuscript of Dvůr Králové* (Rukopis královédvorský), allegedly found in 1817 and inspired, among others, by the Ossian poems. This work of several Czech nationalists, Václav Hanka (1791–1861), Josef Linda (1789 or 1792–1834) and František Horčička, contains both heroic songs in Ossianic style (such as 'Záboj, Slavoj and Luděk')[14] and a number of lyrical folk songs.[15]

More evidence of the mediating role of Scott's verse tale is Čelakovský's own choice of texts for translation. The magazine publication of the first canto of *The Lady of the Lake* was preceded by his Czech rendering of *Carthon*

---

[11]   Here Kamarýt seems to have – at least partially – misrepresented Schiller's theory, according to which Shakespeare was a modern analogue of Homer and a typical representative of 'naive' poetry (Abrams 1958, 238).

[12]   In this German letter to John Bowring from August 1827, Čelakovský uses these terms also for the periodization of the history of Czech literature: while 'the poetry of nature' ('Naturpoesie') had the form of 'heroic songs' ('Heldenlieder') during the first period of the development of Czech literature (until 1350), in the latest period (from 1780) it acquired the form of folk songs, which date back only to the seventeenth century, and became a subject of imitation (1910, 590–91). This association is very important for the connection between *LL* and the Ossian poems established by Čelakovský.

[13]   According to Felix Vodička (1948, 255), this is a paradoxical situation, in which 'a clearly articulated contemporary demand for a specific literature [. . .] can be fully satisfied only by the works of the past and by anonymous authors' ('vyhraněná soudobá představa literární [. . .] může býti plně uspokojována jen díly minulých dob a anonymních autorů').

[14]   The first English translation of this piece was published by Krystjan Lach Szyrma (1791–1866), Bowring's Polish acquaintance and informant ('Zaboy, Slavoy, and Ludeck', 1821). For information on Szyrma and his correspondence with Bowring see Chudoba (1912, 44–56).

[15]   See the detailed account of these manuscripts, and the continued controversies that have raged over their authenticity, in various political contexts, up to the present, in James Porter (2004) 'Literary, Artistic and Political Resonances of *Ossian* in the Czech National Revival', Chapter 11 in Howard Gaskill (ed.) *The Reception of Ossian in Europe*, pp. 209–21.

(Macpherson 1826), one of the Ossian poems.[16] Apart from associating Scott's poetry with ancient Gaelic tradition, Čelakovský might have also intended to contrast the tragic nature of the Ossianic tale, where Clessámmor is separated from his newly wed wife and later kills his unknown son Carthon, with the positive idealizing features of Scott's epic, especially the portrait of Ellen Douglas and the rendering of the picturesque beauties of Loch Katrine.[17]

Despite the efforts to present Scott as a Romantic folklorist, the early Czech reception of his poetry reflects his importance as one of the most prominent representatives of British literature, whose popularity in Central Europe was equal to that of Lord Byron. While the latter was believed to have sung 'of himself alone' ('sám o sobě'), Scott was valued for his representations of 'the feelings of others, their consequences and causes, in such a masterly way that we almost believe we see the described character and hear his words' (Mácha 1972, 259–60).[18] In his first reference to *Ivanhoe* in a letter to Kamarýt of 5 November 1825, Čelakovský compares the role of Scott's work in contemporary Czech literature to that of Ossianic poetry at the time of Goethe's *Werther*, but he simultaneously emphasizes the value of Scott's representation of national history (1907, 266).[19] Because of his superior skills in characterization

---

[16] Both translations were published in the magazine *Poutník slovanský* (Slavonic pilgrim), edited by František Bohumil Tomsa (1793–1857). While *Carthon* appeared in the first issue of the magazine (Macpherson 1826), the first canto of *The Lady of the Lake*, 'The Chase', was published in the second issue (Scott 1826).

[17] This contrast was also noted by another Czech nationalist leader and likewise a translator of Ossian, František Palacký (1798–1876): 'the very contrast between [Ossian's] cold, rocky and misty country and the soft sentimentality of his heroes made an extraordinary impression in many European countries' ('sama protiva mezi jeho studenou skalnatou a mlhovitou zemí a měkkou sentimentálností jeho hrdin učinila zvláštní dojem v mnohých zemích evropských') (Palacký 1898–1903, 3: 554).

[18] 'popisuje [. . .] cizé city, jejich následky a příčiny tak mistrně, že popsanou osobu takořka před očima míti, jednání její viděti a slova její slyšeti se domníváme.' The comment, attributed to a leading Czech Romantic, Karel Hynek Mácha, is of dubious authenticity. It first appeared in a biographical essay on Mácha, written by his friend Karel Sabina (1813–77) and published in 1845 as 'Úvod povahopisný' (Introduction: the Poet's Character).

[19] 'Well, and how do you like *Ivanhoe*? The same question, I trust, as that Werther was asked: "How do you like Ossian?" – If only we could boast at least one such well and thoroughly written original novel. And with a history like ours!! A source one would not exhaust in a hundred years, especially the events of the middle ages. Moreover, if we take our other Slavonic brothers, the Polish – what a theme for novels from the last two centuries [. . .] And what about the Serbians? [. . .] And, finally, the Russians! – These are mighty streams, but who may draw from them, and who is able to do so? Who has such power as Scott, and even if he had it, where are the means of learning about everything thoroughly national in the past.' ('Nu, a jak se líbí Ivanhoe? Věru právě taková otázka, jako onoho, co se tázal Werthera: "Wie gefällt Ihnen Ossian?" – Kýžbychom my, jenom jediným tak vypracovaným původn. románem se vykázati mohli. A naše dějiny k tomu!! Z těch by ani za sto let se nevyčerpal, zvláště z prostředních století. A vezmemeli pak teprv i jiné naše slovanské bratry. Poláky, jakýby to byl předmět k románům z minulých dvou století

and evocation of historical scenes, Scott acquires higher authority than the ancient Gaelic bard: he is elevated to the position of a monarch and a high priest of European literature. Scott's short note to Čelakovský of 19 April 1828, conveying his thanks for a copy of his translation of *LL* and expressing regrets at his inability to read the 'ancient' Czech language (352),[20] is enthusiastically welcomed by Čelakovský as having caused 'more wonder in Prague than if it came from F [that is, the Austrian Emperor Francis I]' (362),[21] and having pleased him more than 'a letter from the Holy Father in Rome' (1910, 604).[22] And Čelakovský's friend Kamarýt shows an even more personal fervour for Scott's novels: 'If anybody starts to blame Walter Scott as a novelist (not as a critical historian), he shall never be my friend' (Čelakovský 1907, 414).[23]

In spite of this general enthusiasm, there were, apart from Čelakovský's translation of *The Lady of the Lake*, only three other works published in Czech before 1875. Josef František Hollmann's (1802–55) rendering of *LLM*

[. . .] Což Srbové? [. . .] A což konečně Rusové! – To jsou toky, ale kdo smí, kdo chce nabírati, a komu taková síla jako Skot. a byt'by i byla, kde k tomu prostředků seznámiti se se vším dokonale národním v času minulém.' The words abbreviated in the Czech original are given in full in the English translation.) According to Vodička this passage is symptomatic of 'a specific problem of the Czech literary revival' ('zvláštní problém českého literárního obrození'), the split between the foreign provenance of 'literary postulates' ('literární postuláty) determined by European 'literary fashion' ('literární módou'), and the 'immanently given realities' ('imanentně dané skutečnosti') incompatible with these 'postulates' (1948, 305). This rather cryptic statement points chiefly to the absence of the novel as a genre in the earlier Czech revival literature. However, Vodička's commentary neglects more important features of Čelakovský's argument: the difficulty of knowing and representing national and Slavonic histories in their supposed extraordinary richness, and the lack of creative power equal to Scott's.

[20]   On 19 April 1828 Bowring wrote to Čelakovský:

I sent your translation of the Lady of the Lake to Sir Walter Scott [. . .] and yesterday I had a conversation with him of which you were the subject.

On the same day, Scott addressed this note to Čelakovský:

Sir!
I am honoured with a copy of your version of the Lady of the Lake, on which you have done the production more honour than the Author could have expected on its behalf. Being, as you will easily suppose, totally ignorant of your ancient language, I can be no judge of the translation which is to me a book closed and a fountain sealed. My sense of gratitude is however the same and I am Sir your most obedient servant

Walter Scott.
London 19. April 1828.

(Čelakovský 1907, 352)

[21]   'v Praze většího divení dosáhl, než kdyby od F. pocházel.'
[22]   'ein Schreiben vom heiligen Vater aus Rom.'
[23]   'Jen at mně někdo pohaní Waltera Sk. v románu (ne v dějině kritické), ten nikdy mým přítelem nebude.'

(Scott 1836) attempted to imitate the iambic metre of the original. Although this was rather unusual in contemporary Czech literature, the book passed almost unnoticed, overshadowed by innovative works of young Czech poets, Karel Hynek Mácha's (1810–36) *Máj* (May) and František Matouš Klácel's (1808–82) *Lyrické básně* (Lyrical poems) (Otruba 1993, 245).

The growth of public interest in the Czech Hussite movement, a highly controversial topic ideologically used by Czechs and Germans (for example, Karl Herlossohn 1802–49), by radicals (Emanuel Arnold, 1800–69), moderates (František Palacký) and conservatives (Václav Vladivoj Tomek, 1818–1905), motivated the choice of *Old Mortality* as the first novel by Scott published in Czech translation under the title *Puritáni* (The Puritans) (Scott 1840, 1843). The translator, Václav Špinka (1796–1842), who ran the Catholic Archepiscopal Press in Prague from 1832 until his death in 1842, could have chosen Scott's novel with a didactic purpose: to demonstrate the excesses of the Cameronians. In his choice of *OM*, Špinka might have been influenced by a circle of Czech intellectuals, called 'Špinka's Academy', who were meeting in his flat. Apart from Čelakovský, the group included conservatively minded writers, Karel Vinařický (1803–69), the secretary of the Archbishop of Prague and the founder of the *Časopis pro katolické duchovenstvo* (Journal for Catholic Clergy, 1828–52), and Jakub Malý (1811–85). Malý was the first Czech translator with a good command of English (known for his renderings of Shakespeare, Goldsmith, Bulwer-Lytton, Dickens, Frederick Marryat, Washington Irving and Polidori's *Vampire* – cf. Procházka 2005, 298), the editor of a popular series Bibliothéka zábavného čtení (The Library of Entertainment, 1835–44), published also by Špinka, and the author of the first Czech textbook of English grammar as well as an essay on translating English authors, especially Shakespeare, into Czech. It is quite likely that the purpose of the Czech translation of *OM* was twofold: to provide a quality entertainment for the lower classes, unfamiliar with German translations, and to enlist the aid of Scott in the fight against radical interpretations of the Hussite movement.

The translation, possibly based on older German renderings, such as *Die Schwärmer* (The Enthusiasts) (Scott 1824), must have been quite popular, since it ran to a second edition within less than three years. The publisher's subtitle, 'Romantická povídka od W. Scotta' (Romantic Tale by W. Scott), shows that Špinka preferred marketing the novel under the reliable label of popular short chivalric narratives and gothic tales (Vodička 1948, 159–70).

In contrast to *OM*, only moderately successful in Britain after its first publication, *I*, one of Scott's bestselling novels despite its high price,[24] had to wait more than thirty years for its first appearance in Czech. The translator, a classical scholar František Šír (1796–1867), completed it in 1833 but published it only in

---

[24] Compared with 33,000 copies of *RR* printed in 1818 only and 32,000 copies of *I* printed between 1819 and 1821, out of which '12,000 copies [were] said to be sold in three volumes despite the high price' (30 s), the four-volume edition of *BD* and *OM*, although the first three editions (6,000 copies) had been sold in two months, had difficulties selling in later editions. The sixth edition (1819) was using 'old sheets' (St Clair 2004, 637, 202).

1865 under the title *Richard Lev a templáři angličtí* (Richard the Lion and the Templars of England) (Scott 1865). In a review of this novel, Jan Neruda (1834–91), a leading Czech poet and critic of the latter half of the nineteenth century, made a bitter tongue-in-cheek comment that the earlier Czech literati simply did not believe that Scott's novels would find a wider readership in their country (Neruda 1911, 190). Unlike them Neruda pointed out the importance of 'entertaining as well as educative' ('zábavným a poučným zároveň') works of literature with a high aesthetic value, such as Scott's, Hugo's or Bulwer-Lytton's novels. Paraphrasing the introductory passage from *Ivanhoe* about the sad condition of the nation, which consists of 'tyrants and slaves' ('tyranů a otroků') only and has 'no commerce and trade, art and knowledge' ('bez obchodu a řemesla, bez umění a vědomostí'), he expected a wide popularity of the novel based on the interest of Czech readers in historical narratives of all kinds (Neruda 1911, 191).

Despite the cogency of his argument, Neruda's anticipations were mistaken: no other Czech translation of *I* was published before 1914, and the novel became popular only in the mid 1920s, when two translations appeared within one year as parts of two competing editions of Scott's work: Romány Waltera Scotta (Walter Scott's Novels), published by a prestigious press J. R. Vilímek,[25] and Vybrané romány Waltera Scotta (Walter Scott's Selected Novels),[26] a series translated by Zdeněk Matěj Kuděj (1881–1955).[27] However, even in the heyday of its popularity, *I* was surpassed by *T*, published during one year in two translations and reprinted a few years later.

In spite of other efforts to present Scott's novels as part of the mainstream nineteenth-century development in European literature – such as the first modern rendering of Scott's novel in Czech culture, *W* (Scott 1875), translated by two women, Dora Hanušová (1841–1920)[28] and Pavla Králová – earlier as well as later readers definitely preferred adaptations to expensive or serious editions of Scott's novels. For instance, Hanušová's following translation of *Kenilworth* appeared in 1877 in the series entitled 'Laciná národní knihovna' (Cheap Czech Books) and was reprinted in 1880 in an abridged form in a popular series, Nejlacinější zábavné čtení (The Cheapest Entertainment Reading). Even in the 1920s, when Scott's popularity reached its peak, some of his novels were labelled as 'adventure' (Scott 1925) and the publishers avoided titles which could not be marketed under this heading, such as *HM*.

---

[25] The series started in 1926 with *T* and *Castle Dangerous* in a single volume, continued with *I*, *RR*, *P*, *Antiquary*, and *WO* and closed with the reprint of the first volume. It superseded a more 'serious' but unsuccessful edition, Spisy Waltera Scotta (Walter Scott's Writings), inaugurated by Vilímek with *I* in 1914 and continued in 1921 with *K*, reprinted in 1930.

[26] This series was published in a single year (1925), and included translations of *W*, *Count Robert of Paris*, *I*, *R* and *QD*, all by Zdeněk Matěj Kuděj.

[27] A friend of Jaroslav Hašek (1883–1923) and likewise a Bohemian, Kuděj at that time became much better known for his translations of Tarzan stories.

[28] Hanušová was one of the first Czech feminists, known also for the introduction of George Eliot's novels into Czech culture.

The tendency to present Scott as a popular adventure writer can be traced back to the first half of the nineteenth century. At that time, Scott's novels were frequently produced as stage adaptations, such as Josef Kajetán Tyl's (1808–52) 'Richard Lev na pahorku svatojirském a Boj u diamantu na poušti' (Richard the Lion on St George's Mound and The Fight at the Diamond of the Desert). The poem was a part of six *tableaux vivantes* inspired by *I* and *T* and produced at the Estates Theatre (Stavovské divadlo) in Prague in 1837 (Hýsek 1926, 114). It retells the main features of the story of *T* (1825), emphasizing the wickedness and corruption of the Templars, the French, the Germans and the Italians, and glorifying the supreme authority and justice of the Eastern ruler, Sultan Saladin (Tyl 1859, 389–95). Another theatrical adaptation of *T*, staged for the first time in 1826 in the Grand Duke's Theatre in Karlsruhe (Auffenberg, 1828), was translated into Czech by Václav Filípek (1811–63) and appeared under the title *Lev kurdistánský aneb Růže na poušti* (The lion of Kurdistan, or, The desert rose) (Filípek, 1835). The popularity of these abridged and substantially modified versions of Scott's novels had cultural as well as economic causes, which were discussed in 1841 in Tyl's introduction to his translation of an extract from *Ivanhoe* in the journal *Vlastimil*. Though Scott was his favourite author, Tyl claimed that he could not publish unabridged translations of his works, since 'the majority of our readership would find it difficult to buy three-volume novels, or, in perusing them, to cope with all the details of such writings'[29] (quoted in Hýsek 1926, 115).[30] In other words, ordinary Czech readers, used to trivial, Gothic or chivalric romances and shorter tales, were thought to be unable to buy and digest the Waverley novels, which in Western Europe became a 'commodity', along with 'gothic thrillers' and 'society romances [. . .] predictable in textual content, uniform in material appearance, and sufficiently materially substitutable to be "consumed" week after week like bottles of wine' (St Clair 2004, 31).

Given the scarcity of Czech translations in the nineteenth and early twentieth centuries[31] and the popularity of the abridgements and adaptations of Scott's

---

[29] 'obtížno by větší části obecenstva našeho bylo romány třídílové kupovati anebo u čtení všemi podrobnostmi spisu takového se probrati.'

[30] In the introduction Tyl also mentioned that he was translating *The Tales of the Crusaders* (possibly *T*) 'to make up for the absence of original historical novel at least by publishing good translations, rather abridged than faithful' ('aby nedostatek původního historického románu nahradil alespoň dobrými překlady, ale ne věrnými, nýbrž ve zkrácené formě': Hýsek 1926, 114). Evidently, Tyl's criteria of a 'good translation' are not derived from its intrinsic quality and relation to the original but from its function in the Czech cultural revival.

[31] Apart from three longer poems ('The Fire-King', *LLM* and *LL*), only five novels (*I*, *K*, *OM*, *QD* and *W*) were translated between 1825 and 1914, three of them appearing in two editions. In contrast to this, the total number of translations between 1918 and 1939 is thirteen novels (see above) and one epic tale (again, *LL*). Between 1945 and the present time eleven novels have been translated and some of them (*I*, *QD*, *T*) have been published in several translations and also as adaptations for children (see below).

In comparison to neighbouring Slovakia, the number of novels translated was still quite high. In 1938, the leading Slovak critic, Alexander Matuška (1910–75) claimed

novels, it is not surprising that for several decades *LL* had been the most important among a handful of Scott's representative works translated into Czech.
Rather than a translation, it was a paraphrase of the original in rhythmical prose,
with the exception of the introductory stanzas to Canto I and inserted songs,
which were given in mostly dactyllic or trochaic rhymed verse, and in stanzas
reminiscent of Czech folksongs. In prose passages Čelakovský used the style
developed in his own translation of *Carthon*. Apart from Sienkiewicz's rendering of the poem, his models were some works of contemporary Czech literature, such as the poems from *The Manuscript of Dvůr Králové*, Josef Jungman's
translation of Chateaubriand's *Atala* (1805), and Josef Linda's historical novel
Záře nad pohanstvem (Radiance over the pagans, 1818). In contrast to the loose
rhythmic patterns of the Polish translation, Čelakovský's paraphrase used paral-
lelisms, antitheses and heroic similes, frequent neither in the original nor in the
Polish version. Čelakovský also changed the meaning of some keywords in the
original and in the Polish translation. For instance, Scott's 'Who for his *country*
felt alone, / And prized her blood beyond his own,' (V.29) (1904, 260) and
Sienkiewicz's 'co tak szlachetnie dla kraju się poświeca' ('who so nobly con-
secrates himself to the country') (Levý 1957, 132) become 'who prizes the
nation's blood beyond his own' ('jenž výše své vlastní pokládá krev *národu*')
(Scott 1880, 106; my emphasis). The substitution of the 'nation', understood
at that time as an ethnic and cultural unity determined mainly by language,
for 'country' as a unity of the people and its territory, is a conspicuous feature
of this stage of Czech nationalism, which was marked by the refusal of traditional 'territorial patriotism' of the Czech aristocracy and the acceptance of
the language-based notion of national identity. More conspicuous features of
Čelakovský's 'cultural translation' (Asad 1986, 156; Procházka 1996, 75–90) are
the stylistic references to the ideology of Panslavism, such as the use of Russian
otyechestvo, instead of a Scots name starting with 'Fitz': 'James FitzJames' is
russified as 'Jakob Jakobovič' (Scott 1880, 132).

It is difficult to accept the opinion of Jiří Levý that 'Čelakovský has very
independently expressed the metrical principle of his model by means of
symmetrical sentence structure' (1957, 133).[32] On the contrary, Čelakovský's

---

that because of a strong anti-Western bias of Slovak nineteenth-century nationalists,
'all of what was happening in Europe went past us' ('všetko, čo sa v Európe dialo, šlo
mimo nás') (Matuška 1938, 23). This partially explains why the first translation of
Scott into Slovak appeared rather late, in 1930. It was *K*, published under the title
Tajná ženba lorda z Leicestru (The secret marriage of the Lord of Leicester). In 1937,
it was followed by *BL* and later by two editions of *T* (1943, 1946) and by a
translation of *I* (1947). *RR* appeared in Slovak first in 1952, followed by *W* (1956),
and the adaptation of *GM* for children (1964). Other novels, such as *HM*, were
translated only in the last quarter of the twentieth century; but most of them, such
as *BD, FMP, FN*, were published as adaptations for children. Among the most
frequently published novels there are *I, BL* and *T*.

[32] 'Čelakovský velmi samostatně vyjádřil základní metrický princip předlohy prost-
ředky větné symetrie.'

symmetrical style, compared to the style of the Polish translation, is closer to the form of the Classical, Greek and Roman epic poem. Another feature of Czech Romantic 'cultural translations' was to emphasize the affinity between the Slavonic and Ancient literatures: the latter were believed to be closest to nature and to represent the original virtues of uncorrupted humanity.

Closer than to Scott's original, Čelakovský's translation was to the classical ideal of heroic epic as well as to the simplicity of folk poetry (133). Although this connection was fully legitimized as 'the poetry of nature' by the Czech nationalist reading of Schiller's aesthetic, some contemporaries found it incongruous: in 1829 Šebestián Hněvkovský (1770–1847), a representative of the first generation of Czech nationalists, noticed that though being 'an excellent *poetical* work', *LL* 'was not so efficient as [Čelakovský's] works in the Slavonic spirit' (Čelakovský 1910, 19).[33] The work implied by Hněvkovský is Čelakovský's collection called *Ohlas písní ruských* (The echo of Russian songs, 1829). Here the influences of Scott's ballads and songs were substantially transformed to serve the purposes of the Panslavic ideology, celebrating, among others, contemporary Russian victories in the Balkan Peninsula.

The late 1820s and early 1830s can be called 'the beginnings of the cult of Walter Scott' ('počátky kultu W. Scotta') in Czech culture (Vodička 1948, 292). Notwithstanding the scarcity of translations of his works, Scott became – like Byron – a great model for all writers of historical fiction. Still in the 1850s Palacký invoked Scott as the saviour of 'the spirit of the Czech nation wading through the slime of everyday drabness' ('mysl národa v kalu všednosti se brodí'), and valued his novels more than the power of Hussite armies: 'a single Walter Scott would now help us more than five Žižka's'[34] ('jediný Walter Scott by nám nyní prospěl nežli pět Žižků') (Hýsek 1926, 112).[35]

Despite all this, Scott's influence on the writers of the first half of the nineteenth century was, with a few exceptions, rather negligible. In the project of literature inherent in the Czech nationalist ideology of that time, Scott's historical novels represented the capacity of Czech authors to draw 'vivid patriotic truths' from 'the book of history [. . .] especially in those parts of it, where the lush and abundant matter cannot be constrained by the narrow walls of a stage' (Hýsek 1926, 112).[36] Rather than the expansion of the metaphor of history as *theatrum mundi*, this statement implies that Czech historical fictions inspired by Scott were to serve as temporary substitutes for the 'complete patriotic history'

---

[33] 'jest výbor *poetické* práce [. . .], však neoučinkuje tolik, co Vaše ostatní v duchu slovenském složené práce.'

[34] Jan Žižka (about 1360–1424) was a legendary Hussite general, who defeated the crusade sent to the Czech lands in 1421 to crush the incipient rebellion.

[35] In 1828 Václav Kliment Klicpera (1792–1859) expressed a similar view: 'In a country, where the histories of glorious ancestors are read, the famous histories of great ancestors are also written' to 'nourish the resolute spirit' ('v které zemi se veliké děje slavných předků čtou, tam se také slavné děje velkých předků píšou [. . .] i tam duch rázný se povzbudí') (Vodička 1948, 307).

[36] 'jenž by otevřev knihu historie vlastenecké živé pravdy z ní čerpal a zvláště v těch oddílech, kde se bujná látka v úzké stěny herny vtěsnati nedá!'

('úplné historie vlastenecké') (112), which at that time was being written by František Palacký.

The works of fiction influenced by Scott in the first half of the nineteenth century were mostly shorter historical tales. The first of them, *Točník* (Točník Castle, 1828), was written by Václav Kliment Klicpera (1792–1859). It tried to mediate between the tradition of early Romantic poetic prose, represented in Czech literature especially by Linda's *Záře nad pohanstvem*, and popular literature based mostly on the German tale of terror and late eighteenth-century versions of chivalric narratives. Although Klicpera introduced a historical character of the pre-Hussite Czech king, Wenceslas IV, he could not bridge the gap between the requirement of historical authenticity of his protagonists and expressive representations of the setting. According to Felix Vodička, in Klicpera's tale:

> the motifs of the outside world preserve their seeming arbitrariness with respect to the situation and internal uniqueness, thus giving a special meaning to other levels of the theme. In this way they create a stage decoration representing the outer world, whose details are focused to produce an expressionist effect. (1948, 311)[37]

This effect, based on the evocative power and dramatic function of individual details, was confirmed by Klicpera himself, who wrote in the introduction to *Točník* (1827): 'For me the whole world resembles a dramatic poem. From all that I read and see, I spontaneously create and design dramatic scenes' (Vodička 1948, 309).[38]

Klicpera had many imitators; the most important of them was Josef Kajetán Tyl, the leader of the younger generation of the Czech nationalists, who published the first tale from Czech history in 1830, and later even planned a historical novel.[39]

Like Tyl, the Romantic poet Karel Hynek Mácha (1810–36) was an avid reader of Scott's novels. Many of his poems, prose fragments and an attempt at a historical novel, *Křivoklad* (Křivoklad Castle, 1834), testify a powerful influence not only of domestic authors, such as Linda and Klicpera, but chiefly of Scott's novels. Thanks to the survival of Mácha's notebooks, we can now reconstruct his reading of Walter Scott, and Mácha's creative use of Scott's motifs. In an early draft of the last volume of his planned historical tetralogy *Kat* (The hangman), of which *Křivoklad* was a part, Mácha almost completely rewrites a passage from the thirteenth chapter of *The Abbot*, preserving only two isolated words or phrases (here in italics) from the German translation:

---

[37] [m]otivy vnějšího světa si uchovávají zdánlivou nahodilost vzhledem k situaci, vnitřní jedinečnost, dodávajíce ostatním plánům tématu zvláštní význam. Tvoří takto kulisu vnějšího světa, detailů, zaostřených k expresionistickému účinu.

[38] 'Mně je celý svět dramatická báseň! Ze všeho, co čtu, ze všeho, co vidím, bezvolně scény spřádám a osnuju.'

[39] Other authors of historical tales influenced by Scott include Jan Jindřich Marek (using the pseudonym Jan z Hvězdy; 1803–53) and Prokop Chocholoušek (1819–64) (Hýsek 1921, 5).

The building, the gardens, etc., *were all dilapidated and ruinous*, the pillars decorated with sculptures had been used as *the doorpost or threshold*, etc. They knocked on the gate and the porter opened it unwillingly and timidly. First the life of the monks is to be described or some activity within the walls of the monastery; only then both of them knock on the door, that is, Vias[il] [the hero of Mácha's planned novel] and the hangman in Zbrasl[av] [the name of the monastery close to Prague]. The Monastery and the condition of the place is to be described. In the church, through which they walk to the tomb, all is destroyed and lying on one heap, etc. (Mácha 1972, 20–21)[40]

While some parts of this text refer to the details of Scott's description (e.g. '*the pillars with sculptures*' point to the following passage: 'Roland saw fragments of Gothic pillars richly carved [. . .] and here and there a mutilated statue, inverted or laid on its side' [Scott 1906, 122], others deal with the narrative strategy (e.g. 'First the life of the monks is to be described or some activity within the walls of the monastery') and still others point to characters in other works of Mácha (the hangman in *Křivoklad*) and to the specific Czech historical locations and monuments (the ruinous monastery at Zbraslav with the tomb of one of the last Přemyslid kings, Wenceslas II). While Mácha strives for an expressive style integrating a few details taken from Scott's text in the dynamic flow of the narrative – this can be exemplified by Mácha's contemporary fragment *Pout' krkonošská* (A pilgrimage to the Krkonoše Mountains) written about 1832 – Scott dwells on static details and ironically recapitulates the causes of the spoil. Where Scott evokes the 'memory' of the place in the context of both the local historical time and the history of the Reformation, Mácha attempts to represent a scene from history as a subjective, dreamy vision. This is typical of Mácha's *Křivoklad* as well as of his fragments of historical tales *Klášter sázavský* (Sázava Monastery, about 1832) or *Valdice* (1836).

In Mácha's works, Scott's fiction functions as an intertext, mediating between available accounts of Czech history (especially the 1541 chronicle by Václav Hájek of Libočany, end of fifteenth century – 1553) and Mácha's draft of his historical fiction.[41] Moreover, Scott's novel here becomes a transformative agent, stimulating both the independent imagination and narrative strategy, and also a revisionist reading of history. Though Mácha does not copy Scott's account of 'idolatry' and 'superstitious devotion of the papists' (1906, 122), he selects the Stuttgart edition, translated by Leonhardt Tafel (Scott 1828), where the passage critical of Catholicism is retained, and does not use the Vienna edition, in which the same passage was deleted by a censor (Mácha 1972, 375).

---

[40]   Das Gebäude, die Gärten etc., *alles war zertrümmert*, die Bildsäulen usw. gebrauchten die Einwohner *als Schwellen* usf. Sie klopften und der Pförtner öffnete leise und furchtsam. Früher ist das Leben der Mönche oder eine Handlung in ihren Mauern zu beschreiben, und dann erst klopfen die beiden an, nämlich Wias[il] und der Henker in Zbrasl[av]. Das Kloster und die Lage des Ortes ist zu beschreiben. In der Kirche, durch die sie zur Gruft schreiten, ist alles zerstört, durcheinander geworfen etc.

[41]   Wellek shows that for Mácha Scott was also 'the intermediary of other influences: the Gothic novel and Shakespeare' (1963, 167).

The later drafts of the historic tetralogy show that the Czech religious reformer Jan Hus would become an important character in it.

Mácha's preoccupation with Scott's novels shows a range of different concerns, which are later articulated in his major works. For instance in the case of *AG* it extends from wild Alpine sceneries to subtle political stratagems.[42] From the fourth and twenty-second chapters of *LM* Mácha draws the fatal scenes of his novel *Cikáni* (The gypsies, 1835) and from *QD* he takes the inspiration to create characters of King Wenceslas IV and his hangman, the descendant of the extinct old royal house of the Přemyslids. In Mácha's only historical novel, *Křivoklad*, Scott's stimuli give rise to proto-existentialist conflicts of late Romanticism, emphasizing the analogy between the individual tragedies of his heroes and the tragic events of Czech medieval history, which seems to move hopelessly toward a still greater decay of the royal power and the feudal state. This is symbolized by the interchangeable identities of the king and his hangman: Mácha's apostrophe 'King Hangman!' [. . .] 'Hangman King!' ('Králi kate!' [. . .] 'Kate králi!') (1961, 24) refers to the hangman's ancestors from the extinct Czech royal house of the Přemyslids, and erases the difference between the heroes.

Perhaps the most inventive transformation of Scott's stimuli can be found in the third and fourth cantos of Mácha's lyrical-epic tale *Máj* (May, 1836). Here, Scott's image of scattered 'bones of men, / In some forgotten battle slain,' (Scott 1904, 229; cf. Mácha 1972, 84–85)[43] in the third canto (III.5) of *LL* is expanded into the string of metaphors on the transience of individual consciousness, lapse of historical time as well as of the discontinuity of time in general:

> The last indignant thoughts of the defeated dead,
> Their unremembered names, the clamour of old fights
> The worn-out northern lights, after their gleam is fled,
> The untuned harp, whose strings distil no more delights,
> The deeds of time gone by, quenched starlight overhead,
> [. . .]

---

[42]   According to Wellek (1963, 166), Mácha links the wild Alpine landscape at the beginning of Scott's novel with the rugged cliff above the monastery of Svatý Jan pod Skalou and the rocky ravine of Šárka, both locations connected with events in Czech sagas, legends and early history. Wellek's conjecture about the connection between Svatý Jan and the castle of Karlštejn (1963, 166), central for 'Karlův Týn', a planned volume of Mácha's historical tetralogy, is quite plausible. It indicates that the volumes of the hangman tetralogy following *Křivoklad* were intended to combine panoramic historical perspective with accounts of minute but symptomatic historical events, dramatic, adventurous scenes and dynamic, powerful landscape descriptions.

[43]   'Aus alter unbekannter Schlacht / so gräßlich in matten Mondesschein, das weiß gebleicht hat Wind und Regen. [. . .] Und manch' Gewürm sich träg bewegt / an diesem bleichenden Gebein, / das einst so flink und stark sich geregt.' Other motifs in the extract, namely the vegetation overgrowing human bones, have inspired other passages of Mácha's in the third and fourth cantos of *Máj*.

As the smoke of burnt-out fires, as the shatter'd bell's chime,
Are the dead years of the dead, their beautiful childhood time.[44]

(Mácha 1965, 61)

Mácha's transformation of Scott's rendering of a strange folk saga about the birth of Brian the Hermit into a text symbolizing different – both individual and collective, apocalyptic and discontinuous – dimensions of time ('the dead years of the dead, their beautiful childhood time'), is a fitting means to close the chapter on Scott's reception in the context of Czech Romantic folklorism. Mácha's catachretic metaphors no longer follow Romantic adaptations of folklore but they anticipate modern reflexive poetry and twentieth-century thought about time. It is not surprising they had an immense influence on Czech modernist poetry from the 1920s to the 1940s (Josef Hora, 1891–1945, František Halas, 1901–49) and later (František Hrubín, 1910–71, Vladimír Holan, 1905–80).

In conclusion, let us return briefly to the period after 1875, when the first modern Czech translations of Scott started to appear. This time coincides with the rise and decline of the Czech historical novel, represented by Václav Beneš Třebízský (1849–84), the author of sentimental, sometimes nostalgic, but also tragic pictures from Czech history, and Alois Jirásek (1851–1930), who followed Scott not only in his interest in historical facts but also in his use of particular and local events to illustrate, interpret (and invent) large-scale historical processes. In contrast to Scott's elegiac representations of the Highlanders and their culture, Jirásek accentuated the central importance of the Hussites for modern Czech history and reinvented this controversial religious movement, which had resulted in a protracted period of military turmoil, as a historical struggle of the Czech gentry and farmers for a powerful nation-state.

With the growth of the ideological importance of Jirásek's novels, Scott's influence on mainstream Czech culture came to an end. While Scott's novels were published as adventure reading in the 1920s, Jirásek was glorified as the successor of Palacký and 'a genuine democrat' ('ryzí demokrat'):

> who was never dazzled by the glamour of court festivities [. . .] and the theatrical bravery of tournaments; beyond everything he saw and above all he valued the people, its soul, its mind, its welfare and suffering.[45] (Frič 1921, 63)

Although Scott is not expressly mentioned in the passage (referring to Van der Velde and Alexandre Dumas, *père*), it is evident that his novels were valued only

---

[44]   takt' jako zemřelých myšlenka poslední,/ tak jako jméno jich, pradávných bojů hluk,/ dávná severní zář, vyhaslé světlo s ní,/ zbortěné harfy tón, ztrhané struny zvuk,/ zašlého věku děj, umřelé hvězdy svit [. . .], vyhasla ohně kouř, slitého zvonu hlas,/ to jestit' zemřelých krásný dětinský čas (Mácha 1959, 45). This passage from the third canto of Mácha's poem repeats itself with some variation in Canto IV.

[45]   Nikdy se nedal oslnit leskem dvorských slavností [. . .] a divadelní statečností rytířských turnajů; za vším a především měl na zřeteli lid, jeho duši, jeho smýšlení, jeho blaho i utrpení.

in historical terms for vivid imagination, which 'awakened enthusiastic love of the past and national character' ('probouzeje lásku i nadšení pro minulost a individualitu národní') (Frič 1921, 61). While Scott is seen as a representative of Romantic historicism, which became one of the catalysts of the National Revival movement, Jirásek is celebrated as the author of 'a true and artistic picture' ('věrný a umělecký obraz') (Hýsek 1921, 6) of Czech history. The 'truth' of this 'picture' was believed to consist in the expression of the 'spirit of the age' ('ducha doby'), the ethos of the Hussite reformation:

> Amidst corrupted Christendom, our Hussite movement fought for better, morally regenerated humanity [. . .] preaching the ideals of new democracy and ethical life.[46] (Hýsek 1921, 6)

Rather than by Palacký's history, these sweeping ideological generalizations were inspired by the thought of the first Czechoslovak president, Tomáš Garrigue Masaryk (1850–1937). In his essay, 'Problém malého národa' (The Problem of a Small Nation, 1901), Masaryk saw the sense of Czech history in the creation of a democratic society based on the ethical ideals of the Hussite Reformation. In this way he attempted to ascribe a universal relevance to the Czech struggle for religious truth and national identity: 'The Czech question is not only ours but of the whole world'[47] (Masaryk 1990, 88).

Despite his political glorification, Jirásek was reconnected with Scott in the 1930s by a leading literary critic, František Xaver Šalda (1867–1937), who saw Scott as a representative of Romantic historicism and Jirásek as his mere follower (1987a, 1:452). As with his repudiation of Byron (Procházka 2005, 2:302), Šalda based his argument on a sharp contrast between Mácha's and Scott's historical fiction. While Scott was 'a passionate local chronicler [. . .] with an excellent knowledge of material aspects of life in the past epochs, [. . ..] his characters are hollow and lifeless; mere conventional puppets in historically very true costumes [. . .]'[48] (Šalda 1987b, 2: 198), Mácha was 'absorbed in psychological enigmas' ('zabírá se rád do dušezpytných záhad') (1987c, 2: 90). Like Scott's historical novel, Jirásek's oeuvre has become completely 'outdated' ('vyžilo se') [. . .], having completely exhausted its narrative energy; to live further in future, it would need purely poetic and creative qualities which it lacks'[49] (1987d, 2: 203).

Šalda's fervent condemnations were true only in the case of Scott's further reputation in Czech culture; he was completely mistaken in Jirásek's case. Zdeněk Nejedlý (1878–1962), whom Šalda criticized for trying to 'galvanize'

---

[46]   Naše husitství bojovalo uprostřed zkaženého křestanství za lepšího, mravně obrozeného člověka [. . .], hlásalo ideály nové demokracie a mravního života.

[47]   'Česká otázka je otázka celého světa, nejen nás.'

[48]   'vášnivý lokální kronikář [. . .] výborný znatel hmotného bytu minulých epoch, [. . ..] nitro jeho figur bývá duté a mrtvé; bývají to konvenční loutky velmi věrně historicky oblečené.'

[49]   'vydalo všechnu svou energii fabulistickou i vyprávěcí; aby žilo ještě dále v budoucnosti, musilo by mít kvality ryze básnické a tvárné, kterých nemá.'

('galvanizovat') Jirásek's dead historical novels (1987d, 2: 203), succeeded in selling Jirásek again to the communist ideologues. Since the 1950s, the communist distortion of these fictions of the Czech past, identifying the Hussite movement with a Marxist scheme of social revolution, made Scott's novels completely irrelevant as representations of history. They continued to appear mostly as adventure readings for children,[50] which is still their major role in the present Czech culture.

---

[50] A number of Czech translations of Scott's novels were published by the Státní nakladatelství dětské knihy (State Publishing House for Children's Books) and its succesor, the Albatros publishers. The exceptions to this rule were for instance *HM* (Scott 1958) and *BL* (Scott 1985). According to Dr Kamila Vránková's unpublished bibliography, between 1947 and 2003 *I, QD,* and *T* appeared in four adaptations. Though these adaptations were not always substantially abridged, such as those in the series 'Favourite Books for Children', including the prose versions of *LL* and *The Lord of the Isles* (Scott 1909), they were introduced in a specific way: as adventure tales, from which young readers can learn about life in the past, and as accounts of history, endorsing its Marxist ideological interpretation. This is true of the passage on chivalry in the translation of *I*: 'on the one hand there is a world full of elevated but mostly hypocritical ideals, the world of seemingly high culture and glamour. On the other hand medieval darkness and obscurantism rule everywhere as an unchangeable law' ('Na jedné straně je tu svět naplněn vznešenými, ale namnoze jen pokryteckými ideály, svět zdánlive vysoké společenské kultury a lesku. Na druhé straně však vládne neúprosným zákonem středověké tmářství') (Nenadál 1989, 447). Another statement of this kind concludes an afterword to *QD*.

11 The Polish Reception of Sir Walter Scott

Mirosława Modrzewska

No serious study of Polish Romanticism (1822–63) can be complete without a discussion of the enormous influence the works of Walter Scott had on Polish literature. The only British author contemporary to Scott who was more visibly influential was Byron, with whom Scott is frequently paired and contrasted. An early example is Stanisław Windakiewicz, *Walter Scott i Lord Byron w odniesieniu do polskiej poezji romantycznej* (Walter Scott and Lord Byron in relation to Polish Romantic poetry), published in Kraków in 1914. The part devoted to Walter Scott starts as follows:

> Walter Scott and Byron influenced the shape and content of the most heartfelt works of the Polish spirit. If it had not been for Scott and Byron, Polish Romanticism would have brought forth different literary works – not *Marya, Konrad Wallenrod, Pan Tadeusz, Beniowski,* or *Dziady.* In discussing Polish Romanticism we continually come across these two names, out of which two commonly used terms have been created: 'walterscottism' and 'byronism'. They appeared in Poland by way of international exchange of thoughts and patterns; they came from far off countries on the wings of renown, recommended by French and German articles and translations. The most local of Scottish authors and the most un-English and cosmopolitan, indeed the most continental of the English poets, they met in the pages of periodicals and were to influence the European literature which were then in the stage of transformation.
>
> Scott and Byron are authors of momentous significance in our literature and their own. (9–10)[1]

---

[1] Walter Scott i Byron wpłynęli na kształt i zawartość najserdeczniejszych dzieł polskiego ducha. Gdyby nie Scott i Byron, romantyzm polski byłby inne dzieła wydał – nie *Marye, Konrada Wallenroda, Pana Tadeusza, Beniowskiego, Dziady.* Roważając romantyzm polski, ciągle zaczepiamy o te dwa nazwiska, z których utworzono nawet utarte termina: walterskotyzm i byronizm. Pojawiły się one w Polsce drogą internacyonalnej wymiany myśli i wzorów; przypłynęły z dalekich krajów na skrzydłach renomy, zalecane przez francuskie i niemieckie artykuły i przekłady. Najbardziej lokalny autor szkocki i najbardziej nieangielski i kosmopolityczny – a właściwie najbardziej kontynentalny z poetów angielskich – spotykali się na łamach czasopism periodycznych i mieli oddziałać na literatury europejskie, które wtedy znajdowały się w studyum przetwarzania.

Scott was recognized as a creative genius by contemporary Polish writers as well as by the reading public of the time, and was a point of reference for a new Romantic style. Adam Mickiewicz's fantastic Lithuanian and Belorussian folk stories and ballads in *Ballady i romanse* caused as much criticism as they aroused enthusiasm, but those who wanted to be complimentary about this new literary event placed Mickiewicz's mysterious world of magic characters and fairies in the context of Scott's 'antiquarian' poetic output. Mickiewicz's friend, Jan Czeczot (1796–1847), an ethnographer who performed great services for Belorussian folk poetry, wrote in his letters to the poet (26 November and 8 December 1822) about the success of Mickiewicz's volume in Warsaw: 'They call you the Walter Scott of Lithuania' (nazywają cię Walterem Scottem litewskim). This must have been a great compliment as elsewhere in the letter he addresses Mickiewicz warmly with the words: 'Well then, dear Walter Scott, send me, if you can, as soon as possible, the materials for the second volume, finish the tale if you can, and at least finish *Forefathers' Eve*' (Otóż, kochany Walterze Skocie, przysyłaj, jak możesz, powieść, a przynajmniej popraw *Dziady*) (Siwicka 2001a, 490). The presence of Walter Scott in the early days of Polish Romanticism was unquestionable.

The first mention of Walter Scott in the Polish press is to be found in *Pamiętnik Warszawski* (The Warsaw Journal) in November 1816 in an article translated from the *Bibliothèque Universelle*, signed with a letter S. and entitled 'Rzut oka na literaturę angielską w ostatnich dwudziestu latach, pismo wyjęte z dziennika: Bibliotheque universelle 1816. Miesiąc Styczeń' (A glance at English literature of the last twenty years, an article extracted from the *Bibliothèque Universelle*. January 1816). Among various names of prominent British authors (Radcliffe, Edgeworth, Byron), Scott is given particular attention. His affinities with medieval poetry and medieval romance are noticed in respect of thematic quality and poetic style; also appreciated are his Romantic and picturesque landscapes and the miscellaneous and imaginative character of his literary output. Scott is declared by the author to be the 'Ariosto of the North' and his readers are encouraged to study English (S., 298–99).

This article was known to Polish poets and writers who studied at the University of Vilnius. It was part of the phenomenon known as *britomania*: a strong interest from student intellectual circles such as the Philomathian Society in German and English literature, as opposed to French literature, which was considered to be 'overburdened' with neo-classical tradition (Ostrowski 1963, 29: 116–17). In the archives of their activity, part of which include correspondence between the years 1815–23, we find information about the growth of *britomania* and the members' efforts to acquaint themselves with English literature, first in French and German, and then in English. One member of the circle, Franciszek Malewski, knew English and his English lessons were in high demand among the Philomaths. Franciszek Malewski and Jan Sobolewski translated from English and were regular readers of the *Bibliothèque Britannique* and the *Bibliothèque Universelle*, as well as the *Edinburgh Monthly Review*.

From Malecki's letters we also know that he was well acquainted with German almanacs with translations from Shakespeare, Scott and Byron. Witold Ostrowski in his article on Scott in Poland in the years 1816–30 (1963) provides a useful collection of quotations from the Philomaths' correspondence, revealing their remarkable motivation to read literatures in the original:

> Malewski was a keen reader of everything that came from England, treating German as a bridge, not only to English literature, but to English in general. In his letter of 9 October 1819 he urges Mickiewicz to: 'get down quickly to German, even at the cost of your Greek or French. Now is the time to do it, so that you can read all the English works in their precise translations; besides, the work you put into it will pave your way to the English language itself.'[. . .]
>   A month later Mickiewicz writes to Jeżowski: 'I have made considerable progress in German' [. . .]. To which Malewski replies (6 April 1821) with a new challenge: 'Now that you have got to know German Leben, Geist and Welt, Adam, it is time to meet English comfort, blessing and grief; I leave it to your consideration' [. . .]. Mickiewicz listens to his friend this time too, so 'Jarosz' (Malewski) writes to him on 13 February 1822: 'Thank God, you have got down to English!'[2]

It is well documented that soon Mickiewicz and his Vilnius university friends were reading *Britische Dichterproben* (German–English versions of British poetry) with the help of Ebers's *New Hand-Dictionary of the English and German Language* (Ostrowski 1963: 118).

In January 1818 Walter Scott became known in Poland via the Geneva monthly magazine *Bibliothéque Universelle* and the French translations of his poetry there. Adam Mickiewicz was delighted by the dark poetics of *LL* and commented on it in his review for the literary students' club of the Philomathian Society (Towarzystwo Filomatów) as the 'best example of serious, chivalric poetry' ('najpiękniejszy wzór poezji rycerskiej, poważnej') pervaded by the spirit of Caledonian bards: 'the same gloominess and atrocity, the same horrifying and wild tenderness' ('taż sama ponurość i okropność, czułość przerażająca i dzika') (Siwicka 2001a 490). From then on, he became a keen reader of Walter Scott in French for the first few years and then slowly discovered Scott in the original. At the time of his stay in Moscow he was glad to find that the numbers of Scott's readers were increasing and that each of his new books was immediately in circulation (Windakiewicz 1914 16–17).

---

[2] Malewski był gorliwym czytelnikiem wszystkiego, co pochodziło z Anglii. Korzystał ze znajomości Francuskiego, niemieckiego i angielskiego, traktując niemiecki jako pomost nie tylko do literatury angielskiej, lecz także i do angielszczyzny. W liście z 9 X 1819 tak zachęca Mickiewicza: 'Weź się co rychło, choćby z ujmą greckiego, francuskiego, do niemczyzny. Teraz jest pora po temu i wszystkie dzieła angielskie mógłbyś czytać w dokładnych tłumaczeniach; prócz tego praca na to wyłożona utrze ci drogę do samego języka angielskiego'. W miesiąc później Mickiewicz pisze do Jeżowskiego: 'W niemczyźnie znacznie postąpiłem'. Na to 6 IV 1821 Malewski odpowiada nowym wezwaniem: 'Czas by teraz, panie Adamie, kiedyś poznał niemieckie Leben, Geist i Welt, poznać angielski comfort, blessing i grief; zostawiam to do namysłu'. Mickiewicz i tym razem słucha kolegi, więc 'Jarosz' pisze 13 II 1822: 'Chwała Bogu, żeś się wziął do angielszczyzny!'.

Polish versions of Scott appeared in literary magazines from 1821, when *LLM* was translated into prose by Kazimierz Brodziński and published in *Pamiętnik warszawski* (The Warsaw Journal) as *Poema ostatniego barda*. In 1822 Karol Sienkiewicz, the librarian of Prince Adam Czartoryski, published his translation of *LL* (Pani Jeziora). Between the years 1822 and 1825, literary magazines published other translations of Scott's poetry into Polish, by E. Odyniec, J. B. Zaleski, W. Malecka, and other anonymous poets. But the time of greatest interest in Scott's creativity was when he became recognized as primarily an author of excellent historical romances. By 1830 three of his poetic tales in verse and seventeen of his novels had been translated into Polish. F. S. Dmochowski, who published a series of Scott's novels in Polish entitled *Wybór Dzieł* (Selected works), used French translations for this purpose; E. Rykaczewski translated Scott from the original (Krajewska 1994, 23).

At first '*walterscottism*' in Polish literary life meant a fashion for imitating old Scottish ballads, with their repertoire of sensational plots, conspiracies, intriguing characters and supernatural motivation of events. Then Scott's tales and romances became a useful treasury of motifs and characters traceable in the works of the most distinguished Polish Romantic poets: Mickiewicz, Seweryn Goszczyński, Bohdan Zaleski, and after 1840 in the works of W. Pol, L. Kondratowicz and C. K. Norwid. But, of course, Scott turned out to be most influential for nineteenth-century prose and the art of story telling. This first became visible in the writing of Michał Grabowski and Henryk Rzewuski. (Krajewska 1994, 24)

The different aspects of Scott's literary output received varying degrees of literary interest depending on the current poetic and philosophical needs and the stage of literary development of Polish Romanticism. After the interest in the poetic ballad and its antiquarian and folk provenance came the fascination with the narrative tale in verse. And although Polish Romantic poets recognized the primacy of Byron in this area, who, they claimed, perfected the genre and gave it a really Romantic and individualist expression (Maciejewski 1994, 750), they nevertheless followed Scott's tales for their historical landscape and local costume. Critics have noticed Scott's influence in some of Mickiewicz's narrative tales in verse, especially *Grażyna* (Grażyna: A Lithuanian tale) (1823) and *Konrad Wallenrod* (Konrad Wallenrod: A Tale from the History of Lithuania and Prussia) (1828).

Grażyna (the name of the eponymous heroine, which was created by Mickiewicz for the tale, comes from a Lithuanian adjective *grażûs*: 'beautiful') is a chivalric story of a lady in armour who heroically defends her own people against the Teutonic Order. The historical background is fourteenth-century Lithuania and the border disputes of the local princes. The tale draws on various literary traditions, including Torquato Tasso's Renaissance epic *Gerusalemme liberata*, and the Romantic cult of Joan of Arc, as well as Polish sources, such as *Jadwiga, królowa polska* (Jadwiga, the Polish Queen) by Julian Ursyn Niemcewicz (1814), and other historical works by the same author. But what Mickiewicz owes to the Scottish writer is the Romantic epic poetic genre, the idea of historical and local colour as a means of speaking poetically about the present; and the elegiac dreaming into the mythologized heroic past, with an embedded didactic patriotic intent.

It is known that at the time of writing *Grażyna* (1823) Mickiewicz was reading many of Scott's works. Stanislaw Windakiewicz finds traces of whole expressions in *Grażyna* that bear similarities to *Marmion*, in the descriptive parts of the poem concerning the knights' armour shining in the western sun, their bugle horn blowing, or the drawbridge of the castle falling noisily. Mickiewicz's description of the valley of Kowno (Lithuanian: Kaunas) echoes Scott's valley of Teesu in Yorkshire from *Rokeby* (Windakiewicz 1914 15–16):

> 'For where the thicket-groups recede,
> And the rath primrose decks the mead,
> The velvet grass seems carpet meet
> For the light fairies' lively feet' (IV.2)[3]

Scott's influence seems to be even more impressively present in *Konrad Wallenrod*. Though the compositional and poetic technique and the shaping of the protagonist as a dark Romantic conspirator with divided conscience places Mickiewicz's tale in the Byronic tradition of narrative tales in verse (Modrzewska 309–310), the setting of the action in a fourteenth-century Lithuania oppressed by the Teutonic Order, and the historicism with which Mickiewicz delineates the details of customs and appearance of medieval chivalry link *Konrad Wallenrod* with Scott's *The Tales of the Crusaders, I* and *T*, all of which Mickiewicz read and knew well. The story is based on an authentic character, Konrad Wallenrod, who was the Grand Master of the Teutonic Knights in the years 1391–93. He had been a ruthless oppressor of Lithuania until 1392, just before the siege of Vilnius, when he unexpectedly deserted his army, causing a disaster. The rumours of his madness and his mysterious death made it all perfect material for an intriguing story (Siwicka 2001, 227–31). In Mickiewicz's literary version of the legend, Konrad Wallenrod, the Grand Master, like many of Scott's characters, turns out to be a person in disguise (a Lithuanian boy, Alf, living among the Knights of the Cross).

Mickiewicz's description of the life and customs (such as the election of the Grand Master) of the order is similar to what we find in the descriptions of the Knights of the Temple by Scott in *I* (ch. XXXVII). One of the

---

[3]   In *Grażyna*:

> 'Widziałem piękną dolinę przy Kownie,
> (I have seen a beautiful valley near Kowno,)
> Kędy Rusałek dłoń wiosną i latem
> (Where fairies' hands in spring and Summer)
> Ściele murawę, kraśnym dzierzga kwiatem;
> (lay the grass, embroider with the red flower;)
> Jest to dolina najpiękniejsza w świecie'
> (It is the most beautiful valley in the world.)
> Mickiewicz 1949, *Dzieła*, II, v. 384–87, p. 19

most important motifs of chivalric life, both in Walter Scott's poetry and in Mickiewicz's *Konrad Wallenrod*, is minstrelsy. *LLM* was one of the most widely known narrative poems, though there are other works by Scott in which the figure of the bard plays an important role. In *T* (1825), also known to Mickiewicz, Richard the Lionheart presents himself as a lover of minstrelsy and listens to his favourite troubadour, Blondel de Nesle. Likewise, Konrad Wallenrod is presented as a singer himself 'brought up' on the prophetic songs of the *wajdelota* (bard), the father figure of Halban. Halban, like Scott's bards, is a key character, playing the role of a medium bringing forth the demonic power of tradition and history, and reminding Wallenrod of his patriotic duty and the necessity of taking revenge on the Teutonic Order in the name of old Lithuanian heroes.

It has been noticed that the 'walterscottian' character of the bard in particular had a crucial influence on the reading style of the contemporary public. The figure of the bard in the fictional world of many Romantic texts represents the point of view of the poet/writer in accordance with the views of the literary epoch on the prophetic/philosophical role of a Romantic author. The relationship between the bard and the characters is, then, a model of the relationship between the Romantic author and his readers: they were to be emotionally involved in the story told and its contents were to be read as past history having direct influence in the present. Poetic imperatives were to be treated seriously: Romantic readers were to become Romantic lovers, conspirators and liberators (Siwicka 1995, 43).

This communicative model between the writer and the reader may clearly be seen in Walter Scott's poem *The Bard's Incantation: Written under the Threat of Invasion in the Autumn of 1804.*

> [. . .]
> Wake ye from your sleep of death,
>   Minstrels and bards of other days!
> For the midnight wind is on the heath,
>   And the midnight meteors dimly blaze:
> The Spectre with his Bloody Hand,
> Is wandering through the wild woodland;
> The owl and the raven are mute for dread,
> And the time is meet to awake the dead!
> [. . .]
> Arise, the mighty strain to tell!
> For fiercer than fierce Hengist's strain,
> More impious than the heathen Dane,
> More grasping than all-grasping Rome,
> Gaul's raving legions hither come!"
> The wind is hush'd, and still the lake –
>   Strange murmurs fill my tinkling ears,
> Bristles my hair, my sinews quake,
>   At the dread voice of other years –
>   (Scott *Poetical Works*, 583–84)

Mickiewicz creates a similar idea of national song/poetry as a link between tradition and the present day, making it possible for modern humans to regain lost greatness and solemnity. In *Konrad Wallenrod* he makes his minstrel Halban sing the famous 'Song of the Wajdelota' to arouse the phantoms of the past and inspire the souls of his listeners/readers to action.

Mickiewicz himself decided to place Halban in the centre of the title page illustration of his book; the lithography was done for him by Gotard Sobański. In a letter to the painter he gave detailed instructions as to the composition of the scene: the bard calmly fixing his hypnotizing gaze on the drunken and angry Konrad Wallenrod, the Grand Master. In Mickiewicz's poem Halban is given the demonic power of a 'lion-tamer', subduing the powerful knight.

Mickewicz's version of Scott's minstrel, imposing patriotic imperatives on his reading public, has attracted considerable critical attention (Siwicka 2001). Probably the first written report of *Konrad Wallenrod* was a denunciation by Nicholas Novosiltsov (March 1828), commissary of the Russian Government in partitioned Poland, in which he wrote about the wickedness of the old minstrel called Halban, who is a 'mask' for Mickiewicz himself. *Konrad Wallenrod* was censored as being extremely dangerous for Tsarist rule. So was Walter Scott's *The Life of Napoleon* (Żywot Napoleona), which could only be legally published at the time after much diplomatic activity (Zielińska 2001, 69–70).

An even greater influence of Walter Scott is generally noticed in another epic poem by Mickiewicz, *Pan Tadeusz* (1834), which is acknowledged in Poland to be the greatest national narrative poem ever written. It was a version of *scottism* understood as the author's desire to preserve in the collective memory an old and, as in Scott's novels, beautiful world, with all its customs. The plot followed romance lines and included similar motifs and characters. As in *W*, *OM*, or *RR* we find in *Pan Tadeusz* a dramatic love plot set on the country estate of a rich but childless uncle. His 20-year-old nephew, Tadeusz Soplica, who comes home having finished his education in Vilnius, unexpectedly meets his young cousin Zosia Horeszko, who has been destined for him as a wife but has not yet been introduced into society. A law suit between the two families of Soplica and Horeszko concerning the ownership of a ruined old castle causes the house to fill with guests. At a family dinner Tadeusz takes Telimena for Zosia, who is Telimena's niece. This is the beginning of the romance intrigue that ends with the happy marriage of Zosia and Tadeusz, which is at the same time a fortunate solution to the dispute over the castle. The romance plot is intertwined with the main story of Jacek Soplica (the father of Tadeusz), who only reveals his true identity on his deathbed and appears in the course of the action as Father Robak ('Worm'). His former identity as Jacek, a violent outlaw who killed the father of his beloved Ewa Horeszko because he was not allowed to marry her, is modelled on a Byronic character. Declared a traitor, he has to flee the country. He comes back hooded as a monk and with a changed name; he organizes an insurrection in Lithuania and takes part in the battle for Soplicowo. He then makes his final confession and gains general forgiveness and rehabilitation as a patriot and the man who saved the life of the last Horeszko by skilfully shooting a bear during a hunt. The romance plot of *Pan Tadeusz*, together with the colourful historical setting, make this long poetic narrative similar to Scott's prose historical romances.

Mickiewicz also created characters who are similar to specific Scott figures, such as, for example, Gerwazy, the faithful servant of the Horeszko family, who, as Stanisław Windakiewicz has noticed, resembles 'the flower of Majordomos', Caleb Balderstone, from the *BL* (1914, 30–35). Gerwazy, like Caleb, is a 'living' testimony to the glorious past of a once great family, preserving their customs and legends, living in the ruins of a castle and still winding the old clocks. As in Scott's novels, Mickiewicz's characters are taken from all walks of life in the traditional society depicted: they include young lovers, distinguished ladies, angry aristocrats, monks, and even peddlers who link various strata. But in Mickiewicz's epic those characters acquire the local colour of Polish Lithuania, or, on the contrary, are clearly shown as having acquired a foreign look, like Count Horeszko and his Italian fashion.

The presence of Walter Scott in the creation of *Pan Tadeusz* was felt by Mickiewicz himself. When he finished Book V, he wrote in a letter to his friend and fellow-poet Edward Antoni Odyniec, a translator of Scott: 'There is no point in sending you excerpts, because you will not learn anything from them. They would be like a few pages torn out of Walter Scott (forgive me the immodest comparison), and the whole thing is too extensive' ('Wyjątki tobie trudno posłać, bo z nich nic się nie dowiesz, jak z kilku kart wyrwanych z Waltera Scotta (wybacz nieskromne porównanie), a całość zbyt jest obszerna'). That a comparison to Walter Scott was the highest of compliments and a recognition of beauty may also be seen in the readers' reaction, especially that of another great poet, Juliusz Słowacki (1809–49), who wrote in a letter to his mother (18 December 1834): 'Adam's new poem (*Pan Tadeusz*) also aroused many sounds of the past in me. It is a very beautiful poem, similar to Walter Scott's romance, written in verse' (Adama nowy poemat obudził także we mnie wiele dźwięków przeszłości: bardzo piękny poemat, podobny do romansu Walter Scotta, wierszem napisanego). (Siwicka 2001, 490–91).

Adam Mickiewicz may have lost his literary interest in Scott's historical romances later in his life during the time of his professorship at the Collège de France (1840–44), when he lectured on Slavonic literatures and accused Scott of lacking all mysticism and not fulfilling the true vocation of literature. In her article 'Walter Scott' in *Mickiewicz. Encyklopedia* (2001) Dorota Siwicka summarizes Mickiewicz's views on *scottism* at this time:

His pronouncements could be unusually harsh. In course II (lesson XV) of his Paris lectures he said: 'The method popularised by Walter Scott has already caused great damage to Slavonic literature, and threatens still worse things'. The criticism, however, did not pertain only to the numerous imitators of the writer, but to the main principle of Scott's work: 'hubris, possibly even greater than that of Byron'. It was hubris – Mickiewicz would say – that allowed writers of this kind to turn great heroes into literary figurines, 'like a conjurer, casting shades for the entertainment of the spectator'. In the same way 'Sir Walter Scott wrote for the amusement of his readers, for the entertainment of his frivolous public'. Art as entertainment, using history or folk song for amusement, all this Mickiewicz considered now a transgression against the sacred vocation of the word. He returns to this issue in course III (lesson XVI), when he clearly states that Scott 'does not know the mystery of the

relationship between heaven and earth', which is revealed in the Slavonic drama.[4]
(2001a, 491)

The controversy about Scott continued. The problem of depicting Polish and
Slav history was also important in post-Napoleonic times and in partitioned
and post-insurrectionist Poland after 1831. *Pan Tadeusz*, written in exile, was
Mickiewicz's last tribute to the idealized past of traditional Lithuania, but literature for him bore great responsibility for shaping the minds of his readers. And
the version of *walterscottation* ('walterskotacje') represented by some Polish
writers of historical romances and their reviewers was a fascination with history
in a politically regressive and conservative spirit. For conservative circles, the
sentimental dwelling upon the great traditions of the nobility provided an antidote to the inevitable process of social disintegration, insurrectionist conspiracy,
and liberal tendencies in contemporary political thought. The novels modelled
on Scott by Michał Grabowski, such as *Stanica hulajpolska* (The Polish Revelry
Watchtower) (1840–41), or by Henryk Rzewuski, such as *Listopad* (November)
(1845–46), followed these lines. They presented the grandeur of hierarchical
culture and taught the necessity of honouring national traditions and the virtues
of Sarmatian heroes (Bachórz 1994, 737).

However ambivalent the attitude of the great Polish Romantics might have
been to the Sarmatian legend of the valiant Polish knighthood of the sixteenth,
seventeenth and eighteenth centuries (the term comes from the notes of
Ancient Roman geographers, who gave the name 'Sarmatia' to lands of what
was later to become the Republic of Poland), the influence of Walter Scott in
the revival of the myth is unquestionable. *Sarmatia* as the republic of the gentry
is recreated in *Pan Tadeusz* with all of its scenery and trappings: a country
manor surrounded by villages inhabited by impoverished nobility, wearing
their traditional costumes (*kontushes*), surrounded by their ancestral heritage
in the shape of furniture, crockery, old clocks and arms of all sorts. Also recalled
are their inherited privileges and customs, in the centre of which was the life
of the family and the neighbourhood, including celebrations and visits, quarrels
and disputes. The characters ranged in type from the amiable and Arcadian
host of a hospitable estate to the litigious reveller, but they shared a common

---

[4] W jego wypowiedziach pojawiły się sądy niezwykle surowe. W kursie II (lekcja
XV) prelekcji paryskich mówił: 'Metoda upowszechniona przez Waltera Scotta
sprawiła już wielkie spustoszenie w literaturze słowiańskiej, a jeszcze większymi
zagraża'. Krytyka nie dotyczyła wszak tylko licznych naśladowców pisarza, lecz
głównej zasady jego twórczości: 'jest nią pycha, większa może jeszcze niż pycha
Byrona'. To pycha – mówił Mickiewicz – pozwala pisarzom tego rodzaju czynić z
wielkich bohaterów historii figurki iterackie: 'Jak kuglarz dla zabawy widzów
rzucający cienie', tak i 'Sir Walter Scott pisał dla zabawienia swych czytelników, dla
zabawienia tłumów próżniaczej publiczności'. Sztuka jako rozrywka, wykorzysta-
nie historii czy pieśni gminnych dla zabawy, wszystko to uważał teraz Mickiewicz
za występki przeciw świętemu powołaniu słowa. Powróci do tej kwestii w kursie III
(lekcja XVI), kiedy powie wyraźnie, iż Scott 'nie zna tajemnicy tego związku
pomiędzy niebem a ziemią', którą objawia dramat słowiański.

belief in the value of freedom, democracy among the gentry, honour and religious piety.

In the history of Polish literature and culture the Sarmatian legend and its ideological heritage came under continual attack as traditionalist, xenophobic and simplistically mystical. It was also criticized for a baroque love of abundance and profusion, which revealed itself in literature of the romance type, with its clear dichotomy of values and characters, complicated plot, richness of detail and ornamental style of language, characteristic of the old gentry story-telling (for example, H. Rzewuski, *Pamiątki Soplicy* [The mementoes of Soplica]). But despite the criticism and many parodies of *sarmatism*, it flourished as a literary theme in the years 1830–40 because of the popularity of Walter Scott's literary method, the antiquarian passion for collecting historical and local details, and the post-insurrectionist (after 1831) interest in ancestral history. All this coincided with the conspiratorial and patriotic activity of the writers in exile and brought about a revival of the chivalric Sarmatian myth, in its sanctified version, based on the patriotic-religious paradigm of the Confederacy of Bar, idealized as the eighteenth-century Polish bid for independence (Nawarecki 1994, 861).

Walter Scott's poetics of the historical romance enjoyed the greatest number of imitators in Polish literature and criticism between the years 1815 and 1850. Among the prose writers usually mentioned there is Julian Ursyn Niemcewicz and his novel *Jan z Tęczyna* (Jan of Tęczyn) (1825), which critics recognized as the first *walterscottian* Polish novel. They noticed in it a variety of motifs borrowed from *W*, in the descriptions of the household and customs, and in the romance technique taken over from *Monastery, BL* and *I* (Ostrowski 1963, 125). Other imitators of Scott's historical romance are Klementyna Hoffman, with female heroes of *Listy Elżbiety Rzeczyckiej* (1824) (The letters of Elżbieta Rzeczycka) and *Dziennik Franciszki Krasińskiej* (1825) (The diary of Franciszka Krasińska); Feliks Bernatowicz, the author of *Pojata córka Lezdejki albo Litwini w XIV wieku* (1826) (Pojata the daughter of Lezdejka, or the Lithuanians of the fourteenth century) and *Nałęcz* (1828) (Nałęcz); Fryderyk Skarbek, the author of *Tarło* (1826) (Tarło) and *Damian Ruszczyc* (1827) (Damian Ruszczyc); Aleksander Bronikowski, the author of *Hipolit Boratyński* (1825–26) (Hipolit Boratyński), *Mysza Wieża* (1826) (The tower of mice), *Zawieprzyce* (1827) (Zawieprzyce), *Kazimierz i Esterka* (1828) (Casimir and Esther), *Jan III Sobieski i dwór jego* (1830) (Jan Sobieski III and his court); Fryderyk Wężyk, the author of *Władysław Łokietek* (1828) (Ladislaus The Elbow-High) and *Zygmunt z Szamotuł* (1829) (Sigmund of Szamotuł); Zygmunt Krasiński, the juvenile author of *Władysław Herman i dwór jego, powieść historyczna z dziejów narodowych XI wieku* (1830) (Władysław Herman and his court, a historical novel on the history of the nation in the eleventh century).

It should be mentioned that despite the tremendous popularity of Walter Scott in nineteenth-century Polish culture, the spectacular development of the historical novel as a genre was not solely dependent on him. The roots of the historical novel go back to eighteenth-century tradition and the Enlightenment's typical interest in the theme of the moral and institutional obligations of a society's collective life, as against individual consciousness. The Romantic phase of the theme, with its 'aestheticized' and mythologized depiction of the past in a romance model of the world, was a fashionable trend and one of the possible options in historical writing. A highly influential nineteenth-century writer of Polish historical prose, Józef Ignacy Kraszewski (1812–87), the author of almost 600 volumes of miscellaneous writings, including a twenty-nine-volume series of historical novels covering all ages of Polish history, started his career as a historiographer with two novels: *Rok ostatni panowania Zygmunta III* (The last year of the reign of Sigismundus III) and *Kościół Święto-Michalski w Wilnie* (St Michael's Church in Vilnius) (1833), which were written with a consciously polemical intent in relation to the literary works of the 'Walterscottians'. Kraszewski dissociated himself from the 'friendly' version of history in their romances and opted for a more 'documentary' version of the genre. His declared attitude was one of critical 'irony'; his historical novels have a 'chronicle'/mimetic quality and a great quantity of well-researched factual detail (Bachórz 1994, 738–39).

But Scott's romance idea of history was to come back in a modified but highly creative form in the historical novels by Henryk Sienkiewicz (1846–1916), winner of the Nobel Prize in 1905 for his novel *Quo vadis* (1896). His neo-Romantic, optimistic vision of the chivalric past was a spectacular success with the readers, partly due to the demand for a 'compensatory myth' (Bujnicki 25) in occupied Poland, but first of all due to the artistic talent of the writer.

Sienkiewicz's *Trylogia* (*Trilogy*) about seventeenth-century Poland comprised *Ogniem i mieczem* (With fire and sword), vols 1–3 (1884); *Potop* (The deluge), vols 1–6 (1886); and *Pan Wołodyjowski* (Colonel Wołodyjowski), vols 1–3 (1887–89). It was written against the background of Polish Positivism (a political and cultural movement emphasizing progress through hard work at the grass-roots level) and 'naturalist' tendencies in prose literature. He clearly declared his literary outlook and purpose:

> May literature at least create for us other worlds, where everything is not so stunted, but great; not so flat but elevated; not so morbid and mortal, but healthy and immortal; not decrepit, but young. Give us some other world and some other spaces, in which breasts made feverish from urban fumes, will, once at least, breathe freely and deeply.[5] (Bujnicki 1990, 26)

His philosophy of writing novels to 'lift people's hearts' ('ku pokrzepieniu serc') was exhibited in 'walterscottian' plot formation with an emphasis on adventure and distinctive characters. The historical background of *The Trilogy* is a series of military disasters of the seventeenth-century Polish Republic, invaded by the Swedes (*Potop*) and the Turks (*Pan Wołodyjowski*) or suffering from civil war, with Hetman Chmielnicki and his Cossack rebellion in the eastern borderlands (*Ogniem i mieczem*). But the collective effort of Polish

---

[5] Niechże choć literatura stworzy nam światy inne, gdzie wszystko nie jest takie karłowate, ale wielkie, nie takie płaskie, ale wzniosłe, nie chorobliwe i śmiertelne, ale zdrowe i nieśmiertelne, nie zgrzybiałe, ale młode. Dajcie nam jakie inne światy i inne jakieś przestrzenie, w których piersi zgorączkowane od miejskich wyziewów odetchną choć raz swobodnie a szeroko.

chivalry and the valiant patriotic stance of individuals turn defeat into final victory. On the one hand, Sienkiewicz's novels exhibit great erudition and are instructive in their antiquarian piety, while on the other hand their world is one of clear spiritual values, in which the fictitious adventures of hyperbolized individuals are interwoven with the historic chain of events in a heroic psychomachic narrative.

> Many scholars have drawn attention to the *syncretic* and polymorphous quality of *The Trilogy*. The coexistence of many elements has been noted in its structure: national epic, fairy tale, the yarn (story-telling) of the gentry, as well as the historical novel paradigms of Scott and Kraszewski. Jan Trznadlowski has coined a useful term, *the historical adventure novel*, which links a fictitious and fast-moving love intrigue (the plot framework of the novel) with historical motifs.[6]

Part of Henryk Sienkiewicz's heart-warming policy in his creation of the chivalric world of seventeenth-century Sarmatia with its colourful baroque style was the strategy of anecdote and humour embedded in the archaic language and the revived seventeenth-century mentality of the permanent nobleman-soldier. The key character in this constructed reality is Zagłoba – modelled on Falstaff and Odysseus, and one of Sienkiewicz's most original achievements. Zagłoba and his 'unbelievable' stories counterbalance the grandeur of history and indirectly pave the way for a new reading and re-editions of Walter Scott's romances.

Sienkiewicz's affinities with the historical writings of Walter Scott are clearly visible in the lack of any clash between the documentary (historical) and the adventure plane of the narration and in the ease with which Sienkiewicz blends the historical and the fictitious. This is largely due to his adoption of the post-Romantic concept of the model of reality in which the historical legend or tale and its narrative poetics of a gentry yarn pervades the 'antiquarian' mode; and the essential quality of the plot is the sensational and humorous aspect of the intrigue. The importance of characters, often hyperbolized, and their individual language in Sienkiewicz's novels is a significant aspect of Sienkiewicz's concept of 'national character'.

> Sienkiewicz, adopting Scott's method and modifying it at the same time, presented in his novel a variety of different communities; they have been endowed with their own 'portraits'. Operating with communities, which where primarily military ones, the writer created powerfully evocative pictures, such as the presentation of

---

[6] Wielu badaczy zwracało uwagę na synkretyzm *Trylogii* i jej wielopostaciowość. Wskazywano na obecność w jej strukturze pierwiastków epopeicznych, baśniowych, związków z gawędą szlachecką i wzorami powieści historycznych Scotta i Kraszewskiego. Jan Trzynadlowski posłużył się trafną nazwą historycznej powieści przygody łączącej fikcyjną, pełną szybko zmieniających się zdarzeń intrygę miłosną (ona określa ramy fabularne powieści) z wątkami historycznymi. (Bujnicki 1990, 28)

Zaporoże cavalry crossing the steppe. Being a background to the activities of individual heroes, the community is to some extent self-contained.[7] (Bujnicki 1973, 101)

It defines the character's natural milieu with all its stereotypical connotations and paradigms of values, which Sienkiewicz, similar to Walter Scott, used so readily in his dialogue with the reader (105).

The post-Sienkiewicz reading style of Walter Scott's novels is clearly visible in the neo-Romantic literary criticism of Andrzej Tretiak (1886–1944), a well-known translator and historian of Polish and English literature. In his introduction to a subsequent edition of *W*, translated by Teresa Świderska (1929), he delineates the most important features of Scott's literary output and the place of his novels in literary tradition. He starts the chapter devoted to 'The Development of National Feeling' ('Rozwój uczucia narodowego') (X–XVII) as follows:

Glorification of the national past is an outcome of conscious patriotism. It is a way of awakening the feeling of patriotism in the readers, of teaching them what they should do in order to live one moment as nobly as once their ancestors lived their whole life, of encouraging them to take part in the chain of glorious national events, and great deeds of the past. The practical end of this activity is the good and the greatness of the nation in the present moment.[8]

Tretiak draws attention to the literary merit of Scott's novels and to their fascination as a source of information on Scottish and English history and the local landscape. He regards their 'antiquarian' quality as a means of patriotic edification for the reader. He also enlarges on the importance of Scott's literary humour:

The sympathy he has for the people (because if, according to Carlyle, he did not reach *their* hearts, he at least gave them *his* heart) endows this humour with the brightness of a happy summer noontime. While reading Scott we feel inclined to unrestrained laughter, and indulge this inclination at every opportunity, knowing

---

[7]   Sienkiewicz przyswajając i zarazem modyfikując metodę Scotta dokonał w powieści prezentacji różnorodnych zbiorowości. I one posiadają swoje "portrety". Operując zbiorowościami – przede wszystkim wojskowymi – pisarz tworzył obrazy o silnej sugestywności, jak np. prezentacja idących przez step oddziałów zaporoskich. Będąc tłem dla działań indywidualnych bohaterów, zbiorowość jest do pewnego stopnia samoistna.

[8]   Gloryfikacja przeszłości narodowej jest wynikiem świadomego patriotyzmu. Jest ona środkiem do rozbudzenia uczuć patriotyzmu w czytelnikach, do nauczenia ich, co mają robić, by jedną chwilę tak górnie przeżyli, jak ich przodkowie niegdyś całe życie', do zachęcenia ich do brania udziału w łańcuchu narodowych chlubnych wydarzeń, wielkich czynów przeszłości. Praktycznym celem tego działania jest dobro i wielkość narodu w chwili współczesnej. (X)

that the laughter will offend no one, irritate no one, hurt no one, and that we are entitled to laugh in the atmosphere created by Scott.[9]

The reception of Walter Scott in Poland was a dynamic process depending on the literary and cultural needs of the Polish reading public, and the phases of enthusiasm and criticism testify to his powerful position in Polish language and culture. A piece of contemporary evidence of this high position is the latest edition of the Polish version of *W* by Teresa Świderska in 2005, in a series of *Biblioteka Gazety Wyborczej* devoted to the classics of nineteenth-century world literature.

---

[9] Sympatia, jaką ma do ludzi – bo jeżeli nie docierał do i c h serca, według Carlyle'a, to dawał im całe swoje serce, – nadaje temu humorowi jasność wesołego letniego południa. Czytając Scotta, czujemy się skłoni do swobodnego śmiechu i korzystamy z każdej sposobności z tego, wiedząc, że ten śmiech nikogo nie obraża, nikogo nie drażni, nikomu nie sprawia przykrości, i że do tego śmiechu mamy w atmosferze scottowskiej prawo. (1927, XLVI)

12 The Rise and Fall of Walter Scott's Popularity in Russia

Mark G. Altshuller, translated by
Neil Stewart

The epoch of Walter Scott (the 1830s)

In Russia, Walter Scott has always been known primarily as an author of historical novels, although his poetry was also extensively translated in the 1820s, the first decade of his fame. This essay will deal primarily with Scott the novelist, the creator of a genre hitherto unknown in world literature.

This is not the place for a detailed analysis of Scott's historico–philosophical concepts. Such an analysis is undertaken in other chapters of the present volume. We will limit ourselves here to those characteristics of Scott's ideology and poetics that were especially important for his Russian followers and imitators.

1. In his works, Scott *combined history with invention*. The most important element of Scott's poetics is the way in which the author suggests the complete (or nearly complete) authenticity of the historical material underlying his narrative. His work is based on a painstaking examination of historical materials; he closely and deliberately links his text to certain historical events. The application of – or pretension to – such scientific standards (in his novel *The Antiquary*, Scott himself good-humouredly mocks his passions and foibles as historian and archaeologist) had not been known in literary fiction before.[1] The readers readily concurred in this 'genuine' historicism and accepted Walter Scott's novels as serviceable models of history. One of I. S. Turgenev's characters, for instance, 'appreciated the English novelist as a

---

[1] In the ancient novel, historical (as well as biological) time is simply non-existent. See M. M. Bakhtin (1986) 'Formy vremeni i khronotopa v romane: Ocherki po istoricheskoi poetike' (Forms of Time and Chronotope in the Novel: Notes on Historical Poetics), in *Literaturno-kriticheskie stat'i*, pp. 121–29. The same can be said about the medieval chivalry novel and the pseudo-historical novels of the seventeenth and eighteenth centuries.

serious, almost scientific, writer'.[2] In creating the genre of the historical novel and describing events from various epochs, Scott, of course, was obliged to recreate on the pages of his novels historical characters familiar to his readers. Here lay another remarkable artistic innovation of his, one that to a considerable extent accounted for the unheard-of popular success of his novels.

2. Familiar historical figures *invariably* appear on the periphery of Scott's novels. They are never at the centre of the action. Even though in their brilliance and vitality they may at times eclipse the colourless portrait of some ideal protagonist, they never become the main narrative driving force of the novel. Scott draws the historical figures into the adventures of his main character. Kings and dukes, chief counsellors and famous statesmen become involved in his fate, play a highly important and often decisive role in his life. Thus figures like Louis XI or Richard the Lionheart, who dwell, as it were, at the roadside of the main narration, take on special depth and plasticity when caught in a passing ray of light.

3. In all European countries, the development of Romanticism sparked an interest in national culture. Scott revealed to the Scottish people their own history and to the whole world the hitherto unknown poetic world of Scotland. Here is just one example of the reception of the poetics of Walter Scott's novels by Russian readers:

> All Nature – the forest, the water, the walls of little huts, the sandy hills – all glows in fiery purple [. . .] and against this purple background is sharply silhouetted a cavalcade of men, riding along a sandy, winding road, accompanying some lady to some gloomy ruin, or hurrying to a safe castle, where wild goat awaits them for supper, an episode from the Wars of the Roses told by a grandfather, and a ballad sung by a young miss to the sound of the lute – images that the pen of Walter Scott so abundantly affords us.[3]

Much later (1852), when Walter Scott's fame had long passed its peak, I. S. Turgenev pointed out the characteristically Romantic national orientation of Scott's Scottish novels, calling one of them 'a spacious, solid building, with an unshakeable foundation, firmly grounded on the national soil' (5: 372).[4]

---

[2] 'Уважал в английском романиете серьезного, чуть не научного писателя'; cf. the story *Klara Milich*, in Turgenev (1852) *Polnoe sobranie sochinenii i pisem*, Moscow; Leningrad: Nauka, 13: 90.

[3] вся природа – и лес, и вода, и стены хижин, и песчаные холмы – все горит точно багровым заревом … по этому багровому фону резко оттеняется едущая по песчаной извилистой дороге кавалькада мужчин, сопутствующиих какой-нибудь леди в прогулках к угрюмой развалине и поспешающих в крепкий замк, где их ожидает эпизод о войне двух роз, расказанный дедом, дикая коза на ужин, да пропетая молодою мисс под звуки лютни баллада – картины, которыми так богато населило наше воображение перо Вальтера Скотта. I. A. Goncharov (1953) *Oblomov*, in *Sobranie sochinenii v 8 tt.*, Moscow, 4: 106–07.

[4] 'пространным, солидным зданием, со своим незыблемым фундаментом, врытым в почву народную'

As we will see, questions of representing national history, the character of a people and its way of life were matters of deep concern to Walter Scott's Russian followers.

4.   The most important characteristic of Walter Scott's novels, and one which stands in favourable contrast to all Russian historical fiction to the present day, was the tolerant attitude of their author. It was noted long ago that Scott loves to describe borderline situations in his novels: an opposition or direct conflict of two nations, cultures, religions, ways of life, and the like. This may be the confrontation of Normans and Saxons, conquerors and defeated (*I*), a clash, an armed conflict on religious grounds (*OM*), religious differences, general differences of lifestyle: food, drink, clothes, armour, forms of matrimony, conceptions of love, etc. (*I, T*).

The protagonists of Scott's novels always find themselves between two mutually hostile parties in diametrical opposition to one another. Scott, however, never gives preference to either of the contestants; both, he says, are right in their own way, both of the warring sides have their merits as well as their failings. The Scottian protagonist, apart from his other noble qualities, is always characterized by moderation and tolerance. Fanaticism is alien to him, and his political convictions are never radical. He is always ready to hear his opponent out. He may not agree with him, but he will acknowledge his subjective position. A human life is always more important to him than national or political disagreements. Therefore the protagonist will so often find himself between two enemy camps, that is in one of the *borderline situations* which are so typical of Scott's novels. 'Scott's position as author excluded partiality in any form whatsoever as a matter of principle'.[5]

The prejudices and intolerance still alive in Europe and dominating in present-day Russia were thus done away with by Scott. Although the fanaticism and violence that have been typical of humankind at all turning points of its history are depicted on the pages of his novels, the author of these novels invariably appears as a disciple of 'wisdom, learning, and moderation'.[6] This cannot be said of the majority of Scott's imitators, who 'found in any historical conflict "us" and "them", right and wrong, the good and the bad, projecting into the past their present sympathies and antipathies' (Dolinin 1988, 227–28).[7] Indeed, this sound scholarly verdict aptly characterizes the Russian imitators of Walter Scott.

---

[5]   'авторская позиция Скотта принципиально исключала какую бы то ни было пристрастность': A. Dolinin (1988) *Istoriya, odetaya v roman: Val'ter Skott i ego chitateli* (History in the guise of a novel: Walter Scott and his readers), Moscow: Kniga, p. 227.

[6]   'мудрости, учености и умеренности'. Scott's words from the essay *Rasskazy traktirshchika*; cf. Val'ter Scott (1960–1965) *Sobranie sochinenii v dvadtsati tomakh*, Moscow; Leningrad: Khudozhestvennaia literatura, 20: 592.

[7]   'в любом историческом конфликте искали и находили «своих» и «чужих», правых и виноватых, добрых и злых, проецируя в прошлое сиюминутные симпатии и антипатии'.

Information on the literary work of Walter Scott appeared relatively late in Russia. His name is first mentioned in print only in 1811. In England he had long been considered a leading poet. In Russia, however, his name was practically unknown. Even the author of the note in the journal 'Vestnik Evropy' (The Messenger of Europe) inadvertently rendered his name as '*William* Scott' (a confusion perhaps with the Edinburgh professor of that name, which wrongly appeared on Scott's own first publication – a translation of Goethe).[8] During the next decade as well Scott remained practically unknown to Russian readers. Even the publication of such famous novels as *W* (1814), *RR* (1819), or *I* (1820) did little to change the general picture. It took the resounding success of Walter Scott's novels in France, where every new novel by 'the author of *Waverley*' was quickly translated into French and greeted with boundless enthusiasm, to make Russian society turn to his novels. Only in the mid-1820s did Walter Scott's novels begin to be published as single volumes in Russian. All these translations were made from Defauconpret's French, and it was precisely this French Scott (either in French or translated from the French) who for many years became a favourite author of Russian readers.[9]

It is interesting to note that some of Scott's novels, although they have been translated from the original, continue to exist in Russian culture under titles given to them 200 years ago by their French translators. In the most authoritative twenty-volume Russian edition of Scott (1960–65) – an edition that we will come back to later – some novels, though they have naturally been translated from the English, retain their French titles. The practically untranslatable title of the famous novel *OM*, for instance, is rendered in the Russian edition as *Puritane*, after the French *Les Puritains de l'Ecosse*. The no less famous novel *HM* is invariably called *Edinburgskaya temnitsa* (The Edinburgh Prison) in Russia.

One of the few to focus their attention on Scott's poetry as early as the mid-1810s and keep an interest in him in the course of their entire lives was the ingenious poet and translator V. A. Zhukovsky, the poetic mentor of Pushkin. Eighty-nine volumes of works by Scott in three European languages are still present in his library (there may have been more originally): most of these are in English, many in French, a few volumes in German, and one in Russian (the two final parts of 'The Edinburgh Prison', 1825).[10] Among Zukhovsky's works there is a brilliant translation of the ballad *The Eve of Saint-John* (1824) – from the poem *Marmion* – under the title 'Sud v podzemele' ('A Trial in the Vaults', 1832).

While in the case of Scott's early novels the publication of a Russian translation would follow that of the original at an interval of ten or more years

[8]   Yu. D. Levin (1975) 'Prizhiznennaya slava Val'tera Skotta v Rossii' (Walter Scott's Fame in Russia during his Lifetime), in *Epokha romantizma: Iz istorii mezhdunarodnykh svyazei russkoi literatury*, Leningrad: Nauka, p. 6.

[9]   Cf. D. Yakubovich (1930) 'Rol' Frantsii v znakomstve Rossii s romanami Val'ter Skotta' ('The Role of France in Russia's Acquaintance with Walter Scott's Novels'), in *Yazyk i literatura* [Leningrad], 5.

[10] Cf. the richly documented essay by E. M. Zhilyakova (1988) 'V. Skott v biblioteke V. A. Zhukovskogo' (W. Scott in V. A. Zhukovsky's library), in *Biblioteka A. Zhukovskogo v Tomske*, Tomsk: Izdatel'stvo Tomskogo universiteta, pp. 300–68.

(*W* 1814 and 1827 respectively, *GM* 1815 and 1824, *A* 1816 and 1826), these gaps became narrower and narrower with his growing popularity (*T* 1825 and 1827, *FMP* 1828 and 1829, *AG* 1829 and 1830), and one of the last novels, *Count Robert of Paris*, was published in Russia in the very same year as in England (1831).

From the early 1820s Scott can be called – without exaggeration – the most popular English writer in Russia, and he has to a considerable extent retained his popularity to the present day. Karamzin and Pushkin, Vyazemsky and Bestuzhev-Marlinsky were equally enthusiastic about Scott. Among the followers of the 'English wizard' there was even Tsar Nicholas I, otherwise totally indifferent to literary fiction, while N. M. Karamzin dreamt of having a statue of Scott erected in his garden. The hero of Pushkin's poem *Count Nulin* returns to Russia carrying 'Walter Scott's latest novel' with him, and Pechorin, the protagonist of M. Lermontov's famous novel *A Hero of Our Time*, spends the night before his duel reading *Old Mortality*, and enchanted by 'the magic of fiction' forgets all about the bloody combat. By the end of the 1820s all Scott's novels had been translated into Russian and republished several times.[11]

Critical statements against Scott were extremely rare at this time. For this reason, a lengthy review of F. Bulgarin's historical novel *Mazepa*, which appeared in 1834, at the height of Scott's fame, attracted general attention. It was written by O. I. Senkovsky, a talented journalist and professor at the University of St Petersburg, an expert in oriental languages and literatures and editor of the journal *Biblioteka dlya chteniya* (The Reading Library). Senkovsky rejected on principle the very genre created by Walter Scott, being probably irritated by what he saw as an inappropriate mixing of science (history) and fiction in one text:

> My soul revolts against embracing this illegitimate child: a historical novel, in my opinion, is but a son born out of wedlock, without family or lineage, the result of an act of adultery committed by history with the imagination [. . .] a bastard generated from two distinct and antagonistic principles [. . .] a treacherous form of beauty [. . .] and a mystification from beginning to end.[12]

While other readers, among them Goethe, were enthusiastic about the variety and vivacity of the human characters in Scott's novels ('The king, the brother of the king, the crown prince, the high dignitary of the Church, the nobility, the magistrate, the burghers and the workers, the highlanders – all are drawn by the

---

[11] Cf. the similarly well-documented essay by Levin.

[12] Душе моей противно брать в руки незаконорожденного ребенка: исторический роман, по-моему, есть побочный сынок без роду и племени, плод соблазнительного прелюбодеяния истории с воображением ... это урод, составленный из двух разнородных и противодействующих начал ... это ложная форма прекрасного ... с начала до конца это мистификация. O. Senkovskii (Baron Brambeus) (1859) '[Review of] Istoricheskii roman: po povodu romana *Mazepa* F. Bulgarina [1833]' (The Historical Novel: On F. Bulgarin's Novel *Mazepa*), *Sobranie sochinenii* [St Petersburg], 8: 44.

same hand and with the same precision'[13]), Senkovsky saw in these novels nothing but monstrosity and formlessness: 'Making use of his brilliant narrative gift, he brings on to the scene hangmen, gypsies, and Jews; he has revealed to the European public a disgusting poetics of gallows, scaffolds, executions, massacres, drunken gatherings, and wild passions'.[14]

Senkovsky's statement attested to his wit and sharpness of thinking and anticipated critical arguments that somewhat later were raised against the French Romantics (Hugo, Vigny, Eugène Sue and others), but was nevertheless greeted with general indignation. Belinsky, Bestuzhev-Marlinsky, Gogol and others came out against it. Senkovsky remained isolated in his time.

The Russian public naturally awaited with impatience a Russian historical novel, the model for which could only be Walter Scott. Writing an entire novel in the manner of Scott did not prove easy, however. Early attempts in that direction were limited to short stories and tales, such as the pieces written in prison by the Decembrist Kornilovich. A professional historian who knew well the epoch he described, Kornilovich portrayed humble protagonists whose happiness is effected by Peter I ('Tatyana Bolotova'). Another example is his story 'Andrei Bezymennyi' (1831). The historicism of these texts – the position of the authentic historical figure on the periphery – without doubt owes much to the work of Walter Scott. The rough exoticism of Baltic Livonia, similar in a way to Scotland, was described by the talented writer Alexander Bestuzhev (Marlinsky) in his stories, which were written in the years 1823–25. Bestuzhev was another Decembrist, exiled first to Siberia and then to the Caucasus, where he perished. He deliberately used certain devices and motifs from Scott's novels, which he knew and loved well. This is especially apparent in the story 'Revelsky turnir' ('The Tournament of Tallinn', 1825), which obviously draws on motifs and devices from Walter Scott's *Ivanhoe*.[15]

Russian writers, however, were as yet unable to present their readers with a whole historical novel in the manner of Scott. The gifted writer I. I. Kireevsky outlined a very interesting plan for a novel modelled on Scott's in his sketch 'Tsaritsynskaya noch' ('The Night in Tsaritsyno', 1827). His hero will accept neither Godunov nor the impostor (*samozvanets*); he broods on the fate of

---

[13] 'Король, брат короля, кронлрииц, князь церкви, дворянетво, магистрат, бюргеры и ремесленники, горцы – все они написаны одинаковой рукой и одинаково метко очерчены.' I. P. Ekkerman (1981) *Razgovory s Gete v poslednie gody ego zhizni* (Johann Peter Eckermann, *Gespräche mit Goethe in den letzten Jahren seines Lebens*), Moscow: [n. pub.], p. 261.

[14] 'Он вывел на сцену, под защитой прелести своего повествовательного дара, палачей, цыган, жидов; он открыл европейской публике отвратительную поэзию виселиц, эшафотов, казней, резни, пьяных сборищ и диких страстей.' O. Senkovskii, p. 49.

[15] For more detailed information see Mark Altshuller (1996) *Èpokha Val'tera Scotta v Rossii (Istoricheskii roman 1830-kh godov)* (The epoch of Walter Scott in Russia [The Historical Novel of the 1830s]), St Petersburg: Akademicheskii proekt, pp. 37–53.

Russia and is finally killed in a fratricidal combat outside the Kremlin.[16] The brilliant plan, however, was not realized: Kireevsky's novel was never written. The problem was not only that such a large new format was difficult to handle at first, it was also generally doubted whether anything in the way of a Walter Scott novel could be constructed on the basis of materials from Russian history. As the 'Westerners' (*zapadniki*) saw it, Russian culture lacked any conception of the meaning and autonomy of the individual subject that was depicted in European literature, and more specifically in European historical novels. At the centre of such a novel there was always 'an individual and family existence, connected to the development of Christian ideas'.[17]

Shortly afterwards, in 1828–29, the idea that Russian history had nothing to offer European civilization was expressed most radically by P. Chaadaev in his *First Philosophical Letter:*

> For us, there is no such thing as philosophical experience; centuries and generations have passed us by without avail [. . .] we have given the world nothing, taught it nothing, we have not contributed a single one to the vast stock of human ideas, have in no way aided the advance of human reason, but rather spoilt whatever we received through this advance.[18]

Nor did the avowed Westerner P. A. Vyazemsky, a famous literary critic and poet, find in the Russian past anything that could in the least interest a novelist:

> It is doubtful whether our materials would be worth anything for novels in the manner of Walter Scott. In our history, at least before Peter the Great, there were no morals, no community, no civil or private virtues – all indispensable elements for a writer on the look-out.[19]

The Slavophiles, who doubted that the reforms of Peter had benefited the country and who looked to pre-Petrine Russia for genuinely Russian values,

---

[16] For a detailed analysis of the Scottian devices in Kireevsky's plan see Altshuller 1996, 61–64.

[17] 'индивидуальное и семейственное существование, связанное с развитием христианских идей.' V. Titov (1828) 'O romane kak predstavitele obraza zhizni noveishikh evropeitsev' (On the Novel as a Representation of the Life Style of Contemporary Europe), *Moskovskii vestnik,* 7: 171.

[18] Йсторический опыт для нас не существует, поколения и века протекли без пользы для нас ... мы ничего не дали миру, ничему не научили его, мы не внесли ни одной идеи в массу идей человеческих, ничем не содействовали прогрессу человеческого разума, и все, что нам досталось от этого прогресса, мы исказили. P. A. Chaadaev (1987) *Stat'i i pis'ma* (Essays and Letters), Moscow: Sovremennik, p. 41.

[19] сомневаемся в богатстве наших материалов для романов вроде Жальтера Скотта. В нашей истории, по крайней мере до Петра Великого ... нет нравов, общежития, гражданственного и домашнего быта: источников необходимых для наблюдателя-романиста. P. A. Vyazemsky, 'Retsenziya na al'manakhi 1827 goda: Severnaya lira i dr.' (Review of Almanacs of the Year 1827: *The Northern Lyre* and Others), *Moskovskii telegraf,* part 3, no. 3/1, p. 245.

thought and argued differently, of course. They contended that the history of Russia was rich in events and ideas and offered a great deal of material for historical novels. In the almanac *The Northern Lyre for the Year 1827*, the well-known historian M. M. Pogodin published his 'Letter on Russian Novels', in which he describes the society at a fictitious evening party discussing Walter Scott. The hostess is convinced that Russian history has nothing to offer for a novel in his style. The narrator vehemently disagrees: ancient Russian history, the relations with the Varangians and the Greeks, the Varangians in Kiev, the baptism of Russia, and so on – all this provided plenty of inspiration for the novelist (note in passing that just shortly afterwards, in 1833, the ancient period of Russian history was indeed depicted in M. Zagoskin's novel *Askold's Grave*). Pogodin (1984, 138) proceeded by naming further turning-points of Russian history that might interest novelists and pointed out with direct reference to Scott that the Russian Old Believers (*raskolniki*) represented a phenomenon by no means less important or interesting than the 'Scottish puritans'.[20]

Even Tsar Nicholas I intervened in this conflict, although he did not, of course, fully understand the literary polemics. He naturally took the side of the Slavophiles. It is significant how severely the Tsar dealt with Chaadaev a few years later for his devastating appraisal of Russian history: he declared the philosopher insane.

Early in 1827 Nicholas, having read a review of the manuscript of Pushkin's historical drama *Boris Godunov*, wrote:

> I believe that the aim of Mr Pushkin would have been better fulfilled if – after the necessary bowdlerization – he had turned his comedy about Tsar Boris into a historical story or novel in the manner of Walter Scott.[21]

Pushkin took offence and refused to revise his play.

Historians have on later occasions reviled Nicholas for his judgement, calling him a despot without any taste. They were not altogether correct. Nicholas indeed did not like or understand literature, but he loved and understood history, and in the case of Walter Scott, whom he knew personally,[22] was prepared to make an exception: these novels were similar to historical writings. In his library there was a good selection of books by the Scottish bard. Nicholas would sometimes spend his evenings reading them in the company of his young wife, who in her turn passed them on to her ladies-in-waiting (Levin 1975, 10). Having noticed that Pushkin's dramatic text in a way resembled the novels he knew and enjoyed, and being the simple-minded reader he was, the emperor

---

[20]   Pogodin, M. M. (1984) *The Northern Lyre for the Year 1827*, Moscow: Nauka.

[21]   'Я считаю, что цель г. Пушкина была бы выполнена, еслиб с нужным очищением переделал комедию свою в историческую повесть или роман на подобие Вальтер Скотта.' Vidok Figlarin; cf. A. I. Reitblat (ed.) (1998) *Pis'ma i agenturnye zapiski F. V. Bulgarina v III otdelenie* (F. V. Bulgarin's Letters and Official Notes to the III. Department), *Novoe literaturnoe obozrenie* [Moscow], p. 97. The manuscript version of the drama was entitled 'A Comedy on Tsar Boris'.

[22]   Cf. Altshuller 1996, 110–11.

wanted to see a historical novel in the manner of Walter Scott – in full accord with the general reading public, who impatiently awaited the appearance of a Russian Scott (it is another side of the matter, however, that this meant that Pushkin's play could not be printed and was published only four years later).

The writers strove to fulfil this public demand. Bulgarin was especially keen, knowing the impatience of the Tsar himself. However, it took another two years for a Russian Walter Scott to emerge, and Bulgarin himself was a few months too late. The first Russian novel à la Walter Scott came out only in 1829. Its author was Mikhail Zagoskin and it was called *Yuri Miloslavsky, or The Russians in 1612*. Zagoskin chose the year 1612 for his novel, the 'Time of the Troubles' (Smuta), when Russia was shaken by inner conflicts, peasant uprisings, and foreign invasions. Later Russian novelists would often turn to that period. Zagoskin studied and analysed the historical material very thoroughly and like Scott pretended to give his readers an authentic picture of a colourful distant past.

The hero of the novel, the young noble Juri Miloslavsky, is also clearly reminiscent of Walter Scott's young heroes. He finds himself between two camps. A member of the old Russian aristocracy, Yuri has sworn allegiance to the Polish crown prince Vladislav, who has been elected by the boyars to the Russian throne. He tries to persuade himself that this choice will put an end to the Polish intervention, the inner conflicts, and the like. But deep down he does not like the Poles. Finally, he renounces his earlier aberrations and heroically fights the Polish usurpers.

As in Scott, the hero of Zagoskin's novel is characterized by a certain passivity: he is put in prison, freed by others, he is wounded (like Ivanhoe), taken away somewhere, etc. The novel also features a band of noble robbers in the chapter on the Cossack Kirsha Danilov, who helps the protagonist (cf. Robin Hood in *Ivanhoe* or Rob Roy in the eponymous novel).

Historical figures also appear: the head of the Nizhnii Novgorod militia, Kozma Minin, and Avramii Palitsyn, the cellarer of the Troitse-Sergievsky monastery and author of the famous *Skazanie* (Tale) about the 'Time of the Troubles'. Unlike Scott's, however, these historical figures do not come off: they remain pale and nondescript. They play an auxiliary role in the main action (a smaller one than in Scott). Minin admonishes the hero to side with the Russians and fight the Poles; Palitsyn sets him free from the oath he has sworn to the Polish crown prince.

As in Scott, Zagoskin's hero finds himself vacillating between two sides, but in this case the resemblance turns out to be a superficial one. The Russian writer does not possess the moderation, tolerance, and impartiality that the great Scotsman displayed in describing political strife, religious wars, and racial conflicts. For Zagoskin, as for the majority of Russian writers, there is only black and white, good and evil: good Russians and their inevitable counterparts: evil Poles, Frenchmen, Jews, Swedes, Old Believers (*raskolniki*), Tatars, and just about everyone who is not Russian.

The absence of the tolerance that had characterized the novels of Scott was to influence the reception of Zagoskin's novel abroad. Shortly after the publication of the novel, the high society lady V. I. Lanskaya and her daughters translated *Juri Miloslavsky* into English. In 1828, Frederic Chamier,[23] captain of the British fleet and later author of popular 'seafarer' novels, happened to be in St Petersburg and apparently made the acquaintance of Lanskaya, who handed over to him her manuscript for publication (and, probably, revision). The translator, who was very well aware of Zagoskin's indebtedness to Scott, very much wanted the great Scotsman to get to know the manuscript, which was also dedicated to him:

> A Russian Lady and her daughters
> The translators of this work
> From their language into English
> (The first [of its] kind ever written in Russia)
> Dedicate it by the author's desire as well as their own
> To sir Walter Scott,
> Hoping that this production will not appear entirely unworthy
> In the eyes of the English reader
> If placed under [the] protection of the Genius of *Waverley*.[24]

Scott had no chance to take notice of the manuscript: he was already seriously ill, suffered two apoplectic strokes in 1831 and died on 21 September 1832. Meanwhile, the publication of the English book was delayed, and one of the main reasons for this delay, it would seem today, was Zagoskin's unconcealed polonophobia. In 1830 a rebellion had broken out in Poland (it should be said in defence of Zagoskin that he had written his novel prior to this event), and the sympathies of the whole of Europe were with the insurgents. A lot of Polish emigrants came to England. As a reviewer put it: '[. . .] the strong popular feeling of this country in favour of the Poles may have played its part in preventing the appearance of this book in English dress.'[25]

When the book finally came out in 1834 in three volumes and under the title *The Young Muscovite, or The Poles in Russia*, it differed considerably from Zagoskin's work. Following the recipes of Scott, Chamier had thoroughly rewritten the novel (he calls his changes 'improvements'), introduced an additional plot, expanded the text to three times its original length (thus bringing it closer to Scott's novels in terms of quantity), added epigraphs, and, most importantly, significantly toned down Zagoskin's obtrusive anti-Polish patriotism. As the aforementioned reviewer had remarked, not without irony, 'patriotism is a virtue that seldom observes the golden mean'. It is this 'golden mean' that Chamier tried to adhere to in the manner of Scott. He strove to

---

[23] For more detailed information on Chamier see Gleb Struve (1949) 'Pushkin in Early English Criticism', *The American Slavic and East European Review* (ASEER), 8.4: 305–08; and Maria L. Danilewicz (1961) 'Chamier's Anecdotes of Russia', *The Slavonic and East European Review* (SEER), 40.94: 85–98.

[24] Cf. M. P. Alekseev (1982) 'Russko-angliiskie literaturnye svyazi (XVIII vek-pervaya polovina XIX veka)' (Anglo-Russian Literary Contacts in the Eighteenth and the First Half of the Nineteenth Century), *Literaturnoe nasledstvo* [Moscow], 91: 358–59.

[25] *Foreign Quarterly Review* (FQR), 1833, 11: 383. On the author of the review (V. G. Leeds) see Struve 1949, 308–13.

depict both sides fairly and correctly and commented that the system of government in Poland was better than that in Russia. If the Russians were daring and patriotic, they were also crueller and less civilized than the Europeanized Poles.[26] Chamier's revised text was successful with the public, who saw it as a well-made imitation of Walter Scott. Between1833 and 1834 it was reprinted twice.[27]

This success inspired Zagoskin, who went on to exploit the newly found genre, devices, and themes. After *Miloslavsky*, there followed two more novels with similar titles: *Roslavlev, or The Russians in 1812* (1831) and *The Russians at the Beginning of the Eighteenth Century* (1848). Together with the first novel they form a kind of trilogy: the Russians in the 'Time of the Troubles', the Russians under Peter I, and the Russians in the war of 1812 (cf. Scott's trilogy *Waverley, Guy Mannering*, and *The Antiquary*). Zagoskin, however, moved further and further away from Scott's tolerance, the 'golden mean'. Both later novels were written in times of uprisings and revolutions: in Poland and France (1830) and in France, Germany, Austria and Hungary (1848), respectively. While they retain several of Scott's devices, both books are characterized by an excess of noisy and vulgar patriotism and monarchism.

A few months after Zagoskin's first historical novel came Faddei Venediktovich Bulgarin. His reputation in the history of Russian literature is that of a police informer, corrupt journalist, etc. This reputation is all-in-all a deserved one, if not always altogether fair. In any case, Bulgarin was not without literary talent, sharpness of mind, and the gift of observation. His novels generally enjoyed a deserved success. Late in 1829 he published his novel *Dmitry Samozvanets* (Dmitry the impostor), the action of which, as indicated by the title, is also situated in the 'Time of the Troubles'. Like Walter Scott, Bulgarin painstakingly studied historical sources and strove for historical plausibility, the description of 'the natural aspect of historical events', blending history with invention in the manner of Scott. In his preface he neatly captures the essence of Walter Scott's approach to the representation of history in a novel:

> All [. . .] the goings-on have been described truthfully, I have allowed myself to invent only in those places where history is silent or has left us nothing but doubts. [. . .] I have used invention merely to tie the authentic historical events together and to reveal secrets that the witnesses had no access to.[28]

In spite of this declaration, Bulgarin moved even further away from the Scottian model than Zagoskin. His malicious protagonist is more reminiscent of

---

[26] Frederic Chamier (1834) *The Young Muscovite: Or the Poles in Russia; in two volumes*, New York: [n. pub.]; cf. Altshuller 1996, 83–85.

[27] cf. Alekseev 1982, 389–90.

[28] Жсе . . . происшествия изображены мною верно, и я позволял себе вводить вымысел там только, где история молчит или представляет одни сомнения . . . Вымыслами я только связал истинные исторические события и и раскрыл тайны, недоступные источникам. Faddei Bulgarin (1830) *Dmitrii Samozvanets*, St Petersburg: [n. pub.], no. 1, pp. vii–viii (separate pagination).

the sinister villain in a Romantic poem by Byron than of Scott's tolerant, calm, and conscientious heroes. He is an agent of evil, a murderer, an egoist with uncontrollable passions, whose language teems with pompous Romantic clichés.

The same defects characterize Bulgarin's second (and last) historical novel *Mazepa* (1833–34). Here we find an abundance of horrors and fatal desires (torture, incest, parricide, the starvation of the hero's love behind iron doors, etc.), more typical of the Gothic novel. At the same time it must be admitted that both of Bulgarin's novels are distinguished by their balanced and objective depiction of the warring sides (Poles, Russians, and Ukrainians), an understanding of historical perspectives and the contradictions of historical development. In this respect, he is closer to Walter Scott than many of his contemporaries, although the following epigram, attributed to Pushkin by mistake, mocks Bulgarin and emphasizes by means of an untranslatable game of words the vast difference between him and his model:

> Everyone says: he's a Walter Scott
> But I am a poet, not a hypocrite.
> He is simply a swine, agreed.
> But a Walter Scott he is not.[29]

One of the most talented Russian novelists of the first half of the nineteenth century was I. Lazhechnikov, the author of three remarkable historical novels, *The Last Page* (1831–1833), *The Ice Palace* (1835), and *The Infidel* (1836). Lazhechnikov was a great admirer of Scott, he knew his novels well and said of their heroes: 'they stand vividly before you: they are like relatives or friends whose traits you will never forget'.[30]

All three novels by Lazhechnikov show the influence of Scott to a greater or lesser extent. The best of these, *The Ice Palace*, must be counted among the best Russian novels there are. It is based on authentic facts, but on facts that are only possible in Russia, with her fierce and prolonged frosts.

The Ice Palace is in many ways similar to *K* (1820) which, incidentally, also lacks the happy ending otherwise typical of Scott. *K* and *The Ice Palace* both depict two conflicting parties at the court. In Lazhechnikov these are the Russians and the Germans. However, in contrast to most other Russian novels, in *The Ice Palace* not all Germans are portrayed as equally evil and not all Russians are necessarily good. The work displays a certain streak of Scottian tolerance in the depiction of two warring sides. The heroes, both energetic

---

[29]   Vse govoryat: on Val'ter Skott, / No ya, poet, ne litsemeryu. / Soglasen ya: on prosto skot, / No, chto on Val'ter Skott, – ne veryu. The Russian word 'skot' means 'cattle' or in a pejoratively figurative sense 'swine' [trans. note]. Quoted in V. E. Vasil'ev, M. I. Gillel'son, N. G. Zakharenko (eds) (1975) *Russkaya epigramma vtoroi poloviny XVII-nachala XX v.* (Russian epigrams from the second half of the seventeenth to the beginning of the twentieth century), Leningrad: Sovetskii pisatel, p. 437.

[30]   'резко выступают перед вами: это ваши родные, ваши друзья, которых черты вы никогда не забудете.' Letter to A. F. Koni (1912) *Russkaya starina* (9), p. 142.

young favourites (Artemii Volynsky and Count Leicester), also resemble each other. The women in love with the protagonists both perish: Lelemiko as well as Leicester's beautiful young wife Amy, whom he has married secretly. And most importantly, in both cases a feast described in great detail is central to the plot of both novels, one held at Castle Kenilworth and the other inside the ice palace. In the course of these celebrations the intricate plots are unravelled, driving the action on to a tragic outcome. From the same work by Scott, Lazhechnikov borrowed the character of a youth for his first novel, *The Last Page*. In Scott this character is called 'Flibbertigibbet'; Lazhechnikov gives him the genuinely Russian name 'Martin'.

Pushkin and Scott

A major part in the development of Russian 'Scotticism' was doubtless played by Pushkin, who thoroughly understood the essential characteristics of Scott's manner and the originality of the Scottish genius's contribution to world literature. Several scattered comments by Pushkin show how clearly he perceived the merits of Scott's novels. Let us remember how enthusiastic the aged Goethe was about the vivid representation of so many characters from different social classes that densely populated these novels. Almost at the same time (1830), Pushkin in an unpublished and unrevised note (written half in Russian and half in French) praises the broadness of Scott's approach to reality, his truthfulness, the historical authenticity of his novels, his true-to-life portraits of characters, be they kings or common men:

> The chief beauty of Walter Scott's novels lies in the fact that we are shown times long gone . . . in a contemporary, down-to-earth perspective . . . The charm of a historical novel is that history appears quite similar to what we see around us. Shakespeare, Goethe, and Walter Scott are not slavish admirers of kings and heroes. Their heroes do not (like the French) resemble slaves mimicking merit and virtue. They just remain true to normal life; there is nothing contrived or theatrical in their language, not even in ceremonial situations, because such situations are familiar to them.[31]

The Russian poet fully understood and greatly appreciated Scott's trick of fusing history and imagination and he formulated this principle in typically

---

[31] Главная прелесть романов Вальтера Скотта состоит в том, что мы знакомимся с прошедшим временем . . . современно, домашним образом . . . очаровывает в историческом ромне – зто то, что историческое в них совершенно подобно тому, что мы видим. Шекспир, Гете, Вальтер Скотт не имеют холопского прстрастия к к королям и героям. Они не походят (как герои французские) на холопей, передразнивающих достоинство и благородство. Они держатся просто в обычных жизненных обстоятельствах, в их речах нет ничего искусственного, театрального, даже в торжественных обстоятельствах, ибо подобные обстоятельства им привычны. A. S. Pushkin (1962) *O literature* (On literature), Moscow, p. 247.

concise, aphoristic fashion: 'These days, by the word *novel* we understand a historical epoch developed into a fictitious narrative. Walter Scott attracted a whole mass of imitators. But how far removed they are from the Scottish wizard!' (1962, 180)[32] It is natural that Pushkin wanted to write a Russian historical novel that would not only not be inferior to 'the great works . . . of the Scottish wizard' but would even surpass them. He set himself this task quite consciously: 'With the help of God I will write a historical novel that will delight even the foreigners', he is cited by Annensky, the author of a very trustworthy biography of Pushkin. He was even franker with his close friend Nashchokin: 'Wait and see, once I've got my act together I will take that Walter Scott to task!'[33]

The first attempt, however, ended unsuccessfully. Pushkin began writing a novel about his ancestor, a negro bought by Peter I, who had personally christened him and given him the name Hannibal. Hannibal was a highly remarkable figure with a romantic biography: a military engineer, he received his education in France, and in Russia became a general. Pushkin's novel in the poetic manner of Walter Scott did not turn out well, however, and having begun work on it in 1826 and written a few chapters, he gave the project up for good in 1828.

A real masterpiece à la Walter Scott was, however, published by Pushkin shortly before his death, in 1836, namely his novel *The Captain's Daughter*. It bore all the traits of Scott's poetics. The action is set in 1773–75, the time of the peasant uprising under Pugachev, that is, about sixty years before the time of writing (cf. the title of Scott's first novel: *Waverley, or 'Tis Sixty Years since*). The protagonist of the novel is a typical Walter Scott character. He is very young and sets off to a strange place (like Osbaldistone in *RR* – a novel with which *The Captain's Daughter* has a particularly large number of parallels[34]). On the way, he meets a stranger, who turns out to be Pugachev (cf. the robber Rob Roy in Scott); he falls in love, fights a duel with his rival, an ugly but clever young officer called Shvabrin, who manages to drive a wedge between him and his father, and blackens his name with the authorities by accusing him of treason, etc. Very similar things happen in *RR*. The hero, as is so often the case in Scott, finds himself between two enemy camps: the insurgent peasants with Pugachev at their head and the government troops. The historic figures of Pugachev and Catherine II have been placed on the periphery of the novel in the manner of Scott. Pugachev helps the protagonist, Catherine helps his beloved Masha. It has

---

[32] 'В наше время под словом роман разумеем историческую эпоху, развитую в вымышленном повествовании. Вальтер Скотт увлек за собой целую толпу подражателей. Но как они все далеки от шотландского чародея!'

[33] 'бог даст, мы напишем исторический роман, на который и чужие полюбуются [. . .] Погоди, дай мне собраться, я за пояс заткну Вальтер Скотта.' P. V. Annenkov (1873) *Pushkin: Materialy dlya ego biografii i otsenki ego proizvedenii* (Pushkin: materials for his biography and criticism of his works), St Petersburg: [n. pub.], p. 191; and P. I. Bartenev (1992) *O Pushkine* (On Pushkin), Moscow, p. 351.

[34] Cf. Altshuller 1996 and Dolinin 1988.

often been noted that the scene in which Masha declares herself to the Tsarina is strangely reminiscent of the final scene in *HM*, where Jeanie meets Queen Caroline. Pushkin indeed shows the empress in a thoroughly 'down-to-earth aspect': taking a morning stroll in the park, clad in a simple dress. *RR* is a particularly good example of the essential characteristic of Scott's novels, which Pushkin describes as representing 'a historical epoch' by means of 'a fictitious narrative'. Scott had prefaced his novel with a long biography of Rob Roy and quoted several historical documents. Pushkin wrote his historical treatise *The History of Pugachev* at the same time as his novel, thus supplementing it with a whole volume of historical documents. There is some reason to believe that *The History of Pugachev* was originally meant as a preface to *The Captain's Daughter*.[35]

The *Captain's Daughter* is many times shorter than Scott's excessively long novels. In this, Pushkin achieved a total triumph. He wrote a brilliant and perfect example of a Russian historical novel (in the mode of Sir Walter Scott), quite successfully 'taking Scott to task'. It was, however, a truly Pyrrhic victory. The contemporaries and the generation that immediately followed saw in *The Captain's Daughter* something long familiar, and they had already tired of certain forms and clichés. They did not realize the depth of Pushkin's historical argument, his marvellous precision, the conciseness and brilliance of his prose, and received *The Captain's Daughter* rather coldly. The true merits of the novel were appreciated only by later generations of readers, critics and scholars.

The well-known and most influential Russian critic V. G. Belinsky, for instance, when subjecting Pushkin's works to a detailed analysis in 1846 (his 'Articles on Pushkin' make up 700 large-format pages altogether), limited himself to just one colourless paragraph on *The Captain's Daughter* – a comparison of Savelich's servant with Caleb from *The Bride of Lammermoor* (1819) (7:577)[36] – even though we will soon see that Belinsky thought rather highly of Walter Scott himself.

Walter Scott from the 1840s to the 1860s

On the threshold of the 1840s, educated Russian society and the reading public cooled off somewhat towards their former Romantic idols Byron and Walter Scott. The influence of German culture superseded that of British. The most famous and radical critic of the first generation after Pushkin, V. G. Belinsky (1811–48), represents something of an exception, however. True, his activity was still closely related to the 1830s: Belinsky had known Walter Scott's novels from his early youth, when that writer was still alive and at the height of his fame. He often mentions him in his early articles and reviews. In unison with Russian as

---

35   Cf. N. N. Petrunina and G. M. Fridlender (1974) *Nad stranitsami Pushkina* (On Pushkin's pages), Leningrad: Nauka, pp. 91–92; N. N. Petrunina (1992) *Proza Pushkina* (Pushkin's prose), Moscow: [n.pub.], p. 351.
36   Belinsky, V. G. (1953–57) *Polnoe sobranie sochinenii* (Complete works), vols 1–8, Moscow: [n. pub.].

well as European literary criticism of the 1830s, he maintained that it had been Walter Scott who 'created, invented, revealed –, or rather: divined – the epos of our time – the historical novel' (1: 133).[37]

In his essay 'Menzel as a Critic of Goethe' (1840), for example, Belinsky places Scott on a par with Byron and Goethe, singling out these three authors as the founders of truly 'modern' (*noveishego*) art. Shortly afterwards, Belinsky formulated his idea of how a novel should be organized in order for the creative intention of the artist 'as a private phenomenon to embody a basic law of global life'.[38] Belinsky illustrated this by the novels of Walter Scott, which contained 'a host of persons, characters, and events' together with a sense of *wholeness* of the novel, its colour, its individual quality, its *something* that words cannot express [. . .] The characters and events of all these novels may already be gone from your memories, but titles like *The Bride of Lammermoor, Ivanhoe, Old Mortality,* etc. will never cease to bring the most varied ideas to mind' (4: 203–4).[39]

It was this 'individual quality' of Scott's novels, their subordination to a single more general idea and *Weltanschauung* that for Belinsky represented the highest ideal of art.

Walter Scott was always included alongside Homer, Shakespeare, Byron, and Cervantes in the list of great names that Belinsky so frequently recited. Nor did he change his attitude to Scott in the last years of his life, when he began his fight against Romanticism in the name of a newly established literary trend, the so-called 'Natural School'. Belinsky declared 'the representation of truth' the most important purpose of literature and preferred the French 'social novel' (George Sand, Balzac, Hugo, Sue) to those of the 'dreamers' from Germany (Hoffmann) and Ireland (Maturin). However, he insisted that the best contemporary authors of social novels were in many ways 'indebted to the geniuses of Walter Scott and Cooper', because 'their novels described not imagined but real life' (10: 106, 140)[40] – and this in spite of the fact that Belinsky was at that time strongly influenced by democratic ideas and considered Walter Scott 'a Tory, a conservative, and an aristocrat by conviction and breeding' (10: 305).

When in 1845 a multi-volume edition of Walter Scott's novels, translated for the first time from the English original, began to be published in Russia (twenty-four volumes were announced) Belinsky, greeting the edition after the publication of the third volume (*The Antiquary*), wrote:

---

[37] 'создал, изобрел, открыл или, лучше сказать, угадал эпопею нашего времени – исторический роман.'

[38] 'в частном явлении могла воплотить основной закон мировой жизни'.

[39] 'множество лиц, характеров и событий. [. . .] зелое романа – его колорит, его индивидуальная особенность, его нечто, для выражения которого нет слова ... Уже и лица всех романов и содержания их Йзгладились из вашей памяти, но со словами: "Ламермурская невеста", "Ивангое", "Шотландские пуритане" и пр. никогда не перестанут для вас соединяться совершенно различные понятия.'

[40] '[лучшие авторы современных социальных романов многим] обязаны гению Вальтер Скотта и Купера [. . .]. В их романах изображена жизнь действительная, а не воображаемая.'

Walter Scott is not one of those writers that you read once and then forget forever [. . .] He remains a true friend all your life, one whose charming company will always provide consolation and pleasure. He is a poet for both sexes and every age [. . .] from early youth to ripe old age. Reading his novels takes one straight into a world of wonderful but realistic phenomena, it fills the soul with a soothing feeling of bravery and modesty at the same time. Captivating the imagination, Walter Scott's art educates one's heart and develops one's reason because it is neither eccentric nor theatrical, neither dreamy nor sickly: it is always here, on earth, in reality. It is a mirror of historical as well as private life. (9: 284)[41]

Meanwhile, Pushkin's younger contemporary M. Lermontov had mocked the readers of Scott's voluminous novels and their 'capacity for suffering' (*terpenie*) even in his youth (1833–34). Not long before Lermontov's death (1840), Belinsky visited him at a police station where the poet was being detained for his involvement in a duel. In the course of their long conversation, Lermontov denied that Scott's novels had any depth or artistic wholeness compared with Cooper's: 'there is little poetry in him. He is dry'.[42] It is true that one chapter of his own classic novel *A Hero of Our Time* – 'Princess Mary' – was written under the direct influence of Scott. Here Lermontov did not draw on the historical novels, however, but rather on the only work by Scott treating a contemporary subject, the 'health resort novel' *St Ronan's Well*.[43] In Lermontov we find the same sort of 'spa society', a similar rivalry in love, a fatal duel, and the like. It is no coincidence that in this same chapter 'Princess Mary' the 'magical fiction' of the Scottish bard is mentioned in a positive context.

Another of Pushkin's younger contemporaries, N. V. Gogol, seems to have been even less influenced by Scott, although he was a fervent admirer of Scott and himself wrote historical (or pseudo-historical) stories. Gogol argued with Senkovsky with zest and vehemence when the latter made his disparaging comments about Scott in the above-mentioned essay opposing the historical

---

41   Вальтер Скотт не принадлежит к числу тех писателей, которые прочитываются раз и потом навсегда забываются . . . Это неизменный друг всей ващей жизни, обаятельная беседа которого всегда утешит и усладит вас. Это поэт всех полов и всех возрастов, от отрочества . . . до глубокой старости. Он для всех равно увлекателен и назидателен. Чтение его романов, унося человека в мир роскошных, хотя и действительных явлений, проливает в его душу какое-то бодрое и вместе с тем кроткое, успокоительное чувство. Очаровывая фантазию, образовывает сердце и развивает ум, потому что поэзия Вальтера Скотта не эксцентрическая, не драматическая, не мечтательная и не болезненная: она всегда здесь, на земле, в действительности. Она – зеркало жизни исторической и частной.

42   'в нем мало поэзии. Он сух.'

43   Cf. D. P. Yakubovich (1935) 'Lermontov i Val'ter Skott' (Lermontov and Walter Scott), *Izvestiya AN SSSR: Otdelenie obshchestvennykh nauk*, 3: 243–72; Mark Altshuller (1992) '*Knyazhna Meri* Lermontova i *Sen-Ronanskie vody*' (Lermontov's *Princess Mary* and *St Ronan's Well*), in Etkind, Efim (ed.) *Norwich Symposia on Russian Literature and Culture: Michail Lermontov, 1814–1989*, Northfield, VT: Russkaia shkola Norvichskogo universiteta, pp. 14–154.

novel. For Gogol, Scott was 'a genius, in whose immortal works life was contained in all its fullness'.[44] Pushkin said of *Taras Bulba*, Gogol's famous historical narrative, that its beginning was 'worthy of Walter Scott'. The famous scholar G. A. Gukovsky has rightly labelled it pseudo-historical: 'The action of the story takes place in ancient times. When exactly remains unknown. There is not a single authentic historical fact in it'.[45] Nor is there a single authentic historical figure. And, what is most important, Gogol's story has nothing in common with Scott ideologically. The Russian writer differs from the English in his total lack of tolerance and his inability to detach himself from the conflict described, to find a possible truth on both sides.

In the story there are two camps: the Cossacks – and everyone else (basically Poles and a few Jews). The former are noble, the latter, especially the Jews, are repulsive. Several additional motifs (reminiscent of *OM* and *I*) serve only to emphasize this difference. Between the warring sides there can be no reconciliation whatsoever. When Taras's son Andrii changes sides out of love for a beautiful Polish girl, Taras kills his son with his own hands. A contemporary commentator has neatly observed that had Walter Scott written this story, the young Cossack would have been allowed to marry his love and Taras Bulba would have feasted merrily at their wedding.[46]

In spite of all these differences, both Lermontov and Gogol made abundant use of one of Walter Scott's favourite devices, namely narration on many levels, with one of the characters telling the story, a second writing it down and the author himself appearing only on a third level (cf. for example Scott's *Tales of my Landlord*). In Lermontov, it is the elderly officer Maxim Maximych who recounts the story of Pechorin while the narrator writes them down and the author publishes them. In Gogol's *Evenings on a Farm near Dikanka*, the various stories are told by unsophisticated, simple and uneducated country folk, while the bee-keeper Rudy Panko writes them down, and the author, who like Walter Scott remains anonymous at first, finally publishes them.

Scott himself commented not without humour on the novelists' device for explaining the appearance of mysterious texts, the manuscripts that someone has apparently thrown into the sea, that someone has used for wrapping their shopping in, or that a dead lodger leaves behind:

> I venture to enrol you in the happy combination of fortuitous circumstances, which usually put you in positions of the works which you have the goodness to bring into public notice. One walks on the seashore, and a wave casts on land a small cylindrical

---

[44] 'великий гений, коего бессмертные создания объемлют жизнь с такою полнотою.' N. V. Gogol (1952) *Polnoe sobranie sochinenii* (Complete works), Moscow: Izdatel'stvo Akademii nauk SSSR (1937–1952), 8: 160.

[45] 'Действие повести протекает в старину, когда именно – неизвестно. Ни одного определенного исторического факта в ней нет.' G. A. Gukovskii (1959) *Realizm Gogolya* (Gogol's Realism), Moscow; Leningrad: Gosudarstvennoe izdatel'stvo khudozhestvennoi literatury, pp. 126, 128.

[46] Anna Elistratova (1984) *Nikolai Gogol and the Western European Novel*, Christopher English (trans.), Moscow: Raduga, pp. 48–49.

trunk or casket, containing a manuscript which is with difficulty deciphered [. . .] Another steps into a chandler's shop, to purchase a pound of butter, and behold! the waste paper on which it is laid is the manuscript of a cabalist. A third is so fortunate as to obtain from a woman who lets lodging the curious contents of an antique bureau, the property of a deceased lodger.[47]

The Russian authors followed Scott's recipe closely. In Lermontov, the officer eagerly gathers up the notes that Maxim Maximych has thrown away. In Gogol, Rudy Panko's wife uses the manuscript of the story about Shponka for pastry-baking, which is why it is printed without an ending.

The borrowing of such artificial motifs does not, however, indicate a substantial influence of Scott's works, nor any special esteem for his methods. The time for Scott was fast running out. This is illustrated by the fate of one of the best Russian historical novels to be deliberately modelled on Scott's work, *Prince Serebryannyi* by A. K. Tolstoy.

The action is set in the time of the *Oprichnina*, of the great terror initiated by Tsar Ivan the Terrible, one of the most ill-fated rulers of Russia. The novel is full, possibly to overflowing, of typical Walter Scott motifs, characters, and situations. Its young hero, the noble, good and somewhat insipid Prince Serebryannyi, is reminiscent of Walter Scott's protagonists. He is torn between the ideal of unconditional allegiance to the Tsar and his complete moral incapability of taking part in the bloody bacchanalia. He is put in prison and freed by a band of robbers, whose leader's life he has once saved (cf. *I, Yuri Miloslavsky, The Captain's Daughter*). There is also a case of 'divine judgement' (cf. *Ivanhoe*), a faithful servant (cf. *BL, The Captain's Daughter*) and much, much more.

The novel took a long time, twelve years, to be written and was published in 1862. It was received as an anachronism and widely ridiculed. The famous satirist M. E. Saltykov-Shchedrin greeted it with a mock review: 'My dearest Count! [. . .] You have brought back my youth to me, reminded me of the publication of *Yuri Miloslavsky* and *Roslavlev*, of the first humble attempts of Lozhechnikov. Those were happy days, my dearest Count.'[48] The review was written in the name of a retired teacher of literature, a poor old devil who was 'overcome by paralysis' before he could finish his assigned work.[49] In spite of possessing a fair number of merits (the quick unfolding of the narrative, the relative conciseness of the narration, the beautiful language, the interesting plot), Tolstoy's intelligent attempt to return to the poetics of Walter Scott's novels and to restore the genre of the historical novel to its former glory was doomed to failure in the 1860s.

---

[47]   Walter Scott (1902) introd. to *The Monastery*, New York: [n. pub.], pp. XLVI–XLVII.

[48]   'Любезный граф! . . вы воскресили для меня мою юность, напомнили мне появление "Юрия Милославского", "Рославлева", напомнили первые попытки робкого еще тогда Ложечникова. Это было счастливое время, любезный граф.' The name of the talented author of *The Ice Palace* has been deliberately distorted, it would seem, and with satiric intention (trans. note: 'Lozhechnikov' suggests 'lozh', that is, 'lie').

[49]   M. E. Saltykov-Shchedrin (1966) *Sobranie sochinenii* (Collected works), Moscow: [n. pub.], pp. 353, 362.

We have quoted above the beginning of Turgenev's enthusiastic remark on the structure of Scott's novels: 'a spacious, solid building, with an unshakeable foundation, firmly grounded on the national soil.' It continues thus: 'Its sprawling prefaces are like a colonnade, with adjoining salons and shady corridors, making communication so much more convenient. In our days, such a novel would be almost impossible. Its time is over, it is no longer up-to-date' (5: 372).[50] In the 1850s, when these lines were written (1852), Russian society underwent substantial changes. Its consciousness began to be dominated by a Positivism that fostered utilitarian conceptions of art and literature. Although Turgenev by no means shared these ideas, he clearly perceived the changes in taste of the Russian reading public.

The ideological leader of the radical Russian *raznochintsy* intelligentsia, N. G. Chernyshevsky, did not accord literary fiction a particularly important role in society: 'The function of literature is to evaluate (and explain) the phenomena of real life, thereby making them accessible to human understanding and catalysing action [. . .].'[51] At best, literature could function as 'a text-book of life', that is, to help to understand and solve this or that contemporary social problem. This is the main thesis of Chernyshevsky's most important work *Esteticheskie otnosheniya isskustva k dejstvitel'nosti* (The aesthetic relations of art to reality). Chernyshevsky's attitude to fiction was generally condescending; he saw it as a secondary product of spiritual activity. Seen from this perspective, the historical novel – a fictitious narrative which distracted the reader from the real, contemporary problems – seemed like a particularly useless plaything.

The genre itself was rejected by the radical intelligentsia. The most popular critic of the 1860s, D. I. Pisarev, remarked: 'Historical novels [. . .] in the majority of cases represent one of the most useless and unattractive forms of literature.'[52] And indeed, as in the 1840s, we see fewer and fewer novels à la Walter Scott published in Russia. The older generation, it seems, had long since read them all, while the younger generation had other interests. At the end of the 1830s, Scott was no longer being re-edited. In the years 1835 and 1838, only two novels by Scott were published, *QD* and *FN* respectively. The readers had stopped buying the books that not long ago had been so popular, and the editions from the 1820s took decades to sell out (Dolinin 1988, 166).

---

[50] 'пространное, солидное зданиее, со своим незыблемым фундаментом, врытым в почву народную, с своими обширными вступлениями в виде портиков, со своими парадными комнатами и темными коридорами для удобства сообщения [. . .] этот роман в наше время почти невозможен: он отжил свой век, он несовременен . . .'

[51] Irina Paperno (1988) *Chernyshevsky and the Age of Realism: A Study in the Semiotics of Behaviour*, Stanford, CA: Stanford University Press, p. 164.

[52] 'исторические романы . . . составляют в большей части случаев один из самых бесплодных и непривлекательных родов литературы.' Pisarev, M. I. (1955–56) 'Frantsuzkii krest'yanin v 1789 godu' (The French Peasant in the Year 1789), in *Sochineniya v chetyrekh tomakh*, Moscow: Gosudarstvennoe izdatel'stvo khudozhestvennoi literatury, 4: 400.

In 1845–46, an attempt to publish a complete critical collection of Scott's works ended in a spectacular disaster. Instead of the usual jumbled, hastily made 'translations' from the French, the edition was to consist of competent translations from the originals, retaining all of Scott's extensive prefaces and annotations. The project was directed by the energetic journalist and publisher A. A. Kraevsky, and prominent members of the contemporary intelligentsia participated, among them B. Botkin, E. Korsh, and N. Ketcher, the well-known translator of Shakespeare. Only four of the thirty-one volumes planned materialized, however, and these came out in rather arbitrary order: volume two (*GM*), volume three (*A*), volume six (*I*), and volume fifteen (*QD*). And here the edition ended. It is worth remarking that 120 years later a similar project on a somewhat humbler scale was completed most successfully. We will come back to this later.

Scott's novels underwent a transformation not uncommon for masterpieces of world literature. Well received by the readers and permanently assigned to the canon of world culture, they are transferred from the grown-ups' bookshelves to the children's library. Between 1866 and 1881, twenty-five volumes of Scott's works were published that had indeed been especially 'revised for the young'. This edition included all the novels of the English writer, and between 1874 and 1877 a parallel ten-volume edition came out.[53] Editions for children continued to be published even when interest in the historical novel had later been rekindled. From 1891 to 1895, the well-known publisher F. Pavlenkov brought out a twenty-four volume edition of 'collected works in abridged [somewhat excessively abridged!] translations by L. Shelgunova', a translator, writer, and member of the Russian radical movement. The abridgements were indeed drastic: the text was cut down to a fifth, sixth, or seventh of its original size. All these 'translations' were about a hundred pages in length, while the average length of Scott's novels was somewhere between five and seven hundred pages. In this form they became accessible to even the youngest children.[54]

The tradition of revising and abridging for children and young people was continued by I. Sytin, another eminent publisher. One of his most popular and best known projects was a journal of adventure and travel stories for young readers: *Vokrug sveta* (Around the world). The journal was published with literary supplements containing the work of the writers that the young readers loved: Mayne Reid, Jules Vernes, Dumas, Conan Doyle, and others.[55] Walter Scott also fell into this category. In 1904–05, a twelve-volume collection of his

---

[53] I. M. Levidova (1958) *Val'ter Skott: bio-bibliograficheskii ukazatel* (Walter Scott: a bio-bibliographical guide), Moscow: Vsesoyuznaya knizhnaya palata, p. 39.

[54] Cf. Levidova, 40; cf. the (somewhat superficial) commentary by E. Vilenskaya and L. Roitberg in N. P. Shelgunov, *Vospominaniya* (Memoirs), (1967), E. Vilenskaya L. Roitberg, and M. L. Mikhailov (eds), Moscow: Khudozhestvennaia literatura, vol. 2: 520.

[55] Cf. S. V. Belov and A. P. Tolstyakov (1976) *Russkie izdateli XIX–nachala XX veka* (Russian publishers of the nineteenth and early twentieth centuries). Leningrad: Nauka, pp. 79–81.

works was published as a supplement. It contained novels in radically abridged and revised form (on the title page of some books there is the remark 'From the novel by Walter Scott, rewritten by E. K.').[56] It should be noted that this edition included some of Walter Scott's less well-known novels, which were not to be republished for a very long time: *Karl Smelyi* ('Charles the Bold': in Russia the novel *Anne of Geierstein, or the Maiden of the Mist* came out under this title), *The Betrothed, Castle Dangerous.*

Scott and Tolstoy

The most important Russian historical novel of all time also made its appearance in the 1860s: L. N. Tolstoy's *War and Peace*. Tolstoy's historico-philosophical argument, the moral problems he grapples with, and the representation of the human character in *War and Peace* are much more profound than in the novels of Scott, whom Tolstoy, in the words of his son, 'did not like'.[57] When revising and shortening his list of authors whose novels should be published in Russian, Tolstoy after some deliberation decided to eliminate Scott (leaving George Sand, George Eliot, Bulwer-Lytton, and a few others[58]). He contrasted Victor Hugo, 'who will remain with all of us forever', with the likes of Byron or Walter Scott, who were destined to be forgotten (61: 139).[59]

The latter remark was written in May 1866, when Tolstoy was finishing work on *War and Peace*. He certainly knew Scott's novels. Composing his historical novel, Tolstoy therefore could not help consciously or unconsciously (it is no coincidence that it was Scott who came to his mind while he was completing his epos) drawing on Scott's achievements (mediated, perhaps, by *The Captain's Daughter*): Scott's conception of the historical process, his devices in the representation of characters and events – all this visibly influenced Tolstoy's grandiose artistic creation.

War and Peace describes events that took place some fifty to sixty years before the time of writing. About the same period of time separates the action described in Scott's novels from their author's present day. Note that Scott called his very first novel *Waverley, or 'Tis Sixty Years Since*. The same temporal distance is kept in the best Russian imitation of Scott, Pushkin's *The Captain's Daughter*. The Pugachev rebellion took place in 1773–75; *The Captain's Daughter* was printed in 1836. Tolstoy adhered to the same principle in constructing the historical setting. According to his son:

---

[56]   'По роману В.Скотта переделала Е.К.' Levidova, 41.

[57]   'не любил': S. L. Tolstoy (1955) *Ocherki bylogo* (Sketches of the Past), in *L. N. Tolstoi v vospominaniyakh sovremennikovm*, N. N. Gusev, V. S. Mishin and K. N. Lomunov (eds.) Seriya literaturnykh memuarov, Moscow: Gosudarstvennoe izdatel'stvovo khudozhestvennoi literatury, 1.1: 171.

[58]   L. N. Tolstoy (1928–1959) *Polnoe sobranie sochinenii* (Complete collected works), 90 vols, Moscow; Leningrad: [n. pub.], 64: 30.

[59]   'всегда и у всех останется'

he talked [in 1878] about his plans to write a novel about the Decembrists, saying that he would write about them now that roughly fifty years had passed since 1825, just as he had written *War and Peace* fifty years after 1812. This period he considered sufficiently long to allow treatment of an epoch in terms of history, but not too far removed in time for the memories to have lost their freshness. (1: 179)[60]

Scott said approximately the same thing about his Scottish novels. In his preface to *Ivanhoe (Dedicatory Epistle to the Rev. Dr. Dryasdust E.A.S.)*, he wrote:

Many now alive [. . .] well remembered persons who had not only seen the celebrated Roy M'Gregor, but had feasted, and even fought, with him. All those minute circumstances belonging to his private life and domestic character, all that gives verisimilitude to narrative and individuality to the persons introduced, is still known and remembered in Scotland.[61]

The importance of the 'Scottian' sixty-year interval for Tolstoy's historical epos has been firmly established in a recent essay by Gareth Jones (2004).[62]

Tolstoy used to say that he liked the idea of the family in *Anna Karenina* and the idea of the people in *War and Peace*. This important remark shows that the depiction of the people (Tolstoy is obviously referring to ordinary people, not to the higher classes of society) as an integrated mass (even though it consisted of separate individuals) was a deliberate element of the author's plans. The depiction of the people plays an important role in Tolstoy's novel, a much more important one than in Scott's. For Tolstoy, the victory over Napoleon was the result of an elemental national uprising that involved the entire population of Russia. However, while the educated people and their spiritual endeavours are portrayed with a profundity and insight into their inner worlds that remain unequalled by any other writer, the ordinary folk form a homogeneous mass, the general ideas of which are represented by the famous character Platon Karataev. In his descriptions of such ordinary people, Tolstoy is clearly inferior to Scott, about whom Goethe, as we have already seen, justly said: 'The king, the brother of the king, the crown prince, the high dignitary of the Church, the nobility, the magistrate, the burghers and the workers, the highlanders – all

---

[60]   он говорил про свое намерение писать роман о декабристах <1878>, что так же, как он писал "Войну и мир" спустя пятьдест лет после двенадцатого года, так теперь он будет писать о декабристах спустя приблизительно пятьдесят лет после 1825 года. Этот срок он считал достаточным для того, чтобы относиться к тому времени, как к истории, и не слишком отдаленным строком, чтобы утратилась свежесть воспоминаний о нем.

[61]   (1902) *The Waverley Novels by Sir Walter Scott: Ivanhoe*, New York, pp. XX, 18, 21.

[62]   W. Gareth Jones (2004) ' "This Sixty Years Since": Sir Walter Scott's Eighteenth Century and Tolstoy's Engagement with History', in Bartlett, Roger and Lindsey Hughes (eds) *Russian Society and Culture and the Long Eighteenth Century: Essays in Honour of Anthony G. Cross*, Münster: Lit Verlag, pp. 185–94. See here for more detail on the (not very voluminous) literature on the literary relationship of Tolstoy and Scott.

are drawn by the same hand and *with the same precision* [my italics]' (Ekkerman, 261).[63]

On the other hand, Tolstoy's intellectual heroes are far more complicated than any of Scott's characters. The positive figures of the latter are just average, ordinary, good people, such as, for instance, the good-hearted and naive Waverley or Osbaldistone in *Rob Roy*. There is actually a hero similar to Scott's in *War and Peace*, namely Nikolai Rostov, a character who is not very bright and devoid of the spiritual depths so clearly marked in his wife Maria Bolkonskaya. The tense, agonizing spiritual quests of his brothers-in-law, Andrei Bolkonsky and Pierre Bezukhov, are quite foreign to him.[64] Indeed, the author appreciates such simple-heartedness, openness, orderliness, and goodness in a way similar to that in which Scott had appreciated these qualities in his positive heroes.[65] The youth Petya Rostov also reminds one of the naive, open, and well-meaning young Scottian protagonists.

Tolstoy faced a formidable artistic task. The main heroes of the epos (the Bolkonskys, the Rostovs, the Besukhovs) were fictitious characters. But in a historical novel that described the events of 1805–12, historical figures like Alexander I, Napoleon, Kutuzov et al. had to appear as well. In solving the problem of how to combine the depiction of fictitious and historical characters, Tolstoy, willy-nilly, had to draw on the experience of Walter Scott, who placed historical figures on the periphery of the main action: a considerable artistic achievement, lending the historical characters, whom the readers knew and remembered, special depth and plasticity.

In Tolstoy's epos, the historical personalities of Alexander I, Napoleon, and Kutuzov are similarly placed on the periphery. We see Tsar Alexander, dejected and alone after the battle of Austerlitz, through the eyes of Nikolai Rostov. The Supreme Commander's aide-de-camp Prince Andrei tells of Kutuzov's wisdom and considers his role in the war. Tolstoy, however, does not have his emperors and military commanders directly influence the protagonists' lives quite as often as Scott. Nor perhaps is there much point in identifying too closely Scott's novelistic imagination with Tolstoy's realistic epos. Still: Napoleon, whom the dying, half unconscious Prince Andrei unexpectedly happens to see celebrating his victory at Austerlitz, plays no smaller role in the inner life of Bolkonsky than do, for example, Richard and Saladin in the biography of the Scottish prince Kenneth (*T*).

---

[63] 'Король, брат короля, кронпринц, князь церкви, дворянство, магистрат, бюргеры и ремесленники, горцы – все они написаны одинаково уверенной рукой и одинакозо метко очерчены.'

[64] Gareth Jones has pointed out a certain similarity between Pierre Bezukhov and Waverley in his essay (191–92).

[65] Cf. the sophisticated treatment of Nikolai Rostov in S. Bocharov (1971) '*Voina i mir* L.N. Tolstogo' (L. N. Tolstoy's *War and Peace*), in S. Bocharov, V. Kozhinov, and D. Nikolaev (eds), *Tri shedevra russkoi klassiki*, Moscow: Khudozhestvennaia literatura, pp. 81–85.

Scott and Dostoevsky

Tolstoy wrote his historical epos because, whether he liked it or not, he eventually had to cross Scott's creative path at some point. A little different and more positive was the attitude of another great Russian writer to Scott: F. M. Dostoevsky. Again, however, there is little reason to speak of any truly substantial influence of the 'Scottish wizard' on his work.

When he was young, almost still a child, 'at the age of twelve during a vacation', Dostoevsky, in his own words, 'read the whole of Walter Scott' (30.1: 211).[66] This reading made such an impression on the boy that it coloured all the years of his youth. Later, fully forty years of age, he recalled (the narrator here is psychologically very close to the author, almost identical with him):

> Long ago, in my youthful fantasies, I loved to imagine myself as Pericles, as Marius, as a Christian in the time of Nero, as a knight in a tournament, as Edward Glendinning from Walter Scott's novel *The Monastery*, etc., etc. The things I would dream up in my youth [. . .]. In my life there have been no fuller, brighter, or more sacred moments. I dreamt away all my youth and after fate had suddenly made me a civil servant I would finish my duties at the office, rush back to my room, put on my ragged dressing-gown [. . .] and dream, get carried away, suffer, [. . .] and imagine [. . .].[67] (1861, 19: 70)

There follows the story of a young girl whom the author calls '[his] Amalia':

> I gave her books by Scott and Schiller [. . .]. We read the story of Clara Mowbray together and indulged in our feelings [. . .]. I would read or retell novels and in exchange for this she mended my old socks and starched my two shirts.[68]

Reminiscing about the time when he began to feel capable of composing truly human histories, to see himself as a writer and creator, Dostoevsky retrospectively linked his status with Walter Scott's world. Two novels in

---

[66]   '12-ти лет в деревне во время вакаций [Достоевский] прочел всего Вальтер-Скотта.' F. M. Dostoevsky (1972–90) *Polnoe sobranie sochinenii v tridtsati tomakh* (Complete collected works in thirty volumes), Leningrad: Nauka.

[67]   Прежде в юношеской фантазии моей я любил воображать себя иногда то Периклом, то Марием, то христианином из времен Нерона, то рыцарем на турнире, то Эдуардом Глянденингом из романа "Монастырь" Вальтер Скотта и проч., и проч. и чего я не перемечтал в моем юношестве . . . Не было минут в моей жизни полнее, святее и чище. Я до того замечтался, что проглядел всю мою молодость, и когда судьба вдруг толкнула меня в чиновники, я только что кончу, бывало, служебные часы, бегу к себе на чердак, надеваю свой дырявый халат . . . и мечтаю, упиваюсь и страдаю . . . и воображаю.

[68]   Я ей давал книги Вальтер Скотта и Шиллера. . . . Мы прочли с ней вместе историю Клары Мовбрай и расчувствовались . . . Она мне за то, что я читал и пересказывал ей романы, штопала старые чулки и крахмалила мои две манишки. Dostoevsky, F. M. (1861) *Peterburgskie snovideniya v stikhakh i proze* (St Petersburg dreams in verse and prose), [n.p.]: [n. pub.], 19: 70.

which the future writer found characters similar to himself and situations reminding him of his own life are mentioned in connection with his artistic coming-of-age.

The Monastery is not one of Scott's better novels. Even in its author's lifetime it was subjected to severe criticism. Dostoevsky remembered it, however, and singled it out among many others that he had read. Among the plethora of complicated and sometimes downright mystical motifs of the novel, what perhaps interested him more than anything else was the contrasting fates of two heroes, two brothers. One of these, Halbert, is a proud and brave knight, who after overcoming many challenges in a series of tournaments finally occupies a place of honour as one of the highest government officials of his time. His brother Edward, who is secretly in love with the girl Halbert marries, remains alone, without a position and awaiting in eternal grief his inevitable consecration as a monk. It is this character of Scott's that impressed Dostoevsky more than any other. He would correlate Edward's bitter sacrifice with his own fate in the days of his poor and hungry youth.

The second novel mentioned, *SRW*, is one of Scott's best and his only non-historical novel, particularly popular with Russian readers of the 1830s and 40s. Dostoevsky refers to it as 'the history of Clara Mowbray' ('истории Клары Мовбрай'), that is, the melancholy story of a girl who is tricked into marrying a man she does not love, the brother of her beloved. In this novel as well, the moral contrast of the respective fates of two brothers forms a central element of the plot. This, however, is a case of cold-blooded deceit versus magnanimous modesty. It is no coincidence that the author recalls how he read this novel of Scott's in the company of 'his Amalia', with whom, of course, he is secretly in love, just as she appears to be with him. But Amalia:

> a good [. . .] kind, modest girl of secret dreams and suppressed passions like mine [. . .] suddenly married one of the poorest creatures in the world, a man of forty-five with a boil on his nose [. . .], who offered Amalia his hand and eternal poverty.[69] (1861, 19:70)

For Dostoevsky, the fate of the St Petersburg Amalia, who loses her beloved and commits herself to a man she does not love, reflected in a complicated way the fate of Clara Mowbray. Remembering these times and his unhappy Amalia, he writes that it was just then that this melancholy story 'flared up before him' ('замерещилась') and 'tore his heart in two' ('глубоко разорвала сердце'). It is this very story, too, that in an originally modified form underlies Dostoevsky's first novel, *Poor Folk* (1845): Varenka corresponds to Amalia, while Makar is a 'poor creature . . . of about forty-five' ('беднейшее существо . . ., лет сорока пяти'). She does not, however, marry him but the strange and immoral Bykov,

---

[69] хорошенькая . . . добрая, кроткая, с затаенными мечтами и с сдавленными порывами, как и я . . . вышла вдруг замуж за одно беднейшее существо в мире, человека лет сорока пяти, с шишкой на носу . . . предложившего Амалии руку и непроходимую бедность.

whom she loves even less. It may well be that we owe the publication of *Poor Folk*, which so impressed his contemporaries, to the highly subtle, scarcely perceptible influence of Scott's novel. Scott may even be said to have sparked off this author's literary career. Dostoevsky himself has encouraged such speculations, at any rate.[70]

The spirit of Walter Scott is also obvious in Dostoevsky's early Romantic love stories: *Poor Folk*, *White Nights*, and *Netochka Nezvanova*. In *White Nights*, the dreamer-protagonist feels attracted to the strong-minded, purposeful heroine of *The Heart of Midlothian* (Effie Deans) and the courageous and resolute Diana Vernon from *Rob Roy*, while young Nastenka prefers the brave Rebecca and the affectionate Rowena from *Ivanhoe*. In his unfinished story *Netochka Nezvanova* (1848–49), his last before his Siberian exile, the sixteen-year-old heroine and her clever tutor read and discuss *Ivanhoe*. Their similar understanding of Scott's novel draws the two lonely, suffering women together.

But this is where Dostoevsky's enthusiasm for Scott seems to have more or less ended. Among the heroes of his *completed* works, there is not one who reads Walter Scott. But the protagonist of the unfinished novel *The Life of a Great Sinner* (Zhitie velikogo greshnika, 1870), a most contradictory character who despises his fellow men but is at the same time magnanimous, good, and proud, passionately yearning sometimes for moral perfection, sometimes for material wealth, 'reads an awful lot' ('ужасно много читал') according to Dostoevsky's draft, namely 'Walter Scott and others' ('Вальтер Скотт и проч') (1972–90, 9: 132). In the notes for his novel *A Raw Youth* from the 1870s, which are to a certain extent connected with those for the subsequently unwritten *Life*, the hero, reproaching himself for his unseemly behaviour, remembers that there exists 'another world, a literary, dreamy one' and characterizes this world thus: 'Walter Scott, fiery inspiration. A dream. Invention is a noble thing' (1972–90, 16: 180).[71] In the final text of *A Raw Youth* Scott, however, is not mentioned.

In his letters and his journalism, the mature Dostoevsky appears to have practically forgotten Scott, and where he is mentioned it is already a different Scott that Dostoevsky refers to. This latter Scott is an author intended primarily for young readers: 'Teach your children Walter Scott' ('Учите Вальтеру Скотту детей ваших') (1972–90, 24: 133). Dostoevsky remembered very well the inflammatory effect Scott once had on his youthful imagination, but in 1880, not long before his death, the ageing sixty-year-old writer considered that influence a positive one:

> I [. . .] read the whole of Walter Scott, and if I developed a powerful imagination and an impressionable mind, I nevertheless channelled these in the right direction [. . .]. I enriched my life with so many beautiful and lofty impressions from this reading [. . .]. I advise you to give Walter Scott to your daughter at this point [. . .] all the more so as he is now completely forgotten by us Russians [. . .] and she may never encounter

---

[70] For more detail on this, see the essay by Elena Dryzhakova (forthcoming) *Dostoevskii i Val'ter Skott* (Dostoevsky and Walter Scott).

[71] 'Вальтер Скотт, Зажечь. Мечта. Придумать благородное дело.'

another opportunity or necessity to acquaint herself with this great writer [. . .]. Walter Scott has great educational value.[72] (1972–90, 30.1: 211–12)

And, as if summing up his thoughts on the 'Scottish wizard', Dostoevsky concludes: Scott stands for 'a grand, sensible, loftier' form of 'reconciliation of the heart' ('великое, осмысленное, высшее сердечное примирение') (1972–90, 24: 133). Here it is no longer the dreamy, fantastic quality of his novels that is appreciated, but rather their serene wisdom and tolerance, their devotedness to family traditions and eternal human values.

Walter Scott and the historical novel at the end of the nineteenth century

The 1880s saw an unexpected flourishing of the Russian historical novel and an unusual popularity of that genre. In the words of a contemporary critic 'the most widely read writer at the end of the nineteenth century, according to sociological data, was Evg. Salias and after him came Vs. Solovev, D. Mordovtsev, and G. Danilevsky'.[73] These were all authors of historical novels.

The unexpected revival of interest in this literary genre can be explained, on the one hand, by the enormous success of the historical and pseudo-historical novels of Hugo and Dumas, who had done away with Scott's conscientious thoroughness, his leisurely and thoughtful narration, and replaced all this with rapidly unfolding plots that abounded in fatal passions and (especially in the case of Hugo) Gothic terrors. These French novelists found a host of imitators in Russia and the market was soon flooded with historical novels.

On the other hand, the success of the historical novel was stimulated by important cultural and ideological circumstances. Since the middle of the nineteenth century, Russian history had been subjected to a fruitful and meticulous investigation. The 1860s and 70s saw the publication of S. M. Solovev's fundamental twenty-nine-volume *History of Russia since Ancient Times* (Istoriya Rossii s drevneishikh vremen) and other works containing an enormous amount of factual material by authors like N. Zabelin, M. Semevsky, N. Kostomarov and many others. They were read widely and with great interest by educated readers of the most diverse political convictions.

---

[72] я . . . прочел всего Вальтер-Скотта, и пусть я развил в себе фантазию и впечатлительность, но зато я направил ее в хорошую сторону . . . захватил с собой в жизнь из этого чтения столько прекрасных и высоких впечатлений . . . Советую и вам дать вашей дочери теперь Вальтер-Скотта, тем более, что он забыт у нас, русских, совсем, и потом . . . она уже и не найдет ни возможности, ни потребности сама познакомиться с этим великим писателем . . . Вальтер-Скотт имеет высокое воспитательное значение.

[73] 'самым читаемым писателем в конце XIX века по социологическим данным был Евг. Салиас, а вслед за ним шли Вс.Соловьев, Д.Мордовцев и Г.Данилевский.' Yuri Belyaev (1988) *Svidaniya cherez veka*, Moscow: Sovremennik, p. 148.

From a Positivist point of view, an important merit of the historical novels lay in the fact that they made historical facts accessible to a large reading public from different social classes, who would read nothing apart from fiction. D. Mordovtsev, one of the most popular authors of the 1880s, was referring to this when he pointed out that when he had written historical treatises merely 'two or three thousand readers' had taken any notice, whereas now that he wrote novels he was read by 'many a thousand more'. And since, from a Positivist or utilitarian point of view, the merit of a work of art lay in its potential usefulness, and learning historical facts was definitely useful, Mordovtsev could proudly claim that through his novels he was of 'considerably greater use to many a thousand more readers'.[74] Moreover, arguing in a vein typical of the followers of Chernyshevsky and Pisarev, with their utilitarian attitude to art, Mordovtsev positively demanded that a historical novel be tendentious, thus deliberately and consistently distancing himself from the principles of Walter Scott. Censorship did not permit one to speak about the present, while the historical novel allowed for greater freedom of speech, and therefore 'it was unacceptable for a historical novel not to serve the needs of the present', which made it a means of propaganda. 'Such a principled [i.e. tendentious] attitude towards the past renders the historical novel a powerful educational factor in the life of society' (1881, 649, 651).[75] This thesis is in full accordance with Chernyshevsky's most famous idea: that art was supposed to function as a textbook of life. Attacking Mordovtsev and his call for tendentious representations of history in the name of a preconceived ideology (be it liberal or conservative), an opponent of his pointed to the novels of Walter Scott, which were written impartially, without the slightest tendentiousness, and to the works of Pushkin (more familiar to the Russian reader).[76] An echo of this renewed interest in the historical novel at the turn of the century was the publication of another large collection of Scott's works alongside the editions for children. Between 1896 and 1899 the editors of the popular and respected journal *Vestnik Inostrannoi Literatury* (Messenger of Foreign Literature) brought out eighteen volumes of Scott's works.

According to surveys among contemporary readers, the most popular writer of the 1880s was Count Evgeny Salias (1840–1908). He mainly wrote historical novels and was most prolific. The collection of his works published between 1894 and 1904 consists of thirty-three volumes (note that in 1991–93, a two-volume and a five-volume edition of his works came out in Moscow). An obituary to the writer openly called him a late literary descendant of Walter Scott.[77]

---

[74] 'пользу значительно большему – на многие тысячи большему числу читателей.' D. Mordovtsev (1881) 'K slovu ob istoricheskom romane i ego kritike (pis'mo k redaktsiyu)' (Concerning a Comment on the Historical Novel and its Criticism [Letter to the Editors]), *Istoricheskii vestnik*, 6.9: 643–44.

[75] 'такое принципиальное отношение к прошлому дает историческому роману силу воспитательного фактора в жизни общества.'

[76] F. Bulgakov (1881) 'V zashchitu istorii v istoricheskom romane (pis'mo v redaktsiyu)' (In Defence of History in the Historical Novel [Letter to the Editors]), *Istoricheskii vestnik*, 6.12: 835–37.

[77] [Anon.] (1909) obituary for Salias, *Istoricheskii vestnik*, 115.1: 425–26.

In fact there are only slight similarities to Scott to be found in Salias's novels, although like all other historical novelists he could not help being influenced to some extent by the English writer.

The voluminous historical novel *Pugachevtsy* (Pugachev's Men) is justly considered Salias's best work. Its idea, as the title indicates, was to describe a large popular movement. The title is reminiscent of one of Scott's best novels, OM. Salias's novel was influenced by Scott either directly or via Pushkin, who, as we have seen, wrote his masterpiece *The Captain's Daughter* under the direct influence of Scott. Salias feels that there is some truth on both sides of the conflict he describes. Such objectivity, which was also characteristic of Scott (and Pushkin), can be seen in the satirical portraits of generals and landowners as well as in the inner goodness that occasionally flares up in the wild and cruel Pugachev. It is also evident in the way that the reader, although neither he nor the author sympathizes with the rebellion that Pushkin called 'senseless and merciless' in *The Captain's Daughter*, is made to understand the reasons why the ordinary people so readily accepted a runaway Cossack as their Tsar and were so willing to join the ranks of his undisciplined troops. Like Walter Scott in 'The Puritans', Salias depicts a popular mass movement. It is no coincidence that his novel is called not 'Pugachev', but *Pugachev's Men*. The truly nightmarish excesses of the popular element begin when Pugachev has left the scene, and countless small bands, each led by its own 'Pugachev', drench Russia in blood.

The novels of Vsevolod Sergeevich Solovev achieved great popularity in the 1870s and 1880s. The son of an eminent historian, he was used from early childhood to dealing with historical materials. His novels, written in a light style and with interesting plots, do not lay any claim to deep analysis of historical facts, but are characterized by historical accuracy and a thorough knowledge of the material. While they may not have any exceptional artistic merit, they were easy reading, were widely read, and occupy a respectable position in Russian historical fiction.

By no means a man of leftist leanings, Solovev was opposed to violent changes of any kind and depicted the horrors of the French Revolution without the slightest sympathy for the frenzy of the masses or the demagogues who exploited this frenzy. In describing Paul I, he made no secret of the Tsar's neurotic pride, but as one of very few historians and writers he drew his noble, chivalrous character with marked compassion.

Solovev's best known work is his nearly ten-volume epos about the Gorbatovs, an old aristocratic family. It was probably written under the impact of such epics as the *Comédie humaine* by Balzac or Zola's *Les Rougon-Macquart*. The moderate and tolerant Solovev by no means exaggerated the achievements of the Russian aristocracy, even hinting at (possibly under the influence of Zola) certain symptoms of its degeneration. He describes satirically the high-society life of St Petersburg and points out certain merits of the emerging *raznochintsy* intelligentsia (not, of course, the revolutionary intelligentsia). At the same time he sympathizes deeply with the honourable and intelligent aristocratic Gorbatovs.

Especially similar to Walter Scott's work is the first novel of the series, *Sergei Gorbatov* (1881). Like so many of Scott's works, the novel is named after its main protagonist (cf. *W* or *GM*). Sergei Gorbatov is very young and leaves home in order to take up military service (like Waverley). In Petersburg he makes the acquaintance of various historical figures (Catherine II, her heir Paul, Bezborodko, and Platon Zubov, the Tsarina's last favourite and the antagonist of the hero). Thus, Walter Scott's method of placing historical characters on the periphery is adopted. Also very much in the manner of Walter Scott, Paul helps the protagonist and arranges his wedding (like King Richard in *T*). There is a faithful servant in the novel (cf. Caleb in *BL*), a type that Pushkin introduced into Russian literature (Savelich in *The Captain's Daughter*). In Solovev it is the dwarf Moska.

In the novel *Sergei Gorbatov*, we even find the two rival heroines that are so typical of Scott. It is well known that Scott often pairs off two beautiful women against each other: a blonde and a brunette (cf. *Waverley*, *The Pirate*, *Ivanhoe*). The hero is first attracted to the hot-blooded brunette, but finally marries the blonde.[78] In the same way Gorbatov, who is engaged to the fair beauty Tanya, falls in love with the Duchess d'Origny and her 'black, fiery eyes' ([c] черными, горячими глазами)[79] in Paris, but having lived through the terrors of the French Revolution finally returns to Russia and marries his Tanya after all.

Walter Scott in the twentieth century

There came the twentieth century, and the catastrophic events of 1917 changed Russian culture forever. It would seem that under the new circumstances there would no longer be room for the conservative, old-fashioned Walter Scott in the reader's consciousness. And this is indeed what happened at first: during the first decade of Soviet rule not a single novel by Scott was published in Russia.

Meanwhile the Bolsheviks devoted a lot of attention to history, which was viewed exclusively in Marxist terms, that is, from the point of view of the class struggle. A strange phenomenon of Soviet ideology manifested itself: in accordance with Marxism the Bolshevists denied the role of the individual in history. But at the same time, as is well known, there was never in the history of Europe (except perhaps in the case of Fascist Germany) a personality cult of similar proportions: never did the worship of a leader assume such phenomenal dimensions.

This paradox influenced in a strange way the development of the Soviet historical novel. Its main protagonists very often *are* historical personalities. The popular masses, the fictitious representatives of these masses, and other fictitious characters were little more than a foil to the activities of the main hero. In this way, the Soviet historical novel abruptly turned its back on the tradition of Walter Scott. Compared with Scott, the characters changed places in the Soviet novel. The historical figures moved from the periphery to the centre of the action, while the fictitious ordinary characters began to play a secondary role.

---

[78]   See Alexander Welsh (1992) *The Hero of the Waverley Novels*, Princeton N.J.: Princeton University Press, pp. 48–55.

[79]   Vsevolod Solovev (1960) *Sergei Gorbatov: Khronika chetyrekh pokolenii* (Sergei Gorbatov: A Chronicle of Four Generations), Washington: Victor Kamkin, 2: 90.

This principal change in the structure of the historical novel was noted by B. M. Eikhenbaum as early as the late 1920s: 'We have entered a new phase in the development of the historical and the biographical novel [. . .] [The emphasis is no longer on] historical events, but rather on excellent persons building their own fates [. . .]'.[80] Eikhenbaum was speaking not only of Russia, but also of Europe, and it was not political leaders he had in mind, but writers and painters. He did, however, perceive the general tendency correctly and clearly.

It is enough to look at the titles of the most popular Soviet historical novels, which speak for themselves: *Peter I.*, *Stepan Razin*, *Emelyan Pugachev*. The historical novels by Yuri Tynyanov (*Kyukhlya*, *Smert' Vazir-Mukhtara* [published in English under the title 'Death and Diplomacy in Persia'], and *Pushkin*) are brilliant examples of historico-biographical novels, but next to nothing remains in them of Walter Scott's poetics.

A definite and most remarkable exception is represented by Mark Aldanov's tetralogy *Myslitel'* ('The Thinker'). Aldanov (1886–1957), as has often and rightly been pointed out, was under the lifelong influence of L. Tolstoy, to whose work he devoted several marvellous studies. This, however, is natural and does not rule out the direct or indirect influence of other authors. It is important to take into account that Aldanov's books were written in exile and that the author was not under any pressure from the official ideology. This allowed him to breathe freely and compose novels that betrayed inspiration by the most diverse writers, among them Walter Scott.

The philosophy of the history of *The Thinker* is defined by a short 'Prolog' of eight pages. In thirteenth-century Paris, several characters meet: a Russian student from Kiev, a monk, a warrior recently returned from a crusade, and a wise sculptor who has just completed an ominous figure for the balustrade of Notre Dame: a thoughtful devil, who serenely and with terrible scepticism surveys the world around him, the ashes of recently burned heretics and 'infidels' and other no less horrible historic events that will be narrated in the tetralogy – the French Revolution, the events of Thermidor, the murder of Tsar Paul I, the Napoleonic Wars, the death of Napoleon, and so on.

It may not be a coincidence that motifs from Walter Scott's novel *The Talisman* have been included in the discussion between the above-mentioned characters: Sultan Saladin, who is mentioned in a similarly positive context as in Scott, and Richard the Lionheart.

But in contrast to Scott, this time it is almost a contemporary of ours who describes the tragic events in the tetralogy (which ends in the late eighteenth century). In Scott, the historical process is generally seen more-or-less optimistically. The system of society, historical excesses notwithstanding, is presented as potentially orderly. The average man is generally able to build his future successfully. This explains the happy endings of most of his novels.

---

[80]   'Мы вступили в полосу нового развития исторического и биографического романа ... Пробладающим материалом являются не исторические события, а выдающиеся люди, строящие свою судьбу.' B. M. Eikhenbaum (2001) *Moi vremennik* (My chronicle), St Petersburg: Inapress, pp. 129–30.

In Tolstoy, the historical process is predetermined, although its laws remain inscrutable to the human mind. At best, a natural man like Kutuzov may be able to divine a few tendencies of this process, which is directed by a higher will – God's.

The sceptic and misanthrope Aldanov polemicized against Tolstoy in his philosophical treatise *Ul'mskaya noch'* (The night at Ulm): there is no regularity whatsoever in history. Everything is decided by chance: the success of the French Revolution no less than that of Thermidor (the execution of Robespierre and the end of the terror), the outcome of the Battle of Borodino as well as the result of the war of 1812. In the novel *Nachalo kontsa* (The beginning of the end), the writer Vermandois, whose views are often close to those of his author, says:

> I do not expect anything intelligent or good from history, it would seem. But time and again, history succeeds in bringing about something so monstrous and horrible that I can only raise my hands [in despair and say]: I did not expect it, I never thought of it, I did not see it coming![81]

These views are reflected by the tetralogy. As in Scott, its main hero is a fictitious character, while the historical figures (Catherine II, Bezborodko, Zorich, Paul I, S. Vorontsov, Pitt, Robespierre and many others) are located on the periphery, although Aldanov is more interested in them than in the fictitious protagonist. The author will sometimes forget about the latter and devote many pages to Catherine or Robespierre (he does not like Catherine and hates Robespierre).

The portrait of the protagonist shows Aldanov's misanthropy. Julius Shtaal, a young man of unknown origin, is outwardly similar to Walter Scott's heroes. He travels from Russia to England and from England to France, he is young, good-looking and inexperienced, and he is unwillingly drawn into historical events and situations. In ethical or moral respects, however, he clearly differs from the Scottish novelist's young men.[82] Since history is nothing but a chaotic ensemble of chance events, there can be no pre-existing ethical norms (i.e. no 'categorical imperative'). Therefore, Aldanov's pallid and weak-willed hero is carried away by the flow of historical events and all too easily drawn into situations in which an honest person should not be involved. He becomes a spy and travels to France (he very much wants to go to Paris) on Pitt's instructions. He seduces his patron's lover. He is drawn into the conspiracy to murder Paul I. In the last novel of the tetralogy, *Svyataya Elena, malen'kii ostrov* (St Helena, little

---

[81]   Ничего умного, ничего хорошего я от истории, кажется, не жду. Но она неизменно выбирает нечто настолько чудовищное по глупости и мерзости, что мне остается лишь разводить руками: не догадался, не подумал, не предвидел! Mark Aldanov (1995) *Nachalo kontsa* (The beginning of the end), in *Novosti*, Moscow: [n. pub.], p. 179. On the autobiographical quality of the portrait of Vermandois see A. Chernyshev (1995) 'Aladanov v 1930-e gg' (Aldanov in the 1930s), ibid., pp. 12–13.

[82]   On possible parallels between Shtaal and Scott's heroes cf. C. Nicholas Lee (1969) *The Novels of Mark Aleksandrovich Aldanov*, The Hague; Paris: Mouton, p. 45.

island), the protagonist is no longer necessary. This novel was the first to be written and was later included in the tetralogy to show the complete senselessness of the historical process in the strange and sad death of Napoleon. Shtaal does not appear at all in this novel. His name features just once: in a strange letter it is mentioned as that of an officer and is accompanied by a brief and rather sceptical comment on his moral qualities. This paragraph was included only in a separate edition in order to link the fourth novel formally to the rest of the tetralogy. From the earlier journal version it is absent.[83]

Meanwhile, in the Soviet Union, under a totalitarian regime and most rigid censorship, classical literature became a curious kind of retreat. The intelligentsia read these books to find refuge from the omnipresent political discourse, and savoured the mastery of the old writers, their objectivity and tolerance. This helps to explain why so many copies of classic works could be printed and sold, many more than would have been conceivable anywhere else in Europe.

As we have pointed out, not a single novel by Walter Scott was republished in the Soviet Union in the decade that followed 1917. But between 1928 and 1930, the publishing house 'Zemlya i Fabrika' (Land and Factory) (ZIF) undertook an edition in fourteen volumes of Walter Scott's 'Collected Novels'. This publisher gave a lot of attention to fantastic and adventure literature. It was here that the journals 'Vokrug sveta' (Around the World) and 'Vsemirnyj sledopyt' (The World Scout), very popular among young readers, were published. The edition of Scott was also aimed at the young reader. It included almost all of his novels. Drawing on the experience of the pre-Revolutionary collections of Scott's works, ZIF published all texts in 'revised' and 're-edited', that is in simplified form, to make them more easily accessible not just to children, but also to the common reader, who was not very well educated. Every volume was accompanied by a 'Preface', mostly written by I. Mashbits-Verov, a very orthodox Marxist critic. His 'Prefaces' were supposed to provide the readers with an antidote to the ideology of the popular but conservative and bourgeois author.

The translators, editors and 'revisers' generally made use of the existing translations. They hurried, since there was always a deadline and little pay. For the sake of the pay, even Osip Mandelstam, who was desperately poor, took part in the project. Translations were his only means to support himself, although 'the fees were always simply beggarly', as the writer's wife recalled, who even 'taught herself how to stitch together such revisions for him'.[84] Mandelstam or his wife revised six of Scott's books for ZIF and the 'Collected Novels': *OM*, *HM*, *I*, *A*, *P*, *FMP* and *GM*. It is interesting to note that in 1992 Mandelstam's version of *FMP* was reprinted in 250,000 copies in Minsk and published together with *BD*.

In the stifling atmosphere of a totalitarian culture, Scott's novels ceased to be a mere reading for children. It is most likely that grown-up readers took no less

---

[83] Cf. Aladanov (1921) *Sovremennye zapiski* (Contemporary notes), 3: 78–79.

[84] 'научилась кропать за него какие-то обработки для ЗиФ'а.' Nadezhda Mandelstam (1972) *Vtoraya kniga* (Second book), Paris; New York: YMCA Press, pp. 296–97.

pleasure in retreating into a world of 'magic imagination', where people were guided by the ideals of goodness and justice rather than by class interests. Even a Soviet critic (B. G. Reizov) has conceded this, although he did so only during the period of the 'Thaw' (*ottepel'*), when the cruel regime had slightly slackened its grip. He formulated all sorts of reservations like 'regardless of all the limitations of his social consciousness', but had to admit that Scott had become 'one of the best loved authors of the Soviet reader' (одним из любимых авторов советского читателя).[85] It is possible that the authorities were aware of the fact that Scott did not fit into their own monstrous world, for they became increasingly suspicious of him: the collected works of 1928–30 were to be the last such collection in the Soviet Union for a long time. Only a few of the most popular novels like *I* or *QD* were published in single editions, but not very often, and mainly after the death of Stalin.

The most important event in the history of Russian 'Scottianism' was the publication of his *Collected Works* in twenty volumes. It fell into the 'Thaw' period: the first volume came out in 1960, the twentieth in 1965. Russia had not seen a comparable edition of Scott until then. Each volume had between 600 and 800 pages and included one or two novels. A part of the nineteenth volume was dedicated to a somewhat scant overview of his poetry, and the twentieth volume contained a few passages from his diaries and essays.

Not all of Scott's works were included in the edition, however. Among those left out were: *R*, *BET*, *SD*, *AG* and *Castle Dangerous*. This is a pity. It should have been possible with a little effort to compose a full Russian edition of his novels at last, all the more so since some of them remain practically inaccessible to the Russian reader to this day.

Although the editors usually left out the highly interesting documents that Scott would sometimes append as historical commentary to his novels (in the edition of *RR*, even the famous manuscripts written by the hand of the robber himself were not included), they preserved Scott's lengthy prefaces and his annotations. The novels were translated, of course, from the original by experienced and competent translators and were accompanied by a high-profile commentary. The edition was a colossal success with the reading public. Although 300,000 copies of the first volume were printed, it proved unusually difficult to subscribe to the collected works. Prospective subscribers had to queue up in long lines in spite of night service and advance signings, nor by any means could all readers be satisfied. The demand for the edition did not fall significantly for five years, and of the last – the twentieth – volume, there were still as many as 298,000 copies printed.

It should be said that the readers' interest in Scott has not lessened much in recent years. After the fall of the communist regime, interest in literary fiction in Russia seriously waned, making Russia in this respect more like other countries.

---

[85]   Val'ter Skott (=Walter Scott) (1960–65) *Sobranie sochinenii v dvadtsati tomakh* (Collected works in twenty volumes), Moscow: Gosudarstvennoe izdatel'stvo khudozhestvennoi literatury, 1: 6.

People prefer to spend less money on books, the prices of which have risen and continue to rise. It is also important to take into account that many members of the intelligentsia, who used to be the main purchasers of fictional literature, have suffered a considerable degree of impoverishment over the last ten to fifteen years, so that less and less of the family budget can be spent on books.

The disappearance of party censorship and ideological guidelines have allowed Scott's novels to retain their respectable position in a crumbling market, although the rampant commercialization and a general disregard for the philological culture that Russian editions were once so famous for have sadly affected most of these publications.

Several attempts have been made (in 1992, 1993, and 1997) to publish new multi-volume editions of Scott's works (in twenty and twenty-two volumes, respectively) that were meant to surpass and supplant the well-known twenty-volume edition from the 1960s. But these attempts have generally been abortive, and in the course of such editions the number of copies printed has been known to fall considerably, sometimes to one-tenth (!) of the number originally planned: from 150,000 to 15,000.

At the same time, as in the nineteenth century, Walter Scott's novels once again occupy the ever-present niche of literature for children and young readers. In order to interest these young readers, book series with attractive titles are published: 'Captains and Pirates', 'The Corsair. Adventures at Sea', 'A Pirate Novel', 'The Buccaneers', 'Kings and Queens', 'For Happiness, Gold, and Fame', 'The World Library of Adventures', 'Adventure Novels', etc. Scott's novels occupy a place of honour in such series: *P*, *BD*, *LM* and others. Every year his most popular novels are re-edited: *I*, *QD*, *T*, and so on.

On the other hand, very few attempts are made to acquaint Russian readers with the novels and other works of Scott that are as yet little known or unknown to them.

In 1994, Walter Scott's novel 'Charles the Bold' was published: it was the novel *AG*, which was published in Russian under this title for the first time in the twentieth century. The editors used, without explanation, the translation of 1893 under this title. Surprised by this 'new' novel of Scott's, other publishers hurriedly included it in their own programmes, so that in the same year 'Charles the Bold' came out three times altogether. *Castle Dangerous* was published once, while the famous novel *R* seems not to have been republished since the early nineteenth century.

In 1995, Scott's most important historical treatise *The Life of Napoleon Bonaparte* appeared. In spite of his patriotism and conservative views, Scott wrote equably and elegantly about the French Revolution and portrayed the main enemy of the British Empire in a true and impartial manner, although he naturally showed little sympathy for him. The book, however, was drastically abridged: the highly interesting and detailed opening account of the French Revolution from 1789 to 1793 was left out, for instance, although it is extremely important for understanding Scott's historical views and his political position. According to the puzzling information on the title page, some editor took upon himself the 'composition' of the book, whereupon someone else performed a 'literary revision' on it. The point of this vivisection, which estranged the text from its original, is as much a mystery to the reader as are its underlying principles, no further explanation being forthcoming. In 2002, Scott's *Letters on Demonology and Witchcraft* was published for the first time in its entirety.

The most remarkable and important event in the history of Scott's Russian reception in recent years, however, was the first full Russian translation of his novel in verse *Marmion* (until then it had only been published in prose form in 1828). Plans to include the text in the large twenty-volume edition had at the time been categorically stalled by the chief editor, Professor P. M. Samarin, because of the author's 'conservative views' and his 'apologia' of two political enemies of Russia: William Pitt the Younger and Charles Fox. So the almost completed translation had to be left unprinted.[86] Forty years later, the text came out in the prestigious series 'Literaturnye pamyatniki' (Literary Monuments), and the well-known poet and translator Vasily Betaki was finally allowed to complete his old work. This solid scientific edition contains the full text of the poem, Walter Scott's own commentary, an essay on *Marmion* and notes by G. Usova. Highly readable and interesting, not just for the Russian reader, is the translator's account of his travels in Scotland, to the places in which the action of the novel is set: 'Po sledam lorda Marmiona' ('In the Footsteps of Lord Marmion').

It may be seen as symbolic that the translation of *Marmion* was published in the year 2000, on the threshold of the third millennium, emphasizing, as it were, that the glorious name of the Scottish bard remains alive in Russia and has not lost its appeal for the Russian reader. And it is with this marvellous edition that I conclude my short account of Walter Scott's fate in Russia.

---

[86] Val'ter Skott (2000) *Marmion: Povest' o bitve pri Floddine v shesti pesnyakh* (Sir Walter Scott: *Marmion: A Tale of Flodden Field in Six Cantos*), ed. V. P. Betaki and G. S. Usova. St Petersburg: Nauka, pp. 5–6.

13 Slovene Reception of Sir Walter Scott in the Nineteenth Century

Tone Smolej

The purpose of this chapter, which refers to one of the most interesting periods of otherwise rather modest Anglo-Slovene literary contacts, is to sketch the reproductive (critical), readers' (passive) and productive reception of Sir Walter Scott in the territory of today's Slovenia, which in the nineteenth century was part of the Austrian Empire.

Reproductive reception

In the Slovene cultural milieu the name of Sir Walter Scott appears for the first time in the first half of the 1820s, in the leading literary magazine *Illyrisches Blatt* (Illyrian Paper), published in Ljubljana, the capital of the former Illyrian kingdom. Even though the magazine was published in German, most of its contributors were Slovene. The magazine's first editor was Franz Xaver Heinrich who, as an excellent grammar school teacher of history, was probably also interested in Scott. At the end of October 1825 *Illyrisches Blatt* published a short biography of the Scottish author, who visited Paris at the time. Scott was described as 'the famous and well-known author', but there was no mention of any of his works. Only in December 1826 did Heinrich publish a longer biography, saying that Scott had translated Bürger's *Lenora*, which was very popular with Slovene literary authors. The article containing references to Scott's poetry and the novel *Waverley* ended with the statement that in English literature Scott's novels had earned him a place near Shakespeare. A week later *Illyrisches Blatt* wrote about Scott's *Napoleon* and at the end of August 1827 the magazine announced to its readers the appearance of *Chronicles of the Canongate*. At the end of the 1820s the magazine published several anecdotes from Scott's life.

While the theatregoers in the neighbouring Klagenfurt could watch German dramatizations of Scott's novels (e.g. *The Talisman*) already in 1829, the public in Ljubljana only had the opportunity to see his *Kenilworth* by a German travelling theatre group at the end of January 1846; the then editor of *Illyrisches Blatt*, critic Leopold Kordesch, did not write extensively on the performance. Nevertheless, if it seems that articles on Scott were scarce, this cannot be said about his readers, who were rather numerous.

The readers' reception

The first reference to reading Scott can be found in a private letter by Matija Čop (1797–1835) to an acquaintance in December 1822. Čop points out that he had recently delighted (naschen) in some contemporary authors. Apart from Manzoni, Lamartine and Byron he also mentions Scott (Čop 1986, 54). One can only guess which work Čop, who was considered the best-educated Slovene humanist of the first half of the nineteenth century and was the mentor of the romantic poet France Prešeren, took delight in. It may be that he was reading *K* and *P* (1821) or *FN* (1822). Be that as it may, polyglot and anglophone Čop read Scott's works in the original; on the list of books from his library made upon his death one can find *Notices and Anecdotes of Sir Walter Scott* and *The Works of Walter Scott*, but it is not known which titles the latter actually contained.

A decade later, the poet Stanko Vraz (1810–51) was reading Scott: a preserved invoice of a Graz bookseller proves that in 1834 he bought *A* in the original (Slodnjak 1950, 80). In Vraz's legacy a two-page fragment was found in which a wounded soldier wonders who was the girl that had taken care of him, and it was assumed that the poet was perhaps considering a historical tale similar to *W*, where the same motif can be found (Bogataj 1982, 23). Vraz never carried out his plan, as he soon began writing only in Croat.

Far less interest in the novelist was demonstrated by Janez Trdina (1830–1905), who was reading Scott in grammar school around 1848, and considered him boring. Nevertheless, in his memoirs written in the second half of the 1860s and published only after the Second World War, Trdina, who by then had read Scott's *Napoleon*, somewhat moderated his opinion:

> An acquaintance once lent me a Walter Scott, declaring that his novels were most highly acclaimed. I had started reading and it made me yawn terribly: there was almost no action but lots of various descriptions of land and habits that were of no interest to me. However, with time, it did whet my curiosity: Walter describes the events in a smooth, logical, and at times classical manner. He really is among the best novelists, but this is exactly why he appears to be bleak and boring to the young who do not yet have any idea about art. Scott is suitable for mature men, not for children and women. (Trdina 1946, 137)[1]

---

[1]   Nek znanec mi posodi Walterja Scotta, rekoč, da so njegovi romani najbolj glasoviti med vsemi. Začnem brati, zeha se mi strašno, ker ne najdem dejanja skoraj nič, veliko pa vsakovrstnih popisov zemlje in navad, ki me niso kar nič zanimali. Toda sčasoma me je začelo vendarle mikati – kar se je godilo, popisuje Walter gladko, logično, sem ter tja klasično. Res je, da spada med najboljše romaniste, toda ravno zato se zdi nekako pust in dolgočasen mladini, ki še nima nobenega smisla o umetnosti. Scott je za zrele možake, ne pa za otroke in babe.

At approximately the same time, the future literary historian Fran Levec (1846–1919) was of a different opinion. In September 1866 he sent Scott's *A* to his girlfriend, advising her to read it carefully in a fortnight and commenting: 'Germans, at least those who like the German blasé emptiness, do not appreciate Scott very much; there are others, however, who adore him. The former say that Scott's narration is too exhaustive and boring, the latter claim that the very fact that he can paint the human character in such detail makes him an excellent writer' (Levec 1967, 17).[2] Presumably, Levec was acquainted with the criticism of the 'Jungdeutschen', which was that such historical novels conveyed the description of clothing rather than the description of persons (Oppel 1971, 49). In the same letter Levec also pointed out that Walter Scott was the 'teacher of Jurčič's' – who was in fact a true 'Scott enthusiast'.

His school friend and future Slavic scholar Fran Celestin (1883, 320) remembered that in grammar school Josip Jurčič (1844–81) was most impressed by Walter Scott and that also later, during his university studies in Vienna, Jurčič was quite keen on the Scottish novelist. Levec (1888, 420) wrote that in 1862, still as a grammar school student, Jurčič found Scott's novels at his friend Ferdinand Ullrich's home: 'He began to read and Scott's writing had such an influence on him that it as good as determined his fate. He would read night and day [. . .]'.[3] Later, documents were found, revealing that Jurčič had read Scott already a year earlier, when he was 17. Around 15 December 1861 he wrote in a notebook, which was found in his legacy,[4] that he read '5, 6 *Redgauntlet*, 16, 17 *Kloster*, 31, 32 *Braut von Lamermoor*, 33 *Herz von Mid-loth*' (Rupel 1968, 327). Jurčič, of course, had no difficulty reading Scott in German translations, because the teaching language in grammar schools at the time was German. One can be quite certain that the numbers in front of the titles indicate the corresponding numbers of the volumes of Scott's texts. In *BL* Jurčič may have been interested in Lucy's tragic feelings before her marriage to a man she did not love. Further to the theme of unfortunate love, Jurčič was also interested in the descriptions of monasteries. In *The Monastery* he must have read the chapters in which The White Lady appears. In *R* the young writer was attracted more by the descriptions of the inn than the search for the abducted person. It has not been known until now that in 1864 Jurčič noted in his notebook the names of two heroes from the same work (Joshua Geddes and Peter Peebles); however, the description of the ambience in the inn is rather less legible.[5] In 1865, Jurčič must have read Scott's novel *Kenilworth*; in his notebook one can

---

[2]   'Nemci, vsaj nekteri, kim je priljubljena nemška blazirana praznota, Scotta ne česte posebno, nekteri pa neizrečeno; prvi pravijo, da je Scott preobširen tedaj tudi predolgočasen popisovalec, drugi pa trde, da ravno to je izvrstno na njem, ker značaj človeški tako natanko narisa.'

[3]   'Začel ga je brati in romani Scottovi so imeli nanj takšen vpliv, da so takorekoč odločili usodo njegovo. Bral ga je noč in dan.'

[4]   National and University Library (Narodna in univerzitetna knjižnica), Ljubljana (NUK). Ms 1447. Map 2. B, No. 1.

[5]   NUK. Ms 1447. Map 2. B, No. 4.

find the Slovene translation of Scott's incipit,[6] which will later play a very important role.

Productive reception

I Scott and Jurčič's early works

In 1864, the twenty-year-old Jurčič was awarded the best story prize for *Jurij Kozjak*, his first work of some length. He situated the narrative in the second half of the fifteenth century, that is, at the time of Turkish incursions into today's Slovene territory. Even though his work was of overtly historical nature, Jurčič is supposed to have followed the example of *GM*, which does not go that far into the past (Kos 1987, 129). Scott's novel was well known in the Slovene milieu and had already been mentioned in 1852 in the popular magazine *Novice*. An anonymous author wrote in the article entitled 'Gypsies and their language' that '[gypsies] were excellently described by the famous Walter Scott in his book *Der Astrologe*'. As is the case in *GM*, in *Jurij Kozjak* gypsies also play an important role:

> Some fifty years before the beginning of our story, gypsies came into our land. Before that time they were unknown in these parts of Europe, and even today we are not certain where they came from. The historians of the old days used to say that a foreign people wandered to Europe, a people of brown skin, unfamiliar costume and strange language. [. . .] However, its tribes soon dispersed around European lands and almost everywhere roused local population by their idle dallying and even more by the fact that they were rather keen on swindling people and only badly distinguished between what was 'ours' and what was 'theirs' (Jurčič 1961, 103).[7]

In both stories disputes occur between local populations and gypsies. In Scott's novel, due to a real war, the Laird of Ellangowan chases gypsies from their encampment and, as a result, a gypsy woman pronounces a curse upon him. In Jurčič's work, Kozjak, the lord of the castle, brutally treats a gypsy boy, who tried to steal his horse, after which the boy's father announces revenge. In both works a nobleman's underage son is abducted. While Scott does not directly describe the act of abduction, Jurčič does so in detail. In the latter's story the abduction is carried out by the vengeful gypsy chieftain, although it is financed by the boy's uncle who wishes to get hold of the property. In Scott's narrative it becomes

---

6   NUK. Ms 1447. Map 2. B, No. 5.
7   Kakih petdeset let popred, preden se je pričela naša povest, prišli so cigani v naše kraje. Popred niso bili znani tod po Evropi in še današnji dan ne vemo za gotovo, od kod so za prvega prišli. Zgodovinopisci tedanjih časov pripovedujejo, da je tuj narod v Evropo priromal – rjave kože, neznane noše in tujega jezika. [. . .] Kmalu pa so se razšli v drhalih po vseh evropejskih deželah, kjer so si skoraj povsod prebivalce razdražili zavoljo svojega lenega pohajkovanja in pa še bolj zavoljo tega, ker so preradi tega ali onega ogoljufali in le slabo ločili, kaj je moje, kaj tvoje.

clear only later that the abduction was part of a broader conspiracy led by Gilbert Glossin, who wants to take possession of Ellangowan's wealth. Both texts are placed in two different time periods between which respectively seventeen and eighteen years pass. In the second part Jurčič moves away from Scott's model. While both youngsters later assert themselves as combatants, Jurij Kozjak is sold to Turkey as janizary (a member of an infantry unit in the Sultan's army) and returns to his land as a hostile Turkish soldier; contrary to Henry, Jurij only reappears at the end of the story. In all likelihood, Jurčič did use Scott's theme of a gypsy abductor who recognizes his former victim and reveals the background of the crime, and the motif of the main conspirator's violent death. Jurij Kozjak's uncle hangs himself just like the diabolical abductor Hatteraick after he has strangled Glossin in jail.

Like *Jurij Kozjak*, *Hči mestnega sodnika* (1866) (The daughter of the town magistrate) is set in the fifteenth century in a time when the inhabitants of Ljubljana were in dispute with the then province governor Georg von Auersperg. While Jurčič's hero Sumerek is a historically attested character, nothing is known about Sumerek's daughter and it can be assumed that the author borrowed various motifs for his narrative from *FMP* (Kos 1987, 129). In both narratives the daughter rejects the suitor, be it for his combativeness (Catharine) or his age (Helena), while both fathers are rather well disposed towards their daughters' admirers. However, while the daydreaming and pious Catharine in no way encourages the courting of the crown prince, Duke of Rothsay, the much more sensual Helena flirts with Auersperg's partner of Italian origin, Ciriani. The following chapters of Jurčič's story show further Scott influence. Just like the Duke of Rothsay, Ciriani also tries to abduct the citizen's daughter at night, but her alleged lover (Henry/Simon) chases the abductors away. In Scott's story the citizens keep the chopped-off hand of one of the abductors, and in Jurčič's tale they take hold of the severely wounded servant himself. In both cases such brutality sparks off a turbulent debate in the town council. As in *Jurij Kozjak*, Jurčič, who also considerably reduced the number of characters, later moved away from Scott's example. Helena approaches Ciriani herself, but he abducts her against her will and presumably dishonours her. When Auersperg, under pressure by the citizens, decides to return Sumerek's daughter, Ciriani stabs her, after which Simon avenges her death. Jurčič's story thus ends on a much more sombre note than Scott's – Catharine lives through all attacks. It needs to be underlined that Jurčič supplemented Scott's opposition between the middle class and aristocracy with the opposition between Slovenes on the one hand and Germans and Italians on the other, with the following clear message: the political future lies in the Slovene middle class (Hladnik 1994, 142).

II Scott and the first Slovene novel: The Tenth Brother

It seems that literary history has not paid enough attention to the incipit of Jurčič's novel *Deseti brat* (The tenth brother), which reads as follows: 'Since long ago, storytellers have had the right, as observed already by the renowned novelist Walter Scott, to begin their story in an inn, the meeting place of all travellers, where various natures can reveal themselves to each other directly and without restraint − which complements the well known saying "There is truth in wine" ' (Jurčič 1965, 141).[8] The incipit was, of course, modelled on the beginning of Scott's *Kenilworth*: 'It is the privilege of tale-tellers to open their story in an inn, the free rendezvous of all travellers, and where the humour of each displays itself, without ceremony or restraint' (Scott 1999, 1). In the sentence following the incipit Jurčič refers to Scott again: 'We also intend to use this right, as we are of the opinion that our Slovene inns and innkeepers, in spite of their much simpler appearance in the countryside, are just as original as those old English ones in Scott's writings' (Jurčič 1965, 141).[9] In other words, one should follow Scott's principles, since they are useful in describing Slovene places and people, which deserve no less to be put into words. Furthermore, Jurčič's incipit is also a kind of initial tribute to the admired literary model, which would assist the author in the creation of the very first Slovene novel − *The Tenth Brother* (1866). From *K* Jurčič took the so-called 'static incipit' (*incipit statique*), which gives quite a lot of information to the reader without, however, starting *in medias res* (Del Lungo 2003, 174). This type of incipit was favoured by the novelists in the first half of the nineteenth century, as it introduced the reader into the story gradually. On the other hand, in *A*, which impressed Jurčič so much (Levec 1888, 422) and is of key importance for the creation of *The Tenth Brother*, Scott begins the story *in medias res*.

It is worth pointing out that both *A* and *The Tenth Brother* begin with the motif of an unknown young stranger arriving in an obscure place and encountering difficulties with transportation. In *A* a young man of genteel appearance (Lovel) is joined by an older, spirited gentleman (the antiquary Oldbuck), who quarrels with the carriage owner because her diligence is obviously coming late. In Jurčič's novel, on the other hand, the older and the younger man step from a carriage. The younger and very handsome man (Kvas) wishes to continue his way to avoid the nightfall, and the older man (Doctor Vencelj) has to persuade the innkeeper to lend Kvas a horse.

From that point onwards, the journeys of the two heroes are rather different. While the reasons for Lovel's stay in Fairport are mysterious, the Slovene narrator tells us that Kvas is a secondary-school graduate who is coming to the castle of Slemenice as a tutor to earn the money for his future university studies in Vienna. In Fairport, Lovel meets his former acquaintance Isabella Wardour, who hardly wishes to recognize him. When he saves her from drowning during high tide, the girl warns him that he should stop dreaming, for she would not marry him without her father's permission. According to Isabella's father, Sir Arthur,

---

[8] 'Pripovedovalci imajo, kakor trdi že sloveči romanopisec Walter Scott, staro pravico, da svojo povest začno v krčmi, to je v tistem shodišču vseh popotnih ljudi, kjer se raznovrstni značaji naravnost in odkrito pokažejo drug drugemu poleg pregovora: "v vinu je resnica." '

[9] 'Da se torej tudi mi te pravice poprimemo, izvira iz tega, ker menimo, da naše slovenske krčme in naši krčmarji, čeravno imajo po deželi veliko preprostejšo podobo, niso nič manj originalni ko staroangleški Scottovi.'

Lovel as an illegitimate child is not a suitable bridegroom for their respectable family. At the castle of Slemenice, Kvas meets the landlord's daughter Manica and before long falls in love with her. In a letter to a friend the young tutor reflects on the foolishness of his feelings:

> The world judges a man by what he has, by what he is and by how he is. And since the world is old, this has become an old habit: if one was to negate it, one would be alone in so doing; if one was to oppose it, one would have to roll the rock up a steep hill. She is the daughter of a well-to-do, one may say a wealthy landowner, she will bring a nice dowry, and even if her father is not a nobleman, she comes from a respected, distinguished family. And myself! – I have nothing, I am worth nothing, I am nothing! (Jurčič 1965, 217).[10]

Just as Lovel can never be acceptable to Wardour, Kvas can never be acceptable to the Slemenice family. Here it needs to be pointed out that Kvas's social rank is lower than Lovel's. The Slovene hero is not a respectable officer but only a tutor – nevertheless, the landlord's daughter is rather fond of him. Through the use of this motif and the introduction of letters Jurčič came close to Rousseau's model in his novel *Julie ou la Nouvelle Héloïse*.

Beside the theme of a socially unequal couple there is, in both novels, the motif of a love triangle leading to quarrels. In Scott's novel the story is complicated by the visit of Oldbuck's nephew Hector M'Intyre. Just as Lovel feels uneasy about M'Intyre, Kvas is uneasy about his landlord's neighbour Marijan Piškav, who is a wealthy and favoured suitor; the reader, however, soon learns that Manica does not love him. There is no duel in Jurčič's novel, but the two characters do have a bitter quarrel during a hunt. Marijan, whom Manica has decidedly turned down, threatens Kvas and orders him to leave – or else he will shoot him. In this context there is another association with Scott. As if he had anticipated something, Doctor Vencelj, with whom Kvas had arrived, warns the young man to beware of quarrels. In similar vein Oldbuck warns his former fellow traveller to pay attention to his feelings, since 'your life has been given you for useful and valuable purposes'. After Kvas has left, Marijan, in a fury, fires a bullet at the beggar Spak; the latter, however, succeeds in hitting him back with a rifle butt and Marijan falls down, wounded. Later the reader finds out that the fight was, in fact, a settling of accounts between Cain and Abel.

One of the most important elements Jurčič included in his novel under Scott's influence is a horrendous story, which in fact represents a prelude to both novels. In *A*, the old Elspeth, immediately after the death of the Earl of Glenallan's mother, confesses to him and accepts a part of responsibility because she knew that the Earl's mother, fearing loss of property and title, falsely proclaimed her son's fiancée Eveline to be a daughter of her own husband; as a

---

[10] Svet sodi človeka po tem, kar ima, kar je in kakršen je. Svet je pa že star, torej tudi ta navada v starosti utrjena; kdor bi jo hotel ovreči, ta bi sam stal, kdor bi ji hotel ravnati nasproti, moral bi skalo v strm klanec valiti. Ona je edina hči premožnega, lahko rečem bogatega graščaka, imela bo lepo doto, in dasi oče njen ni plemenitnik, ima vendar češčeno, poznano ime. In jaz! – Nimam nič, ne veljam nič, nisem nič!

consequence, the young woman went insane and committed suicide, persuaded that she was pregnant by her own brother. An analogous story appears in Jurčič's work, even though the plot is quite different: here, the narrator is an innocent victim, not an accomplice. The mortally wounded Spak confides to Kvas that Piškav, Marijan's father, had seduced a girl and married her. When, after the death (that he caused himself) of a relative of hers, he found out that she was poor, he left her, pregnant. Just like the Countess of Glenallan, Piškav also manipulated some documents: his marriage with the young woman was invalid, since the priest who conducted the ceremony had been ousted beforehand. While there is no doubt in Jurčič's text that Spak is Piškav's child from that marriage, the fate of the baby that was born immediately after Eveline's suicide, but had disappeared before the Countess was able to get rid of it, is unclear. Only with Oldbuck's assistance does Glenallan become aware that his lost son is in fact Lovel. Being of appropriately high rank he can, after all, marry Isabella. In *The Tenth Brother* there is also a solution for the poor Kvas: Spak discovers that the young tutor is in fact Piškav's nephew. Marijan must follow his father's will and surrender his home to the former rival; after having taken a doctor's degree at Vienna university, Kvas can, finally, marry Manica.

Literary history (Šanda 1905) has focused on the character of the beggar, Spak, who is also the title hero of Jurčič's novel (according to a popular legend the tenth brother, or rather the tenth son in a family had to leave home, but was praised as a kind of bard). Spak was usually compared to Scott's minor character, Edie Ochiltree. Like Edie, who in *A* sets off to see Glenallan, Spak, in *The Tenth Brother*, also heads to a mysterious castle – not as a messenger but as a black-mailer. He then declares the money he has received as his hidden treasure; Edie, too, displays interest in fictitious treasures. Both beggars also offer precious assistance to a young stranger (Lovel/Kvas). In addition, while Ochiltree helps Lovel to run away after the duel, Spak brings Kvas the necessary wealth. The two characters are nevertheless of very different natures. While Edie is a spirited and good-humoured companion to the main characters, Spak is a vengeful and restless eternal wayfarer. After the novel ends, Edie's vagrancy continues; Jurčič's hero, on the contrary, is killed by his own brother.

In literary history, attention has already been drawn to the fact that Jurčič also followed Scott's example in relation to the narrative manner (Koblar 1936, 38). Like the Scottish novelist, he addresses the reader from time to time and indi-cates, for example, that the story is continuing in the next chapter. In both novels, this is used in the narration of the horrendous story from the past. Scott interrupts his story with the following words: 'The tenor of communication is disclosed in the following chapter' (Scott, 361). Jurčič employs a similar procedure: 'Martinek's story is rather long, and the gentle reader will find its continuation in the next chapter' (Jurčič 1965, 309).[11] Koblar (1936, 28) points out that Jurčič also emulated Scott's romantic irony, through which the author would remind the reader that the entire novel was only an illusion.

---

[11] 'Ker je povest Martinkova precejšno dolga, stavimo jo blagovoljnemu bralcu v naslednji odstavek.'

There are, however, some elements mentioned by Jurčič's narrator to which Slovene literary history has not paid adequate attention. In Chapter IV of *The Tenth Brother* the narrator ridicules the numerous scholars who overemphasize the etymological significance of proper names for their country's history, and ponders amusingly on the possible Sanskrit origin of the name of the Slovene village of Obrhek: 'Perhaps some good-natured antiquary will help me with a possible second edition of *The Tenth Brother* and free me from my perplexity by adding a short commentary at the bottom of this page' (Jurčič 1965, 172).[12] This is as if the Slovene novelist was calling upon Scott's good-humoured antiquary Oldbuck, who was intensely involved in such issues. One cannot but recall his fervent interpretation in Chapter XIV that the name of 'Quickensbog' is of Saxon origin. Both Scott's and Jurčič's narrators are keen on quoting examples from Cervantes's *Don Quixote*. The narrator in *A* reveals that Oldbuck did not buy books 'at the enormous prices of modern times, which are sufficient to have appalled the most determined [. . .] bibliomaniac upon record [. . .] Don Quixote de la Mancha', who was stated 'to have exchanged fields and farms for folios and quartos of chivalry' (Scott s. a, 30). The narrator in *The Tenth Brother*, on the other hand, justifies Marijan's hot-tempered nature with the fact that the young man read a lot of the novels that Don Quixote criticized (Jurčič 1965, 285).

Koblar (1936, 30) had already pointed out that under Scott's influence Jurčič put a motto from a song at the beginning of every chapter. Scott often used quotations from Shakespeare's plays; and in novels, which Jurčič must have been acquainted with, they are quite numerous – in *HM* and *K* more than a third of the total number. It is not unlikely that when using quotations from some of Shakespeare's plays (*The Tempest* and *Hamlet*) Jurčič was also influenced by Scott.

After 1866 the reception of Scott in Slovenia became closely connected with the name of Josip Jurčič. Nevertheless, this relationship was interpreted in quite a number of different ways. Two years after the publication of *The Tenth Brother*, Fran Levec (1868, 19) characterized Jurčič as 'our Walter Scott'. Ten years later the critic Josip Stritar (1877, 63) put forward the idea, which still gets repeated, that Jurčič had learned from Scott but never imitated him. Later, Levec (1888, 422), who – being a contemporary of Jurčič – remembered the writer reading *A*, suggested that there were quite a lot of reminiscences of Scott's novel in *The Tenth Brother*. However, Šanda (1905, 77) rejected the term 'reminiscence', asserting that in fact Jurčič had simply copied the essential moments from Scott. Reflections like these reveal the basic dilemmas of comparative literature. Although Scott's influence on Jurčič is indisputable, there are, even today, scholars who deny any foreign effect on him and maintain the idea that Jurčič was an 'autochthonous' national writer (e.g. Kmecl 1981, 38, 49).

---

[12] 'Morda mi bo kak dobrovoljen starinoslovec pri mogoči drugi izdaji Desetega brata tu iz zadrege pomagal ter mi pod črto tega lista napravil majhen komentarček.'

Conclusion

Despite the absence of notable critical reviews and translations, the Slovene reception of Sir Walter Scott was quite fruitful; this was mainly due to Josip Jurčič. Under the influence of the Scottish novelist, Jurčič started writing historical prose. However, the Slovene author described different places and events, which may be the reason why Scott's influence is more obvious at the level of fundamental motifs, be they Gothic (abductions, conspiracies, sexual violence, dark histories from the past) or sentimental (love triangles, impossible love). In the 1870s, Jurčič started moving away from Scott's model to approach realism, but was, nevertheless, still introducing themes that were characteristic of Scott (e.g. rebellion against the ruler, a noble criminal). Despite the fact that after Jurčič's premature death literary critics marvelled at his fondness for Scott and even quoted Zola in *Les romanciers naturalistes*, where he described the Scottish novelist purely as a good decorator, appreciated predominantly by young women (Celestin 1883, 320), Scott's novels continued to be widely read in Slovenia in the second half of the nineteenth century. Regrettably, these novels were only German translations, as can be seen from numerous advertisements and reviews of the then new German illustrated edition. Scott's impact on the development of Slovene prose is immeasurable. At the beginning of the Slovene novel stands the name of Josip Jurčič and at the beginning of Jurčič's novel stands the name of Sir Walter Scott.

14 'His pirates had foray'd on Scottish hill': Scott in Denmark with an Overview of his Reception in Norway and Sweden[1]

Jørgen Erik Nielsen

Interest in English literature had manifested itself in Denmark in the second half of the eighteenth century, and translations had appeared. But familiarity with contemporary English literature was slow to establish itself in the first two decades of the nineteenth century, for political reasons. The Treaty of Tilsit in July 1807 prompted Britain to demand an alliance with Denmark and the Danish navy as a pledge. Denmark refused, which resulted in the bombardment of Copenhagen in early September and war with Britain till January 1814. Denmark had then become a small and impoverished state: the year 1813 had seen the bankruptcy of the state, and the peace treaty terminated the old union with Norway. Among the wealthy merchants of that country, familiarity with England and the English language was common (Schnitler 1911, 13–18), but during the war Norway had experienced famine, the background of Henrik Ibsen's poem *Terje Vigen* (1861). From 1814 to 1905 Norway was, with its own constitution, united with Sweden, which came out of the Napoleonic wars as an ally of Britain and Russia.

The earliest reference to Scott in Danish printed material would seem to be found in the periodical *Kjøbenhavnske lærde Efterretninger* (Copenhagen Learned Intelligence 1802, 15, 236–37), in a review, translated from the French, of M. G. Lewis's *Tales of Wonder*; Scott and Southey are mentioned as contributors to the book. In Sweden a periodical mentions him in 1811 (Lindström 1925, 102).

In the years 1812–14 Abrahamson, Nyerup and Rahbek published a new edition of Danish medieval ballads in five volumes: *Udvalgte Danske Viser fra*

---

[1] The quotation is from *Harold the Dauntless*, I/ii/4. All translations from Nordic languages are by the author, and the place of publication is Copenhagen unless stated otherwise.

Middelalderen (Selected Danish ballads from the Middle Ages). In its fifth volume, the preface dated 1 October 1813, Nyerup refers (10–14) to Thomas Percy's *Reliques of Ancient English Poetry* (1765), Robert Jamieson's *Popular Ballads and Songs* (1806) and Scott's *Minstrelsy of the Scottish Border* (1803). Jamieson's work had appeared one year before the beginning of hostilities between Britain and Denmark, and at it first seems surprising that Nyerup, though he knew English, should have been able to keep abreast of contemporary literature to that extent. In this case, however, we know how he got the book: an acquaintance of his was the Danish man of letters Andreas Andersen Feldborg (1782–1838), who lived in England from 1802 to 1816 and for a period of time after 1821. In the summer of 1810 he managed to pay a visit to Denmark and Norway and became acquainted with Christian Molbech (1783–1857), historian, man of letters and linguist. In the following years the two men kept up a correspondence, apparently thanks to the clandestine traffic between Tønningen in south-western Slesvig and Heligoland or Harwich. In a letter of 8 February 1811 Feldborg asks Molbech to give his regards to a number of friends in Copenhagen, among them Professor Nyerup, with the promise soon to send him 'Jamieson's Ballads, Songs etc'.[2] In Sweden the poet Per Daniel Amadeus Atterbom (1790–1855) mentions Scott as a ballad collector in his *Poetisk kalender* (Poetical calendar) for 1816 (Lindström 102).

Soon after the restoration of peace in 1814, notices about contemporary English literature began to appear in Danish newspapers. The first translated samples appeared in *Nytaarsgave for begge Kiøn: 1817* (New Year's offering for both sexes: 1817), also entitled *Asterkrandsen* (The aster garland), translated and edited by Professor Knud Lyne Rahbek (1760–1830). The book, small and modest, is a collection of short poetical translations from a number of languages, about one-third from English, among them two poems by Byron, two by Campbell and three by Scott ('The Last Words of Cadwallon; or the Dying Bard', 'The Palmer', and 'The Resolve'). Very few modern English books had come to Denmark so soon after the war, and Rahbek had undoubtedly read them in C. R. W. Wiedemann's English-language anthology *Modern English Poems*, I–II (Kiel, 1815–16).

Rahbek was perfectly aware of the change in contemporary English poetry and comments on it in an essay called 'Strøetanker' ('Stray Thoughts') in his periodical *Tilskueren* (The Spectator) on 6 June 1820. The classical English poets 'from the days of Queen Anne: Pope, Addison, Swift, their predecessor Dryden et al. have witnessed the fading of their aura face to face with that of the modern Romantics: Byron, Walter Scott, Thomas Moore et al.'[3]

In 1820–21 Rahbek published in his periodical *Hesperus* six articles under the headline 'Om Englands nyere poetiske Litteratur' (On the contemporary

---

[2] Letter in the Royal Library, Copenhagen, call number 'Ny kgl. S., 3000–4' (Nielsen 1986).

[3] 'fra Dronning Annas Tid, Pope, Addison, Swift, deres Forgiænger Dryden, o.fl. have seet deres Nimbus falme og blegne for de nyere Romantikers, Byrons, Walter Scotts, Thomas Moores o.fl.'

poetic literature of England). His source of information was F. J. Jacobsen's book *Briefe an eine deutsche Edelfrau über die neuesten englischen Dichter* (Letters to a German noblewoman on contemporary English poets) (Altona, 1820). Jacobsen was a lawyer in Altona, then the biggest town in Holstein. At the end of his fifth article Rahbek informed his readers that he now intended to turn to Scott, his favourite poet among the contemporaries, whose complete poetical works he had access to from a friend; but the sixth article (in *Hesperus*, IV/3) is all about the development of English literature from 1066 to Pope. Rahbek produced a number of small translations of poems by Scott, but his strength failed when he was to include him in his useful survey.

Nineteenth-century translations

The first novel by Scott to appear in Danish was *Røde Robin* I–II (1821), Caspar Johannes Boye's translation of *RR*. The novel, which bears Scott's name, has been translated from Lindau's German version (1819), so naturally the abridgements in the German edition are found in the Danish edition too. Boye did know English and in 1822 published translations of *The Heart of Midlothian* and *Ivanhoe*, but in his preface to *Røde Robin* he regrets that he had for months been waiting in vain for the English original.

Rahbek had announced *Røde Robin* as forthcoming in *Tilskueren* (The Spectator) on 16 May 1820, and at the back of the book the impending appearance of a Danish translation of *I* is mentioned. Such advance notices could give translators a warning of possible competition, and it worked in the case of *Napoleon Bonaparte*. Andreas Peter Liunge and Hans Georg Nicolai Nyegaard had in May 1826 announced their translations as forthcoming, and on 27 May Liunge printed a prospectus in *Nyt Aftenblad* (The New Evening Journal), but on 21 July 1827 he informed the public in *Kjøbenhavnsposten* (The Copenhagen Mail) that only one translation was due. The work (in nine volumes) appeared as a joint enterprise in 1827–30 and was available by subscription in both Denmark and Norway. A different translation by Frederik Julius Schaldemose (1828) is an abridged one. But advance notices did not always prevent rival translations in the fairly limited market of Denmark. By 1832 all of Scott's novels were available in Danish, and in most cases he is mentioned as the author on the title page.

Four of Scott's metrical tales appeared in prose translations, undoubtedly done from the German, in the years 1824–29. Some translators, Rahbek and Liunge among them, published extracts in metrical translation, but not till 1836 did a complete metrical tale appear in translation: *Pigen ved Søen*, Peter Diderik Ibsen's translation of *The Lady of the Lake*.

Scott's drama *Halidon Hill* came out in 1822, and Rahbek's translation of it appeared in that same year. In his periodical *Tilskueren* (1822, 13) he explains in 'Brev fra Senior om en Brevveksling med W. Scott' (Letter from Mr Senior about a Correspondence with W. Scott) how he had sent with an acquaintance going to Edinburgh a letter to Scott and a copy of the above-mentioned edition of medieval Danish ballads. Scott thanked Rahbek in a letter of 30 June 1822, assuring him that he was the 'proud possessor' of Peder Syv's old edition of

1695 and that he would have to learn Danish in order to fully appreciate the new edition. In his 'letter' in *Tilskueren* Rahbek says that he intends to send his forthcoming translation of the drama to Scott, so that he can use it as a primer of Danish. Scott scarcely spent much time learning Danish, but the book is found in the library at Abbotsford.[4]

The year 1832 saw the appearance of a new translation of *Waverley*, translated by Schaldemose, as volumes I–II of Scott's *Samlede Skrifter* (Collected works). That edition, whose last volume came as late as in 1858, contains twenty Scott novels, not all in new translations, besides Schaldemose's translation of the spurious *Allan Cameron* (1841). The edition was available by subscription in both Denmark and Norway.

Spurious novels appeared in Danish too, one of them a fabrication produced in Denmark entitled *Lord Sydenham, Historisk Roman af Walter Scotts efterladte Papirer* (1835, L.S. Historical novel from the posthumous papers of Walter Scott), translated by S. J. Bang. However, that book is a translation from 1831 of Lee Gibbons's *The Cavalier*. Presumably, this translation had not sold well, so four years later the publisher attributed it to Scott, invented a different title and a spurious translator and had a new title page printed.

In Norway translations of Fielding and Smollett, *The Life of Napoleon Bonaparte* and five of the novels appeared in Christiania, now Oslo, between 1827 and 1834; but written Norwegian and written Danish were in those days very similar, and Danish translations were in general use. In Sweden most of the novels were translated from 1821, other than *Paul's Letters to His Kinsfolk*, which has never appeared in Danish.

The Swedish translations came in for much criticism from reviewers (Lindström 1925, 110–11), but so did many of their Danish counterparts. Not all that criticism was just of course, but what could you expect? The demand for translations from English was great, and many translators had insufficient familiarity with the language.

Most Danish Scott translations from this period are complete, with occasional abridgments, but including mottoes and inset poetry. Few notes were translated, and neither were the introductions, but then most of this material was not in the editions available to the early translators.

Those translators certainly had their abilities tested, and clearly their merits are varied, but many of the novels posed a problem that these translators could not solve: linguistic individualization with various degrees of Scots dialect. There was no tradition for translating dialect to rely on. Consequently the difference of rank between the Queen and Jeanie Deans in *HM*, Chapter 36 becomes less apparent in Boye's translation, though Jeanie's respectful addresses to the unknown lady are clear enough even in translation.

Boye appears to be the first translator to have preserved the title 'laird'. In Hviding's translation of *Guy Mannering* (1823) Bertram Ellangowan is 'Herren' ('the master'), but in his 1837 version Schaldemose adopts 'laird', even declining

---

[4]   *The Letters of Sir Walter Scott*, 7: 202–10. Scott's letter is preserved in The Royal Library in Copenhagen, call number 'Ny kgl. S. 1455'. Harvey Wood, 249.

it like a normal Danish noun ('Lairden'='the Laird'), though at the first appearance of this title at the beginning of Chapter 2 it is explained a few lines further down, where the word is translated into 'Herremanden' ('the squire'). The use of this title in translations imparts a Scottish flavour to the Danish text, but on the other hand Boye consistently calls Jeanie 'Johanne', possibly to facilitate the pronunciation for his readers.

A new edition of Scott's *Samlede Romaner* (Collected novels) in twenty volumes appeared in the years 1855–71, not all in new translations; for example, Boye's old reliable versions reappeared. A novel like *I* was in very great demand and was printed more than once. Illustrated editions began to appear in the 1880s and editions prepared for youthful readers, the first one being *Udvalgte Fortællinger: Bearbejdede for Ungdommen* (Selected tales: prepared for youthful readers), 1881–82, with illustrations, consisting of *T* and *QD*. Norwegian and Swedish bibliographies tell a similar story.

Booksellers and libraries

Booksellers' catalogues tell us that Scott's novels were already for sale in Copenhagen bookshops in the early 1820s; from bookshops outside the metropolis very few catalogues are preserved. The Danish translations were there of course, but also a great number of German translations and some French ones. Scott's novels in English are listed too, so big bookshops at least must have counted on some demand for them. Most editions in English were Continental reprints, which were much cheaper than the originals (there were no Danish reprints with the exception of texts intended as textbooks for the study of English). Scott's poetry and non-fictional prose were on the shelves too, but in much smaller numbers. Library catalogues confirm Scott's popularity: his novels were found in club and circulating libraries both in and outside Copenhagen, and, not surprisingly, modest circulating libraries had little besides the novels which were primarily in Danish translation.

In Norway we have precise information about the University Library in Christiania (now Oslo), the only public library of importance to possess Scott novels before 1830. The registers of that library demonstrate a dramatic rise in loans of Scott between 1825 and 1835 (Tysdahl 1983: 475 and 1988: 169–72). An amusing example of how interest in Scott continued, at least among young people, is furnished by a catalogue of the Cathedral School library of Christiania (1883). The headmaster complains that a number of volumes in a Scott edition were completely worn out because of their popularity.

Danish criticism

The appearance of Danish Scott translations called forth reviews, the most important ones in *Dansk Litteratur-Tidende* (Danish Journal of Literature), where nine Scott novels and *The Castle of Pontefract* were discussed in eight reviews between 1821 and 1827. These reviews are unsigned, but many similarities in tone and content make it reasonable to think that the same reviewer has been busy. An increasing familiarity with Scott is felt; thus in the first review in 1821 (of *RR*) the critic has relied entirely on Jacobsen's *Briefe an eine deutsche Edelfrau* for background information, whereas in his review of *I* and *GM* (1823) he can refer to novels that have not yet appeared in Danish. Scott's novels are praised for the verisimilitude in their depictions of the past. The appearance of Scott as a novelist is explained as dependent on the spirit of the age, but in his discussion of *Rob Roy* the reviewer does not mention historical change. He praises Scott for his unstudied descriptions of the contrast between Bailie Jarvis and the Highlanders, unlike E. T. A. Hoffmann's descriptions of philistinism versus poetry, but does not mention that Rob Roy says to Frank in Chapter 35 that he is 'vexed' to think of his sons 'living their father's life'. The uncertainty about their future expressed in that utterance is also found in the abridged Danish 1821 edition.

The best Danish Scott criticism from this early period is Molbech's, written in reviews of Danish literature. The most well-known example, the one considered here, is his review of the poet and novelist Bernhard Severin Ingemann's novel *Valdemar Seier* (Valdemar the Victorious)[5] in *Nordisk Tidsskrift for Historie, Literatur og Konst* (Nordic Journal of History, Literature and Art 2, 260–308 (1828),). Whereas the reviews in *Dansk Litteratur-Tidende* are rather short, Molbech's articles are long and repetitive, but extremely instructive. Molbech is not blind to the existence of a Scott vogue, but he is convinced of the merits of the Scotsman's novels. A historical novel, he argues, is a work of fiction in which the author 'without sacrificing poetry must not violate history' (267).[6] Scott, he thinks, had succeeded in that in his novels, whereas Ingemann had not in *Valdemar Seier*. Molbech also emphasizes verisimilitude in Scott's novels, one instance being the foregrounding of ordinary people instead of great historical figures. It is quite credible that Molbech may have been influenced in his Scott criticism by Anglophone criticism, such as Jeffrey's (Lindström 1925, 121–22; Nielsen 1976, I: 313), but altogether, he managed in these reviews to point to a number of characteristics of Scott's novels which later critics, for example Lukács and Daiches, have described and discussed as among Scott's major contributions to the development of the novel. As late as 1849, Molbech tells Atterbom in a letter that he has come to detest historical novels, but adds: 'I remain faithful to W. Scott only.'[7]

In 1833 Johan Ludvig Heiberg (1791–1860), poet and critic, published a small book *Om Philosophiens Betydning for den nuværende Tid* (On the importance of philosophy for the present age), in which he sees poetry becoming philosophy in didactic poems such as Dante's and Calderon's. English literature, he says, cannot boast 'one single speculative head.' ('Et eneste speculativt Hoved'). 'England's new Shakespeare too, Walter Scott, blind to the present age and living in the past only, is completely realistic, because he is entirely national,

---

[5] The second word, meaning 'victory', is now always written 'sejr', and is in later editions of the novel too.

[6] 'uden at bortgive *Poesien*, ikke maa krænke *Historien*'.

[7] 'Kun W. Scott bliver jeg tro' (Borup 1956, III: 41).

even provincial'(43).[8] As Heiberg sees it, his national character prevented Scott from expressing ideas. In that same year the poet Adam Oehlenschläger (1779–1850) published in his periodical *Prometheus* IV the treatise 'Om det Musikalske, det Philophiske, det Maleriske og det Historiske i Poesien' (On the musical, the philosophical, the picturesque and the historical in poetry). He praises Scott as a great immortal poet, a painter of historical portraits: 'Is there not in Walter Scott's historical portraits greater penetration into the many-sided tendencies of the human spirit than in Byron's monotonous proud egoism?'[9]

Already in Scott's lifetime there had been competitors for the readers' favour, and now after his death it was the time to take an overall view of his life and works, as new writers arrived on the scene. In Carl Bagger's novel *Min Broders Levnet* (The life of my brother, 1835) the narrator uses a quotation from 'Walter Scott's Literary Heir and Successor'.[10] That quotation is from the Danish translation (1834) of Bulwer-Lytton's novel *Paul Clifford*: Danish critics had already called him 'Scott's successor'.

Scott was in the 1830s already a classic to refer to or to compare new authors with. Bulwer-Lytton was soon eclipsed by Dickens, and in April 1844 the journal *Ny Portefeuille* (The new portfolio) published Dickens's portrait with an article on his life and works. We are told here that Dickens often 'has his characters with great drastic effect speak the language of the lower ranks, but never oversteps the line of beauty, an asset which both Bulwer and Marryat, indeed Walter Scott himself, might envy him.'[11]

Swedish criticism

Much of the early Swedish Scott criticism resembles what we have seen in Denmark (Lindström, 99–142). In *Swensk literatur-tidning*, 1821 (50: 789) the critic Vilhelm Frederik Palmblad (1788–1852) mentions in an article on contemporary Swedish literature that English poets like Scott, Byron and others have 'struck notes for which the one-sided admirers of Addison and Pope have no ear' (Lindström, 104). Rahbek wrote something very similar, but the Swedish periodical makes the point that those 'notes' are surprisingly similar to what you find in contemporary German literature.

In the periodical *Heimdall* the critic and linguist Johan Erik Rydqvist (1800–77), its editor from 1828–32, frequently discussed Scott in his articles, as

---

[8] 'Ogsaa Englands nye Shakespeare, Walter Scott, blind for det Nærværende og blot levende i det Forbigangne, er aldeles realistisk, fordi han er national, ja endog provinciel.'

[9] 'er der i de Walter Scottske historiske Portrætter ikke en større Indtrængen i den menneskelige Aands fleersidige Retninger, end i Byrons monotone stolte Egoismus?'

[10] 'Walter Scotts litteraire Arving og Successor' (Bagger 1928, IX: 73).

[11] 'Han lader sine Personer ofte med stor drastisk Virkning tale de lavere Stænders Sprog, men overskrider aldrig Skjønhedslinien, et Fortrin, hvorfor baade Bulwer og Marryat, ja selv Walter Scott kunne misunde ham.'

he had already done in a prize paper. To Rydqvist, contemporary literature attempts to unite descriptions of outward and inward movements, and Scott's treatment of the individual, the national, the historical and the local are examples ready at hand. He emphasizes, not surprisingly, Scott's poetical treatment of history and his objectivity. Rydqvist was familiar with English literary criticism and with Molbech's reviews. The Dane was the friend of some of the new Swedish men of letters; we have already seen him as the correspondent of Atterbom.

We must also mention Erik Gustaf Geijer (1783–1847), poet and from 1817 professor of history at Uppsala, who in his *Litteratur-bladet* (1839: 2) published a review of Lockhart's biography with a respectful attitude to Scott and his oeuvre, a poetry that is derived from life itself and with an emphasis on reality.

Private letters and memoirs. Influence in Denmark

From private letters and memoirs we have ample evidence of Scott's popularity. Like Rahbek, Oehlenschläger exchanged some letters and books with Scott, using Feldborg as his courier, and from his first letter, dated 7 May 1822, it seems clear that he was already acquainted with twelve of the Waverley novels (Preisz III: 194–99).

The writer Bernhard Severin Ingemann (1789–1862) praises Scott's depictions of situations and characters in a letter of 10 September 1822 to the German poet Ludwig Tieck, but, he says, he often misses in the novels, 'a pervading great general idea'.[12] Ingemann was an established poet already, steeped in German Romanticism, but in the 1820s he turned to national themes when he produced his fictional accounts of Danish medieval history: the metrical tale *Valdemar den Store og hans Mænd* (Valdemar the Great and his men, 1824), the novels *Valdemar Seier* (Valdemar the Victorious, 1826), *Erik Menveds Barndom* (The childhood of Erik Menved, 1828), *Kong Erik og de Fredløse* (King Erik and the outlaws, 1833) and *Prins Otto af Danmark og hans Samtid* (Prince Otto of Denmark and his contemporaries, 1835), concluded by the metrical tale *Dronning Margrethe* (Queen Margrethe, 1836). *I* was clearly a source of inspiration and instruction for him, not least perceptible in parts of *Kong Erik og de Fredløse*, and he admitted his indebtedness to Scott's craftsmanship, but in the preface to *Prins Otto af Danmark* he emphasizes that he wants to take his own path, aiming at the attention of his compatriots, relying on information from old chronicles and ballads and foregrounding historical, not fictional characters. Recent scholarship has argued that in *I* the difference between Scott and Ingemann is not conspicuous, as King Richard could be regarded as the hero (Hjørnager Pedersen). Ingemann's purpose in writing his historical novels is clear from *Valdemar den Store* (I,12), where he calls upon the people of bygone ages to 'show us where your salvation came from' ('vis os, hvorfra din Frelse

---

[12]   'eine durchgehende grosze Totalidee', here quoted from Galster 1922: 30.

kom!'). Ingemann and his contemporaries still lived in the aftermath of war and defeat.

Carsten Hauch (1790–1872) was a poet and a scientist. During a study tour in Southern Europe he developed an inflammation in his right foot, which was amputated in Naples in 1825. In his *Minder fra min første Udenlandsreise* (Recollections of my first journey abroad, Copenhagen, 1871) he recounts how a friend brought him books, primarily Anglophone ones, on his sickbed, so he could 'become better acquainted with Byron and with such works by Walter Scott as I had formerly not read in the original' (113–14).[13] Like Ingemann, Hauch, who is today primarily remembered as a lyric poet, began to write historical novels. In *Vilhelm Zabern* (1834), his first novel, we are told that Hauch has got hold of the fictional Vilhelm Zabern's memoirs in manuscript and reproduced them in nineteenth-century Danish. The scene is laid in early sixteenth-century Norway and Denmark, and Zabern, born in Norway like Hauch, becomes intimately acquainted with King Christian II and his court. We witness the Reformation of the Church, and Hauch uses supernatural machinery as Scott does in *The Monastery*, set in Scotland in the same period.

Steen Steensen Blicher (1782–1848) had published poems and a translation of Ossian, when he became acquainted with Scott's novels and in his vicarage in Jutland began to write his short stories (Nørvig 246–48), which have secured his place in Danish literature. In his youth he had taught himself English, but the British bombardment in September 1807 destroyed the young student's earthly possessions in the metropolis and not unnaturally did some damage to his anglophilia. Like Scott, Blicher was familiar with his native soil: the then extensive heaths in central Jutland with the inhabitants' local speech, local legends and traditions, which furnished the material for his best short stories. Blicher's change to writing primarily prose was apparently stimulated by his familiarity with Scott, though it should not be forgotten that the interest in traditional lore was in the air in the age of Romanticism.

If Blicher's literary performance bears the mark of Scott's influence, it is no surprise to find echoes of the Scotsman in his stories. Thus Langemargrethe in 'Fjorten Dage i Jylland' ('Fourteen Days in Jutland') is Blicher's depiction of an eighteenth-century robber woman, but she bears a strong resemblance to Meg Merrilies in *GM*. Elsewhere, there is a parallel with *The Antiquary*.

As in Scott there is much realism in Blicher's descriptions. Both had their roots in the eighteenth century, and in Blicher's story 'Røverstuen' (The Robber's Nest) he parodies shallow Romanticism. Chapter 2 of that story opens with some sarcastic remarks on attempts always to look for foreign influence on Danish literature. But detailed descriptions in Scott's manner 'pay better in other countries than here, where books are borrowed rather than bought'.[14] Blicher was always in straitened circumstances.

---

[13] 'gjøre nærmere Bekjendtskab med Byron og med de Arbeider af Walter Scott, som jeg tidligere ikke havde læst i Originalsproget.'

[14] 'bedre betale sig i andre Lande end her, hvor man hellere laaner Bøger end køber dem'.

An amusing illustration of the rush to get hold of a Scott novel, and a reminder to us not to forget the existence of private loans, is furnished by the poet Christian Winther (1796–1876), who in his youth spent three years studying divinity at his stepfather's vicarage far from the temptations of the metropolis. In a letter of 10 October 1821 to a fellow student in Copenhagen he wrote: 'I did not lend your Kerker in Edinburgh to Rosenkilde, Krøyer did, and I don't know where it has gone since.'[15] On 16 August 1825, after his return to Copenhagen, he wrote to another friend of his regretting that he could read the English poets in translation only (Borup 1974, I: 41).

A slightly younger man was Hans Christian Andersen (1805–75), who in 1822 left Odense to seek his fortune in Copenhagen. In *Mit Livs Eventyr* (The fairy-tale of my life; I: 75) he tells how in 1822 he read Scott for the first time; his novels were 'a new world I looked into; I forgot here the need of reality around me and gave to the circulating library what I was to buy a midday meal for'.[16] According to Andersen's *Levnedsbog*, 89–90, some unfinished memoirs not published till 1926, the novel in question was Boye's translation of *HM*, which had appeared in March 1822. Young Andersen 'felt a holy shudder at the thought of the delight of being a poet'.[17] In 1823 he received some Scott novels as Christmas presents, and there are, not surprisingly, in Andersen's works and letters many references to the Scotsman.

The influence of Scott is found in two of Andersen's novels at least: *O.T.* (1836) and *De to Baronesser* (The two baronesses, 1848), most demonstrable in the latter, where Elisabeth, the young heroine, under the influence of Jeanie Deans leaves her home on one of the Frisian islands, till 1864 part of the United Monarchy, and travels all the way to Copenhagen to save the life of a friend, who has been reported to have murdered a fellow sailor. Like Scott (and Blicher) Andersen gives precise descriptions of places at the time in question and draws on much local tradition.

Altogether, Danish readers enjoyed Scott's novels, though they often found his descriptions too long. His non-fiction is occasionally referred to in private letters too, above all *The Life of Napoleon Bonaparte*, which revived the sad memories of the year 1807, but also his works on older English authors.

Private letters and memoirs. Influence in Norway

The period of early Scott reception was also the period when Norwegian fiction was establishing itself, now that the country's cultural capital was no longer Copenhagen. A pioneer in that process was the schoolmaster and writer Maurits (or 'Mauritz') Christopher Hansen (1794–1842). His few novels, the

---

[15] 'Din *Kerker in Edinburgh* har ikke *jeg* men Krøyer laant til Rosenkilde, og siden veed jeg ikke, hvor den er kommet hen' (Borup 1974, I: 14).

[16] 'en ny Verden, jeg saae ind i; jeg glemte her Virkelighedens Trang omkring mig og gav til Leiebiblioteket, hvad jeg skulde kjøbe Middagsspise for.'

[17] 'følte en hellig Gysen ved Tanken om det Herlige at være Digter.'

first one from 1819, and his numerous prose stories are scarcely read today, but they have secured him a place in literary history as an innovator who introduced features from contemporary European literature, both popular and more refined, into Norwegian fiction. A recent study is Tysdahl 1988, with its precursor Tysdahl 1983.

On 14 September 1823 Hansen mentions Scott, whom he has been reading, in a letter to his friend C. N. Schwach. In a letter of 20 July 1824 he writes to his friend about a novel he is working on called *Keadan eller Klosterruinen* (Keadan or the monastery ruin), which appeared in 1825: 'The treatment, which you do not know, shall – risum teneto – be Walter Scottish.'[18]

Hansen had published poems, a novel and a number of short stories, when he became acquainted with Scott in the early 1820s and began writing primarily stories for periodicals, which was probably more remunerative than producing poems and novels. Scott's example may have confirmed him in his decision to concentrate on writing prose, but the Scotsman did not prompt him to turn to historical themes; for example in *Keadan* the scene is Norway and Copenhagen in Hansen's own days. What then can be adduced to argue for Scott's influence on Hansen's writings? In his deep-probing analysis of them, Bjørn Tysdahl has pointed to some new departures in Hansen's writing after he became acquainted with Scott. He now wrote few stories with a classical or medieval background. He began to use more space on descriptions of the Norwegian countryside, and he learnt to represent the countryside as seen from the point of view of one character. The landscapes he depicts are dominated by man's activities. Country people appear in the stories in their own right and are occasionally allowed to speak in their own dialect. Taken together, all those points clearly sound 'Walter Scottish'.

The poet Henrik Wergeland (1808–45) read Scott in Danish translations, not only novels, but also *The Life of Napoleon Bonaparte*, from which book he probably derived the impression of Bonaparte as the liberator of the peoples and the enemy of the princes, which he develops in his poem 'Napoleon' (1827).[19]

In the oeuvre of Andreas Munch (1811–84), history plays a prominent part. After his appearance on the literary scene with a volume of poetry in 1836, he later produced some historical plays and may have had Scott in mind in his depictions of conflicts in Norwegian history. Like anybody else of his generation he had read Scott. As a schoolboy in Christiansand he borrowed novels by Scott and Ingemann from a circulating library (Munch 1874).

Scott's impact is obvious in Munch's novel *Pigen fra Norge* (The maid of Norway, 1861). Even the subtitle 'Historisk-romantisk Fortælling' ('Historical-romantic tale') is reminiscent of many Danish Scott translations, where identical or similar subtitles are used, clearly attempts to render the English word 'romance'. The story opens: 'One evening at the beginning of the month of

---

[18] 'Behandlingen som du ikke kjender, skal – risum teneto – være Walter Scottisk' (Tysdahl 1983: 478 and 1988: 97).
[19] Wergeland, *Samlede Skrifter* I: 177–90. Beyer, 2: 21 and 97–99.

May in the year AD 1300', one year after the accession to the throne of Haakon V, who had immediately got rid of some of his predecessor's trusted men.[20] One of them, Bjarne Lodinssøn, the former chancellor, appears in Chapter 1, where he is on his way to the castle of Audum Hugleiksson, 'The fallen Noble' ('Den faldne Stormand'), as the title of Chapter 2 goes. Audum is introduced in a detailed historical account at the beginning of Chapter 2.

Thus the story is laid precisely in time; it incorporates much historical fact, which is occasionally elucidated in footnotes; it contains some historical characters, who play a more prominent part than in Scott's novels; and Norwegian natural scenery is described in all its splendour. The maid of Norway is Margrethe, King Haakon's niece, who was reported dead in the Orkney Islands many years earlier. Rumours among the common people would have it that she is not dead, but grew up in humble surroundings in Lübeck. She is now grown-up, and the fallen nobles would like to see her as heir to the throne of Norway. But they fail in their attempt. At a trial she is declared an impostor, and she is burnt at the stake. Audun is found hanged, but Bjarne Lodinssøn, a scheming, repulsive politician, changes sides, denounces her as an impostor, and saves his skin (the historical Bjarne died in 1311). The Scotsman Ronald Glennorrin, a fictitious character, is an inexperienced young man who falls victim to the machinations of Bjarne and Audun.

Munch sent copies of his new book to Hauch and Ingemann, who commended it in their letters of thanks. Hauch makes a comparison with Ingemann, but neither of them mentions Scott (Munch 1954:103–6). But then, twenty-nine years had passed since the Scotsman's death, and so many historical novels had appeared in that period.

On 16 January 1871 Munch wrote a letter to the Danish poet Christian K. F. Molbech (1821–88) about a work he was engaged on: a translation of *The Lady of the Lake* (123–24). He writes that as far as he knows Scott's metrical tales have not been translated, so he cannot have been aware of P. D. Ibsen's 1836 translation. Munch's translation, entitled *Pigen ved Søen* like Ibsen's, was published in 1871. Both have preserved the original's octosyllabic iambic lines and furnish explanatory notes, mostly built on those of the original. Both have kept close to the original, but Munch, appreciably a poet, frequently moves more freely; for example he expands the text and uses sixteen lines where Scott and Ibsen confine themselves to fourteen.

In the second half of the nineteenth century Norwegian literature reached a peak, not least in the dramas of Henrik Ibsen (1828–1906). Ibsen had read Scott in his youth, and may well have had the Scotsman in mind when he depicted national emergencies in his dramas. But Ibsen was also an admirer of Maurits Hansen's stories, and may have learnt from him too, perhaps an indirect Scott influence. Another important figure in Norwegian literature is Bjørnstjerne Bjørnson (1832–1910). On 23 December 1877 Mrs Augusta Marie Hall in Denmark wrote a letter to him, mentioning Clara, a character in his play *Kongen* (The King, 1877): 'she reminds me of Walter Scott's female characters, give us

---

[20] 'En Aften i Begyndelsen af Mai Maaned, Aar efter Christi Byrd 1300'.

more in that direction.'[21] Mrs Hall may be right, but after half a century Scott's female characters will have been appreciated and perhaps imitated by many later writers.

Private letters and memoirs. Influence in Sweden

In 1828 the Swedish periodical *Heimdall* informed its readers that 'a university teacher in Uppsala intended to give us a Swedish novel in the manner of Walter Scott.'[22] That university teacher was Gustaf Wilhelm Gumælius (1789–1877), and his novel *Thord Bonde eller slutet av Konung Albrechts regering*, I (Thord the Peasant or the end of King Albrecht's reign, I) appeared later in 1828. Albrecht was both Duke of Mecklenburg and King of Sweden, and the German influence was not popular with the Swedish nobles. In 1389 he was defeated and taken prisoner by the Danish Queen Margrethe. Stockholm remained true to the King and was assisted by the Vitalie Brethern, freebooters whose ships harassed the Baltic.

The story opens one night on board one of those ships. Thord, the protagonist, is there as the prisoner of the freebooters, is taken to their camp and is dramatically liberated at the end of the volume; but a second volume never appeared. The 'first Swedish original attempt in this branch of literature',[23] as the preface has it, remained unfinished.

The title of the book is reminiscent of *Waverley*, and Thord is the young courageous hero who is caught up in the turmoil of war. Lüdiger, the captain of the ship, appears similar to Dirk Hatteraick in *Guy Mannering*, whose oath 'Donner and hagel' in Chapter 47 may have led to Gumælius having Lüdiger say 'Dunder och blixt' (p. 21).

Another historical novel is *Snapphanarne: Gammalt nytt om Skåne från sjuttonde seklet* (The guerrillas: old news about Scania from the seventeenth century, 1831) by the pseudonymous 'O.K'. 'Svenskt original' ('Swedish Original'), the title page says, to assure us that this is not a translation. The descriptions of the horrors of guerrilla warfare, in which pro-Danish guerrillas try to harm the Swedish army as much as possible, are realistic, and, like Scott, the author tries to be fair to both parties.

The year 1832 saw the appearance of the novel *Den siste friseglaren* (The last freebooter), I–III by Pehr Sparre, colonel and writer. The period is the end of the sixteenth century, when the Polish King Sigismund was also King of Sweden, and there was a war between him and Duke Karl, the regent.. As in *W* the conflict is both political and religious. The narrator's attitude is emphatically anti-Catholic, and the first seven pages are devoted to a historical

---

[21] 'hun minder mig om Walter Scotts Quindetegninger, giv os flere i samme Retning' (Anker, Bull and Nielsen I: 119).

[22] 'en Academisk lärare i Upsala hade i sinnet, at gifva oss en Svensk roman à la Walter Scott' (Lindström 186).

[23] 'det första svenska originalförsök i detta vitterhetsslag'.

elucidation of the discrepancy between the northern mentality and Catholicism. Sparre is meticulous in his treatment of historical facts. Each volume ends with explanatory notes, and in I: 8 he opens his story almost overprecisely: 'At the beginning of the month of August O.S. in the year 1598 two men sat conversing animatedly at Stålboda Manor, situated in the northern part of the province of Jönköping.'[24]

A Swedish novelist of greater stature than the three historical novelists is Fredrika Bremer (1801–65). On 6 October 1834 she wrote to her friend Böklin: 'Walter Scott! Dear B, how I love him. . . . Reading Walter Scott I feel vividly that the direction the novel and the drama have taken in several countries towards the ugly and uncanny is really bad.'[25] As examples she mentions Bulwer-Lytton's novels about criminals and Balzac's 'talented' depictions of everyday life. A few months after this declaration of love for Scott she published her epistolary novel *Grannarne* (1837), in which the scene is laid in her own time, but as in the case of Maurits Hansen she may have been stimulated by Scott to produce realistic novels.

Interestingly, in a review in *Dansk Litteratur-Tidende* 1835 (23: 362) of Thomasine Gyllembourg's (1773–1856) *Nye Fortællinger* (New tales), literary language is said to have developed immensely in the previous decades, one of the important factors being Scott. Gyllembourg's novels and tales are not historical ones, neither are Hans Christian Andersen's novels *Improvisatoren* (The improvisatore) and *O. T.*, but a reviewer of those two novels in *Maanedsskrift for Litteratur* (The Monthly Literary Journal) 1837 (18: 63) emphasizes the healthy impact on literature of Scott's depictions of the world his characters live in.

Theatrical performances

The Scott vogue in the 1820s and 1830s is apparent on the stage as well. In January 1824 *Tempelherre-Retten* (The Templars' Court), C. J. Boye's translation of Lenz's German adaptation for the stage of *Ivanhoe* was on in Copenhagen. On 29 January 1829 the Royal Theatre in Copenhagen celebrated the King's birthday with the first performance of *Pigen ved Søen*, Rossini's ballad opera *La donna del lago* (*LL*) in Johan Ludvig Heiberg's Danish translation of the Italian libretto. Heiberg's text had appeared in print in 1828. Hans Christian Andersen adapted two Scott novels for the stage: *Bruden fra Lammermoor* (The Bride of Lammermoor) to the music of Ivar Frederik Bredal (performance and printed edition, 1832) and *Festen paa Kenilworth* (The Celebration at Kenilworth) to the music of Christoph Ernst Frederik Weyse (performance and printed edition of songs, 1836). Marschner's opera and Wohlbrück's libretto in Thomas Overskou's

---

[24] 'I början af Augusti månad, efter gamla stilen, år 1598, sutto på Stålboda Herregård belägen i norra delen af Jönköpings Län, tvenne män under ett liffligt samtal.'

[25] 'Walter Scott! Min goda B hvad jag älskar honom . . . Läsande Walter-scott känner jag klart att den rigtning roman och Theaterlitteraturen i flera länder tagit till det otäcka och ohyggliga, verkligen är skadlig' (Johanson and Kleman I: 304).

translation, *Tempelherren og Jødinden* (The Templar and the Jewess), another adaptation of *Ivanhoe*, had its first performance in Copenhagen on 21 April 1834. In 1842–43 an Italian opera company gave several performances of *Lucia di Lammermoor* in the Court Theatre in Copenhagen.

Scott's last days

In the summer of 1832 Scott's journey home from Italy, his ominous illness and his return to Abbotsford were reported on. His death was announced in the newspapers in early October, and in the following months his funeral, the settlement of his debt and other biographical details were described or mentioned. But trees do not grow into the sky, and politically antagonistic criticism found expression in two notices in *Nyeste Morgenpost* (The Newest Morning Post) 9, 28/1 1833 and *Allernyeste Skilderie af Kjøbenhavn* (The Very Latest Picture of Copenhagen) 10, 1/2 1833. In both cases the source is a German article. Scott the old reactionary, we are given to understand, died appropriately after the passing of the Reform Bill, which he opposed. As an antidote readers could at the same time read Bulwer-Lytton's sympathetic 'Death of Sir Walter Scott' in *The New Monthly Magazine* 35: 300–04 (1832), in which the author, ideologically distant from Scott, asserts that the Scotsman's depictions of common people were more beneficial to their cause than the writings of such poets as Byron, Shelley and Moore. That obituary was printed in Danish translation under the title 'Walter Scott. Skizze af Bulwer' ('Walter Scott. Sketch by Bulwer') in *Nyeste Repertorium for Moerskabs-Læsning* (The Newest Magazine for Leisure Reading) 1, on 5 January 1833. Not all those items were of Danish origin, but they belong to the impressions that Danish readers received of Scott.

Late nineteenth-century criticism: Georg Brandes

A comprehensive discussion of British literature in the early decades of the nineteenth century was delivered by the critic Georg Brandes (1842–1927) in his lectures on French, German and English literature in that period. Brandes delivered his lectures at the University of Copenhagen, beginning on 3 November 1871. Having obtained a doctoral degree he was entitled to teach at the university, where he aspired to the Chair of Aesthetics, but failed in his attempt. The lectures, which were delivered over a number of years, were later published under the title *Hovedstrømninger i det nittende Aarhundredes Litteratur* (Main currents in nineteenth century literature), which has run through a number of editions and been translated into several languages His work is literary scholarship and also propaganda for 'free thought', and in the preface to the sixth edition of the entire work (1923) he argues that its design is 'political, not literary' ('politisk, ikke literært' (I: 3)). Brandes's influence was considerable in bringing about what came to be known as 'the modern transition' ('det moderne Gennembrud') in Danish literature in its swerve away from post-Romanticism.

Brandes's lectures on English literature were delivered in the spring of 1874 and the autumn of 1875 and appeared in print as volume 4 of the entire work under the title *Naturalismen i England* (Naturalism in England, 1875), originally with the subtitle *Byron og hans Gruppe* (Byron and his group), a clear indication of who his hero was. English literature, he argues, shook off the fetters of Classicism, and the threat of Napoleonic hegemony led to nationalism in many countries. In Britain these forces found expression in 'Naturalism', love of nature and Realism, and Naturalism led to Radicalism, to 'a gigantic revolt against religious and political reaction' ('et mægtigt Oprør mod religiøs og politisk Reaktion') (5). Scott is clearly not an exponent of Radicalism, but Brandes respects him as a noble character, who could in his turn respect men whose attitudes were vastly different from his own.

Among the novels Brandes discusses only a few in some detail, and he rightly emphasizes the novelty of Scott's depicting specific countries at specific periods. But Brandes, adopting a rather facile evolutionism, adds: 'If we look back from the height of our age to his second period of composition, that of prose, and the long sequence of novels, we are unable to see them in the light they stood in to his contemporaries'[26] (191). They were bound to gratify readers, as they never caused offence, and were moral as well as poetical. In modern literature, Brandes argues, we can 'without exaggeration set up the law that an author must be thought immoral and cause offence to one generation at least among his contemporaries, if he is not to be regarded as dull and narrow-minded already by the next generation' (191).[27] The reader, Brandes says, enjoys the delineation of characters and the lively dialogue, but the novels lack ideas. And Brandes concludes his chapter on Scott with another touch of evolutionism: 'It brings its own punishment on a poet in the present century to be unaffected by the march of modern science and scholarship' (195).[28] Scott was *unaffected*, and consequently he has with his followers and kindred spirits in all the countries of Europe 'become the favourite author of boys and girls around the age of fourteen, a poet whom all adults have read and no adult ever reads' (196).[29] Brandes does not dispute Scott's importance in literary history, but believes that as an author his days are over.

Twentieth-century reception

There is no denying the truth in Brandes's concluding words: Scott is no longer read by adults. The vast majority of Danish editions of Scott since the 1870s are intended for children.

---

[26] 'See vi fra vor Tids Høide tilbage paa det andet Tidsrum af hans Digtning, Prosa-Perioden, og den hele lange Rækkefølge af Romaner, saa er det een ikke muligt at see dem i samme Lys, hvori de stode i hans Samtid.'

[27] 'uden Overdrivelse opstille den Lov, at en Skribent *maa* gjælde for umoralsk og maa vække Anstød idetmindste hos een Generation af sin Samtid, hvis han ikke allerede skal forekomme den ham nærmest følgende Generation triviel og bornert.'

[28] 'Det hævner sig i dette Aarhundrede paa en Digter at være uberørt af den hele moderne Videnskabs Gang.'

[29] 'bleven Yndlingsdigteren for Drenge og Piger omkring Fjortenaarsalderen, en Digter, som alle Voxne *have* læst og ingen Voxen nogensinde læser.'

An attempt to make children aware of Scott as an interesting man and the author of a great number of exciting novels was made by Josepha Martensen in her *Walter Scott: En Fortælling om hans Liv* (Walter Scott: A story of his life, 1920). An elderly lady here gives her grandchildren a detailed account of the life of Scott, the good Christian, and she gives vivid synopses of a number of the novels.

The translations prepared for youthful readers are abridged ones, and in some cases they are abridgments of an old translation. P. V. Grove's translation of *I* came out in 1883, and in 1899 he published it in an abridged version, on the title page indicated as such, but apparently not intended as a translation for children. In 1944 *I* appeared in an edition 'abridged and adjusted for youthful readers by Henrik Madsen, Headmaster'. No translator is mentioned, but it is clearly Grove's translation. Today Scott is primarily thought of as the author of *I*, also available as strip cartoons, and, to a much lesser degree, of *QD* and *T*.

However, *I*, *QD* and *GM* appeared, in 1976, 1978 and 1987 respectively, in modern unabridged translations, the first two by Svend Jensen, the third by Luise Pihl. This undertaking would appear financially risky, but Hernov's publishing house had, as in its other editions of classical Anglophone novels in translation, allied itself with the Nyt Dansk Litteraturselskab (New Danish Literary Society), which helps to supply public libraries with good literature. It seems credible that the choice of two quite well-known novels and an eminently entertaining one to open the new Scott edition was done with an eye to its marketability; but only those three Scott translations have appeared.

These three novels are beautifully embellished with old British illustrations. The translations include mottoes, inset poetry and many footnotes, but not prefaces or long end-notes. Svend Jensen has adopted easily-read modern Danish with a suitable tinge of the past. In Luise Pihl's *GM* there are occasional unfortunate translations, but she has been careful to preserve the Scottish character (e.g. 'laird'), and she has done well in preserving the linguistic characterization, substituting Jutlandish dialect for Scottish.

A glance at Norwegian and Swedish catalogues of books gives a very similar impression of Scott's status. It is perhaps not surprising that nothing by him is included in the Swedish poet Gunnar Harding's marvellous presentation in Swedish translation of Anglophone Romantic literature, mostly poetry. These translations with introductions and interpretation are found in three volumes that appeared in 1997, 2000 and 2002.

Scott on the stage was marvellously revived in June 2003, when the Royal Theatre produced *Ivanhoe*, by Jørgen Ljungdalh and Jokum Rohde on the basis of Scott's novel, as an open-air performance in Dyrehaven, a wood north of Copenhagen. A lavish performance saw mail-clad knights on live horses, and Torquilstone, here called Mørkeborg (Castle of Darkness), going up in flames in the darkening wood. Although Scott survives only slenderly in modern editions and scholarship, this was a welcome revisiting of a world that was for a long span of years 'foray'd' by Scandinavians avid for every word issuing from the Laird of Abbotsford.

15 European Reception of Scott's Poetry: Translation as the Front Line

Tom Hubbard

'Behold the Tiber!' the vain Roman cried,
Viewing the ample Tay from Baiglie's side;
But where's the Scot that would the vaunt repay,
And hail the puny Tiber for the Tay?
(Scott 1904, 832)

Heading the first chapter of *The Fair Maid of Perth* (1828), this 'motto' offers an irreverent take on reciprocally directed comparisons between diverse lands and cultures. The north–south polarity is apt, given nineteenth-century European perceptions of Scotland as a distant, exotic outpost; next stop, Thule. Walter Scott was initially received as a poet, and as the successor to an earlier Scottish poet, James Macpherson. Macpherson (1736–96) – in his persona of Ossian – was perceived by many, including the Hungarian poet János Arany, as the north's preferred (and preferable) counterpart to the south's Homer. South Europeans did not always go out of their way to dispute this; twelve years after the death of the Wizard of the North, the Spaniard Vicente Boix published a turgid verse memorial, retrospectively praising Scott 'que entre las nobles sombras / De Fingal y de Ossian eterno vives' (Boix 1845). As will become clear in the following pages, other southerners were not quite so generous.

The most celebrated theorist of literary reception, Wolfgang Iser, has written of the processes of familiarization and defamiliarization in the act of reading, of how we bring our accumulation of existing experience and consciousness to bear on the new text before us. An expository text, as befits its function and content, requires utilitarian clarity; a literary text, however, invites and (indeed constantly) attracts the reader as active participant, as co–creator of its potentially multiple meanings. Iser invokes Gestalt psychology as he analyses the activity of reading, which 'can be characterized as a sort of kaleidoscope of perspectives, preintentions, recollections' (1988: 215). The reader's responses constantly metamorphose as he/she reads, as their preconceptions undergo modification as each stage of the text is negotiated, above all as he/she faces the challenge of 'indeterminacy' in that text – which 'indeterminacy' exists only in literary, and not expository, works. Such indeterminacy, which Iser calls the 'gaps' and 'blanks' in interpretation – our 'not-knowing' – serve only to excite the reader's curiosity; whatever meanings he/she lacks induces their acquisition. Take this further: the case of a newly encountered literature/language culture – as also the author's œuvre – within which an individual text is situated. Here, the desire of Self for Other operates on a more expansive plane than that of the individual text per se, and it is here that Iser's original reader-response theory opens into his concept of 'literary anthropology'. In other words, the dialectic between reader and text implies a significance beyond the narrowly 'literary', with implications for human communication generally, and our need to communicate in the first place with those who are not ourselves, and upon matters that have not originally 'belonged' to us. 'We appear to want to be ourselves', writes Iser, 'and simultaneously outside ourselves. If that seems to be a basic human situation – a way of extending ourselves – then this question of assembling an array of conventions horizontally in the literary text might be a way of looking at the regulatory functions according to which human beings conduct their lives' (Iser 1997–98: 6). Within literature, it is the translator who can arrange such intercultural meetings, meriting praise as international diplomat or risking blame as international pimp. To emphasize the obvious, the translator precedes the reviewer; he or she is at the front line of reception.

In Scott's case, this is not to downplay Macpherson/Ossian as precursor, especially as regards popular European preconceptions of Scottish landscape and 'atmosphere'. It's a commonplace that *LL* created the Scottish tourist industry, clarifying as it did existing 'Ossianic' notions – but not clarifying too much: Scott's Trossachs are depicted with sufficient vagueness to excite visitors to come and see for themselves. Theodor Fontane, in 1858, came to Scotland as both tourist and literary professional – the two need not be mutually exclusive – and noted that it was 'really quite sensible that on the breakfast tables of Stirling you should find, alongside the latest newspapers, considerable quantities of gilt-edged copies of *The Lady of the Lake* in red and green bindings' (Fontane 1965 [1860], 104).

The poems' accumulated charisma could lead other Continental visitors into embarrassing misapprehensions. During the early 1820s the French writer Charles Nodier visited Loch Katrine, doubtless mindful of the iconic scene where James Fitz-James encounters the young boatwoman, Ellen Douglas, as she rows ashore. Nodier himself encountered a Loch Katrine boatwoman who sang for him a Gaelic song. Nodier was so moved that he went on to publish an account of his epiphanic moment. Some time later, however, a Gaelic speaker wrote to *Blackwood's Magazine*, claiming that he knew both the boatwoman and her song, which was not the noble chant that Nodier thought it was. It was in fact a satire on a local laird and his exercising of his presumed *droits de seigneur* with all the comely wenches in the vicinity of the loch (Roe 1953, 67–68).

Nodier's compatriot and friend, Amédée Pichot, was a prolific translator of Scott's works, including the poetry, into French. In his *Vues pittoresques de l'Ecosse* (Paris: Gosselin, 1826), Pichot solemnly advises us that one visits Loch Katrine with a copy of *The Lady of the Lake* in one's hand, just as one visits Lake Avernus with a copy of Virgil's *Aeneid*. Pichot is aware that there are at least two

European countries competing in the picturesque stakes, and declares that 'The Switzerland of William Tell [. . .] has found a rival in the Scotland of Wallace'. Now, in 1826, according to Pichot, there are as many pilgrims at Loch Katrine as there are at the Lake of Geneva (quoted in Bisson 1943, 329).

Commodities or Icons?

Towards the end of Scott's life, from the late 1820s on, his shorter poems were appearing in French translation in 'keepsakes', a form of periodical – more precisely, an almanac – originating in Britain. A 'keepsake' was published as an attractive little volume to be given as a present; it would be printed on paper of high quality, and adorned with steel engravings. These publications carried such titles as *Album littéraire: receuil de morceaux choisis de littérature contemporaine, Livre de jeunesse et de beauté, Le chansonnier de graces, Almanach dédié aux demoiselles, Hommage aux dames*: there is no need to labour the point about the intended market and readership (Lachèvre 1929). For Anglophone readers of Scott, the pieces chosen belong to the most obscure corners of his œuvre, but they were often light lyrics, literary collectables as it were, such as 'The Cypress Wreath'. This piece, which appears in *Rokeby*, is not one of the most celebrated parts of that long narrative poem, but it served its effete purpose readily enough: 'O Lady, twine no wreath for me,/ Or twine it of the cypress-tree!/ Too lively glow the lilies light,/ The varnish'd holly's all too bright' (Scott 1904, 357) is presented in the *Almanach des dames, pour l'an 1828* as 'La couronne de cypress. Imité de Walter Scott', the first line reading 'Le lis a trop d'éclat pour mon pâle visage' (The lily has too much brilliance for my pale face).

However, one detects elsewhere a certain weariness with this kind of packaging of Scott abroad, this culture of miscellanies, digests, of 'morceaux choisis'. A writer in a literary review based in Liège, Belgium, declared that Scott was an author whose worth it was difficult to judge by means of extracts, however well-chosen; to present, say, Shakespeare and Homer in gobbets would be to give a false idea of their stature (*Le Mathieu Laensbergh* 14 July 1825, quoted in Charlier 1949, 103). This more than hints at the core contradiction of the mainland European reception of Scott's poetry: the implied (and/or actual) readers are either consumers or citizens, and these two roles are not easily compatible.

However, while acknowledging that it was not altogether impossible to be both consumers and citizens, one can detect a spectrum of keepsake collectors at one end and cultural (even political) nationalists at the other. Scott himself, Tory Unionist that he was, could make statements eminently deployable as rallying calls for the champions of small countries against devouring empires. Take, for instance, the following remark to Washington Irving in 1817: 'A real old Scottish song is a cairn gorm, [. . .] a precious relic of old times, that bears the national character stamped on it, – like a cameo, that shows what the national visage was in former days, before the breed was crossed' (Quoted in Zug 1978, 229).

Literary intellectuals of east-central Europe were ripe to respond. Poland was in the early decades of what was to be its century-long partition between the powers of Prussia, Russia and Austria. Adam Mickiewicz (1798–1855), Poland's 'national' poet and the advocate of his country's 'Messianic' role in a future Europe, was a student at the University of Wilno (Vilnius), where he and his comrades, around 1820, shared their enthusiasm for the poetry of Scott (Krzyżanowski 1933–34, 181). Krystyn Lach-Szyrma (1791–1866), tutor to the Czartoryski princes, whom he accompanied on their Grand Tour, arrived in Edinburgh in 1820; he went on to take his doctorate at its university and to travel across Scotland. As a fluent writer of English, he was able to contribute to *Blackwood's Edinburgh Magazine*, his articles later comprising his book *Letters Literary and Political in Poland, Comprising Observations on Russia and Other Sclavonian Nations and Tribes* (Edinburgh, 1823). Through him the readers of *Blackwood's* learned of the rich hoard of Slavonic traditional poetry which, he reported, had been published in collections but which had not been as well served as the ballads in Scott's *Minstrelsy of the Scottish Border* (1802–03). Lach-Szyrma writes with passion, and at climactic points in his text he seems to be addressing his compatriots – albeit in English! – rather than the subscribers to the magazine: 'There should be born Sir Walter Scotts, to recal[l] from beneath the mountain-tombs (Kurhany), overgrown with moss and weeds, the bold spirit of the old Sclavonian chivalry' (Lach-Szyrma 1823, 15). Much later he sounds a sombre note: 'The Poles have reason [. . .] to brood [. . .] with far more mournful recollections than the Scots. The wrongs sustained by the Poles were heavier, as they rendered them strangers in their own country' (148–49). For present purposes his most intriguing comment is the claim that, according to the consensus, 'the most *popular* of all Scottish poets is undoubtedly Burns, and the most *national*, Sir Walter Scott' (1823, my italics).

Again we have a pair of concepts which are not mutually exclusive and are indeed mutually enhancing: Burns's popularity ensures his status as national icon, and while Scott's poetry may not be as well loved as that of Burns, insofar as it is Scottish in tone and content it has enjoyed a considerable following in the homeland. 'Popularity' is the factor common to both reader-as-consumer and reader-as-citizen. As the nineteenth century proceeded, it was the former which predominated. The failed Polish Insurrection of 1863–64 marked the decline of Romantic Messianism and, as elsewhere in Europe, the trend was towards scientific Positivism and economic individualism. Scott's compatriot Samuel Smiles, the author of *Self-Help* (1859), became the new pan-European bestseller in translation, and Scott himself became worthily exciting fare for children and young people.

In the early decades of the century, however, Lach-Szyrma's 'national' Walter Scott focused minds on the need for a struggling language-culture to acquire a corpus of creative literature. The Czechs, like the Poles, rediscovered Slavonic ballads, but enlarged their hoard by turning Scottish ballads into their own idiom. It is well known that a 'new' literature establishes itself partly by importing foreign works on the basis of permanent loan. A work of Scottish literature can become a work of Polish or Czech literature (and, hopefully, vice versa). The quarry for European literary nationalists was, initially, Bishop Thomas Percy's *Reliques of Ancient English Poetry* (1765), followed more emphatically by Scott's *Minstrelsy of the Scottish Border*, and indeed by Scott's original poetry, some of which was included in the *Minstrelsy*. Even as late as 1898 Jaroslav

Vrchlický (1853–1912), composer of original ballads and Professor of Comparative Literature at the Charles University, Prague, was publishing his Czech versions of Scott's shorter poems, together with a sizeable extract from *The Lady of the Lake*, in his anthology *Moderní básníci angličti* (Modern English poetry).

Ballad-traffic

It is worth dwelling on the continental response to the *Minstrelsy*'s contents, initially on those supplied by Scott as editor, and then on those supplied by Scott as author – bearing in mind that, in this case, the two functions are blurred, given Scott's creative enhancement of many of the ballads in his care. Ironically enough, the *Minstrelsy* was especially well travelled in German, the language of oppressors of central Europe; however, this could hardly render Germanophone writers any less sensitive to the poetry of the common people. Indeed, it was Johann Gottfried von Herder (1744–1803) who had so eloquently championed the particularity of each language culture against the bland universalism that had been assumed by Neoclassicism. Herder himself translated a few Scottish ballads, but it was Henriette Schubart who in 1817 brought out a German version of Scott's *Minstrelsy* as *Schottische Lieder und Balladen von Walter Scott* (Leipzig and Altenburg: Brockhaus). Four years earlier, Wilhelm Grimm had published translations of three Scottish songs, two of which he had found in the *Minstrelsy*, but he confessed later that although he had intended to translate the whole of Scott's anthology, Frau Schubart's work had overtaken him and he did not wish to crowd the market (Michaelis-Jena 1975, 46). Later German luminaries who translated Scottish ballads, together with the more ballad/folk-song-like poems of Scott, include the major poet and writer Annette Droste-Hülshoff (1797–1848) and Ferdinand Freiligrath (1810–76), poet and important translator of Burns and the English Romantic poets, as well as a revolutionary comrade of Karl Marx. The *Minstrelsy* strongly influenced the original ballad poetry of Theodor Fontane (1819–98), to whom reference has already been made, and long before he was to emulate the realism of Flaubert's *Madame Bovary* in his novel *Effi Briest* (1895), he produced in 1861 a German version of one of the *Minstrelsy*'s starkest examples of Scottish ballad realism, 'The Twa Corbies'. In Hungary, the original ballads of János Arany (1817–82) took their cue from Scott's anthology, and his version of 'Sir Patrick Spens' (1853) is a classic of Hungarian poetry in its own right, and thus a supreme example of the 'permanent loan' phenomenon.

It was a short step from the *Minstrelsy*'s anonymous contributors to the editor's own productions therein. One of his most translated pieces was 'The Eve of Saint John', and the Russian translation by Vasily Andreevich Zhukovsky (1783–1852) is of note for the very Russian nature of its publication history. When the text was submitted to the censor, objection was taken to 'the irreligious title and the lack of any "moral purpose" ' (Simmons 1935, 245). Zhukovsky was obliged to change the title to 'Zamok Smal'golm' (The Castle of Smailholm) and to modify a number of the verses [v. Altshuller].

It could not be claimed that the new title, by naming the scene of the action (a tower near Kelso), could in any way transform the piece into an accurate representation of Borders topography and culture, even if that were possible or even desirable in a Russian context. Scott's ballad is a taut, acerbic tale of illicit sex and the posthumous return of the lady's lover-warrior. When Zhukovsky's version appeared in the *Nevsky Al'manakh na 1828 god* (St Petersburg 1827, 9–16) it was accompanied by an engraving of the tryst between the lady and her ghostly paramour. At the top of the steps leading to the door is a crucifix of Russian Orthodox form, the lower of the two cross-bars at the traditional acute angle to the main bar. Such bizarre meta-morphoses are not unusual in the passage from Scottish originals to their Russian renderings: S. B. Davis (1991) has demonstrated how Scott's peasant characters had become misrepresented in Russian versions made via the unreliable intermediary agency of Defauconpret's French translations. Gogol, in particular, was an admirer of Scott, and he may have relied on these ver-sions which would present their readers not with an example of 'the best educated [i.e. Scottish] peasantry in Europe' but with a character more akin to a backward *muzhik*, like the bee-keeper in Gogol's short stories with Ukrainian settings.

'The Eve of Saint John' undertakes another strange voyage, into Dutch, as guided by Jacob van Lennep (1802–68). In his version 'De Sint Jans Nacht', van Lennep transposes the action from the Scottish Borders to the Low Countries: the first reference to Brabant appears in the third stanza (Lennep 1872 [1826], 379–81). By contrast, his compatriot Nicolaas Beets (1814–1903) remains faith-ful to the original setting: 'Vroeg zit de Heer van Smaylho'm op [. . .]'; 'Hij zoekt geen troepen van Buccleuch [. . .]' (Beets 1876 [1834], 80–88). Lennep's practice, however, was that of a confessed plagiarist; he would carry over a good number of Scott's poems without acknowledging (at least initially) their prov-enance. He would therefore feel no obligation to observe Scottish topography. The results might lead us to consider that an imaginative thief offers attractions wanting in the faithful plodder.

Dutch translators had no problem in reproducing the Scots/English ballad metre in their own, related, language. French versification requires much more of a departure, as is evident in 'La nuit de la Saint-Jean' by Antoine Fontaney (1803–67), included in his *Ballades, melodies et poésies diverses* (Paris: Hayet, 1829). The metrical 'gap' between Scots/English and French reveals Fontaney's mis-understanding of the pronunciation of the trisyllabic place-name Dryburgh: 'Il est près de Dryburgh, dans un saint monastère,/ Une Sœur qui jamais ne regarde les cieux [. . .]' ('There is a nun in Dryburgh bower,/ Ne'er looks upon the sun [. . .]' (Fontaney 1829, 25; Scott 1904, 667). In fairness to Fontaney, it must be said that the English usually pronounce the suffix – *burgh* as one syllable, and it is unlikely that the translator ever heard the place-name from Scottish lips. It is possible, even probable, that Fontaney assumed it was pronounced 'Dry-burg', but, if so, he still extended the courtesy – not always forthcoming from his compatriots – of spelling it correctly.

Clearly, issues of versification as they relate to divers target languages can illuminate comparisons of the choices made by translators, for whom 'Lochinvar' was a favourite. What follows is the first verse of the original poem, followed by van Lennep's adaptation and an anonymous Finland-Swedish version.

> O, young Lochinvar is come out of the west,
> Through all the wide Border his steed was the best;
> And save his good broadsword he weapons had none,
> He rode all unarm'd, and he rode all alone.
> So faithful in love, and so dauntless in war,
> There never was knight like the young Lochinvar.
>   (Scott 1904, 142)

> O! Culemburgs Heer kwan gereden met spoed:
> Geen paard aan de Lek als het zijne zoo goed;
> Geen wapenen droeg hy dan 't heupzwaard alleen:
> En zonder gevolg kwam hy voorwaart gereên.
> Zoo trouw aan zijn liefste en zoo kloek in 't geweer,
> Was nimmer een Ridder als Culemburgs Heer.
>   (van Lennep 1872, 71)

> O, ung Lochinvar far ut just som bäst;
> Af alla på gränsen är snabbast hans häst.
> Hans bredsvärd vid sedan, det skramlar så smått
> För öfrigt oväpnad och ensam han gått.
> Ack, ingen så tapper och trogen dock var
> I strid och i kärlek, som ung Lochinvar!
>   ('Ung Lochinvar' 1860, 349–50)

Quite apart from matters of fidelity to the original *meaning*, van Lennep again clearly 'transposes' the action, unlike his Swedish counterpart. That van Lennep is guilty of plagiarism is at best arguable; after all, he is making a new, very Dutch poem, albeit with considerable stimulus from Scott. However, the metre and rhythm of the Dutch and Swedish versions are remarkably close to those of the original English, and are models of how this can be achieved between languages which belong to the same broad family, whatever the very substantial differences between them.

Danish is much closer to Swedish than is Dutch. We would expect a Danish version, therefore, to go along with the consensus. However, Frederik Schaldemose, who was one of the leading Danish translators of Scott (of the novels as well as the poetry), opts to rework 'Lochinvar' into that form known to Scottish and English readers as the 'ballad stanza'; he does this for the first four lines of each verse, then his Danish music, so to speak, takes on a life of its own:

> Fra Norden kommer Lochinvar
> Alt paa sin Ganger god;
> I Haanden draget Sværd han har,
> I Hjertet freidigt Mod;
> Saa rider flux [?] han under Øe,
> At vinde sig sin tabte Mø,
> Og fast i Sadlen sidder
> Den fagre Nordlands Helt.
>   (Schaldemose 1826, 66–68)

Schaldemose changes the geographical polarities of the poem: in the original, Lochinvar comes 'out of the west', but here he comes from the north ('fra Norden'). Could it be that Schaldemose, as a Dane, the citizen of a northern country, is marking out Scotland as on the same latitude? It is as if there is a perception, conscious or otherwise, of a geocultural affinity.

By now it will be clear that I consider the most revealing aspects of translation-as-reception to be present in the shorter rather than the longer poems. I have cited a number of first appearances of pieces in periodicals, and of course periodicals favour short poems or cogent extracts. It is here that we can trace the very beginnings of mainland European interest in Scott. Before moving on to *LL*, that longer work which established Scott's reputation, it remains to undertake a couple of case studies of ballad-like poems which were published later than the *Minstrelsy* but which remind Scott's readers of the origins of his poetic imagination and practice.

'The Palmer', dating from 1806, is composed in the traditional ballad metre; equally traditional is Scott's reluctance to use 'he/she said' intrusions to what must be a briskly told narrative. Ballads are miniature theatre-pieces – the word 'ballad' is etymologically related to 'ballet' – and the reader must visualize, on his mind's stage as it were, which character is making a particular speech. The first stanza of 'Sir Patrick Spens' is often cited as the archetype of the ballad technique. Similarly, in 'The Palmer', from the very beginning we hear of the eponymous character's plight, and in his own words:

> O open the door, some pity to show,
>   Keen blows the northern wind!
> The glen is white with the drifted snow,
>   And the path is hard to find.

The door-keeper, so addressed, does not himself speak in the poem, nor indeed does he open the door, with tragic results. However, Antony-Béraud, in his French translation of 1835, performs on Scott's poem the kind of action which Scott himself performed on the ballads he collected: that is to say, Antony-Béraud adds his own stanzas, expanding the original ten to twenty-five. He transforms this into a dialogue between 'le pélerin' and 'le chatelain', thereby reinforcing the *theatrical* dimension of the ballad.

Antony-Béraud's change of title to 'La nuit de décembre' is not only gratuitous but unsubtle: a good ballad does not state the obvious. Freiligrath's German version, 'Der Pilger' (1877 [1844], 73–74) is more faithful to the original. We would expect a special regard on the part of a German translator towards a Scott poem, given that Scott's first literary efforts included translations of German ballads, including Bürger's 'Lenore'. A Dutch translation, 'De Pelgrim' (1827), signed A. H. and appearing in the Rotterdam-based periodical *Apollo* on 25 December that year, is similarly close to the original, even metrically, as with the Freiligrath. Again, there appears to be greater ease of translation between broadly related languages than between those which are not.

Scott's ballad of 'Rosabelle', to give it its popularly applied title, has enjoyed more of a following – domestically and abroad – than the larger poem of which it is a part, *The Lay of the Last Minstrel* (1805). In that context, in the course of the sixth and last canto, it is sung by the minstrel Harold. The Castle of Ravenscraig, or Ravensheuch as Scott calls it, stands on a crag overlooking the Firth of Forth, on the Fife side. 'The lovely Rosabelle' is addressed by a nurse, servant or gentlewoman – true to the ballad technique, the narrator does not specify – and warned to rest in the castle, 'Nor tempt the stormy firth to–day' (Scott 1904, 44–45). Rosabelle, however, is determined to cross the estuary to Roslin, with the inevitably tragic outcome.

This ballad attracted the attention of Karolina Pavlova (1807–93), who is now considered Russia's greatest woman poet of the nineteenth century. In her lifetime she was hounded by many of her literary peers for several reasons: for being part-German; for presuming, as a woman, to be a professional rather than a dilettante writer; for a perception that she was a representative of art-for-art's-sake. Her accomplishments, however, were astonishing, especially in terms of the number of languages at her command. It was inevitable that she would become a translator – indeed, it was financially necessary for her. Her closest literary friend and colleague, Count Alexei Konstantinovich Tolstoy (1817–75), himself a translator of the Scottish ballad 'Edward, Edward' and of Byron and Goethe, praised her thus: 'I've never encountered such a memory as yours. I've never encountered, neither in the present nor in the past, *such a translator* as you. You do not translate – you create for the second time, and often excel the original' (quoted in Sendich 1974, 542).

This is how she tackles the second stanza, quoted above, of 'Rosabelle' ('Rozabella' in her version):

> Nazad, grebtsy, nazad lad'ei!
> Ostan'sya v vernom zamke, deva!
> Ne otpravlyaisya v put' nochnoi,
> Ne iskushai morskogo gneva! [. . .]
>   (Pavlova 1839, 131–33)

She does not specify the name of the castle – Ravensheuch – although she does cite Roslin. One would have thought 'Ravensheuch', with its last consonant no stranger to Russian ears (it's the *ch* as in *loch*), to be far from off-putting to a woman at home in so many languages. She settles, however, on a declined form of *zamok* (castle); it would appear that she took the poetic, and probably metrical, decision not to include the name. However, a Danish translator finds that the name actually helps him along poetically, with its promise of a rhyme:

> Din Baad du Søgut diærv fortøi:
>   O dvæl i Dag du skiønne Mø!
> Hvil du paa Borgen Ravnehøi,
>   Frist ei i Dag oprørte Sø.
> ('Skiald Harolds Sang' 1821, 158–60)

The closeness of Scots and Danish allows for an easy transition from Ravensheuch to Ravnehøi. Another Dane, Hans Christian Andersen, was not quite so assured when he visited the castle in 1847, and confused it with Ravenswood in *The Bride of Lammermoor* (Andersen 1955 [1855], 161).

The Lady of the Lake

So far we have not mentioned Italy, whose relationship with Scott's works has been well documented in several studies, critical and bibliographical (Benedetti 1974; Jack 1972; Ruggieri Punzo 1975). Rossini's opera, *La donna del lago*, based (however freely) on *LL*, was a sensation from its première at the Teatro San Carlo, Naples, in 1819; high praise for the production came from no less a luminary than the novelist Stendhal (see Mitchell 1977 and 1996; Tambling).

However, in this country, the hold of Neoclassicism was still strong. The *Biblioteca italiana, ossia Giornale di letteratura scienze ed arti* (Italian Library, or Journal of Literature, Sciences and Arts), published in Milan, carried a long review of two translations of *LL* by the Cavaliere Pallavicini (presented at the time only as 'Cav. P.') and the medical doctor Giuseppe Indelicato. The reviewer objects to much in the poem which will baffle conservative Italian readers. In particular, it is claimed, the opening of the poem is too diffuse and deflects the reader from the main action: the stag is receiving more attention than the principal (human) actors of the tale. Perhaps the English find beauty in such digressiveness; Italian readers, however, favour more economy in the conduct of a poem.

Despite the splendid title, continues our reviewer, the poem does not come up to the level of Homer, Virgil, Ariosto or Tasso; Scott's poem is a pygmy compared with these giants ('un pigmeo messo al confronto d'un gigante'). If Scott had called his work a 'novella' rather than a 'poema' that would have caused less offence: a 'novella' implies no claim for the high tone expected of a 'poema'. As Mary E. Ambrose (1972) notes, however, Scott had his Italian admirers among those of a disposition more sympathetic to Romanticism. She cites one critic who explicitly challenged the *Biblioteca italiana* reviewer, expressing his preference for Indelicato's version to that of 'Cav. P.' The *Biblioteca italiana* had favoured the latter.

Ambrose points out that Indelicato saw Scott as a perfect example of the 'poet as painter' (1972, 78). It is curious that while Scott judged himself to be lacking in the skills of a visual artist, and indeed appeared more than a little 'Neoclassical' in his predilection for general rather than precise description, critics were lavish in their praise for his descriptive power. It is arguable that this derives more from the music of his verse, especially in its onomatopoeic movement, than from tableaux which may actually feed very little to the eye. Be that as it may, the Dutchman Jacob Geel (1789–1862) translated two extracts from *LL*. Geel 'also saw in him [Scott] the picturesque narrator of the past' (Geel 1822, 441ff; Vissink 1922, 131–32). Unfortunately, Dutch historical novels, taking their cue from Scott, were on the whole mediocre; the Netherlands' past was narrated more effectively and 'picturesquely' by a well-known foreign heir of Scott – Alexandre Dumas, in *La tulipe noire* (1850), which sets a private tale of the Dutch tulip craze within the troubled political context of the 1670s.

The Slav countries varied widely in their response to *LL*. Certainly the 1822 Polish version by Karol Sienkiewicz, librarian to the Scotophile Czartoryski princes, was a landmark, as was the 1828 version by František Čelakovský, who was in personal correspondence with Scott himself. At this time, Čelakovský (1799–1852) was much in contact with the writers of Slovenia, but that country was comparatively little occupied with Scott, and nothing remains on the record here apart from a few notices of Čelakovský's translation in the review *Slovenska bčela*. (Klančar 1948–49, 224) As late as 1867, 'Zora', a Serbian students' society, based in Vienna, commissioned a medical student, Radmilo Lazarevic, to translate *The Lady of the Lake*; he read his version, *Jezerkinje vile*, to the members of 'Zora' (Klančar, 219–20). The 1860s also saw Croatian versions of Scottish ballads and Scott poems by Velimir Gaj and Franjo Marković (1845–1914). Klančar explains that in the Balkan Slav countries Romanticism lacked a literary dimension: dominated variously by the Turkish and Hapsburg empires, Balkan leaders felt impelled to devote themselves to political rather than intellectual aspirations (227). This claim reads oddly in the light of the evidence that literary-linguistic activity was far from negligible in the region.

If Klančar's utterance were supportable, it would still beg the question as to how Poland and Bohemia, themselves in the clutches of major powers, were able to deploy literature – including foreign literature, and Scott in particular – in the struggle for national identity. The relative lack of Scott activity in the Balkans remains a mystery. The collected translations of Stanko Vraz (1810–51), a leading poet of both Croatian and Slovenian loyalties, includes Burns, Byron, Gavin Douglas, William Drummond, William Dunbar and even minor Scottish poets such as Alexander Hume, William Miller, Alexander Rodger and William Thom, but no Scott (Vraz 1868). It is all the more curious as Scott himself did not neglect the Balkans: one of his earliest works was an English version, via Goethe's intermediary German, of the Bosnian ballad 'Hasanaginica'. It tells of a woman who faces separation from her children because of the patriarchal tyranny of her husband and her brother, a not unfamiliar scenario in the ballads of Scott's own Border country.

The poetry or prose debate

A casual survey of the records for Scott's poetry in BOSLIT, the Bibliography of Scottish Literature in Translation, would reveal that the passage from one language to another often entails the less inspiring passage from poetry into prose. For its part the *Bibliothèque universelle* of Geneva claimed that French translation of Scott was impossible: vagaries of language, custom, history, local colour and taste were barriers to the French reader. The journal went on to quote the conventional wisdom that if it was necessary to learn Spanish in order to read Cervantes, it followed that one would need to learn English to understand Scott, and even that was not enough: Scotland and its history must be studied, in order to familiarize oneself with the places which he described (Pictet de Rochemont 1816, 9). That did not prevent the *Bibliothèque universelle* from going on to print translated extracts from nine works by Scott over the next few years. These include the poems, turned into prose, and in the case of 'Rosabelle' the venture was all too pedestrian, especially if we quote the version of the stanza already presented above in Russian and in Danish:

Enchainez, enchainez la barque, brave matelots! Reste,
reste ô noble Dame! repose en sûreté dans le château de
Ravensheuch. Ne t'expose point aujourd'hui à une mer
orageuse.

(Le dernier barde 1821, 312)

In mitigation, the translator or translators have not shied away from the name Ravensheuch. I write 'translators' because Charles Pictet, the *Bibliothèque universelle*'s man in charge of dealing with Anglophone texts, was assisted by his family; his wife, daughters and nieces were examples of those Genevan citizens who so irritated Napoleon because they knew English so well (Bridel and Francillon 1998, 222).

The arguments for and against translation of poetry into prose can throw into sharper relief the contention that translation works best between languages belonging to the same family. Bayard Taylor (1825–78), the American translator of Goethe's *Faust*, is robust in his demand that the translator rise to a poetic challenge. In translating from German to English and from English to German it is not only possible but imperative to follow the same metre as the original, and Taylor quotes Freiligrath's version of Scott's 'Pibroch of Donal Dhu' as a triumphant vindication of this principle:

Kommt, wie der Wind kommt,
Wenn Wälder erzittern!
Kommt, wie die Brandung
Wenn Flotten zerspittern!
Schnell heran, schnell herab,
Schnellen kommt Al'e! –
Häuptling und Bub' und Knapp,
Herr und Vasalle!

(Taylor 1875, ix)

(Come as the winds come, when
    Forests are rended,
Come as the waves come, when
    Navies are stranded:
Faster come, faster come,
    Faster and faster,
Chief, vassal, page and groom,
    Tenant and master.)

(Scott 1904, 731)

However, the decision to turn a Scott poem into poetry or prose is not necessarily determined by a target language's proximity to or distance from the host language. Portuguese translators may understandably opt to make a prose version of the ballad 'The Fire King' ('O Rei das chamas', *O Correio das damas, 2* [1837]), and do likewise for an extract from Canto 3 ('The Fiery Cross') of *The Lady of the Lake* ('O Fanaticó selvagem, ou a Cruz de fogo e a maldição',

O Mosaico, 1 [1837], 150), but the north Europeans do not always share Bayard Taylor's confidence regarding reciprocal transfer between Germanic languages. In Danish, Frederik Schaldemose's *Marmion* (1824) is a prose version, as is C. F. Holm's 1828 *Rokeby*. However, Schaldemose's *Harold den Uforfærdede* (Harold the Dauntless, 1825) is in both prose and verse, and in an 1827 Swedish version of *Rokeby* (*Mathilda Rokeby, eller Rofwarekulan i Scargill*), the main narrative strophes of the poem are in prose, while the songs and lyrics are in verse. The latter example seems to confirm the pattern of translators' bias towards the Scott of the shorter pieces, which would be perceived as more 'poetic' than those lines whose primary function is to develop the 'big' story. The macro-narrative, as it were, almost inevitably lacks the allure of the micro-narrative of ballad or ballad-like poem.

Another Danish peculiarity is an interest in the prose appendages to the poems, particularly the notes to *The Lay of the Last Minstrel*. In its issue for 5 May 1820, the periodical *Tilskueren* (The Spectator) printed translations of notes 28, 30 and 31, all pertaining to the medieval wizard and scientist Michael Scot, who fascinated his near-namesake as both a legendary and historical figure. Knud Lyhne Rahbek (1760–1830) translated both extracts and notes from the *Lay*: Jørgen Erik Nielsen (1983, 468–69) remarks that Rahbek's interest in the notes reflects his interest in the history and folklore of both Scotland and Scandinavia; he and Scott entered into a correspondence which reveals a mutual personal and professional regard (Scott's own interest in matters Scandinavian is well documented by Paul Robert Leeder [1920]).

There exists at least one example of Scott's *prose* translated as poetry: the poet and playwright Josef Kajetán Tyl (1808–56) 'elevated' a number of extracts from *The Talisman* into Czech verse (Mánek 1996, 94).

Song-settings of Scott's poems

Professor Jeremy Tambling is contributing on opera to the present volume, so I shall confine myself to song-settings. A composer is unlikely to set a prose translation if a good poetic one is at his disposal. In the preface to his version of *Faust*, Bayard Taylor (1875, vii) quotes Beethoven's confession of his intense sensitivity to poetry: 'Goethe's poems exercise a great sway over me, not only by their meaning, but also by their rhythm. It is a language which stimulates me to composition.' Franz Schubert, in the most celebrated of all Scott settings, was fortunate in being able to avail himself of Adam Storck's *Das Fräulein vom See* (Essen: Bädeker, 1819). Schubert addressed himself to seven of the lyrical interludes to *LL*, and turned Ellen's 'Ave Maria' into one of the best known examples of the German *Lied* (Einstein 1971, 296–97).

At the other extreme, the most obscure song-setting of Scott may be by Mikhail Glinka (1804–57), the first of the great nineteenth-century Russian composers. His masterpieces are generally reckoned to be his operas *Ivan Susanin* (known in the Anglophone world as *A Life for the Tsar*, 1836), and *Ruslan and Lyudmila* (1842). However, he did much to establish the Russian art song and in this respect he was the precursor of Borodin, Mussorgsky, Tchaikovsky and Rimsky-Korsakov. Glinka's setting of 'The Harp' in Canto 5 of *Rokeby* played no part in this process; the text, by Konstantin Aleksandrovich Bakhturin (1809–41), condenses the original's seven stanzas into one, reducing it to the point where it bears only the very faintest relationship to Scott's poem. As with many of the operas based on Scott's novels, the original work is no more than a starting point. Glinka had contemplated an opera based on *Rokeby*, and that it never materialized is probably not to be regretted.

There are many occasions when the hazards of a cultural gap are agreeably absent for the receiving agents, when a familiarization process is inherent in the original work itself. An obvious example is Schaldemose's 1825 Danish version of *Harold the Dauntless*, with its Danish protagonist. For its Anglophone readers, *The Vision of Don Roderick* (1811) is one of the most minor of the longer Scott poems, but by virtue of its subject matter it possessed a special appeal for the Spanish and Portuguese; as regards the former, this is attested by the Spanish poet and critic Manuel Milá y Fontanals (1818–84), himself a translator as well as an essayist on Scott (Churchman and Peers 1922, 262). Scott composed the poem as a fundraiser for the 'Committee of Subscribers for Relief of the Portuguese Sufferers', that is to say, Portuguese victims of the Peninsular war. Translated Portuguese extracts from the poem appeared during the same year that the original was published, in the London-based exiles' journal *O Investigador portuguez em Inglaterra*, no. 6, December 1811, 151–62. A freely rendered Spanish version did not appear until 1829, from a Barcelona publisher; according to Churchman and Peers (1922, 271), 'the translator, in his preface, says that he has modified his work to suit Spanish Catholic taste'.

In 'To a Louse' Robert Burns wrote: 'O wad some Power the giftie gie us/ To see oorsels as ithers see us!' For Scottish readers of Scott, an encounter with his mainland European reception must lead to surprises. 'Proud Maisie', a ballad-like poem from *HM*, is a staple of anthologies of Scottish poetry, and radiates the inevitability and familiarity of an anonymous folk song to its many admirers, comparatively few of whom will have read the novel in which it appears. Other pieces from the novels exist in translation in their own right, quite independently of the novels (which are not necessarily cited as their source); 'Proud Maisie', however, is conspicuous by its absence from the records of early translations of Scott. This contrasts bizarrely with the overseas popularity (with translators, at any rate) of poems which to Scottish readers are obscure, unread, and perhaps unreadable, such as 'The Violet' or 'The Maid of Toro'. The latter piece even makes an appearance as 'Fecioara de la Toro' in the Bucharest periodical *Literatorul* (1 [1880], 31), as translated by Bonifaciu Florescu (1848–99), who also made Romanian translations of Burns. Admittedly, this is to look at the situation from the perspective of twentieth- and twenty-first century taste, which is not best known for excitement over Scott's work generally. However, that 'Proud Maisie' could be overlooked by cultures which warmed to *The Minstrelsy of the Scottish Border*, and from there to Scott's original poetry, may be explicable by the poem's being embedded in a novel, and its concomitant non-inclusion in the *Minstrelsy* and other poetry collections.

Whereas a perception of 'Scottishness' may have predisposed a translator of Macpherson or Burns to tackle Scott and the ballads, it is wise not to exaggerate instances of this. An interest in 'English' poetry generally would sweep up these poets together with their peers south of the border; the concept of 'Scottish literature' as a distinct tradition (or set of traditions) did not penetrate the European mainland until well into the twentieth century, and it still has a long way to go before it establishes itself within and beyond academia.

Translation and new creation

So far, we have been discussing a process that would be conventionally and unambiguously described as 'translation' (though as a practitioner I personally prefer the term 'transcreation' as more appropriate to the transference of poetry, and would restrict 'translation' to the process involving expository texts). However, there is one major aspect of reception which does not involve translation as such, although at times it inhabits an almost indefinable frontier area between that and what we call 'influence'. We could even think in terms of a spectrum between translation and influence, along which there could be wild oscillations within a particular text.

Certain major European poets did not set out to translate Scott's poetry, but in terms of narrative and thematic situations the debt to him is strikingly evident. *Hjortens Flugt* (1855), a long narrative poem by the Dane Christian Winther (1796–1876), owes much to Byron's *Mazeppa*, but Nielsen (1988, 472) finds an echo of the chase in *The Lady of the Lake*. Aleksandr Pushkin (1799–1837) considered Scott's poetry to be 'food for the soul', and it was well represented in his library. From Nicolas-Louis Artaud's French translation of the *Minstrelsy, Chants populaires des frontiers méridionales de l'Ecosse* (1826), Pushkin took a version of the ballad 'The Twa Corbies' and turned it into Russian ('Dva vorona', *Severnye tsvety na 1829 g* [St Petersburg, 1828], 31–32) – which text Edwin Morgan has since re-translated into Scots (1988: 259)! Melita Grinsbergs (1954, *passim*) has traced strong influences from Scott poems on works by Zhukovsky, Pushkin and Mikhail Lermontov (1814–41). As well as the translation of 'The Eve of Saint John', discussed above, *Marmion, The Lady of the Lake*, and 'The Gray Brother' appear in synopsis or paraphrase in original poems by Zhukovsky. The setting and character of Mazeppa in Pushkin's *Poltava* (1828) draw on *Marmion* (as well as, notably, Byron's narrative poem about the Ukrainian hero), and Dr Grinsbergs identifies the scene with the expiring steed in *Boris Godunov*, also by Pushkin, as well as the episode with the stag, appearing in his 'Shumit Kustarnik' ('The Soughing Bush') as being from *The Lady of the Lake*.

Lermontov was aware of his Scottish ancestry: he was descended from the Learmonths of Balcomie Castle in Fife. In one poem, 'Zhelanie' ('A Wish'), he imagines himself as a raven, migrating westward from the steppes to a crumbling Scottish castle. He admired the work of Ossian/Macpherson. In her thesis Dr Grinsbergs discusses a rich field of Scott influences, and we shall limit ourselves to the major ones, above all in the long narrative poem *Izmail Bey* (1832) which displays elements of *Marmion*, 'The Fire King' (the theme of religious apostasy) and *LL*; in the last case there is the iconic episode with the stag but, even more intriguingly, Izmail-Bey's offer of hospitality to a Russian officer who is fleeing from a posse of Cherkessians – the people to whom Izmail-Bey belongs. The two enemies pass the night under the same tent, and in the morning Izmail conducts his guest almost to the Russian lines, warning him that if they meet on the field, he can expect no mercy. Even allowing for laws of hospitality common to both Cherkessian and Highland warriors, the similarities between this encounter and that of Fitz-James with Roderick Dhu are too close to be coincidental (Duchesne 1910, 292–94).

It is rarer to find connections between single short poems bearing no clear 'translation' relationship to each other, but the Scoto-Russian Lermontov provides perhaps the most convincing example, as noted by both Duchesne and Grinsbergs: Scott's 'Lullaby of an Infant Chief' and Lermontov's 'Kazach'ya kolybel'naya pesnya' (Cossack Cradle Song, 1840). Compare the last verse of the Scott with the first four lines of Lermontov's third stanza:

> O hush thee, my babie, the time soon will come
> When thy sleep shall be broke by trumpet and drum;
> Then hush thee, my darling, take rest while you may,
> For strife comes with manhood, and waking with day.
>   (Scott 1904, 729)

> Sam uznaesh', budet vremya,
>   Brannoe zhit'ë;
> Smelo vdenesh' nogu v stremya
>   I vozmësh' ruzh'ë.

(The time will come – you will get to know for yourself the soldier's way of life; boldly you will put your foot into the stirrup and take up your gun.)
>   (Obolensky 1965, 161)

The Swedish poet Gustaf Fröding (1860–1911) takes us into a late phase of reception, by which time Scott's poetry had declined sharply in favour of the novels. A victim of poor mental and physical health, exacerbated by alcoholism, Fröding is Sweden's *poète maudit*, with Nietzschean and Symbolist leanings which many would consider dubious symptoms in themselves. During the 1880s Swedish literature was dominated by realism and Zolaesque naturalism; the paramount urban realist novel is Strindberg's *Röda Rummet* (The red room, 1879), whose Stockholm setting is so accurate that one can follow the action with recourse to a city map. The 'nittitalisterna', to use the Swedish term for the writers of the 1880s, reacted strongly against the previous decade, and 'turned to history rather than the current social debate, to the individual rather than society, to the provinces rather than the cities, to a sense of nation rather than class, to nature rather than civilisation, to folk culture rather than high culture, to poetry rather than prose' (Graves 2000, 8). To this counter-*Zeitgeist* belongs Fröding; his concomitant preference for a heroic past to a utilitarian present accounts for his passionate devotion to the work of Walter Scott. One might have expected this major translator of Burns to have taken up at least the slighter lyrics and ballads of Scott, but for Fröding that vogue has passed beyond revival. Instead he composes his own original poetry on themes from Scott's life and oeuvre generally, and like so many invalids – including Scott himself – celebrates physical courage in wild landscapes. If one wishes to grasp the nature of Swedish national Romanticism at the turn of the nineteenth century, one needs to take an indirect route via Scott's Scotland.

Finally, and this must remain speculative *pro tem*, there is a possible link between episodes in *Marmion* and the drama *Maria Stuart* (1832) by the Polish poet Juliusz Słowacki (1809–49), whose dates reveal him to be an exact contemporary of Chopin. In Act 5 the Scottish queen feels guilt for her responsibility in the assassination of her husband Lord Darnley. To cheer her, her page sings the Scottish ballad 'Edward' (which is included in Percy's *Reliques* but not in Scott's *Minstrelsy*). As that poem concerns a son who accuses his mother of having had his father murdered, the page's performance has the effect opposite to that which he intended. Instead of feeling consoled, Mary experiences even greater guilt.

It is a masterful stroke for Słowacki the dramatist, an example of shrewd literary borrowing. The situation, however, has a precedent in Canto 3 of *Marmion*, where the protagonist's page sings a melancholy song which disturbs Marmion's conscience ('Well might he falter! By his aid/ Was Constance Beverley betray'd' [Scott 1904, 119]). We would require evidence to determine whether or not Słowacki, consciously or otherwise, borrowed more than a ballad for his 'Scottish' play.

Hans Christian Andersen (1805–75) also inserted a translation of a Scottish ballad in a drama with a Scottish setting. Here we are on firmer ground as Andersen was a declared admirer of Scott and the ballad 'The Twa Corbies' is taken from the *Minstrelsy*. Moreover, the drama – actually an opera, or three-act 'Syngespil' with music by Ivar Frederik Bredal (1800–64) – is based on a Scott novel. *Bruden fra Lammermoor* was premiered in Copenhagen in May 1832, complete with kilted performers and similar trappings: Andersen wanted the opera to look Scottish, and 'The Twa Corbies' was appropriated to reinforce the sense of place.

It is that sense of place, albeit with a 'Scottish' atmosphere often lacking in the topographical precision to which Scott himself made no claim, which excited European imaginations. In the poetry, Scott left a large artistic space allowing for almost infinite negotiations between original text and translation – if we can widen the definition of 'translation' to include adaptation, song-setting, illustration and like modes. In a sense, by virtue of their greater length and tendency to spell out whatever in the poetry was tantalizingly suggestive, the novels reduced that artistic space. There remain the caveats, already made, that not all reception of the poetry showed an awareness of its Scottishness, and often entailed a certain *bizarrerie* when it did. It can be confidently advanced, however, that Scott the poet provided not only the initial entry point to Scott the novelist but (*pace* Ossian/Macpherson) to the very nation of Scotland itself.

16 Scott's 'Heyday' in Opera

Jeremy Tambling

The history of 'Scott in Europe' includes much that was influential in opera in the nineteenth century – and almost exclusively then: virtually no operas derived from Scott were written in the twentieth century. Scott's impact on opera was strongest in Italy (Ambrose 1981, 58–78), in the same way that he influenced the most representative of Italian nineteenth-century novels, Manzoni's *I promessi sposi* (The betrothed, 1827). In Italy, a shift from those classical libretti associated with the eighteenth century, which had come from Metastasio (1698–1782), meant a change towards operas based on events perceived as having more 'reality'. In that sense, Italian opera provides, in the 1820s to 1840s particularly, just before the time of Verdi, another chapter in what Donald Davie in 1961 called 'the heyday of Sir Walter Scott'. The subject of how many operas have been derived from Scott has been well documented (Forbes 1968; Mitchell 1977; Mitchell 1996; Fiske 1998), although with none of these writers does the subject take wing. Perhaps a clue to this lies in considering that Verdi never set Scott (though his interest in Scotland appears in *Macbeth*), nor did Berlioz, nor Puccini; Bizet's *Fair Maid of Perth* is far from his *Carmen*; Mussorgsky's *Boris Godunov*, though Pushkin-based, is historical in a way remote from Scott, and the nearest Wagner came to Scott was in *Rienzi*. The implications of these absences we will consider at the end.

Scott's relation to music appears in his collecting Border ballads in *Minstrelsy of the Scottish Border* (1802); ballads appear in those verse romances giving him an international reputation: *LLM* (1805), *M* (1808), and *LL* (1810), translated into French in 1813, and Italian in 1821 (Ambrose 1972, 74–82). The first London version, by Thomas Dibdin, of *LL* appeared in 1810, with musical numbers. A year later, Henry Bishop (1786–1855), musical director at Covent Garden, then Drury Lane, and also Vauxhall Gardens, who added ballads and musical numbers to plays, produced *LL* (1811) as *The Knight of Snowdoun*; but Jerome Mitchell in his analysis does not count this as opera (1977, 10–19), partly on the basis that none of the major characters sing. Nine years later Rossini (1792–1868) set the poem as *La donna del lago* for the Teatro San Carlo in Naples, where he was music director, in a version by the Neapolitan librettist Andrea Leone Tottola (d. 1831); it was one of the earliest adaptations of a Scott text as opera. Rossini had already written a classic Scott-like opera: *Elisabetta, Regina d'Inghilterra* (Elizabeth, Queen of England, 1815), centred on the Earl of Leicester, and with a pre-*Kenilworth*-like plot. The source was Sophia Lee's eighteenth-century novel, *The Recess: A Tale of Other Times*, which had become a stage play in 1814. The overture for *Elisabetta* had appeared before, for *Aureliano in Palmira* (1813), and it is very familiar, because it was to be used again for *Il Barbiere di Siviglia* (The Barber of Seville, 1816). *Elisabetta* had its own newness – for example, the Naples management sent off to England for historically accurate costumes, and the music aimed at more continuity (less like episodic eighteenth-century *opera seria*) by having recitatives accompanied by strings, or by the whole orchestra; the device was made famous in Bellini's *Il pirata* (1827). *Elisabetta* makes the point that it is not necessarily helpful to think of Scott as a point of origin, but in relation to the Romantic Primitivism which drew on Scotland and also on the medieval, in an 'invention of tradition' whose result, in several Scott operas, was certainly kitsch (Trevor-Roper 1983, 15–41; Pittock 1999, 36–38, 41). Scott's texts came out of an historical interest running throughout Europe, as much as his novels created material that would form nineteenth-century European opera. Stendhal's *Life of Rossini* (1824), writing of *Elisabetta*, suggests the power of the representation of Elizabeth in nineteenth-century Italian opera: 'a queen in whose nature the noblest virtues of a great sovereign are from time to time eclipsed by the human weakness of a beautiful woman gazing regretfully at the shadow of her departing youth' (Stendhal 1956, 152). This image, in Italian romantic opera, proves as powerful as that of the abandoned bride.

Scott's *W* appeared in 1814, and *GM* in 1815 (set by Bishop the following year), before his visit to Waterloo and Paris. *The Antiquary* (1816), set by Bishop in 1820, was succeeded by *Tales of My Landlord* (1816): *BD* and *OM*. The former was set by Charles Edward Horn (1786–1849) as *The Wizard, Or, The Brown Man of the Moor*, in London in 1817, in conditions similar to those of Bishop; while Bishop set the latter novel as *The Battle of Bothwell Bridge* (1820). There followed in 1817 *RR*, which, as *Rob Roy MacGregor, or, Auld Lang Syne* appeared as a melodrama by Isaac Pocock and John Davy (incidentally, popularising 'Auld Lang Syne') at Covent Garden in 1818. Songs from Scott were set to music (for example by Schubert) and sung in bourgeois drawing rooms: dramatization and making the novels into operas was an obvious follow-through. The second series of *Tales of My Landlord* gave *HM* (1818), the third *BL* and *LM* (1819) (the second made a drama by Dibdin, with the subtitle, *The Spectre at the Fountain*; the last set by Bishop).

The year of Rossini's opera, 1819, was the year of *I*, where the interest shifted from Scotland's recent history to England in the Middle Ages. One of *I*'s first appearances was through Bishop, as *Maid Marian*; but this novel's vicissitudes in opera must be discussed later. There followed *The Monastery* and *The Abbot* (1820), *K* and *P*, *FN* (set by Bishop) and *PP* (1822) (set by Horn). *QD* and *SRW* followed (1823), and then *R* (1824). In 1825, *Tales of the Crusaders* appeared, comprising *The Betrothed* and *T* (1825) (another source for Bishop). The year of *WO*, Scott's bankruptcy, and his wife's death, 1826, saw his second visit to Paris, where Antonio Pacini presented a *pasticcio* version of *I*, made up of Rossini's music, which was performed in Scott's presence in Paris. Of later work, it suffices to mention *FMP*, which Bizet set in 1867 in a libretto by J. H. Vernoy de Saint-Georges and J. Adenis (Dean 1975, 177–85).

When Scott died in 1832, he had completed a tour through the Mediterranean, Italy and Germany, while several of his works had already become operas, or had been put together as the basis of an opera, as with *The Monastery* and *GM*, which the librettist Eugene Scribe (1791–1861) wrote as *La Dame Blanche* (The white lady). It was set in 1825 by the French composer Adrien Boieldieu (1775–1834) as a Romantic *opera comique* which, influenced by Weber, in turn influenced Wagner. Set in Scotland in 1753, the woman in white, thought to be a ghost, is Anna, who had previously, in Hanover, nursed and loved the English officer Georges Brown, who is about to buy the deserted Scottish Gothic castle in which she lives, and where she is harassed by the wicked steward Gaveston, who wishes to possess the castle and its treasure. Brown buys the castle, and proves that he is Julien Avenel, the long-lost heir, by being able to complete a folk song, 'Robin Adair', which the Scottish clansmen are singing. Indeed, Georges has been dimly aware that he has seen the castle before, and the opera focuses then on his returning memory, so anticipating the interest that Bellini (1801–35) has in unconscious states (as in *La sonnambula* ([The sleepwalker] 1831), while 'the woman in white' theme persists in his and Donizetti's interest in abandoned brides. The work ends with the union of the two, and the treasure found.

In considering Scott operas, a distinction must be noted between those which exploited Scotland, and those which preferred the English historical background. It has been argued that Italy used Scotland for settings because it was so distant that events taking place in it, however political, could not be regarded as a threat to the rulers of Bourbon Naples, who otherwise might have been sensitive to the representation of politics, particularly those of the Risorgimento (Black 1984, 23, 78, 82, 134, 167). Another distinction is between those which do or do not exploit the abandoned bride theme, which in Scott associates itself with Blanche's song in *LL* (IV.22), and gives the key to much that follows in operatic versions, turning ballad and folk themes into bourgeois music performed with no sense of place, but giving opportunity for musical display.

The first Italian opera to be considered here is Rossini's *La donna del lago*, where there appears the fascination felt through Europe for Scotland, which had made Macpherson and *Ossian* important, and deriving also from Herder's translations of border ballads from Percy's *Reliques*. Anselm Gerhard sees *La donna del lago* as an early instance of the treatment of the history of the previous 300 years – as opposed to classical history or mythology – on the operatic stage: he thinks the first Rossinian opera fully to engage with history is *Le Siège de Corinthe* (The siege of Corinth, 1826), and its apogee *Guillaume Tell* (William Tell, 1829) – *La donna del lago* has often been compared with the latter (Gerhard 1998, 73–74). We can approach the opera through Stendhal, who had been to Scotland, and considered that Edinburgh had never 'been the seat of a powerful monarch and, like St Petersburg, the centre of a rich and idle aristocracy', which for him explained the absence of Scottish music, despite the powerful ballad music which was 'native to the soil from which it sprang'. Stendhal went on to justify the necessity for patronage by comparing the destinies of Haydn and Burns. He also compares Rossini and Scott, whom he admired, saying that Rossini uses a device which Scott invented: 'just as Rossini uses his orchestral harmony to prepare the way for, and to reinforce, his passages of vocal music, so Walter Scott prepares the way for, and reinforces, his passages of dialogue and narrative by means of description' (Stendhal 1956, 57). Stendhal refers for illustration to the opening pages of description of *Ivanhoe*, and points to a new tendency in Rossinian opera, that the music should relate to the subject-matter, rather than be, as heretofore, autonomous (with the ability to exchange overtures, for instance). Stendhal, suggestively for the limits of both, finds Rossini and Scott alike in their tricks of writing and enabling their prolificity (169–70), and says of both that neither of them portrays deep emotion, one of Scott's distinctive features being to dispense with love scenes: 'the theme of serious love is as foreign to Rossini as it is to Walter Scott' (206).

La donna del lago has features which are meant to recall Ossian, as with the male chorus of bards who conclude Act I to the accompaniment of harps (Scott's text has only one bard). Stendhal describes how 'the décor of the opening scene showed a wild and lonely loch in the Highlands of Scotland, upon whose waters, the lady of the lake, true to her name, was seen gliding gracefully along, upright beside the helm of a small boat. The mind turned instantly towards Scotland and waited expectantly for the magic of some Ossianic adventure. Signorina Colbran, who contrived to display considerable grace at the tiller of her skiff, managed to put up quite a creditable performance in her opening aria' (377). The aria, 'O mattutini albori' ['O morning dawn'], succeeds a chorus of huntsmen – a staple of nineteenth century opera, as in *Lucia di Lammermoor* and *Tristan und Isolde*. The episode leads into a long sequence with the disguised James, and is perhaps one of the strongest parts of the opera. As Kimbell says of the opening (there is no overture): 'the blending in the first tableau of hunting party and barcarolle is in the highest degree picturesque, and the use of six on-stage hunting horns, spatially distributed to facilitate echo effects, seems a direct attempt to translate one of Scott's couplets into theatrical terms: 'faint, from further distance borne / were heard the clanging hoof and horn' (Kimbell 1991, 451–52). The literary reference is the end of the first stanza of Scott's poem; the barcarolle effect appeared also in Rossini's *Otello* (also 1819). Here it should be noted that Scott's importance was like that of Shakespeare's for the Italian Romantics, and that Scott was admired because he was taken to be like Shakespeare. Scott and Shakespeare together show how much Rossini was a Romantic, but Kimbell argues cogently also for Rossini's scepticism towards Romanticism. The opera ends in Stirling Castle with a theme which is repeated three times, with a powerful coloratura for the soprano as she sings: 'Fra il padre e fra l'amante / oh quel beato istante! / Ah! chi sperar potrà / tanta felicità' (Between father and lover, what a happy moment; ah, who could hope for such happiness), and Herbert Lindenberger interestingly finds in this climax evidence of more aggression in Rossini's female characters than in his male: the contrast, is, of course, with Donizetti and Bellini, as well as with Scott (1998, 100).

Rossini was at the front of those who set Scott, but the most memorable year for Scott in Europe was 1835, which saw works by Donizetti (1797–1848) and Bellini. The first, composer of over sixty-five operas (four a year for his working life of twenty-five years), was born and died in Bergamo. He worked in Naples (1822–38), Palermo (1825–26) and Rome, but the opera to make his reputation was *Anna Bolena* (Milan, 1830). It was a Scott-like theme, which must be discussed as belonging to what Scott had legitimated. *Anna Bolena* succeeded *Elisabetta al castello di Kenilworth* (1829, from Scott), an *opera seria*, to words provided by Tottola. Behind this libretto was a play by Gaetano Barbieri, and behind that was Scribe's libretto for Daniel Auber's (1882–71) opera *Leicester, ou Le Château de Kenilworth* (Leicester, or, the Castle at Kenilworth 1823). And Donizetti's version of *Kenilworth* was not his first use of English history: in 1823, Tottola had supplied him with the libretto for *Alfredo il grande* (Alfred the Great), which Ashbrook thinks was derived from one that Simon Mayr (1763–1845), Donizetti's teacher, had set in 1818 (Ashbrook 1982, 537). (Mayr's interest in English history showed in his having previously set *La Rosa bianca e la rosa rosso* [The white rose and the red], an *opera seria* on the Wars of the Roses, for Genoa in 1813.)

Donizetti's version of *Kenilworth* was his first opera with dominant roles for two women, Elizabeth, and Amelia, to whom Leicester is secretly married. *Enrico VIII, ossia Anna Bolena* (Henry VIII, or, Ann Boleyn, Turin 1816), from a French play by Marie-Joseph de Chenier of 1791, and another by Count Alessandro Pepoli (Venice, 1788) were the sources for the librettist, Felice Romani. *Anna Bolena* has only one dominant role, taken at the premiere by the soprano Giuditta Pasta (1797–1865). Anna Bolena is disturbed by the king's new attentions to Giovanna Seymour. Her first love, Percy, played by the tenor Rubini, has returned, in a trap set by Enrico (bass), who hopes thereby to gain grounds for dissolving his marriage, so that he can wed the third wife. In 1836, Mazzini, who thought Donizetti had in this opera approached epic poetry in music, said that Enrico was Donizetti's exposure of the tyrant (Ashbrook 1982, 67). In the last scene, Anna is delirious: it is, essentially, the abandoned bride theme. In the condemned cell, her mind wanders to her early love for Percy, 'Ah dolce guidami castel natio' (O sweet native place, guide me). Her fellow prisoners appear: Percy, Rochefort, her brother, and Smeton, her household musician, in love with her (a mezzo-soprano). Asking Smeton to play for her, she sings Donizetti's setting of 'Home sweet home' ('Cielo, a' miei lunghi spasimi') with chamber-orchestra acompaniment, and as the crowd offstage proclaims the new Queen, sings a cabaletta 'Coppia iniqua' where she refuses to curse the royal couple, At the end she swoons. This 'ultima scena' was one of madness, deriving from Bellini's for Imogene in *Il pirata* (1828).

Donizetti returned to British history and Elizabeth (whom he wrote into three different operas in all) with *Maria Stuarda* (1834) and *Roberto Devereux ossia Il conte di Essex* (Robert Devereux, or, The Earl of Essex 1837). The first, performed with Maria Malibran in the title role, showed the meeting of Elizabeth and Mary Stuart, which Schiller had made part of his play of 1800 (translated by Andrei Maffei in 1830). Elizabeth punishes the Scots Queen with death because of her jealousy over the Earl of Leicester (tenor), whom both women love, while Mary calls Elizabeth 'vil bastarda' to her face. The second, to a libretto by Salvatore Cammarano (1801–52), after a play by Francois Ancelot, called *Elisabeth d'Angleterre* (1832) drew also on Romani's libretto for the opera by Saverio Mercadante (1795–1870), *Il conte d'Essex* (1833).

This investment in the past of Britain may be related to a larger interest in historical themes, and interest in history, for which Scott was the primary focus, but which then extended beyond him. In French opera, it received its decisive expression in an opera already mentioned: Rossini's *Le Siège de Corinth* (Paris, 1826), which depicted the fall of Corinth to the Turks in 1458, giving the sense of a society undergoing violent transition. The lovers, from opposite sides, are doomed because of the political collapse. This historical opera laid the ground-work for the development of such grand operas as *La Muette de Portici* (The dumb girl of Portici, Auber 1828), *Guillaume Tell* (Rossini's last opera, [1829], after which he retired from composing), *Robert le Diable* (Meyerbeer, 1831), *La Juive* (The jewess: another title which remembers Scott, though the action is set in sixteenth-century Spain: Halévy 1835) and *Les Huguenots* (1836) and *Rienzi* (Wagner, Dresden, 1842, based on Bulwer-Lytton, himself influenced by Scott). Auber, already mentioned for *Leicester*, is mainly famous for *La Muette de Portici*, which was also to Scribe's libretto; its Brussels production in 1830 initiated revolution in Belgium. Drawing, in its historical subject-matter, on Masaniello's revolt in Naples in 1647, it was unthinkable without Scott's influence; yet 'grand opera' (opera with ballet included) would exceed in its sense of national display (opera as an art form advertising the nation-state) what Scott had legitimated.

In 1835, Donizetti was writing for Paris, Europe's centre for grand opera: invited by Rossini, who had moved to Paris ten years before, he presented *Marino Faliero*, based on Byron's play of that name, at the Théâtre Italien. In Naples, on 26 September of that year, he put on *Lucia di Lammermoor*, with the librettist Cammarano. He had nine more years of composition in him before being diagnosed with syphilis, which paralysed him, its symptoms long apparent in his frenzied activities, journeyings, sexual adventures, obsessiveness, and mel-ancholia. His last years formed a chapter in the history of madness, and his death in the 'year of revolutions' was symbolic, for Donizetti was no 'reformer'. Many of his operas concern family honour (father and daughter are central) and are costume drama. It was 'Romantic' opera, divided into 'numbers' separated by recitative, sometimes *recitativo semplice* (using a harpsichord), then recitative with strings or the full orchestra, until the recitative becomes *arioso*, which breaks down the distinction between conversation where action happens, and solo aria (reflection and feeling).

Lucia di Lammermoor, the opera which, above all, uses the wronged bride as motif, had been set several times already before Donizetti came to it, in several countries, for instance, by the French composer of *opéra comique* Adolphe Adam (1803–56), and then by three Italian composers: in 1827, by the Neapolitan and Rossinian Michele Carafa (1787–1872); as *Le nozze di Lammermoor* (The wed-ding of Lammermoor), by Luigi Rieschi (1831) with the title *La fidanzata di Lammermoor*, (The betrothed woman of Lammermoor); and, with the same name, by Mazzucato in Padua in 1834, to a libretto by Beltrame. The heroine is implicitly unstable throughout, starting with her telling Alisa that she has seen in the fountain a vision of her ancestress, murdered by an ancestor of Edgardo's: her music conveys this instability. Her mad scene requires a soprano with much ability in vocal ornamentation (*fioritura*). Edgardo must sing top C, and since he brings the opera to a close, it has been seen as a work principally for a tenor. Lucia and Edgardo have a duet, 'Ah! Verranno a te sull'aure', which is recalled in the mad scene. Lucia Ashton loves Edgardo, the enemy of her brother, Enrico, for the parts of her father and her brother are fused into one character here. The brother / sister relationship has its own non-patriarchal, but potentially sexual dynamic, and appropriately, the opera also omits the mother, so central to the novel and its motivations. Lucia is persuaded to making a

marriage with Arturo Bucklaw which will rescue her brother's political for-
tunes. If at the heart of this opera is insanity, it continues a line of interest that
Donizetti had explored with Anna Bolena, and with Torquato Tasso and
Lucrezia Borgia in other operas. This interest, which makes the opera what
Deidre O'Grady (1991, 142–52) calls 'psychological drama', is much developed
out of Scott, distant from the text, attenuating what is in the novel – even if James
Kerr finds in Scott's novel Edward's entry into the hall after Lucy has betrothed
herself to another 'operatic' (Kerr 1989, 97). Part of the afterlife of this opera,
which is therefore the afterlife of Scott, and which could be explored further, is
its role in *Madame Bovary, Anna Karenina* and *Where Angels Fear to Tread*.

Apart from Donizetti, the most interesting use of Scott is in a work which
influenced *Lucia*, Bellini's ultimately non-tragic opera, *I Puritani di Scozia* (The
puritans of Scotland, 25 January 1835). Bellini's librettist had been the Genoese
Felice Romani (1788–1865), resident at La Scala, who wrote for Rossini,
Donizetti, Meyerbeer (1791–1864), Mercadante (1795–1870) and Pacini.
Bellini liked particularly in Romani the beauty of the verses. In Bellini's
response to the feeling of words, indeed, to the importance of words, lay the
reason for his style being called 'filosofico' (philosophical). Bellini's sense of
dramatic situations, his replacement of recitative by arioso, his slow and long
melodies, and the increasing break-up of single arias by dialogue while
the melodic line is held by the orchestra, are all central to his opera writing.
They compare with his interest in the unconscious, or madness, or dream-states,
which produce in him a fidelity to vocal music emphasizing 'naturalness' of
feeling. Whereas Rossini produced *canto fiorito*, Bellini's style allowed for more
declamation of words in a style regarded as more natural: *canto spianato* (smooth,
level singing). This gives primacy to the woman's voice, a feature of 'bel canto',
so that Bellini's operas characteristically show repressed women clinging to
secrets which will kill them, like Norma, the Druid priestess whose lover is
Pollione, the Roman officer, by whom she has had children, and whom, in a
Medea-like moment, she thinks of killing. As with Queen Elizabeth in Scott
operas, Norma's sympathies are split politically, and sexually: her lover now
loves another Druid priestess, Adalgisa. *I Puritani* is a free rendering of Scott, for
the plot, set in Plymouth during the Civil War, has little to do with *OM*. It came
after a break with Romani, and a visit to Paris, where Bellini met Heine and
Chopin, and aided by Rossini, signed a contract at the Théâtre Italien for an
opera, whose libretto was provided by Carlo Pepoli, a Republican in exile who
would have politicized the theme. Bellini's letters to him, however, describe the
task of opera as that of 'moving people to tears by singing [. . .] opera must
make people weep, shudder and die through singing [. . .] poetry and music, to
be effective, demand naturalness and nothing else' (Rosselli 1996, 43). The
Scott-inspired scale of *I Puritani* is bigger than previous operas of Bellini, but,
rather than moving towards French 'grand opera', and continuing its political
and public associations, Bellini intended revising it towards something more
Italian, for Naples, with the Spanish mezzo-soprano Maria Malibran (1808–36)
singing in it; but he died in Puteaux, outside Paris, that same year.

One focus of interest is the typical irresolute hero of Scott's novels, who later
appears in French grand opera (he is Arnaldo in the Schiller-based *Guillaume
Tell*). We have discussed some of the Scott-land based operas, though there should

also be mention of Carafa's 1833 setting of *HM* (to a libretto by Scribe), and another by Federico Ricci (1809–77) in 1838. The first was called *La Prison d'Edimbourg*, the second, *La prigione di Edimburgo* (both: The prison of Edinburgh). Yet the enthusiasm to set Scott seems to have contained a slight preference overall for the non-Scottish works. *K*, which Beethoven had planned to set, was made into an opera some eleven times in the nineteenth century. *T* was also set, by the Rossinian composer Giovanni Pacini (1796–1867) in 1829, with the title, *Il talismano, ovvero La terza crociata in Palestina* (The Talisman, or, the third crusade in Palestine), and by Adam in 1843, as *Richard en Palestine*, and, later, by Michael Balfe (1808–70), composer of the ballad-opera *The Bohemian Girl* (1843), who had tried to create an English national opera. His Italianate version appeared posthumously, as *The Knight of the Leopard* (1874). *WO* was an early work of Friedrich von Flotow (1812–83), who set it as *Alice* (1837); he also set *RR*. *I* was set some ten times, for instance by Marshner (1795–1861: *Der Templer und die Jüdin* [The Templar and the jewess] 1829, Leipzig); in 1832, by Pacini (who in 1843 wrote an opera about Mary Tudor, *Marina, regina d'Inghilterra* [Mary, Queen of England] after Victor Hugo, maintaining the Italian practice of using British history); and the German composer Nicolai (1810–49) in 1840 as *Il templario* (The Templar). Nicolai had previously written *Rosomonda d'Inghilterra* (Rosamond of England, 1838), a subject also treated by Donizetti, and he continued with Tudor England in *Die lustigen Weiber von Windsor* (The Merry Wives of Windsor, 1849).

Perhaps most famously, *I* was set by Sir Arthur Sullivan (1842–1900) as the 'grand opera' he had never composed. He had written a cantata, *Kenilworth: A Masque* for Birmingham in 1864, and an overture to *Marmion* (1867); *The Yeomen of the Guard* (1888) is also Scott-like. To words by Julian Sturgis, and dedicated to Victoria, *Ivanhoe* (1891) opened the Royal English National House, built by Richard D'Oyly Carte, running for a continuous 160 performances. Since then, it has gone completely from the repertory. Taking the emphasis off Rowena, it made Rebecca the heroine, relied on scenes of comedy between Richard and Friar Tuck, and, disastrously for its structure, Ivanhoe did not appear in the second of the three acts (Lamb 1973, 475–78).

Ivanhoe's glorification of Anglo-Saxon virtues identified with Britain's most imperialist decade. Yet it failed, as an anachronism, and the reason says something about what happened to Scott and opera. Sullivan has often been seen as Rossini-like, but Rossini, whom we have compared to Scott, retired in 1829, with nearly forty years of musical inactivity to go. Scott was then still alive, but his 'heyday' was the 1830s; Verdi, whose opera career began in 1839, acts as the caesura here. Rossini's retirement, much discussed, seems to have been in part a retreat from a modernity he associated with the French composers whom he brought on; subsequent grand opera was more spectacular, more visual, more intense than what had gone before (Gerhard 1998, 114–57). Artistic decline in setting Scott maps onto that. Nineteenth-century realism in music learned from Scott, but its interest in modernity and increasing use of opera for national display meant that it wrote different histories for its operas, finding new forms of kitsch, newer forms of musical nationalism.

17 'Seeing with the Painter's Eye': Sir Walter Scott's Challenge to Nineteenth-Century Art

Beth S. Wright

In 1810 a British reviewer of *LL* marvelled:

> Never, we think, has the analogy between poetry and painting been more strikingly exemplified than in the writings of Mr. Scott. He sees every thing with a painter's eye. Whatever he represents has a character of individuality, and is drawn with an accuracy and minuteness of discrimination which we are not accustomed to expect from verbal description.[1]

'Seeing with the painter's eye' has several significant implications when we consider visual responses to Scott. Scott's vivid anecdotes of action meant that his works could easily inspire painters, graphic artists and illustrators. His meticulous description of architecture, artifacts, costume and landscape settings and his antiquarian knowledge of medieval history and culture assisted scholars as well as artists and architects. In 1844 Thackeray, reviewing art exhibitions in London, wrote:

> It would be worth while for someone to write an essay showing how astonishingly Sir Walter Scott has influenced the world; how he changed the character of novelists, then of historians, whom he brought from their philosopher to the study of pageantry and costume, how the artists then began to fall back into the middle ages and the architecture to follow.[2]

The ground-breaking innovation of Scott's conception of history, which as Thackeray notes had an 'astonishing' impact on historians as well as novelists, would influence the visual arts in many ways. In this chapter I shall examine the reasons why Scott's works were so enthusiastically received and why themes from them were so frequently translated into visual forms. I shall also examine

---

[1] *Quarterly Review* 1810, 512, cited in Allentuck 1973, 190.
[2] Thackeray, 'May Gambols, or Titmarsh in the Picture Galleries', *Fraser's Magazine* [Paris], June 1844, cited in Gordon 1988, 146–47.

why they also posed almost insurmountable challenges to the visual arts, and how a genius such as Delacroix was able, nonetheless, to create visual art that equalled Scott's text in its insight and presentation of content.

'The route to glory is the route to riches'

On the occasion of Scott's death in 1832 the journal *L'Artiste* (devoted to a fraternal relationship between literature and the arts) described him as having renewed 'every creative medium: literature, painting, sculpture, architecture' in modern Europe.[3] There were economic repercussions to this enormous impact. As early as 1820 a reviewer commented that Scott was '[o]ne of those happy mortals for whom the route to glory is the route to riches.'[4] 'If we only consider Walter Scott's significance according to his impact on the economy, haven't gold pieces and money flooded into our coffers?' a journalist queried (rhetorically) in an article entitled 'On Walter Scott's influence on modern society's wealth, morality and happiness.'[5] Thousands of paintings and prints (at times reproduced for *Keepsakes* or *Beauties*), illustrated editions (often both expensive and extensive, incorporating maps, frontispieces and vignettes), foreign translations, theatrical adaptations, fashions and furnishings were produced. Often these products travelled throughout Europe; this very article was originally published in Britain, reprinted in France and then in Spain.

The enthusiastic response to Scott's works in every European nation transformed every aspect of modern society. In 1887 a French critic contrasted the universal rage for Scott's works c.1820–35 with the current appreciation of Tolstoy, Dostoevsky and Gogol by an elite group of specialists, when the whole nation 'from the academician to the little provincial bourgeois, from the great lady to the grisette' read Scott; Scott took possession 'of our drawing-rooms, our theatres, our studios, our exhibitions of painting'.[6] What was the reason for this extraordinary enthusiasm? *L'Artiste* (1832, 114) described his birth as

---

[3] 'sa mission, qui devait renouveler toutes les formes de la fantaisie, la littérature, la peinture, la sculpture, l'architecture' (1832b, 114). Unless otherwise noted all translations from the original French are my own.

[4] 'Walter Scott est un de ces mortels heureux pour qui la route de la gloire est la route de la fortune' (1820, [n. page]).

[5] 'A ne considérer l'apparition de Walter Scott que sous le rapport économique, l'or et l'argent n'ont-ils pas coulé à flots chez nous?' (1833, 181). After Andrew Monnickendam and I recognized the similarity of this article to one which appeared in Spain in 1838, he and Paul Barnaby pursued its origin. Dr Barnaby has established that this French article, published anonymously, was compounded of sections written by Philarète Chasles and freely translated by him from essays by Harriet Martineau (1833) and William Maginn (1832), and that this sentence was by Chasles. See Monnickendam, p. 79, n. 39.

[6] 'c'était la France tout entière, depuis l'académicien jusqu'au petit bourgeois de province, depuis la grande dame jusqu'à la grisette [. . .] Il s'était emparé de nos salons, de nos théâtres, de nos ateliers, de nos expositions de peinture.' Pontmartin 1881–90, 8 (1887): 230–31; English trans. in Partridge 1970, 124.

'providential,' for his talents and experiences were ideally suited to the needs of the age. Having lived through the French Revolution and Napoleonic wars, the people of modern Europe understood historical causation differently from their parents. Scott's historical conception, which combined a lawyer's knowledge of precedent and practice, an antiquarian's knowledge of archival and concrete remains and a poet's and a novelist's power of invention, helped redefine both historical literature (factual, fictional, and dramatic) and historical art.

Scott's historical conception was particularly significant for those whose sympathies lay with the populace rather than the court and who were seeking to establish modern nations on cultural rather than dynastic foundations: Saint-Simonians, Liberals, Carbonarists and those taking part in Italy's Risorgimento. In Italy Scott was 'read obsessively by almost all Italian reformers' (Boime 1993, 41). His Italian followers created historical novels and paintings which could celebrate the achievements of medieval and Renaissance Italian republics while evading the censors, such as Manzoni's *I promessi sposi* (1827: The betrothed), describing seventeenth-century Lombardy under Spanish rule. Art works representing such subjects (including subjects from Scott) were understood in the context of Carbonarist political engagement in the 1820s and as part of the Risorgimento's campaign of 1859–70 to unify the Italian peninsula as an independent nation-state. The historical subjects with contemporary political allusions by Francesco Hayez (1791–1882) included three versions of *I Vespri Siciliani* (Sicilian vespers, 1821–22; 1826–27; 1844–46), describing Sicilian resistance to French rule in the thirteenth century. Hayez, praised by the politician Giuseppe Mazzini in 1841 as a patriotic painter (Mazzocca 1996, 267), took part in the struggle for Italian independence in 1848. It is not surprising, given *Ivanhoe*'s themes of cultural conflict and the need to build a modern nation-state, that Hayez produced a suite of twenty-two lithographs illustrating Scott's *Ivanhoe* (Milan: Giuseppe Vassalli, 1828–29; Milan, Biblioteca Nazionale Braidense). He exhibited the first six in 1828 in Milan to critical praise and brisk sales, despite their high price of thirty-six lire (Gozzoli and Mazzocca 1983, 349–51).[7] In the next generation Telemaco Signorini (1835–1901) and Giovanni Fattori (1825–1908) also exhibited works inspired by Scott, and participated in the Risorgimento.[8]

Ary Scheffer and his brothers Henry (a painter) and Arnold (a journalist, art critic and historian) were members of a circle of radical politicians and historians who hailed Walter Scott as the founder of the modern historiography because he presented history as cultural dynamic rather than dynastic succession.[9]

---

[7] Gozzoli and Mazzocca 1983, 349–51, catalogue # 198: *Soggetti tratti dall'Ivanhoe romanzo storico di Walter Scott composti et disegnati da Hayez*; see Scott, *Ivanhoe* [1983], trans. Dettore, intro. Praz. See Mazzocca 1994, 190–91, catalogue # 127; Mazzocca 1996; Castellaneta 1971; Pinto 1973.

[8] See Pinto 1973; Dini 1987; Boime 1993, 10–11, 87–88; Troyer 1996.

[9] In 1818 Arnold Scheffer was expelled from France after publishing a critique of the Bourbon government. In 1821 he became a Carbonarist agent, responsible for organizing the Midi. All three Scheffer brothers participated in the Belfort garrison uprising in 1822. See Wright 1997, 143–44, 232–33.

Augustin Thierry (1820) reviewed Scott's *Ivanhoe* as a history of the impact of the Norman conquest, the subject of his own *Histoire de la Conquête de l'Angleterre* (1825).[10] Reviewing QD in 1823, the historian Félix Bodin insisted that Scott was 'not a novelist who one fine day decided to become a historian; he is in truth a historian whose novels are nothing but history itself'.[11] In 1826, the Saint-Simonian historian Bazard, assessing Scott's impact on conceptions of history as well as on historical fiction, described Scott as 'the founder and leader of the most significant and best known faction of the modern historiographic school' because he linked individual with societal passions, placing them in their political and geographical context.[12] At the same time, Scott's portrayals of suffering Stuart monarchs were eagerly read by members of the French audience who wished to establish political analogies between on the one hand the Stuarts in the sixteenth and seventeenth centuries – particularly Mary Stuart, who was featured in *The Abbot*; Charles II, who appeared in *WO* and *PP*; and Charles Edward Stuart, who appeared in *W* and *R* – and on the other hand the Bourbons who had suffered and perished in the French Revolution or who had abdicated or mounted unsuccessful rebellions after 1830 (Wright 1984; Wright 1997, 35–38, 91–104). Members of every historiographic school and political faction respected his work.

Thus Scott was in the enviable position of being praised by leading intellectuals for his ground-breaking innovations while becoming one of the first 'best-selling' authors. The publisher Charles Gosselin, who negotiated an agreement with Scott's British publishers which meant that French translations could appear simultaneously with the original English language versions, boasted that his firm alone had been responsible for publishing 1,400,000 volumes of Scott.[13] In 1830, editions of Scott accounted for three-quarters of the British novels, and more than one-third of *all* the novels published in France. Of the 111 novels by British authors published in France, 82 were by Scott (Devonshire [1967], 6).

Not surprisingly this popularity resulted in frequent visual representations of his subjects. More than 300 artists exhibited more than 1,000 works in Great Britain between 1814 and 1900 in the Royal Academy, British Institution, and

---

[10]   See Wright 1997, 131–32, 135, 137.

[11]   'Sir Walter n'est pas un romancier qui s'avise un beau jour de devenir historien: c'est réellement un historien, qui, en voulant faire des romans, ne fait pas autre chose que de l'histoire' (Bodin 1823, 454).

[12]   'le romancier Walter Scott n'en doit pas moins d'être considéré comme le fondateur et le chef de la faction le plus considérable et la seule connue, de l'école historique moderne' (St.-A. B.' 1826, 393).

[13]   Lyons examined provincial 'déclarations des imprimeurs' as well as *the Bibliographie de la France*; these data are incomplete. After 1813 the *Bibliographie de la France* ceased to provide print runs, and printers (negligent or evasive) failed to provide a copy to the 'dépôt légal' for some of their works. F18 for the provinces gives the printer's name, but not always the publisher (or even the author at times). Lyons does not include works published in languages other than French. See also Samuels 2004, 162–86.

Royal Scottish Academy exhibitions, almost half of them between 1830 and 1850 (Gordon 1988, 141; Altick 1985, 429–30). In 1843 Scott inspired more works (thirty) than Shakespeare (twenty-five).[14] The same held true in France, where more than thirty paintings, sculptures, and lithographs were exhibited in the Paris Salon of 1831; more works were inspired by Scott than by the Bible and mythology combined (Heine 1833, 328). Between 1822 and 1863 more than 297 individual items of works from Scott were offered for exhibition in Paris and the French provinces; the years of greatest activity were between 1827 and 1850.[15] In France twenty to thirty works were presented for exhibition every year between 1827 and 1840, apart from 1832 when there was an epidemic of cholera. Between 1841 and 1863 (when statistics ceased to be collected by Wright and Joannides), at least one work was present virtually every year.

Once we scrutinize the records more closely, as has been done for the French artists, the difficulties in mapping the patterns become apparent. First, a single item might contain multiple works. Antoine and Tony Johannot exhibited their watercolours for the Furne edition illustrations in the Paris Salon of 1831 as two framed sets of eight.[16] Second, the same design in watercolour or oil, which might appear in a subsequent exhibition as a graphic work, also affected a mass audience through its publication. In 1833 and 1834 Mauduit and Caron exhibited their engraved vignettes after the Johannot Furne illustrations.[17] Third, the same artwork might be exhibited in several places over several years, considerably enlarging Scott's impact. De Rudder, for example, exhibited his painting *John Balfour de Burley* (from *Old Mortality*) in Lyons (1843), Strasburg (1846), and both Dijon and Lyons in 1858.[18] The impact of individual works was often compounded.

---

[14] Catherine Gordon allowed me to study her records when I was engaged in research for my dissertation (Wright 1978). Gordon 1988 provides information only for works accepted into these three exhibitions, a fraction of the works produced.

[15] See Wright 1978; Wright and Joannides 1984, 1985; Wright 1987; Wright 2010. Wright 1978 provides information from the Archives du Louvre (including dimensions) for paintings offered for exhibition at the Paris Salon, works exhibited in Paris sites such as the Musée Colbert, and provincial art exhibitions in France, as well as lithographs and engravings and illustrated editions published in France. Wright and Joannides 1984 provide a chronology of works offered for exhibition in France. Wright and Joannides 1985 organize works exhibited by thematic source.

[16] Salon 1831 #1124 A. Johannot 'un cadre contenant plusieurs sujets tirés de Walter Scott'; Salon 1831 #1127 T. Johannot 'un cadre de sujets tirés de Walter Scott'.

[17] Salon 1833 #2792 Mauduit 'vignettes d'après MM. A. et T. Johannot, pour les oeuvres de M. de Chateaubriand, de Walter Scott, de Byron, etc.' Salon 1834 #2179; Caron, 'gravure. sujet tiré du Monastère de Walter Scott d'après A. Johannot, vignettes, Furne'.

[18] In 1833 in France thirty-five individual works were exhibited or presented for exhibition for a total forty-eight exhibitions that year; sixty-three times in all. See Wright and Joannides 1984, 127–28, updated. And, of course, the works exhibited were only a fraction of the works produced (works refused exhibition are included in Wright 1978).

In Britain and France the preferred sources follow slightly different patterns. In Britain the most popular novel as a pictorial source was *Ivanhoe* (approximately 100 paintings are recorded by Gordon and Altick). *HM* and *BL* inspired eighty works; *OM* approximately sixty; and *K*, *AB*, and *A* between forty and fifty each.[19] In France these seven novels were also extremely popular, but there were not the extreme disparities between them, and others were as popular or even more so.[20] *QD*, possibly because of its French setting and protagonist (Louis XI), was more popular than any of the previously mentioned novels, and inspired twenty works. After this were *I* (eighteen); *AB* (sixteen); *K*, *BL* and *WO* (thirteen); *HM* (twelve); and *MO* (eleven). In the next tier were *P* (eight); *T* (seven); *A*, *FMP*, and *LM* (six); and *OM* and *PP* (five). The poem *LL* and the history *Tales of a Grandfather* inspired four works. The fewest works were inspired by *RR* and *W* (three); *FN*, *GM*, and *R* (two); and *AG*, *BET*, and *M* (one).

Within these sources certain episodes drew particular attention because an easily visualized anecdote contained a clear action imbued with strong emotion, as in the signing of the marriage contract in Chapter 33 of *BL* (three works of thirteen), or a well-known historical act was described, as when Walter Raleigh laid down his cloak for Queen Elizabeth in Chapter 15 of *K* (three works of thirteen). Of the twenty works inspired by *QD* three portrayed the scene in Chapter 13 in which Louis XI consulted Galeotti. *Ivanhoe*'s Chapter 28 (Ivanhoe nursed by Rebecca) and Chapter 33 (Rebecca abducted from Torquilstone) inspired three and four works each out of a total of eighteen for the entire novel. Of *WO*'s thirteen works, three were of Cromwell at Windsor contemplating Van Dyck's portrait of Charles I (from Chapter 8). *The Abbot*'s Chapter 31, describing Mary Stuart in captivity in Lochleven, was depicted four times out of sixteen. This scene resonated with past and present French experiences; it could be seen as alluding to the captivity of Marie-Antoinette during the French Revolution and the Duchesse de Berry in 1832, after the uprising supporting her son Henri was quelled by Louis-Philippe's government (Wright 1984; Russcol 1990). References to pre-existing imagery were a stimulus. Half of the six works illustrating *LM* described Chapter 6's scene of Annette Lyle playing the harp, visually allied to Ossianic imagery from the late eighteenth and early nineteenth century. Three works of *P*'s eight portrayed Chapter 28, in which Magnus Troil and his daughters visit Norna. This episode was sometimes paired in graphic works with the sequel of Norna awakening Minna and Brenda, an episode which Achille Devéria offered as a pendant to the brutal awakening of sleeping princes described in Shakespeare's *Richard III* (Wright 1981).

Illustrated texts became a 'sizeable industry' (Altick 1985, 427). Commercial stimuli included the need for increased sales of Cadell's 'Magnum Opus' edition of the Waverley Novels in forty-eight volumes (1829–33) to repair the bankruptcy of Scott's publishers Constable & Co. and printer Ballantyne (Gordon

---

[19]   Altick 1985, 424–36, p. 433.

[20]   Wright and Joannides 1985, organized by novel or poem subdivided into chapter or canto. Unfortunately, works offered for exhibition often did not have an identifying literary source beyond 'sujet tiré de Walter Scott'.

1971, 308).[21] As in any industry, a range of products were produced: from the primarily textual (editions with a frontispiece or multiple vignettes) to the primarily visual, ranging from Gonin's ten coloured plates commemorating an *Ivanhoe* costume ball given by the Prince and Princess of Orange in Brussels in 1823 (Gozzoli and Mazzocca 1983, 351) to books of images with a textual accompaniment and graphic works with quotations in their captions.

The most significant French illustrated editions were published by Gosselin (illustrations primarily by Alexandre-Joseph Desenne [1785–1827]) and by Furne (illustrations by the brothers Charles-Henri-Alfred Johannot [1800–37] and Antoine [known as Tony] Johannot [1803–52]).[22] Sales of Scott's works are even more impressive when we consider average salaries during this period. The high prices for such luxurious illustrated editions as Gosselin's collected works (1826–28) in seventy-two volumes with thirty maps and seventy-five copper-plate engravings meant that skilled male artisans were paying the equivalent of one day's wages (approximately four francs) for each volume; many workers earned far less. Collectors of engravings spent even more; twenty-five francs before text was added (Samuels 2004, 183).

Anglo-French collaboration continued throughout the 1830s, especially in 'Keepsake' compendia of illustrations; *The Literary Gazette* urged that this 'commixture of foreign and native art' in 'friendly union' be repeated more frequently (1830, 754). In Britain the most significant illustrated editions were commissioned by Robert Cadell, who was convinced that this was 'the age of graphically illustrated Books'.[23] Cadell's 'Magnum Opus' edition illustrations were commissioned from more than thirty leading artists, including John Martin, Landseer, Wilkie and Bonington.[24] Turner was repeatedly commissioned to illustrate Scott's works. In 1831 Cadell calculated that Turner's illustrations were capable of selling an additional 5,000 copies of Scott's *Poetical Works*.[25] Turner contributed twelve designs of the final fifty-two views (sixty-five had

---

[21] See the appendix of illustrated editions in France in Wright 1978, 578–81.

[22] *Oeuvres Complètes de Walter Scott*, trans. Defauconpret, sixty vols in 8 with designs by Desenne assisted by Eugène Lami and Alfred and Tony Johannot and engraved by Heath, Wedgwood, J. R. West, W. Ensom and others (Paris: Charles Gosselin, 1822–29); separate ed. of forty vignettes 1824; luxury edn with thirty maps and seventy-five copper-plate engravings, eighty-four vols in 12 (Paris: Gosselin, 1826–28); *Oeuvres Complètes de Walter Scott*, trans. Defauconpret, thirty-two vols in 8 (Paris: Furne, 1830–32) with thirty vignettes by Alfred and Tony Johannot. Later significant illustrated works or editions include: *Oeuvres Complètes de Walter Scott*, trans. Louis Vivien, thirty-six vols (Paris: Pourrat frères, 1836–39) with sixteen plates by Denis Auguste Raffet (1804–60); three editions 1837–42; *Quentin Durward*, trans. Louis Vivien (Paris: Pourrat, 1838) with vignettes by Théophile-Evariste-Hippolyte-Etienne Fragonard (1806–1876); *Oeuvres de Walter Scott*, trans. Defauconpret (Paris: Barba, 1844) with forty plates by Charles Emile Jacque (1813–94).

[23] Finley 1980, 184, citing Cadell's 'Notice' prefacing the Abbotsford Edition of the Waverley novels (1842–46).

[24] See Noon 2003, 271 catalogue #178 Landseer, *The Bride of Lammermoor* (1828; Philadephia Museum of Art).

[25] Gordon 1971, 309 citing Scott, *Letters*, 11: 485 note by Cadell to Scott.

been planned) for the Arch edition of Scott's *Provincial Antiquities and Picturesque Scenery of Scotland* (Scott 1826), twenty-four designs for Cadell's edition of Scott's poetry (Scott 1833–34), and forty for the companion edition of his non-fictional works in prose (Scott 1834–36), as well as several designs for the first and second edition of Lockhart's memoirs of Scott's life (Lockhart 1839).[26] Turner's images were also solicited for suites of 'illustrations with textual accompaniment'; he produced six of the ninety designs for G. N. Wright's *Landscape – Historical Illustrations of Scotland and the Waverley Novels* (1836). Charles Tilt specialized in such works, working with Turner and others, including Richard Westall and George Cattermole.[27] Comparable French publications included Pichot's *Vues pittoresques de l'Ecosse* (1826), a guidebook to the sites described in Scott's novels, in which extensive quotations accompanied François-Alexandre Pernot's topographical views of contemporary landscape peopled with minuscule staffage; vignettes of scenes of action from the novels were provided by Eugène Lami, Richard Parkes Bonington, Paul Delaroche and other artists.[28]

The watercolour and oil preparatory designs for these illustrations were considered art works, not commercial works, and were highly praised. 'These vignettes are paintings', 'D.' wrote (*L'Artiste* 1833, 46) of the Johannot brothers' watercolours for the Furne illustrations when they were exhibited in the Paris Salon for art (not industry).[29] Their purchase in 1832 by Princesse Marie d'Orléans was noted in the *Journal des Débats* (20 December 1832).[30]

Another factor deserves comment before we consider the unique characteristics of the visual response to Scott: the ease with which these media reached a wide audience, across media boundaries and across national boundaries. In art works (unlike texts which were either in the original language or translated into a native language), the images produced from well-known texts were immediately recognizable, as we shall see, to their international audience, and they were often exhibited several times in several countries. Graphic works (sometimes with bilingual texts) were published and sold in a multinational market.[31]

---

[26]   On Turner and Scott see Holcomb 1971, 1973; Finley 1980; Altick 1985, 427.
[27]   *Landscape Illustrations* (1832); *Landscape Illustrations* (1833); *Portraits of the Principal Female Characters* (1833). See Finley 1980, 229–31.
[28]   Pichot published prose translations of Scott's poems that included a biography of Scott (1820), an assessment of his works (1821) and an account of his tour of Great Britain (1825). See Macmillan 2001; Morris, 2005, 52.
[29]   'ces vignettes sont des tableaux.' 'D.' 1833, 46. See Wright 1978, 196–97.
[30]   See Kolb 1937b, 174 and 207; Janin 1832, 1833, 1837, 1866; Marie 1925.
[31]   Henri Gaugain's print shop and exhibition gallery, the Musée Colbert, played a major role. In 1829–30 he and his successor Ardit published a suite of more than 20 lithographs in Paris and London with textual citations in French and English with subjects from *Rokeby*, *The Talisman*, *The Fair Maid of Perth*, *Ivanhoe*, *Kenilworth*, *The Antiquary*, *The Abbot*, *The Bride of Lammermoor*, and *Rob Roy*; see Wright 1990, Wright 2010. Bulla (Paris) published a suite by Nicolas-Eustache Maurin (1799–1850) (six scenes from *Ivanhoe*, 1836) and Napoléon Thomas (active 1831–48) (six scenes from *The Talisman*, 1844) with texts in French and Spanish. In 1854 Maurin's lithographs from *The Talisman* (captions in French and Spanish) were sold in Paris and London, with the reissued *Ivanhoe* suite. See Wright 1987, 15–18. See Abad 1984 on Scott's influence on Spanish Romantic medievalism.

Prints carried titles (even chapter or page citation) in their legend; exhibition catalogues offered the same information and sometimes included lengthy citations from the text. Works with subjects from Scott's novels or poems would assist a foreign artist in capturing the attention of a British audience. Fradelle, who studied first in Paris and then in Italy before settling in London in 1816, exhibited scenes from Scott simultaneously in Paris and London between 1825 and 1832.[32]

In addition to leaping over linguistic obstacles Scott permeated multiple media with his exceptionally vivid narrative style, which had the ability to present 'pictures of past days, which what is commonly called History had neglected to afford', as a reviewer of the illustrated Magnum Opus edition noted in 1832.[33] As Ann Rigney has pointed out, he demonstrated this ability during a period when the very 'representability' of history was at issue, whether in historiography, historical fiction or historical imagery. Furthermore, Scott's works appeared during a period in which Romantic expressiveness predominated, rather than mimesis or formalism, a period which investigated synaesthetic correspondences and promoted such collaborative media as tableaux vivants and operas. Scott's audience, attuned to such subjective qualities in his works as local colour and religious or political biases, was eager to visualize the invisible as well as translate the concrete from one medium to another. Given these factors it was only to be expected that his texts would be translated into hundreds of graphic and pictorial works, as well as adapted into theatrical, operatic and musical works.[34] But as Scott himself acknowledged in *LM*, intermedial transference was not always seamless, and could pose problems. There the artist Dick Tinto, affronted when his friend Peter Pattieson admitted that he was unable to admire Tinto's painting without fully understanding its subject, challenged him to narrate the entire story from the notes he supplied (on pages in which words were interwoven with caricatures and landscape sketches). What benefits and challenges did these visual responses to Scott's works offer for illustration, painting, and graphic art?

---

[32] Henri Jean-Baptiste Victoire Fradelle (1778–1865), *The Earl of Leicester's Visit to Amy Robsart at Cumnor Place*, exhibited British Institution 1825 (# 81), engraved in Paris 1827 by Jazet & Aumont. Fradelle's *Rebecca treating Ivanhoe's wounds*, exhibited British Institution 1826 (# 382), exhibited Paris Salon 1827 (# 410), engraved in London 1830 by T. Lupton; possibly re-exhibited 1830 in Paris at the Musée du Luxembourg (3rd supplement, # 364), with *The Black Knight and the Clerk of Copmanhurst* (3rd supplement, # 363), previously exhibited British Institution 1829 (# 147); engraved in London 1830 by W. Say; Paris Salon 1831 (# 826). Fradelle's *Queen Elizabeth and Lady Paget*, exhibited British Institution 1828 (# 324) engraved in London 1828 by Ackerman; exhibited Paris Salon 1831 (# 825) and Musée Colbert 1832 (1832a, 28). See Graves 1908, 196; Wright 1978, 501–504. Fagan/Stonard 2008.

[33] [Lister] 1832, 77 in Rigney 2001, 53. See Rigney's Chapter 1 'Hybridity: The Case of Sir Walter Scott', 13–58.

[34] See White 1927; Mitchell 1977.

'He sees everything with the painter's eye'

Scott's own visual imagination, while acute, was replicative rather than expressive. He himself struggled, unsuccessfully, to learn watercolour, oil painting and sketching techniques, so that he could create a lasting memento of a site on which a historical event had occurred. 'After long study and many efforts, I [. . .] was obliged to relinquish in despair an art which I was most anxious to practice.'[35] Despite his visual sensitivity, the artist Charles Leslie recalled:

> He talked of scenery as he wrote of it – like a painter, and yet for pictures, as works of art, he had little or no taste, nor did he pretend to any. To him they were interesting merely as representing some particular scene, person or event; and very moderate merit in their execution contented him.[36]

Scott admitted as much; he appreciated visual works for their impact on memory more than on the senses or emotions. They were means of 'fixing attention' rather than independent aesthetic creations:

> Pictures and prints I have found in my family lectures a very good mode of fixing attention – indeed I am so convinced of this that I would have a gallery of portraits annexed to every great school – it is not to children alone that such illustrations are useful.[37]

The impact of Scott's vividly descriptive manner of writing was very different when it dealt with landscape locality, antiquarian interest and illustrative invitation.

Scott's interest in landscape and the picturesque combined aesthetic theory and historical content with practice.[38] Describing landscape, for Scott himself or for the artists responding to him, meant describing the site's historical significance as intrinsically linked to its topography. As a result, Scott's readers often became tourists, who took part in 'historical' or 'picturesque pilgrimages' throughout Europe to the sites described by him, and who would be eager to purchase 'picturesque itineraries' in illustrated books, landscape paintings and prints.[39]

---

[35]   Scott, *Journal* (1 March 1826); Lockhart, *Life*, 1:51, cited in Allentuck 1973, 188. James Skene's architectural sketches of Plessis-les-Tours helped inspire *Quentin Durward*; see Whiteley 2010, 25

[36]   Leslie 1860, 62, cited in Holcomb 1973, 202. p.35.

[37]   Scott to Lord Montague, October 1823, *Letters* 8:103, cited in Murdoch 1972, 35. On the pedagogic use of visual images see Wright 2000.

[38]   In 1818, Scott became a shareholder in *Provincial Antiquities and Picturesque Scenery of Scotland*, on condition that the original paintings and drawings enter his collection. Scott's 'On Landscape Gardening', *Quarterly Review* March 1828; reprinted in *Miscellaneous Prose Works*, 21: 77–151. See Allentuck 1973, 190.

[39]   The artist Gigoux recalled that Scott, who had made the Middle Ages 'a craze', influenced him to go on a 'historical pilgrimage' to Switzerland to see the sites described in *Anne of Geierstein* (1885, 13–14).

As a result of what Pichot described as a 'revolution in curiosity' in his *Vues pittoresques de l'Ecosse* (1826), Scotland became a popular tourist destination.[40] By 1835 a French art periodical calculated that Scott's influence had caused a reversal of interest from the Mediterranean to northern Europe: while six out of ten landscapes of an Italian site had been exhibited between 1805 and 1815, between 1820 and 1829 eight out of ten landscapes presented Highlanders in tartan in Scottish sites (1835, 27–28).

Scott's impact on tourism extended beyond the numerous voyagers wishing to see sites described in his poems, novels or history. Explaining how place was the incarnation of time and history, he transformed their expectations of such views. Now the viewer of ruins in remote geographical sites was also a viewer of the distant past and its lost cultural institutions:

castles left to moulder in massive ruins; fields where the memory of ancient battles still lives among the descendants of those by whom they were fought or witnessed [. . .] bear [. . .] witness to the remoteness of its date; and he who traverses these peaceful glens and hills to find traces of strife, must necessarily refer his researches to a period of considerable antiquity.[41]

Charles Nodier (1823) praised Scott's texts for encouraging a sense of 'national piety' in Great Britain, a 'religion of names and of monuments'.[42]

It is difficult to track the exhibition of landscape scenes of sites made famous by Scott. In some cases they were identified merely as a landscape in the catalogue; the Scott reference was mentioned in critical assessment.[43] Works were called 'Landscape, subject taken from Walter Scott' or were given only a tangential reference to a particular theme or text: 'Interior of a forest (Charles II taking refuge at Woodstock)'.[44] At times the landscape site was tied to its historical significance, which Scott had described in more than one text. Pernot's

---

[40] 'cette révolution de curiosité, on ne peut le nier, ce sont les poèmes et les romans de Walter Scott qui seuls l'ont produite'. Pichot 1826, iii–viii.

[41] Walter Scott, 'The Border Antiquities', introduction to *Provincial Antiquities and Picturesque Scenery of Scotland, Prose Works* (1834–6) 7: 4, cited in Finley 1980, 206–7.

[42] 'En Angleterre [. . .] il y a des champs que la piété nationale a protegé d'une enceinte [. . .] c'est sur cette espèce de religion de noms et de monuments que l'auteur de Waverley a fondé en partie l'empire qu'il exerça avec tant de droits sur les lecteurs de son pays' (Nodier 1823).

[43] An unspecified landscape (Salon 1824 #858) by Antoine Guindrand (1801–1843) was titled *La comtesse de Croye confiée par Louis XI à la garde de Quentin Durward, et poursuivie par Dunois et le duc d'Orléans* in a review (1824, 4). See Wright 1978, 213.

[44] Salon 1831 #233 Alexis-François Boyenval (b.1784), *Paysage, sujet tiré de Walter Scott*; Salon 1831 #255 Philippe Budelot (active 1810–41), *Sortie de forêt* (Marie Stuart au château de Lochlenven); Salon 1831 #256 Budelot, *Intérieur de forêt* (Charles II réfugié à Woodstock); Salon 1831 #1970 Goutay [Michel Goutay-Riquet (b.1804)], *Paysage composé, sujet tiré du Monastère, de Walter Scott*.

Salon catalogue description for Inversnaid's waterfall (1845) cited both *Waverley* and *Rob Roy*.[45]

Just as his 'picturesque' descriptions of distant places were admired, so were his descriptions of the physical aspects of distant times: artifacts, costume, architecture and furniture. For Pichot Scott was the 'poet of chivalry':

> he depicts feudal mores in the most brilliant colours [. . .] we see the characters, costumes, horses, hunts, combats [. . .] the talent of Walter Scott is an eminently picturesque one.[46]

Many readers were convinced that he was permitting them to 'see back' into the past. This approach could decline into mere bric-à-brac; verbal pedantry resulting in visual clutter (one jaundiced reviewer commented that *Kenilworth* could serve as a magazine of sixteenth-century fashion).[47] The vivid description of artifacts only provided the substratum of appeal for his visual interpreters.

'A ready-made painting which only needs to be reproduced'

The attribute which had the greatest significance for artists was Scott's ekphrastic approach; he had already 'turned readers into viewers' (Samuels 2004, 167).[48] A French critic in 1824 wrote admiringly 'His pages speak as clearly to the mind as the most practiced paintbrush would to the eyes.'[49] Scott himself often solicited this comparison between text and image by prefacing a descriptive passage with 'It was a scene such as Wilkie could have painted' (or Raphael, or Salvator Rosa), immediately providing a verbal description of each figure's demeanour, pose and costume. *L'Artiste*, a Parisian journal founded to support the fraternity of the arts, urged artists in 1834 to profit from this:

---

[45] Salon 1845 #1318 François-Alexandre Pernot (1793–1865), *Vue de la cascade d'Invernaid, sur les bord du lac Lomond.* C'est au-dessus de cette cascade, plus près de l'extremité occidentale du lac, et au pied du ben Lomond, qu'est la caverne de Rob-Roy (Mac-Gregor). On croit qu'elle a été aussi la refuge d'un prince malheureux; car on lit sur un rocher le nom de Charles Edouard. (Voir *Waverley* et *Rob-Roy*, par Sir Walter Scott). Wright 1978, 545.

[46] 'il trace le tableau de mœurs féodales et l'anime des plus riches couleurs [. . . .] On a sous les yeux tous les personnages, les costumes, les chevaux, les chasses, les combats [. . . .] Le talent de Walter Scott est éminement pittoresque.' (Pichot 1821, 20–22).

[47] 'son roman serait au besoin un excellent Journal des Modes du XVIe siècle.' Pétigny 1821, 143.

[48] As Samuels points out (2004, 64), Scott's ekphrastic envisioning of the past was even more impressive because earlier novelists (such as Madame de Genlis) had 'eschewed the visual as part of an aesthetic and moral program to instruct readers in the dangers of appearances [while] Scott transformed history into something to see'.

[49] Ch. du R., 'Variétés' [review of *Les eaux de Saint-Ronan*], *Gazette de France*, 20 January 1824, 1, cited in Samuels 2004, 167.

Lord Byron and Walter Scott [. . .] have drawn, you know how beautifully and how accurately, all the main scenes of their novels and poems. Each of their pages is a ready-made painting which only needs to be reproduced; but, in the name of heaven, why don't artists reproduce them?[50]

In 1837 *L'Artiste* repeated this advice, insisting that verbal text was equal to visual image:

Walter Scott, in France and in England, has seen his works' descriptions and characters portrayed thousands of times. One could say that he has in the arts as in literature broken new historical ground – With Walter Scott, artists need only follow the text line by line to make their work come to life in every visual and expressive detail. The text gives them as it were a ready-made painting. The costume, the pose, the gesture, everything is prepared and perfectly clear, and they only need to copy it exactly.[51]

L'Artiste's advice was commercially valid, but it ignored aesthetically troubling factors. First, artists were directed toward illustrative support *of* the text rather than pictorial inspiration *from* the text. Second, reproducing the text placed artists in an impossible situation: either they succeeded – at doing nothing more than repeating previously determined items – or they failed, since they had not been completely faithful to the text. Members of the audience were ready to compare their own well-thumbed edition. Wachsmuth prepared for such scrutiny when he exhibited a painting of a Scott subject in Cambrai in 1828, describing it in the catalogue as 'Scene from *Quentin Durward*. Walter Scott, volume 1, page 142, chapter 4'. In 1834 a critic in Lille defended Roqueplan's *Death of the Spy Morris* as being no more horrific than Scott's *Rob Roy*: 'We have studied this painting while comparing it to the passage in the novel which we were holding in our hand.'[52] Artists might well prefer not to submit to scrutiny, which subordinated pictorial achievement to textual fidelity.

A far more serious drawback was that the factor central to Scott's popularity – his innovative view of history – resisted visualization in historical art as it had been understood heretofore. For conservative artists and critics the modern historical novel was a noxious influence: 'the leper of modern times'.

---

[50] 'Lord Byron et Walter Scott [. . .] ont dessiné, vous savez avec quel bonheur et quelle exactitude, toutes les scènes principales de leurs romans et de leurs poèmes. Chacune de leurs pages est un tableau tout fait qu'on n'a qu'à reproduire; mais, au nom de ciel! pourquoi ne les reproduit-on pas?' (1834, 240–41).

[51] Walter Scott, en France et en Angleterre, a vu mille fois reproduire les descriptions et les personnages de ses livres. On pourrait dire qu'il a tracé aux arts comme à la littérature une route nouvelle dans l'histoire. – Avec Walter Scott les artistes, pour donner à leur œuvre une expression juste, une vérité vivante, n'ont qu'à suivre le texte ligne par ligne; ils y trouvent, pour ainsi dire un tableau déjà complet qu'il leur suffit de copier exactement. Le costume, la pose, le geste, tout y est marqué, prévu et parfaitement défini. (1837, 132).

[52] 'Nous avons étudié ce tableau en le comparant au passage du roman que nous tenions à la main' ('B.' 1834, 12).

'The novel, leper of modern times'

We must remember that according to conservative aesthetics historical painting was predicated on creative, not historical, literature. In his *Poetics*, Aristotle had placed poetry, philosophy, and tragedy above historiography. These creative works demonstrated irresistible causation and promoted catharsis. They were not chronicles of mere coincidence, set into chronological sequence.[53] Similarly genre painting, which was representational and informative, was deemed to be of lesser significance and merit than historical painting (more accurately 'intellectual painting' since it included subjects from religion, mythology, and fictional literature), which was elevating as well as enlightening.

As the purpose of historical painting was spiritual and intellectual elevation, its visual language was predicated on abstract significance and meaning, not concrete objects. History painters needed to select elevating subjects and describe them so that their meanings – eternally valid moral precepts – would be immediately clear to a universal audience. Thus a Classical or Neoclassical historical painter would place major protagonists in the centre of the composition with strong light, clean boundary lines and large areas of simplified colour. Subsidiary episodes would be given less visual emphasis; placed in shadow, in the corners, in neutral tones. In contrast, genre painting's purpose was information rather than elevation; since it replicated people and objects as they could be seen in the world, it permitted a greater degree of visual complexity and the sequential viewing of anecdotes and artifacts. In 1819 the art critic Etienne-Jean Delécluze (a Neoclassical painter who was Jacques-Louis David's pupil) credited Aristotle for his definition of the difference between history painting and genre painting. The history painter painted a sorrowful or charming action (set in a historical period and place). In contrast, the genre painter was an 'observer of customs, who makes use of an action to [. . .] depict mores.'[54] These mores, presented with full descriptive details, were of secondary importance to the history painter; visual pedantry would distract attention and dilute emotional reaction. As early as 1822 Delécluze argued that modern Troubadour painting's composite *genre historique*, like the historical novel, was fundamentally flawed because it confounded two irreconcilable enemies: *peinture de genre* and *peinture d'histoire*. The Troubadour approach (which he called 'romantic' since it was based on the medieval *romaunt*) was incompatible with history painting's 'poetic' approach, which was predicated on exalted sentiments and eternal truths. Delécluze warned that the historical novel's influence in the arts as well as in literature was noxious, and called the novel the 'leper of modern times'.[55]

---

[53]   Aristotle, *The Poetics*, in Aristotle 1958, 18. See Gossman 1990, 231–38; Wright 1997, 15–18.

[54]   'curieux observateur des coutumes [. . .] [il] se sert d'une action pour [. . .] peindre les moeurs.' ('E. J. D.' [Delécluze] 1819, 186–87).

[55]   'Depuis nombre d'années, on entretient dans les lettres, et par suite dans les arts, une erreur fâcheuse: c'est de confondre le *romanesque* avec le *poétique*, et de vouloir allier ces deux choses qui sont nées ennemies irréconciliables. [. . .] Le ROMAN, cette lèpre des tems modernes obstrue toutes nos idées, fausse tous nos jugemens.' E. J. D. [Delécluze] 1822, 859–60.

Scott's historical novels, contemporary critics charged, took a parallel approach. Instead of highlighting a unique hero in the foreground, Scott was preoccupied by the cultural background. As one critic wrote in 1825:

> For Walter Scott, the accessory is everything and the action nothing more than a frame into which he places an epoch, with its mores, opinions, costumes.[56]

In 1855, looking back on Scott's impact in literature, Delécluze assessed it as intellectually significant and successful with a wide audience of readers but a dangerous influence for the visual arts because Scott preferred 'to depict mores rather than acts'.[57]

Thus – paradoxically – Scott's works posed two, opposite problems for visual translation: he was both hyper-visual and anti-visual. His texts presented an extremely detailed material record of past history. At the same time he conceived of history as a dynamic clash of cultures, religious sects, or social classes: factors which might be easier to convey in language than in gesture, costume, or artifact. Simultaneous narratives occurring in different places, mores vocalized so that dialect and deliberately archaic words represented religious beliefs, clan allegiances, social class – these would pose almost insurmountable challenges to visual representation.[58] Nevertheless Romantics like Amédée Pichot were willing to see a new form of historical painting: 'if we lose a canto of the Iliad, we may gain a novel by Walter Scott.'[59] And Romantic artists were able to address these challenges successfully, as we see in works by Ary Scheffer, Richard Parkes Bonington, and Eugène Delacroix.

---

[56] Pour Walter Scott, tout est dans [. . .] l'accessoire: son action ne lui emporte en rien; c'est un cadre où il jette toute une époque, avec ses moeurs, ses opinions, ses costumes. Review of Kératry's novel *Les derniers des Beaumanoir, Le Globe*, 2 May 1825, cited in Massmann 1972, 47.

[57] 'Scott [. . .] préparait, grâce au point de vue dont il a envisagé l'histoire, une révolution importante dans les esprits, même les plus sérieux. [. . .] Déplaçant l'intérêt, concentré jusqu'à lui sur les événements [. . .] il le porte plus particulièrement sur les personnages, peignant les mœurs de préférence aux faits' (Scott [. . .] stimulated a significant shift in everyone's thinking, even leading intellectuals, because of his conception of history [. . .]. Until his arrival, interest had been concentrated on events [. . .] he emphasized characters, preferring to depict mores rather than acts) Delécluze 1855, 387.

[58] 'les traductions ne peuvent donner qu'une idée trés-incomplète du talent et de l'esprit de ce brillant romancier. Il est impossible de faire passer dans notre langue une foule de traits piquans dont tout le sel est, ou dans les vieux langage anglais, ou dans le dialecte écossais [. . .] Walter Scott [. . .] est l'un des plus grands peintres de moeurs qui aient jamais existé' (translations can only give a partial idea of this brilliant novelist's talent and style. It is impossible to translate into our language a myriad of piquant aspects taken from archaic English or Scottish dialect [. . .]. Walter Scott is [. . .] one of the greatest painter of mores who has ever lived.) 1822, 3. On vocalizing mores see Wright 1997, 140–43; Wright 2000.

[59] Reviewing the exhibition at the Royal Academy, Pichot wrote: 'si nous perdions un chant de l'Iliade, nous pourrions gagner un roman à la Walter Scott' (Pichot 1825, 1: 180–81).

'Scintillating with ideas'

Ary Scheffer's *The Death of the Fisherman's Son* (1823; ?St. Petersburg: Hermitage) came from a description by Scott of 'a scene which Wilkie alone could have painted' in Chapter 31 of *The Antiquary*.[60] This was Scott's first reference to Wilkie, whom he had met in April 1809 in London at the home of his publisher John Ballantyne (Marks 1998, 352).[61] Wilkie portrayed Scott at Abbotsford surrounded by family, friends and dogs in a costume conversation piece, *The Abbotsford Family* (1817; Edinburgh, Scottish National Portrait Gallery), and included him in *The Entrance of George IV at Holyrood House* (1830, Her Majesty Queen Elizabeth II), an event in George IV's ceremonial visit to Edinburgh in 1822, which had been planned by Scott.[62]

On their first meeting Wilkie (who shared Scott's interest in ethnographic description) had been impressed by Scott's 'very rich mind' and his anecdotes about Highlanders under the feudal system.[63] Admiring *A* and *OM*, Wilkie took a three-month tour of Scotland in 1817 in order to gather picturesque material regarding the 'lives and manners of the common people' of Scotland.

Wilkie's scenes of peasant life were accurate descriptions of localized and class-specific mores. His analysis of culture as seen in physiognomy and costume paralleled Scott's approach, as when in Chapter 20 of *RR* (which Wilkie called a 'work of genius') Frank Osbaldistone and Andrew Fairservice visit the cathedral at Glasgow. Scott identifies the Highlanders in this congregation of Lowlanders (possibly there for a cattle fair) by their wearing of the tartan and their lack of familiarity with the language in which the sermon is preached. He introduces his description of the congregation's individualized responses by making a visual comparison: to Raphael's tapestry cartoon representing St Paul preaching at Athens. In the same way, *A* (and Scheffer's *Death of the Fisherman's Son* inspired by it) present a variegated group offering individualized reactions conditioned by age, relationship, profession, and class to the same stimulus: Steenie's death.

In Chapter 11 Maggie Mucklebackit had reminded Jonathan Oldbuck: 'It's no fish ye're buying – it's men's lives.' In Chapter 34 Steenie Mucklebackit's father, forced to mend the same boat in which his son has perished so that his other children will not starve, exclaims bitterly to Oldbuck:

---

[60]   Ary Scheffer (1795–1858), *L'enterrement du jeune pêcheur, sujet tiré de l'Antiquaire, de Walter Scott* (Salon 1824 #1541), exhibited Musée Colbert 1829 (#28), lithographed for Engelmann in *Croquis lithographiques by Scheffer aîné. 1er cahier* (1826). See Kolb 1937a, 471; Ewals 1987, 2:234.

[61]   David Wilkie (1785–1841) described his participation in illustrating the Magnum Opus in 1826 as 'repaying a debt of obligation' for Scott's mention of him in *The Antiquary* (Brown 1985, 375). Scott refers to Wilkie in *The Heart of Midlothian* (1818) in Chapter 42 and in *The Bride of Lammermoor* (1819) in Chapter 1.

[62]   See Brown 1985; Russell 1987, catalogue 227, 90–91; Chiego 1987; Errington 1988; Marks 1998; Tromans 2002.

[63]   Diary of Wilkie, cited in Cunningham 1843, 1: 232–33. See also Morris 2005, 60–61.

It's weel wi' you gentles, that can sit in the house wi' handkerchers at your een when ye lose a friend; but the like o' us maun to our wark again, if our hearts were beating as hard as my hammer.[64]

Scheffer retains this agonized exclamation (though it occurs in a future chapter) in his portrayal of the scene in Chapter 31 in which Oldbuck hesitantly enters the cottage to pay his respects to the family just after Steenie's death. Oldbuck's polite sadness is very different from the family's agony:

> the lower orders are less restrained by the habit of suppressing their feelings [. . .] The antique force and simplicity of their language [. . .] give pathos to their grief, and dignity to their resentment.[65]

Ary Scheffer, who described themes from Scott throughout his career, would have been particularly interested in this aspect, since presenting peasants' grief with pathos and dignity is a characteristic of many of his contemporary works, such as his *Burning of a Village in Alsace in 1814* (1827).[66]

Scott and Scheffer offer the greatest possible range of emotions in the clearest possible physical signs, from the father's face (contorted with anguish) and the mother's bosom wracked by sobs to the young children's greedy appreciation of the funeral feast. Scheffer does, however, depart from Scott's description of the senile grandmother Elspeth's pose so that his description of her significance as 'a being in whom the light of existence was already obscured by the encroaching shadows of death' would be more evident.[67] In the novel her distaff had been taken from her and she could see the corpse. Scheffer places her in the darkness, turned away from the company and holding her distaff and thread like one of the Fates who cut the thread of life.

Scheffer's challenge was to visualize this range of differentiated emotional states within one crowded room without distracting spectators and diminishing the emotional impact. Though the critic 'M★★★' (1825, 344–47) praised his painting as 'scintillating with ideas', he feared that it would be impossible for a visual work to convey all the text's meaning, episodically multiplied, subjectively

---

[64]   Scott 1969, Chapter 34, 307.

[65]   Scott 1969, 'Advertisement', 1.

[66]   Ary Scheffer, *Sujet tiré des Puritains d'Ecosse* (1826), painting exhibited Paris, Société des Amis des Arts May 1826, #161, lithographed in Engelmann's *Croquis lithographiques par Scheffer aîné. 1er cahier* as no. 6 *Morton*, sold in the Coutan collection sale March 8, 1829 (69) (*Old Mortality*, Chapter 33); see Kolb 1937a, 471, 481. Lost painting c.1824 from *Old Mortality*, Chapter 13 (Ewals 1987, 2:234). Paintings *Effie et Jeanie Deans à la prison d'Edimbourg* (c.1832; Dordrecht Museum) from *The Heart of Midlothian* (Ewals 1987, 2: 245–46); *Robert Bruce. Episode de la retraite de Bruce aux îles Hebrides* (from *Tales of a Grandfather*) and *La Fiancée de Lammermoor*, both exhibited Caen, 1846; lost. The exhibition catalogue describes the latter subject as Lucy, bloodstained and crouching near the chimney, after having stabbed her husband; see Kolb 1937a; Wright 1978, 564–66.

[67]   Scott, *The Antiquary*, Chapter 31; Everyman Edition, 1969, 286.

driven, and predicated on mores rather than action.[68] Flocon and Aycard (1824, 49) doubted that any painter could adequately depict this heartbreaking passage, depending as it did on 'an infinite number of incidents which the novelist piles one on the other'.[69] This challenge may have been one reason why Scheffer cited Poussin's *Death of Germanicus* (1627). This respected academic artist advocated the expression of individualized emotion through legible gestures in an additive rather than a centralized composition; his painting *The Israelites Gathering Manna in the Desert* (1637–39) and commentary on it were well known.[70]

Scott often evoked pre-existing parallels for his fictional situations, and his quotations from Shakespeare or Schiller in chapter headings signalled his desire for readers to recognize them. Artists capitalized on these parallels by visually citing known images of parallel situations, as Scheffer had cited Poussin. In Achille Devéria's lithograph (Paris: Gaugain, 1829) of Chapter 4 in *The Abbot* (1820), Roland Graeme is berated by the Protestant minister Henry Warden for his threatened use of a knife.[71] Devéria emphasizes not only Roland's rage but the anger and humiliation of his protector, the Catholic Lady Mary Glendinning of Avenel. Devéria recognized the source of Scott's episode: John Knox's harangue of Mary Stuart. To make this apparent in visual terms he cited Robert Smirke's *Mary Queen of Scots Reproved by Knox*, engraved by Thomas Holloway in 1800 for the Bowyer Historic Gallery. For Mary Stuart and for Lady Mary of Avenel, Protestant ministers blame Catholic women for their supporters' ostentation, arrogance and violence. The violent brawl at the island castle of Avenel, factions oriented by religion, a lonely maternal figure: these prefigure what will occur in Edinburgh. Roland's street brawls (and political intrigues at Holyrood) will lead the Earl of Murray (Regent of Scotland) to send him to Lochleven, to keep Mary Stuart under surveillance. But Roland's loyalty to his Queen, the influence of his Catholic grandmother, and his love for Catherine Seyton will convince him to assist in Mary's escape. Devéria's print shows us a private moment which hints that an ordinary lad will be capable of changing the course of history at a future time, on a public stage.

In Bonington's and Delacroix's paintings inspired by *QD* (1823) we see a similar naive hero who must learn to navigate through political shoals, this time in fifteenth-century France, where a modern nation-state is beginning to rise from the ruins of feudalism. Bonington's *Quentin Durward at Liège* (1827; Nottingham City Museums and Galleries) reveals his understanding of Scott's conception of history as cultural clash.[72] Chapter 19 begins with Quentin's 'strange vacancy and chilliness of the heart' because he is separated from Isabelle

---

68   'papillottent par les idées'. M★★★ (1825, 344–47).
69   'une infinité d'incidens que le romancier ajoute les uns aux autres.' Flocon and Aycard 1824, 49.
70   See Duro 1997, 122–28.
71   Achille-Jacques-Jean-Marie Devéria (1800–1857). See Wright 1987, 1990, 2010.
72   Richard Parkes Bonington (1802–1828). See Cooper 1946; Kemp Wright 1973; Noon 1991, 274–75, catalogue #143; 2003, 130, catalogue #58; Noon 2008, 454–457, catalogue #414.

de Croye, his 'lodestar'. Bonington follows Scott's characterization of his 'love melancholy' as numbness; his Quentin is wooden, self-absorbed and, easily disoriented, will be swept along by Liège's citizens, when they realize that he is a Scots archer in Louis XI's guard, and intuit the king's support for their uprising against Charles the Bold of Burgundy.

When Scott introduces the burghers they appear beneficent, even comic: Pavillon, 'a jolly, stout [. . .] respectable man [with a] velvet cloak and gold chain' and 'Rouslaer [. . .] a corpulent dignitary [. . . with a] belly, like a battering-ram' (Scott 1963, 270–71). But as they conduct him to the Stadhouse, where the city leaders wish to welcome him with a banquet, Quentin realizes that he is in danger. The burghers pinion his arms as he walks behind Nikkel Blok, head of the butcher's guild, who brandishes a 'death-doing axe [. . .] smeared with blood and brains'. Claus Hammerlain, drunken head of the ironworkers' guild, is followed by 'at least a thousand unwashed artificers of his class.' Frightened, Quentin is swept along by an 'unsavoury tide' (Scott 1963, 273).

Scott shows us class conflict as well as geographical conflict. The rising self-confidence of artisans, which frightens the burghers, provides the subtext for Chapter 21 after Quentin has rescued Isabelle and seeks to escape. Pavillion's lieutenant Peterkin Geislaer warns him that the bishop is in danger, and that 'Nikkel Blok the butcher and all the rabble of the suburbs take part with William de la Marck [. . .] partly for old envy towards us, who are the craftsmen and have privileges' (297–98).

Delacroix's *The Murder of the Bishop at Liège* (1829; Paris, Musée du Louvre) presents Chapter 22's 'fearful revel', the ferocious orgy in the sacked castle of Schonwaldt, the bishop's palace.[73] In an 1823 review, Delacroix's friend Hugo praised this as one of the best chapters of the novel.[74] This 'orgy' is not a scene in which everyone takes a similar part, feeling the same emotions. On the contrary, everyone is torn between two points of view. The uneasy Liègeois burghers fear both Charles's soldiers and their own neighbours, the drunken Liègeois artisans 'of lower education, or a nature more brutal' (Scott 1963, 304). The once-gallant William de la Marck has become, through violence and debauchery, the bestial Wild Boar of the Ardennes. Louis of Bourbon, Bishop of Liège, though dragged into the hall by ruffians is 'composed and undismayed' (308); first irresolute, then haughty, even as he faces death.

---

[73] Eugène Delacroix (1798–1863); Paris, Musée Colbert December 1829, #108; Paris, Musée Colbert February 1830, #58; London, Royal Academy 1830 #328 (as *The Boar of Ardenne*); Paris Salon 1831 3rd supplement #2949; Paris Exposition Universelle 1855, #2923; London, Universal Exhibition 1862, #256. Delacroix admired Wilkie's sketch for *The Preaching of Knox* (1832) in 1825 when he visited London. See Toupet 1963; Wright 1978, 480–82; Gordon 1979, catalogue #8, 16; Johnson 1 (1981): 131–34, catalogue #135; Elliott 1984; Wright and Joannides 1985, 108; Macmillan 1993; Wright 1997, 122, 224; Jobert 1998, 114–18; Moreau 1998, 174–76; Macmillan 2001; Hannoosh 2009; Allard 2011; Siegfried 2013, 115–117.

[74] Hugo 1823a, reprinted in Hugo 1934, 344–45; Hugo 1823b, reprinted in Hugo 1934, 116–22.

Will the bishop become a 'Christian martyr' before the reader–viewer's eyes? Scott describes at some length the execution earlier of a cowardly soldier who claimed part of the booty without having fought for it. His corpse hung on iron bars 'intercepting the pale moonbeam, [which] threw on the castle-floor an uncertain shadow' (305). But only two sentences describe the bishop's murder in mid-sentence. While he remonstrates, William de la Marck rises wordlessly, lifts a finger and uses Blok as Blok uses his bloodstained cleaver; 'the murdered bishop sank without a groan at the foot of his own episcopal throne' (308).

Shocked Liégeois shout their denunciations of the act and promise vengeance. Each of de la Marck's soldiers 'mingled as they were among their late allies [. . .] had, in an instant, his next neighbour by the collar, while his right hand brandished a broad dagger that glimmered against lamplight and moonshine' (310). Then Quentin Durward makes de la Marck's son, Carl Eberson, his hostage and the balance of power shifts once again. He acknowledges that he is Louis XI's representative. When the Liègois shout their defiance, vowing to live or die with Durward, de la Marck pacifies them, inviting them to return to carousing.

Thus although the title of Delacroix's great painting refers to Blok's execution of the bishop, its real subject is fluctuating mood and political alliance: 'the citizens and the soldiers [. . .] scarce knew whether they were friends or foes' (310). Delacroix represents Scott's content, not simply Scott's actions: class conflict and shifting loyalties. His insight into the text enabled him to make these subjective states and vacillating moods visible through the metaphor of wavering light which Scott repeatedly uses: the 'dagger that glimmered against lamplight and moonshine', the corpse that intercepted a 'pale moonbeam' and 'threw [. . .] an uncertain shadow'. The crux of the work for Delacroix, his friend Villot tells us, was the tablecloth which 'blazed up and illuminated the orgy', against which Quentin stands out in bold silhouette.[75] The result is, as Baudelaire wrote in 1855, an 'admirable translation of Walter Scott, a potent description of a mob, turmoil, light'.[76]

Conclusion: Scott's part in the transformation of modern art

In 1840, Thackeray recognized Scott's impact on the modern school of French painting when he reviewed exhibitions in Paris: Scott offered artists an encyclopaedic thematic repertory, with subjects ranging from ancient Byzantine to modern European history. He offered vivid anecdote rather than lapidary precept. He enabled artists, readers and spectators to see the past, reconstructed in every antiquarian detail and to have insight into its thoughts and emotions. In great part Scott was a catalyst for modern art.

---

[75] Jobert 1998, 118 citing Frédéric Villot, catalogue of Villot sale (11 February 1865), 1.

[76] 'admirable traduction de Walter Scott, pleine de foule, d'agitation et de lumière' (1998, 103).

18 'Scotland is Scott-Land': Scott and the Development of Tourism

Alastair Durie

Introduction

The importance of Scott to the development of tourism in Scotland has long been taken for granted. Most visitors to Edinburgh in the nineteenth century, for example, would have made their way not just to the castle and the palace, but also to a small cottage beneath the Crags, important only because it was popularly supposed to be Jeanie Deans'. It was part of a Scott trail, with many stopping points in Edinburgh and elsewhere in Scotland. Now, of course, the cottage is gone, as indeed is so much of the fascination with Scott. The once detailed knowledge of Scott's writing and its relationship to the Scottish countryside has faded. While he has still some general presence in the images of the country (and from the 1960s on Scottish banknotes), it can no longer be said, as it once was frequently by visitors and promoters alike, that Scotland is 'Scott-land'.[1] That is now largely shrunk to just Abbotsford, which as a literary shrine is firmly part of a tourist's schedule while on tour in the Borders.

Yet there is no dispute that the emergence of tourism in Scotland was very much linked to Scott. 'Scott wrote the script for the promotion of Scottish tourism', concludes one recent significant study of Scottish tourism (Gold and Gold 1995, 83).

This study starts therefore by examining what Scott contributed to the birth and development of the tourism industry in Scotland, and reviews how long his influence lasted. Leaving aside the debate as to whether the way in which Scott, whom Craig calls 'that great fabricator of the Scottish past' (McIlvanney and Ryan 2005, 47), portrayed Scotland formed or deformed Scottish culture,[2] the 'tartan-wrapped Scotland', to use Janet Adam Smith's tart phrase (1963, 189),

---

[1] This phrase was used by the American traveller Bayard Taylor in 1844 (1859) and cited in Lockwood 1981, 70.
[2] This issue is reviewed in McCrone, Morris and Kelly 1995, 60–61.

the focus here is firstly on his writings' appeal to, and effect on, outsiders and their patterns of travel within Scotland.

This chapter will look at what Scott's writing may have done for tourism in other parts of Britain, Ireland or indeed Europe. Olcott has concluded that the 'true "Scott country" is limited strictly to Scotland, England and Wales' (1913, 337), and that once he stepped outside the ground he knew well, his writing and his appeal alike were very limited. But this present volume demonstrates that this was not the case. It is, however, true that his influence on tourism and tourist numbers is most apparent in direct terms for his home territory of Scotland, and to a more restricted extent in a few parts of England (of which Kenilworth is an example). W. H. Hutton's study, *Highways & Byways in Shakespeare's Country*, which first appeared in 1914, argued that it was 'with Scott for guide that one must visit Kenilworth' (1926, 373).[3] But the further his writing was placed from Scotland, the weaker the pull. *Quentin Durward* had no impact on French tourism, despite its setting.[4]

Scott and tourism in Scotland

It is clear that Scott's writing led to tourists visiting specific places. There is no more powerful illustration and corroboration of the immediate impact of Scott's writing on tourism than the way that the publication of *LL* in May 1810 led to a remarkable surge in tourists over the following months and years to Callander and the Trossachs (although one must be cautious in that these were already holiday destinations). A Stirling physician, Dr Lucas, noted in his diary on 28 August 1810 that many strangers were 'passing through the town in their way to the Trossachs, a very wild romantic part of the country'.[5] And what was producing this 'mania', as he dubbed it, was Scott's poem. Within weeks of its appearance, travellers were making their way north: Mrs Grant of Laggan had received warning early in June that two English ladies of her acquaintance were set on a trip to Loch Catherine (Katrine), and mid September found her accompanying them from Stirling to the Trossachs, 'where all the world are going to disturb the wood-nymphs and emulate Walter Scott'. She may have drawn evidence from the visitors' book, but she may also have been exaggerating for effect when she reported from the inn at Callander: 'Five hundred chaises have been here this summer.'[6]

Sir John Sinclair was of like mind as to the increase of tourists and its cause. In November he wrote to Scott after a visit to Loch Katrine to acknowledge that 'you have increased the number of visitors beyond measure'. He went on – not for nothing was he known as 'Statistical' Sir John – to state that his was the

---

[3]   He adds that 'all modern Kenilworth is due to Scott'.
[4]   'We find him floundering about in a sea of gazetteers, atlases, histories and geographies' (Olcott 1913, 37).
[5]   Stirling Archives, PD 16/4/2 Diary of Dr Lucas.
[6]   Letter CVII, Stirling, 17 September 1810 (Grant 1844, 1: 267–69).

297th coach in the course of the year 'when there had never previously been above 100'.[7] Sir John's objective in writing to Scott was to persuade him to set a sequel to *LL* – to be called *The Lady of the Sea* – in Sinclair's native Caithness, in the hope of attracting like numbers of tourists to that remote locality.

That writing could sell a place was a lesson that others drew; Washington Irving heard in August 1817 from Scott of an aged woman at whose inn 'with but little custom' he was pausing for refreshment (1835, 186). Her attention to him was first-rate, but what lay behind it was that she had heard that he was the gentleman who had written 'a bonnie book about Loch Katrine'. Could he not write a little about their lake also, she begged, as it had done the inn at Loch Katrine a 'muckle deal of good'?

While Loch Katrine and the Trossachs stand out as prime beneficiaries of Scott, there were other places in Scotland that also benefited, though none, perhaps, to the same extent. And this was recognized by contemporaries. In the *Edinburgh Evening Courant*'s obituary of Scott, full recognition was given to his role in the promotion of tourism.[8] The case was made, and accepted in Scottish circles that indeed Scott was without rival in terms of the effects on tourism and travel that his literature produced:

> Cervantes has done much for Spain, and Shakespeare for England, but not a tithe of what Sir Walter Scott has accomplished for us. In each of these great writers we find many localities sanctified by their genius, in their respective countries; but that of Scott pervades every corner of his native land.

It is perhaps unnecessary to suggest that the obituarist's enthusiasm had outstripped reality, with the claim that every corner of Scott's native land had felt his touch. Some areas benefited more than others, and for longer, of which the Borders, the Trossachs and the Western Isles stand out. Certainly Scott was given much of the credit by contemporaries for putting these areas on the map for tourists. In 1818, the artist William Daniell dedicated his superb collection of prints to Walter Scott. There was a fulsome tribute to Scott for the way that his genius as shown in his 'last great poem', *The Lord of the Isles*, had rescued from what he called 'obscurity' the western coast and isles of Scotland (Daniell 1818, 1). The popular *Scottish Tourist and Itinerary*, first published in 1825 and quickly reprinted several times within a few years, was also dedicated to him (Durie 2003, 50), as were many other guides. Certainly places, councils and commercial interests were quick to exploit any connection to Scott's writing, real or arguable; Auchmithie (near Arbroath) was still making much eighty years on of its setting within *A. J. M. Bailey* complained after a tour through the Scottish Borders in 1878 that he had seen about 500 old castles and that what he wanted was a ruin that Sir Walter Scott hadn't written about – 'but I don't know where to find it' (1879, 284). And it is true that those places that Scott had not written about felt themselves disadvantaged. It was a complaint of St Andrews that it was

---

[7] Scott to Joanna Baillie, 31 December 1810 (Grierson 1952, 419–20).
[8] As reported in the *Stirling Journal*, 28 September 1832.

relatively overlooked in the 1820s and 1830s by 'fashionable visitors' because neither Scott nor Burns or Byron had written about it (Durie 2003, 47). But that Scott had written about a place or locality did not guarantee that tourists would follow; the use of the Northern Isles in *The Pirate* led to no flood of visitors from the south. The doings of Mordaunt Mertoun and Magnus Troil made nothing like the impact in terms of draw as those of Roderick Rhu or Baillie Nicol. Indeed, the authoritative *Guide to the Highlands*, compiled by Robert and Peter Anderson of Inverness in the 1830s, heads the tour section on the Orkney and Zetland Islands with a quotation not from Scott but from Shakespeare! *The Pirate* is referred to only once in the context of Papa Stour.[9]

In the first phase of Scott's impact on Scotland as a tourist destination, it was mainly either domestic or English readers who were drawn by his writing. Continental or American visitors were few. They came to see the sights and the scenes made familiar to them, to discover at first hand what they had seen through the page. Amongst their ranks there were those, of course, the equivalent of 'loco spotters', who came to check the topographic accuracy and to delight in any inaccuracies they could unearth. An English visitor, Thomas Babbington from St Albans, in 1864 betook himself to the Borders and to Melrose. He was curious to know whether Scott in the poem *The Eve of St John* was to be found 'slipping in accuracy' with regard to the celebrated vantage point of Smailholm Tower. Could, he wondered, the Baron of Smailholm's lady really have seen all she was supposed to have seen on the eve of St John's?[10] This kind of topographical obsession was not untypical.

Anticipation was not always matched by reality. A Swedish lady on a coach tour through the Trossachs found her neighbour, a Belgian count, completely bored; when she asked him why he was travelling, he replied that it 'was the modish thing to do' (Kramer 1870, 58). Scott certainly was to draw foreign visitors to Scotland, with his writing reinforced by plays and operas such as Rossini's *La Donna del Lago* that was premiered in Naples in 1819. Hubbard quotes Stendhal's enthusiasm for the set, which showed a wild and lonely loch in the Highlands of Scotland upon which the Lady was gliding along at the helm of a small boat. 'The Mind turned instantly towards Scotland' (Hubbard 2000). Peace after 1815 and better transport led to the numbers of English, Continental and American tourists in Scotland increasing dramatically. A visitor in 1822 to an inn near the Trossachs, perhaps in Callander, noted from an inspection of its visitors' register that the guests gave addresses in Italy, Spain, the United States, the West and East Indies, and China.[11]

It is, of course, impossible to put any firm figures on the industry's growth, as no record was kept by government or any other agency of visitors to Scotland,

---

[9] 'We have no room for a description of it, and must refer our readers to Sir Walter Scott's Pirate and Dr Hibbert's minute account' (1850, 748).

[10] Glasgow City Archives, TD 1/913: Thomas Babbington to Mrs Archibald Smith, 15 October 1864: 'One ought when there [the Border land] to have all the notes to Scott's poems by heart.'

[11] William Pearson cited in Grenier 2005, 53.

but a guesstimate would be that the numbers of tourists crossing into Scotland rose from a few hundred each year in the later eighteenth century to several thousand by the 1820s. The coming of the steamship and then the railway in the 1840s was thereafter greatly to expand the flow. Domestic tourism, Scots travelling within Scotland, also developed, but it is even harder to assess its scale.

Enthusiasm for Scott was stronger and lasted longer amongst foreigners than locals. One such visitor was the educated and clever Pole, Krystjan Lach Szyrma, who was tutor and escort to three young upper-class Poles and spent two years at Edinburgh University in the early 1820s. He heard Scott for himself speaking at a dinner, and liked him. More than that he admired his work, as his reminiscences show, and a tour round the Highlands in 1824, which brought him to Loch Katrine, prompted this reflection:

> The genius of Sir Walter Scott has taken these places out of oblivion, deserted and unknown beforehand, they are now swarming with people who come from many distant parts, anxious to see their beauty. (2004)

It is tempting to assume that all tourists in Scotland were literary and cultural because their letters and journals have survived, and there is an almost total absence of any other systematic tourist source data as to the numbers of visitors, or their origins or their interests,. This is not the case. But if one were to use only their evidence it would certainly seem that the great majority after 1810 or so were drawn at least in part by Scott. This is particularly true of Continental or American visitors from Meissner through Mendelssohn to Fontane and Stowe (Hiley 1996, 29–38).[12]

As an enthusiast for Scott, ('no author has filled me more'), Hans Christian Andersen had fully intended a visit to Abbotsford during his tour in Scotland during August 1847. Circumstances prevented this, but he did have the consolation of lunch with J. G. Lockhart and Miss Lockhart, Scott's son-in-law (himself a literary power in the land) and granddaughter, from whom he was to get a Scott autograph (Brendsdorff 1975, 191–195).

Yet one must be cautious. That European and other visitors commented on places and scenes in Scotland made significant to them through Scott does not prove that Scott was their reason for coming to Scotland. Karl Friedrich Schinkel was a first-rate Prussian artist and architect, responsible for many of the finest buildings in Berlin in his day, on a technical mission through Britain in 1826, and though he knew Scott's work (he refers to *The Pirate*),[13] what seems to have shaped the Highland leg of his Scottish itinerary was a fascination with Ossian. Moreover, enthusiasm for Scott, however real, did not always convert into an actual visit to Scotland; the reading may have been a substitute for, rather than a stimulus to, travel. And many, however keen, could not necessarily muster

---

[12]   Hiley cites (33) the comment of Meissner on the boats laid on to ferry visitors to Ellen's Isle on Loch Katrine: 'that which was only reality in the poet's imagination has now become historical fact to these people'.

[13]   On his visit to Staffa: 'I was reminded of Walter Scott's descriptions in the Pirate' (1993, 170).

either the time or the finance to visit Scotland in person. Queen Victoria's German dresser, who had been born in Baden, came to Scotland in 1858 en route to Balmoral, and took advantage of some free time in Edinburgh to sightsee, which, she reported, made her speechless with delight. Her mother, back in Germany, had been the one to inspire her with a love of Scott, and she went to see the Scott Monument:

> Sir Walter Scott needs no stone monument in order to live in our memory: his characters come to life for anyone who has travelled in Scotland. I declare freely and openly to all whom I have often heard describing his novels as tedious and rambling, that they have failed to understand and absorb the profound truth, the pure natural poetry of his language. He who can write in such a way that his whole story comes to life as soon as one breathes the air in which it was written, is indeed great, immortal! I respect my dear mother much more for having always admired Sir Walter Scott so much, since I have been in Scotland, and I only wish she could come once to see Edinburgh, with its dread dungeon, as her just reward! (Stoney and Wellzen 1994).

Yet as the visitors' books for Abbotsford show, visitors from France or Germany, for all their high profile, were few in number, a handful each year before 1850. Baron James Rothschild from Paris, and someone who simply signed himself Bellanger 'Architect', also from Paris, were the only foreign visitors there in August 1843.[14]

Abbotsford may not give the whole picture, but it is surely indicative of patterns within the flow of cultural tourists, and despite the greater distance that they had had to come, Americans were much more numerous in Scotland than European visitors. There was to be a marked increase in both constituencies in the later nineteenth century, but while Alexander Smith, writing in the early 1860s, described crowds of chattering Frenchmen and stolid Germans at Oban, they were just two ingredients in a hugely mixed throng waiting for the steamer (1912, 68).[15]

Sport was what put Scotland on the summer itinerary for an increasing number of visitors. While Victorian Scotland, with its deer forests, grouse moors and salmon fishing, was to become Europe's sporting playground for the wealthy, already by the later eighteenth century there was a stream of sporting tourists from the south, with whom Scott was familiar. 'They came here occasionally as sportsmen to shoot moor game, without any idea of looking at scenery' (Willis 1835, 78). While there were just a few, there were no great problems; as for example, the understanding extended to Scott's neighbour, the Cornish gentleman who had settled in Selkirkshire for the sake of the fishing.[16]

But the grouse shooting in the north was a growing attraction, with some Highland inns packed to overflowing on the eve of the Glorious Twelfth of

---

[14] Rothschild was there with his brother Lionel from London. Abbotsford House, Visitor Book 5.

[15] The first edition was published in 1865.

[16] Scott to George Ellis, 27 August 1803 (Lockhart 1900, 343).

August when the season began. Scott understood the appeal of field sports for tourists, but his writing did not often directly promote it (the deer hunt in the *LL* is one of the exceptions), although later depictions (such as Prince Albert's using the traditional leister to fish) may derive from the scene where the hero uses that method in *R*. The popularity of field sports was a critical element in the conversion of tourism to a commercial industry. Scott observed in 1810 that 'The number of English travellers have of late years made the Highland tours tolerable which they were not in my former visits to the mountains – so that we have no tales of hardships or even privation to tell you.'[17] Such change had to be financed. Scott was the tipping point, when tourism moved from custom to commerce.

A key figure in catering for, and helping to develop this new clientele, was Thomas Cook, whose development of the package tour was one of the most significant innovations in nineteenth-century tourism. And while his early trips were in the Midlands and then North Wales, his 'Tartan Tours' were the making of his business and his reputation. It is noticeable how Scott was utilized in Cook's promotion from the first expedition north in 1846:

> No laboured description of natural beauties, no far-fetched historical notices are required to invest a trip to Scotland with popularity [thanks to] [t]he piper who has played in our streets, the tales we learnt in our childhood, the historical associations of the productions of 'Nature's Poet'. (Cook 1846, 14)[18]

The 'land of Scott' was a draw that Cook exploited, and Abbotsford was a regular calling place for his parties. When he brought a party of influential Americans in 1873, Abbotsford was one of their few stopping points in a hectic schedule, and they much appreciated it. Cook acknowledged in July 1868 how much he owed to Scott: 'Sir Walter Scott gave a sentiment to Scotland as a tourist country, and we have spent nearly twenty three seasons in attempts to foster and develop that sentiment.' It is arguable that without his Scottish success, the operations of his firm might never have developed as they did; Scotland (unlike Ireland) was a steady banker.

Cook was not alone in his use of Scott as the iconic image of Scotland. The Scottish Railway Companies made play with his name and work to attract visitors. Edinburgh station, previously the North Bridge Station, was renamed sometime in the early 1860s as Waverley.[19] The North British Railway Company advertised its new direct route (which opened in 1862 between Edinburgh and Carlisle via Hawick) as the Waverley route, which 'it was at pains to identify with

---

[17] Scott to George Ellis, 29 July 1810 (Grierson 1952).
[18] See also Brendon 1991, Chapter 3: 'Tartan Tours'.
[19] There is considerable uncertainty as to when this change of name actually occurred. The nearby bridge across the railway, the Little Mound, was renamed Waverley Bridge in or around 1844 when the Scott monument was completed nearby.

Sir Walter Scott in every way possible.'[20] An engine was named 'Abbotsford'. Posters in their thousands were issued to promote this direct but picturesque route under the title of 'The Home and haunts of Sir Walter Scott', with Scott's image in the centre surrounded by views of Abbotsford, Dryburgh and Melrose Abbeys and of course, the Scott Monument (Cole and Durack 1990, 38).[21] Nor indeed were the tourism and the transport industries the only beneficiaries of Scott. The rise of the Borders' woollen industry owed much to the Scott-inspired popularity of tweed.

Scott and tourism in Europe

The occasional British visitor did make their way while travelling in the Loire to the ruins of the Chateau at Plessis-les-Tours because of Scott's *QD*, and it was a literary connection to which reference was made in all the standard British guidebooks. But did any French or other European enthusiasts follow their lead? Late Victorian and Edwardian guides for British visitors such as Cook's *Handbook to Normandy and Brittany* did mention Scott (Cook 1904, 253), but Baedeker, the main European guide, does not. Recent writing about European tourism has tended to focus on key topics such as the growth of the spas, the rise of the Riviera, the phenomenon of Lourdes and the development of Normandy with but relatively little on either domestic tourism or literary tourism.[22] The effect of Byron (and Rousseau, in whose footsteps Byron walked) has, however, recently been traced.[23]

Yet there may have been indirect effects, in that the kind of writing associated with Scott had parallels on the Continent, and there had been and was a similar quarrying of the past which led for example to the exploitation of the William Tell story, made familiar by Schiller's well-known play amongst others. Lucerne was certainly seen as a place for British tourists to visit on account both of its scenery and the historical recollections associated with William Tell, a classic region, in Murray's words 'the reputed sanctuary of freedom' (1970, 52). Scott was part of the process by which tourism became an industry in nineteenth-century Europe, created by a shift in consumer preferences which radiated out from Britain where this orientation of expenditure took earliest and deepest root. After Scott, the question for many, perhaps most, people with time and

---

[20]   Thomas states that the name Waverley Route first appears in the minute books of the North British Railway Company without any indication of why it was chosen or who made this inspired choice. He is inclined to think that it was the choice of Richard Hodgson, the Chairman of the Company (1976, 60).

[21]   The Glasgow and South-Western Railway Company was making similar efforts to promote Ayrshire as the Land of Burns.

[22]   Two important recent collections of essays on European tourism are Berghoff and others 2002, and Anderson and Tabb 2002.

[23]   See Ernest Giddey (2004) ' "A Meteor in the Sky of Literature": Byron and Switzerland', in Cardwell, Richard (ed.) *The Reception of Byron in Europe*, 2 vols, London: Continuum, 1: 71–79.

money to spare — and there were more and more of them — was not whether they would travel but where. Once their appetite was whetted, the travellers looked for other areas to visit. As one traveller summed it up, 'where shall we go next?' (*Miss Jemima's Swiss Journal* [1863] 1963, xiii).

Tourism had become part of the annual schedule, a habit to be fed. The impulse, fed in many cases first by Scott's writing, to visit the Trossachs, led later to the Rhine and other locations. It survives in the influence of film on tourism.

Conclusion

Scott did, therefore, play an important part in the promotion of tourism in Scotland and as a European industry. For Scotland, although Ossian, Burns ('The land of Burns' at Ayr and Alloway)[24] and later Barrie (Angus) are not without significance, Scott's influence stood head and shoulders above any other writer's, an influence that was to work both in general terms for the country as a whole and for particular locations. And it generated employment and income for others: he has 'put money into the pockets of Scottish hotel-keepers, Scottish tailors, Scottish boatmen, and the drivers of Highland mails' (Smith 1912, 11).

The growth of tourism was, however, a development about which Scott was far from completely enthusiastic. He did not set out to promote tourism; it was a kind of by-product of his work. Wordsworth produced a *Guide to the Lakes* for the use of 'tourists and residents',[25] and later Hardy wrote a guide to Dorset. Scott did not. He disliked the flow of travellers who came to 'see ruins and spend money' for what that did to the character of the common people. He objected, as others have done, to the cultural corrosion of tourism, when showing rocks and ruins became a trade,[26] what once had been a matter of courtesy and hospitality became commercialized. But other areas blamed their lack of tourism on the absence of a comparable writer. It was still worthwhile just before the First World War for the shipping firm, David MacBrayne, whose steamers served the coastal trade of the Clyde and the West, to sponsor an illustrated 'West Highland edition' of Scott's *The Lord of the Isles*, along with *A Voyage to the Hebrides*, the diary that he kept of his tour north in August and September 1814.[27] They commissioned the well-known Scottish travel writer, George Eyre-Todd, to provide an introduction. The volume concludes with

---

[24] Poster of the Glasgow & South Western Railway Company, 1914: '*To see the Land of Burns Travel by the Midland and G & S. W. Rlys.*' (Cole and Durrack 1990, 63).

[25] Simmons says that this first appeared in obscure form in 1810, to be reprinted as a *Description of the Scenery of the Lakes*, in 1822 (Murray 1970, 9–10). See also Nicholson 1995, 156–59.

[26] '[They] are as greedy as Italian cicerones. They look upon the English as so many walking money bags; the more they are shaken and poked, the more they will leave behind them' (Irving 1835, 78).

[27] Internal evidence suggests a publication date in the summer of 1913. The illustrators were J. W. and John Carey.

advertisements for steamer tours through the scenery described by Scott. Scott was a potent force, without which tourism in Scotland might not have grown as fast or in the same directions, or indeed tourism in Europe have developed as quickly from an enthusiasm of the few into an industry for the many.

Bibliography

Introduction

Aaron, Jane and Chris Williams (eds) (2005) *Postcolonial Wales*, Cardiff: University of Wales Press.

Ahier, John and Alistair Ross (eds) (1995) *Social Subjects within the Curriculum: Children's Social Learning in the National Curriculum*, London; Washington: Falmer.

Eagleton, Terry (2000) *The Idea of Culture*, Oxford: Blackwell.

Gamer, Michael (2000) *Romanticism and the Gothic*, Cambridge: Cambridge University Press.

Hazlitt, William (1910) *Lectures on English Poets and The Spirit of the Age*, London: J. M. Dent.

Johnson, Edgar (1970) *Scott: The Great Unknown*, 2 vols, London: Hamish Hamilton.

McCann, Andrew (1999) *Cultural Politics in the 1790s: Literature, Radicalism and the Public Sphere*, Basingstoke: Macmillan.

McCaw, Neil (ed.) (2004) *Writing Irishness in Nineteenth-Century British Culture*, Aldershot: Ashgate.

Mansel, Philip (1983) *The Influence of the Later Stuarts and Their Supporters on French Royalism 1789–1840*, Royal Stuart Papers XXI, Huntingdon.

Manzoni, A, (1972 [1827]) *I promessi sposi*, Harmondsworth: Penguin.

Pittock, Murray G. H. (2003a) 'Historiography', in Broadie, Alexander (ed.) *The Cambridge Companion to the Scottish Enlightenment*, Cambridge: Cambridge University Press, pp. 258–79.

— (2003b) 'Scott and the British Tourist', in Carruthers, Gerry and Alan Rawes (eds) *English Romanticism and the Celtic World*, Cambridge: Cambridge University Press, pp. 151–66.

— (2004) 'Enlightenment Historiography and its Legacy: Plurality, Authority and Power', in Brocklehurst, Helen and Robert Phillips (eds) *History, Nationhood and the Question of Britain*, Basingstoke: Palgrave Macmillan, pp. 33–44.

Prentis, Malcolm D. (1983) *The Scots in Australia*, Sydney: Sydney University Press.

Scott, Sir Walter (1972) *The Journal of Sir Walter Scott*, ed. W. E. K. Anderson, Oxford: Clarendon Press.

Toda, Fernando (2005) 'Multilingualism, language contact and translation in Walter Scott's Scottish novels', in Delabastit Dirk and Rainier Grutman (eds) *Fictionalising Translation and Multilingualism, Linguistica Antverpiensia 4*, Antwerp: Hogeschool Antwerpen.

Chapter 1: Scott in France

Arrous, Michel (ed.) ([n.d.]) *Alexandre Dumas: une lecture de l'histoire*, [n. place]: Masinneuve et Larosse.
Auerbach, Erich (1957) *Mimesis: The Representation of Reality in Western Literature*, trans. Willard Trask, New York: Anchor Books.

Balzac, Honoré (1970) *L'Envers de l'histoire contemporaine*, ed. Samuel S. DeSacy, introd. Bernard Pingaud, Paris: Gallimard.
— (1999) *Le Cabinet des antiques*, ed. Nadine Satiat, Paris: Gallimard.
Barbey d'Aurevilly, Jules (1964–66) *Oeuvres Romanesques Complètes*, ed. Jacques Petit, 2 vols, Paris: Gallimard.
Baudelaire, Charles (1961) *Oeuvres Complètes*, ed. Claude Pichois, Paris: Gallimard.
Bony, Jacques (1990) *Le récit nervalien: une recherche des forms*, Paris: José Corti.

Casanova, Pascale (1999) *La République mondiale des lettres*, Paris: Seuil.
Chateaubriand, François René (1951) *Mémoires d'Outre-Tombe*, eds Maurice Levaillant and Georges Moulinier, 2 vols, Paris: Gallimard.

Kimbell, David (1991) *Italian Opera*, Cambridge: Cambridge University Press.

Dumas, Alexandre (1989) *Mes Mémoires*, 2 vols, Paris: Robert Laffont.

Flaubert, Gustave (1964) *Madame Bovary: Moeurs de province*, New York: Dell Publishing, The Laurel Language Library.
— (1965) *Madame Bovary*, trans. Paul de Man, New York: Norton Books.
— (1973–98) *Correspondance*, ed. Jean Bruneau, 4 vols, Paris: Gallimard.

Garside, Peter (1999) 'Walter Scott and the "Common" Novel, 1808–1819', *Cardiff Corvey: Reading the Romantic Text 3*, September.
Gautier, Théophile (2002) *Romans, contes et nouvelles*, ed. Pierre Laubriet, Paris: Gallimard.

Hook, Andrew (2003) 'The French Taste for Scottish Literary Romanticism', in Dawson, Deirdre and Pierre Morère (eds) *Scotland and France in the Enlightenment*, Lewisburg: Bucknell University Press, pp. 90–107.
Hugo, Victor (1967) *Notre-Dame de Paris*, ed. Léon Cellier, Paris: Garnier-Flammarion.

Lacroix, Paul [Jacob le bibliophile] (1829, 1831) *Soirées de Walter Scott à Paris*, 2 vols, Paris: Eugène Renduel.
Lamartine, Alphonse (1963) *Oeuvres poétiques*, ed. Marius-François Guiard, Paris: Gallimard.
Lukács, Georg (1983) *The Historical Novel* [1947], trans. Hannah and Stanley Mitchell, Lincoln: University of Nebraska Press.

Maigron, Louis (1970 [1898]) *Roman historique à l'époque romantique: essai sur l'influence de Walter Scott*, Geneva: Slatkine Reprints.

Manning, Susan (2003) ' "*Peine forte et dure*": Scott and France', in Dawson, Deirdre and Pierre Morère (eds) *Scotland and France in the Enlightenment*, Lewisburg: Bucknell University Press, pp. 108–27.

Maxwell, Richard (2001) 'Inundations of Time: A Definition of Scott's Originality', *English Literary History*, 68: 419–68.

— (2002) 'Phantom States: *Cleveland, The Recess*, and the Origins of Historical Fiction', in Cohen, Margaret and Caroline Dever (eds) *The Literary Channel: The Inter-National Invention of the Novel*, Princeton: Princeton University Press, pp. 151–82.

Merimée, Prosper (1969) *Chronique du règne de Charles IX*, ed. Pierre Josserand, Paris: Gallimard.

Michelet, Jules (1952) *Histoire de la Révolution française*, ed. Gérard Walter, Paris: Gallimard.

Mitchell, Jerome (1977) *The Walter Scott Operas: An Analysis of Operas Based on the Works of Sir Walter Scott*, [Tuscaloosa]: University of Alabama Press.

Nerval, Gérard de (1989) *Oeuvres complètes*, eds Jean Guillaume and Claude Pichois, 3 vols, Paris: Gallimard.

Nodier, Charles (1961) *Contes*, Paris: Garnier frères.

Pichot, Amédée (1826) *Vues pittoresques de l'Ecosse*, Paris: Charles Gosselin, Lami-Denozan.

— (1834) *Le Perroquet de Walter Scott: Esquisses de voyages; Légendes, romans, contes biographiques et littéraires*, 2 vols, Paris: A. Everat.

Prévost, Antoine (1810) *Oeuvres choisies*, 38 vols, Paris: Leblanc.

Proust, Marcel (1987–89) *A la recherche de temps perdu*, ed. Jean-Yves Tadié, 4 vols, Paris: Gallimard.

Quinet, Edgar (1995) *The Story of a Child*, trans. Rosemary and Peter Ganz, London: Duckworth.

Sainte-Beuve, Charles (1956) *Oeuvres*, 2 vols, Paris: Gallimard.

Scott, Walter (1830) *Oeuvres complètes*, trans. Auguste-Jean-Baptiste Defauconpret, 30 vols, Paris: Fumes.

— (1830–32) *Oeuvres*, trans. Albert Montémont, 32 vols, Paris: Armand-Aubrée.

— (1838–39) *Oeuvres complètes*, trans. Louis Vivien, 25 vols, Paris: P.-M. Pourrat.

— (1848) *Oeuvres*, trans. Léon de Wailly, Paris: Charpentier.

— (1849–57) *Oeuvres complètes*, trans. Louis Barré, 32 vols, Paris: J. Bryaîné.

— (1862) *Ivanhoé*, trans. Alexandre Dumas, 2 vols, Paris: Michel-Lévy frères.

Stendhal (1824) *Vie de Rossini*, Paris: Auguste Boulland.

— (1952) '*Sur Le Rouge et le noir*': *Romans et nouvelles*, ed. Henri Martineau, Paris: Gallimard, 1: 700–14.

— (1959) *Selected Journalism from the English Reviews*, ed. Geoffrey Strickland, New York: Grove Press.

Welsh, Alexander (1968) *The Hero of the Waverley Novels*, New York: Atheneum.

Vallès, Jules ([n.d.]) 'Les Victimes du Livre', in Labouret, Denis (ed.) *Les Victimes du livre: Ecrits sur la littérature*, Jaignes: La Chasse au Snark.

— (1975) *Oeuvres*, ed. Roger Bellet, 2 vols, Paris: Gallimard.

— (1877) *Les Indes-Noires*, Paris: J. Hetzel.

— (1989) *Voyage à reculons en Angleterre et en Ecosse*, ed. Christian Robin, Paris: le cherche midi.

Vigny, Alfred (1950) *Oeuvres complètes*, ed. F. Baldensperger, Paris: Gallimard.

Chapter 2: Another Tale of Old Mortality: The Translations of Auguste-Jean Baptiste Defauconpret in the French Reception of Scott

Alciatore, Jules C. (1954) 'Stendhal et Scott', *Symposium* [Syracuse University], 8: 147–50.

— (1966) 'Quelques remarques sur Stendhal et les héroines de Walter Scott', *Stendhal-Club* [Grenoble], 8: 339–45.

Ancelot, J.-A.-F.-P. and X. B. Saintine (1833) *Têtes rondes et cavaliers: drame historique en 3 actes, mêlé de chants*, Paris: J.-N. Barba.

Baldensperger, Fernand (1927) 'La grande communion romantique de 1827: sous le signe de Walter Scott', *Revue de littérature comparée* [Paris], 47–87.

Balzac, Honoré de (1976–81) *La Comédie Humaine*, ed. Pierre-Georges Castex, 12 vols, Paris: Galllimard.

— (2001) 'Etudes sur M. Beyle', in Victor Del Litto (ed.) *Stendhal sous l'oeil de la presse contemporaine*, Paris: Champion, pp. 758–804.

Benani, Agnès (1993) 'Auguste-Jean Baptiste Defauconpret, ou, L'Ecrivain et son double', *GRAAT: Publication des Groupes de Recherches Anglo-Americaines de l'Université Francois Rabelais*, 10: 189–201.

Benedetti, Anna (1974) *Le traduzioni italiane da Walter Scott e i loro anglicismi*, Florence: Olschki.

Béreaud, Jacques G. A. (1971) 'La Traduction en France à l'époque romantique', *Comparative Literature Studies*, 8: 224–44.

Bisson, L. A. (1942) *Amédée Pichot: A Romantic Prometheus*, Oxford: Blackwell.

Brémond, Henri (1924) 'Le Romantisme conservateur', in *Pour le romantisme*, Paris: Bloud & Gay, pp. 65–173.

Conner, Wayne (1980) 'Scott and Balzac', *Scottish Literary Journal*, 7: 65–72.

Crouzet, Michel (1981) 'Avertissement', in Scott, Sir Walter, *Waverley; Rob-Roy; La Fiancée de Lammermoor*, ed. Michel Crouzet, trans. A.-J.-B. Defauconpret, Paris: Laffont, p. 5.

Dargan, E. Preston (1934) 'Scott and the French Romantics', *Publications of the Modern Language Association of America*, 49: 599–629.

Davis, S. B. (1991) 'From Scotland to Russia via France: Scott, Defauconpret and Gogol', *Scottish Slavonic Review*, 17: 21–36.

Defauconpret, A.-J.-B. (1833) Introduction to Cunningham, Allan, *Notice biographique et littéraire sur Sir Walter Scott: suivie d'une notice bibliographique sur les diverses éditions de la traduction de M. Defauconpret*, trans. A.-J.-B. Defauconpret, Paris: C. Gosselin, [1]–16.

Del Litto, Victor (1971) 'Stendhal et Walter Scott', *Etudes anglaises* [Paris], 24: 501–08.

Draper, F. W. M. (1923) *The Rise and Fall of the French Romantic Drama: With Special Reference to the Influence of Shakespeare, Scott and Byron*, London: Constable.

Garnand, Harry Jennings (1926) *The Influence of Walter Scott on the Works of Balzac*, New York: Publications of the Institute of French Studies.

Gordon, R. K. (1928) 'Sir Walter Scott and the *Comédie Humaine*', *Modern Language Review*, 23: 51–55.

Green, F. C. (1957) 'Scott's French Correspondence', *Modern Language Review*, 52: 35–49.

Greene, Militsa (1965) 'Pushkin and Sir Walter Scott', *Forum for Modern Language Studies*, 1: 207–15.

Haggis, Donald (1973) 'Scott, Balzac, and the Historical Novel as Social and Political Analysis: *Waverley* and *Les Chouans*', *Modern Language Review*, 68: 51–68.

— (1974) 'Fiction and Historical Change in *La Cousine Bette* and the Lesson of Walter Scott', *Forum for Modern Language Studies*, 10.4 (1974).

— (1985) 'The Popularity of Scott's Novels in France and Balzac's *Illusions perdues*', *Journal of European Studies*, 15: 21–29.

Hartland, Reginald William (1928) *Walter Scott et le roman 'frénetique': contribution à l'étude de leur fortune en France*, Paris: Champion.

Hennig, John (1956) 'Goethe's Translation of Scott's Criticism of Hoffmann', *Modern Language Review*, 51: 369–77.

Hersant, Patrick (1999) 'Defauconpret, ou, Le demi-siècle d'Auguste', *Romantisme*, 29.106: 83–88.

Hugo, Victor (1976) 'Sur Walter Scott à propos de *Quentin Durward*', in *Littérature et philosophie mêlées*, ed. Anthony R. W. James, Paris: Klincksieck, 2: 27–47.

J. P. F. (1855) 'Defauconpret (Auguste-Jean-Baptiste)', in *Nouvelle biographie générale: depuis les temps les plus reculés jusqu'à nos jours*, Paris: Firmin Didot, 13: 349.

Lyons, Martin (1984) 'The Audience for Romanticism: Walter Scott in France, 1815–51', *European History Quarterly*, 14: 21–46.

Maigron, Louis (1898) *Le Roman historique à l'époque romantique: essai sur l'influence de Walter Scott*, Paris: Hachette.

Massmann, Klaus (1972) *Die Rezeption der historischen Romane Sir Walter Scotts in Frankreich, 1816–1832*, Heidelberg: Carl Winter Universitätsverlag.

M'Crie, Thomas (1817) Review of *Tales of My Landlord*, *Edinburgh Christian Instructor*, 14: 41–73, 100–140, 170–201.

Mérimée, Prosper (1969) *Chronique du règne de Charles IX*, pref. Pierre Josserand, Paris: Gallimard.

Meschonnic, Herni (1999) *Poétique du traduire*, Paris: Verdier.

Ostrowski, Witold (1965) 'Walter Scott in Poland, Part II: Adam Mickiewicz and Walter Scott', *Studies in Scottish Literature*, 3: 71–95.

Pichot, Amédée (1825) *Voyage historique et littéraire en Angleterre et en Ecosse*, 3 vols, Paris: Lavocat & Gosselin.

Quérard, Joseph-Marie (1828) *La France littéraire, ou, Dictionnaire bibliographique des savants, historiens et gens de lettres de la France, ainsi que des littérateurs étrangers qui ont écrit en français, plus particulièrement pendant les XVIIIe et XIXe siècles*, Paris: Firmin Didot, II.

Rémusat, Charles de (1883–86) *Correspondance de M. de Rémusat pendant les premières années de la Restauration*, ed. Paul de Rémusat, 6 vols, Paris: C. Lévy.

Richardot, J. (1965) 'Defauconpret (Auguste-Jean-Baptiste)', in *Dictionnaire de biographie française*, Paris: Letouzey, 10: 515.

Ruggieri Punzo, Franca (1975) *Walter Scott in Italia: 1821–1971*, Bari: Adriatica.

Scott, Walter (1816) *Tales of My Landlord, Collected and Arranged by Jedediah Cleishbotham, Schoolmaster and Parish-Clerk of Gandercleugh*, 4 vols, Edinburgh: William Blackwood; London: John Murray.

Steiner, George (1975) *After Babel: Aspects of Language and Translation*, London: Oxford University Press.

Stendhal (1959) *Selected Journalism from the English Reviews: With Translations of Other Critical Writings*, ed. Geoffrey Strickland, London: J. Calder.
— (1962–68) *Correspondance*, ed. Henri Martineau and V. del Litto, 3 vols, Paris: Gallimard.
— (1970) *Racine et Shakespeare: études sur le romantisme*, Paris: Garnier-Flammarion.
Streeter, Harold Wade (1936) *The Eighteenth-Century English Novel in French Translation: A Bibliographical Study*, New York: Institute of French Studies.

Ward, Nicole (1980) 'The Prison-House of Language: *The Heart of Midlothian* and *La Chartreuse de Parme*', *Comparative Criticism*, 2: 93–107.
West, Constance B. (1932) 'La Théorie de la traduction au XVIIIe siècle: par rapport surtout aux traductions françaises d'ouvrages anglais', *Revue de littérature comparée*, 12: 330–55.

Translations

The following is not an exhaustive list of all French translations. Under each heading it records the *first* French translation of individual works by Scott in chronological order.

1. Fiction

Where the first translation of a work is not by A.-J.-B. Defauconpret, the first edition of Defauconpret's version is also listed. Where rival translations of the same novel are published in the same year, all are listed (alphabetically by translator), with no attempt made to establish which appeared first.

GM
(1816) *Guy Mannering, astrologue: nouvelle écossaise*, trans. Joseph Martin, 4 vols, Paris: Plancher.
(1821) *Guy Mannering, ou, L'Astrologue*, trans. A.-J.-B. Defauconpret, 4 vols, Paris: H. Nicolle.

BD; OM
(1817) *Les Puritains d'Ecosse, et, Le Nain mystérieux: contes de mon hôte, recueillis et mis au jour par Jedediah Cleisbotham*, trans. A.-J.-B. Defauconpret, 4 vols, Paris: H. Nicolle; (1821) 2nd edn, Paris: H. Nicolle; (1830) 4th edn, Paris: Lecointe.

A
(1817) *L'Antiquaire*, trans. Mme Maraise, 4 vols, Paris: Renard.
(1821) *L'Antiquaire*, trans. A.-J.-B. Defauconpret, 4 vols, Paris: H. Nicolle.

RR
(1818a) *Rob-Roy*, trans. A.-J.-B. Defauconpret, 4 vols, Paris: H. Nicolle.
(1818b) *Robert-le-Rouge Mac-Grégor, ou, Les Montagnards écossais*, trans. H. Villemain, 4 vols, Paris: Dentu.

HM
(1818) *La Prison d'Edimbourg: nouveaux Contes de mon hôte, recueillis et mis au jour par Jedediah Cleisbotham, maître d'école et sacristain de la paroisse de Gandercleugh*, trans. A.-J.-B. Defauconpret, 4 vols, Paris: H. Nicolle.

W

(1818) *Waverley, ou, L'Ecosse il y a soixante ans: roman historique, contenant les principaux événements de l'expédition du prince Edouard en 1745*, trans. Joseph Martin, 4 vols, Paris: Mme Peronneau.

(1826) *Waverley, ou, Il y a soixante ans*, trans. A.-J.-B. Defauconpret, 4 vols, Paris: C. Gosselin.

BL

(1819) *La Fiancée de Lammermoor: contes de mon hôte, recueillis et mis au jour par Jedediah Cleishbotham, maître d'école et sacristain de la paroisse de Gandercleugh*, trans. A.-J.-B. Defauconpret, 3 vols, Paris: H. Nicolle.

LM

(1819) *L'Officier de fortune: épisode des guerres de Montrose: contes de mon hôte, recueillis et mis au jour par Jedediah Cleishbotham, maître d'école et sacristain de la paroisse de Gandercleugh*, trans. A.-J.-B. Defauconpret, 2 vols, Paris: H. Nicolle.

I

(1820) *Ivanhoé, ou, Le Retour du Croisé*, trans. A.-J.-B. Defauconpret, 4 vols, Paris: H. Nicolle.

MO

(1820) *Le Monastère*, trans. A.-J.-B. Defauconpret, 4 vols, Paris: H. Nicolle.

AB

(1820) *L'Abbé: suite du 'Monastère'*, trans. A.-J.-B. Defauconpret, 4 vols, Paris: H. Nicolle.

K

(1821a) *Kenilworth*, trans. Fanny Angel Collet, 4 vols, Paris: Lerouge.

(1821b) *Kenilworth: précédé d'une Notice historique sur le château de Kenilworth et sur le comte de Leicester*, trans. A.-J.-B. Defauconpret, 4 vols, Paris: H. Nicolle.

(1821c) *Le Château de Kenilworth: orné du portrait de la reine Elisabeth, et d'un plan du château: et accompagné d'une Notice historique sur Kenilworth et sur le comte de Leicester*, trans. Jacques-Théodore Parisot, 4 vols, Paris: Corréard.

P

(1822a) *Le Pirate*, trans. A.-J.-B. Defauconpret, 4 vols, Paris: Ch. Gosselin; Ladvocat.

(1822b) *Le Pirate, ou, Les Filibustiers*, trans. anon., 4 vols, Paris: Librairie nationale et étrangère.

FN

(1822a) *Les Aventures de Nigel*, trans. Fanny Angel Collet, 4 vols, Paris: Ch. Gosselin; Ladvocat. Commissioned by publishers Haute-Coeur & Gayet, this edn was bought and published by Gosselin to eliminate competition (see Quérard 1836, 565).

(1822b) *Les Aventures de Nigel*, trans. A.-J.-B. Defauconpret, 4 vols, Paris: Ch. Gosselin; Ladvocat.

PP

(1823) *Peveril du Pic*, trans. A.-J.-B. Defauconpret, 5 vols, Paris: Ch. Gosselin.

QD
(1823) *Quentin Durward, ou, L'Ecossais à la Cour de Louis XI*, trans. A.-J.-B. Defauconpret, 4 vols, Paris: Gosselin; Ladvocat.

SRW
(1824a) *Les Eaux de Saint-Ronan*, trans. Fanny Angel Collet, 4 vols, Paris: Mme de Wincop; Delaunay.
(1824b) *Les Eaux de Saint-Ronan*, trans. A.-J.-B. Defauconpret, 4 vols, Paris: Ch. Gosselin; Ladvocat.

R
(1824) *Redgauntlet: histoire du XVIIIe siècle*, trans. A.-J.-B. Defauconpret, 4 vols, Paris: Ch. Gosselin.

T, TBET
(1825) *Histoires du temps des Croisades*, trans. A.-J.-B. Defauconpret, 6 vols, Paris: Ch. Gosselin.

WO
(1826) *Woodstock, ou, Le Cavalier: histoire du temps de Cromwell, année 1651*, trans. A.-J.-B. Defauconpret, 4 vols, Paris: Ch. Gosselin.

CC
(1827) *Chroniques de la Canongate*, trans. A.-J.-B. Defauconpret, 4 vols, Paris: Ch. Gosselin.

FMP
(1828) *La Jolie Fille de Perth, ou, Le Jour de Saint-Valentin: roman historique, avec des notes explicatives*, trans. A.-J.-B. Defauconpret, 4 vols, Paris: Ch. Gosselin.

AG
(1829a) *Anne de Geierstein, ou, La Vierge des brouillards*, trans. J. Cohen, 4 vols, Paris: Boulland.
(1829b) *Charles-le-Téméraire, ou, Anne de Geierstein, la fille du brouillard: roman historique*, trans. A.-J.-B. Defauconpret, 5 vols, Paris: Ch. Gosselin.

TC, MAMM, 'On the Supernatural in Fictitious Composition', 'Phantasmagoria'
(1829) *Le Miroir de la tante Marguerite, et, La Chambre tapissée: contes par sir Walter Scott: précédé d'un 'Essai sur l'emploi du merveilleux dans le roman', et suivis de 'Clorinda, ou, Le Collier de perles'*, trans. Mme Charles Gosselin, Paris: Ch. Gosselin.

CRP
(1831) *Robert, comte de Paris: roman du Bas-Empire*, trans. A.-J.-B. Defauconpret, 4 vols, Paris: Ch. Gosselin.

CD
(1831) *Le Château périlleux: roman écossais du XIVe siècle*, trans. A.-J.-B. Defauconpret, 4 vols, Paris: Ch. Gosselin.

2. Poetry

LL
(1813) *La Dame du Lac: roman, tiré du poème de Walter Scott*, trans. Elisabeth de Bon, 2 vols, Paris: Galignani.

M
(1820) *Marmion, ou, La Bataille de Flodden-Field*, trans. Amédée Pichot, 2 vols, Paris: Ladvocat; H. Nicolle (Romans poétiques, 4–5).

RO, HD
(1820) *Mathilde de Rokeby, suivi de, Harold l'intrépide*, trans. Amédée Pichot, 2 vols, Paris: Ladvocat; H. Nicolle (Romans poétiques, 2–3).

LLM
(1821) *Le Lai du dernier ménéstrel: précédé d'une Notice historique sur Sir Walter Scott et sur ses écrits, et orné de son portrait*, trans. Amédée Pichot, Paris: H. Nicolle; Ladvocat (Romans poétiques, 1).

LI
(1821) *Le Lord des îles*, trans. Amédée Pichot, Paris: H. Nicolle; Ladvocat (Romans poétiques, 6).

BT
(1821) *La Dame du lac, et, Les Fiançailles de Triermain*, trans. Amédée Pichot, 2 vols, Paris: H. Nicolle (Romans poétiques, 7).

VDR, FW, 'Thomas the Rhymer', Selected Poems
(1821) *La Vision de don Roderick; Le Champ de bataille de Waterloo; Thomas-le-Rimeur; Ballades; Mélanges de poésies légères*, trans. Amédée Pichot, 2 vols, Paris: H. Nicolle (Romans poétiques, 8).

MSB: Selections
(1825) *Ballades, légendes et chants populaires de l'Angleterre et de l'Ecosse*, ed. and trans. A. Loève-Weimars, Paris: A. A. Renouard.

MSB: Complete
(1826) *Chants populaires des frontières méridionales de l'Ecosse*, trans. Nicolas-Louis Artaud, Paris: Ch. Gosselin; Sautelet.

There is not space here to list translations of shorter poems by Scott. For further information, consult BOSLIT (Bibliography of Scottish Literature in Translation) <http://boslit.nls.uk>. Most are eventually collected in the following edn of Scott's collected works:

(1849–57) *Oeuvres complètes de Walter Scott*, trans. Louis Barré, 32 vols, Paris: J. Bry aîné.

3. Drama

HH
(1822) *Halidon Hill: esquisse dramatique, tirée de l'histoire d'Ecosse*, trans. A.-J.-B. Defauconpret, Paris: Ch. Gosselin; Ladvocat.

HA
(1830) *La Maison d'Aspen: tragédie*, trans. Louise Swanton Belloc, *Le Keepsake français* [Paris], 1: 179–213.

MC
(1833) *La Croix de Mac-Duff: esquisse dramatique*, trans. Louise Swanton Belloc, *Le Panorama littéraire de l'Europe* [Paris], 1: 81–91.

AU, DD, IB
(1857) *La Maison d'Aspen: tragédie; Halidon Hill: drame; Auchindrane: tragédie; La Croix de Macduff: scène dramatique; Devorgoil; Il Bizzarro; Poésies inédites*, trans. Louis Barré, Paris: J. Bry aîné.

4. *Miscellaneous Prose*

PLK
(1822) *Lettres de Paul à sa famille: écrites en 1815; suivi de, La Recherche du bonheur: conte*, trans. Amédée Pichot, 3 vols, Paris: Ch. Gosselin; Ladvocat.

LN
(1825) *Biographie littéraire des romanciers célèbres: depuis Fielding jusqu'à nos jours*, trans. anon., 4 vols, Paris: Ch. Gosselin.

MJD
(1825) *Vie de John Dryden: renfermant l'histoire de la littérature anglaise, depuis la mort de Shakespeare jusqu'en 1700*, trans. anon., 2 vols, Paris: Ch. Gosselin.

MJS
(1826) *Mémoires politiques et littéraires sur la vie et les ouvrages de Jonathan Swift, doyen de Saint-Patrice*, trans. anon., 2 vols, Paris: Ch. Gosselin.

'Romance', 'Chivalry', 'Drama'
(1826) *Essais historiques et littéraires*, trans. anon., 2 vols Paris: Ch. Gosselin.

NB
(1827) *Vie de Napoléon Buonaparte, empereur des Français*, trans. A.-J.-B. Defauconpret and others, 10 vols, Paris: Ch. Gosselin; Treuttel et Würtz.

RD
(1828) *Sermons*, trans. anon., Paris: Ch. Gosselin.

TG1
(1828) *Histoire d'Ecosse: racontée par un grand-père à son petit-fils: première série*, trans. Charles-Auguste Defauconpret, 3 vols, Paris: Ch. Gosselin.

TG2
(1828) *Histoire d'Ecosse: racontée par un grand-père à son petit-fils: seconde série*, trans. Mme Charles Gosselin, 4 vols, Paris: Ch. Gosselin.

TG3
(1830) *Histoire d'Ecosse: racontée par un grand-père à son petit-fils: troisième série*, trans. A.-J.-B. Defauconpret, 4 vols, Paris: Ch. Gosselin.

TG4
(1831) *Histoire de France: racontée par un grand-père à son petit-fils*, trans. A.-J.-B. Defauconpret, 4 vols, Paris: Ch. Gosselin.

LDW
(1832a) *Histoire de la démonologie et de la sorcellerie*, trans. A.-J.-B. Defauconpret, 2 vols, Paris: Ch. Gosselin
(1832b) *La Démonologie, ou, Histoire des démons et des sorciers*, Albert de Montémont, Paris: Arm. Aubrée.

HS
(1833–35) 'Ecosse', in Scott, Sir Walter, Sir James Mackintosh and Sir Thomas Moore, *Histoire générale des îles Britanniques*, trans. A.-J.-B. Defauconpret, 3 vols, Paris: Ch. Gosselin.

Chapter 3: The Reception of Sir Walter Scott in Spain

Alonso, Amado (1984) *Ensayo sobre la novela histórica: el modernismo en 'La gloria de Don Ramiro'*, Madrid: Gredos.
Álvarez-Rodríguez, Román (1983) *Origen y evolución de la novela histórica inglesa*, Salamanca: Universidad de Salamanca.

Cabo-Pérez, Gemma de (2001) '*Kenilworth* 1821–¿1999?', in Cabanillas, Isabel de la Cruz and others (eds) *La Lingüística Aplicada a finales de siglo: ensayos y propuestas*, Alcalá de Henares: A.E.S.L.A. and Universidad de Alcalá de Henares, 2: 789–95.
Churchman, Philip Hudson and Edgar Allison Peers (1922) 'A Survey of the Influence of Sir Walter Scott in Spain', *Revue hispanique* [Paris], 40: 2–86; 55: 227–310.

Ferreras, Juan Ignacio (1976) *El triunfo del liberalismo y de la novela histórica (1830–1870)*, Madrid: Taurus.

García-González, José Enrique (2005) 'Traducción y recepción de Walter Scott en España: estudio descriptivo de las traducciones de *Waverley* al español' (doctoral thesis, University of Seville; forthcoming on CD-ROM).
González-Palencia, Ángel (1927) *Walter Scott y la censura gubernativa*, Madrid: Imp. Municipal.

Lloréns, Vicente (1989) *El romanticismo español*, rev. 2nd edn, Madrid: Castalia.
López-Folgado, Vicente and Lucía Mora-González (1987) 'La primera traducción de *The Bride of Lammermoor*, de W. Scott', in Santoyo, Julio-César and others (eds) *Fidus interpres: Actas de las Primeras Jornadas Nacionales de Historia de la Traducción*, León: Universidad de León and Diputación Provincial, 1: 349–53.

Marrast, Robert (1988) 'Ediciones perpiñanescas de Walter Scott en castellano (1824–1826)', in *Romanticismo (La narrativa romantica: Atti del IV Congreso sul Romanticismo spagnolo e ispanoamericano; Bordighera, 9–11 aprile 1987)*, Genoa: Biblioteca di Lett., 3–4: 69–80.
Martín, Félix (1988) 'El siglo XIX', in Pérez-Gallego, Cándido (dir.) *Historia de la literatura inglesa*, Madrid: Taurus, 2: 133–300.
Menéndez-Pelayo, Marcelino (1940) *Historia de las ideas estéticas en España*, ed. Enrique Sánchez-Reyes, 5 vols, Santander: Consejo Superior de Investigaciones Científicas.

Milá y Fontanals, Manuel (1892a) 'Las aguas de San Román, por Sir Walter Scott', in *Obras completas: Opúsculos literarios*, Barcelona: Librería de Álvaro Verdaguer, 4: 38–41.

— (1892b) 'Poemas de Sir Walter Scott', in *Obras completas: Opúsculos literarios*, Barcelona: Librería de Álvaro Verdaguer, 4: 198–208.

Montesinos, José F. (1980) *Introducción a una historia de la novela en España en el siglo XIX: seguida del esbozo de una bibliografía española de traducciones de novelas (1800–1850)*, 4th edn, Madrid: Castalia.

Murphy, Martin (1995) 'The Spanish *Waverley*: Blanco White and *Vargas*', *Atlantis*, 17.1–2 (November): 165–80.

Peers, Edgar Allison (1926) 'Studies in the Influence of Sir Walter Scott in Spain', *Revue Hispanique* [Paris], 68: 1–160.

— (1967) *Historia del movimiento romántico español*, trans. José María Gimeno, 2nd edn, 2 vols, Madrid: Gredos.

Pujals, Esteban (1969) *El Romanticismo inglés: orígenes, repercusión europea y relaciones con la literatura española*, Santander: Universidad Internacional Menéndez Pelayo.

Rabadán, Rosa (ed.) (2000) *Traducción y censura inglés-español: 1939–1985: Estudio preliminar*, León: Universidad de León.

Regalado-García, Antonio (1966) 'Galdós y Walter Scott', in *Benito Pérez Galdós y la novela histórica española: 1868–1912*, Madrid: Ínsula, pp. 133–56.

Ruiz-Casanova, José Francisco (2000) *Aproximación a una historia de la traducción en España*, Madrid: Cátedra.

Santoyo, Julio-César (2000) 'Traducción y censura: Mirada retrospectiva a una historia interminable', in Rabadán, Rosa (ed.) *Traducción y censura inglés-español: 1939–1985: Estudio preliminar*, León: Universidad de León, pp. 291–308.

Soldevila, Ferrán (1926) 'Walter Scott y el Renacimiento literario catalán', *Bulletin of Spanish Studies*, 3.10: 88–90.

Stoudemire, Sterling A. (1950) 'A Note on Scott in Spain', Sterling A. Stoudemire Papers: 1920s–1990s [MSS], University of North Carolina Library, pp. 3–6.

Varela-Jacome, Benito (1974) *Estructuras novelísticas del siglo XIX*, Barcelona: José Bosch.

Zavala, Iris M. (1971) *Ideología y política en la novela española del siglo XIX*, Salamanca: Anaya, pp. 15–39.

Translations

(1823–24) 'Retazos de la novela inglesa intitulada Ivanhoe', trans. and ed. José María Blanco-White, *Las Variedades, o El Mensajero de Londres* [London], 1 (January 1823): 31–38; 2 (January 1824): 173–76; 3 (April 1824): 206–14.

(1825) *Ivanhoe*, 2 vols, trans. José Joaquín de Mora, London; Mexico City: Ackermann.

(1826a) *Los Puritanos de Escocia & El enano misterioso*, 4 vols, trans. D. F. A. y G. [Don Francisco Altés y Gurena], Perpignan: Alzine.

(1826b) *El Talismán*, 2 vols, trans. José Joaquín de Mora, London; Mexico City: Ackermann.

(1826c) *El Talismán, ó Ricardo en Palestina*, 3 vols, trans. Juan Nicasio Gallego and Eugenio de Tapia, Barcelona: Piferrer.

(1827a) *El oficial aventurero: episodio de las guerras de Montrose*, 2 vols, trans. B. C., Bordeaux: Beaume.

(1827b) *Quintín Durward, ó el escocés en la corte de Luis XI*, 4 vols, trans. D. F. A. y G. [Don Francisco Altés y Gurena], Perpignan: Alzine.

(1828a) *El anticuario*, 4 vols, trans. anon., Bordeaux: Beaume.

(1828b) *La pastora de Lammermoor o la desposada*, 2 vols, trans. D. L. C. B., Madrid: Sanz.

(1828c) *Rob Roy*, trans. V. F. D. M., Bordeaux.

(1829a) *Matilde de Rokeby. Novela histórico-poética*, trans. Mariano Rementería y Fica, Madrid: Moreno.

(1829b) *Visión de don Rodrigo*, trans. A. Tracia, Barcelona: Viuda e hijos de Brusi.

(1830a) *La dama del lago. Novela histórica & Los desposorios de Triermain o El valle de San Juan*, 2 vols, trans. Mariano Rementería y Fica, Madrid: Moreno.

(1830b) *El espejo de la tía Margarita and El aposento entapizado*, trans. anon. Madrid: Moreno.

(1830c) *El lord de las islas*, trans. anon Madrid: Moreno.

(1830d) *El pirata*, 4 vols, trans. anon., Madrid: Moreno.

(1831a) *Las cárceles de Edimburgo*, 4 vols, trans. anon., Madrid: Moreno.

(1831b) *Carlos el Temerario o Ana Geierstein, hija de la niebla*, 2 vols, trans. anon., Madrid: Jordán.

(1831c) *El castillo de Kenilworth*, 4 vols, trans. Pablo de Xérica, Bordeaux: Beaume.

(1831d) *Woodstock o El caballero*, 4 vols, trans. anon., Madrid: Jordán.

(1833) *Waverley, ó Ahora sesenta años*, 3 vols, trans. José María Heredia, Mexico: Galván.

(1833–34) *Redgauntlet*, 5 vols, trans. D. F. de O., Barcelona: Bergnes.

(1834) *Roberto, Conde de París*, 4 vols, trans. anon., Barcelona: Bergnes.

(1835) *Guy Mannering o El Astrólogo*, 4 vols, trans. Pablo de Xérica, Paris.

(1836a) *Las aventuras de Nigel*, 4 vols, trans. Pablo de Xérica, Paris: Rosa.

(1836b) *El día de San Valentín o La linda doncella de Perth*, 4 vols, trans. J. M. Moralejo, Paris: Rosa.

(1836c) *Peveril del Pico*, trans. W. Montes, 5 vols, Paris: Rosa.

(1840a) *El abad*, 4 vols, trans. anon., Paris: Rosa.

(1840b) *El castillo peligroso*, 2 vols, trans. Pedro Mata, Paris: Rosa; Mexico City: Galván.

(1840c) *Los desposados o sea El condestable de Chester*, 3 vols, trans. Pedro Mata, Paris: Rosa; Mexico City: Galván.

(1840d) *El monasterio*, 4 vols, trans. Eugenio de Ochoa, Paris: Rosa; Mexico City: Galván.

(1841a) *Las aguas de San Ronan*, 4 vols, trans. Eugenio de Ochoa, Paris: Rosa; Mexico City: Galván.

(1841b) *Quintín Durward, episodio de la historia de Luis XI*, 5 vols, trans. anon., (pub. in fascicles), *El Panorama* [Madrid], Sunday edn.

(1843) *Canto del último trovador: Poema en seis cantos*, trans. Pablo Piferrer, Barcelona: Oliveres.

(1882) *Los boyeros*, trans. Joaquín Riera y Bertrán, Barcelona: C. Verdaguer.

(1907) *Las crónicas de la Canongate*, 2 vols, trans. Rafael Mesa López, Paris: Garnier.

(2004) *Defensa de la nación escocesa: las cartas de Malachi Malagrowther*, trans. Fernando Toda, Málaga: Universidad de Málaga.

Chapter 4: Ivanhoe, a Tale of the Crusades, or Scott in Catalonia

Aribau, Bonaventura Carles (1833) 'La patria: Trobes', *El Vapor* [Barcelona], 26 March, 3–4.

Ayguals de Izco, Wenceslao (1833) 'El patriotismo en ciencias y artes', *El Vapor* [Barcelona], 26 March, 4.

Bergnes de las Casas (1835) 'Influjo que ha ejercido y está ejerciendo Walter-Scott en las riquezas, la moralidad y la dicha de la sociedad moderna', *El Museo de las Familias*, 354–59.

Bertrán de Amat, Felipe (1891) *Del origen y doctrinas de la Escuela Romántica y de la participación que tuvieron en el adelantamiento de las bellas artes en esta capital los señores d. Manuel y d. Claudio Lorenzale*, Barcelona: Imprenta Barcelonesa.

Brown, Reginald F. (1945) 'The Romantic Novel in Catalonia', *Hispanic Review*, 13: 293–323.

Buendía, Felicidad (ed.) 'Prologo', in *Antologia de la novela historica española*, Madrid: Aguilar, pp. 44–47.

Churchman, Philip H. and E. Alison Peers (1922) 'A Survey of the Influence of Sir Walter Scott in Spain', *Revue Hispanique*, 55: 227–310.

'Influencia de las obras de Walter Scout en la generacion actual' (1833), *El Vapor* [Barcelona], 2 November, 1–2.

Jorba, Manuel (1984) *Manuel Milà i Fontanals en la seva època: trajectòria ideològica i profesional*, Barcelona: Curial.
— (1991) *Manuel Milà i Fontanals*, Barcelona: Curial Edicions Catalanes.

Juretschke Hans (1973–74) 'Alemania en la Obra de Milá y Fontanals, *Boletín de la Real Academia de Buenas Letras de Barcelona*, 35: 5–66.

Juretschke Hans (1989) *L'Obra crítica i erudita de Manuel Milà i Fontanals*, Barcelona: Curial.

King, Edward L. (1962) 'What is Spanish Romanticism?', *Studies in Romanticism*, 2.1: 1–11.

López Soler, Ramon (1823a) 'Análisis de la cuestion agitada entre románticos y clasicistas', *El Europeo* [Barcelona], 29 November, 207–14.
— (1823b) 'Conclusion del análisis de la cuestion agitada entre románticos y clasicistas', *El Europeo* [Barcelona], 6 December, 29: 254–59.

Menéndez Pelayo, Marcelino (1908) *El Doctor Manuel Milá y Fontanals: semblanza Literaria*, Barcelona: Gustavo Gili.

Milà Fontanals, Manuel (1844) *Compendio del arte poética*, Barcelona: D. J. M. de Grau.
— (1854a) 'Poemas de Walter Scott I', *Diario de Barcelona*, 9 February, 976–77.
— (1854b) 'Poemas de Walter Scott II', *Diario de Barcelona*, 15 February, 1130–33.
— (1892a) 'Las Aguas de San Ronan por Sir Walter Scott', in *Las obras completas del doctor Manuel Milá y Fontanals coleccionadas por Marcelino Menéndez y Pelayo*, 4: 38–41.
— (1892b) 'Moral literaria. Contraste entre la escuela escéptica y Walter Scott' in *Las obras completas del doctor Manuel Milá y Fontanals coleccionadas por Marcelino Menéndez y Pelayo*, 4: 6–10.
— (1892c) 'Un párrafo de historia literaria' in *Las obras completas del doctor Manuel Milá y Fontanals coleccionadas por Marcelino Menéndez y Pelayo*, 4: 249–53.
— (1912a) 'Cervantes y el romanticismo', *Homenatje a Milà y Fontanals – Acció*, 6–7.
— (1912b) *Manual d'historia crítica de la literatura catalana moderna – primer part 1823–1900*, Barcelona: Editorial Pedagògica.

Montoliu, Manuel de (1936) *Aribau y la Catalunya del seu temps*, Barcelona: Institut d'Estudis Catalans.

[n. title] (1823) *El Europeo* [Barcelona], 27 December, 351.
'Noticias literarias' (1824) *El Europeo* [Barcelona], 14 February, 198–99.

Par, Alfonso (1935) *Shakespeare en la literature española*, vol. 3, Madrid: Biblioteca Balmes.
Peers, E. Allison (1920) 'Some Provincial Periodicals in Spain during the Romantic Movement', *Modern Language Review*, 15: 374–91.
— (1926a) 'Literary Ideas in Spain from 1839 to 1854', *Modern Language Review*, 21: 44–54.
— (1926b) 'Studies in the Influence of Sir Walter Scott in Spain', *Revue Hispanique*, 1–156.
— (1967) *Historia del Movimiento Romántico Español*, 2nd edn, Madrid: Gredos.
Piferrer Pablo (1839) *Recuerdos y bellezas de España*, Barcelona: Joaquin Verdaguer.

Rubió Lluch, Antonio and Cosme Parpal Marqués (1919) *Milá y Fontanals y Rubió y Ors: Discursos escritos para la solemne sesión conmemorativa del centenario del nacimiento de dichos ilustres profesores*, Barcelona: Pedro Ortega.

Serrahima, Maurici and Maria Teresa Boada (1996) *La novel'la històrica en la literatura catalana*, Barcelona: Publicacions de l'Abadia de Montserrat.

Tubino, Francisco Mᵃ (2003) *Historia del renacimiento literario contemporáneo de Cataluña, Baleares y Valencia*, Pamplona: Urgoiti Editores.

Zellars, G. G. (1931) 'Influencia de Walter Scott en España', *Revista de filología española*, 18: 149–62.

Chapter 5: The Reception of Walter Scott in Nineteenth-Century Austria

Alexis, Willibald (1821) [Review of] *The works of the right honourable Lord Byron* and *The works of Walter Scott* [German reprint edns, Zwickau: Schumann 1819/20 and 1819, respectively], *Jahrbücher der Literatur*, 15: 105–45.
— (1823) 'The Romances of Walter Scott' [German reprint edn, Zwickau: Schumann], *Jahrbücher der Literatur*, 22: 1–75.

Bachleitner, Norbert (1990) *Quellen zur Rezeption des englischen und französischen Romans in Deutschland und Österreich im 19. Jahrhundert*, Tübingen: Niemeyer.
— (1991) ' ". . . der so nachtheiligen Romanen-Lektüre ein Ende zu machen": Der historische Roman und die österreichische Zensur im Vormärz, am Beispiel von Walter Scotts *Woodstock*', *Sprachkunst*, 22.1: 35–48.
— (1999) *Kleine Geschichte des deutschen Feuilletonromans*, Tübingen: Narr.
Bauerfeld, Eduard von (1844) 'Einleitung', *Die hinterlassenen Papiere des Pickwick-Club* [. . .] von Boz (Charles Dickens), vol. 1, Vienna: Mausberger, I–XVI; repr. in Bachleitner (1990), pp. 323–28.
Breier, Eduard (1871) *Mein literarisches Wirken!*, Vienna: [n. pub.].

Eder, Beatrix (1934) 'Grillparzers Verhältnis zur englischen Literatur' (unpublished doctoral thesis, University of Vienna).

Feuchtersleben, Ernst von (1836a) 'Scott und Bulwer', *Wiener Zeitschrift für Kunst, Literatur, Theater und Mode*, 629–30, 637–39.
— (1836b) 'Moderne poetische Literatur', *Blätter für Literatur, Kunst und Kritik*, 117.20: 121–23, 125–26.
— (2002) *Sämtliche Werke und Briefe*, vol. 6, ed. Barbara Otto, Vienna: Österreichische Akademie der Wissenschaften.

Grillparzer, Franz ([n.d.]) *Sämtliche Werke*, ed. August Sauer, part 3, vol. 2, *Briefe und Dokumente*, part 2, Vienna: Schroll.
— ([n.d.]) *Werke in sechs Bänden*, vol. 6, *Erinnerungsblätter*, Vienna: Österreichische Staatsdruckerei.

Hammer-Purgstall, Joseph Freiherr von (1940) *Erinnerungen aus meinem Leben 1774–1852*, ed. Reinhart Bachofen von Echt, Vienna; Leipzig: Hölder-Pichler-Tempsky.
Holzner, Johann, Elisabeth Neumayr and Wolfgang Wiesmüller (2000) 'Der Historische Roman in Österreich 1848–1890', in Amann, Klaus, Hubert Lengauer and Karl Wagner (eds) *Literarisches Leben in Österreich 1848–1890*, Vienna; Cologne; Weimar: Böhlau, pp. 455–504.

Jahrbücher der Literatur (1820), 12: 124–55.

Klieneberger, Hans R. (1986) 'Stifters *Witiko* und die Romane Walter Scotts', *Adalbert-Stifter-Institut des Landes Oberösterreich Vierteljahresschrift*, 35: 145–55.
Kucher, Primus-Heinz (2002) *Ungleichzeitige/verspätete Moderne: Prosaformen in der österreichischen Literatur 1820–1880*, Tübingen; Basle: Francke.

Lechner, Silvester (1977) *Gelehrte Kritik und Restauration: Metternichs Wissenschafts- und Pressepolitik und die Wiener 'Jahrbücher der Literatur' (1818–1849)*, Tübingen: Niemeyer.
Lengauer, Hubert (1989) *Ästhetik und liberale Opposition: Zur Rollenproblematik des Schriftstellers in der österreichischen Literatur um 1848*, Vienna; Cologne: Böhlau.
Literarischer Anzeiger (1821a), 3: 14–16.
Literarischer Anzeiger (1821b) 'Linien zu Schriftstellerbildnissen. No. 11. Walter Scott', 3: 415–18.
'Literatur' (1825) *Wiener Zeitschrift für Kunst, Literatur, Theater und Mode*, 1022–24.
'Literatur' (1827) *Wiener Zeitschrift für Kunst, Literatur, Theater und Mode*, 210–12.

Martino, Alberto (1990) *Die deutsche Leihbibliothek: Geschichte einer literarischen Institution (1756–1914)*, Wiesbaden: Harrassowitz.

Pichler, Caroline von (1893) 'Briefe an Therese Huber', *Jahrbuch der Grillparzer-Gesellschaft*, 3: 269–365.
— (1914) *Denkwürdigkeiten aus meinem Leben*, ed. Karl Blümml, 2 vols, Munich: Müller.
Ritter, Alexander (2000) 'Die Bekannten und die beiden "großen Unbekannten": Scott, der historische Roman und sein Einfluß auf Charles Sealsfield', in Bachleitner, Norbert (ed.) *Beiträge zur Rezeption der britischen und irischen Literatur des 19. Jahrhunderts im deutschsprachigen Raum*, Amsterdam; Atlanta: Rodopi, pp. 443–77.
'Romantische Literatur' (1825) [report on Strauß edn of Scott's complete works], *Der Sammler*, 76.
'Romantische Literatur' (1826) [report on Strauß edn of Scott's complete works], *Der Sammler*, 212.

Schöll, Adolf (1836) 'Joseph Freyherr von Eichendorff's Schriften', *Jahrbücher der Literatur*, 75: 96–139.

Scott, Walter (1871) *Woodstock or the Cavalier: A Tale of the Year Sixteen Hundred and Fifty-One*, Edinburgh: Black.

Sealsfield, Charles (1835) *Lebensbilder aus beiden Hemisphären: Die große Tour*, Zurich: Orell, Füßli & Co. [title of later edns: *Morton oder die große Tour*].

Seidlitz, Julius (1836) *Die Poesie und die Poeten in Österreich im Jahre 1836*, Grimma: [n.p.].

Stifter, Adalbert (1929) *Sämmtliche Werke*, vol. 19, ed. Gustav Wilhelm, Reichenberg: Kraus.

— (1979) *Sämtliche Werke*, vol. 25, *Erzählungen*, 3: *Gedichte und Biographisches*, ed. Klaus Zelewitz, Hildesheim: Gerstenberg.

'Der Traum, Bericht von Walter Scott' (1829), *Der Sammler*, 274–76.

'Walter Scott und seine Romane' (1827) *Wiener Zeitschrift für Kunst, Literatur, Theater und Mode*, 1171–74.

Wiener Allgemeine Literaturzeitung (1813), 1647 49.

Wiener Allgemeine Literaturzeitung (1815), 679–86.

Wiesmüller, Wolfgang (1981) 'Adalbert Stifters Reflexionen über den historischen Roman', in Holzner, Johann, Michael Klein and Wolfgang Wiesmüller (eds) *Studien zur Literatur des 19. und 20. Jahrhunderts in Österreich: Festschrift für Alfred Doppler zum 60. Geburtstag*, Innsbrucker Beiträge zur Kulturwissenschaft: Germanistische Reihe 12, Innsbruck: Universität Innsbruck, Institut für Germanistik, pp. 43–53.

— (1995) 'Geschichte als Kassandra? Zum Verhältnis von Historie und Dichtung bei Adalbert Stifter', in Holzner, Johann and Wolfgang Wiesmüller (eds) *Ästhetik der Geschichte*, Innsbrucker Beiträge zur Kulturwissenschaft: Germanistische Reihe 54, Innsbruck: Universität Innsbruck, Institut für Germanistik, pp. 61–75.

Wild, Rupert (1935) 'Die historischen Romane der Caroline Pichler mit Rücksicht auf die Einflüsse Walter Scott's' (unpublished doctoral thesis, University of Vienna).

Translations

(1819) 'Alix Brand, Ballade aus der *Lady of the Lake* von Walter Scott' (Alice Brand, Ballad from *The Lady of the Lake*), trans. Caroline Pichler, *Aglaja* [Vienna], 253–58.

(1820–21) *Die Schwärmer*, trans. W. A. Lindau, 3 vols, Brünn: Traßler [Old Mortality].

(1821) 'Das Schloß der sieben Schilde', from Scott's *Harold the Dauntless*, trans. Joseph von Hammer, *Wiener Zeitschrift für Kunst, Literatur, Theater und Mode*, 477–78.

(1825a) *Kenilworth*, ed. Friedrich Böhmer, Brünn: Traßler.

(1825b) *Die Flucht nach Kenilworth*, Tragödie in fünf Acten, nach Walter Scott's Roman Kenilworth von Johann Reinhold Lenz, Mainz: [n. pub.].

(1825–30) *Walter Scott's Werke*, 93 vols, Vienna: Mausberger.

(1825–31) *Auserlesene Werke*, neueste verbesserte Ausgabe mit Nachrichten über des Verfassers Lebensumstände, 74 vols, Vienna: Strauß.

(1826a) *Woodstock, eine romantische Darstellung aus den Zeiten Cromwell's*, trans. C. F. Michaelis, Leipzig: Herbig.

(1826b) Songs from *The Lady of the Lake*, trans. Adam Storck, composed Franz Schubert: Ellen's Gesang I (op. 52, no. 1), Ellen's Gesang II (op. 52, no. 2), Bootgesang (op. 52, no. 3), Coronach (op. 52, no. 4), Normans Gesang (op. 52, no. 5), Ellen's Gesang III (Hymne an die Jungfrau, 'Ave Maria'; op. 52, no. 6), Lied des gefangenen Jägers (op. 52, no. 7).

(1827a) *Woodstock, eine romantische Darstellung aus den Zeiten Cromwell's*, trans. C. F. Michaelis, (Walter Scott's auserlesene Werke 58–60), Vienna: Strauß.

(1827b) *Maria Stuarts erste Gefangenschaft*, Drama in vier Aufzügen nach W. Scott von Johann Wenzel Lembert, *Dramatische Neujahrsgabe für 1827*, Vienna: [The Abbot].

(1827–34) *Walter Scott's Werke*, neu übersetzte, verbesserte Ausgabe, 78 vols, Grätz: Kienreich.

(1828) *Das Fräulein vom See: ein Gedicht in sechs Gesängen*, trans. Ferdinand Haas, Vienna: Gerold [The Lady of the Lake].

(1829) *Über das Leben und die Werke der berühmtesten englischen Romandichter*, trans. Ludwig Rellstab, Vienna: Schade [Lives of the Novelists].

(1845) *Kenilworth: historisch-romantisches Schauspiel in fünf Aufzügen*, nach Walter Scott's gleichnamigen Romane für die Bühne bearbeitet von Johann Wilhelm Lembert [Johann Wenzel Tremler], Vienna: [n. pub.].

Chapter 6: The Reception of Sir Walter Scott in German Literary Histories *c*1820–*c*1945

Ackermann, Richard (1902) *Kurze Geschichte der englischen Litteratur in den Grundzügen ihrer Entwicklung*, Stuttgart; Zweibrücken: Lehmann.

Allemann, Beda and Erwin Koppen (eds) (1975) *Teilnahme und Spiegelung: Festschrift für Horst Rüdiger*, Berlin; New York: de Gruyter.

Ammon, Hermann (1929) *Deutsche Literaturgeschichte in Frage und Antwort von Luther bis zur Gegenwart*, Berlin; Bonn: Dümmler.

Andermatt, Michael (2000) ' "Engelland" als Metapher: Walter Scott, Augustin Thierry und das mittelalterliche England in Conrad Ferdinand Meyers Novelle *Der Heilige*', in Stark, Susanne (ed.) *The Novel in Anglo-German Context: Cultural Cross-Currents and Affinities; Papers from the Conference Held at the University of Leeds from 15 to 17 September 1997*, Amsterdam; Atlanta: Rodopi, pp. 195–212.

Aust, Hugo (1994) *Der historische Roman*, Stuttgart: J. B. Metzler.

Bachleitner, Norbert (1989) ' "Übersetzungsfabriken": Das deutsche Übersetzungswesen in der ersten Hälfte des 19. Jahrhunderts', *Internationales Archiv für Sozialgeschichte der deutschen Literatur*, 14: 1–49.

— (2000a) 'Die deutsche Rezeption englischer Romanautorinnen des neunzehnten Jahrhunderts, insbesondere Charlotte Brontës', in Stark, Susanne (ed.) *The Novel in Anglo-German Context: Cultural Cross-Currents and Affinities*, Amsterdam; Atlanta: Rodopi, pp. 173–94.

— (ed.) (2000b) *Beiträge zur Rezeption der britischen und irischen Literatur des 19. Jahrhunderts im deutschsprachigen Raum*, Amsterdam; Atlanta: Rodopi.

Bandow, Karl (1876) *Charakterbilder aus der Geschichte der Englischen Litteratur*, Berlin: Robert Oppenheim.

Bartels, Adolf (1905) *Geschichte der Deutschen Literatur*, 2 vols, Leipzig: Avenarius.

Biesalski, Ernst-Peter (1991) *Die Mechanisierung der deutschen Buchbinderei 1850–1900*, Frankfurt a.M.: Buchhändler-Vereinigung.

Bleibtreu, Karl (1887) *Geschichte der englischen Litteratur im neunzehnten Jahrhundert*, Leipzig: Wilhelm Friedrich.

Bode, Emil (1927) *Einführung in die Geschichte der englischen Literatur besonders der Neuzeit*, Bielefeld; Leipzig: Velhagen & Klasing.

Bölling, Rainer (1983) *Sozialgeschichte der deutschen Lehrer: Ein Überblick von 1800 bis zur Gegenwart*, Göttingen: Vandenhoeck & Ruprecht.

Brandes, Georg Morris Cohen (1876) *Der Naturalismus in England: Die Seeschule Byron und seine Gruppe*, Berlin: Duncker.
— (1872–78) *Hauptströmungen der Literatur des neunzehnten Jahrhunderts: Vorlesungen, gehalten an der Kopenhagener Universität*, trans. Adolf Strodtmann, 6 vols, Berlin; Leipzig: Duncker; Barsdorf.
— (1905) *Main Currents in Nineteenth Century Literature*, 6 vols, London: Heinemann.

Craig, Gordon A. (1997) *Über Fontane*, trans. Jürgen Baron von Koskull, Munich: Beck.
Cunningham, Allan (1834a) *Biographical and Critical History of the British Literature of the Last Fifty Years*, Paris: [n. pub.].
— (1834b) *Biographische und kritische Geschichte der englischen Literatur von Samuel Johnson's bis zu W. Scott's Tode*, trans. Alexander Kaiser, Leipzig: Weidmann'sche Buchhandlung.

Dietschreit, Frank (1988) *Lion Feuchtwanger*, Stuttgart: Metzler.
Durrani, Osman and Julian Preece (eds) (2001) *Travellers in Time and Space: The German Historical Novel / Reisende durch Zeit und Raum· Der deutschsprachige historische Roman*, Amsterdam; Altanta: Rodopi.

Eggert, Hartmut (1971) *Studien zur Wirkungsgeschichte des deutschen historischen Romans 1850–1875*, Frankfurt a.M.: Klostermann.
Eggert, Hartmut, Ulrich Profitlich, and Klaus R. Scherpe (eds) (1990) *Geschichte als Literatur: Formen und Grenzen der Repräsentation von Vergangenheit*, Stuttgart: Metzler.
Eichhorn, Johann Gottfried (1808) *Geschichte der schönen Redekünste in den neuern Landessprachen: Zweite Abtheilung*, Göttingen: Vandenhoek & Ruprecht.
Einhundert Jahre Velhagen Klasing 1835–1935 (1935), Bielefeld: Velhagen & Klasing.
Engel, Eduard (1883) *Geschichte der Englischen Literatur von den Anfangen bis zur Gegenwart; Mit einhem Anhang: Die nordamerikanische Literatur*, Leipzig: Elischer.
— (1902) *A History of English Literature (600–1900)*, trans. Hamley Bent, London: Methuen.
— (1913) *Geschichte der Deutschen Literatur von den Anfängen bis in die Gegenwart*, vol. 2, Vienna: Tempsky; Leipzig: Freytag.
— (1915) *Geschichte der Englischen Literatur von den Anfängen bis zur Gegenwart; Mit einem Anhang: Die nordamerikanische Literatur*, Leipzig: Brandstetter.
Engler, Balz and Renate Haas (eds) (2000) *European English Studies: Contributions towards the History of a Discipline*, [Leicester]: English Association.
Erbach, Wilhelm (1908) *Ferdinand Freiligrath's Uebersetzungen aus dem englischen [sic] im ersten Jahrzehnt seines Schaffens*, Bonn: Foppen.

Fehr, Bernhard (1931) *Die englische Literatur des 19. und 20. Jahrhunderts: Mit einer Einführung in die englische Frühromantik*, Potsdam: Akademische Verlagsgesellschaft Athenaion.
Fohrmann, Jürgen (1989) *Das Projekt der deutschen Literaturgeschichte: Entstehung und Scheitern einer nationalen Poesiegeschichtsschreibung zwischen Humanismus und Deutschem Kaiserreich*, Stuttgart: Metzler.
Führer durch die Tauchnitz Edition mit 'Series for the Young' und 'Collection of German Authors' (1927), Leipzig: Tauchnitz.

Gätschenberger, Stefan (1874) *Geschichte der Englischen Dichtkunst nebst einer Skizze der wissenschaftlichen Literatur England's*, London: Wohlauer.
Geppert, Hans Vilmar (1976) *Der 'andere' historische Roman: Theorie und Strukturen einer diskontinuierlichen Gattung*, Tübingen: Niemeyer.

— (2000) 'Ein Feld von Differenzierungen: Zur kritisch-produktiven Scott-Rezeption von Arnim bis Fontane', in Bachleitner, Norbert (ed.) *Beiträge zur Rezeption der britischen und irischen Literatur des 19. Jahrhunderts im deutschsprachigen Raum*, Amsterdam; Atlanta: Rodopi, pp. 479–500.

Glauning, Friedrich (1898) 'Englisch', in Zange, Friedrich (ed.) *Didaktik und Methodik der einzelnen Lehrfächer; Erste Hälfte: Evangelischer Religionsunterricht [. . .]* Geschichte, vol. 6, Munich: Beck.

Göres, Jörn (ed.) [1977] *Lesewuth, Raubdruck und Bücherluxus: Das Buch in der Goethe-Zeit*, Düsseldorf: [Goethe-Museum].

Groß, Konrad, Kurt Müller and Meinhard Winkgens (eds) (1994) *Das Natur/Kultur-Paradigma in der englischsprachigen Erzählliteratur des 19. und 20. Jahrhunderts*, Tübingen: Narr.

Haas, Renate (2000) '1848 and German English Studies/German Philology', in Engler, Balz and Renate Haas (eds) *European English Studies: Contributions towards the History of a Discipline*, [Leicester]: English Association, pp. 293–311.

Habitzel, Kurt and Günter Mühlberger (1996) 'Gewinner und Verlierer: Der historische Roman und sein Beitrag zum Literatursystem der Restaurationszeit (1815–1848/49)', *Internationales Archiv für Sozialgeschichte der deutschen Literatur*, 21: 91–123.

Hackenberg, Fritz (1913) *Elise von Hohenhausen: Eine Vorkämpferin und Übersetzerin englischer und nordamerikanischer Dichtung*, Münster: Regensbergsche Buchdruckerei.

Haenicke, Gunta (1979) *Zur Geschichte der Anglistik an deutschsprachigen Universitäten 1850–1925*, Augsburg: Universität Augsburg.

Haenicke, Gunta (1982) *Zur Geschichte des Faches Englisch in den Prüfungsordnungen für das Höhere Lehramt 1831–1942*, Augsburg: Universität Augsburg.

Hasubek, Peter (2000) 'Das Geheimnis des schwarzen Ritters oder Scott und Immermann', in Stark, Susanne (ed.) *The Novel in Anglo-German Context: Cultural Cross-Currents and Affinities; Papers from the Conference Held at the University of Leeds from 15 to 17 September 1997*, Amsterdam; Atlanta: Rodopi, pp. 117–28.

Hausmann, Frank-Rutger (2003) *Anglistik und Amerikanistik im 'Dritten Reich'*, Frankfurt a.M.: Klostermann.

Höfle, Frieda (1937) *Cottas 'Morgenblatt für gebildete Stände' und seine Stellung zur Literatur und zur literarischen Kritik*, Berlin: Gutenberg.

Holzner, Johann and Wolfgang Wiesmüller (1997–2002) *Projekt Historischer Roman* <http://histrom.literature.at/start.html> [accessed 25 August 2005].

Keiderling, Thomas (2000) 'Leipzig als Vermittlungs- und Produktionszentrum englischsprachiger Literatur zwischen 1815 und 1914', in Bachleitner, Norbert (ed.) *Beiträge zur Rezeption der britischen und irischen Literatur des 19. Jahrhunderts im deutschsprachigen Raum*, Amsterdam; Atlanta: Rodopi, pp. 3–76.

Klippel, Friederike (1994) *Englischlernen im 18. und 19. Jahrhundert: Die Geschichte der Lehrbücher und Unterrichtsmethoden*, Münster: Nodus.

Knorr, Herbert (1961) 'Theodor Fontane und England', 2 vols (unpublished thesis, University of Göttingen).

Korff, H. A. and Wilhelm Linden (eds) (1930) *Aufriß der deutschen Literaturgeschichte nach neueren Gesichtspunkten*, Leipzig; Berlin: Teubner.

Körting, Gustav (1910) *Grundriss der Geschichte der englischen Literatur von ihren Anfängen bis zur Gegenwart*, Münster: Schöningh.

Kosch, Wilhelm (1925–31) *Die deutsche Literatur im Spiegel der nationalen Entwicklung von 1813 bis 1848*, 3 vols, Munich: Partus & Co.

Leixner, Otto von (1883) *Illustrirte Geschichte der fremden Literaturen: Das Schriftthum der altorientalischen und altklassischen sowie der neueren Völker*, 2 vols, Leipzig; Berlin: Spamer.

Leixner, Otto von (1899) *Geschichte der fremden Literaturen*, Leipzig; Berlin: Spamer.

Luther, Arthur (1940) *Deutsche Geschichte in deutscher Erzählung: Ein literarisches Lexikon*, Leipzig: Hiersemann.

Meyer, Michael (1973) 'Die Entstehung des historischen Romans in Deutschland und seine Stellung zwischen Geschichtsschreibung und Dichtung: die Polemik um eine "Zwittergattung" (1785–1845)' (unpublished doctoral thesis, University of Munich).

Michael, Ian (1993) *Early Textbooks of English: A Guide*, Reading: Colloquium on Textbooks, Schools and Society.

Mühlberger, Günter and Kurt Habitzel (2001) 'The German Historical Novel from 1780 to 1945: Utilising the Innsbruck Database', in Durrani, Osman and Julian Preece (eds) *Travellers in Time and Space: The German Historical Novel / Reisende durch Zeit und Raum: Der deutschsprachige historische Roman*, Amsterdam: Rodopi, pp. 5–23.

Müllenbrock, Heinz-Joachim (1994) 'Natur und Geschichte im historischen Roman Sir Walter Scotts', in Groß, Konrad, Kurt Müller and Meinhard Winkgens (eds) *Das Natur/Kultur-Paradigma in der englischsprachigen Erzählliteratur des 19. und 20. Jahrhunderts*, Tübingen: Narr, pp. 23–34.

Mundt, Theodor (1842) *Geschichte der Literatur der Gegenwart: Vorlesungen*, Berlin: Athenaeum.

Murray, Kathleen (1921) *Taine und die englische Romantik*, Munich; Leipzig: Duncker & Humblot.

Neuhaus, Stefan (2000) ' "Sechsunddreißig Könige für einen Regenschirm": Heinrich Heines produktive Rezeption britischer Literatur', in Bachleitner (2000b), pp. 409–42.

— (2001) 'Zeitkritik im historischen Gewand? Fünf Thesen zum Gattungsbegriff des Historischen [sic] Romans am Beispiel von Theodor Fontanes *Vor dem Sturm*', in Durrani and Preece (2001), pp. 209–25.

— (2002) *Das Spiel mit dem Leser: Wilhelm Hauff; Werk und Wirkung*, Göttingen: Vandenhoeck & Ruprecht.

Paul, Adolf (1934) *Der Einfluß Walter Scotts auf die epische Technik Theodor Fontanes*, Breslau: Priebatsch's Buchhandlung.

Perthes, Friedrich (1924) *Der deutsche Buchhandel als Bedingung des Daseins einer deutschen Literatur*, Gotha; Stuttgart: Perthes.

Price, Lawrence Marsden (1953) *English Literature in Germany*, Berkeley: University of California Press.

Reitemeier, Frauke (2001) *Deutsch-englische Literaturbeziehungen: Der historische Roman Walter Scotts und seine deutschen Vorläufer*, Paderborn: Schöningh.

Ritter, Alexander (2000) 'Die Bekannten und die beiden "großen Unbekannten": Scott, der historische Roman und sein Einfluß auf Charles Sealsfield', in Bachleitner (2000), pp. 443–77.

Salomon, Ludwig (1887) *Geschichte der deutschen Nationallitteratur des neunzehnten Jahrhunderts*, Stuttgart: Levy & Müller.

Scheler, Manfred (1987) 'Berliner Anglistik in Vergangenheit und Gegenwart', in Scheler, Manfred (ed.) *Berliner Anglistik in Vergangenheit und Gegenwart 1810–1985*, Berlin: Colloquium Verlag, pp. 3–159.

Scherer, Wilhelm ([1929]) *Geschichte der Deutschen Literatur*, ed. Heinz Amelung, Berlin: Th. Knaur Nachfolger.

Scherr, Johannes (1874) *Geschichte der Englischen Literatur*, Leipzig: Wigand.
— (1881) *Allgemeine Geschichte der Literatur: Ein Handbuch in zwei Bänden*, 2 vols, Stuttgart: Conradi.
— (1882) *A History of English Literature*, trans. M. V., London: Sampson Low, Marston, Searle, & Rivington.
Schirmer, Walter Franz (1937) *Geschichte der englischen Literatur von den Anfängen bis zur Gegenwart*, Halle a.d.Saale: Niemeyer.
Schirmer, Walter Franz (1948) *Kurze Geschichte der englischen Literatur von den Anfängen bis zur Gegenwart*, Halle a.d.Saale: Niemeyer.
Schlegel, Friedrich von (1841) *Geschichte der alten und neuen Literatur: Vorlesungen, gehalten zu Wien im Jahre 1812*, Berlin: Athenaeum.
Schlösser, Anselm (1937) *Die englische Literatur in Deutschland von 1895 bis 1934 mit einer vollständigen Bibliographie der deutschen Übersetzungen und der im deutschen Sprachgebiet erschienenen englischen Autoren*, Jena: Biedermann.
Schmid, Susanne (2000) 'Bewunderung, Kritik und Vielstimmigkeit: England und englische Literatur im *Magazin für die Literatur des Auslandes* von 1832 bis 1849', in Bachleitner (2000), pp. 107–17.
Schmidt, Hartmut ([1977]) 'Der deutsche Buchhandel 1755–1835: Verlags- und Urheberrecht; Buchhandelspraxis; Der Büchernachdruck; Werbung im Buchhandel', in Göres, Jörn (ed.) *Lesewuth, Raubdruck und Bücherluxus: Das Buch in der Goethe-Zeit*, Düsseldorf: [Goethe-Museum], pp. 9–147.
Schrey, Helmut (1982) *Anglistisches Kaleidoskop: Zur Geschichte der Anglistik und des Englischunterrichts in Deutschland*, Sankt Augustin: Hans Richarz.
Schröder, Konrad (1969) *Die Entwicklung des englischen Unterrichts an deutschsprachigen Universitäten bis zum Jahre 1850: Mit einer Analyse zu Verbreitung und Stellung des Englischen als Schulfach an den deutschen höheren Schulen im Zeitalter des Neuhumanismus*, Ratingen: Henn.
Schulz, Gerhard (1989) *Die deutsche Literatur zwischen Französischer Revolution und Restauration*, 2 vols, Munich: Beck.
Schüren, Rainer (1969) 'Die Romane Walter Scotts in Deutschland' (unpublished doctoral thesis, Free University Berlin).
Sigmann, Luise (1918) *Die englische Literatur von 1800–1850 im Urteil der zeitgenössischen deutschen Kritik*, Heidelberg: Winter.
Spalding, William (1854) *Geschichte der englischen Literatur nebst Proben aus den bedeutenderen Schriftstellern und einer Entwickelungsgeschichte der englischen Sprache*, trans. [E. Schröder], Halle: Graeger.
Stark, Susanne (ed.) (2000) *The Novel in Anglo-German Context: Cultural Cross-Currents and Affinities*, Amsterdam; Atlanta: Rodopi.
Steinecke, Hartmut (1975a) '*Wilhelm Meister* oder *Waverley*? Zur Bedeutung Scotts für das deutsche Romanverständnis der frühen Restaurationszeit', in Allemann, Beda, Erwin Koppen, Dieter Gutzen and Joachim Krause (eds), *Teilnahme und Spiegelung: Festschrift für Horst Rüdiger*, Berlin; New York: de Gruyter, pp. 340–59.
— (1975b) *Romantheorie und Romankritik in Deutschland: Die Entwicklung des Gattungsverständnisses von der Scott-Rezeption bis zum programmatischen Realismus*, 2 vols, Stuttgart: J. B. Metzler.
Stierstorfer, Klaus (2000) *Konstruktion literarischer Vergangenheit: Die englische Literaturgeschichte von Warton bis Courthope und Ward*, Heidelberg: Winter.

Taine, Hippolyte (1880) *Die Neuzeit der englischen Literatur*, trans. Gustav Gerth, Leipzig: Ernst Julius Günther Nachfolger.
— (1906) *History of English Literature*, trans. H. van Laun, 4 vols, London: Chatto & Windus.

ten Brink, Bernhard (1891) *Über die Aufgabe der Litteraturgeschichte. Rede gehalten am 1. Mai 1890 dem Stiftungstage der Kaiser-Wilhelms-Universität Straβburg*, Strasburg: Heitz & Mündel.

Tippkötter, Horst (1971) *Walter Scott: Geschichte als Unterhaltung. Eine Rezeptionsanalyse der Waverley Novels*, Frankfurt a.M.: Vittorio Klostermann.

Tschischwitz, Benno (1876) 'Einleitung', in Scott, Walter, *Quentin Durward*, trans. and ed. Benno Tschischwitz, Walter Scotts Romane 1, Berlin: Grote, pp. vii–xiv.

Uerlings, Herbert (2001) 'Die Erneuerung des historischen Romans durch interkulturelles Erzählen: Zur Entwicklung der Gattung bei Alfred Döblin, Uwe Timm, Hans Christoph Buch und anderen', in Durrani and Preece (2001): 129–54.

Uhlig, Claus (1982) *Theorie der Literarhistorie: Prinzipien und Paradigmen*, Heidelberg: Winter.

Vilmar, August Friedrich Christian (1894) *Geschichte der Deutschen National-Litteratur*, Marburg; Leipzig: Elwertsche Verlagsbuchhandlung.

Walter, Anton von (1982) *Zur Geschichte des Englischunterrichts an höheren Schulen: Die Entwicklung bis 1900 vornehmlich in Preuβen*, Augsburg: Universität Augsburg.

Walzel, Oskar (1929) *Die deutsche Literatur von Goethes Tod bis zur Gegenwart*, Berlin: Askanischer Verlag.

Wegmann, Carl (1910) *Theodor Fontane als Übersetzer englischer und schottischer Balladen*, Münster: Westfälische Vereinsdruckerei.

Weimar, Klaus (1990) 'Der Text, den (Literar-) Historiker schreiben', in Eggert, Hartmut, Ulrich Profitlich, and Klaus R. Scherpe (eds) *Geschichte als Literatur: Formen und Grenzen der Repräsentation von Vergangenheit*, Stuttgart: Metzler, pp. 29–39.

Wenger, Karl (1905) *Historische Romane deutscher Romantiker: (Untersuchungen über den Einfluss Walter Scotts)*, Berne: Francke.

Westenfelder, Frank (1989) *Genese, Problematik und Wirkung nationalsozialistischer Literatur am Beispiel des historischen Romans zwischen 1890 und 1945*, Frankfurt a.M.: Lang.

Wittmann, Reinhard (1999) *Geschichte des deutschen Buchhandels*, Munich: Beck.

Wülcker, Richard (1896) *Geschichte der Englischen Litteratur von den ältesten Zeiten bis zur Gegenwart*, Leipzig; Vienna: Bibliographisches Institut.

Zange, Friedrich (ed.) (1898) *Didaktik und Methodik der einzelnen Lehrfächer: Erste Hälfte; Evangelischer Religionsunterricht [. . .] Geschichte*, Munich: Beck.

Zapp, Franz Josef, and Konrad Schröder (eds) (1983) *Deutsche Lehrpläne für den Fremdsprachenunterricht 1900–1970: Ein Lesebuch*, Augsburg: Universität Augsburg.

Translations

(1817) *Schottische Lieder und Balladen von Walter Scott*, trans. Henriette Schubart, Leipzig; Altenburg: Brockhaus.

(1822) *Die Jungfrau vom See: Ein Gedicht in sechs Gesängen von Walter Scott*, trans. Willibald Alexis, 2 vols, Zwickau: Schumann.

(1823) *Kenilworth: Roman nach Walter Scott*, trans. Georg Lotz, 3 vols, Hanover: Hahn.

(1826) *Der Alterthümler*, trans. *r, Leipzig: Gleditsch.

(1864) *Der Herr der Inseln von W. Scott*, trans. W. Hertzberg, Bremen: Geisler.

(1876) *Quentin Durward*, trans. and ed. Benno Tschischwitz, Walter Scotts Romane 1, Berlin: Grote.

(1883) *Waverley*, trans. Ludwig Proescholdt, 3 vols, Stuttgart: Spemann.

([1900]) *Ivanhoe*, trans. and ed. Adam Stein, Leipzig: Oehmigke.

(1908) *Ivanhoe: Ein historischer Roman von Walter Scott*, trans. and rev. Albert Geyer, Leipzig: Abel & Müller.

(1915) *Ivanhoe*, ed. Fritz Meyer, Kiel; Leipzig: Lipsius & Tischer.

Chapter 7: The Reception of Walter Scott in East, West and Reunified Germany (1949–2005)

Baadke, Friedrich (1978) 'Nachwort' to *Old Mortality*, trans. Rudolf Schaller, Berlin: Rütten & Loening, pp. 543–50.

— (1982) 'Nachwort' to *Das Herz von Midlothian*, trans. Walter Wilhelm, Berlin: Rütten und Loening, pp. 691–704.

— (2004a) letter to author, 5 November.

— (2004b) letter to author, 10 November.

Barck, Simone, Martina Langermann and Siegfried Lokatis (1997) *'Jedes Buch ein Abenteuer': Zensur-System und literarische Öffentlichkeit in der DDR bis Ende der sechziger Jahre*, Berlin: Akademie Verlag.

Berger, Christian (2003) letter to author, 27 February.

Berger, Friedemann (2003) letter to author, 18 February.

'Die Braut von Lammermoor' (1968) review in *Ihre Brigitte*, June, [n. page].

Deutsche Bibliothek Catalogue <www.ddb.de> [accessed 30 November 2005].

Dienel, Traude (1974) 'Nachwort' to *Im Auftrag des Königs: die gefährlichen Abenteuer des Quentin Durward*, trans. T. Oelckers (1831), ed. Edgar Pässler, Frankfurt a.M.: Insel-Verlag, pp. 596–608.

Dietschreit, Frank (1988) 'Nachwort' to *Der Talisman*, trans. Wilhelm Sauerwein (c. 1850), Frankfurt a.M.; Berlin: Ullstein, pp. 314–20.

— (1989a) 'Nachwort' to *Eine Sage von Montrose*, trans. Franz Kottenkamp, ed. Frank Dietschreit, Frankfurt a.M.; Berlin: Ullstein, pp. 221–23.

— (1989b) 'Nachwort' to *Der schwarze Zwerg*, trans. Franz Kottenkamp (1852), ed. Frank Dietschreit, Frankfurt a.M.; Berlin: Ullstein, pp. 157–60.

Emmerich, Wolfgang (1996) *Kleine Literaturgeschichte der DDR* [1989], Frankfurt a.M.: Luchterhand Literaturverlag.

Ernst, Paul (1984) 'Nachwort' (1911) to *Ivanhoe*, trans. Leonhard Tafel, ed. Ernst, Frankfurt a.M.: Insel-Verlag, pp. 615–17.

Gamerschlag, Kurt (1978) *Sir Walter Scott und die Waverley Novels: Eine Übersicht über den Gang der Scottforschung von den Anfängen bis heute*, Darmstadt: Wissenschaftliche Buchgesellschaft.

— (1982) 'Nachwort' to *Waverley oder's ist sechzig Jahre her*, trans. Gisela Reichel, notes, chronology and bibliography Gamerschlag, Munich: Deutscher Taschenbuch Verlag, pp. 553–71.

— (2003) letter to author, 19 March.

Hillhouse, James T. (1968) *The Waverley Novels and Their Critics* [1936], 2nd edn, New York: Octagon Books.

Ilberg, Werner (1965) 'Nachwort' to *Ivanhoe*, trans. Christine Hoeppener, Berlin: Verlag Neues Leben, pp. 541–45.

'Der junge Waverly [*sic*]' (1972) review in *Der Morgen*, 28 October, [n. page].

Kaiser, Bruno (1952) 'Nachwort' to *Ivanhoe*, trans. Christine Hoeppener, Berlin: Rütten & Loening, pp. 678–80.

Klein, Michael (1999) 'Nachwort' to *Das Leid von Lammermoor*, trans. W. Sauerwein, ed. Michael Klein, Blieskastel: Gollenstein, pp. 427–41.

Klotz, Günther (1959) 'Vorwort' to *Das Herz von Midlothian*, trans. Walter Wilhelm, Berlin: Aufbau Verlag, pp. 5–6.

— (1997) 'Nachwort' to *Ivanhoe*, trans. C. Hoeppener, Stuttgart: Verlag Das Beste, pp. 569–75.

Krenn, Ruth (1957) 'Nachwort' to *Quentin Durward*, trans. Theodor Oelckers (1831), ed. Ruth Krenn, Berlin: Kinderbuchverlag, pp. 378–85.

Küfner, Hans (1970) 'Nachwort' to *Im Auftrag des Königs: die gefährlichen Abenteuer des Quentin Durward*, trans. T. Oelckers (1831), ed. Ruth Krenn, Würzburg: Arena-Verlag, pp. 406–07.

Links, Roland (2003) letter to author, 14 March.

Lukàcs, Georg (1989) *The Historical Novel* [1947], trans. Hannah and Stanley Mitchell, London: Merlin Press.

McInnes, Edward (1990–91) 'Realism, History and the Nation: The Reception of the Waverley Novels in Germany in the 19th Century', *New German Studies*, 16.1: 39–51.

Maes, Elke (2003) letter to author, 17 January.

Mandelartz, Carl (1949) 'Nachwort' to *Ivanhoe*, trans. Carl Mandelartz, Düsseldorf: Hoch, pp. 253–54.

Ochojski, Paul M. (1960) 'Walter Scott and Germany: A Study in Literary Cross-Currents' (unpublished doctoral thesis, Columbia University).

— (1973) 'Waverley ueber Alles: Sir Walter Scott's German Reputation', in Bell, Alan (ed.) *Scott Bicentenary Essays*, New York: Barnes & Noble, pp. 260–70.

Pleticha, Heinrich (1998) 'Nachwort' to *Ivanhoe*, trans. B. Tschischwitz, ed. G. Geisler, Stuttgart: Thienemann/Erdmann, pp. 409–13.

— (2003) letter to author, 21 March.

Reichel, Gisela (1972) 'Nachwort' to *Waverley oder's ist sechzig Jahre her*, trans. Gisela Reichel, Leipzig; Weimar: Kiepenheuer, pp. 553–74

Schüren, Rainer (1969), 'Die Romane Walter Scotts in Deutschland' (unpublished doctoral thesis, Free University Berlin).

Schulz, Elisabeth (1955) 'Nachwort' to *Das Herz von Midlothian*, trans. Walter Wilhelm, Berlin: Rütten und Loening, pp. 831–75.

— (1956) 'Nachwort' to *Kenilworth*, trans. Benno Tschischwitz (19th century), ed. Elisabeth Schulz, Berlin: Rütten & Loening, pp. 645–68.

Schwachhofer, René (1965) 'Nachwort' to *Die Braut von Lammermoor*, Weimar: Kiepenheuer, pp. 497–501.

Szudra, Klaus Udo (1972) 'Nachwort' to *Ivanhoe*, trans. Christine Hoeppener, Berlin: Rütten & Loening, pp. 599–617.

Tippkötter, Horst (1971) *Walter Scott: Geschichte als Unterhaltung; Eine Rezeptionsanalyse der Waverley Novels*, Frankfurt a.M.: Vittorio Klostermann.

'Vorwort' to *Das Herz von Midlothian* (1987), trans. Walter Wilhelm, trans. copyright

Rütten und Loening, Reinbek bei Hamburg: Rowohlt Taschenbuch Verlag, pp. 8–9.

'Waverley' (1980) review in *Ostsee-Zeitung*, 29 March, [n. page].

Translations in East Germany

BL
(1965) *Die Braut von Lammermoor*, ed. and epilogue René Schwachhofer, Weimar: Kiepenheuer.

FMP
(1960) *Das schöne Mädchen von Perth*, trans. anon. ('an old translation edited and abridged'), Berlin: Neues Leben.

HM
(1955) *Das Herz von Midlothian*, trans. Walter Wilhelm, epilogue Elisabeth Schulz, Berlin: Rütten und Loening.
(1959) *Das Herz von Midlothian*, trans. Walter Wilhelm, epilogue Günther Klotz, Berlin: Aufbau Verlag.
(1982) *Das Herz von Midlothian*, trans. Walter Wilhelm, epilogue Friedrich Baadke, Berlin: Rütten und Loening.

I
(1952) *Ivanhoe*, trans. Christine Hoeppener, Berlin: Rütten & Loening.

K
(1956) *Kenilworth*, trans. Benno Tschischwitz (19th century), ed. and epilogue Elisabeth Schulz, Berlin: Rütten & Loening.
(1975) *Kenilworth*, old anon. trans., Berlin: Verlag Neues Leben.
(1979) *Kenilworth*, trans. anon., Berlin: Verlag Neues Leben.

OM
(1954) *Old Mortality*, trans. Rudolf Schaller, Berlin: Rütten & Loening
(1978) *Old Mortality*, trans. Rudolf Schaller, epilogue Friedrich Baadke, Berlin: Rütten & Loening.

QD
(1957) *Quentin Durward*, trans. Theodor Oelckers [1831]; ed. and epilogue Ruth Krenn, Berlin: Kinderbuchverlag

RR
(1957) *Rob Roy*, trans. C. Hoeppener, Berlin: Rütten & Loening.

T
(1983) *Der Talismann: Erzählung aus der Zeit der Kreuzfahrer*, old anon. trans., Berlin: Verlag Neues Leben

W
(1972) *Waverley oder's ist sechzig Jahre her*, trans. and epilogue Gisela Reichel, Leipzig; Weimar: Kiepenheuer.

Translations in West Germany

AG
(1974) *Anna von Geierstein oder die Tochter des Nebels*, trans. E. Elsenhaus [1851], Frankfurt a.M.: Goverts.

BD
(1989) *Der schwarze Zwerg*, trans. Franz Kottenkamp [1852], ed. and epilogue Frank Dietschreit. Frankfurt a.M.; Berlin: Ullstein.

BL
(1975) *Die Braut von Lammermoor*, trans. W. Sauerwein [1851], Frankfurt a.M.: Goverts.

HM
(1987) *Das Herz von Midlothian*, trans. Walter Wilhelm, epilogue anon., Reinbek bei Hamburg: Rowohlt Taschenbuch Verlag.

I
(1949) *Ivanhoe*, trans. Carl Mandelartz, Düsseldorf: Hoch Verlag.
(1953) *Ivanhoe: Eine Geschichte von verwegenen Rittern aus d. Zeit d. Richard Löwenherz*, trans. anon., Wuppertal: Kolibri-Verlag.
(1957) *Ivanhoe*, trans. anon., Hamburg: Verlag Internationale Klassiker.
(1963) *Ivanhoe: Ein treuer Ritter seines Königs*, trans. anon., Munich: Südwest-Verlag.
(1964) *Ivanhoe*, trans. Elisabeth Ciccione, Hamburg: Tessloff-Verlag.
(1967) *Ivanhoe*, trans. and ed. Paul Frischhauer, Wiesbaden: Vollmer.
(1968) *Ivanhoe*, trans. and ed. Inge Lehmann, Rastatt: Favorit-Verlag.
(1969) *Ivanhoe*, trans. Benno Tschischwitz [1880], ed. Joachim Brückmann, Munich: Heyne.
(1970) *Ivanhoe*, trans. and ed. Rudolf Hermann, Stuttgart: Spectrum-Verlag.
(1975) *Ivanhoe*, trans. Ernst Susemihl [1860], Frankfurt a.M.: Goverts.
(1976) *Ivanhoe, der enterbte Ritter*, trans. and ed. Katerina Horbatsch, Göttingen: Fischer.
(1981) *Ivanhoe, der schwarze Ritter*, trans. anon., Nuremberg: Germania-Buch.
(1983) *Ivanhoe*, ed. Burkhard Busse modernizing a 19th-century trans., Cologne: Lingen.
(1984) *Ivanhoe*, trans. Leonhard Tafel [19th century], ed. and epilogue Paul Ernst [1911], Frankfurt a.M.: Insel-Verlag.

K
(1985) *Kenilworth*, eds R.W. Pinson and Heinz Reck, Kettwig: Magnus-Verlag.

LM
(1989) *Eine Sage von Montrose*, trans. Franz Kottenkamp, ed. and epilogue Frank Dietschreit, Frankfurt a.M.; Berlin: Ullstein.

QD
(1964) *Quentin Durward*, trans. and abr. A. Merkelbach-Pinck, further ed. Jürgen Rauser, Freiburg i.Br.: Alsatia-Verlag
(1967) *Quentin Durward: Des Königs Schildknappe*, trans. and ed. Jochen Schatte Balve: Engelbert-Verlag.
(1970) *Im Auftrag des Königs: die gefährlichen Abenteuer des Quentin Durward*, trans. T. Oelckers [1831], ed. Ruth Krenn, epilogue Hans Küfner, Würzburg: Arena-Verlag
(1974) *Im Auftrag des Königs: die gefährlichen Abenteuer des Quentin Durward*, trans.

T. Oelckers [1831], ed. Edgar Pässler, epilogue Traude Dienel, Frankfurt a.M.: Insel-Verlag.
(1981) *Quentin Durward im Dienste des Königs*, trans. anon., Stuttgart: Spectrum-Verlag.
(1982) *Im Auftrag des Königs*, ed. L. M. Mattis-Brandau, Bayreuth: Gondrom.
(1987) *Quentin Durward im Dienste des Königs*, anon. trans. [19th-century], illus. anon., (Neubearbeitung unter Verwendung e. Übers. aus d. 19. Jh. mit 8 zeitgenöss. Ill.), Rastatt: Moewig.

RR
(1957) *Rob Roy*, trans. anon., Hamburg: Verl. Internationale Klassiker.
(1978) *Robin, der Rote*, 'freely retold' Herbert Kranz, Würzburg: Arena.

T
(1977) *Der Talismann*, trans. Sophie May [19th century], ed. Hanna Bautze, Ravensburg: Maier.
(1983) *Der Talismann: Erzählung aus der Zeit der Kreuzfahrer*, old anon. trans., Berlin: Verlag Neues Leben
(1988) *Der Talisman*, trans. Wilhelm Sauerwein [ca 1850], epilogue Frank Dietschreit, Frankfurt a.M.; Berlin: Ullstein.

W
(1974) *Waverley oder vor sechzig Jahren*, trans. C. Herrmann [1851], Frankfurt a.M.: Goverts.
(1982) *Waverley oder's ist sechzig Jahre her*, trans. Gisela Reichel, epilogue Kurt Gamerschlag, Munich: Deutscher Taschenbuch Verlag.

Translations in reunified Germany

BL
(1991) *Die Braut von Lammermoor*, trans. [W. Sauerwein], Berlin: Verlag Neues Leben.
(1999) *Das Leid von Lammermoor*, trans. W. Sauerwein, ed. and epilogue Michael Klein, Blieskastel: Gollenstein.

I
(1991) *Ivanhoe*, trans. C. Hoeppener, Berlin: Rütten & Loening.
(1992) *Ivanhoe*, trans. C. Mandelartz, Würzburg: Arena.
(1992) *Ivanhoe*, trans. anon., ed. Sybil Gräfin Schönefeldt, Stuttgart: Hoch.
(1993) *Ivanhoe*, trans. L. Tafel, ed. and epilogue P. Ernst, Frankfurt a.M.: Insel.
(1993) *Ivanhoe*, trans. anon., Schönau: [n. pub.].
(1994) *Ivanhoe*, trans. C. Mandelartz, Würzburg: Arena.
(1996) *Ivanhoe*, trans. L. Tafel, ed. and epilogue P. Ernst, Frankfurt a.M.: Insel.
(1997) *Ivanhoe*, trans. C. Hoeppener, epilogue G. Klotz, Stuttgart: Verlag Das Beste.
(1998) *Ivanhoe*, trans. B. Tschischwitz, ed. G. Geisler, epilogue H. Pleticha, Stuttgart: Thienemann/Erdmann.
(2003) *Ivanhoe*, trans. C. Hoeppener, Belin: Aufbau-Verlag.
(2004) *Ivanhoe*, trans. anon., Erftstadt: Unipart.
(2004) *Ivanhoe*, trans. anon., Augsburg: Weltbild.
(2004) *Ivanhoe*, trans. C. Mandelartz, Würzburg: Arena.

OM
(1991) *Old Mortality*, trans. Rudolf Schaller, epilogue F. Baadke, Berlin: Aufbau Taschenbuch.

QD
(2004) *Im Auftrag des Königs: Die gefährlichen Abenteuer des Quentin Durward*, trans. T. Oelkers, Warendorf: Hoof.

RR
(1995) *Rob Roy*, trans. anon, Munich: Deutscher Taschenbuch Verlag.
(1997) *Rob Roy*, trans. anon., Schönau: [n. pub.].

T
(1993) *Richard Löwenherz*, trans. Theresia Leitner, Klagenfurt: Kaiser.

Chapter 8: The Hungarian Reception of Walter Scott in the Nineteenth Century

Bajza, József (1823) letter to Toldy, 15 December 1823, in Bajza, József and Ferenc Toldy (1969) *Bajza József és Toldy Ferenc levelezése*, ed. Oltványi Ambrus Budapest: Akadémiai, p. 72.
— (1830) letter to Toldy, 15 July 1830, in Bajza and Toldy (1969), p. 105.
— (1832) 'Scott Walter írói jövedelme', *Társalkodó*, 35.5: 2.
— (1836) 'A kárpitos szoba', in *Pillangó: Külföldi válogatott elbeszélések zsebkönyve*, Buda: Széplaki Erneszt [Bajza József], [n. page].
— (1899a) 'A regényköltészetről', in Badics, Ferenc (ed.) *Bajza József Összegyűjtött Munkái*, Budapest: Franklin Társulat, 4: 102–135.
— (1899b) *Bajza József elbeszélései és fordításai*, in Badics, Ferenc (ed.) *Bajza József Összegyűjtött Munkái*, vol. 2, Budapest: Franklin Társulat.
Bart, István (1980) *Walter Scott világa*, Budapest: Európa.
Bényei, Miklós (1970) 'Eötvös József könyvtára', *Magyar Könyvszemle*, 182–92.
Bölöni, Farkas Sándor (1984) *Napnyugati utazás: Napló* [1834], Budapest: Helikon.

Czuczor, Gergely (1835) 'Szellemi mozgás Angliában, s annak haladása, tekintettel más európai nemzetekre', *Tudománytár*, 5: 28–60 (44–46).

Döbrentei, Gábor (ed.) (1831–34) *Közhasznú Esmeretek Tára a Conversations-Lexicon szerént Magyarországra alkalmaztatva*, 12 vols, Pest: Wigand; entries: 'angol irodalom' (1: 292), 'román' (10: 222–24) and 'Walter Scott' (10: 402–03).

Elek, Oszkár (1938) 'Scott Walter a magyar irodalmi köztudatban', *Irodalomtörténet*, 12–24.
Eötvös, József (1847) *Magyarország 1514-ben*, Pest: Hartleben.

Fábri, Anna (1987) *Az irodalom magánélete*, Budapest: Magvető.
Fenyő, István (1983) *Haza s emberiség*, Budapest: Akadémiai, pp. 118–24.
Ferencz, Lenke and Zsolt Tasnádi (2002) 'John Paget János angol és magyar világa', *A Természet Világa*, 133 5.
Ferenczi, Zoltán (1915) 'A századéves Waverley', *Budapesti Szemle*, 164.
Fleming, John and John M. Leighton (1830) *Select Views on the River Clyde*, engrav. Joseph Swan, Glasgow: Swan; London: Moon, Boys & Graves.
Fried, István (1986) 'Az "Abafi" előzményeihez', *Irodalomtörténeti Közlemények*, 3: 222–29.
Fülöp, Géza (1978) *A magyar olvasóközönség a felvilágosodás idején és a reformkorban*, Budapest: Akadémiai.

Gaal, József (1835) 'Gyűlölség és szerelem', in *Rajzolatok*, Pest: Heckenast.
Gaal, József (1836) *Szirmay Ilona*, Pest: Heckenast.
Gorove, István (1844) *Nyugot: Utazás külföldön*, Pest: Heckenast.
György, Lajos (1941) *A magyar regény előzményei*, Budapest: Magyar Tudományos Akadémia.
Gyulai, Pál (1857) *Egy régi udvarház utolsó gazdája*, Pest: [n. pub.].

Hegedűs, Sámuel (1837) 'Walter Scotthoz', *Poétai Próbái* [Kolozsvár], 61–69. *Honművész* (1835), 2: 653.

Jakabfi, László (1941) *Az angol irodalom és a Vörösmarty-Bajza-Toldy triász*, Budapest: A Szerző.
Jókai, Mór (1846) *Hétköznapok*, Pest: Hartleben.
— (1852) *Erdély aranykora*, Pest: Emich.
— (1853a) *Egy magyar nábob*, Pest: Emich.
— (1853b) *Török világ Magyarországon*, Pest: Müller.
— (1854) *Janicsárok végnapjai*, Pest: Számvald.
— (1854) *Fehér rózsa*, Pest.
— (1860) *Szegény gazdagok*, Pest: Emich.
— (1862) 'Úti levelek', 'More Patrio (Regényes kóborlások)', in *Magyarhon szépségei*, Pest: Heckenast.
— (1883) *Bálványosvár*, Budapest: Athenaeum.
Jósika, Miklós (1836) *Abafi*, Pest: Heckenast.
— (1858) *Regény és regényítészet*, Pest: Emich.
— (1865) *Emlékirat*, 4 vols, Pest: Heckenast.

Kazinczy, Ferenc (1890–1911) *Kazinczy Ferenc levelezése*, ed. János Váczy, 21 vols, Budapest: Magyar Tudományos Akadémia.
Kemény, Zsigmond (1855–57) *Özvegy és leánya*, Pest: Szilágyi & Emich.
— (1858) *A rajongók*, Pest: Pfeifer.
— (1862) *Zord idő*, Pest: Pfeifer.
Kisfaludy, Károly (1823) 'A vérpohár', *Auróra*.
— (1825) 'Tihamér', *Auróra*.

Murányi, Lajos (1993) *A reformkori Fejér vármegye olvasáskultúrája: A székesfehérvári kaszinók és a Fejér Megyei Olvasótársaság (1838–1849)*, Székesfehérvár: Fejér Megyei Levéltár & Vörösmarty Mihály Megyei Könyvtár.
Muzárion (Majláthról) (1833) 1: 89.

Nagy, László (1836) 'Ida', *Regélő*, 35: 273–77.
Nagy, Miklós (1968), *Jókai*, Budapest: Szépirodalmi.

Oltványi, Ambrus (1969a) note to Toldy's letter to Bajza 9 Dec 1823, in Bajza and Toldy, p. 549.
— (1969b) note to Toldy's letter to Bajza 12 Dec 1828, in Bajza and Toldy, p. 650.

Paget, John (1839) *Hungary and Transylvania*, 2 vols, London: Murray, 1: 120–21.
Papp, Miklós (1857) 'Scott Walter öccse (Valódi angol történet)', *Hölgyfutár*, 746, 750.
Petrichevich, Horváth Lázár (1836) *Az elbujdosott, vagy egy tél a fővárosban*, Kolozsvár: Tilsch.
— (1843) 'Jósika Miklós regényeiről s a regényirodalomrúl általában', *Honderű*, 1: 125.

Péter, Károly (1847), 'Halál szerelemért', *Honderű*, 1: 469–70.

Riedl, Frigyes (1877) 'Kemény Zsigmond és Walter Scott', *Pesti Napló*, Esti kiadás (evening issue), 1 June, 136: 142.

Sárosi, Gyula (1857) 'Három tövis'. I. 'Scott Walternek Napoleon című megbukott hőskölteményére' (from English), *Hölgyfutár*, 231: 931.
'W. S. életéből néhány vonások' (1823) *Hasznos Mulatságok*, 2: 323–26.
'Scott Walter halála' (obituary) (1832) *Társalkodó*, 8 December, 98: 391–92.
'Scott Walter, IV. György koronáztatása napján' (1838) *Társalkodó*, 15: 60.
Szana, Tamás (1875) 'A történelmi regény és Walter Scott', in *Vázlatok*, Budapest: Zilahy, pp. 42–61.
Szegedy-Maszák, Mihály (1995) 'Az összehasonlító irodalomkutatás időszerűsége', *Studia Litteraria*, 125.
Széchenyi, István (1830) *Hitel*, Pest: Trattner & Károlyi, p. 60.
— (1925–39) *Gróf Széchenyi István naplói*, ed. Gyula Viszota, 2 vols, 3, 4 Budapest: Magyar Történelmi Társulat.
Szemlélő (Kassa) (1837) 84, 165 66, 181–82, 185, 193–95.
Szinnyei, Ferenc (1925–26) *Novella- és regényirodalmunk a szabadságharcig*, 2 vols, Budapest: Magyar Tudományos Akadémia.
— (1939–41) *Novella- és regényirodalmunk a Bach-korszakban*, 2 vols, Budapest: Magyar Tudományos Akadémia.

Toldy, Ferenc (1823a) letter to Bajza, 29 November, in Bajza and Toldy (1969), p. 67.
— (1823b) letter to Bajza, 9 December, in Bajza and Toldy (1969), p. 70.
— (1828) letter to Bajza, 12 December, in Bajza and Toldy (1969), p. 454.
— (1829) letter to Bajza, 11 April, in Bajza and Toldy (1969), p. 455.
Tornay [Szontagh Gusztáv] (1837) 'Románok és novellák', *Figyelmező*, 1: 14–16, 18, 20; 4: 11, 18, 25; 5: 9, 23.z.

Viszota, Gyula (1925–39) notes, *Gróf Széchenyi István naplói*, ed. Gyula Viszota, 3 vols, 4, Budapest: Magyar Történelmi Társulat.

Walsh, Robert (1832) *Narrative of a Journey from Constantinople to England*, London: Westley & Davies, p. 302.

Zentai, János (1942) *A magyarországi németség angol műveltsége (1830-ig)*, Debrecen: [n. pub.].
Zilahy Imre (1847) 'A történeti regény', *Magyar Szépirodalmi Szemle*, 16: 241–45; 17: 264–69.

Nineteenth-century translations

BL
(1874) *Lammermoori menyasszony*, trans. L. Lajos Pálóczy, Budapest: Ráth Mór.

I
(1829) *Ivanhoe*, trans. András Thaisz, Pest: Landerer.

LL
(1896) 'Gyászdal "A tó tündére" című költői beszélyből (Lady of the Lake)', trans. Béla Szász, *A vasárnapi újság*, 819.

PP

(1874) *Peveril lovag*, trans. János Frecskay, Budapest: Athenaeum.

Other

(1836) 'Kárpitos szoba' (Tapestried Chamber) trans. József Bajza, in *Pillangó: külföldi válogatott elbeszélések zsebkönyve*, Buda: Széplaki Erneszt.
(1871) 'Esküvő' (Jock of Hazeldean) trans. Károly Sükei, *A Vasárnapi Újság*, 427.
(1888) 'Lodogár' (Lochinvar?) trans. Gusztáv Jánosi, *Budapesti Szemle*, 54: 270–71.
(1890) 'Tűzkirály' (Fire-king) trans. Gusztáv Jánosi, *Budapesti Szemle*, 62.161: 284–89.
(1898) 'Kárpitozott szoba' (Tapestried Chamber) trans. Dáni Ede, Ungvár: [n. pub.].

Chapter 9: The Canonization of Walter Scott as the Inventor of the Historical Novel in Twentieth-Century Hungarian Reception

Bart, István (1974) 'Postscript', in Scott, Walter, *A fekete törpe*, Budapest: Európa, 433–44.
—— (1977) 'Postscript', in Scott, Walter, *A Lammermoori nász*, Budapest: Európa, 401–10.
—— (1980) *Walter Scott világa*, Budapest: Európa.
Berinkey, Irma P. (1933) 'Az Aranykorporsó', *Nyugat* [Budapest], 4: 253–55.

Carlyle, Thomas (1873) 'Walter Scott', trans. Ferencz Baráth, *Budapesti Szemle* [Budapest], 6: 225–76.
Csetri, Lajos (1967) 'Regény és történelem', *Tiszatáj* [Szeged], 2: 155–61.

Elek, Oszkár (1938) 'Scott Walter a magyar irodalmi köztudatban', *Irodalomtörténet* [Budapest], 1–2: 12–24.

Ferenczi, Zoltán (1915) 'A százéves Waverley', *Budapesti Szemle* [Budapest], 194: 82–105.

Gyáni, Gábor (2004) 'Történelem és regény: a történelmi regény', *Tiszatáj* [Szeged], 4: 78–97.

Hegedűs, Géza (1971) 'Walter Scott születésének kétszázadik évfordulójára', *Nagyvilág* [Budapest], 8: 1229–332.
Hites, Sándor (2004) 'Sir Walter Scott és az Ivanhoe magyar fordítói', *A múltnak kútja*, Budapest: Ulpius ház, pp. 143–69.

Laczkó, Géza (1935) 'Walter Scott Ivanhoe' in Véber, Károly (ed.) (1981) *Öröklés és hódítás*, Budapest: Szépirodalmi kiadó, pp. 477–80.
—— (1937) 'A történelmi regény', *Nyugat* [Budapest], 10: 239–57.
Lóránd, Imre (1967) 'Históriai belletrisztika-történelemszemlélet', *Tiszatáj* [Szeged], 8: 775–81.
Lukács, Görgy (1962) *The Historical Novel* [1947], trans. Hannah and Stanley Mitchell, London: Merlin Press.

MSZMP (1966) 'Az irodalom és a művészetek hivatása társadalmunkban', *Társadalmi Szemle* [Budapest], 7–8: 29–58.

Nagy, László (1968) 'Gondolatok a történelmi regényről', *Tiszatáj* [Szeged], 2: 170–75.

Pomogáts, Béla (1966) 'Lektűr-giccs- álművészet', *Kritika* [Budapest], 11: 36–37.
Prónai, Antal (1927) *A magyar irodalom története*, Budapest: Szent István Társulat.

Szana, Tamás (1871) 'Walter Scott', *Figyelő* [Budapest], 31: 365–67.
Szász, Imre (1963) in Scott, Walter, *Talizmán*, Budapest: Szépirodalmi Könyvkiadó,
     pp. 285–90.
Szász, Károly (1875) 'A történelmi hűségről a költészetben', *Budapesti Szemle* [Budapest],
     18: 225–47.
Szathmáry, Györgyné (1967) 'A történelmi regény egy könyvtár gyakorlatában', *Tiszatáj*
     [Szeged], 6: 583–88.
Szegedy-Maszák, Mihály (1982) *Kubla kán és Pickwick úr*, Budapest: Magvető.
Szegedy-Maszák, Mihály and others (2003) *Irodalom*, Budapest: Krónika nova.
Szenczi, Miklós and Tibor Szobotka (1972) *Az angol irodalom története*, Budapest:
     Gondolat.
Szerb, Antal (1935) *A magyar irodalom története*, Budapest: Révai.
— (1941) *A világirodalom története*, Budapest: Magvető.
Szinnai, Tivadar (1959) 'Translator's Postscript', in Scott, Walter, *Rob Roy*, Budapest:
     Móra, pp. 458–62.
Szinnyei, Ferenc (1926) *Novella- és regényirodalmunk a szabadságharcig*, Budapest: MTA.

Ungvári, Tamás (1964) 'Preface', in Scott, Walter, *Puritánok utódai*, Budapest: Európa,
     pp. 1–19.

Voinovich, Géza (1921) 'Scott Walter', in *Regényírók*, Budapest: Franklin-társulat,
     pp. 131–46.

Wéber, Antal (1959) *A magyar regény kezdetei*, Budapest: MTA.
Wellek, René (1963) *Concepts of Criticism*, New Haven: Yale University Press.

Yolland, Arthur (1913) 'Walter Scott's influence on Jósika', *The Hungarian Spectator*
     [Budapest], 2.
— (1928) *Szemelvények a XIX.század angol remekíróiból: Angol olvasókönyv*, Budapest:
     Franklin-társulat.

Zsigmond Ferenc (1913) 'Scott és Jósika', *Irodalomtörténet* [Budapest], 3: 129–42; 4:
     217–27.

Twentieth-century translations

BL
(1967) *A lammermoori nász*, trans. Ilona Kulin, Bratislava: Tatran.
(1967) *A lammermoori nász*, trans. Ilona Kulin, Budapest: Európa.
(1977) *A lammermoori nász*, trans. Ilona Kulin, Budapest: Európa.

FN
(1975) *Nigel jussa*, trans. Ágota Kászonyi, Európa: 1975.

HM
(1980) *Midlothian szíve*, trans. Gy. László Horváth, Budapest: Európa.

I

(1906) *Ivanhoe*, trans. Ilona Győry, Budapest: Révai.

(1935) *Ivanhoe*, trans. Ernő Salgó, Budapest: Az Est, Pesti Napló.

(1955) *Ivanhoe*, trans. Tivadar Szinnai, Bratislava: Csehszlovákiai Magyar Kiadó.

(1955) *Ivanhoe*, trans. Tivadar Szinnai, Budapest: Ifjúsági.

(1962) *Ivanhoe*, trans. Tivadar Szinnai, Budapest: Szépirodalmi.

(1964) *Ivanhoe*, trans. Tivadar Szinnai, Budapest: Móra.

(1966) *Ivanhoe*, trans. Tivadar Szinnai, Budapest: Európa.

(1975) *Ivanhoe*, trans. Tivadar Szinnai, Bukarest: Kriterion.

(1976) *Ivanhoe*, trans. Tivadar Szinnai, Budapest: Móra.

(1980) *Ivanhoe*, trans. Tivadar Szinnai, Budapest: Móra.

(1993) *Ivanhoe*, trans. István Bart, Budapest: Európa.

(1993) *Oroszlánszívű Richárd (The Talisman)* trans. Zoltán Majtényi, Budapest: Pesti Szalon.

(1997) *Ivanhoe*, trans. Judit Varga, Budapest: Juventus.

(2000) *Ivanhoe*, trans. Tivadar Szinnai, Budapest: VAL-ART-LA.

K

(1971) *Kenilworth*, trans. Balázs László, Budapest: Európa.

(1981) *Kenilworth*, trans. Balázs László, Budapest: Európa.

OM

(1964) *Puritánok utódai*, trans. Tivadar Szinnai, Budapest: Európa.

(1979) *Puritánok utódai*, trans. Szinnai, Bratislava: Madách.

(1979) *Puritánok utódai*, trans. Szinnai, Budapest: Európa.

PP

(1978) *A lovag (Woodstock)* trans. György Szegő, Bratislava: Madách.

(1978) *A lovag (Woodstock)* trans. György Szegő, Budapest: Európa.

(1979) *A lovag (Woodstock)* trans. György Szegő, Budapest: Európa.

QD

(1905) *Quentin Durward*, trans. Béla Telekes, Budapest: Révai.

(1928) *Quentin Durward*, trans. Kámán Csillay, Budapest: Regények-regényei.

(1957) *Quentin Durward*, trans. Elek Máthé, Budapest: Szépirodalmi.

(1966) *Quentin Durward*, trans. Elek Máthé, Budapest: Európa.

(1982) *Quentin Durward*, trans. Ágnes Katona, Budapest: Európa.

(1999) *A skót íjász-Quentin Durward*, trans. Elek Máthé, Debrecen: Aquila.

R

(1972) *Redgauntlet*, trans. István Bart, Budapest: Európa.

RR

(1959) *Rob Roy*, trans. Tivadar Szinnai, Budapest: Móra.

(1987) *Rob Roy*, trans. Ágnes Katona, Budapest: Európa.

(1990) *Rob Roy*, trans. Tivadar Szinnai, Bratislava: Madách.

(1990) *Rob Roy*, trans. Tivadar Szinnai, Budapest: Móra.

T

(1929) *A talizmán / A titkos házasság*, trans. Pál Forró, Budapest: Légrády.

(1963) *A talizmán*, trans. Imre Szász and Miklós Vajda, Budapest: Szépirodalmi.

(1963) *A talizmán*, trans. Imre Szász and Miklós Vajda, Bratislava: Szlovák Szépirodalmi Kiadó.

(1963) *A talizmán*, trans. Imre Szász and Miklós Vajda, Bucharest: Irodalom és Művésze.
(1999) *A talizmán*, trans. Pál Forró, Pécs: Mecsek Express.

W
(1949) *Waverley*, trans. János Bókay, Budapest: Révai.
(1958) *Waverley vagy hatvan évvel ezelőtt*, trans. János Bókay, Budapest: Zrínyi.
(1976) *Waverley*, trans. István Bart, Budapest: Európa.
(1986) *Waverley*, trans. István Bart, Budapest: Európa.

Other

(1921) *A fekete törpe (The Black Dwarf)* trans. Sándor Bíró, Budapest: Ifjúsági.
(1974) *A fekete törpe*, trans. György Donga, Hanna Udvarhelyi, Budapest: Európa.
(1981) *A fekete törpe*, trans. Istvàn Bart, György Donga, Hanna Udvarhelyi, Budapest: Európa.
(1982) *A kárpitos szoba*, trans. Istvàn Bart, György Donga, Hanna Udvarhelyi, Budapest: Kriterion.
(1994) *A fekete törpe*, trans. György Donga, Szentendre: Interpopulart.
(1995) *A fekete törpe*, trans. György Donga, Szentendre: Interpopulart.

Chapter 10: From Romantic Folklorism to Children's Adventure Fiction: Walter Scott in Czech Culture

Abrams, M. H. (1958) *The Mirror and the Lamp: Romantic Theory and the Critical Tradition*, New York: W. W. Norton.
Asad, Talal (1986) 'The Concept of Cultural Tradition in British Social Anthropology', in Clifford, James and George Marcus (eds) *Writing Culture: The Poetics and Politics of Ethnography*, Berkeley: University of California Press, pp. 149–68.
Auffenberg, Joseph, Freiherr von (1828) *Der Löwe von Kurdistan: ein romantisches Schauspiel in fünf Acten, nach W. Scott's Talisman bearbeitet . . .*, Würzburg: in der Ettlinger'schen Buch- und Kunsthandlung.

Čelakovský, František Ladislav (1907) *Korespondence a zápisky Frant. Ladislava Čelako-vského. Dopisy 1818–1829* [vol. 1], ed. František Bílý, Prague: Česká akademie císaře Františka Josefa pro vědy, slovesnost a umění.
— (1910) *Korespondence a zápisky Frant. Ladislava Čelakovského II.*, ed. František Bílý, Prague: Česká akademie císaře Františka Josefa pro vědy, slovesnost a umění.
Chudoba, František (ed.) (1912) *Listy psané Johnu Bowringovi ve věcech české a slovanské literatury*, Prague: Královská česká společnost náuk.

Filípek, Václav (1835) *Lev kurdistánský aneb Růže na poušti*, Prague: Václav Špinka.
Frič, Jan (1921) *Život a dílo Aloisa Jiráska*, Prague: Gustav Voleský.

Gaskill, Howard (ed.) (2004) *The Reception of Ossian in Europe*, The Athlone Critical Traditions Series: The Reception of British Authors in Europe, series ed. Elinor Shaffer, London; New York: Continuum.

Hýsek, Miloslav (1921) *Alois Jirásek*, Prague: Státní nakladatelství.
— (1926) *Josef Kajetán Tyl*, Prague: Zlatoroh.

Levý, Jiří (1957) *České theorie překladu*, Prague: SNKLHU (Státní nakladatelství krásné literatury, hudby a umění).

Mácha, Karel Hynek (1959) *Máj*, in *Básně a dramatické zlomky: Spisy Karla Hynka Máchy*, ed. Karel Janský, vol. 1, Prague: SNKLHU.
— (1961) *Křivoklad, in Próza: Spisy Karla Hynka Máchy*, eds Karel Janský, Karel Dvořák and Rudolf Skřeček, vol. 2, Prague: SNKLHU.
— (1965) *May*, trans. Edith Pargeter, Prague: Artia.
— (1972) *Literární zápisníky, deníky, dopisy: Spisy Karla Hynka Máchy*, eds Karel Janský, Karel Dvořák and Rudolf Skřeček, vol. 3, Prague: Odeon.
Macpherson, James (1826) 'Karthon', trans. František Ladislav Čelakovský, *Poutník slovanský* [Prague], 1: 77–96.
Masaryk, Tomáš Garrigue (1990) 'Problém malého národa', in Navrátil, Josef (ed.) *Ideály humanitní*, Prague: Melantrich, pp. 67–98.
Matuška, Alexander (1938) 'Česká a slovenská literatúra', *Přítomnost* [Prague], 10.20: 150–60.

Nenadál, Radoslav (1989) 'Líc a rub rytířství v příběhu o statečném Ivanhoeovi', in *Ivanhoe*, trans. Jaroslav Kraus, Prague: Albatros, pp. 442–48.
— (1990) 'Walter Scott a jeho román Quentin Durward', in *Quentin Durward*, trans. Milan Rejl, Prague: Albatros, pp. 469–73.
Neruda, Jan (1911) 'Richard Lev a Templáři angličtí', in Ignát Herrmann, Ladislav Quis and Karel Rožek, (eds) *Kritické spisy Jana Nerudy*, Prague: František Topič, 7.2: 190–92.

Otruba, Mojmír (1993) 'Josef František Hollmann', in Forst, Vladimír (ed.) *Lexikon české literatury*, Prague: Academia, 2.1: 245–46.

Palacký, František (1898–1903) *Spisy drobné*, eds Leander Čech, V. J. Nováček and Bohuslav Rieger, Prague: Bursík a Kohout, 3: 554.
Procházka, Martin (1996) 'Romantic Revivals: Cultural Translations, Universalism and Nationalism', in Bassnett, Susan and Martin Procházka (eds) *Cultural Learning: Language Learning*, Prague: The British Council and Charles University, pp. 75–90.
— (2005) 'Byron in Czech Culture', in Cardwell, Richard (ed.) *The Reception of Byron in Europe, Volume 2: Northern, Central and Eastern Europe*, 2 vols, The Athlone Critical Traditions Series: The Reception of British and Irish Authors in Europe, series ed. Elinor Shaffer, London; New York: Continuum, pp. 283–304.

Šalda, František Xaver (1987a) 'Dvojí dějepisectví', in *Z období Zápisníku*, ed. Emanuel Macek, vol. 1, Prague: Odeon, pp. 443–55.
— (1987b) 'Alois Jirásek čili mýtus a skutečnost', in *Z období Zápisníku*, ed. Emanuel Macek, vol. 2, Prague: Odeon, pp. 197–201.
— (1987c) 'Mácha snivec i buřič', in *Z období Zápisníku*, ed. Emanuel Macek, vol. 2, Prague: Odeon, pp. 83–90.
— (1987d) 'Zdeněk Nejedlý o Aloisovi Jiráskovi', in *Z období Zápisníku*, ed. Emanuel Macek, vol. 2, Prague: Odeon, pp. 202–03.
Scott, Walter (1904) *The Poetical Works of Sir Walter Scott*, ed. J. Logie Robertson, London: Henry Frowde, pp. 637–40, 653.
St Clair, William (2004) *The Reading Nation in the Romantic Period*, Cambridge: Cambridge University Press.

Tyl, Josef Kajetán (1859) 'Richard Lev na pahorku svatojirském a Boj u diamantu na poušti', in *Sebrané spisy J. K. Tyla*, ed. Václav Filípek, Prague: Kober a Markgraf, 14: 389–95.

Vodička, Felix (1948) *Počátky krásné prózy novočeské*, Prague: Melantrich.

Wellek, René (1963) 'Mácha and English Literature', in *Essays on Czech Literature*, Slavistic printings and reprintings 43, The Hague: Mouton, pp. 148–78.

'Zaboy, Slavoy and Ludeck' (1821) trans. Krystjan Lach Szyrma, *Blackwood's Edinburgh Magazine*, 10.55: 147–51.

Translations

(1822–29) *Walter Scott's Romane*, Taschenbibliothek der ausländischen Klassiker, 108 vols, Zwickau: Schumann.

(1824) *Die Schwärmer*, Leipzig: Hartmann.

(1825) 'Ohenník', trans. Simeon Karel Macháček, *Čechoslav* [Prague], 6: 161–63.

(1825–30) *Walter Scotts Werke*, 93 vols, Vienna: Mausberger.

(1825–31) *Auserlesene Werke: Neueste verbreitete Ausgabe mit Nachrichten über des Verfassers Lebensumstände*, 74 vols, Vienna: Strauß.

(1826) *Panna jezerní*, Zpěv první, Lov, trans. František Ladislav Čelakovský, *Poutník slovanský* [Prague], 2: 16–28.

(1826–32) *Walter Scott's sämmtliche Werke: Neu übersetzt*, vols 1–150, 163–69, Stuttgart: Franckh.

(1826–34) *Walter Scott's sämmtliche Werke: Vollständige Ausgabe der prosaischen Werke*, Abtheilung 1 (43 vols), Abtheilung 2 (14 vols), Abtheilung 3 (2 vols), Gotha: Hennings und Hopf.

(1827–34) *Walter Scotts Werke: Neuübersetzt, verbreitete Ausgabe*, 93 vols, Grätz [Graz]: J. A. Kienreich.

(1828) *Der Abt, Walter Scott's sämmtliche Werke: Neu übersetzt*, vols 85–89, trans. Leonhardt Tafel, Stuttgart: Franckh.

(1836) *Píseň posledního skotského Barda. Báseň v šesteru zpěvu, od Waltera Skotta sepsaná a v češtinu převedená od J. F. P. Hollmanna*, trans. Josef Hollmann, Prague: Tomáš Tábor.

(1840–1843) *Puritáni*, trans. Václav Špinka, Prague: Arcibiskupská tiskárna.

(1875) *Waverley aneb Před šedesáti lety*, trans. Dora Hanušová and Pavlína Králová, Prague: T. Mourek.

(1880) *Panna jezerní: Báseň Waltera Scotta*, trans. František Ladislav Čelakovský, 3rd edn, Prague: I. L. Kober.

(1909) *Panna jezerní a Pán ostrovní*, Dětem nejmilejší knihy s obrázky, Prague: Kočí.

(1925) *Hrabě Pařížský: Dobrodružný román*, *Vybrané romány W. Scotta*, trans. Zdeněk Matěj Kuděj, vol. 2, Prague: A. Svěcený.

(1958) *Srdce Edinburku*, trans. Jarmila Fastrová, Prague: Mladá fronta.

(1985) *Nevěsta z Lammermooru*, trans. Jarmila Fastrová, Prague: Odeon.

Chapter 11: The Polish Reception of Sir Walter Scott

Bachórz, Józef (1994) 'Powieść', in Bachórz, J. and A. Kowalczykowa (eds) *Słownik literatury polskiej XIX wieku*, Wrocław: Ossolineum, pp. 733–49.

Bartoszyński, Kazimierz (1963) *O powieściach Fryderyka Skarbka*, Warsaw: Państwowy Instytut Wydawniczy.

Bujnicki, Tadeusz (1973) *Trylogia Sienkiewicza na tle polskiej powieści historycznej*, Wrocław: Ossolineum.

Bujnicki, Tadeusz (1990) *Polska powieść historyczna XIX wieku*, Wrocław: Ossolineum.

Grabowski, Michał (1840) *Literatura i krytyka*, Wilno: Wenman.

Krajewska, Wanda (1994) 'Angielsko-polskie związki literackie', in Bachórz, J. and A. Kowalczykowa (eds) *Słownik literatury polskiej XIX wieku*, Wrocław: Ossolineum, 1994, pp. 22–26.

Maciejewski, Marian (1994) 'Powieść poetycka', in Bachórz, J. and A. Kowalczykowa (eds) *Słownik literatury polskiej XIX wieku*, Wrocław: Ossolineum, pp. 749–55.

Mickiewicz, Adam (1925) *Konrad Wallenrod and Other Writings of Adam Mickiewicz: Translated from the Polish by Jewell Parish, Dorothea Prall Radin, George Rapall Noyes and Others*, Berkeley: University of California Press.

—— (1949) *Dzieła: Wydanie narodowe*, vol. 2, *Powieści poetyckie*, ed. Konrad Górski, Cracow: Czytelnik.

Nawarecki, Aleksander (1994) 'Sarmatyzm', in Bachórz, J. and A. Kowalczykowa (eds) *Słownik literatury polskiej XIX wieku*, Wrocław: Ossolineum, pp. 858–62.

Ostrowski, Witold (1963) 'Walter Scott w Polsce 1816–1830', *Zeszyty Naukowe Uniwersytetu Łódzkiego*, 29: 115–32.

S. (1816) 'Rzut oka na literaturę angielską w ostatnich dwudziestu latach, pismo wyjęte z dziennika: Bibliotheque universelle 1816. Miesiąc Styczeń.', *Pamiętnik warszawski*, Warsaw: Drukarnia Rządowa, 6 (September–December): 289–308.

Siwicka, Dorota (1995) *Romantyzm: 1822–1863*, Warsaw: Wydawnictwo Naukowe PWN.

—— (2001a) 'Scott Walter', in Rymkiewicz, J. M., D. Siwicka, A. Witkowska, and M. Zielińska (eds) *Mickiewicz: Encyklopedia*, Warsaw: Grupa Wydawnicza Bertelsmann Media.Horyzont, pp. 490–91.

—— (2001b) 'Halban' in Rymkiewicz, J. M., D. Siwicka, A. Witkowska, and M. Zielińska (eds) *Mickiewicz: Encyklopedia*, Warsaw: Grupa Wydawnicza Bertelsmann Media.Horyzont, pp. 184–85.

Scott, Walter ([n.d.]) *Scott's Poetical Works*, London; Glasgow: Collins' Clear-Type Press.

Tazbir, Janusz (1994) 'Historia w powieści', in Bachórz, J. and A. Kowalczykowa (eds) *Słownik literatury polskiej XIX wieku*, Wrocław: Ossolineum, pp. 336–45.

Tretiak, Andrzej (1947) introd. to Walter Scott, *Rob Roy: Powieść historyczna z XVIII wieku*, trans. Teresa Świderska, Warsaw; Poznań: Księgarnia Św. Wojciecha.

Windakiewicz, Stanisław (1914) *Walter Scott i Lord Byron w odniesieniu do polskiej poezji romantycznej*, Cracow: Drukarnia Uniwersytetu Jagiellońskiego.

Zielińska, Marta (2001) 'Cenzura', in Rymkiewicz, J. M., D. Siwicka, A. Witkowska, and M. Zielińska (eds) *Mickiewicz: Encyklopedia*, Warsaw: Grupa Wydawnicza Bertelsmann Media.Horyzont, pp. 68–70.

Translations

BL

(1930) *Narzeczona Lammermoor*, trans. anon., 3 vols, Warsaw: Biblioteka Rodzinna.

(1965) *Narzeczona Lammermoor*, trans. Włodzimierz Lewik (poems) and Krystyna Tarnowska, 3 vols, Warsaw: [n. pub.].

FMP

(1979) *Piękne dziewczę z Perth*, trans. Krystyna Tarnowska, Warsaw: Nasza Księgarnia.

I
(1829) *Ivanhoe, czyli powrót krzyżowca*, trans. Franciszek Salezy Dmochowski, Warsaw: Gazeta Przewodnika Polskiego.
(1948) *Talizman*, trans. Teresa Tatarkiewicz, Warsaw: [n. pub.].
(1972) *Ivanhoe*, trans. Teresa Tatarkiewicz, Warsaw: Nasza Księgarnia.
(1978) *Ivanhoe*, trans. Teresa Tatarkiewicz, Warsaw: Nasza Księgarnia.
(2003) *Ivanhoe: powrót krzyżowca*, trans. Agnieszka Ślusarczyk and Marta Stępkowska, Cracow: Zielona Sowa.

K
(1828) *Tajemnica zamku Kenilworth*, trans. Janina Colonna Wawelska, Warsaw: Biblioteka Nowości.
(1874) *Kenilworth: romans historyczny*, trans. Erazm Rykaczewski, Warsaw: S. Lewental.
(1967) *Kenilworth*, trans. Erazm Rykaczewski, Łódź: Wydawnictwo Łódzkie.

LLM
(1842) *Pieśń ostatniego Minstrela*, trans. Edward Odyniec, Wilno: [Wenman].
(1874) *Pieśń ostatniego Minstrela: Ballady i baśnie*, trans. Edward Odyniec, Warsaw: Gebethner i Wolff.

QD
(1991) *Kwintyn Durward*, trans. anon., 3 vols, Gdansk: Grott.

RR
(1830) *Rob-Roy*, trans. anon., Warsaw: Biblioteka Nowych Romansów.
(1926) *Rob Roy: Powieść historyczna z XVIII wieku*, trans. Teresa Świderska, introd. Andrzej Tretiak, Poznań: Księgarnia Św. Wojciecha.
(1947) *Rob Roy: Powieść historyczna z XVIII wieku*, trans. Teresa Świderska, introd. Andrzej Tretiak, Poznań: Księgarnia Św. Wojciecha.
(1956) *Rob Roy*, trans. Teresa Świderska, ed. Stefan Garczyński, introd. Zdzisław Ryłko, Warsaw: Nasza Księgarnia.
(2003) *Rob Roy*, trans. Michał Grubacki, Cracow: Zielona Sowa.

W
(1929) *Waverley*, trans. Teresa Świderska, introd. Andrzej Tretiak, Cracow: Krakowska Spółka Wydawnicza.
(2005) *Waverley*, trans. Teresa Świderska, introd. Andrzej Tretiak, Biblioteka Gazety Wyborczej, EU: Mediasat Group, S.A.

Other

(1822) *Pani jeziora: Poema Waltera Scotta*, Warsaw, trans. Karol z Kalinówki (Sienkiewicz), Warsaw: [n. pub.].
(1826) *Czarny Karzeł*, trans. anon., 2 vols, Warsaw: [n. pub.].
(1826) *Pan dwóchset wysep: Romans poetyczny Waltera Scotta*, trans. Wanda Malecka, Warsaw: A. Brzezina.
(1826) *Ryszard Lwie Serce*, trans. Franciszek Salezy Dmochowski, 3 vols, [n.p.]: [n. pub.].
(1827) *Więzienie w Edynburgu*, trans. Franciszek Salezy Dmochowski, Warsaw: [n. pub.].
(1828) *Antykwaryusz: romans*, E . . . G . . . [Henryk Emanuel Glüksberg], 3 vols, [n.p.]: [n. pub.].
(1828) *Dugald Dalgetty rycerz najemny*, trans. Karol Korwell, Wilno: Wenman.
(1829) *Hetman z Cherter*, trans. Franciszek Salezy Dmochowski, 3 vols, Warsaw: [n. pub.].

(1830) *Klasztor: powieść*, trans. anon., 2 vols, Warsaw: Biblioteka Nowych Romansów.
(1830–32) *Opat: romans*, trans. Franciszek Salezy Dmochowski, 4 vols, Warsaw: [n. pub.].
(1838) *Dziewica z jeziora*, trans. Edward Odyniec, vols 1 & 2, Lipsk: Breitkopf I Haertel.
(1874) *Dziewica z jeziora*, trans. E. Odyniec, Warsaw: Gebethner i Wolff.
(1875) *Czarny Karzeł*, trans. anon, Warsaw: Nakład Redakcji Tygodnika Mód i Powieści.
(1925) *Ryszard Lwie Serce*, trans. A. Lange, 4 vols, Warsaw: Wydanie Biblioteki Groszowej.
(1948) *Czerwona rękawica*, trans. Wanda Peszkowska, Wrocław: [n. pub.].
(1949) *Na zamku*, trans. Erazm Rykaczewski, ed. Irena Doleżał Nowicka, Warsaw: Stanisław Cukrowski.
(1949) *Tajemnica Opactwa: Romans historyczny*, trans. Rykaczewski, ed. Irena Doleżał Nowicka, introd. Stanisław Helsztyński, Warsaw: Stanisław Cukrowski.

Chapter 12: The Rise and Fall of Scott's Popularity in Russia

Monographs

Alekseev, M. P. (1958) *Val'ter Skott i 'Slovo o polku Igoreve'*, Moscow; Leningrad: Akademii Nauk SSSR.
Al'tshuller, Mark (1996) *Epokha Val'tera Skotta v Rossii: istoricheskii roman 1830–kh godov*, St Petersburg: Akademicheskii proekt.

Bel'skii, A. A. (1958) *Val'ter Skott: ocherk tvorchestva*, Moscow: Obshchestvo po rasprostraneniiu politicheskikh i nauchnykh znanii RSFSR

Eishiskina, N. M. (1959) *Val'ter Skott; kritiko-biograficheskii ocherk*, Moscow, Gosudarstvennoe izdatel'stvo detskoi literatury ministerstva prosveshcheniia RSFSR

Levidova, I. M. (1958) *Val'ter Skott : bio-bibliograficheskii ukazatel' k 125-letiyu so dnya smerti*, Moscow: Vsesoyuznaya knizhnaya palata.
Levin, Yurii D. (1975) 'Prizhiznennaia slava Val'tera Skotta v Rossii (Istoricheskii roman 1830-kh godov)', in *Epokha romantizma: Iz istorii mezhdunarodnykh svyazei russkoi literatury*, Leningrad: Nauka.

Orlov, S. A. (1960) *Istoricheskii roman Val'tera Skotta*, Gorky: Gor'kovskii gosudarstvennoi universitet.

Pinskii, L. E. (1989) *Magistral'nyi syuzhet: F. Viion, V. Shekspir, B. Grasian, V. Skott*, Moscow: Sovetskii pisatel'.

Reizov, B. G. (1965) *Tvorchestvo Val'tera Skotta*, Leningrad: Khudozhestvennaya literatura.

Struve, Gleb (1945) *Scott Letters Discovered in Russia*, Manchester: Manchester University Press.

Monographs in translation

Daiches, David (1987) *Ser Val'ter Skott i ego mir* [Sir Walter Scott and His World], ed. and trans. V. Skorodenko, Moscow: Raduga.

Elze, Carl Friedrich (1894) *Ser Val'ter Skott* [Sir Walter Scott], St Petersburg: zhurnal 'Panteon Literatury'.

Pearson, Hesketh (1978) *Val'ter Skott* [Walter Scott: his life and personality], trans. V. Skorodenko, Moscow: Molodaya gvardiia.

Articles

Alekseev, M. P. (1975) 'Prizhiznennaia slava Val'tera Skotta v Rossii', in *Epokha romantizma*, Leningrad: Nauka, pp. 5–67.

Boborykin, P.D. (1895) 'Angliiskoe vliyanie v Rossii', *Severnyi vestnik*, 10: 177–98.

Kirpichnikov, A. I. (1891) *Val'ter Skott i Viktor Giugo: dve publichniia lektsii, chitannaya v Odesse v 1890 g*, St Petersburg: N. A. Lebedev – zhurnal, Panteon literatury'.

Mann, Yury (1993) 'Russian Attitudes to the Aesthetics of Walter Scott', in Henry, Peter, Jim MacDonald and Halina Moss (eds) *Scotland and the Slavs*, Nottingham: Astra Press, pp. 15–23.

Nikolyukin, A. (1971) 'Val'ter Skott v Rossii', *Moskovskii komsomolets*, 15 August, 7.

Orlov, S. A. (1971) 'Russkie druz'ya Val'tera Skotta', *Literaturnaya gazeta*, 11 August, 14.

Parker, W. M. (1967) 'Scott and Russian Literature', *Quarterly Review*, 305: 172–78.

Simmons, Ernest-J. (1935) 'Walter Scott and the Russian Romantic Movement' in his *English Literature and Culture in Russia 1553–1840*, Harvard Studies in Comparative Literature, vol. 12, Cambridge, MA: Harvard University Press, pp. 237–68.
Struve, Gleb (1950) 'Russian Friends and Correspondents of Sir Walter Scott', *Comparative Literature*, 2: 307–26.
Struve, Peter (1932/1933) 'Walter Scott and Russia', *Slavonic and East European Review*, 11: 397–410.

West, James (1978) 'Walter Scott and the Style of Russian Historical Novels of the 1830s and 1840s', in Birnbaum, Henrik (ed.), *American Contributions to the Eighth International Congress of Slavists, Zagreb and Ljubjlana, September 3–9, 1978*, Columbus: Slavica, pp. 757–72.

Papers

Zholkovsky, Alexander (2000) 'Tri vstrechi s vlastitelem: Val'ter-Skottovskii motiv u Pushkina, L'va Tolstogo i Fazili Iskandera', *Pushkin Bicentennial Conference: Alexander Pushkin and Humanistic Study; Methodological Assumptions, Issues of Translation, East-West Dialogue*, Stanford University, April 12–17.

Scott and Bestuzhev-Marlinskii

Vatsuro, V. E. (1995) 'Iz istorii "goticheski romana" v Rossii: A. A. Bestuzhev-Marlinskii', *Russian, Croatian and Serbian, Czech and Slovak, Polish Literature*, 38.2: 207–26.

Scott and Denis Davydov

Novikov, A. (1942) 'Denis Davydov and Walter Scott', *Russian Literature and Art*, August 1: 4.

Rozov, Zoja (1940) 'Denis Davydov and Walter Scott', *Slavonic and East European Review*, 19: 300–03.

Scott and Gogol

Altshuller, Mark (1989) 'The Walter Scott Motifs in Nikolay Gogol's Story "The Lost Letter" ', *Oxford Slavonic Papers*, 22: 81–88.

Davis, S. B. (1991) 'From Scotland to Russia via France: Scott, Defauconpret and Gogol', *Scottish Slavonic Review*, 17: 21–36.

Elistratova, Anna Arkad'evna (1984) *Nikolai Gogol and the West European Novel*, Moscow: Raduga, pp. 43–53.

Kornblatt, Judith Deutsch (1989) ' "Bez skotov oboidemsia": Gogol and Sir Walter Scott', in Clayton, J. Douglas (ed.) *Issues in Russian Literature before 1917*, Ohio: Columbus, pp. 75–84.

Pikulyk, Romana Myroslawa Bahrij (1979) 'Taras Bul'ba and The Black Council: The Adherence to and Divergence from Walter Scott's Historical Novel Pattern' (unpublished doctoral thesis, University of Michigan).

Scott and Dostoevsky

Dryzhakova, Elena (forthcoming) *Dostoevskii i Val'ter Skott*.

Scott and Kyukhel'beker

Levin, Yurii D. (1964) 'V. K. Kyukhel'beker o poezii Val'tera Skotta', *Russkaia literatura*, 7.2: 95–101.

Scott and Lermontov

Al'tshuller, Mark (1992) '*Knyazhna Meri* Lermontova i *Sen-Ronanskie vody*' (Lermontov's *Princess Mary* and *St Ronan's Well*), in Etkind, Efim (ed.) *Norwich Symposia on Russian Literature and Culture: Michail Lermontov, 1814–1989*, Northfield, VT: Russkaia shkola Norvichskogo universiteta, pp. 14–154.

Jakubovich, D. L. (1935) 'Lermontov i Val'ter Skott', *Izvestiia AN SSSR, Seriia 7, Otdelenie obshchestvennykh nauk*, 3: 243–72.

Matiash, S. A. (1992) 'O evropeiskom i russkom istochnikakh "Borodina" Lermontova', *Russkaia literatura*, 3: 112–21.

Scott and Pushkin

Altshuller, Mark (1988) 'Motifs in Sir Walter Scott's *The Fair Maid of Perth* in Aleksandr Pushkin's "Tazit" ', *Slavic and East European Journal*, 32: 41–54.

Frazier, Melissa (1993) '*Kapitanskaia dochka* and the Creativity of Borrowing', *Slavic and East European Journal*, 37: 472–89.

Greene, Militsa (1965) 'Pushkin and Sir Walter Scott', *Forum for Modern Language Studies*, 1 207–15.

Hoisington, Sona Stephan (1981) 'Pushkin's "Belkin" and the Mystifications of Sir Walter Scott', *Comparative Literature*, 33: 342–57.

Kropf, David Glenn (1994) *Authorship as Alchemy: Subversive Writing in Pushkin, Scott, Hoffmann*, Stanford: Stanford University Press.

Raleigh, John Henry (1981) 'Scott and Pushkin', in Mintz, Samuel I., Alice Chandler and Christopher Mulvey (eds) *From Smollett to James: Studies in the Novel and Other Essays Presented to Edgar Johnson*, Charlottesville: University Press of Virginia, pp. 48–83.

Vries, Gérard de (1997) 'Nabokov, Pushkin and Scott', *Revue de littérature comparée*, 71.3: 307–22.

Yakubovich, D. P. (1930) 'Rol' Frantsii v znakomstve Rossii s romanami Val'ter Skotta' ('The Role of France in Russia's Acquaintance with Walter Scott's Novels'), in *Yazyk i literatura* [Leningrad], [n. pages].
— (1940) '*The Captain's Daughter* and the novels of Walter Scott', *Pushkin*, 4–5: 165–97.
Yakubovich, D. P. and V. D. Rak (2004) 'Scott Walter', *Pushkin and World Literature: Materials to Pushkin Encyclopedia (Pushkin i mirovaia literatura: Pushkinskaia entsiclopedia), Pushkin: Materials and research (Pushkin: Matyerialy i issledovania)*, St Petersburg, 18–19: 311–16 (Bibliography, pp. 314–16).

Scott and Shakhovskoi

Gozenpud, A.A. (1966) 'Val'ter Skott i romanticheskie komedii A. A. Shakhovskogo', in *Russko-evropeiskie literaturnye svyazi: sbornik statei k 70-letiyu so dnya rozhdeniya akademika M.P. Alekseeva*, Moscow: Nauka, pp. 38–48.

Scott and Tolstoy

Christian, R. F. (1988) 'Sir Walter Scott, Russia and Tolstoy', *Scottish Slavonic Review*, 10: 75–91.

Jones, W. Gareth (2004) ' "This Sixty Years Since": Sir Walter Scott's Eighteenth Century and Tolstoy's Engagement with History', in Bartlett, Roger and Lindsey Hughes (eds) *Russian Society and Culture and the Long Eighteenth Century: Essays in Honour of Anthony G. Cross*, Münster: Lit Verlag, pp. 185–94.

Scott and Turgenev

Parker, W.M. (1939) 'Burns, Scott and Turgenev', *Notes and Queries*, 176: 291–92.

Waddington, Patrick (1980) *Turgenev and England*, London, pp. 207–14.

Zhekulin, Nicholas G. (1976) 'Turgenev in Scotland, 1871', *Slavonic and East European Review*, 54.3: 355–70.

Scott and Zagoskin

Altshuller, Mark (1995) '*Roslavlev*: roman i popytka romana: M. Zagoskin, A. Pushkin i Ser Val'ter Scott', *Canadian American Slavic Studies*, 29: 285–99.

Holman, John (1997) 'The Influence of Sir Walter Scott on the First Russian Historical Novel' (unpublished doctoral thesis, University of Pennsylvania).

Scott and Zhukovsky

Hewton, Ainslie (1973) 'A Comparison of Sir Walter Scott's "The Eve of St. John" and Zhukovsky's Translation of the Ballad', *New Zealand Slavonic Journal*, 11: 145–50.

Reizov, Boris G. (1966) 'V. A. Zhukovskii, perevodchik Val'tera Skotta: "Ivanov vecher"', in *Russko-evropeiskie literaturnye svyazi: sbornik statei k 70-letiyu so dnya rozhdeniya akademika M. P. Alekseeva*, Moscow: Nauka, pp. 439–66.

Zhilyakova, E. M. (1988) 'V. Skott v biblioteke V. A. Zhukovskogo' (W. Scott in V. A. Zhukovsky's library), in *Biblioteka A. Zhukovskogo v Tomske*, Tomsk: Izdatel'stvo Tomskogo universiteta

Other Studies in Russian Monographs

Dolinin, A. A. (1988) *Istoriia, odetaia v roman: Val'ter Skott i ego chitateli*, Moscow: Kniga.
Dubashinskii, I. A. (1993) *Val'ter Skott: ocherk tvorchestva*, Daugavpils: Izdatel'stvo Daugavpilsskogo pedagogicheskogo instituta.

Paevskaya, A. (1891) *Val'ter Skott: ego zhizn i literaturnaya deyatelnost biograficheskii ocherk*, St Petersburg: [n. pub.].
Pinskii, L. E. (1989) *Magistral'nyi siuzhet: F. Viion, V. Shekspir, B. Grasian, V. Skott.* Moscow: Sovetskii pisatel'.

Reizov, B. G. (1965) *Tvorchestvo Val'tera Skotta*, Leningrad: Khudozhestvennaya literature.

Socié, Albert (1977) 'Génèse et fonction du héros fictif dans *La Fille du capitaine* de Pouchkine', in Apel-Muller, Michel and others (eds) *Recherches sur le roman historique en Europe XVIIIe–XIXe siècles*, Paris: Annales littéraires de l'Université de Besançon, 1: 287–309.

Val'ter Skott: bio-bibliofraficheskii ukazatel' k 125-letiiu so dnia smerti (1958) Moscow: Vsesoiuznoi Knizhnoi Palaty.

Articles

Barskova, V. S. (1977) 'Shotlandskaya narodnaya legenda v balladakh V. Skotta', *Filologicheskie nauki*, 19.2: 32–41.
Bel'skii, A. A. (1968) 'O literaturno-esteticheskikh vzglyadakh V. Skotta (v svyazi s problemoi tvorcheskogo metoda', *Uchenye zapiski Penzenskogo pedagogicheskogo instituta*, 157: 106–32.
Bunin, P. (1971) 'Val'ter Skott', *Komsomol'skaya pravda*, 15 August, 2.

Chechtko, M. V. (1996) ' "Roman o vodakh" v tvorchestve Dzhein Osten i Val'tera Skott: puti khudozhestvennogo analiza deistvitel'nosti', *Vestnik Moskovskogo Universiteta*, 9.1: 9–19.

Diakonova, Nina (1976) 'The Aesthetics of Walter Scott', *Zeitschrift für Anglistik und Amerikanistik*, 24: 5–21.

Elistratova, A. (1967) 'Val'ter Skott: nash sovremennik?', *Voprosy literatury*, 2: 220–25.

Guseinov, Gasan (1971) 'Na rodine velikogo romantika', *Literaturnyi Azerbaidzhan*, 8: 133–34.

Koleznikov, B. I. (1980) 'Devid Lindsei i Val'ter Skott', in *Problemy realizma v zarubezhnoi literature XIX–XX vekov*, Moscow: Moskovskii oblastnoi pedagogicheskii institut im N. K. Krupskoi, pp. 109–12.
Krutov, Yu. I. (1975) 'Istorizm i nekotorye zhanrovye osobennosti romana Val'tera Skotta', *Voprosy romantizma*, 2: 102–15.

Mikhal'skaya, N. P. (1971) 'Val'ter Skott: k 200-leityu so dnya, rozhdeniya pisatelya', *Literatura v shkole*, 4: 88–92.

Reizov, Boris G. (1971) 'Istoriia i vymysel v romanakh Val'tera Skotta', *Izvestiia Akademii Nauk S.S.S.R.*, 30: 306–11.
— (1974) 'History and Fiction in Walter Scott's Novels', *Neohelicon*, 2: 165–75.
Rogov, V. (1971) 'Val'ter Skott', *Detskaya literatura*, 8: 44–46.

Serdyukov, A. I. (1966) 'Obshchestvenno-istoricheskie vzglyady Val'tera Skotta', *Uchenye zapiski Azerbaidzhanskogo gosudarstvennogo universiteta*, 7: 92–7.
— (1969) 'Literaturnaya sreda Val'tera Skotta', *Uchenye zapiski Azerbaidzhanskogo gosudarstvennogo universiteta*, 1–2: 131–6.
— (1970) 'Poemy Val'tera Skotta', *Uchenye zapiski Azerbaidzhanskogo universita*, 5–6: 83–9.
— (1975) 'Tipologicheskie priznaki romanov Val'tera Skotta', *Uchenye zapiski Azerbaidzhanskogo gosudarstvennogo universiteta: Seriya yazyka i literatury*, 1: 64–69.
Sidorchenko, L. V. (1976) 'Problema krestovykh pokhodov v romanakh V. Skota', *Problemy metoda, zhanra i stilya v progressivnoi literature zapada XIX–XX vv*, 2: 58–70.
— (1978) 'Roman V. Skotta *Graf Robert Parizskij*: problema istoricheskoi lichnosti', *Vestnik Leningradskogo Universiteta*, 20: 58–65.

— (1979) 'Problema zavoevaniia v tvorchestve Val'tera Skotta 1819–1831 gg.', *Problemy istorii zarubezhnoi literatury*, 1: 80–88.

Sokolyans'kii, M. G. (1967) 'Tvorchestvo Val'tera Skotta', *Inozemna filologiya*, 12: 159–

Translations

(1823) *Kenil'vort, istoricheskii roman Sira Val'tera Skotta, s prisovokupleniem preduvedomitel-'nogo zamechaniya o Kenil'vosrtskom zamke i zhizneopisaniya grafa Leichestera*, I–IV, Moscow.

(1824) *Mannering, ili Astrolog, sochinenie Sira Val'tera Skotta, perevod s frantsuzskogo, izdannyi Vladimirom Bronevskim*, I–IV, Moscow.

(1824) *Tainstvennyi karlo. Povest' Sira Val'tera Skotta*, I, II, Moscow.

(1824) *Shotlandskie puritane, povest' traktirshchika, izdannaya Kleishbotemom, uchitelem i klyucharem v Gander-Kleige. Istoricheskii roman, sochinenie Val'tera Skotta*, trans. Vasily Sots, I–IV, Moscow: Tipografiia Selivanovskogo.

(1824) *Vysluzhivshiisya ofitser, ili Voina Montroza, istoricheskii roman. Soch[inenie] Val'tera Skotta, avtora Shotlandskikh puritan, Rob Roya, Edimburgskoi temnitsy i proch* I–IV, Moscow.

(1825) *Edinburgskaya temnitsa, iz sobraniya novykh skazok moego khozyanina, izdannyikh Dzhedediem Kleishbotom, ponomarem i uchitelem Gender-Klyufskogo prikhoda. Sochinenie Sira Val'tera Skotta*, I–IV, Moscow.

(1825) *Abbat, ili nekatorye cherty zhizni Marii Stuart, korolevy shotlandskoi. Sochinenie Sira Val'tera Skotta*, I–IV, St Petersburg

(1825/1826) *Antikvarii, sochinenie Sir Val'tera Skotta*, III, IV, Moscow.

(1826) *Ivangoe, ili vozvrashchenie iz Krestovykh pokhodov. Sochinenie Val'tera Skotta, I–IV*, St Petersburg.

(1826–27) *Kanten' Dyurvard, ili Shotlandets pri dvore Lyudovika XI. Istoricheskii roman Sira Val'tera Skotta*, I–IV, Moscow.

(1827) *Veverlei, ili Shest'desyat let nazad. Sochineniie Sira Val'tera Skotta*, I–IV, Moscow.

(1827) *Nevesta Lammermurskaya. Novye skazki moego khozyanina, sobrannye i izdannye Dzhedediem Kleishbotamom, uchitelem i klyucharem Gander-Kleigskogo prokhoda. Sochinenie Sira Val'tera Skotta*, I–III, Moscow.

(1827) *Talisman, ili Rishard v Palestine. Iz istorii vremenen krestovykh pokhodov. Val'tera-Skotta*, I–III, Moscow.

(1828) *Sen-Ronanskie vody. Sira Val'tera Skotta*, I–VI, Moscow.

(1828) *Redgontlet (Krasnaya perchatka). Povest' os'magonadesyat' stoletiya. Sochinenie Sira Val'tera Skotta*, I–IV, Moscow.

(1828) *Konnetabl' Chesterskii, ili Obruchennye (Iz vremen krestovykh pokhodov). Sochinenie Sira Val'tera Skotta*, I–III, St Petersburg.

(1829) *Vudstok ili Vsadnik. Istoriya Kromvelevykh vremen. 1651 dog. Soch[inenie] Sira Val'ter Skotta*, I–IV, St Petersburg.

(1829) *Morskoi razboinik. Sochinenie Sir Val'tera Skotta*, I–IV, Moscow.

(1829) *Priklyucheniya Nigelya. Sochinenie Sira Val'tera Skotta*, I–IV, Moscow.

(1829) *Rob–Roi: Sochinenie Val'tera Skotta. S istoricheskim izvestiem o Rob-Roe mark-Gregore Kambele i ego semeistve*, I–IV, Moscow.

(1829) *Monastyr': Sochinenie Sira Val'tera Skotta*, I–IV, Moscow.

(1829) *Pertskaya krasavitsa, ili Prazdnik sv. Valentina. Istoricheskii roman Sira Val'tera Skotta*, I–IV, Moscow.

(1830) *Karl Smelyi, ili Anna Geiershteinskaya, deva mraka. Soch[inenie] sira Val'ter Skotta*, I–V, St Petersburg.

(1830) *Peveril', istoricheskii roman Sira Val'tera Skotta*, I–V, Moscow.

(1830) *Doch' shotlandskogo lekarya. Sochinenie sira Val'tera Skotta*, I–II, Moscow.

(1831) *Graf Robert Parizhskii. Roman Vostochnoi imperii: Soch[inenie] Sira Val'ter-Skotta*, I–IV, St Petersburg.

(1833) *Opasnyi zamok. Poslednee sochinenie sira Val'ter-Skotta*, I–II, St Petersburg.

(1960) *Aivengo; Ivanhoe*, trans. E. Beketovaya, ed. and trans. V. Ivanov, introd. R. Samarin, Moscow: Gosudarstvennoi izdatel'stvo detskoi literatury.

(1960–65) *Sobranie sochinenii v dvadtsati tomakh*, trans. N. D. Vol'pin, A. S. Kulisher, E. G. Beketovaya and others, vol. 1: Ueverli; vol. 2: Gai Mennering; vol. 3: Antikvarii; vol. 4: Chernyi karlik. Puritane; vol. 5: Rob Roi; vol. 6: Edinburgskaia temnitsa, vol. 7: Lammermurskaia nevesta. Legenda o Montoze; vol. 8: Aivengo; vol. 9: Monastyr'; vol. 10: Abbat; vol. 11: Kenilvort; vol. 12: Pirat; vol. 13: Prikliu cheniia Naidzhela; vol. 14: Peveril Pik; vol. 15: Kventin Dorvard; vol. 16: Sent-Ronanskie vody; vol. 17: Vudstok, ili Kavaler; vol. 18: Pertskaya krasavitsa, ili Valentinov den'. Rasskazy; vol. 19. Talisman. Poemy. Stikhotvoreniia: Ballady. Raznye stikhotvoreniia. Pokaianie. Sud v podzemel'e. Valentinov den'. Rasskazy; vol. 19: Talisman. Poemy. Stikhotvoreniia: Ballady. Raznye stikhotvoreniia. Pokaianie. Sud v podzemel'e. Razboinik; vol. 20: Graf Robert Parizhskii. Stat'i i dnevniki, trans. and ed. B.G. Reizov, R. M. Samarin and B. B. Tomashevskii, Moscow: Gosudarstvennoe izdatel'stvo khudozhestvennoi literatury.

(1968) *Aivengo*, trans. E. Beketovaya, Kishinev: Lumina.

(1991) 'Abbatstvo koshmarov', in *Komnata s gobelenami: angliiskaia goticheskiia proza*, ed. and trans. N. A. Solov'ev, Moscow: Pravda.

(2000) *Marmion: Povest' o bitve pri Floddine v shesti pesnyakh*, ed. V. P. Betaki and G. S. Usova. St Petersburg: Nauka

Chapter 13: Slovene Reception of Sir Walter Scott in the Nineteenth Century

Bogataj, Jože (1982) *Sir Walter Scott in slovenska zgodnja pripovedna proza*, B-diplomska naloga.

Celestin, Fran (1883) 'Naše obzorje V.', *Ljubljanski zvon*, 3: 320–27.
Čop, Matija (1986) *Pisma 1*, Epistolae Slovenorum illustrium 6.1, Ljubljana: Academia scientiarum et artium slovenica.

Del Lungo, Andrea (2003) *L'incipit romanesque*, Paris: Seuil.

Hladnik, Miran (1994) 'Slovenska zgodovinska povest v 19. stoletju', *Seminar slovenskega jezika, literature in kulture*, 30: 127–52.

Jurčič, Josef ([n.d.]) *Der zehnte Bruder*, trans. Ferdinand Kolednik, Regensburg: Verlag Josef Habbel.
— (1953) *George Koziak: A Slovenian Janizary*, trans. Ferdinand Kolednik, Montreal: Industrial School for the Deaf.
Jurčič, Josip (1961) 'Jurij Kozjak', *Zbrano delo 1*, Ljubljana: Državna založba Slovenije.
— (1965) 'Deseti brat', *Zbrano delo 3*, Ljubljana: Državna založba Slovenije.
— (1967) 'Hči mestnega sodnika', *Zbrano delo 4*, Ljubljana: Državna zložba Slovenije.

Klančar, Anthony J. (1946) 'Josip Jurčič, the Slovene Scott', *The American Slavic and East European Review*, 5: 19–33.
Kmecl, Matjaž (1881) *Rojstvo slovenskega romana*, Ljubljana: Mladinska knjiga.

Koblar, France (1936) 'Uvod', in Jurčič, Josip, *Deseti brat*, Celje: Družba sv. Mohorja, [n. page].
Kos, Janko (1987) *Primerjalna zgodovina slovenske literature*, Ljubljana: Znanstveni inštitut Filozofske fakultete.

Levec, Fran (1868) 'Josip Jurčič', *Novice*, 26: 19.
— (1888) 'Spomini o Josipu Jurčiči', *Ljubljanski zvon*, 8: 418–29.
— (1967) *Pisma 1*, Epistolae Slovenorum illustrium 4.1, Ljubljana: Academia scientiarum et artium slovenica.

Oppel, Horst (1971) *Englisch-deutsche Literaturbeziehungen II: Von der Romantik bis zur Gegenwart*, Berlin: Erich Schmidt Verlag.

Rupel, Mirko (1961) 'Opombe', in Jurčič, Josip, *Zbrano delo 1*, Ljubljana: Državna založba Slovenije, [n. page].

Scott, Walter ([n.d.]) *The Antiquary*, London: The Waverley Book Company.
— (1968) *Guy Mannering*, London: Dent.
— (1999) *Kenilworth*, London: Penguin Classics.
Slodnjak, Anton (1950) 'O Stanku Vrazu kot slovenskem pesniku', *Slavistična revija*, 3: 65–90.
Stritar, Josip (1877) 'Josip Jurčič', *Zvon*, 3: 63.
Šanda, Dragan (1905) 'Jurčič-Scott', *Dom in svet*, 18: 76–83.

Trdina, Janez (1946) 'Spomini', *Zbrano delo 1*, Ljubljana: Državna založba Slovenije.

Vraz, Stanko (1952) 'Začetek izvirne povesti', *Slovenska djela II*, Zagreb: Jugoslavenska akademija znanosti i umjetnosti, 169–171.

Chapter 14: 'His pirates had foray'd on Scottish hill': Scott in Denmark with an Overview of his Reception in Norway and Sweden

Abrahamson, Werner Hans Frederik, Knud Lyne Rahbek and Rasmus Nyerup (eds) (1812–14) *Udvalgte danske Viser fra Middelalderen 1–5*, Copenhagen: Beeken.
Alexander, J. H. and David Hewitt (eds) (1983) *Scott and his Influence: Papers of the Aberdeen Scott Conference 1982*, Aberdeen: Association for Scottish Literary Studies.
— (1993) *Scott in Carnival*, Aberdeen: Association for Scottish Literary Studies.
Andersen, Hans Christian (1832) *Bruden fra Lammermoor*, Musiken komponeret af J. Bredal, Copenhagen: Reitzel.
— (1836) *Sangene i Festen paa Kenilworth*, Musiken af Weyse, Copenhagen: Reitzel.
— (1951) *Mit Livs Eventyr I–II*, ed. H. Topsøe-Jensen, Copenhagen: Gyldendal.
— (1962a) *Levnedsbog*, ed. H. Topsøe-Jensen, Copenhagen: Schønberg.
— (1962b) *O.T.*, ed. Henning Fonsmark, Copenhagen: Reitzel.
— (1962c) *De to Baronesser*, ed. Henning Fonsmark, Copenhagen: Reitzel.
Anker, Øgvind, Francis Bull and Torben Nielsen (1953) *Bjørnstjerne Bjørnsons Brevveksling med Danske 1875–1910*, I: Copenhagen; Oslo: Gyldendal.

Bagger, Carl (1928) *Udvalgte Skrifter*, ed. Oskar Schlichkrull, Copenhagen: Holbergselskabet af 23. September.
Beyer, Edvard (ed.) (1974) *Norges litteraturhistorie 2*, Oslo, Cappelen.
Bjørnson, Bjørnstjerne (1877) *Kongen*, Copenhagen: Gyldendal.

Blangstrup, Christian (ed.) (1926) *Salmonsens Konversationsleksikon* XXI, 2nd edn, Copenhagen: Schultz.

Blicher, Steen Steensen (1964–65) *Samlede Noveller og Skitser,* 1–5, Copenhagen: Rosenkilde og Bagger.

Borup, Morten (ed.) (1956) *Christian Molbechs brevveksling med svenske forfattere og videnskabsmænd, I–III,* Copenhagen: Rosenkilde og Bagger; Lund: Gleerup.

— (ed.) (1974) *Breve fra og til Christian Winther I–IV,* Copenhagen: Reitzel.

Brandes, Georg (1873–90) *Hovedstrømninger i det 19de Aarhundredes Litteratur,* 1–6. 4: Naturalismen i England (1875), Copenhagen: Gyldendal.

— (1923) *Hovedstrømninger i det nittende Aarhundredes Literatur,* 1–6, 6th edn, Copenhagen: Gyldendal.

Bremer, Fredrika (1837) *Grannarne,* Christianstad: Schmidt & Co.

Clausen, Julius (ed.) (1898–1901) *Illustreret Verdens-Litteraturhistorie, I–III,* Copenhagen: Gyldendal.

Elze, Karl (1878) *Sir Walter Scott,* trans. K. Kroman, Copenhagen: Schubothe.

Frykman, Erik (1983) 'Galt and Scott – Dependence and Independence', in Alexander and Hewitt (1983): 312–20.

Galster, Kjeld (1922) *Ingemanns historiske Romaner og Digte,* Copenhagen: Aschehoug.

Gibbons, Lee (1821) *The Cavalier,* London: Longman.

Gumælius, Gustaf Wilhelm (1828) *Thord Bonde eller slutet af Konung Albrechts regering,* Uppsala: Palmblad.

Gyllembourg, Thomasine (1835) *Nye Fortællinger,* Copenhagen: Reitzel.

Hansen, Adolf (1902) *Den engelske og nordamerikanske Litteraturs Historie i Omrids,* Copenhagen: Gyldendal.

Hansen, Mauritz (1969) *Fortællinger,* Bergen: Eide.

Harding, Gunnar (1997) *En katedral av färgat glas. Shelley – Byron – Keats och deras epok,* trans. Ingrid Ingemark and Gunnar Harding, Stockholm: Gedins.

— (2000) *Och drog likt drömmar bort. Coleridge – Wordsworth och deras epok,* trans. Ingrid Ingemark, Jesper Högström and Gunnar Harding, Stockholm: Wahlström & Widstrand.

— (2002) *Där döda murar står. Lord Byron och hans samtida,* trans. Ingrid Ingemark and Gunnar Harding, Stockholm: Wahlström & Widstrand.

Hartveit, Lars (1983) 'Affinity or Influence? Sir Walter Scott and J. G. Farrell as Historical Novelists', in Alexander, J. H. and David Hewitt (eds) (1983), pp. 414–20.

— (1993) 'A Reading of *The Pirate* in the Light of Scott's Views on the Craft of Fiction', in Alexander, J. H. and David Hewitt (eds) (1983), pp. 332–44.

Hauch, Carsten (1834) *Vilhelm Zabern,* Copenhagen: Reitzel.

— (1871) *Minder fra min første Udenlandsrejse,* Copenhagen: Reitzel.

Heiberg, Johan Ludvig (1828) *Pigen ved Søen.* Syngespil i tre Acter med Musik af Rossini, Copenhagen: Reitzel.

— (1833) *Om Philosophiens Betydning for den nuværende Tid,* Copenhagen: Reitzel.

Ingemann, Bernhard Severin (1824) *Valdemar den Store og hans Mænd,* Copenhagen: Reitzel.

— (1826) *Valdemar Seier,* Copenhagen: Reitzel.

— (1828) *Erik Menveds Barndom,* Copenhagen: Reitzel.

— (1833) *Kong Erik og de Fredløse,* Copenhagen: Reitzel.

— (1835) *Prins Otto af Danmark og hans Samtid*, Copenhagen: Reitzel.
— (1836) *Dronning Margrethe*, Copenhagen: Reitzel.

Jacobsen, Friedrich Johann (1820) *Briefe an eine deutsche Edelfrau, über die neuesten englischen Dichter*, Altona: [n. pub.].
Johanson, Klara and Ellen Kleman (1915) *Fredrika Bremers brev samlade och utgivna Del I 1821–1838*, Stockholm: Norstedt.

K., O. (1831) *Snapphanarne. Gammalt nytt om Skåne, från sjuttonde seklet*, Stockholm: Hjerta.

Lindström, Erik (1925) 'Walter Scott och den historiska romanen och novellen I Sverige intill 1850', *Göteborgs Högskolas Årsskrift*, XXXI, ii, Gothenburg: Wettergren & Kerber.

Martensen, Josepha (1920) *Walter Scott. En Fortælling om hans Liv*, Copenhagen: Frimodt.
Munch, Andreas (1861) *Pigen fra Norge*, Christiania: Tønsberg.
— (1874) *Barndoms- og Ungdoms-Minder*, Christiania: Aschehoug.
Munch, Anna E. (1954) *Et nordisk Digterhjem: Andreas og Amalia Munch 1862–1884; Breve og Erindringer*, Copenhagen: Fischer.

Nielsen, Jørgen Erik (1976–77) *Den samtidige engelske litteratur og Danmark 1800–1840 I–II*, Publications of the Department of English University of Copenhagen 3–4, Copenhagen: Nova.
— (1983) 'Sir Walter Scott's Reception in Nineteenth-Century Denmark', in Alexander, J. H. and David Hewitt (eds) (1983), pp. 467–74.
— (1986) 'Andreas Andersen Feldborg: in Denmark English, in England Danish', *Angles on the English Speaking World* [Copenhagen], 1: 51–63.
— (1993) 'Scott's Use of Two Danish Ballads in *The Lady of the Lake*', in Alexander, J. H. and David Hewitt (eds) (1993), pp. 89–96.
Nørvig, Johannes (1943) *Steen Steensen Blicher. Hans liv og værker*, Copenhagen: Munksgaard.

Pedersen, Viggo Hjørnager (1983) 'Walter Scott in Denmark: The Transfer of Literary Form as Exemplified by a Comparison of *Ivanhoe* and *Valdemar Sejr*', in Engelberg, Karsten (ed.) *The Romantic Heritage: A Collection of Critical Essays*, Copenhagen: Publications of the Department of English, University of Copenhagen, 12: 185–200.
Preisz, Daniel (ed.) (1955) *Breve fra og til Adam Oehlenschläger 1809–1829 III*, Copenhagen: Gyldendal.

Rahbek, Knud Lyne (1817) *Nytaarsgave for begge Kiön: Asterkrandsen; Samling af poetiske Oversættelser efter det Tydske, Svenske, Engelske, Italienske og Franske*, trans. K. L. Rahbek, Copenhagen: Beeken.

Schnitler, Carl W. (1911) *Slegten fra 1814*, Studier over norsk embedsmandskulturi klassicismens tidsalder 1814–1840: Kulturformene, Christiania: Aschehoug.
Schück and Warburg (1985) *Illustrerad svensk litteraturhistoria 6*, 3rd rev. edn, Stockholm: Gidlunds.
Sparre, Pehr (1832) *Den siste friseglaren I–III*, Stockholm: Hjerta.

Tysdahl, Bjørn (1983) 'Sir Walter Scott and the Beginnings of Norwegian Fiction, and a Note on Ibsen's Early Plays', in Alexander, J. H. and David Hewitt (eds) (1983), pp. 475–84.

— (1988) *Maurits Hansens fortellerkunst*, Oslo: Aschehoug.
— (1993) 'Unifying and Disruptive Imagery in Old Mortality', in Alexander, J. H. and David Hewitt (eds) *Scott in Carnival*, (1993), pp. 172–83.

Wergeland, Henrik (1918) *Samlede Skrifter I*, ed. Herman Jæger, Christiania: Steen.
Wiedemann, Christian Rudolph Wilhelm (ed.) (1815–16) *Modern English Poems I–II*, Kiel: Hesse.
Wohlbrück, W. A. (1834) *Tempelherren og Jødinden: Musiken af Heinr. Marschner*, trans. Th. Overskou, Copenhagen: Det kgl. Teaters repertoire nr. 102.
Wood, E. H. Harvey (1973) 'Scott's Foreign Contacts', in Bell, Alan (ed.) *Scott Bicentenary Essays*, Edinburgh; London: Scottish Academic Press, pp. 238–59.

Danish translations

HH
(1822) *Halidon Hill*, trans. K. L. Rahbek, Copenhagen: Beeken.

GM
(1823) *Guy Mannering eller Stjernetyderen I–III*, trans. C. W. Hviding, Copenhagen: Gyldendal.
(1837) *Guy Mannering eller Stjærnetyderen I–II*, trans. F. Schaldemose, Copenhagen: Møller.
(1987) *Guy Mannering eller astrologen*, trans. Luise Pihl, Copenhagen: Hernov.

HM
(1822) *Midlothians Hjerte eller Fængslet i Edinburgh I–IV*, trans. C. J. Boye, Copenhagen: Gyldendal.

I
(1822) *Ivanhoe I–III*, trans. C. J. Boye, Copenhagen: Gyldendal.
(1883) *Ivanhoe*, illus. and trans. P. V. Grove, Copenhagen: Philipsen.
(1899) *Ivanhoe*, illus., trans. and abr. P. V. Grove, Copenhagen: Det Nordiske Forlag.
(1944) *Ivanhoe*, adapt. and abr. H. Madsen, Copenhagen: Gyldendal.
(1976) *Ivanhoe*, trans. Svend Jensen, Copenhagen: Hernov.

K
(1885) *Kenilworth*, illus. and trans. F. Winkel Horn, Copenhagen: Philipsen.

NB
(1827–30) *De Franskes Keiser, Napoleon Bonapartes Levnet: Med en indledende Udsigt over den franske Revolution I–IX*, trans. H. G. N. Nyegaard and A. P. Liunge, Copenhagen: Steen.
(1828) *Napoleon Buonapartes Levned I–II*, trans. and abr. F. Schaldemose, Copenhagen: Møller.

QD
(1884) *Quentin Durward*, illus. and trans. F. Winkel Horn, Copenhagen: Philipsen.
(1978) *Quentin Durward. Den skotske bueskytte*, trans. Svend Jensen, Copenhagen: Hernov.

W
(1832) *Waverley eller det er tresindstyve Aar siden I–II*, trans. F. Schaldemose, Copenhagen: Møller.

Other

(1821) *Røde Robin I–II*, trans. C. J. Boye, Copenhagen: Gyldendal.
(1832–56) *Samlede Skrifter I–XXXIX*, various trans., Copenhagen: Møller.
(1835) *Lord Sydenham* [spurious], trans. S. J. Bang, Copenhagen: translator.
(1836) *Pigen ved Søen*, trans. P. D. Ibsen, Copenhagen: translator.
(1841) *Allan Cameron I–II* [spurious], trans. F. Schaldemose, Copenhagen: Møller.
(1855–71) *Samlede Romaner I–XX*, various trans., Copenhagen: Philipsen.
(1871) *Pigen ved Søen*, trans. A. Munch, Copenhagen, Forlagsbureauet.
(1881–82) *Udvalgte Fortællinger bearbejdede for Ungdommen I–II*, illus. and adapted M. Barack, Copenhagen: Nyt dansk Forlagskons.

Swedish translations

(1830–33) *Morfars sagor eller berättelser ur Skottlands historia*, vols 1–3, Norrköping: Collin & K and Schmidt & K.
(1832–33) *Morfars berättelser ur Frankrikes historia*, vols 1–3, Norrköping: Schmidt & Koch Bohlin.
(1833–34) *Grefve Robert av Paris*, 4 vols, Stockholm: L. J. Hierta.
(1835) *Det farliga slottet*, Uppsala: [n. pub.].
(1853–58) *Romaner i svensk öfversättning*, vols 1–26, Stockholm: F. & G. Beijer; this edn is a revision of the translations from the 1820s.
(1877–83) *Romaner: Illustr. uppl.*, [vols] 1–16, Stockholm: F. & G. Beijer. '1–16' indicates novels, perhaps not vols; seemingly 1st illus. Swedish edn.

Chapter 15: European Reception of Scott's Poetry: Translation as the Front Line

Ambrose, Mary (1972) 'La donna del lago: the First Italian Translations of Scott', *Modern Language Review*, 67: 74–82.
Andersen, Hans Christian (1955 [1855]) *The Mermaid Man: the Autobiography of Hans Christian Andersen*, new abr. trans. Maurice Michael, London: Arthur Barker.
Antony-Béraud (1835) 'La nuit de décembre: ballade (imitation de Walter Scott)', *Revue du XIX siècle poétique*, 2: 48–52.
Arany, János (1853) 'Sir Patrick Spens', *Szépirodalmi lapok* [Pest], no. 21.
Artaud, Nicolas-Louis (1826) *Chants populaires des frontières méridionales de l'Ecosse*, Paris: C. Gosselin.
Ascherson, Neal (1995) *Black Sea*, London: Cape.

Beets, Nicolaas (1876 [1834]) *Dichtwerken* [. . .] 1830–1873, vol. 1, Amsterdam: W. H. Kirberger.
Benedetti, Anna (1974) *Le traduzioni italiane da Walter Scott e i loro anglicismi*, Florence: L. S. Olschki.
Biblioteca italiana (1822), 25: 183–91.
Bisson, L. A. (1943) *Amédée Pichot: a Romantic Prometheus*, Oxford: Basil Blackwell.
Boix, Vicente (1845) 'A la memoria de Walter Scott', *El fenix* [Valencia], 23 November.
BOSLIT [Bibliography of Scottish Literature in Translation] <http://boslit.nls.uk>
Bridel, Yves and Roger Francillon (1998) *La bibliothèque universelle (1815–1924): miroir de la sensibilité romande au XIXe siècle*, Lausanne: Payot.

Čelakovský, František Ladislav (1828) *Panna jezerní*, Prague: [n. pub.].

Charlier, Gustave (1949) *Le mouvement romantique en Belgique, 1815–1850: I : La bataille romantique*, Brussels: La Renaissance du Livre.

Churchman, Philip E. and E. Allison Peers (1922) 'A Survey of the Influence of Sir Walter Scott in Spain', *Revue hispanique*, 55: 227–310.

Davis, S. B. (1991) 'From Scotland and Russia via France: Scott, Defauconpret and Gogol', *Scottish Slavonic Review*, 17: 21–36.

'Le dernier barde' (1821), *Bibliothèque universelle* [Geneva], 16: 312.

Duchesne, E. (1910) *Michel Iouriévitch Lermontov: sa vie et ses œuvres*, Paris: Plon.

Einstein, Alfred (1971) *Schubert*, trans. David Ascoli, London: Panther.

Exposição comemorativa (1971) do II centenario de Walter Scott: Suplemento ao catálogo: traduções portuguesas, teses de licenciatura e estudos críticos, Lisbon: Insituto Británico em Portugal.

Fontane, Theodor (1861) 'Die zwei Raben', in *Balladen*, Berlin: Hertz.

— (1965) *Across the Tweed. Notes on Travel in Scotland, 1858* [1860], trans. Brian Battershaw, London: Phoenix House.

Fontaney, Antoine (1829) *Ballades, melodies et poesies diverses*, Paris: Hayet.

Freiligrath, Ferdinand (1877) *Ferdinand Freiligrath's Gesammelte Dichtungen* [1844], expanded edn, vol. 2, Stuttgart: G. J. Göschen.

Geel, Jacob (1822) 'Proeve eener navolging van de Lady of the Lake van Walter Scott', *Magazijn voor Wetenschaften, Kunsten en Letteren* [Amsterdam], 1: 441ff.

Graves, Peter (2000) *Fröding, Burns and Scott*, Edinburgh: Lockharton Press.

Grinsbergs, Melita (1954) 'Some Aspects of Scottish Authors in Russian Literature in the First Half of the Nineteenth Century' (unpublished doctoral thesis, University of Edinburgh).

Iser, Wolfgang (1988) 'The Reading Process: a Phenomenological Approach', in Lodge, David (ed.) *Modern Criticism and Theory: a Reader*, London: Longman, pp. 212–28.

— (1997–98): Richard van Oort, 'The Use of Fiction in Literary and Generative Anthropology: an Interview with Wolfgang Iser', *Anthropoetics*, 3.2 (Fall 1997/ Winter 1998) <http://www.humnet.ucla.edu/humnet/anthropoetics/ap0302/ Iser_int.htm> [accessed 25 August 2005]

Jack, R. D. S. (1972) *The Italian Influence on Scottish Literature*, Edinburgh: Edinburgh University Press.

Klančar, Anthony J. (1948–49) 'Scott in Yugoslavia', *Slavonic and East European Review*, 27: 216–27.

Krzyżanowski, Julian (1933–34) 'Scott in Poland', *Slavonic and East European Review*, 12: 181–89.

Lach-Szyrma, Krystyn (1823) *Letters Literary and Political in Poland, Comprising Observations on Russia and Other Slavonian Nations and Tribes*, Edinburgh: [n. pub.].

— (2004) *From Charlotte Square to Fingal's Cave: Reminiscences of a Journey Through Scotland 1820–1824*, ed. and introd. Mona Kedslie McLeod, trans. Helena Brochowska, East Linton: Tuckwell Press.

Lachèvre, Frédéric (1929) *Bibliographie sommaire des Keepsakes et autres recueils collectifs de la période romantique, 1823–1848*, 2 vols, Paris: L. Giraud-Badin.

Leeder, Paul Robert (1920) 'Scott and Scandinavian Literature: the Influence of Bartholin and Others', *Smith College Studies in Modern Languages*, 2: 8–57.
Lennep, Jacob van (1872 (1826)) *Poëtische Werken*, vol. 1, The Hague: Martinus Nijhoff.

Mánek, Bohuslav (1996) 'Changing Roles of Czech Translators of English Poetry in the Nineteenth Century', in *Litteraria Pragensia: Perspectives*, Prague: The British Council, pp. 91–99.
Michaelis-Jena, Ruth (1975) 'Early Exchanges on Oral Tradition: Two Unpublished Letters by Robert Jamieson and Wilhelm Grimm', *Folklore*, 86: 42–47.
Mitchell, Jerome (1977) *The Walter Scott Operas*, [Tuscaloosa]: University of Alabama Press.
— (1996) *More Scott Operas*, Lanham, MD: University Press of America.
Morgan, Edwin (1988) 'Scots Sang', *Scottish Slavonic Review*, 10 (Spring): 259.

Nielsen, Jørgen Erik (1976, 1977) *Den Samtidige Engleske Litteratur og Danmark 1800–1840*, 2 vols, Copenhagen: Nova. Vol. 2 (1977) is the bibliography.
— (1983) 'Sir Walter Scott's Reception in Nineteenth Century Denmark', in Alexander, J. H. and David Hewitt (eds) (1983) *Scott and His Influence: Papers of the Aberdeen Scott Conference 1982*, Aberdeen: Association for Scottish Literary Studies, pp. 467–74.

Obolensky, Dimitri (ed.) (1965) *The Penguin Book of Russian Verse, [. . .] with plain prose translations of each poem*, rev. edn, Harmondsworth: Penguin.

Pavlova, Karolina (1839) 'Rozabella', *Otechestvennye zapiski*, 7 (12): 131–33.

'De Pelgrim' (1827) *Apollo* [Rotterdam], 25 December, 32.

Pictet de Rochemont, Charles (1816) 'Coup d'œil sur la littérature anglaise en 1815', *Bibliothèque universelle* [Geneva], 1: 9.
Punzo, Franca Ruggieri (1975) *Walter Scott in Italia: 1821–1971*, Bari: Adriatica Editrice.

Roe, F. C. (1953) 'La découverte de l'Ecosse entre 1760 et 1830', *Revue de littérature comparée*, 27: 59–75.

Schaldemose, Frederik (1826) 'Ridder Lochinvar (Efter Walter Scott), *Telegraphen* [Copenhagen], 1: 66–68.
Schubart, Henriette (1817) *Schottische Lieder und Balladen*, Leipzig: Brockhaus.
Scott, Walter (1869) *Minstrelsy of the Scottish Border*, London: Alex. Murray.
— (1904) *The Poetical Works of Sir Walter Scott*, ed. J. Logie Robertson, London: Oxford University Press.
Sendich, Munir (1974) 'Twelve Unpublished Letters of Karolina Pavlova to Alexey Tolstoy', *Russian Literature Triquarterly*, 9: 541–58.
Sienkiewicz, Karol (1822) *Pani jeziora: poema Waltera Skotta*, trans. Karol Z. Kalinowki [Karol Sienkiewicz], Warsaw: N. Glücksberg.
Simmons, Ernest J. (1935) *English Literature and Culture in Russia (1552–1840)*, Cambridge, MA: Harvard University Press.
'Skiald Haralds Sang [. . .] af W. Scott' (1821) *Tilskueren* [Copenhagen], nos 19 and 20: 158–60.

Taylor, Bayard (1875) 'Preface' to trans. of *Faust: A Tragedy by Johann Wolfgang von Goethe; The First Part*, trans. in original metres, Boston: James R. Osgood.

Tytler, Alexander Fraser (Lord Woodhouselee (1907)) *Essay on the Principles of Translation*, London: Dent.

'Ung Lochinvar (Efter Walter Scott)' (1860) *Papperslyktan* [Helsinki], no. 44, 29 October, 349–50.

Vissink, Hendrik (1922) *Scott and His Influence on Dutch Literature*, Zwolle: W. J. Berends.
Vraz, Stanko (1868) *Razlike pjesme: prevodi*, Zagreb: Brzotiskom Dragutina Albrechta.
Vrchlický, Jaroslav (1898) *Moderní básníci angličtí*, Prague: Jos. R. Vilímek.

Weintraub, Wiktor (1954) *The Poetry of Adam Mickiewicz*, The Hague: Mouton.

Zhukovsky, Vasil (1827) 'Zamok Smal'golm', *Nevskiř al'manakh na 1828 god* [St Petersburg], book 4: 9–16.
Zug, Charles G., Jr. (1978) 'The Ballad as History: the Case for Scott', *Folklore*, 89: 229–42.

Chapter 16: Scott's 'Heyday' in Opera

Ambrose, Mary E. (1972) '*La donna del Lago*: The First Italian Translations of Scott', *Modern Language Review*, 67: 74–82.
— (1981) 'Walter Scott, Italian Opera and Romantic Stage Setting', *Italian Studies*, 36: 58–78.
Ashbrook, William (1982) *Donizetti and his Operas*, Cambridge: Cambridge University Press.

Black, John (1984) *The Italian Romantic Libretto: A Study of Salvatore Cammarano*, Edinburgh: Edinburgh University Press.

Dean, Winton (1975) *Bizet*, London: Dent.

Fiske, Roger (1998) Entry for *Scott* in *The New Grove Dictionary of Opera*, ed. Stanley Sadie, 4 vols, London: Macmillan.
Forbes, Elizabeth (1968) 'Sir Walter Scott and Opera', *Opera*, 119: 872–78.

Gerhard, Anselm (1998) *The Urbanization of Opera: Music Theatre in Paris in the Nineteenth Century*, trans. Mary Whittall, Chicago: University of Chicago Press.

Kerr, James (1989) *Fiction Against History: Scott as Story-teller*, Cambridge: Cambridge University Press.
Kimbell, David (1991) *Italian Opera*, Cambridge: Cambridge University Press.

Lamb, Andrew (1973) '*Ivanhoe* and the Royal English Opera', *Musical Times*, 114: 475–78.
Lindenberger, Herbert (1998) *Opera in History: From Monteverdi to Cage*, Stanford: University of Stanford Press.

Mitchell, Jerome (1977) *The Walter Scott Operas: An Analysis of Operas based on the Works of Sir Walter Scott*, [Tuscaloosa]: University of Alabama Press.
— (1996) *More Scott Operas: Further Analyses of Operas Based on the Works of Sir Walter Scott*, Lanham, MD: University Press of America.

O'Grady, Deidre (1991) *The Last Troubadours: Poetic Drama in Italian Opera, 1597–1887*, London: Routledge.

Pittock, Murray G. H. (1999) *Celtic Identity and the British Image*, Manchester: Manchester University Press.

Rosselli, John (1996) *The Life of Bellini*, Cambridge: Cambridge University Press.

Stendhal (1956) *Life of Rossini*, trans. Richard N. Coe, London: John Calder.

Trevor-Roper, Hugh (1983) 'The Invention of Tradition: The Highland Tradition of Scotland', in Hobsbawm, Eric and Terence Ranger (eds) *The Invention of Tradition*, Cambridge: Cambridge University Press.

Chapter 17: 'Seeing with the Painter's Eye': Sir Walter Scott's Challenge to Nineteenth-Century Art

Abad, Vicente Maestre (1984) 'Recuerdos y Bellezas de España: Su origen ideológico, sus modelos', *Goya* [Madrid] 181–182 (July–October): 86–93.

Allard, Sébastien and others (2011) *Delacroix: De l'idée à l'expression (1798–1863)*, exhibition at the La Caixa Foundation organized in collaboration with the Musee du Louvre.

Allentuck, Marcia (1973) 'Scott and the Picturesque: Afforestation and History', in Bell, Alan (ed.) *Scott Bicentenary Essays*, Edinburgh; London: Scottish Academic Press, pp. 188–98.

Altick Richard D. (1985) *Paintings from Books: Art and Literature in Britain, 1760–1900*, Columbus, OH: Ohio State University Press.

Aristotle [1958] *On Poetry and Style*, trans. G. M. A. Grube, Indianapolis: Bobbs-Merrill.

'B.', extract from 'Gazette de Flandre et d'Artois,' repr. *Exposition de Lille en 1834: Visite au Salon* (Lille, 1834), p. 12.

B., St.-A. (1826) [Saint-Amand Bazard], 'Considérations sur l'Histoire', *Le Producteur: Journal philosophique de l'industrie, des sciences et des beaux-arts* [Paris], 4: 390–415.

Baudelaire, Charles (1998) 'Exposition Universelle 1855. Beaux-Arts – Eugène Delacroix', *Le Pays* (1855) in *Charles Baudelaire, Théophile Gautier: Correspondances Esthétiques sur Delacroix*, Paris: Editions Olbia, pp. 100–07.

'Beaux-Arts. Exposition de 1824, 14ᵉ article' (1824), *Le Drapeau blanc* [Paris], 11 December, 4.

Bodin, Félix (1823) 'Du Nouveau roman de Walter Scott [*Quentin Durward*]', *Mercure du XIXe siècle* [Paris] 1: 450–60.

Boime, Albert (1993) *The Art of the Macchia and the Risorgimento. Representing Culture and Nationalism in Nineteenth-Century Italy*, Chicago; London: University of Chicago Press.

Brown, David Blayney (1985) 'Scottish History in Paint and Prose, David Wilkie and Walter Scott', *Country Life* [London], 8 August, 375ff.

Castellaneta, Carlo and Sergio Coradeschi (1971) *L'opera completa di Hayez*, Milan: Rizzoli.

'Chronique' (1835) *L'Art en Province* [Paris], 1: 27–28.

Chiego, William (1987) (ed.) *Sir David Wilkie of Scotland*, catalogue for exhibition at Yale Center for British Art and North Carolina Museum of Art, Raleigh, NC: Museum of Art.

Cooper, Douglas (1946) 'Bonington and *Quentin Durward*', *Burlington Magazine*, (May), 112–17.

Cunningham, Allan (1843) *The Life of Sir David Wilkie: With His Journals, Tours, and Critical Remarks on Works of Art: and a Selection from his Correspondence*, 3 vols London: J. Murray.

'D.' (1833) 'Vignettes pour les Oeuvres de Walter Scott, d'après les tableaux de MM. Alfred et Tony Johannot, gravées par MM. Blanchard, Cousin, Pourvoyeur, etc., publiées par Furne', *L'Artiste* [Paris], 5: 46–47.

'E. J. D.' (1819) [Delécluze, Etienne-Jean] 'Septième Lettre au Rédacteur du Lycée Français sur l'exposition des ouvrages de peinture, sculpture, etc. des Artistes vivans', *Le Lycée Français* [Paris], 2: 182–92.

— (1822) [Delécluze, Etienne] 'Salon de 1822. 10e article', *Le Moniteur universel* [Paris], 18 June, 859–60.

Delécluze, Etienne (1855) *David, son école et son temps. Souvenirs*, Paris: Didier.

Devonshire, M. G. (1967) *The English Novel in France, 1830–1870* [1929], New York: Octagon.

Dini, Piero (1987) *Telemaco Signorini 1835–1901*, exhibition catalogue Villa Forini, Montecatini Terme.

Duro, Paul (1997) *The Academy and the Limits of Painting in Seventeenth-Century France*. New York; Cambridge; Melbourne: Cambridge University Press.

Elliott, Bridget J. (1984) 'The Scottish Reformation and English Reform: David Wilkie's *Preaching of Knox* at the Royal Academy Exhibition of 1832', *Art History* [London], 7.3 (September): 313–28.

Errington, Lindsay (1988) *David Wilkie 1785–1841*, Edinburgh: National Galleries.

Ewals, Leonardus Josephus Ignatius (1987) 'Ary Scheffer: Sa Vie Son Oeuvre' (unpublished doctoral thesis, Katholieke Universiteit te Nijmegen).

'Exposition à la galerie Colbert: 4e article' (1832), *Journal des Artistes* [Paris], 8 January, 1: 28.

Fagan, L. A., rev. John-Paul Stonard (2008) 'Henri Jean-Baptiste Victoire Fradelle (1778–1865)', *Oxford Dictionary of National Biography*, Oxford: Oxford University Press.

'Fine Arts: New Publications' (1830), *Illustrations of le Keepsake Français* and *The Talisman*', *The Literary Gazette* [London], 20 November, p. 754.

Finley, Gerald (1980) *Landscapes of Memory: Turner as Illustrator to Scott*, Berkeley; Los Angeles: University of California Press; London: Scolar Press.

Flocon, Ferdinand and Marie Aycard (1824) *Le Salon de 1824*, Paris: Leroux.

Gigoux, Jean-François (1885) *Causeries sur les Artistes de Mon Temps*, Paris: C. Lévy.

Gordon, Catherine (1971) 'The Illustration of Sir Walter Scott: 19th Century Enthusiasm and Adaptation', *Journal of the Warburg and Courtauld Institutes* [London], 34: 297–317.

— (1979) *The Lamp of Memory – Scott and the Artist*, exhibition catalogue Buxton Museum and Art Gallery, Derby: Derwent Press.

— (1988) ' "We do not envy the sun: Sir Walter Scott" ', in *British Paintings of Subjects from the English Novel 1740–1870*, New York; London: Garland, pp. 140–96; catalogue pp. 286–358.

Gossman, Lionel (1990) 'History and Literature: Reproduction or Signification?' [1978] in *idem, Between History and Literature*, Cambridge, MA: Harvard University Press, pp. 227–56.

Gozzoli, Maria Cristina and Mazzocca, Fernando (1983) *Hayez*, exhibition catalogue Milan Palazzo Reale and Accademia Pinacoteca Biblioteca di Brera: November 1983–February 1984, Milan: Electa.

Graves, Algernon (1908) *The British Institution 1806–1867: A Complete Dictionary of Contributors and their Work from the Foundation of the Institution*, London: George Bell & Sons and Algernon Graves.

Hannoosh, Michèle (2009) *Eugène Delacroix: Journal: Nouvelle édition intégrale établie par Michèle Hannoosh*, 2 vols, Paris: José Corti.

Heine, Henri (1833) 'Salon de 1831', in *De la France*, Paris: Eugène Renduel, pp. 285–347.

Holcomb, Adele M. (1971) 'Turner and Scott', *Journal of the Warburg and Courtauld Institutes* [London], 34: 386–97.

— (1973) 'Scott and Turner', in Bell, Alan (ed.) *Scott Bicentenary Essays*, Edinburgh; London: Scottish Academic Press, pp. 199–212.

Hugo, Victor (1823a) '*Quentin Durward ou l'Ecossais à la cour de Louis XI* par sir Walter Scott', *La Muse Française* [Paris], July, pp. 25–39; in Hugo (1934), pp. 344–45.

— (1823b) 'Sur Walter Scott à propos de *Quentin Durward*', in Hugo (1934), pp. 116–22.

— (1934) *Littérature et Philosophie Mêlées* Paris: A. Michel.

'L'Influence exercée par Walter Scott sur la richesse, la moralité et le bonheur de la société actuelle' (1833) *La Revue Britannique* [Paris], March, 69–83.

Janin, Jules (1832) 'Les frères Johannot', *L'Artiste* [Paris], 4: 153–56.

— (1833) 'Notice biographique sur MM. Johannot frères', *L'Artiste* [Paris], 5: 146–48.

— (1837) 'Alfred Johannot', *Journal des Débats* [Paris], 11 December

— (1866) 'Alfred Johannot', *L'Artiste* [Paris], 1 February, 49–51.

Joannides, Paul (2001) 'Delacroix and Modern Literature', in Wright, Beth S. (ed.) *The Cambridge Companion to Delacroix*, New York; Cambridge: Cambridge University Press, pp. 130–53.

Jobert, Barthelemy (1998) *Delacroix*, trans. Terry Grabar and Alexandra Bonfante-Warren, Princeton: Princeton University Press.

Johnson, Edgar (1970) *Sir Walter Scott: The Great Unknown*, 2 vols, New York: Macmillan.

Johnson, Lee (1981–89) *The Paintings of Eugène Delacroix: A Critical Catalog*, 6 vols, New York: Oxford University Press.

Kemp, Martin (1973) 'Scott and Delacroix, with some Assistance from Hugo and Bonington', in Bell, Alan (ed.) *Scott Bicentenary Essays*, New York: Barnes & Noble, pp. 213–27.

Kolb, Marthe (1937a) *Ary Scheffer et son temps 1795–1858*, Paris: Boivin.

— (1937b) *Une Correspondance inédite de la princesse Marie d'Orléans duchesse de Wurtemberg*, Paris: Boivin.

Landscape Illustrations of the Waverley Novels with Descriptions of the Views (1832) 2 vols, London: Tilt.

Landscape Illustrations of the Novels of the Author of Waverley; with Portraits of the Principal Female Characters (1833) 3 vols, London: Tilt.

Leslie, Charles Robert (1860) *Autobiographical Recollections by the Late Charles Robert Leslie R. A.*, Boston: Ticknor and Fields.

Lockhart, John Gibson (1839) *Memoirs of the Life of Sir Walter Scott*, 2nd edn, 10 vols, Edinburgh: Cadell.

Lyons, Martyn (1984) 'The Audience for Romanticism: Walter Scott in France, 1815–51', *European History Quarterly* [London; Beverly Hills; New Delhi], 14 (January): 21–46.

M★★★ (1825) *Revue critique des productions de peinture, sculpture, gravure exposés au Salon de 1824*, Paris: Dentu.
Macmillan, Duncan (1993) 'Sources of French narrative painting: Between three cultures', *Apollo* [London], May, 297–303.
— (2001) ' "A journey through England and Scotland": Wilkie and other influences on French art of the 1820s', *The British Art Journal*, 2.3: 28–35.
Marie, Aristide (1925) *L'Art et la Vie Romantique: Alfred et Tony Johannot, Peintres, Graveurs et Vignettistes*, Paris: Floury.
Marks, Arthur S. (1998) 'Testaments to a Friendship: David Wilkie's Portraits of Walter Scott', *Studies in Romanticism*, 37 (Fall): 351–93.
Massmann, Klaus (1972) *Die Rezeption der historischen Romans Sir Walter Scotts in Frankreich: 1816–1832*, Studia Romantica 24, Heidelberg: Carl Winter Universitätsverlag.
Mazzocca, Fernando (1994) *Francesco Hayez: Catalogo ragionato*, Milan: Federico Motta.
— (1996) 'Francesco Hayez', in Turner, Jane Shoaf (ed.) *The Dictionary of Art*, London: Macmillan, 14: 264–67; also *The Grove Dictionary of Art Online* (Oxford University Press, 2003) <http://www.groveart.com> [accessed 20 March 2004].
'Mélanges' (1820) *Journal des Débats* [Paris], 15 July, [n. page].
Mitchell, Jerome (1977) *The Walter Scott Operas: An Analysis of Operas on the Works of Walter Scott*. Birmingham, AL: Alabama University Press.
Moreau, Véronique (1998) 'Delacroix lecteur de Walter Scott', in *Delacroix en Touraine*, exhibition catalogue Musée des Beaux-Arts Tours, pp. 145–84.
Morris, Edward (2005) *French Art in Nineteenth-Century Britain*, New Haven; London: Yale University Press.
Murdoch, J. D. W. (1972) 'Scott, Pictures and Painters', *Modern Language Review*, 67: 31–43.

Nodier, Charles (1823) '*Oeuvres Complètes* de Walter Scott, 2ᵉ article', *La Quotidienne*, 17 October, [n. page].
Noon, Patrick (1991) *Richard Parkes Bonington: On the Pleasure of Painting*, exhibition catalogue Yale Center for British Art, New Haven, and Petit Palais, Paris.
— (2003) *Constable to Delacroix: British Art and the French Romantics*, exhibition catalogue Tate Britain, London; Minneapolis Institute of Arts; New York Metropolitan Museum of Art, London: Tate Publishing.
— (2008) *Richard Parkes Bonington: The Complete Paintings*, New Haven; London: Yale University Press.

Partridge, Eric (1970) *The French Romantics' Knowlege of English Literature (1820–1848) according to contemporary French memoirs, letters and periodicals*, reprint *Revue de littérature Comparée* [Paris] (1924), Freeport, NY: Books for Libraries Press.
Pétigny, J. de (1821) 'Le Château de Kenilworth', *Annales de la littérature et des arts* [Paris], 28 April, 143.
Pichot, Amédée (1820) *Sir Walter Scott, Romans poetiques, traduits de l'anglais (en prose) par le traducteur des oeuvres de Lord Byron*, Paris: Ladvocat and Nicolle.
— (1821) *Notice sur Sir Walter Scott et ses écrits*, Paris: Ladvocat and Nicolle.
— (1825) *Voyage historique et littéraire en Angleterre et en Ecosse*, 3 vols, Paris: Ladvocat and Charles Gosselin.
— (1826) *Vues pittoresques de l'Ecosse*, Paris: Gosselin and Lami-Denozan.

Pinto, Sandra, Pacia Barocchi and Fiamma Nicolodi (1973) *Romanticismo Storico*, exhibition catalogue Palazzo Pitti, Florence: December 1973–February 1974.

Pontmartin, Armand de (1881–90) *Souvenirs d'un vieux critique*, 10 vols, Paris: Calmann Lévy.

Portraits of the Principal Female Characters in the Waverley Novels; To Which Are Added Landscape Illustrations of the Highland Widow, Anne of Geierstein, Fair Maid of Perth, Castle Dangerous (1833) London: Tilt.

Praz, Mario (1983) *Ivanhoe: Walter Scott con le incisioni de Hayez*, Milan: Rizzoli.

'Preface du Salon' (1845) *Journal des Artistes* [Paris], 9 February, p. 48.

Russcol, Diane (1990) 'Le thème de la reine prisonnière', *Revue du Louvre*, 40.2: 123–28.

Russell, Francis (1987) *Portraits of Sir Walter Scott: A Study of Romantic Portraiture*, London: White Brothers.

'Salon de 1837, 6e article' (1837) *L'Artiste* [Paris], 13: 129–34.

'Salon de 1845, 14e article' (1845) *Journal des Artistes* [Paris], 4 May, 157.

Samuels, Maurice (2004) *The Spectacular Past: Popular History and the Novel in Nineteenth-Century France*, Ithaca, NY: Cornell University Press.

Scott, Walter (1826) *Provincial Antiquities and Picturesque Scenery of Scotland*, 2 vols, London: J. and A. Arch.

— (1833–34) *Poetical Works*, ed. J. G. L[ockhart], 12 vols, Edinburgh: Cadell.

— (1834–36) *The Miscellaneous Prose Works of Sir Walter Scott*, 28 vols, Edinburgh: Cadell.

— (1932–37) *The Letters of Sir Walter Scott*, ed. H. J. C. Grierson, 12 vols, London: Constable.

— (1963) *Quentin Durward* [1823], Signet Classic edn, New York: New American Library.

— (1969) *The Antiquary* [1816], Everyman edn, London: Dent; New York: Dutton.

— (1972) *The Journal of Sir Walter Scott*, ed. W. E. K. Anderson, Oxford: Clarendon Press.

Siegfried, Susan (2013) 'Alternative Narratives', *Art History* [London], 36.1 (February): 100–27.

Thackeray, William Makepeace (1904) 'On the French School of Painting: With Appropriate Anecdotes, Illustrations and Philosophical Disquisitions, in a Letter to Mr. MacGilp of London', *The Paris Sketchbook* [1840] in *Works of William Makepeace Thackeray*, 32 vols, New York: Scribner, 17: 53–78.

Thierry, Augustin (1820) 'Sur la Conquête de l'Angleterre par les Normands: A propos du roman *Ivanhoe*', *Censeur Européen* [Paris], 20 May, [n. page]; reprint. *Dix Ans d'Etudes historiques*, Paris: Just Tessier, pp. 131–40.

— (1825) *Histoire de la Conquête de l'Angleterre par les Normands: de ses causes, et de ses suites jusqu'à nos jours, en Angleterre, en Ecosse, en Irlande et sur le continent*, 3 vols, Paris: Firmin Didot.

Toupet, Michèle (1963) 'L'Assassinat de l'Evêque de Liège par Eugène Delacroix', *Revue du Louvre*, 83–94.

Tromans, Nicolas (2002) *David Wilkie: Painter of Everyday Life*, exhibition catalogue Dulwich Picture Gallery.

Troyer, Nancy Gray (1996) 'Telemaco Signorini', in Turner, Jane Shoaf (ed.) *The Dictionary of Art*, London: Macmillan, 28: 704–07; also *The Grove Dictionary of Art Online* (Oxford University Press, 2003) <http://www.groveart.com> [accessed 20 March 2004].

'Le Vicaire de Wakefield' (1834), *L'Artiste* [Paris], 7: 240–41.

'De Walter Scott et de ses Traducteurs' (1822) *Miroir des Spectacles* [Paris], 16 June, 3.

'Walter Scott' (1832) *L'Artiste* [Paris], 4: 114–15.

White, Henry Adelbert (1927) *Sir Walter Scott's Novels on the Stage* Yale Studies in English, No. 76. New Haven; London: Yale University Press.

Whiteley, Linda (2010) 'The Sense of the Past', in Bann, Stephen and Linda Whiteley with John Guy, Christopher Riopelle and Anne Robbins, *Painting History: Delaroche and Lady Jane Grey*, London: National Gallery, catalogue for exhibition, pp. 24–33.

Wright, Beth S. (1978) 'The Influence of the Historical Novels of Walter Scott on the Changing Nature of French History Painting, 1815–1855' (unpublished doctoral thesis, University of California at Berkeley).

— (1981) 'Scott and Shakespeare in Nineteenth Century France: Achille Devéria's Lithographs of *Minna et Brenda* and *Les Enfans d'Edouard*', *Arts Magazine*, 55 (February): 129–33.

— (1984) 'The Auld Alliance in Nineteenth Century French Painting: The Changing Concept of Mary Stuart 1814–1833', *Arts Magazine*, 58 (March): 97–107.

— (1987) 'Walter Scott et la gravure française: A propos de la collection des estampes "scottesques" conservée au Département des estampes, Paris', *Nouvelles de l'Estampe* [Paris], 93 (July): 6–18.

— (1990) 'Henri Gaugain et le Musée Colbert: l'entreprise d'un directeur de galerie et d'un éditeur d'art à l'époque romantique', *Nouvelles de l'Estampe* [Paris], 114 (December): 24–31.

— (1996) 'Walter Scott and French Art: Imagining the Past', in Tscherny, Nadia and Guy Stair Sainty (eds) *Romance & Chivalry: History and Literature Reflected in Early Nineteenth-Century French Painting*, London; New York: Matthiesen Fine Art and Stair Sainty Matthiesen, pp. 180–93.

— (1997) *Painting and History during the French Restoration: Abandoned by the Past*, New York; Cambridge: Cambridge University Press.

— (2000) ' "That Other Historian, the Illustrator": Voices and Vignettes in Mid-Nineteenth Century France', *Oxford Art Journal*, 23:1 (Spring): 113–36.

— (2010) ' "A Better Way to Read Great Works": Lithographs by Delacroix, Roqueplan, Boulanger, and the Devéria Brothers in Gaugain's Suite of Scott Subjects (1829–1830)', *Word & Image*, 26.4 (Oct.– Dec.): 337–63.

— (ed.) (2001) *The Cambridge Companion to Delacroix*, New York; Cambridge: Cambridge University Press.

Wright, Beth S. and Paul Joannides (1984) 'Les romans historiques de Sir Walter Scott et la peinture française, 1822–1863 (première partie)', *Bulletin de la Société de l'Histoire de l'Art Français* [Paris], année 1982: 119–32.

— (1985) 'Les romans historiques de Sir Walter Scott et la peinture française, 1822–1863 (deuxième partie)', *Bulletin de la Société de l'Histoire de l'Art Français* [Paris], année 1983: 95–115.

Wright, G. N. (1836) *Landscape: Historical Illustrations of Scotland and the Waverley Novels*, 2 vols, London; Paris; America: Fisher and Co.

Chapter 18: 'Scotland is Scott-Land': Scott and the Development of Tourism

Anderson, George and Peter (1850) *Guide to the Highlands and Islands of Scotland*, Inverness; Edinburgh: Adam & Charles Black.

Anderson, Susan and Bruce H. Tabb (eds) (2002) *Water, Leisure and Culture: European Historical Perspectives*, Oxford; New York: Berg.

Andrews, Malcolm (1989) *The Search for the Picturesque: Landscape, Aesthetics and Tourism in Britain, 1760–1800*, Stanford: Stanford University Press.
Arnold, Frieda (1994) *My Mistress the Queen: The Letters of Frieda Arnold, Dresser to Queen Victoria, 1854–59*, eds Benita Stoney and Heinrich C. Weltzien, trans. Sheila de Bellaigue, London: Weidenfeld & Nicolson.

Bailey, J. M. (1879) *England from a Back Window*, Boston: Lee & Shepard.
Bain, Margaret L. (1931) *Les voyagers français en Ecosse, 1770–1880, et leurs curiosités intellectuelles*, Paris: Champion.
Battiscombe, Georgina and Marghanita Laski (eds) (1965) *A Chaplet for Charlotte Yonge*, London: Cresset Press.
Berghoff, Harmut and others (eds) (2002) *The Making of Modern Tourism: The Cultural History of the British Experience 1600–2000*, Basingstoke and New York: Palgrave.
Brander, Michael (1973) *A Hunt Round the Highlands: On the Trail of Colonel Thornton*, Bath: Standfast Press.
Brendon, Piers (1991) *Thomas Cook: 150 Years of Popular Tourism*, London: Martin, Secker & Warburg.
Brendsdorff, Elias (1975) *Hans Christian Andersen: The Story of his Life and Work, 1805–75*, London: Phaidon.

Charteris, M. (1887) *Health Resorts at Home and Abroad*, London: J & A Churchill.
Clyde, Robert (1995) *From Rebel to Hero: The Image of the Highlander 1745–1830*, East Linton: Tuckwell.
Cockburn, Lord (1983) *Circuit Journeys*, Hawick: Byway Books.
Cole, Beverley and Richard Durack (1990) *Happy as a Sandboy: Early Railway Posters*, London: HMSO.
Connolly, S., R. Houston and R. J. Morris (eds) (1995) *Conflict, Identity and Economic Development: Scotland and Ireland 1600–1939*, Preston: Carnegie Publishing.
Cook, Thomas (comp.) (1846) *Handbook of a Trip to Scotland*, Leicester: [n. pub.].
— (1904) *Handbook to Normandy and Brittany*, London: Simpkin, Marshall, Hamilton, Kent.

Daniell, William (1818) *A Voyage round Great Britain Undertaken in the Summer of the Year 1813*, London: Longman.
Durie, Alastair J. (1998) ' "Unconscious benefactors": Grouse shooting in Scotland, 1780–1914', *International Journal of the History of Sport*, 15.3: 57–73.
— (2003) *Scotland for the Holidays: Tourism in Scotland c1780–1939*, East Linton: Tuckwell Press.

Eyre-Todd, George (ed.) ([c.1913]) *The Lord of the Isles & A Voyage to the Hebrides*, Glasgow: David MacBrayne.

Gaskill, Howard (ed.) (2004) *The Reception of Ossian in Europe*, The Athlone Critical Traditions Series: The Reception of British Authors in Europe, series ed. Elinor Shaffer, London; New York: Continuum.
Gold, John R., and Margaret M. Gold (1995) *Imagining Scotland: Tradition, Representation and Promotion in Scottish Tourism since 1750*, Aldershot: Scolar Press
Grant, Mrs (1844) *Memoir and Correspondence of Mrs Grant of Laggan*, ed. J. P. Grant (her son), 3 vols, London: Longman, Brown, Green and Longmans.
Grenier, Kathleen Haldane (2005) *Tourism and Identity in Scotland, 1770–1914: Creating Caledonia*, Aldershot and Burlington: Ashgate.
Grierson, H. J. C. (1952) *The Letters of Sir Walter Scott 1808–1811*, London: Constable.

Hiley, Alison (1985) 'German-speaking Travellers in Scotland: 1800–1860', 3 vols (unpublished doctoral thesis, University of Edinburgh).
— (1996) ' "Scotland's name is poetry to our ears": German Travellers in Scotland c1800–1860', *Scottish Archives* [Glasgow], 2: 24–38.
Hubbard, Tom (2000) '1800: Scottish Literature's Grand Tour', unpub. conference paper Association for Scottish Literary Studies, 18 November.
Hutton, W. H. (1926) *Highways and Byways in Shakespeare's Country*, London: Macmillan.

Inland Watering Places: Being Descriptions of the Spas of Great Britain and Ireland (1891) London: L. Upcott Gill.
Irving, Washington (1835) *Abbotsford and Newstead Abbey*, London: John Murray.

Johnson, Edgar (1970) *Sir Walter Scott: The Great Unknown*, London: Hamilton.

Kramer, Lotten von (1870) *Bland Skotska Berg och Sjöar* [Among Scottish Mountains and Lakes], Stockholm: Samson & Wallis.

Lach-Szyrma, Krystyn (2004) *From Charlotte Square to Fingal's Cave: Reminiscences of a Journey Through Scotland 1820–1824*, ed. Mona Kedslie McLeod, East Linton: Tuckwell.
Lockhart, D. G. (1900) *Memoirs of Sir Walter Scott*, London: MacMillan.
Lockwood, Allison (1981) *Passionate Pilgrims: The American Traveler in Great Britain 1800–1914*, London; East Brunswick: Cornwall Books & Assoc. University Presses.

McCrone, David, Angela Morris and Richard Kelly (1995) *Scotland the Brand: The Making of Scottish Heritage*, Edinburgh: Edinburgh University Press.
McIlvanney, Liam and Ray Ryan (eds) (2005) *Ireland and Scotland: Culture and Society 1700–2000*, Dublin: Four Courts.
MacLeod, Donald (1877) *A Memoir of Norman MacLeod D.D.*, London: Daldy Isbister.
Miss Jemima's Swiss Journal: The First Conducted Tour of Switzerland, Proceedings of the Junior United Alpine Club 1863 (1962) written for private circulation, London: Putnam for T. Cook and Co.
Mulvey, Christopher (1983) *Anglo American Landscapes: A Study of Nineteenth Century Anglo-American Travel Literature*, Cambridge: Cambridge University Press.
Murray, John (1970) *Handbook for Travellers in Switzerland* [1838], introd. Jack Simmons, Leicester: Leicester University Press.
Murray, Sarah (1982) *A Companion and Useful Guide to the Beauties of Scotland* [1799], Hawick: Byways Press.

Nicholson, Norman (1995) *The Lakers: The Adventures of the First Tourists*, Milnthorpe: Cicerone Press.
Normington, Susan (2001) *This Infernal Woman: Lady Caroline Lamb*, London: Stratus.

Olcott, Charles S. (1913) *The Country of Sir Walter Scott*, London: Cassell.

Scarfe, Norman (2001) *To the Highlands in 1786: The Inquisitive Journey of a Young French Aristocrat*, Woodbridge: Boydell Press.
Schinkel, Karl Friedrich (1993) *The English Journey: Journal of a Visit to France and Britain in 1826*, eds David Bindman and Gottfried Riesman, New Haven; London: Yale University Press.

Sinclair, Sir John (ed.) (1793) *The Statistical Account of Scotland*, Edinburgh: William Creech.

Smith, Alexander (1912) *A Summer in Skye* [1865], Edinburgh: Nimmo, Hay & Mitchell.

Smith, Janet Adam (1963) 'The Sir Walter Scott Lectures for 1963: Scott and the idea of Scotland', *University of Edinburgh Journal*, 21 (4): 188–92.

Taylor, Bayard (1859) *Views Afoot; or, Europe as seen with Knapsack and Staff*, New York: G. P. Putnam.

Thomas, John (1976) *Forgotten Railways of Scotland*, Newton Abbott: David & Charles.

Thomson, Katrina (1999) *Turner and Sir Walter Scott*, Edinburgh: National Galleries of Scotland.

Where Shall We Go? A Guide to the Healthiest and Most Beautiful Places in the British Islands (1868), Edinburgh: A. & C. Black.

Withey, Lynne (1997) *Grand Tours and Cook's Tours. A History of Leisure Travel 1750 to 1915*, New York: William Morrow & Company.

Wordsworth, Dorothy (1997) *Recollections of a Tour Made in Scotland*, ed. Carol Kyros Walker, New Haven and London: Yale University Press.

Index

References to Sir Walter Scott and his works, status and ideas are grouped under **Scott**; references to journals and periodicals, publishers and translators are grouped under **Periodicals**, **Publishers**, **Translators**. See also the **Timeline**.

Lightning Source UK Ltd.
Milton Keynes UK
UKOW04f0715020514

230993UK00003B/3/P